The **Rough Guide** to

# Bali & Lombok

written and researched by

## Lesley Reader and Lucy Ridout

ROUGH
GUIDES

NEW YORK • LONDON • DELHI

www.roughguides.com

# Contents

◄◄ The Gili Islands ◄ Gunung Batur, Bali

# BALI

Senggigi (Lombok)   Lembar (Lombok)

BALI SEA

LOMBOK STRAIT

Lombok

INDIAN OCEAN

Lombok Strait

Badung Strait

Bali Strait

Java

Ketapang
Gilimanuk
Cekik
Labuan Lalang
Pulau Menjangan (Deer Island)
BALI BARAT NATIONAL PARK
Pemuteran
Negara
Medewi
Pura Rambut Siwi
Pekutatan
Pura Agung Pulaki
Seririt
Buddhist Monastery
Dencarik
Lovina Beach
Kubutambahan
Air Sanih
Bukti
Singaraja
Munduk
Pupuan
Wongayagede
Pura Luhur Batukau
Gunung Batukau
Bedugul
Penebel
Antosari
Lalang Linggah
Yeh Gangga Beach
Pura Tanah Lot
Krambitan
Tabanan
Mengwi
Pura Taman Ayun
Sangeh Monkey Forest
Jatiluwih
Penelokan
Kintamani
Toya Bungkah
Gunung Batur
Songan
Gunung Batur
Tejakula
Ponjok Batu
Bondalem
Kubu
Gunung Agung
Besakih
Culik
Tulamben
Amed
Jemeluk
Lipah Beach
Aas
Amlapura
Tirtagangga
Tenganan
Candi Dasa
Padang Bai
Klungkung
Bangli
Gunung Kawi
Tampaksiring
Pejeng
Bedulu
Gianyar
Petulu
Ubud
Tegalalang
Pujung Kelod
Sayan
Teges
Mas
Batuan
Sukawati
Batubulan
Sakah
DENPASAR
Sanur
Benoa Harbour
Tanjung Benoa
Nusa Dua
Jimbaran
Bualu
Pecatu
Pura Luhur Uluwattu
Ngurah Rai Airport
Kuta
Legian
Seminyak
Ubung
Pelaga
Pura Batur
Nusa Lembongan
Jungutbatu
Ped
Buyuk Harbour
Sampalan
Nusa Penida
Toyapakeh

N

20km

highway under construction

| feet | metres |
|------|--------|
| 9000 | 2743 |
| 7000 | 2134 |
| 5000 | 1524 |
| 3000 | 914 |
| 2000 | 610 |
| 1000 | 305 |
| 500 | 152 |
| 250 | 76 |
| 0 | 0 |

Bali
Java
Lombok

# LOMBOK

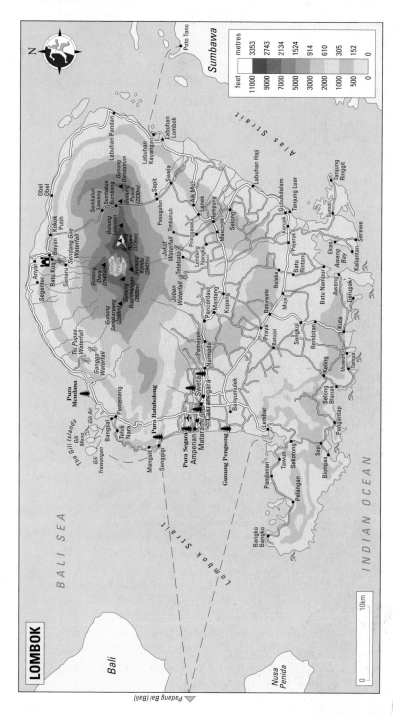

**Bali**

BALI SEA

Lombok Strait

INDIAN OCEAN

Nusa Penida

Padang Bai (Bali)

Sumbawa

Alas Strait

Poto Tano

| feet | metres |
|------|--------|
| 11000 | 3353 |
| 9000 | 2743 |
| 7000 | 2134 |
| 5000 | 1524 |
| 3000 | 914 |
| 2000 | 610 |
| 1000 | 305 |
| 500 | 152 |
| 0 | 0 |

N

The Gili Islands
Gili Meno
Gili Air
Gili Trawangan

Mangsit
Senggigi
Bangsal
Teluk Nara
Pemenang

Pura Meninting
Pura Batubolong
Pura Segara
Ampenan
Mataram
Cakranegara
Sweta
Lakramegara
Narmada
Gunung Pengsong
Banyumulek

Anyar
Segenter
Batu Koq
Senaru
Bayan
Kokok Putih
Obel Obel

Sendang Gile Waterfall
Gunung Leuktan
Rinjani
Gunung Rinjani (3726m)
Danau Segara Anak
Gunung Daya (2914m)
Gunung Buahnangge (2895m)
Gunung Sengkareang (2588m)
Gunung Kondo (2947m)

Sembalun Lawang
Sembalun Bumbung
Gunung Dundatum
Gunung Pusuk (2330m)

Labuhan Pandan

Labuhan Lombok

Labuhan Kayangan

Sapit
Swela
Aik Mel
Pringgasela
Timbanuh
Pesugulan
Lenek
Rempung
Masbagik
Selong
Labuhan Haji

Tiu Pupas Waterfall
Gangga Waterfall

Jukut Waterfall
Jeteluk
Joben Waterfall
Jeteluk
Pancordau
Mantang
Kopang
Pemepek
Pemejek

Lendang Nangka
Batu Rintang
Pejeruk
Korrok
Gubukdalam
Tanjung Luar
Sunut
Tanjung Ringgit

Serewe
Kaliantan
Gerupak
Kuta
Ekas
Awang Awang Bay
Batu Nampur
Batujai
Praya
Batunyale
Muja
Beleka

Selong Blanak
Penganatap
Pengantap
Blongas
Sapi
Sekotong
Tawun
Pandanan
Lembar

Koling
Rembitan
Sengkol
Mawun
Tampa

Bangko Bangko
Pelangan

10km

Introduction to

# Bali & Lombok

**The islands of Bali and Lombok are part of the Indonesian archipelago, a 5200-kilometre-long string of over thirteen thousand islands, stretching between Malaysia in the west and Australia in the east. Sandy beaches punctuate the dramatically rugged coastlines, and world-class surf pounds both shorelines.**

Located just east of the island of Java, Bali and Lombok, its eastern neighbour, have long been the prime destinations in Indonesia's tourist industry. Both islands are small (Bali extends less than 150km at its widest point, Lombok a mere 80km), volcanic, and graced with swathes of extremely fertile land, much of it – particularly on Bali – sculpted into terraced **rice-paddies**. Culturally, however, Bali and Lombok could hardly be more different. Bali remains the only **Hindu** society in Southeast Asia, and exuberant religious observance permeates every aspect of contemporary Balinese life; the Sasak people of Lombok, on the other hand, are **Muslim**, like the vast majority of other Indonesians.

With a tourist industry that dates back over seventy years, the tiny island of **Bali** (population 3.1 million) has become very much a mainstream destination, offering all the comforts and facilities expected by better-off tourists, and suffering the predictable problems of congestion, commercialization and breakneck Westernization. However, its original charm is still much in evidence, its stunning temples and spectacular festivals set off by the gorgeously lush landscape of the interior. Although tourist arrivals plummeted after the Kuta bombing in 2002, causing an island-wide recession that continues to bite, foreign visitors are returning in their previously high numbers (1.4 million in 2004). Meanwhile, **Lombok** (population 2.4 million) plays host to far fewer foreign visitors and boasts only a handful of burgeoning tourist resorts, retaining its reputation as a more adventurous destination than its neighbour, with plenty of unspoilt beaches, wide-open spaces and extensive areas that have yet to be fully explored by visitors.

> **Bali's stunning temples and spectacular festivals are set off by its gorgeously lush landscape**

Until the nineteenth century, both Bali and Lombok were divided into small **kingdoms**, each domain ruled by a succession of rajas whose territories fluctuated so much that, at times, parts of eastern Bali and western Lombok were joined under a single ruler. More recently, both islands endured years of colonial rule under the Dutch East Indies government, which only ended with hard-won **independence** for Indonesia in 1949. Since then, the Jakarta-based government of Indonesia has tried hard to foster

▲ Morning market

## Fact file

• Bali and Lombok are part of the Republic of Indonesia, an ethnically diverse democracy of 206 million people. Everyone over the age of 17 is eligible to vote in the national elections, held at least every five years. The electorate votes first for the 550 members of the House of Representatives (DPR), and subsequently for the president and vice-president.

• As one of 27 self-contained provinces (*propinsi*) of Indonesia, Bali is overseen by a governor; the current incumbent, Drs. I Dewa Made Beratha, was elected by Bali's Regional House of Representatives (DPRD) for a second five-year term in 2003. The province is divided into eight districts, or *kabupaten* (reflecting the borders of the old regencies), and one municipality, Denpasar.

• Lombok and its eastern neighbour, Sumbawa, together form the province of Nusa Tenggara Barat (West Nusa Tenggara), which has been governed by Drs. Lalu Serinata since 2003 from Lombok's capital, Mataram.

• Both islands are volcanic and subject to earthquakes. The last major eruption was in 1963, when 100,000 Balinese homes were destroyed (see p.250). But volcanic ash is also a life-enhancer – both an exceptionally rich medium for growing crops and an excellent fertilizer when carried down the hillsides by rivers. The highest peak in Bali's spine of volcanoes is Gunung Agung (3142m). Lombok's highest point, amidst a cluster of volcanoes topping 2300m, is the summit of Gunung Rinjani (3726m). Separating the two islands is the Lombok Strait – just 35km wide, but 1300m deep in places.

## Rice farming

Emerald-green rice terraces, or *sawah*, are one of the most memorable sights on Bali and Lombok, and you'll see them almost everywhere – ranged in steps up hillsides, tumbling down steep-sided river valleys, and encircling villages. The fertile volcanic soil, plentiful sunshine and regular downpours create ideal growing conditions that sustain at least two crops a year, and an ancient system of *subak* irrigation co-operatives (see p.493) ensures that neighbours help each other where possible – rice farming is unrelenting, back-breaking work, nearly all of it done by hand, from the painstaking planting of the seedlings to the harvesting and threshing of the paddy. Spiritual help is also enlisted from the beloved rice goddess, Dewi Sri, who is courted with numerous rituals and worshipped at tiny shrines in every expanse of *sawah*.

a sense of national identity among its extraordinarily diverse islands, both by implementing a unifying five-point political philosophy, the Pancasila, and through the mandatory introduction of Bahasa Indonesia, now the lingua franca for the whole archipelago. Politically, Bali is administered as a province in its own right, while Lombok is the most westerly island of Nusa Tenggara, a chain of islands stretching east as far as Timor, which is divided into two provinces, West Nusa Tenggara and East Nusa Tenggara.

# Where to go

Bali's best-known resort is **Kuta**, an eight-kilometre sweep of golden sand whose international reputation as a hangout for weekending Australian surfers is enhanced by its numerous restaurants, bars, clubs and shops. Travellers seeking more relaxed alternatives generally head across the southern peninsula to **Sanur** or, increasingly, to peaceful **Candi Dasa** further east, or the black volcanic sands of **Lovina** on the north coast. Quieter, but more upmarket, seaside options can be found at **Jimbaran** in the south and **Pemuteran** in the northwest. On Lombok, the **Senggigi** coastline offers the widest range of accommodation, while the nearby and rapidly developing **Gili Islands** have long been a favourite with backpackers. All these resorts make comfortable bases for **divers** and **snorkellers**, within easy reach of the islands' fine reefs; Bali also boasts an unusually accessible wreck dive. **Surfers** on Bali head for the famed south-coast swells (particularly around Uluwatu) and the offshore island breaks of Nusa Lembongan, though less experienced wave-riders find Kuta and Medewi more manageable. There's also plenty of surfing potential off Lombok's south coast.

Despite the obvious attractions of the beach resorts, most visitors also venture inland to experience more traditional island life. On Bali, the once-tiny village of **Ubud** has become a hugely popular cultural centre, still charming but undeniably commercialized, where traditional dances are staged every night of the week and the streets are full of arts and crafts galleries. **Tetebatu** on Lombok occupies a similarly cool position in the foothills, although, like the island as a whole, it lacks the artistic heritage of Bali. In general, the villages on both islands are far more appealing than the towns, but Bali's capital, **Denpasar**, its former capital, **Singaraja**, and Lombok's **Ampenan–Mataram–Cakranegara–Sweta** conurbation are all worth a day-trip for their museums, markets and temples.

## Surfing

Bob Koke, co-founder of one of Kuta's first hotels, claims to have started Bali's surfing craze in 1936: he'd learnt to surf in Hawaii and, once established in Kuta, began to make his own boards and to teach his staff and guests the rudiments. Since then, Bali's surf breaks have become a major draw for enthusiasts from Australia, Japan and beyond – and local people have taken up the sport with equal zeal, perfecting a distinctive Bali style that even 6-year-olds execute with finesse. Bali's most awesome, and challenging, breaks are at Uluwatu and Padang Padang, though experts rate Lombok's Desert Point even higher. For more on surfing in Bali and Lombok, see p.67.

9

## Garden bathrooms

Perhaps inspired by the traditional use of the outdoors for ablutions (some villagers still bathe in the river every evening), some losmen and many hotels design their bathrooms with garden features. You may simply find a couple of shrubs and an artistically mossed-over stone-carving in your smallest room, or you may be greeted with elegant creations of riverbed pebbles, bamboo shower-spouts, miniature ponds and waterfalls, and perhaps even a sunken bathtub (with Jacuzzi in the poshest places). Many garden bathrooms have a partially open roof – never compromising your privacy, of course, but ideal for star-gazing or even a private shower in the rain.

Bali's other big draw is its proliferation of elegant Hindu **temples**, particularly the spectacular island temple of Tanah Lot and the extensive Besakih complex on the slopes of Gunung Agung. Temple **festivals** are also well worth attending: held throughout the island and at frequent intervals during the year, most are open to tourists.

Both islands hold a number of hiking possibilities, many of them up **volcanoes**. The best is undoubtedly the climb to the crater lake of Lombok's **Gunung Rinjani** – one of the highest peaks in Indonesia – though the ascent to the summit of Bali's

▼ In the shadow of Gunung Batur

10

▲ Padang Bai

**Gunung Batur** is less arduous and therefore more popular. Bali's sole **national park**, Bali Barat, has relatively few interesting trails, but is a rewarding place for **bird-watching**, as is the area around Danau Bratan in the centre of the island. Even if you don't want to go hiking, it's worth considering a trip to the northern hills for the change of scenery and refreshing temperatures; the little village of **Munduk** makes a satisfying focus.

> Despite the attractions of the beach resorts, most visitors also venture inland to experience more traditional island life

# When to go

L ocated in the **tropics**, just eight degrees south of the equator, Bali and Lombok enjoy fairly constant year-round temperatures, averaging 27°C in coastal areas and the hills around Ubud, and 22°C in the central volcanoes around Kintamani. Both islands are hit by an annual **monsoon**, which brings rain, wind, and a sometimes unbearable 97-percent humidity from October through to March.

The **best time to visit** is outside the monsoon season, from May to September, though monsoons are, like many other events in Indonesia, notoriously unpunctual, and you should be prepared to get rained on in Ubud at any time of year. However, the prospect of a daily rainstorm shouldn't put

11

you off: you're far more likely to get an hour-long downpour than day-long drizzle; mountain-climbing, though, is both unrewarding and dangerous at this time of year. You

should also be aware of the peak **tourist seasons**: resorts on both islands get packed out between mid-June and mid-September and again over the Christmas–New Year period, when prices rocket and rooms can be fully booked for weeks in advance.

## Average monthly temperatures and rainfall

|  | Jan | Feb | Mar | Apr | May | Jun | Jul | Aug | Sep | Oct | Nov | Dec |
|---|---|---|---|---|---|---|---|---|---|---|---|---|
| **Kintamani** | | | | | | | | | | | | |
| °C | 22 | 22 | 22 | 22 | 22 | 21 | 21 | 21 | 22 | 22 | 22 | 22 |
| mm | 444 | 405 | 248 | 174 | 72 | 43 | 30 | 21 | 35 | 50 | 166 | 257 |
| **Kuta** | | | | | | | | | | | | |
| °C | 28 | 28 | 28 | 28 | 27 | 27 | 26 | 26 | 27 | 27 | 28 | 28 |
| mm | 394 | 311 | 208 | 115 | 79 | 67 | 57 | 31 | 43 | 95 | 176 | 268 |
| **Mataram** | | | | | | | | | | | | |
| °C | 27 | 27 | 26 | 26 | 26 | 25 | 25 | 25 | 26 | 27 | 27 | 27 |
| mm | 253 | 254 | 209 | 155 | 84 | 67 | 38 | 21 | 36 | 168 | 250 | 209 |
| **Singaraja** | | | | | | | | | | | | |
| °C | 27 | 27 | 27 | 27 | 28 | 28 | 27 | 27 | 28 | 29 | 28 | 28 |
| mm | 318 | 318 | 201 | 123 | 57 | 36 | 31 | 7 | 21 | 54 | 115 | 180 |
| **Ubud** | | | | | | | | | | | | |
| °C | 27 | 27 | 27 | 27 | 27 | 26 | 26 | 26 | 26 | 27 | 27 | 27 |
| mm | 412 | 489 | 274 | 224 | 101 | 172 | 128 | 132 | 142 | 350 | 374 | 398 |

▼ Early morning, Pura Lempuyang Luhur

# 31

## things not to miss

*It's not possible to see everything that Bali and Lombok have to offer in a single trip — and we don't suggest you try. What follows is a selective and subjective taste of the islands' highlights: memorable places to stay, outstanding beaches, spectacular hikes and exquisite crafts. They're arranged in five colour-coded categories, so you can browse through the very best things to see, do, buy and experience. All highlights have a page reference to take you straight into the Guide, where you can find out more.*

**01 Wongayagede** Page **353** • A cool retreat secluded high in the foothills of Gunung Batukau, close by the atmospheric temple of Pura Luhur Batukau.

**02 South Lombok beaches** Page **433** • Some of the most glorious coastline on the islands features sweeping bays and pristine coves between dramatic headlands.

**04 Bali Museum, Denpasar** Page **101** • A good ethnological introduction to traditional life on the island.

**03 Nusa Penida's south coast** Page **263** • Stunning limestone cliffs rise sheer from the crashing ocean.

**05 Sunrise from Gunung Batur** Page **302** • Pre-dawn climbers of Gunung Batur are rewarded by a fabulous sunrise silhouetting Abang, Agung and Rinjani to the east.

**06 Rice-paddies of Iseh and Sidemen** Page **282** • Among the most beautiful of the many sweeping, soaring terraces carved from the hillsides that adorn the islands.

**08 Pemuteran** Page **370** • Appealingly low-key beach haven on the northwest coast, close to some of Bali's most spectacular reefs.

**09**

**Kerta Gosa paintings, Klungkung** Page **242** • Intricate and superbly crafted examples of classical Balinese paintings.

## 10
### South Bali nightlife
Page **130**

Start off in one of Kuta's boisterous Aussie pubs before moving on to a sophisticated DJ-bar in trendy Seminyak.

## 11
### Gunung Agung
Page **251**

A perfectly conical summit, impressively visible from much of Bali.

## 12
### Temple festivals
Page **64**

Every one of Bali's 20,000 Hindu temples holds at least one annual festival to entertain the gods with processions, offerings and music.

**13 Tirtagangga Water Palace** Page **279** • Soothing pools amidst pretty gardens, surrounded by ricefields and impressive mountains.

**14 Street food** Page **56** • Spicy fruit salad, chicken saté and noodle soup are just a few of the local specialities sold from handcarts and food stalls on nearly every street corner.

**16 Gili Islands** Page **399** • Pure white sand, crystal-clear turquoise waters and a laid-back atmosphere make these perennial favourites well worth a visit.

**15 Seafood barbecues, Jimbaran** Page **138** • Fresh fish grilled to order on the beach.

**17** **Ubud** Page **179** • The arty heart of Bali has it all: beautifully sited accommodation, great restaurants, masses of craft shops, and rice fields in every direction.

**18** **Kecak dance** Page **475** • Unforgettable spectacle starring an *a cappella* chorus of at least fifty men.

**19** **Lombok crafts** Page **387** • Textiles, pottery, basketware, carving, furniture... great-value crafts for even the most avid shopper.

**20** **Sanur** Page **151** • Sumptuous hotel gardens and a distinct village atmosphere make this one of south Bali's nicest resorts.

**21** **Shopping** Page **76** • A tantalizing range of goodies, including fashions in Kuta, homewares in Seminyak, arts and crafts in Ubud, and pottery on Lombok.

**22 Gamelan music** Page **468** • The frenetic syncopations of the Balinese xylophone provide the island's national soundtrack.

**23 Diving and snorkelling** Page **70** • Teeming shallow reefs, submerged canyons and visiting oceanic sunfish are just a few of the underwater attractions.

## 24 Learning to paint, carve, cook or dance

Page **214** • Ubud is the best place to take short, tourist-oriented courses in Balinese crafts and performing arts.

## 25 Spas Page **73** •

Pamper yourself with some of the local beauty treatments, including the famous *mandi lulur* turmeric scrub.

## 26 Tanah Lot Page **344** •

Bali's most photographed temple sits serenely atop its own tiny island.

**27 Climbing Rinjani** Page **417** •
The most challenging and rewarding climb on the islands takes in forest, rocky peaks and a dramatic crater-lake.

**28 Pura Meduwe Karang**
Page **319** • A wonderfully exuberant example of Bali's highly ornate northern temple architecture.

**29 Nusa Lembongan** Page **254**
• Laid-back island life, surf-breaks, diving and snorkelling sites and great beaches are all just a short boat ride from the mainland.

**30 Barong-Rangda dance**
Page **474** • This theatrical enactment of the battle between good and evil makes for a gripping show.

24

**31** **Neka Art Museum, Ubud** Page **198** • A breathtaking selection of the finest paintings in Bali, from seventeenth-century narratives to 1960s' expressionism and contemporary abstracts.

# Basics

# Basics

# Getting there

There's no shortage of international and domestic flights to Bali's only airport, Ngurah Rai Airport – sometimes referred to as being in Denpasar, though it's actually 3km south of Kuta and 11km south of Denpasar (see p.114 for full details). Lombok's Selaparang Airport, 2km north of Mataram, is much less busy, served mainly by domestic Indonesian carriers, but also by the Singapore Airlines subsidiary Silk Air.

The most expensive times to fly to Bali and Lombok are during **high season**, which on most airlines runs from the beginning of July through to the middle or end of August and also includes most of December and the first half of January. Flights get booked solid during these peak periods and should be reserved several weeks in advance. Prices drop considerably at other times of the year.

You can often cut costs by going through a specialist **flight agent** – either a consolidator, who buys up blocks of tickets from the airlines and sells them at a discount, or a discount agent, who may also offer insurance and tours, or even a few nights' free accommodation. Periodic **special offers** (direct from airlines, through flight agents, or on the Web) are invariably good deals, although they may come with restrictions. Many airlines and discount travel **websites** offer you the opportunity to book your tickets, hotels and holiday packages online, cutting out the costs of agents, but beware of non-refundable, non-changeable deals. Almost all airlines have their own websites,

offering flight tickets that can sometimes be just as cheap, and are often more flexible.

If Bali or Lombok is only one stop on a longer journey, you might want to consider buying a **Round-the-World** (RTW) ticket. Some travel agents can sell you an "off-the-shelf" ticket that will have you touching down in up to six cities (Denpasar is on many itineraries); others will tailor-make one for you. The only way to include Lombok on such a ticket is to go via Bali.

## Organized tours and packages

Options with tour operators are varied, including small group trips, private itineraries, resort holidays, activity trips and stops in Bali or Lombok as part of a multi-centre trip around Asia. Inevitably, package tours are more expensive and less spontaneous than travelling independently, but if you have limited time or want everything organized for you, they can be useful. You may be able to add some independent travel onto your organized trip and fly back at a later date – check with the operator.

## Tying the knot

Plenty of companies offer packages catering for those wishing to **get married** in Bali, taking care of all the practical details and advising on the necessary (and considerable) paperwork and formalities ahead of the wedding day. Prices vary enormously and it's important to check exactly what is and isn't included. Bali Weddings International (Ⓦ www.baliweddingsinternational.com) and Bali Paradise Weddings (Ⓦ www.baliparadiseweddings.com) get good reports. Some top-class hotels, including the *Bali Intercontinental Resort* at Jimbaran Bay, will also plan the entire event for you; many boutique hotels (see Basics, p.54) are happy to host wedding parties and some, like *Puri Taman Sari* in Mengwi (Ⓦ www.balitamansari .com), also arrange traditional wedding processions and entertainment. For something unusual, Bali International Diving Professionals (Ⓦ www.bidp-balidiving .com) arrange **underwater weddings**.

With all organized packages a large chunk of the price goes on the flight, and the range of accommodation on offer tends to be from the mid to the top end of the market taking in extremely good-value, no-frills places up to some of the plushest hotels on the islands. The majority of hotels used by tour operators are in the Sanur, Legian, Tuban and Nusa Dua areas on Bali, with some available in Ubud, and on Lombok in Senggigi, the *Oberoi* or *Novotel Lombok*. In addition to operators who sell package deals, there are also plenty of tailor-made specialists who will assemble a trip to your specifications and make all the arrangements for you.

Walking and hiking tours, activity trips and tours based on art, crafts and culture have become especially popular in Bali, and there's a range of surf or dive packages at every level of ability, experience and budget.

## From the UK and Ireland

There are no non-stop flights **from the UK or Ireland** to Bali. Singapore Airlines and Qantas/British Airways (code share) usually offer the fastest, most comfortable London–Denpasar flights; both require a (short) transfer in Singapore, but can get you to Bali in as little as 17hr. They are often very competitively priced against the other major airlines that serve Bali, most of which require longer transit times at airports en route, sometimes pushing journey times up to around 22hr. All fares quoted below include tax.

From London, **low-season fares** cost from £500, but in **high season** you're usually looking at a minimum of £700. Flying from elsewhere in the UK, you'll need to add on the return fare to London; from Ireland, it may be cheaper to go via Amsterdam or Frankfurt.

Many travellers stop in Denpasar en route between London and **Australia**: most Qantas/BA tickets should allow you to do this for free, with prices from £625 return to Perth or £700 to Sydney. A typical one-year open **RTW ticket** from London taking in Bangkok, Denpasar, Sydney and Los Angeles can cost as little as £800.

### To Lombok

The most convenient way of getting **to Lombok** is to fly non-stop London–Singapore with Singapore Airlines and then change on to their subsidiary carrier, Silk Air, for the non-stop flight to Mataram (3 weekly; 3hr); the entire trip can be done in 17hr. The complete return journey from London costs around £680 in low season, £820 at peak times. You can buy the return Singapore–Mataram flight direct from the Silk Air website for about £155, but it's hard to find a London–Singapore flight for under £500. Alternatively, take the cheapest available flight to Bali, from where a flight to Mataram costs about £30 return, a bus from £5 return, a tourist boat £13 return or a ferry from £2 return. For full details on getting from Bali to Lombok, see p.380.

### Airlines in the UK and Ireland

**British Airways** UK ☎0870/850 9850, Republic of Ireland ☎1890/626 747, ⊛www.britishairways.com.

**Cathay Pacific** UK ☎020/8834 8888, ⊛www.cathaypacific.com/uk.

**Garuda Indonesia** UK ☎020/7467 8600, ⊛www.garuda-indonesia.com.

**KLM** UK ☎0870/507 4074, ⊛www.klm.com.

**Malaysia Airlines (MAS)** UK ☎0870/607 9090, Republic of Ireland ☎01/676 1561, ⊛www.mas.com.my.

**Qantas** UK ☎0845/774 7767, ⊛www.qantas.co.uk.

**Royal Brunei Airlines** UK ☎020/7584 6660, ⊛www.bruneiair.com.

**Silk Air** Contact via Singapore Airlines ⊛www.silkair.com.

**Singapore Airlines** UK ☎0870/608 8886, Republic of Ireland ☎01/671 0722, ⊛www.singaporeair.com.

**Thai Airways** UK ☎0870/606 0911, ⊛www.thaiair.com.

### Flight agents in the UK and Ireland

**Apex Travel** ☎01/241 8000, ⊛www.apextravel.ie.

**Austravel** ☎0870/166 2020, ⊛www.austravel.com.

**Bridge the World** ☎0870/814 4400, ⊛www.bridgetheworld.com.

**Lee Travel** ☎021/427 7111, ⊛www.leetravel.ie.

**North South Travel** ☎01245/608291, ⊛www.northsouthtravel.co.uk.

**Quest Worldwide** ☎0870/442 3542, ⊛www.questtravel.com.

**STA Travel** ☎0870/160 0599, ⊛www.statravel.co.uk.

**Trailfinders** UK ☎0845/058 5858, ⊛www.trailfinders.com, Republic of Ireland ☎01/677 7888, ⊛www.trailfinders.ie.

Travel Bag ☎0870/890 1456, ⓦwww.travelbag.co.uk.

USIT Northern Ireland ☎028/9032 7111, Republic of Ireland ☎01/602 1904, ⓦwww.usit.ie.

## Online

cheapflights.com ⓦwww.cheapflights.com.
ebookers ☎0800/082 3000, ⓦwww.ebookers.com.
expedia.co.uk ⓦwww.expedia.co.uk.

## UK tour operators

**The Adventure Company** ☎01420/541007, ⓦwww.travelbag-adventures.co.uk. Offers small-group adventures on Bali and Lombok that get well off the beaten track.

**Audley** ☎01869/276200, ⓦwww.audleytravel.com. Tailor-made specialists, with lots of itinerary suggestions for Bali and Lombok, plus ideas on extending to other islands.

**Explore** ☎0870/333 4001, ⓦwww.explore.co.uk. Established adventure holiday company specializing in overland trips.

**Footprint Adventures** ☎01522/804929, ⓦwww.footprint-adventures.com. Trekking, wildlife and birding specialist offering small-group trips including Bali together with Java, Kalimantan, Sulawesi and Sumatra.

**Hayes and Jarvis** ☎0870/366 1636, ⓦwww.hayes-jarvis.com. A range of beach-based holidays in Bali and Lombok, mostly in the resorts in the south and multi-centre trips in various locations around the islands.

**Holidays 4 Less** ☎020/7400 7060, ⓦwww.holidays4less.co.uk. A good range of holidays in south Bali beach hotels or Ubud, with often extremely good deals at three-star hotels and above.

**Imaginative Traveller** ☎0800/316 2717, ⓦwww.imaginative-traveller.com. Imaginative trips that get off the beaten track – including one with a trek to the crater rim on Rinjani – optional diving and snorkelling, and jungle and beach walking.

**Kuoni Travel** ☎01306/740500, ⓦwww.kuoni.co.uk. Hotel-based holidays in Bali and Lombok that can be combined with stays in other parts of Asia or Australia, or with a Bali Experience Tour exploring the island.

**Magic of the Orient** ☎0117/311 6050, ⓦwww.magicoftheorient.com. Holidays based in fine hotels on Bali and Lombok that can be combined with a five-day Bali Discovery itinerary or a cruise east to Komodo.

**Silk Steps** ☎01278/722460, ⓦwww.silksteps.co.uk. Tailor-made specialist with a large and appealing selection of itineraries including Bali and Lombok alongside Java, Kalimantan, Sulawesi and Komodo.

**Symbiosis Expedition Planning** ☎0845/123 2844, ⓦwww.symbiosis-travel.com. Mostly tailor-made holidays, which can include diving, trekking, white-water rafting, mountain biking or anything to do with the arts. They also operate small-group specialist trips including cycling, bird-watching and art tours.

# From the US and Canada

There's a big choice of flights to Bali **from North America**, although none goes direct. Continental is the only North American carrier currently serving Bali. Flights leaving from the **west coast** cross the Pacific to Asian and Australasian hubs such as Taipei, Seoul, Tokyo, Hong Kong or Sydney, from where there are flights on to Bali. The best journey times are around 24 hours (crossing the Pacific on one hop), although considerably more than this is not unusual; slower journeys put down midway, perhaps in Honolulu and/or Guam, while some schedules involve overnighting en route. There are occasional offers below US$900, but typically you'll be looking at a **fare** of $1300 in low season and $2000-plus in high.

From the **east coast**, check out airlines that take a northern trajectory 'over the top'; for example, China Airlines' New York–Anchorage–Taipei route is just 16 hours' flying time. It's also worth looking at routes via one of the major European gateways – typically London, Frankfurt or Amsterdam. These also work out, at best, around 24 hours' journey time, but you'll need to look carefully at how many stops there are. **Fares** are around $2000 minimum in the low, $2700 in the high season.

**RTW tickets** put together by consolidators can cost about the same as the return prices quoted above and typically start from New York or Los Angeles and include combinations of Sydney, Denpasar, Jakarta, Singapore, Bangkok, Rome, Milan, London or Paris. More limited multi-stop tickets with about six stops in Asia can be even cheaper. Yet another possibility, which could also work out cheaper, is Cathay Pacific's "**All Asia Pass**", which costs from $1299 including flights from North America to Hong Kong with stops in all or some of 17 cities over 21 days. High season adds $350 to the cost, and you can buy extra time.

If Lombok is your destination, you'll either fly from Denpasar on a local airline, or to Singapore with Singapore Airlines and then take the three-hour flight to Mataram on their subsidiary Silk Air.

## Airlines in the US and Canada

**Cathay Pacific** ☎1-800/233-2742, ⓦwww
.cathay-usa.com.
**China Airlines** ☎1-800/227-5118, ⓦwww
.china-airlines.com.
**Continental Airlines** ☎1-800/231-0856,
ⓦwww.continental.com.
**EVA Airways** ☎1-800/695-1188, ⓦwww.evaair
.com.
**Garuda Indonesia** US ☎1-800/342-7832,
Canada ☎1-800/663-2254, ⓦwww
.garuda-indonesia.com.
**Japan Airlines** ☎1-800/525-3663, ⓦwww.jal
.co.jp.
**Qantas** ☎1-800/227-4500, ⓦwww.qantas.com.au.
**Singapore Airlines** US☎1-800/742-3333,
Canada ☎1-800/387-8039 or 1-800/663-3046,
ⓦwww.singaporeair.com.

## Flight agents in the US and Canada

**Air Brokers International** ☎1-800/883-3273,
ⓦwww.airbrokers.com.
**Airtreks** ☎1-877/AIRTREKS, ⓦwww.airtreks.com.
**Educational Travel Center** ☎1-800/747-5551 or
608/256-5551, ⓦwww.edtrav.com.
**Long Haul Travel** ☎1-866/548-4548 or 416/360-
7711, ⓦwww.longhaultravel.com.
**STA Travel** US ☎1-800/329-9537, Canada ☎1-
888/427-5639, ⓦwww.statravel.com.
**TFI Tours** ☎1-800/745-8000 or 212/736-1140,
ⓦwww.lowestairprice.com.
**Travel Cuts** US ☎1-800/592-CUTS, Canada ☎1-
888/246-9762, ⓦwww.travelcuts.com.
**Travelosophy** US ☎1-800/332-2687, ⓦwww
.itravelosophy.com.
**Worldtek Travel** ☎1-800/243-1723, ⓦwww
.worldtek.com.

### Online

ⓦwww.cheapflights.com (in US), ⓦwww
.cheapflights.ca (in Canada)
ⓦwww.cheaptickets.com
ⓦwww.expedia.com (in US), ⓦwww.expedia
.ca (in Canada).
ⓦwww.hotwire.com
ⓦwww.priceline.com
ⓦwww.site59.com
ⓦwww.skyauction.com
ⓦwww.travelocity.com (in US), ⓦwww
.travelocity.ca (in Canada)

## Tour operators in the US and Canada

**Absolute Asia** ☎1-800/736-8187, ⓦwww
.absoluteasia.com. Private custom-designed trips.

They can put together themed, country-specific or
multi-country trips around particular activities or
special interests.
**Adventure Center** ☎1-800/228-8747 or
510/654-1879, ⓦwww.adventure-center.com.
Hiking and "soft adventure" specialists offering
moderate activities including trekking and snorkelling.
**Asian Pacific Adventures** ☎1-800/825-1680 or
818/881-2745, ⓦwww.asianpacificadventures
.com. Special small-group tours including "Bali:
Through an Artist's Eye", a fourteen-day trip based
in Ubud concentrating on art and crafts, and "An
Indonesian Cultural Odyssey" covering Bali, Borobudur
and Sulawesi in fifteen days.
**Backroads** ☎1-800/462-2848 or 510/527-1555,
ⓦwww.backroads.com. Cycling, hiking and multisport tours; the nine-day "Bali Multisport" includes
cycling, hiking and snorkelling.
**Goway Travel** ☎1-800/387-8850, ⓦwww.goway
.com. Canada-based operator with plenty of ideas for
Bali and Lombok trips that can include other Asian
destinations.
**Nature Expeditions International** ☎1-800/869-
0639, ⓦwww.naturexp.com. Experts in adventure trips
that include a large element of culture. "Treasures of Bali
and Java" lasts twelve days and includes white-water
rafting, cycling in the Batur area and learning gamelan.
Lectures are included and extensions are possible to
Borneo, Komodo and Sumatra.
**Pacific Delight Tours** ☎1-800/221-7179,
ⓦwww.pacificdelighttours.com. Specialists in
deluxe tours. Their fifteen-day "Asian Vistas" trip
combines Bali with Hong Kong, Singapore and
Bangkok.

# From Australia and New Zealand

**From Australia**, both Australian Air (a Qantas subsidiary) and the Balinese airline Air
Paradise run non-stop flights to Denpasar
(5hr 30min from Sydney, 4hr from Perth, 2hr
from Darwin). Low-season fares from Sydney, Melbourne, Brisbane, Cairns or Adelaide
average A$1050 plus tax; in high season,
prices start at A$1310 plus tax. From Perth,
expect to pay A$980/1270 plus tax; from
Darwin reckon on A$930/990 plus tax.

There are no non-stop flights from **New
Zealand** to Bali, but Garuda run two weekly
flights from Auckland via Brisbane, or you
can fly with Qantas to Australia from Auckland, Christchurch or Wellington, changing
on to the Qantas subsidiary, Australian Airlines, in either Sydney, Melbourne or Perth
for connections to Bali. Through-fares start

from NZ\$1270 in low season, NZ\$1560 high, or an extra NZ\$200–300 from Christchurch or Wellington.

There are no direct **flights to Lombok** from either country, so you'll either need to change in Bali on to a half-hour domestic Denpasar–Mataram flight (cheapest if booked through a travel agent in Kuta, Denpasar or Sanur; see p.33 for details of domestic airlines) or take one of the cheaper ferry routes, as described on p.380.

## Airlines in Australia and New Zealand

**Air Paradise** Australia ☎13 66 66, ✆www.airparadise.com.au.
**Australian Airlines** Australia ☎13 13 13, ✆australianairlines.com.au.
**Garuda** Australia ☎02/9334 9970, New Zealand ☎09/366 1862, ✆www.garuda-indonesia.com.
**Qantas** Australia ☎13 13 13, New Zealand ☎0800/808767, ✆www.qantas.com.au.

## Flight agents in Australia and New Zealand

**Destinations Unlimited** New Zealand ☎09/414 1680, ✆www.travel-nz.com.
**Flight Centre** Australia ☎13 16 00, ✆www.flightcentre.com.au; New Zealand ☎0800/243544, ✆www.flightcentre.co.nz.
**Harvey World Travel** Australia ☎13 27 57, ✆www.harveyworld.com.au; New Zealand ☎09/478 7118, ✆www.harveyworld.co.nz.
**STA Travel** Australia ☎1300/360 960, ✆www.statravel.com.au; New Zealand ☎0508/782 872, ✆www.statravel.co.nz.
**Trailfinders** Australia ☎02/9247 7666, ✆www.trailfinders.com.au.
**Travel.com** Australia ☎02/9249 5444 or 1300/120482, ✆www.travel.com.au; New Zealand ☎0800/468332, ✆www.travel.co.nz.
**Travel Online** New Zealand ✆www.travelonline.co.nz.
**Travelshop** Australia ☎1300/767908, ✆www.travelshop.com.au.

## Tour operators in Australia and New Zealand

**Allways Dive Expeditions** Australia ☎1800/338239, ✆www.allwaysdive.com.au. Dive and accommodation packages to some of the best sites in Bali (from A\$990 per week plus flights) plus liveaboard trips east to Komodo.
**Bali Travel Service** Australia ☎02/9264 5895. Range of ever-changing accommodation package deals.

**Golden Bali Travel** Australia ☎08/8227 1522, ✆www.goldenbali.com. Flights, accommodation, tours and weddings.
**Intrepid Adventure Travel** Australia ☎1300/360 887, ✆www.intrepidtravel.com.au. Well-regarded small-group adventure tour operator that uses local transport and traveller-style accommodation. Their fifteen-day Islands of the Gods (A\$630/NZ\$715 plus flights) includes Ubud, Lovina and Gunung Batur, the Gili Islands, and Tetebatu and Senggigi on Lombok.
**Plan It Holidays** Australia ☎03/9245 0747, ✆www.planit.com.au. Discounted flights and accommodation packages (four nights from Perth for A\$660) to the main resorts in Bali.
**San Michele Travel** Australia ☎1800/222 244, ✆www.asiatravel.com.au. Famous Bali specialist whose eleven-night "Bali Experience" (A\$295) includes accommodation in Sanur, Ubud, Lovina and Kuta, plus all transfers.
**Surf Travel Company** Australia ☎1800/687 873, New Zealand ☎09/473 8388, ✆www.surftravel.com.au. Flights and accommodation packages to the best surf spots in Bali and Lombok, including seven nights all-in to Uluwatu for A\$1135, or \$750 for a six-night yacht charter from Bali to the breaks off Nusa Lembongan, Lombok and Sumbawa.
**Travelshop** Australia ☎1800/108 108, ✆www.travelshop.com.au. Good-value all-in "Hot Bali" flight-plus-hotel deals; from \$660 for four nights in Kuta.

# Travel from Southeast Asia

It's relatively easy to fly to Bangkok and then continue your journey to Bali or Lombok overland via Malaysia and Singapore.

There's a choice of **train** routes from Bangkok to Singapore, via Penang or Kuala Lumpur (KL), described in detail on ⓦwww.seat61.com/Malaysia.htm; for the current timetable and ticket prices, see the Malaysian Railways website ⓦwww.ktmb.com.my (48hr; about £29/US$53 for a second-class sleeper). **Buses** and share-taxis from Hat Yai in south Thailand to Penang run throughout the day (about £9/$13 per person; 6hr). There are also long-distance buses and minibuses from the tourist centres of Krabi, Phuket and Surat Thani to Penang, KL and Singapore.

From Malaysia and Singapore, you have a choice of **ferry** routes into Indonesia. A variety of slow ferries and high-speed boats connect Penang with Medan in northern Sumatra (4–14hr), and Melaka with Dumai, south of Medan (2hr 30min). You can reach the islands of Batam, Bintan and Karimun, in Indonesia's Riau archipelago, from Johor Bahru in southern Malaysia or from Singapore.

Singapore Airlines and Garuda each **fly** Singapore–Denpasar at least once a day, and Silk Air, a Singapore Airlines subsidiary, operate three flights a week from Singapore to Lombok.

## From around Indonesia

The visa situation will determine the feasibility or otherwise of a leisurely journey **through Indonesia** to Bali or Lombok, taking in several other islands en route, though with excellent air links supplementing land and sea routes across the archipelago, the number of possible routes is almost limitless. Details on ferry crossings between Java and Bali are given on p.361, Bali and Lombok on p.380, and Sumbawa and Lombok on p.426.

When booking flights or working out bus and ferry connections, remember that the Indonesian archipelago spans three **time** zones: Sumatra, Java, West Kalimantan and Central Kalimantan are on Western Indonesian Time (GMT+7); Bali, Lombok, the Nusa Tenggara islands, Sulawesi, South Kalimantan and East Kalimantan are on Central Indonesian Time (GMT+8); and West Papua and Maluku are on Eastern Indonesian Time (GMT+9).

## "Overland"

Travelling **"overland" from Java**, the easiest and cheapest option is to buy a through-ticket on a public bus to Denpasar (Ubung terminal) or the Bertais/Mandalika/Sweta terminal on the eastern edge of the Mataram-Ampenan-Cakranegara-Sweta conurbation on Lombok. Passengers stay on the same bus all the way through, including the ferry crossing. From Jakarta, reckon on paying around Rp250,000–275,000 for air-conditioning and reclining seats to Denpasar (24hr) or Lombok (32hr); from Yogyakarta, Rp165,000–200,000 (15hr/22hr). For the hardy, there are services from further afield, including Medan on Sumatra (72hr/84hr). There are also direct Surabaya–Singaraja buses, which pass through Lovina in north Bali.

Travelling **from Australia** and then overland from eastern Indonesia, the most popular route begins in Kupang or Dili, from where you can island-hop all the way to Lombok and Bali or get a Pelni ferry (see below). There are direct buses from Flores – Ruteng (36hr) and Labuhanbajo (24hr) – and Sumbawa – Sape (14hr), Bima (12hr), Domphu (10hr), Sumbawa Besar (6hr) and Taliwang (5hr) – to Lombok where you can then connect to Bali.

## By sea

The national shipping company is Pelni (ⓦwww.pelni.co.id), which runs a fleet of passenger ships, each completing a fortnightly circuit of different inter-island routes. However, timetables can be confusing (and are reissued frequently), so before you travel you should definitely contact one of the Pelni offices (see below). On Bali, the Pelni port is at **Benoa Harbour** (Pelabuhan Benoa; see p.166) southwest of Sanur; on Lombok, it's at **Lembar** (see p.392). Each ship has four cabin classes and one deck class (actually a large air-con lounge), and all rates include meals. **Fares** in the most luxurious class cost considerably more than airfares, while the cheapest are about 25 percent of this. Children pay two-thirds of the adult fare. Booking ahead is vital. There are two Pelni services serving Bali and Lombok: *KM AWU* run Benoa–Lembar–Waingapu–Ende–Kupang–Kalabahi–Maumere–Makassar–Pare-Pare–Berau–Tarakan–Nunukan–Larantuka and return. *KM Tilongkabila* run Lembar–Bima–Labuanbajo–Makasar–Bai-Bau–Raha–Kendari–Kolonedale–Luwuk–Bitung and back.

## By air

There are a multitude of **domestic airlines** connecting Bali and the rest of Indonesia and several hopping between Bali and Lombok. Fares tend to be competitive, but it's always worth shopping around – easily done at Ngurah Rai Airport where all of the airlines below have ticket offices. **Fare** structures are incredibly complicated and largely unfathomable; however, expect to pay around Rp700,000 between Denpasar and Jakarta, Rp380,000 between Denpasar and Surabaya, and Rp245,000 between Denpasar and Mataram – all one-way. See p.86 for departure taxes.

### Domestic airlines

Unless otherwise stated, telephone numbers are for Ngurah Rai Airport counters, Bali.

**Adam Air** ☎0361/227999. Flies Denpasar–Jakarta.
**Awair** ✆www.awairlines.com. National call centre ☎08041/333333. Denpasar–Jakarta.
**Batavia** ☎0361/254955, ✆www.batavia-air.co.id. Denpasar–Jakarta.
**Bouraq** ☎0361/241397. Denpasar–Surabaya–Jakarta.
**Citilink** Selaparang Airport ☎0370/622987 ext 246 and at *Hotel Lombok Raya*, Jl Panca Usaha 11, Cakranegara ☎0370/649999. Mataram–Yogyakarta–Jakarta, Mataram–Surabaya–Jakarta.
**Garuda** ☎0361/751011 ext 5204, ✆www.garuda-indonesia.com. Bali: *Sanur Beach Hotel* ☎0361/288011 ext 158; *Kuta Paradiso* hotel in Tuban ☎0361/761414; Jl Melati 61, Denpasar ☎0361/254747. Lombok: Garuda, Selaparang Airport ☎ & ✆0370/6646846 and at *Hotel Lombok Raya*, Jl Panca Usaha 11, Cakranegara ☎0370/638259. Denpasar–Surabaya, Denpasar–Yogyakarta, Denpasar–Jakarta.
**GT Air** ☎ & ✆0361/759768. Denpasar–Labuhanbajo.
**Kartika Airlines** ☎0361/7405412. Denpasar–Ende–Kupang.
**Lion Air** ☎0361/23666, ✆www.lionair.co.id. Jl Teuku Umar 15a, Denpasar ☎0361/263787, *Sahid Legi Mataram* hotel ☎0370/629111, ✆636213. Denpasar–Yogyakarta, Denpasar–Jakarta, Denpasar–Ujung Pandan–Manado.
**Mandala** ☎0361/751011. Jl Diponegoro No 98 Blok D23, Komplek Pertokoan Kerta Wijaya Plaza, Denpasar ☎0361/222571. Denpasar–Surabaya–Jakarta, Denpasar–Yogyakarta.
**Merpati** ✆www.merpati.co.id. Bali: Jl Melati 51, Denpasar ☎0361/23535. Lombok: Jl Pejanggik 69 ☎0370/621111. Selaparang Airport ☎0370/633691. Denpasar – Mataram.
**Pelita** ✆www.pelita-air.com. Bali and Lombok: book through travel agents. Denpasar–Waingapu–Maumere–Kupang, Denpasar–Bima–Ende–Kupang, Denpasar–Waingapu–Ende–Kupang, Denpasar–Surabaya.
**Sriwijaya Air** ☎0361/745 2727. Jl Teuku Umar 97B, Denpasar ☎0361/228461. Denpasar–Jakarta.
**Star Air** ☎0361/753775. Denpasar–Jakarta, Denpasar–Kupang, Denpasar–Surabaya.
**Wings** Contact at Lion Air. Denpasar–Mataram.

# Visas and red tape

Visa requirements for Indonesia tightened considerably in February 2004, but caused such widespread condemnation that they may be revised again soon: check embassy websites for the latest details.

At the time of writing, only citizens of eleven countries are eligible for **visa-free visits** to Indonesia. Citizens of 35 other countries, including Britain, Ireland, most European states, Australia, New Zealand, Canada, the USA and India, are able to buy thirty-day visas on arrival (VOA). Citizens of all other countries, including the Netherlands and Sweden, must buy their visas in advance.

For citizens of eligible countries, visas for **stays of up to thirty days** can be bought **on arrival** if entering and exiting Indonesia via one of the country's 35 **designated gateway ports**. In Bali, the visa-issuing gateways are Ngurah Rai Airport and Padang Bai port; in Lombok, it's just Selaparang Airport. The fee of US$25 is payable in almost any currency; your passport must be valid for at least six months and you must be able to show proof of onward travel (a return or onward ticket). If you're staying seven days or fewer, the fee is US$10. The seven-day and thirty-day visas on arrival are non-extendable.

If you're not on the list of 35 countries, if you're entering via a non-designated gateway, or if you want to **stay for up to sixty days**, you must buy a **visa in advance** from an Indonesian embassy or consulate. Forms and detailed lists of requirements can be downloaded from most Indonesian embassy websites (see below). Fees for single-entry sixty-day visas are £35/US$35/AUS$60; for multiple entry £125/US$75/AUS$165. In addition, you will need two passport photos and proof of onward travel (a return or onward ticket), and your passport must be valid for at least six months, or one year if applying for a multiple-entry visa. Many but not all visa-issuing embassies also require a recent bank statement showing a minimum balance of £1000 and a recent letter from your employer, educational establishment, bank manager, accountant or solicitor cer-tifying your obligation to return home/leave Indonesia by the designated date.

Penalties for **overstaying your visa** are severe. On departure, you'll be fined $20 for each day you've overstayed up to a limit of sixty days. If you've exceeded the sixty-day barrier you're liable for a five-year prison sentence or a fine of Rp25,000,000.

The Denpasar government **immigration office** (*kantor immigrasi*) is in Renon, at the corner of Jalan Panjaitan and Jalan Raya Puputan (Mon–Thurs 8am–3pm, Fri 8–11am, Sat 8am–2pm; ☎0361/227828). The Lombok *kantor immigrasi* is at Jl Udayana 2, Mataram (same hours; ☎0370/632520).

## Indonesian embassies and consulates abroad

**Australia** 8 Darwin Ave, Yarralumla, Canberra, ACT 2600 ☎02/6250 8600, ⓦwww.kbri-canberra.org.au; 20 Harry Chan Ave, Darwin, NT 0801 ☎08/8941 0048; 72 Queen Rd, Melbourne, VIC 3004 ☎03/9525 2755, ⓦwww.kjri-melbourne.org; 134 Adelaide Terrace, East Perth, WA 6004 ☎08/9221 5858, ⓦwww.kri-perth.org.au; 236 Maroubra Rd, Maroubra, Sydney, NSW 2035 ☎02/9344 9933, ⓦwww.kjri-sydney.org.

**Canada** 55 Parkdale Ave, Ottawa, ON K1Y 1E5 ☎613/724-1100, ⓦwww.indonesia-ottawa.org; 129 Jarvis St, Toronto, ON M5C 2H6 ☎416/360-4020, ⓦwww.indonesiatoronto.org; 1630 Alberni St, Vancouver, BC V6G 1A6 ☎604/682-8855, ⓦwww.indonesiavancouver.org.

**Malaysia** 233 Jl Tun Razak, 50400 Kuala Lumpur ☎03/245 2011, ⓦwww.kbrikl.org.my; 723 Jl Anyer Molek, 80000 Johor Bahru ☎07/221 2000; 467 Jl Burma, 10350 Penang ☎04/227412; Lorong Kemajuan, Karamunsing, Kota Kinabalu, Sabah 88817 ☎088/218600.

**New Zealand** 70 Glen Rd, Kelburn, Wellington ☎04/475 8697, ⓦwww.indonesianembassy.org.nz; 2nd floor, Beca Carter Hollings Femer Ltd, 132 Vincent St, Auckland ☎09/308 0842.

Singapore 7 Chatsworth Rd, Singapore 249761
☏ 6737 7422, ⊛ www.kbrisingapura.com.
Thailand 600 Petchaburi Rd, Bangkok 10400
☏ 02/252 3135–40, ⊛ www.kbri-bangkok.com; 19
Sadao Rd, Songkhla 90000 ☏ 074/311 544.
UK and Ireland 38 Grosvenor Sq, London
W1X 9AD (personal callers: 38 Adams Row, W1)
☏ 020/7499 7661, ⊛ www.indonesianembassy.org
.uk. Recorded visa information ☏ 0906/550 8962.
USA 2020 Massachusetts Ave NW, Washington
DC 20036 ☏ 202/775-5200, ⊛ www.
embassyofindonesia.org; 72 E Randolph St,
Chicago, IL 60601 ☏ 312/345-9300, ⊛ www.
indonesiachicago.org; 10900 Richmond Ave,
Houston, TX 77057 ☏ 713/785-1691; 3457 Wilshire
Blvd, Los Angeles, CA 90010 ☏ 213/383-5126; 5 E
68th St, New York, NY 1002 ☏ 212/879-0600–15;
1111 Columbus Ave, San Francisco, CA 94133
☏ 415/474-9571, ⊛ www.kjrisfo.org.
Worldwide listings at ⊛ www.deplu.go.id.

## Foreign embassies and consulates

Most countries maintain an **embassy** in the
Indonesian capital, Jakarta, and some also
have **consulates** in Bali. Your first point of
contact should always be the Bali consulate.

Australia Consulate in Bali: Jl Hayum Wuruk 88b,
Denpasar ☏ 0361/241118, ⊜ bali.congen@dfat
.gov.au. Embassy: Jl H.R. Rasuna Said Kav C15–16,
Kuningan, Jakarta ☏ 021/2550 5555, ⊛ www
.austembjak.or.id.
Canada Contact the Australian consulate in
Denpasar first. Embassy: World Trade Centre, 6th
floor, Jl Jen Sudirman, Kav 29, Jakarta ☏ 021/2550
7800, ⊛ www.dfait-maeci.gc.ca/jakarta.
Ireland Contact the UK consul in Sanur first.
Netherlands Consulate in Bali: c/o KCB Tours, Jl
Raya Kuta 127, Kuta ☏ 0361/751517, ⊛ www
.kcbtours.com/consulate.babon. Embassy: Jl H.R.

Rasuna Said Kav S-3, Kuningan, Jakarta ☏ 021/524
8200, ⊛ www.netherlandsembassy.or.id.
New Zealand Contact the Australian consulate in
Denpasar first. Embassy: Gedung BRII, 23rd floor,
Jl Jen Sudirman, Kav 44, Jakarta ☏ 021/570 9460,
⊜ nzembjak@cbn.net.id.
UK Honorary consul in Bali: Jl Tirta Nadi 20A, Sanur
☏ 0361/270601, ⊜ bcbali@dps.centrin.net.id.
Embassy: Jl M.H. Thamrin 75, Jakarta ☏ 021/315
6264, ⊛ www.britain-in-indonesia.or.id.
USA Consulate in Bali: Jl Hayam Wuruk 188, Renon,
Denpasar ☏ 0361/233605, ⊜ amcobali@indosat
.net.id Embassy: Jl Merdaka Selatan 5, Jakarta
☏ 021/3435 9000, ⊛ www.usembassyjakarta.org.

## Customs regulations

Indonesia's **customs regulations** allow foreign nationals to import one litre of alcohol,
200 cigarettes or 50 cigars or 100g of tobacco, and a reasonable amount of perfume.
Cars, typewriters, TV sets and video cameras
are supposed to be declared on entry and
re-exported on departure. Import restrictions
cover the usual banned items, including narcotics, weapons and pornographic material,
and foreigners are also forbidden to bring in
any printed matter written in Chinese characters, Chinese medicines, and amounts of
Rp5,000,000 or more in Indonesian currency.
Indonesia is a signatory to the Convention on
International Trade in Endangered Species
(CITES), and so forbids import or export of
products that are banned under this treaty,
which include anything made from turtle flesh
or turtle shells (including tortoiseshell jewellery
and ornaments), as well as anything made
from ivory. Indonesian law also prohibits the
export of antiquities and cultural relics, unless
sanctioned by the customs department.

# Information, websites and maps

Following the economic crisis of the late 1990s, Indonesia closed all its overseas Indonesian Tourism Promotion Offices, but there are plans to reopen three – in Australia, Japan and China – by the end of 2005, and these will be run by local PR companies. Otherwise, there's plenty of information about Bali and Lombok on the Internet and in locally produced, free magazines.

## Tourist offices

On Bali and Lombok, you'll find **government tourist offices** (Mon–Thurs 8am–3pm, Fri 8–noon; those in the main tourist centres keep longer hours) in the regency capitals, but though staff should be able to answer straightforward questions they're generally not particularly traveller-oriented; you may get more help from the smaller, locally run information centres in the biggest tourist centres. Kanwil Depparpostel offices are run by the Jakarta-based directorate-general of tourism and give Indonesia-wide information; Diparda offices are run by each of the provinces of Indonesia; and there are smaller concerns operated by the individual districts.

Wherever you go, you'll see signs offering tourist information – but these are usually private operators selling their own tours or renting out transport.

## Tourist publications

A wealth of **free tourist magazines** fills the gap left by the absence of useful tourist information offices. The main half dozen are widely available in mid-range and upmarket hotels and some big-name restaurants and tourist attractions across Bali as well as in Lombok's main tourist centres.

For **Bali**, the most extensive **listings** for upcoming cultural and sporting events, as well as cinema schedules, are carried by the weekly *What's Up? Bali* (Ⓦ www.whatsupbali .com). The fortnightly *the beat* (Ⓦ www.beat mag.com) focuses on Bali's nightlife and carries listings for gigs, parties, clubs, bars and restaurants. The monthly *Bali Plus* (Ⓦ www .baliplus.com) always lists the month's festivals and dance performances, and also recommends selected restaurants, clubs, spas and tourist activities as well as offering general Bali travel advice. The fortnightly newspaper *Bali Travel News* (Ⓦ www.bali-travelnews.com) also details upcoming temple festivals and film schedules, and carries a long directory of useful contacts, but is of most interest for its short but weighty features on Balinese culture and its distinctive Bali-Hindu editorial voice. Cultural and travel articles are the mainstay of several free, large-format monthly glossies, including the recommended *Hello Bali*. On **Lombok**, the monthly *Lombok Times* is the only tourist-oriented newspaper, covering general info on all aspects of visiting Lombok, plus some small features and maps.

## Websites

Only general tourist-oriented **websites** are listed below: online accommodation-booking services are listed on p.54, and other, specialist, sites are mentioned in their relevant sections in Basics.

### General sites

**Bali Blog** Ⓦ www.baliblog.com. An expat blogs his Bali experiences – hiking up Batur, getting married, going surfing – answers questions and offers all sorts of Bali-related advice.

**Bali Paradise Online** Ⓦ www.bali-paradise .com. Wide-ranging site covering everything from traditional architecture to nightlife recommendations – and the weather forecast. Also has a travellers' forum.

**Bali Tourism Authority** Ⓦ www.balitourism authority.net. The official tourist authority site is of most interest for its detailed calendar of temple and cultural festivals.

**Bali Tourism Board** Ⓦ www.bali-tourism-board .com. The official site of nine Balinese tourism associations introduces the island and its culture and covers basic travel necessities.

**Bali Travel News** @ www.bali-travelnews.com.
Short, serious articles on cultural and religious topics
in this online version of the fortnightly free newspaper.
**Gili Islands News** @ news.giliislands.com. Plenty
of short, up-to-date articles on what's happening on
the islands.
**Lombok Hotels** @ www.lombok.com. Small site
featuring a general introduction to tourist spots, plus
links to Lombok hotels.
**Lombok Sumbawa** @ www.lomboksumbawa
.com. General tourist info from the Lombok Sumbawa
Toursim Promotion Board, plus events listings.

## Travellers' forums

**Bali Forum** @ www.baliforum.com
**Bali Travel Forum** @ www.balitravelforum.com
**Lombok and Bali Travel Forums**
@ www.travelforum.org/bali
**Lombok Lovers Forum**
@ groups.msn.com/LombokLovers
**Lonely Planet Thorn Tree**
@ thorntree.lonelyplanet.com
**Mic's Bali Forums** @ micbali.proboards21.com
**Rough Guides Travel Talk**
@ roughguides.atinfopop.com

## Online publications

**Inside Indonesia** @ www.insideindonesia.org.
Web version of the hard-hitting quarterly magazine,
full of articles about political, social and environmental
issues across the archipelago.
**Jakarta Post** @ www.thejakartapost.com.
Domestic Indonesian news.
**Tempo Interactive** @ www.tempointeractive.com.
Online version of Indonesia's respected weekly news
magazine (English-language edition), with headline
stories.

## Government websites

**Australian Department of Foreign Affairs**
@ www.dfat.gov.au
**Canadian Foreign Affairs Department**
@ www.dfait-maeci.gc.ca
**Irish Department of Foreign Affairs**
@ www.irlgov.ie/iveagh
**New Zealand Ministry of Foreign Affairs**
@ www.mft.govt.nz
**UK Foreign and Commonwealth Office**
@ www.fco.gov.uk
**US State Department** @ travel.state.gov

## Maps

There are plenty of **maps** of Bali available
abroad, but it's harder to find maps of Lombok. If you're intending to rent your own
transport, a detailed road map is vital.

For **Bali**, the best options are Periplus
Travel Maps (1:250,000) and *Bali Pathfinder*
(1:200,000; published annually). Both include
some city plans and area maps, but neither
is perfect. *Bali Pathfinder* is only available in
Bali, chiefly in Ubud bookshops; the Periplus
map is on sale worldwide. Periplus also produce the impressive *Bali Street Atlas*, which
is exhaustively indexed and for the most
part very useful, though it's hard to locate
an indexed town or village without knowing which regency it's in. Recommended
regional maps are mentioned in the relevant
guide accounts. One attractive souvenir map
of the whole island is by Studio Satumata
(1:74,000), which shows the mountainous
contours with exceptional clarity; it's sold at
Ganesha Bookstore in Ubud.

For **Lombok**, go for the Periplus Travel
Maps sheet covering Lombok and Sumbawa (1:200,000); it's easier to find abroad
or in Bali than on the island itself.

### Map outlets

#### UK and Ireland

**Blackwell's Map Centre** 50 Broad St, Oxford OX1
3BQ ☏ 01865/793 550, @ maps.blackwell.co.uk.
Branches in Bristol, Cambridge, Cardiff, Leeds,
Liverpool, Newcastle, Reading and Sheffield.
**The Map Shop** 30a Belvoir St, Leicester LE1 6QH
☏ 0116/247 1400, @ www.mapshopleicester.co.uk.
**National Map Centre** 22–24 Caxton St, London
SW1H 0QU ☏ 020/7222 2466, @ www.mapstore
.co.uk.
**National Map Centre Ireland** 34 Aungier St,
Dublin 2 ☏ 01/476 0471, @ www.mapcentre.ie.
**Stanfords** 12–14 Long Acre, London WC2E 9LP
☏ 020/7836 1321, @ www.stanfords.co.uk.
Also at 39 Spring Gardens, Manchester M2 2BG
☏ 0161/831 0250, and 29 Corn St, Bristol BS1 1HT
☏ 0117/929 9966.
**The Travel Bookshop** 13–15 Blenheim Crescent,
London W11 2EE ☏ 020/7229 5260, @ www
.thetravelbookshop.co.uk.
**Traveller** 55 Grey St, Newcastle-upon-Tyne NE1
6EF ☏ 0191/261 5622, @ www.newtraveller.com.

## US and Canada

**110 North Latitude** US ☎336/369-4171, ⓦwww.110nlatitude.com.

**Book Passage** 51 Tamal Vista Blvd, Corte Madera, CA 94925, and in the San Francisco Ferry Building ☎1-800/999-7909 or ☎415/927-0960, ⓦwww.bookpassage.com.

**Distant Lands** 56 S Raymond Ave, Pasadena, CA 91105 ☎1-800/310-3220, ⓦwww.distantlands.com.

**Globe Corner Bookstore** 28 Church St, Cambridge, MA 02138 ☎1-800/358-6013, ⓦwww.globecorner.com.

**Longitude Books** 115 W 30th St, #1206, New York, NY 10001 ☎1-800/342-2164, ⓦwww.longitudebooks.com.

**Map Town** 400 5 Ave SW #100, Calgary, AB T2P 0L6 ☎1-877/921-6277 or 403/266-2241, ⓦwww.maptown.com.

**Travel Bug Bookstore** 3065 W Broadway, Vancouver, BC V6K 2G9 ☎604/737-1122, ⓦwww.travelbugbooks.ca.

**World of Maps** 1235 Wellington St, Ottawa, ON K1Y 3A3 ☎1-800/214 ⓦwww.worldofmaps.com.

## Australia and New Zealand

**Mapland** 372 Little Bourke St, Melbourne, Vic 3000 ☎03/9670 4383, ⓦwww.mapland.com.au.

**Map Shop** 6–10 Peel St, Adelaide, SA 5000 ☎08/8231 2033, ⓦwww.mapshop.net.au.

**Map World** 280 Pitt St, Sydney, NSW 2000 ☎02/9261 3601. Also at 65 Northbourne Ave, Canberra, ACT 2601 ☎02/6230 4097 and 1981 Logan Road, Brisbane, Qld 4122 ☎07/3349 6633, ⓦwww.mapworld.net.au.

**Map World** 173 Gloucester St, Christchurch ☎0800/627967, ⓦwww.mapworld.co.nz.

# Insurance

Before travelling to Bali or Lombok, it is important to take out **travel insurance**. A typical policy provides cover for medical expenses due to illness or injury, the loss of baggage, tickets and – up to a certain limit – cash or cheques, plus cancellation or curtailment of your journey. Most exclude so-called dangerous sports unless an extra premium is paid: in Bali and Lombok, this can mean scubadiving, kayaking and white-water rafting.

Before buying a policy, check that you're not already covered. Your home-insurance policy may cover your possessions against loss or theft even when overseas, or you can extend cover through your household-contents insurer. Many charge cards include some form of travel cover, and very limited medical cover is sometimes included if you pay for your trip with a credit card. Many private medical schemes also include cover when abroad. In Canada, provincial health plans usually provide partial cover for medical mishaps overseas, while holders of official student/teacher/youth cards in Canada and the US are entitled to meagre accident coverage and hospital in-patient benefits. Students

may find that their student health coverage extends during the vacations and for one term beyond the date of last enrolment.

After exhausting the possibilities above, you might want to contact a specialist travel insurance company, or consider the travel insurance deal we offer (see box, opposite). Many policies can be chopped and changed to exclude coverage you don't need – for example, sickness and accident benefits can often be excluded or included at will. If you do take medical coverage, ascertain whether benefits will be paid as treatment proceeds or only after return home, and whether there is a 24-hour medical emergency number (which you should carry with you at all times

## Rough Guides Travel Insurance

**Rough Guides** has teamed up with Columbus Direct to offer you travel insurance that can be tailored to suit your needs.

Readers can choose from many different travel insurance-products, including a **low-cost backpacker option** for long stays; a **short-break option** for city getaways; a typical **holiday package option**; and many others. There are also **annual multi-trip** policies for those who travel regularly, with variable levels of cover available. Different sports and activities (trekking, skiing, etc) can be covered if required on most policies.

Rough Guides travel insurance is available to the residents of 36 different countries with different language options to choose from via our website – ⓦwww .roughguides.com – where you can also purchase the insurance.

Alternatively, UK residents should call ☏0800/083 9507; US citizens should call ☏1-800/749-4922; Australians should call ☏1 300/669 999. All other nationalities should call ☏+44 870/890 2843.

while you are away, along with the policy number). Always make a note of the policy details and leave them with someone at home in case you lose the original. When securing baggage cover, make sure that the per-article limit – typically under £500/ US$900 – will cover your most valuable possession.

It can be more economical for couples and families travelling together to arrange joint insurance. Older travellers or anyone with

health problems is advised to start researching insurance well in advance of their trip.

If you need to make a claim, you should keep receipts for medicines and treatment, and, if possible, contact the insurance company before making any major payment (for example, on additional convalescence expenses). In the event you have anything stolen, you must obtain an official report from the police.

# Health

Travelling in Bali and Lombok, most people end up with nothing more serious than a bout of traveller's diarrhoea ("Bali belly").

However, illness and accidents (including motorbike accidents and surfers' mishaps) can't be ruled out. In the event of serious illness or accident, you'll need to be evacuated to Singapore or back home, so it is vital to have adequate **health insurance** before you travel.

Discuss your trip with your **doctor** or a specialist travel clinic (see pp.43–44) as early as possible to allow time to complete courses of inoculations. Although no **inocu-**

**lations** are legally required for entry into Indonesia (unless you've come directly from a country that is infected with yellow fever, in which case you'll need to have been immunized and carry a certificate to prove it), vaccinations for hepatitis A, polio, tetanus and typhoid are recommended, and it's also worth asking about inoculations against rabies, Japanese encephalitis, hepatitis B, tuberculosis and diphtheria (see the sources of information on p.43 or *The Rough Guide*

## A traveller's first-aid kit

Items you might want to carry with you include:

- Antiseptic cream
- Insect repellent
- Plasters/bandaids
- Water sterilzation tablets or water purifier
- Lint and sealed bandages
- Knee supports
- Rehydration sachets
- Emergency diarrhoea treatment
- Paracetamol/aspirin/Tylenol
- Multivitamin and mineral tablets

*to Travel Health*). If you have any medical conditions or are travelling with children, you'll need to be particularly careful to get appropriate advice. If you need regular medication, carry a certificate from your doctor detailing your condition – it can be handy if you encounter overzealous customs officials. It's also wise to get a dental check-up before you leave home.

### Treatment in Bali and Lombok

You'll find pharmacies (*apotik*), village health posts and doctors across the islands, although only in the main tourist areas will staff speak English. **Pharmacies** sell a wide range of medicines, many of which you would need a prescription to buy back home. In the **village health posts**, staff are generally well-meaning, but ill-equipped to cope with serious illness. Most Balinese use these together with traditional healers (*balian*) as they believe that physical symptoms are a sign of spiritual illness (see p.495 for more on this).

If you need an English-speaking **doctor**, seek advice at your hotel (some of the luxury ones have in-house doctors). For more serious problems, you'll find a public **hospital** in each district capital and in larger towns such as Denpasar and Singaraja; these are supplemented by private hospitals, many of which operate an accident and emergency department. There are **tourist-friendly clinics** in the main resorts. Most function 24 hours a day, are staffed by English-speak-

ing doctors and nurses and offer consultations (from Rp100,000), emergency call-out (Rp250,000–400,000), ambulances, minor surgery and dental services. The widest range of facilities is in Denpasar, which is also the location of the only **recompression chamber** on the island (see p.107). For full details, see the "Listings" section of each city account. A couple of places on the outskirts of Kuta also have good reputations for dealing with expat emergencies: Bali International Medical Centre (BIMC), Jl Bypass Ngurah Rai 100x ☎0361/761263, ✆www.bimcbali.com; and International SOS, Klinik SOS Medika, Jl Bypass Ngurah Rai 505X ☎0361/720100, ✆www.sos-bali.com.

There are plenty of **dentists** (*doktor gigi*) in Lombok (see p.388) and in Bali services are available in Denpasar (see p.107) and at clinics in Kuta (see p.134), Sanur (see p.164) and Ubud (see p.215). In other areas, it's probably best to get a recommendation from a local tourist office if you need treatment.

### Major diseases

There are several types of **hepatitis**, but the symptoms of all of them are a yellow colouring of the skin and eyes, extreme exhaustion, fever and diarrhoea. It's one of the most common illnesses that afflicts travellers to Asia and can last for several months. Treatment involves rest and complete abstinence from alcohol. The most common types are hepatitis A and hepatitis B, both caused by viruses; vaccines can offer some protection against them. Hepatitis A is transmitted via contaminated food and water or saliva. Hepatitis B is more serious and is transmitted via sexual contact or by contaminated blood, needles or syringes, which means that medical treatment itself can pose a risk if sterilization procedures are not up to scratch.

Many Western travellers will have had routine inoculations against **polio, diphtheria and tuberculosis**. These illnesses are far more common throughout Asia than in the West, and travellers should check that they are still covered against them. **Typhoid** is passed through contaminated food or water and can be lethal. It produces an extremely high fever accompanied by abdominal pains, headaches, diarrhoea and red spots on the body. **Cholera** is an extremely dangerous illness transmitted through contaminated food and water, with symptoms of severe watery diarrhoea, cramps, weakness and vomiting. Dehydration is the danger here, so take rehydration salts and get medical help urgently. The vaccine is considered to be so ineffectual and short-lived that it is not recommended. **Tetanus** (or lockjaw) is potentially fatal and is picked up through contaminated wounds: if you cut or puncture yourself on something dirty, you will be at risk. You should make sure your jabs are up to date before leaving home. **Japanese encephalitis** is a serious viral illness causing inflammation of the brain. It is endemic across Asia and is transmitted from infected birds and animals via mosquitoes. Those planning extended periods of travel in rural areas are most at risk.

Avoid contact with all animals, no matter how cute. **Rabies** is spread via the saliva of infected animals, most commonly cats, dogs or monkeys, and is endemic throughout Asia. If you get bitten, wash the wound immediately with antiseptic and get medical help. Treatment involves a course of injections, but you won't need all of them if you have had a course of pre-departure jabs.

## Malaria

Both Bali and Lombok are within **malarial zones**, although current advice seems to be that there's little risk of the disease in the most popular tourist resorts on Bali. If you're visiting Lombok, you should take full precautions. However, information regarding the prevalence, prevention and treatment of malaria is being constantly updated so you must seek medical advice at least a couple of weeks before you travel. Be sure to let them know if you're visiting other parts of Indonesia or Asia, even in transit. The latest information shows an increase in the most serious form of malaria across Asia and there are reports of resistance to certain drug treatments by some strains. Pregnant women and children need particular advice on dosage and the different drugs available.

Malaria, which can be fatal, is caused by a parasite in the saliva of the anopheles **mosquito**, which is passed into humans when they're bitten by the mosquito. The appropriate prophylactic drug regime depends on your destination but all must be taken to a strict timetable beginning before you go and continuing after leaving the area. If you don't follow instructions precisely, you're in danger of developing the illness. The symptoms are fever, headache and shivering, similar to a severe dose of flu and often coming in cycles, but a lot of people have additional symptoms. Don't delay in seeking help: malaria progresses quickly. If you develop flu-like symptoms any time up to a year after returning home, you should inform a doctor of the areas you have been travelling in and ask for a blood test.

Many of the drugs used in **prevention** have proved fairly effective, with a reasonably low incidence of side effects, over many years of use. However, none is one hundred percent effective and it is vital equally to try to stop the mosquitoes biting you: sleep under a **mosquito net** – preferably one impregnated with an insecticide especially suited to the task – burn mosquito coils, and use **repellent** on exposed skin. The strongest repellents will need to be purchased before you leave home and will probably contain DEET, which is powerful stuff (it melts plastic) and can irritate sensitive skin. However, natural alternatives are available containing citronella, eucalyptus oil or neem oil.

## Dengue fever

Another important reason to avoid getting bitten by mosquitoes is **dengue fever**, caused by a virus carried by a different species of mosquito, which bites during the day. There is no vaccine or tablet available to prevent the illness – which causes fever, headache and joint and muscle pains among the least serious symptoms, and internal bleeding and circulatory system failure among the most serious – and no specific drug to cure it. Reports indicate that the disease is on the increase across the tropics and sub-tropics in recent years. It is vital to get an early medical diagnosis and obtain treatment to relieve symptoms.

## AIDS/HIV

Bali, Java and West Papua are the three most affected places in Indonesia for **AIDS and HIV** infection. Many people with HIV are also infected with hepatitis. **Condoms** can be bought on both islands, but it's as well to bring your own.

## General precautions

**Precautions** while you are travelling can reduce your chances of getting ill. Be scrupulous about **personal hygiene** and treat even small cuts or scrapes with antiseptic. Wear flip-flops or thongs in the bathroom rather than walk around barefoot.

Avoid **food** that has sat around in the heat and always opt for freshly cooked meals; food prepared in fancy tourist places is just as likely to be suspect as that from simple streetside stalls. **Ice** is supposedly prepared under carefully regulated conditions in Indonesia, but it's impossible to be sure how it has been transported or stored once leaving the factory. If you're being really careful, avoid ice in your drinks – a lot easier said than done in the heat.

### Water hygiene

Although **water** may look clean, it can contain a huge population of disease-causing microorganisms. Do not drink untreated tap water on Bali or Lombok. **Bottled water** is available just about everywhere and there are several methods of treating either tap water or natural ground water to make it safe for drinking (and this also avoids creating mountains of waste with your empty plastic water bottles); the most traditional method is boiling, although this isn't practical when you're travelling. However, **water purifying tablets**, **water filters** or **water purifiers** are all available in travel clinics (see pp.43–44) and specialist outdoor-equipment retailers.

## Heat and skin problems

Travellers are at risk of **sunburn** and **dehydration**. Limit your exposure to the sun in the hours around midday, use high-factor sunscreen and wear dark glasses and a sun hat. You sweat a great deal in the heat, so make sure that you drink enough. If you're urinating very little or your urine turns dark (this can also indicate hepatitis), increase your fluid intake. When you sweat you lose salt, so make sure your intake covers this: add some extra to your food or take oral rehydration salts (see below).

A more serious result of the heat is **heat-stroke**, indicated by high temperature, dry skin and a fast, erratic pulse. As an emergency measure, try to cool the patient off by covering them in sheets or sarongs soaked in cold water and turn the fan on them; they may need to go to hospital, though. Heat rashes, **prickly heat** and fungal infections are also common; wear loose cotton clothing, dry yourself carefully after bathing and use medicated talcum powder or anti-fungal powder if you fall victim.

Some travellers get persistent, long-lasting, itchy red rashes from sitting bare-legged on cane or bamboo chairs. Apparently, this is caused by cane mites, and can be alleviated by Silver Clove cream, available in local pharmacies, markets and supermarkets.

## Intestinal trouble

The priority with an **upset stomach** is not to get dehydrated. Start drinking **rehydration salts** as soon as the attack starts, even if you're vomiting as well, and worry about a diagnosis later. Rehydration salts are widely available in pharmacies but it makes sense to carry some with you. There are several brands available in Bali and Lombok – Oralit and Pharolit are two. The home-made form of these is eight teaspoons of sugar and half a teaspoon of salt dissolved in a litre of clean water.

Stomach upsets can either be a reaction to a change of diet, or can signal something more serious. You should seek medical advice if the attack is particularly severe, lasts more than a couple of days or is accompanied by constant, severe abdominal pain or fever. Any blood or mucus in your diarrhoea is a sign you may have bacillic or amoebic **dysentery** and you should see a doctor at once. **Giardia** is another intestinal illness that produces, among other things, smelly farts and burps; it requires medical treatment.

In general, drugs such as Lomotil and Imodium, which stop diarrhoea, should only be used if you get taken ill on a journey or must travel while ill; they are not a cure, and simply paralyse your gut, temporarily plugging you up, at a time when your insides need to get rid of the toxins causing the problem.

## Cuts, bites and stings

If you're contemplating **diving**, you should familiarize yourself with the potential dangers and what first-aid measures are required, although you're probably more at risk from the cold and scrapes from coral than from tangling with hazards like sharks, barracuda, sea snakes, stingrays, scorpionfish, jellyfish, stinging hydroids and sea urchins. All cuts should be cleansed thoroughly, disinfected immediately, covered and kept dry until healed.

On the land, **snakes** are shy and are only likely to attack if you step on them. Take extra care when in jungle areas: wear long thick socks to protect your legs when trekking and walk noisily. If you're bitten, try to remember what the snake looked like, move as little as you can and send someone for medical help. Under no circumstances should you try doing anything heroic with a Swiss army knife. There are also a few poisonous **spiders** in Bali and Lombok, and if you're bitten by one you should also immobilize the limb and get medical help. If you get **leeches** attached to you while trekking in the jungle in the rainy season, use a dab of salt, suntan oil, or a cigarette to persuade them to let go, rather than just pulling them off.

## Medical resources for travellers

### Online

ⓦ **health.yahoo.com** Information on specific diseases and conditions, drugs and herbal remedies, as well as advice from health experts.

ⓦ **www.cdc.gov** The US government's official site for travel health.

ⓦ **www.fitfortravel.scot.nhs.uk** Scottish NHS website carrying information about travel-related diseases and how to avoid them.

ⓦ **www.istm.org** The website of the International Society for Travel Medicine, with a full list of clinics specializing in international travel health. Publishes outbreak warnings, suggested inoculations, precautions and other background information for travellers.

ⓦ **www.tmvc.com.au** Contains a list of all Travellers' Medical and Vaccination Centres throughout Australia, New Zealand and Southeast Asia, plus general information on travel health.

ⓦ **www.tripprep.com** Travel Health Online provides an online-only comprehensive database of necessary vaccinations for most countries, as well as destination and medical-service-provider information.

### UK and Ireland

**British Airways Travel Clinics** 213 Piccadilly, W1 (Mon–Fri 9.30am–5.30pm, Sat 10am–4pm, no appointment required; ☎0845/600 2236); 101 Cheapside, London EC2V 6DT (Mon–Fri 9am–4.30pm, by appointment only; ☎0845/600 2236). ⓦwww.ba.com/travelclinics.

**Dun Laoghaire Medical Centre** 5 Northumberland Ave, Dun Laoghaire, County Dublin ☎01/280 4996, ⒻM01/280 5603. Advice on medical matters abroad.

**Hospital for Tropical Diseases Travel Clinic** 2nd floor, Mortimer Market Centre, off Tottenham Court Rd, London WC1E 6AU (Mon–Fri 9am–5pm by appointment only; ☎020/7388 9600, ⓦwww .thehtd.org). A recorded Health Line (☎0906/133 7733; 50p per min) gives written information tailored to your journey.

**Liverpool School of Tropical Medicine** Pembroke Place, Liverpool L3 5QA ☎0151/708 9393, ⓦwww.liv.ac.uk/lstm/lstm.

**MASTA (Medical Advisory Service for Travellers Abroad)** Twenty-five regional clinics; call ☎0870/606 2782 for the nearest, or see ⓦwww.masta.org. Also operates a pre-recorded 24-hour Travellers' Health Line (UK ☎0906/550 1402, £1 per min), giving written information tailored to your journey, which is also available online.

**Nomad Pharmacy** ⓦwww.nomadtravel.co.uk. Operates travel clinics in its five UK stores, plus a telephone helpline ☎0906/863 3414 (60p per min).

**Travel Medicine Services** PO Box 254, 16 College St, Belfast BT1 6BT ☎028/9031 5220. Offers medical advice before a trip and help afterwards in the event of a tropical disease.

**Tropical Medical Bureau** ⓦwww.tmb.ie. Information on eleven clinic locations across Ireland.

### US and Canada

**Centers for Disease Control** 1600 Clifton Rd NE, Atlanta, GA 30333 ☎1-800/311-3435 or 404/639-3435, ⓦwww.cdc.gov. Publishes a vast amount of information for travellers. Travelers' Health Hotline on ☎1-877/394-8747.

**International Association for Medical Assistance to Travellers (IAMAT)** ⓦwww .iamat.org. Offices in Canada and the US. A nonprofit organization supported by donations. Publishes a variety of information and a list of English-speaking doctors overseas.

**MEDJET Assistance** ☎1-800/963-3538 or 205/595-6626, ⊛www.medjetassistance.com. Annual membership programme for travellers that, in the event of illness or injury, will fly members home or to the hospital of their choice in a medically equipped jet.

**Travel Medicine** ☎1-800/872-8633, ⊛www.travmed.com. Providing information and selling travel-related equipment, plus details of travel clinics in North America.

### Australia and New Zealand

**Travellers' Medical and Vaccination Centres** ⊛www.tmvc.com.au. Twenty-two travel clinics throughout Australia and New Zealand.

# Costs, money and banks

Foreign tourists visiting Bali and Lombok, wherever they come from, invariably find that hotel rooms at all levels of comfort, goods and services are relatively inexpensive when compared with their home countries. However, the range of

## Giving something back

Despite the glossy tourist veneer, Bali is part of a poor country with limited resources to provide good-quality education and health care to its citizens, whose opportunities, quality of life and very survival are compromised as a result. The 2002 bomb brought extra hardship to many. Below are some suggestions for **charities** who would welcome help in some way from visitors.

**AdoptA** ⊛www.pacungbali.com/adopta. A dressmaking and jewellery cooperative run by and for women who were widowed by the 2002 Kuta bomb; they have a small shop in Kuta (see p.132).

**Crisis Care Foundation** ☎0362/42286 or 081/2377 4649, ⊛balicrisiscare.org. Provides free health care for local people both in the clinic in Lovina and as outreach and is run entirely on charitable donations, which are always needed. The clinic is in the hamlet of Lebah; the turning in Kaliasem is signed, and the clinic is a couple of kilometres up on the left. The driving force is an Englishwoman, Gloria, and if the clinic is closed, visitors are welcome to visit her at home nearby; local people will give directions. You can also drop donations at the *Bali Dynasty* hotel in Tuban (see p.120). There's more information and a Wish List on the website.

**East Bali Poverty Project** ☎0361/410071, ⊛www.eastbalipovertyproject.org. Helps isolated mountain villages on the arid slopes of Gunung Agung and Gunung Abang in a number of ways, including setting up projects in sustainable and organic agriculture, establishing schools and health centres, and running awareness programmes on nutrition and sanitation.

**Gili Meno Clinic** ✉j.byrneabroad@hotmail.com. Money has been raised to build and start up a medical clinic on Gili Meno – prior to this, islanders had to travel to the mainland for all health care. Money is now needed for equipment and running costs (including arranging for a doctor to visit) to make sure it stays open. Donations to Wira at *Villa Nautilus*, Joan at Blue Marlin or Bob at Tao' Kombo', all on Gili Meno.

**IDEP Foundation** ⊛www.idepfoundation.org. A Bali-based NGO that promotes sustainable-living programmes across Indonesia. It has been especially active in Bali since the 2002 bomb, encouraging self-sustaining projects that do not entirely depend on tourism. At their HQ in Ubud, their handicrafts shop, Bali Cares (see accommodation, restaurants and other opportunities means that it is just as easy to have a fabulously extravagant experience as a budget one.

Many tourist businesses quote for their goods and services in **US dollars**; in the Guide, prices are given in dollars where this is the case. This includes hotels, dive operators, tour agents and car rental outlets, particularly in the larger resorts. Even where prices are displayed in US dollars, though, you're usually given the option of paying with cash, travellers' cheques, credit card or rupiah.

## Currency

The Indonesian currency is the **rupiah** (abbreviated to "Rp"). Notes come in denominations of Rp100 (red), Rp500 (green), Rp1000 (blue), Rp5000 (green and brown), Rp10,000 (browny-purple), Rp20,000 (green and black, or plain green), Rp50,000 (grey, blue and green) and small, plastic-like, non-tearable Rp100,000 (pastel shades). They are all clearly inscribed with English numbers and letters. Be warned that most people won't accept ripped or badly worn banknotes, so you shouldn't either. **Coins** are useful for public telephones and bemos. They come in five denominations: Rp25 (silver), Rp50 (silver-coloured plastic), Rp100 (silver-coloured plastic), Rp500 (larger, round, bronze), Rp1000 (large, round, bronze with silver rim).

At the time of writing (mid-2005), the **exchange rate** was US$1 to Rp9400, and £1 to Rp17,000. For the current rate, see the Bank Internasional Indonesia at ⊛bii.intnet. co.id/p_r/today_exchange_rates_e.asp. Alternatively, check out the useful "Travellers

p.212), and the adjacent café help fund the work of eleven Balinese charities.

**Kupu-Kupu Foundation** ⊛www.yamp.org/kupukupu. Encourages volunteers to help improve the lives of the 13,000 physically and mentally disabled children and adults in Bali. Sells inexpensive, high-quality handicrafts and jewellery made by disabled craftspeople at its shop in Ubud (see p.212).

**Mitra Bali Fair-Trade Arts and Crafts NGO** ⊛www.mitrabali.com. Welcomes visitors to its HQ in Lodtunduh near Ubud (see p.175) to learn more about its work supporting Balinese craftspeople through fair trade. Also has a fair-trade shop on the Tegalalang road (see p.222) and another in the Bali Discovery Shopping Mall in Tuban, south Kuta.

**Panti Asuhan Kristen (Christian Orphanage)** Jl Jempiring 20, Klungkung ⊛0366/21367. Has been helping orphans from all over Indonesia since 1972. Children range from two years old upwards, staying until they find employment and can support themselves. Visitors wishing to see the work of the orphanage should come after 4pm when the children are home from school; donations of clothes, toys, books and money are all needed. To reach the orphanage, head south from Klungkung town centre (see p.241) along Jalan Puputan. After about 500m, there's a large junction marked by a family statue on the corner; Jalan Jempiring is the road to the right.

**Pondok Pekak Library and Learning Centre** ⓔpondok@indo.net.id. A free library service in Ubud that offers all local children access to books. The centre also holds regular children's activities, such as multi-language singing, dancing, and drawing (see p.215). There is an excellent adult-oriented library of English-language books here and a second-hand books outlet (see p.215). Visitors can support the children's library by using the adult library, by taking cultural classes here (see p.214), by donating children's and adults' books (in English or Indonesian), or by donating funds.

**Vibe (Volunteers and Interns for Balinese Education) Foundation** ⊛www .vibefoundation.org. Ubud-based organization that works to provide outreach educational opportunities for adults and children. Offers four-month volunteer placements in English-teaching and developmental projects; two- and three-week placements are also available in English-teaching and special skills-based projects and at an orphanage. Also welcomes donations of books, art supplies and office stationery.

Currency Cheat Sheets" at ⓦ www.oanda
.com.

## Costs

If you're happy to eat where the local people do, use the public transport system
and stay in simple accommodation, then
you could scrape by on a **daily budget** of
£7/US$12 per person (less if you share a
room). Food and lodgings are a little more
costly in the larger resorts like Kuta (Bali)
and Senggigi, and there's more to spend
your money on in these places, too. For
around £16/$30 a day (less if you share
a room), you'll get quite a few extra comforts, like the use of a swimming pool and
possibly hot water and air-conditioning as
well, three good meals and a few beers.
Staying in luxury hotels and eating at the
flashiest restaurants, you're likely to spend
a minimum of £80/$150 per day. The sky's
the limit at this end of the market, with
$1000-a-night accommodation, helicopter
charters, dive or surf safaris, and fabulous
gourmet meals all on offer.

Most government-run **museums** and
archeological sites charge Rp3100 or
Rp4100 per person (half price for under-
14s); the major private art museums charge
Rp20,000. Youth and student discounts are
very rarely offered in Bali and Lombok. Only
a few temples have entry prices (usually
Rp3100–4100), but all visitors to any temple,
whatever the size or status, are expected
to give a small donation (about Rp5000),
which, in the most popular temples, generally includes sarong and sash rental.

### Bargaining

**Bargaining** is one of the most obvious
ways of keeping your costs down. Except
in supermarkets, restaurants and bars, the
first price given is rarely the real one, and
most stallholders expect to engage in some
financial banter before finalizing the sale; on
average, buyers will start their counterbid
at about 30 to 40 percent of the vendor's
opening price and the bartering continues
from there. Pretty much everything, from
newspapers and cigarettes to woodcarvings and car rental is negotiable, and even
accommodation rates can often be knocked
down, from the humblest losmen through to

the top-end places where potential guests
ask about "low-season discounts".

Bargaining is an art, and requires humour
and tact – it's easy to forget that you're quib-
bling over a few cents or pennies, and that
such an amount means a lot more to an
Indonesian than to you. We've quoted prices in the book to give you a guide, but do
remember that they will go up.

## Cash and travellers'
## cheques

Before you leave home, exchange facilities
should be able to get some **cash** rupiah for
you but order at least a week ahead of your
departure, as there is always a shortage of
rupiah stocks outside Indonesia. However,
rates are poor and you don't really need it;
there are exchange counters at Bali's Ngurah Rai Airport (where there are also ATMs),
Lombok's Selaparang Airport and inside
Jakarta's Sukarno Hatta Airport (domestic
and international terminals), which all open
for arriving passengers. Some cash in **US
dollars** can be useful to take with you, but
take crisp new notes and avoid $100 bills,
which can be hard to exchange.

Most people carry at least some of their
money as **travellers' cheques**, which are
widely accepted at banks and exchange
counters across Bali and in the tourist centres of Lombok (Senggigi, the Gili Islands and
the four-cities area of Mataram-Ampenan-
Cakranegara-Sweta). Outside these areas on
Lombok, facilities are much rarer, so be sure
to carry enough cash. The best cheques to
take are those issued by the most familiar
names, particularly American Express in US
dollars or pounds sterling, though numerous other currencies are accepted in the
largest resorts. Take the **receipt** (or proof of
purchase) that you get when you buy your
travellers' cheques, as banks and exchange
counters may ask to see it. Be aware that
if you lose your passport your travellers'
cheques will be useless as you can't encash
them, so a back-up access to funds (a credit
or debit card) in case of emergency is useful.

In tourist centres, **exchange counters** are
the most convenient places to cash your
cheques. They open daily from around 8am
to 8pm and rates compare favourably with
those offered by the banks. However, be

## Money-changing scams

Some unscrupulous exchange counters try to rip customers off, and there are several well-known **money-changing scams** practised in the bigger resorts, in particular in Kuta and Sanur on Bali.

### Some common rip-offs

• Confusing you with the number of **zeros**. With over Rp10,000 to every pound it's easy for staff to give you Rp100,000 instead of Rp1,000,000.
• Giving you your money in Rp10,000 **denominations**, so that you lose track.
• Tampering with the **calculator**, so that it shows a low sum even if you use it yourself.
• **Folding notes** over to make it look as if you're getting twice as much as you are.
• Turning the lights out or otherwise **distracting** you while the pile of money is on the counter.
• **Stealing** some notes as they "check" it for the last time.
• Once you've rumbled them and complained, telling you that the discrepancy in the figures is due to "**commission**".

### Some advice

• **Avoid** anywhere that offers a ridiculously good rate. Stick to banks or to exchange desks recommended by other travellers.
• Work out the **total amount** you're expecting beforehand, and write it down.
• Always ask whether there is **commission**.
• Before signing your cheque, ask for notes in **reasonable denominations** (Rp10,000 is unreasonable, Rp50,000 is acceptable), and ask to see them first.
• **Count your money** carefully, and never hand it back to the exchange staff, as this is when they whip away some notes without you noticing. You should be the last person to count the money.
• So long as you haven't already **signed** a travellers' cheque, you can walk away at any point. If you have signed the cheque, stay calm, don't get distracted, and count everything slowly and methodically.

wary of money-changing scams (see box above), particularly in Kuta and Sanur.

Normal **banking hours** are Monday to Thursday 8am to 2pm, Friday 8am to noon and, in some branches, Saturday 8 to 11.30am, but these do vary. However, in many banks the foreign-exchange counter only opens for a limited period. Banks in smaller towns don't have foreign-exchange facilities.

### Plastic

Major **credit cards**, most commonly Visa and MasterCard, are accepted by most mid- to top-end hotels and tourist businesses. However, outlets often add to your bill the entire fee that is charged to them (currently four percent), bumping costs up.

In Bali's and Lombok's biggest tour- ist centres (Kuta, Sanur, Nusa Dua, Ubud, Candi Dasa, Lovina and Senggigi – but not

in Amed) and cities (Denpasar, Gianyar, Klungkung and Mataram), you'll find **ATMs** that accept international cards, both Visa and MasterCard as well as **debit cards** on the Cirrus network. Remember that all cash advances on credit cards are treated as loans, with interest accruing daily from the date of withdrawal and, possibly, a transac-

## Lost or stolen credit cards

**American Express** Room 1113 inside the *Inna Grand Bali Beach* in north Sanur (Mon–Fri 9am–5pm; ☏0361/283970). Toll-free numbers in Indonesia for lost cards ☏0800/111 2233 and cheques ☏0800/182 1777. International number ☏001-800-440176.
**MasterCard** ☏001-803-1-887-0623
**Visa** ☏001-803-1-933-6294

tion fee on top. Debit-card withdrawals are not liable to interest payments but check the flat transaction fee your bank will charge. See the relevant sections of resort and city accounts for ATM locations; for an up-to-the-minute list, check ⓦwww.mastercard .com and ⓦwww.visa.com. Be careful when using your card – unlike machines at home, some of the Bali and Lombok machines only return your card *after* they've dispensed your cash, making it easier to forget your card. American Express's Travelers Check Card (see ⓦwww.americanexpress.com) acts as a **combination** of travellers' cheques and plastic – it's a pre-paid card that you can use like a debit card in ATMs, hotels and other businesses, topping it up as and when you wish.

### Wiring money

Wiring money through a specialist agent is a fast but expensive way to **receive money abroad** and should be considered as a last resort. Money should be available for collection in local currency, from the company's local agent within twenty minutes of being sent via Western Union or Moneygram; both charge on a sliding scale, so sending larger amounts of cash is better value. Money can

be sent via the agents, telephone or, in some cases, the websites (see below). **Western Union** has a large network of agents in Bali and Lombok; many post offices and Bank Mandiri branches are agents. **Moneygram** has about eight agents across the islands. Check the websites for locations and opening hours.

It's also possible to have money wired **directly** from a bank in your home country to a bank in Indonesia, but this can be tortuous. If you think you'll use it, check with your bank before travelling to see which branch of which bank they have reciprocal arrangements with, and precisely what details they'll need in order to complete the transaction.

### Agents

**Moneygram** US ☎1-800/666-3947, Canada ☎1-800/933-3278, UK ☎0800/8971 8971, Ireland and New Zealand ☎00800/666 3947, Australia ☎0011800/666 3947, ⓦwww.moneygram.com.
**Western Union** US and Canada ☎1-800/325-6000, UK ☎0800/833 833, Republic of Ireland ☎66/947 5603, Australia ☎1800/173 833, New Zealand ☎0800/005 253, ⓦwww.westernunion .com (customers in the US, Canada and the UK can send money online).

# Getting around

Bali and Lombok are both small enough to traverse in a couple of hours by road (there's no rail transport on either island), although the lack of road or route numbers can make things confusing if you are driving yourself. The major roads are good, carrying at least two-way traffic, and are fairly well maintained, although they see a lot of large trucks. On less-frequented routes, the roads are narrow and more likely to be potholed, while off the beaten track they may be no more than rough tracks.

The state of the road is a reasonable indication of the frequency of **public transport**, which is generally cheap, but offers little space or comfort. In addition to the public transport system, **tourist shuttle buses**

operate between major destinations on Bali and Lombok, and although these are considerably more expensive, they are convenient. If you prefer to drive yourself, bicycles, motorbikes, cars and jeeps are available to rent throughout the islands, or you can rent cars or motorbikes with a driver.

Getting **between Bali and Lombok** is easy by plane or boat. For details, see p.380.

## Bemos and buses

On both Bali and Lombok, public transport predominantly consists of buses and bemos. **Bemos** are minibuses of varying sizes: tiny ones scurry around local routes, while larger versions travel further afield. **Buses** operate long-distance routes such as Denpasar to Singaraja, Denpasar to Amlapura, and Ampanan-Mataram-Cakranegra-Sweta to Labuhan Lombok.

You can pick up a bus or bemo from the bus or bemo **terminal** in bigger towns or flag one down on the road. Fares are paid to the driver or conductor, if there is one. You can't buy tickets in advance – except for inter-island trips, such as from Bali to Java or Lombok.

No local person negotiates a **fare**. When they want to get off they yell "Stoppa", hop out and pay the fixed fare. The extent to which this system is accessible to tourists is variable. Some bemo drivers won't let you get in without agreeing the price beforehand; tourists are usually charged several times the local fare. At some of the main terminals in Denpasar there are fare charts of prices to major destinations, but it can be hard to find them – in reality, there's no substitute for asking a few local people what the fare should be. It's useful to carry coins and small notes with you to pay the exact fare. If you sit with your luggage on your knees, you should not be charged extra for it.

## Tourist shuttle buses

The longest-established firm of **tourist shuttle buses** is Perama (ⓦwww.peramatour.com). They have offices in major tourist destinations and a leaflet and website outlining all their routes. Fares are four or five times that of public transport, but their service is a lot more convenient and luggage isn't a problem; there's also room for wheelchairs, baby buggies and surfboards. Sample prices are Rp20,000 from Kuta to Ubud (3 daily); Rp30,000 Candi Dasa to Kuta (3 daily); Rp50,000 Ubud to Lovina (daily). You usually need to book the day before, but from

popular destinations you can sometimes get a seat the same day. Phone bookings are usually acceptable, and pick-ups and drop-offs at hotels are available (Rp5000 for each). The section "Travel details", at the end of every guide chapter, lists routes. Perama also run a tourist-boat service between Bali and Lombok (see p.380 for details).

There are several **rival companies** to Perama operating on both Bali and Lombok, including Gora and Anjani. They advertise throughout the tourist areas and offer a similar service, but are not as high profile. These are worth checking out if, for example, the Perama office is inconveniently far from the town centre (as in Lovina and Ubud): a rival company may drop you more centrally. They can also make for a far calmer arrival: every hotel tout on Bali and Lombok knows when and where the Perama bus arrives and waits to entice passengers to their lodging. This has advantages when beds are limited but a crowd of thirty touts gathering to accost new arrivals can be an unpleasant entrance anywhere. Other, smaller companies attract less notice.

## Tourist boat

Perama also operate a **tourist boat service** between Padang Bai on Bali and Sengiggi and the Gili Islands on Lombok. It is extremely convenient, faster than using public services, and ties in with the tourist shuttle bus schedules between Padang Bai and other Bali destinations (see p.380).

## Taxis

Metered **taxis** – with a "Taxi" sign on the roof – cruise for business in Denpasar, Nusa Dua, Jimbaran and Kuta on Bali, and Ampenan-Mataram-Cakranegara-Sweta, Lembar and Senggigi on Lombok and are not expensive. It's usual to round the fare up to the nearest Rp1000 when paying.

On Bali, there are several companies, the most common being the light-blue Kuta Blue Bird or Bali Taxis (ⓣ0361/701111, ⓦwww.bluebirdgroup.com) and the white Ngurah Rai Airport Taxis (ⓣ0361/724724). Always check that the meter is turned on when you get in. As an example of fares, to get from Jalan Dhyana Pura in Seminyak to Bemo Corner in Kuta should cost around Rp15,000.

On Lombok, the light-blue Lombok Taxis (☎0370/627000, ⊕www.bluebirdgroup.com) have similar charges: to get from Mataram to central Senggigi will cost Rp15,000–20,000.

As an alternative, you can simply flag down an empty bemo and charter it like a taxi, although you'll have to bargain hard before you get in.

## Dokar/cidomo

The traditional form of transport on the islands is **horse and cart**. The horses wear heavy leather harnesses adorned with silver bells that jingle as they move, so you'll hear them coming. Called **dokar** on Bali and **cidomo** on Lombok, they tend to ply the back routes, often transporting heavy loads. They're also used for city transport in Denpasar and Ampenan-Mataram-Cakranegara-Sweta and as tourist vehicles in Kuta and Senggigi. Negotiate a price before you get in; as a tourist, you won't get far for less than Rp5000.

## Rental vehicles

You need to think about what you're **planning** to do before you decide on a vehicle. If you're heading into the mountains, you need power to cope with the slopes; on rougher terrain you need clearance. Wherever you get the vehicle from, take a telephone contact number to get in touch in case of breakdown.

On both islands you'll need to produce an **international drivers' licence** or **tourist driving licence** before you rent. Be warned that on major holidays (like Galungan and Nyepi) vehicles are snapped up quickly by Balinese going home for the festivities. Rental vehicles need to have both Balinese and Lombok registration to travel on both islands, so you must tell the rental agency if you intend to take the vehicle between the islands, and check with them exactly what paperwork is required.

The multinational **car rental agencies** Hertz (⊕www.hertz.com) and Avis (⊕www.avis.com) have offices on Bali, but not on Lombok – although with prices around US$400 per week, it's more economical to rent a car from local outlets after you arrive. More expensive local agents such as JBA in Sanur (see p.154) charge $25 per day for a Suzuki Jimney, which can fit two people in the front and up to four on bench seats in the back (or $20 per day for four or more days), $35 ($30) for a more comfortable Jeep-like 1600cc Toyota Kijang, and an extra $12 for a driver. Motorbikes go for Rp65,000. However, smaller places and those outside the southern resort areas charge thirty to forty percent less than this. All prices exclude fuel, and note that a "one day" rental normally means twelve hours. Rates drop considerably if you rent for a week or more.

Some outfits offer partial **insurance** as part of the fee; typically, the maximum you'll end up paying in the event of any accident will be $150–500. The conditions of insurance policies vary considerably and you should make certain you know what you're signing. Bear in mind that under this system, if there is minor damage – for example if you smash a light – you'll end up paying the whole cost of it. You can organize your own (expensive) car insurance through Asuransi Jasa Indonesia (⊕www.jasindo.co.id), either via their office in Denpasar at Jl Surapati 22 (☎0361/235357, ⓔdenpasar@jasindo.net) or through certain rental outlets; third-party liability, with an excess of Rp40,000,000, costs Rp168,500 per day.

Before you take a vehicle, **check** it thoroughly and get something in writing about any damage that has already been done, or you may end up being blamed for it. Most vehicle rental agencies keep your passport as security, so you don't have a lot of bargaining power in the case of any dispute.

### Tourist driving licences

If you don't have an international driving licence it's possible to obtain a **tourist driving licence**, which allows you to drive. They are available for cars or motorbikes (Rp150,000) from Pelayan Sim Tourist (Mon–Fri 8am–3pm, Sat 8am–1pm; ☎0361/243939) inside the Kantor Bersama Samsat on Jalan Cok Agung Tresna in the Renon district of Denpasar. Take a passport and home driving licence.

### On the road

Traffic in Indonesia drives **on the left**. There's a maximum speed limit of 70kph. Fuel costs Rp2400 a litre, but may well rise.

Foreign drivers need to carry an **international driving licence** or **tourist driving licence** and the **registration documents** of the vehicle or you're liable to a fine. Seatbelts must be used. All motorcyclists, both drivers and passengers, must wear a helmet; these will be provided by the rental outlet, but most aren't up to much. The police carry out regular spot checks and you'll be fined for any infringements.

In south Bali in particular, some roads change during the day from two-way to one-way. This isn't publicized in any way that is comprehensible to foreigners, but if you're caught you'll be fined. In recent years, there have been reports of police stopping foreign drivers for supposed infringements and "fining" them on the spot – accepting only foreign currency – in what is essentially an extortion racket. Official clean-up campaigns have followed; if it happens to you the best advice is to keep calm and have a small amount of easily accessible notes well away from your main stash of cash if you have to hand some over.

It's worth driving extremely defensively. Accidents are always unpleasant, disagreements over the insurance situation and any repairs can be lengthy, and many local people have a straightforward attitude to accidents involving tourists – the visitor must be to blame. Don't drive at **night** unless you absolutely have to, largely because pedestrians, cyclists, food carts and horse carts all use the roadway without any lights. There are also plenty of roadside ditches.

## Chartered transport

Hundreds of drivers in tourist areas offer **chartered transport** – this means you rent their vehicle with them as the driver. Most have cars or Jeeps, but you can usually find somebody with a motorbike. You're expected to pay for the driver's meals and accommodation if the trip takes more than a day, and you must be very clear about who is paying for fuel, where you want to go and stop, and how many people will be travelling. With somebody driving who knows the roads, you've got plenty of time to look around and fewer potential problems to worry about, but it's very difficult to guarantee the quality of the driving. You'll pay

Rp250,000–300,000 for the vehicle, driver and fuel, but you'll need to bargain. For first-hand recommendations of good drivers, check the Bali and Lombok Travel Forum ⓦwww.travelforum.org/bali.

## Motorbike and bicycle rental

**Motorbikes** available for rent vary from small 100cc Yamahas to more robust trail bikes. Prices start at Rp30,000 per day without insurance (Rp40,000 in the bigger resorts), with discounts for longer rentals. You'll need to show an international motorcycle licence or tourist driving licence. Conditions on Bali and Lombok are not suitable for inexperienced drivers, with heavy traffic on major routes, steep hills and difficult driving off the beaten track. There are increasing numbers of accidents involving tourists, so don't take risks.

In most tourist areas, it's possible to rent a **bicycle** for around Rp20,000 a day; check its condition before you set off and carry plenty of water, as it's hot and thirsty work. Ubud is a popular area for cycling day-trips and guided rides (see p.187), but if you're planning to tour the island by bike, bear in mind that, should you get tired or stranded somewhere, bemos will be extremely reluctant to pick you and your bike up.

## Planes

**Bali's** domestic terminal is adjacent to the international one at Ngurah Rai Airport, 3km south of Kuta; **Lombok's** shares the Selaparang Airport runway in Mataram with the handful of international flights. Domestic airlines have ticket sales counters in the domestic terminal at Ngurah Rai Airport, at Selaparang Airport and/or offices in nearby cities (see p.33 for details).

## Luxury air transport

For special occasions or fantasy journeys – or if you're not counting the rupiah – it's possible to get around the islands by **helicopter**. Air Bali (ⓣ0361/767466, ⓦwww.air-bali.com) offer sightseeing trips of the south or centre of the island – you'll be looking at about $1000 per hour for either sightseeing or chartered transport to one of the dozen or so helipads that are now dotted around the island.

# Accommodation

Whatever your budget, the overall standard of accommodation in Bali and Lombok is high. Even the smallest and most inexpensive lodgings are enticing, nearly always set in a tropical garden and with some kind of outdoor seating area on a covered communal veranda or shaded terrace. Interiors can be a bit sparse, but the terraces encourage you to do as local people do, and spend most of your leisure time in the open air.

The majority of cheap places to stay are classed as **losmen**, a term that literally means homestay, but is most commonly used to describe any fairly small-scale and inexpensive accommodation, be it in the grounds of the family home or not. Nearly everything else comes into the **hotels** category, most of which offer air-conditioning and a swimming pool. **Villas** are private holiday homes, usually pretty luxurious, catering for couples, small groups and families. **Check-out time** in losmen and hotels is usually noon.

Most losmen and all hotel rooms have ensuite **bathrooms** (*kamar mandi*), though in a few of the older homestays you might have to share a communal one. Except in the most basic places, **toilets** (*wc*, pronounced *way say*) are usually Western-style, but flushing is sometimes done manually, with water scooped from the pail that stands alongside. The same pail and scoop is used by the Balinese to wash themselves after going to the toilet (using the left hand, never the right, which is for eating), but most tourist bathrooms also have toilet paper.

Many Balinese and Sasak people still **bathe** in the rivers and public bathing pools, but indoor bathing is traditionally done by means of the scoop and slosh method, or **mandi**. Bathroom water is often stored in a huge basin, but this is not a bath, so never get in it; all washing is done outside it and the basin should not be contaminated by soap or shampoo. Many losmen and all hotels in the bigger resort areas provide showers as well as mandi. Outside the bigger resorts, the very cheapest rooms may not have hot water (*air panas*).

In the more stylish places, bathrooms can be delightful, particularly if they are designed with open roofs and bedecked with plants. These **"garden bathrooms"** often have showers and mandi fed by water piped through sculpted flues and floors covered in a carpet of smooth, rounded pebbles.

## Prices

On the whole, both losmen and hotels are inexpensive. For the simplest double room, **prices** start at around Rp40,000 in the least visited areas, including the Rinjani area and Kuta on Lombok, and Rp60,000 in the smaller resorts such as Lovina, Nusa Lembongan, Candi Dasa and Padang Bai. In Kuta, Ubud, Gili Trawangan and Senggigi, you will find a handful of places charging Rp35,000–50,000, but these fill up very fast, so you should be prepared to pay a minimum of Rp70,000.

During **off-season** (Feb–June and Sept–Nov) you can often negotiate up to fifty percent off the published rate in some of the moderate and expensive hotels; at the very least you should get the service tax deducted or an extra night thrown in for nothing.

Things are rather different in **peak season** (Jan, July, Aug & Dec), when rates can be hiked at whim and rooms are at a premium. During these months it's worth reserving ahead and, if appropriate, asking to be picked up from Bali's Ngurah Rai Airport, a service offered free of charge by many hotels. Losmen, unfortunately, often won't take advance bookings, so at the height of the season it may be worth listening to the touts who hang around the transport terminals in the main resort areas, as they'll guarantee to find you a room, albeit potentially at a slightly inflated rate.

## Accommodation price codes

All the accommodation listed in this book has been given one of the following price codes, corresponding to the **cheapest double room** in high season excluding tax. Rates in low season may be up to fifty percent lower and booking online at any time will give you (often significant) discounts. Nearly all losmen and hotels quote their rates exclusive of the obligatory government **tax** (ten or eleven percent); many of the more expensive hotels add an extra ten percent **service charge** (in hotel-speak, these supplements are usually referred to as "plus-plus").

In general, losmen in the ❶–❹ categories post their prices in **rupiah**. The most upmarket hotels quote their rates in **US dollars**, and usually accept cash, travellers' cheques or credit cards, but will also convert to rupiah. Credit-card transactions are always in rupiah, so check the in-house exchange rate. Unless otherwise indicated, hotels in the ❾ category charge $150–250 for their standard rooms.

❶ under Rp55,000
❷ Rp55,000–105,000
❸ Rp105,000–155,000
❹ Rp155,000–205,000
❺ Rp205,000–305,000; US$20–30

❻ Rp305,000–505,000; US$30–50
❼ US$50–80
❽ US$80–150
❾ US$150–250

## Losmen

While most **losmen** (generally ❶–❸) provide far more sophisticated facilities than the "homestay" tag implies, many are still family-run operations with an emphasis on friendly service and simple, inexpensive accommodation. Rooms tend to be in single-storey detached or semi-detached "cottages" (sometimes known as "bungalows"), which can be anything from whitewashed concrete cubes to artful rattan and bamboo structures built to resemble traditional rice barns. Some are even embellished with woodcarvings and set in their own walled gardens. Furnishings tend to be fairly stark: hard beds and even harder bolsters are the norm, and you may or may not be provided with a light blanket. Most losmen rooms come with fans and netted windows (sticky tape comes in handy for repairing holes), and nearly all have attached (sometimes cold-water only) bathrooms. Certain losmen offer a range of rooms, charging more for hot water, air-conditioning and a prime location, and possibly even a swimming pool as well.

The best losmen provide a complimentary flask of tea, and some include **breakfast** (*makan pagi*) in the price of the room. If you're lucky, this might run to fruit salad and banana pancakes, or may simply comprise toast and coffee.

Very few losmen offer **single rooms** (*kamar untuk satu orang*), so lone travellers will normally get put in a double room at about 75 percent of the full price, which rarely works out at less than Rp30,000.

## Hotels

The least attractive type of lodgings on Bali and Lombok are the **cheap urban hotels** (❶–❺) such as those in Denpasar and Singaraja, which cater for short-stay Indonesian businesspeople and can feel rather soulless and lonely. Nonetheless, they are usually clean enough and tend to be located near transport terminals.

Accommodation in **moderately priced hotels** (❹–❻) is often in "cottages" or "bungalows" and facilities generally include air-conditioning and a swimming pool (*kolam renang*). Of all the **expensive hotels** (❼–❾) on Bali and Lombok, only one is high-rise – the nine-storey *Inna Grand Bali Beach* in Sanur. This caused such consternation when built that a local law was subsequently passed forbidding any other hotel to be taller than a coconut palm. As a result, even the massive international hotels such as Sanur's *Bali Hyatt* and Senggigi's *Sheraton* are low-rise structures, many of them designed to evoke traditional Balinese palaces (*puri*) and temples (*pura*). This *puri-pura* style, dubbed

## Booking accommodation online

Many hotels in Bali and Lombok have a Web page hosted by one or more of the main **online accommodation services** listed below, where you can see photos and usually get a discounted rate. Most of the following online accommodation agents offer **discounts** of up to fifty percent on the published rates of standard and upmarket hotels (US$20 and upwards).

**Access Bali Villas** Ⓦ www.villas-bali.com
**Bali Hotels** Ⓦ www.balihotels.com
**Bali Hotels and Accommodations Company** Ⓦ www.travelideas.net/bali.hotels
**Bali Online Hotels** Ⓦ www.indo.com/hotels
**Bali Resorts** Ⓦ www.baliresorts.com
**Bali RoomFinder** Ⓦ www.baliwww.com/bali/roomfinder
**Hostel World** Ⓦ www.hostelworld.com
**Lombok Hotels** Ⓦ www.lombokhotels.com

**Bali baroque** or Baliesque because of its excessive use of ornamentation, works better in some buildings than others, but certainly adds a distinct character to the upmarket resorts. Their grounds are designed in similarly grand style, with waterfalls, endless lawns and borders of tropical shrubs, and many include a series of free-form swimming pools as well.

If you're looking for smaller-scale places with more character, opt for those that classify themselves as **boutique hotels**. Some comprise as few as half a dozen rooms, and they're generally stylish and luxurious; many are well priced, too. Outstanding examples include *The Watergarden* and *Kubu Bali* in Candi Dasa, *Damai Lovina Villas* in Lovina, *Cabé Bali* in Tirtagangga, *Alam Jiwa* and *Tegal Sari* in Ubud, *Prana Dewi* in Wongayagede, *Gajah Mina* in Lalang Linggah, *Zen Lifestyle Energy Resort* in Ume Anyar, *Sanda Butik Villas* in Sanda and *Cempaka Belimbing* in Belimbing. They are rarer on Lombok but *Vila Ombak* and *Desa Dunia Beda* on Gili Trawangan and *Villa Nautilus* on Gili Meno fit the bill.

An increasing number of Bali's and Lombok's **super-luxury hotels** (US$250–700) are designed in chic modern-Asian style and often comprise private garden-compounds, sometimes with personal plunge-pools as well. We've detailed some of these places, most notably the *Four Seasons Resort* in Jimbaran, the *Tugu* in Canggu, the *Amandari* in Ubud, Candi Dasa's *Alila*, and the *Oberoi* near Tanjung in Lombok.

### Villas

If you want posh accommodation for a family or small group, or extremely private accommodation for a couple, it's worth considering a **villa**. Sometimes the home of an expat, rented out for most of the year, or sometimes purpose-built for holiday rentals, villas are usually designed in appealing Balinese style and equipped with a private pool and kitchen. They can be rented, often at quite reasonable rates, by the day or the week, and prices (from around $180 per night for four people) often include the services of a housekeeper and cook. See Private Vacation Villas in Bali (Ⓦ www.balivillas.com) for some ideas. Be aware, though, that some hotels advertise their bungalows as "villas" even though they don't have kitchens and lack the privacy of genuine holiday homes. For weekly and monthly rental opportunities, see "Long-term accommodation", below.

### Camping

The availability of inexpensive losmen near almost every decent beach on Bali and Lombok means that it's hardly worth lugging a tent and sleeping bag all the way around the islands. To **camp** in Bali Barat National Park you need a permit and must be accompanied by a park ranger; you will also have to supply your own bag and tent. It's considered inappropriate to camp on the slopes of Bali's most sacred mountains, although camping on Lombok's Gunung Rinjani is normal practice and tents, sleeping bags and cooking equipment can be rented for the climb.

## Balinese gardens

Blessed with rich volcanic soil, abundant rivers, lots of sunshine and plenty of hearty downpours, Bali blooms year-round with stunning displays of tropical flora. Roadsides are planted with a rainbow of decorative and shade-giving trees, including scarlet **flame trees** (*flamboyan*), fiery orange **African tulip trees** (*kacret-kacretan*), banyans, and red, pink and white **oleanders** (*kenyeri*), as well as hedges of **croton**, **cordyline** and **coleus shrubs** in variegations that run from burgundy and scarlet through amber and lime. The clustered heads of the red **Javanese ixora** (*soka*) and the pink and orange **lantana** (*kerasi*) are common sights, as are purple and white **bougainvillea** (*kertas*), and the trumpet blossoms of the white **datura** (*kecubung bali*) and the yellow **allamanda**. The two woody **frangipani** shrubs (*jepun jawa* and *jepun bali*) are a staple feature of temple courtyards, as their scented white, pink and yellow blossoms are, like the scarlet blooms of the ubiquitous **hibiscus** (*pucuk*), used in offerings and for decorating religious statues. Many households also cultivate fruit trees such as **papaya**, **banana**, **guava**, **mango** and **coconut**. Even the exotic-looking flame-tipped **heliconia** is not uncommon sights in public and private gardens around the island, and the myriad foliage plants can be equally stunning, not least the large, white-veined, heart-shaped leaves of the **crystal anthurium**.

You'll find all this and more in Bali's **hotel gardens**, whose designers have taken inspiration from the horticultural principles of the traditional courtyard garden, which strives to create a balance of "abundance" and "stillness", and embellished the concept to often breathtaking effect. Perhaps the most famous Balinese hotel garden is the thirty-six acres of the *Bali Hyatt* in Sanur (see p.156), designed by the prolific expat architect and landscape gardener Made Wijaya to evoke a tropical park, complete with coconut groves, contemplative vistas, and the all-important series of pools and ponds, interlaced with shrine-like lanterns and artfully sited mossy-green statues. **Water** is an essential feature of any Balinese garden, and even the smallest losmen courtyard is likely to harbour a few pink **lotus flowers** (*tunjung*) or a couple of white **water lilies** (also known as *tunjung*) in an earthenware water jar. At the most refined end of the spectrum, the bungalows at *The Watergarden* hotel in Candi Dasa (see p.265) are an exquisite example of harmony in an aquatic garden. Other outstanding hotel gardens in Bali and Lombok include the stepped terraces at *Hotel Tjampuhan* in Ubud (see p.191); the innovative integration of an elegant pond and a small, working ricefield into the hotel landscape at *Ananda Cottages*, also in Ubud (see p.191); and the lush extravaganza that falls just this side of wilderness at the *Sheraton* in Senggigi (see p.395). There are many fine small-scale hotel gardens, too, often the product of a single gardener's enthusiasm, as at *Flamboyant* losmen in Candi Dasa (see p.266). For a selection of inspirational and educational **books** on Balinese gardens and tropical plants, see p.505.

## Long-term accommodation

Many losmen are happy to rent out rooms **long-term**, and several establishments in Legian and Ubud provide kitchen facilities and reasonable monthly rates as an incentive. Seminyak, Sanur and the Ubud area are the most popular for larger, more salubrious long-term rentals, and a number of local **real-estate agents** advertise their properties in English with the foreign visitor in mind; see p.134 for leads on places in Kuta–Legian–Seminyak, and p.215 for the Ubud area. For the lease and sale of both villas and land all over the island, try Bali Paradise (Ⓦwww.bali-paradise.com/properties), Bali Real Estate Agents (Ⓣ0361/284069, Ⓦwww.balirealestateagents.com), House of Bali (Ⓣ0361/739541, Ⓦwww.houseofbali.com) or In Touch (Ⓣ0361/731047, Ⓦwww.intouchbali.com). The fortnightly *Bali Advertiser* (Ⓦwww.baliadvertiser.biz) always carries a page or two of property ads, and is available from some hotels, restaurants and tourist offices. If you're thinking about **buying** or building a house in Bali, check out the advice on Owning Property in Bali (⊛www.baliproperties.com). Be very wary of any **time-share** **deal**: many tourists fail to read the small print and have found themselves making unwise investments and unable to claim back their money. See p.75 for related cons.

# Eating and drinking

If you come to Bali or Lombok expecting the range and exuberance of the cooking elsewhere in Southeast Asia, you'll be disappointed. Somehow the ingenuity and panache don't seem to have reached this far, or maybe they've been elbowed out of the way by pizzas, hamburgers and French fries. However, there's a considerable variety of food available, cooked in a range of styles. Ironically, the most elusive cuisines on the islands are the native Balinese and Sasak.

At the inexpensive end of the scale, you can get a bowl of *bakso ayam* (chicken soup with noodles) for Rp5000 or less from one of the **carts** (*kaki lima*) that ply their wares around the streets or line the sidewalks and bus stations during the day and congregate at night markets after dark. Slightly upmarket are **warung** or *rumah makan* (eating houses), which range from a few tables and chairs in a kitchen to fully fledged restaurants. There's usually a menu, but in the simplest places you'll probably just find rice and noodle dishes on offer. Most places that call themselves **restaurants** cater for a broad range of tastes, offering Western, Indonesian and Chinese food, while others specialize in a particular cuisine such as Mexican, Japanese or Italian. The multinational fast-food chains have also arrived in the tourist and city areas.

**Vegetarians** get a good deal, with plenty of tofu (*tahu*) and *tempeh*, a fermented soybean cake, alongside plenty of fresh vegetables.

Restaurant **etiquette** is pretty much the same as in the West, with waiter service the norm. Most places will have a washbasin in a corner so you can wash your hands before eating. If you're eating with friends, don't count on everyone's meal arriving together;

there may be just one gas burner in the kitchen.

**Prices** vary dramatically depending on the location rather than the quality of the meals. In the humblest *rumah makan*, a simple rice dish such as nasi campur is about Rp5000, while tourist restaurants charge Rp8000–30,000 for their version of the same dish. If you choose non-Indonesian food such as pizza, pasta and steak, prices start at around Rp20,000 in tourist restaurants. We've classified all restaurants that we've reviewed as inexpensive, moderate or expensive. **Inexpensive** means you will get a satisfying main dish for less than Rp20,000, **moderate** means it'll be Rp20,000–60,000, and **expensive** implies Rp60,000 and over. Bear in mind that restaurants with more expensive food also have pricier drinks and, in addition, most places add anything up to 21 percent to the bill for tax and service.

See pp.516–518 for a menu reader of dishes and common terms.

## Styles of cooking

The most abundant style of cooking available on both Bali and Lombok is **Indonesian** rice- and noodle-based meals, followed closely by Chinese (essentially Cantonese) food, as well as a vast array of Western food in the resorts. Native Balinese food on Bali, and Sasak food on Lombok, is something you'll need to search out. Should you wish to learn more about local food, cookery schools for visitors are available; see p.86.

## Indonesian food

Based on rice (*nasi*) or noodles (*mie* or *bakmi*), with small side dishes of vegetables, fish or meat, **Indonesian food** is flavoured with chillies, soy sauce (*kecup*), garlic, ginger, cinnamon, turmeric and lemongrass. You'll also find chilli sauce (*sambal*) everywhere.

One dish available in even the simplest warung is **nasi campur**, boiled rice with small amounts of vegetables, meat and fish, often served with a fried egg and *krupuk* (huge prawn crackers). The accompanying dishes vary from day to day, depending on what's available. Another staple is **nasi goreng**, fried rice with vegetables, meat or fish, also often with egg and *krupuk*. The noodle equivalent – *mie* or **bakmi goreng** – is also commonly available. The other mainstays of the Indonesian menu are **gado-gado**, steamed vegetables served with a spicy peanut sauce, and **sate**, small kebabs of beef, pork, chicken, goat or fish, barbecued over a fire and served on a bamboo stick with spicy peanut sauce.

Inexpensive and authentic Sumatran or **Padang** fare is sold in *rumah makan Padang*, which you'll find in every sizeable town. Padang food is cold and displayed on platters. There are no menus; when you enter you either select your composite meal by pointing to the dishes on display, or just sit down, the staff bring you a selection, and you pay by the number of plates you have eaten from at the end. The food is tradition-

ally fiery. Dishes you may encounter include boiled *kangkung* (water spinach), *tempeh*, fried eggplant with chilli, boiled eggs in curry sauce, fried whole fish or fish steaks, meat curry, squid or fish curry, potato cakes, beef brain curry and fried cow's lung.

## Balinese food

The everyday **Balinese** diet is a couple of meals based on rice, essentially nasi campur, eaten whenever people feel hungry, supplemented with snacks such as *krupuk*. The full magnificence of Balinese cooking is reserved for festivals and ceremonies when all the stops are pulled out. One of the best dishes is **babi guling**, spit-roasted pig, served with *lawar*, a spicy raw-meat mash. Another speciality is **betutu bebek**, smoked duck, cooked very slowly – this has to be ordered in advance from restaurants.

Although the Balinese tend not to eat desserts, *bubuh injin*, **black rice pudding**, named after the colour of the rice husk, is available in tourist spots. The rice itself is pink and served with a sweet coconut-milk sauce, fruit and grated coconut. Rice cakes (*jaja*) play a major part in ceremonial offerings but are also a daily food.

## Sasak food

According to some sources, the name "Lombok" translates as "chilli pepper" – highly appropriate considering the savage heat of traditional **Sasak food**. It's not easy to track down, however, and you'll find Chinese and Indonesian food far more widely available on Lombok. Traditional Sasak food uses rice as the staple, together with a wide variety of vegetables, a little meat (although no pork), and some fish, served in various

## Betel

One habit that you'll notice in Bali and Lombok, and generally throughout Southeast Asia, especially among older people, is the chewing of **betel**. Small parcels, made up of three ingredients – areca nut wrapped in betel leaf that has been smeared with lime – are lodged inside the cheek. When mixed with saliva, these are a stimulant as well as producing an abundance of bright red saliva, which is regularly spat out on the ground and eventually stains the lips and teeth red. Other ingredients can be added according to taste, including tobacco, cloves, cinnamon, cardamom, turmeric and nutmeg. You may also come across decorated boxes used to store the ingredients on display in museums.

sauces, often with a dish of chilli sauce on the side in case it isn't hot enough already. Anything with *pelecing* in the name is served with **chilli sauce**. Taliwang dishes, originally from Sumbawa, are also available on Lombok, consisting of grilled or fried food with a chilli sauce. All parts of the animals are used, and you'll find plenty of offal on the menu. There's also a wide range of sticky desserts, many of them served wrapped in leaves.

## Fine dining

Just as it's possible to get by spending a dollar or less for a decent meal in Bali or Lombok, you can also enjoy some superb **fine dining** experiences on the islands. Plenty of innovative chefs, some Western, some Asian, have imported and adapted modern international gourmet cooking and seasoned the resulting melange with local tastes and produce. They offer menus that are creative and imaginative and, best of all, taste great. Restaurants serving this food are invariably stylish, with excellent service, charging US$30–50 per head. This can seem a lot in the context of Indonesian prices, but when compared with restaurants of a similar standard in London or New York, it's decidedly good value. Top choices include the restaurants at *Damai Lovina Villas* in the north of the island (see p.331), *Kafé Warisan*, *Ku dé Ta* and *The Living Room*, all in Seminyak (see p.129), *Mozaic* in Ubud (see p.209) and *Alila* in Candi Dasa (see p.266).

### Fresh fruit

The range of **fresh fruit** available on Bali and Lombok is startling. You'll see **banana**, **coconut** and **papaya** growing all year round, and **pineapple** and **watermelon** are always in evidence in the markets. Of the citrus fruits, the giant **pomelo** is the most unusual to visitors – larger than a grapefruit and sweeter. **Guava**, **avocado** (served as a sweet fruit juice with condensed milk), **passion fruit**, **mango**, **soursop** and its close relative, the **custard apple**, are all common. Less familiar are the seasonal **mangosteen** with a purple skin and sweet white flesh; the hairy **rambutan**, closely related to the lychee; the **salak** or **snakefruit**, named after its brown scaly skin; and the **starfruit**, which

is crunchy but rather flavourless. **Jackfruit**, which usually weighs 10–20kg, has firm yellow segments around a large stone inside its green bobbly skin. This is not to be confused with the **durian**, also large but with a spiky skin and a pungent, sometimes almost rotten, odour. Some airlines and hotels ban it because of the smell, but devoted fans travel large distances and pay high prices for good-quality durian fruit.

## Drinks

**Bottled water** is widely available throughout the islands (Rp1800–4000 for 1.5 litres in supermarkets), as are familiar international brands of **soft drinks** (around Rp2000 per bottle); you'll pay higher prices in restaurants. There are also delicious **fruit drinks** on offer, but be a bit cautious, as you can't always be sure of the safety of the water or ice (for more, see p.42). Many restaurants automatically add sugar to their juices so you'll need to specify if you don't want that. Moderately priced restaurants charge Rp6000–8000 for juice drinks, excluding tax and service.

Indonesians are great **coffee** (*kopi*) and **tea** (*teh*) drinkers. Locally grown coffee (*kopi Bali* or *kopi Lombok*) is drunk black, sweet and strong. The coffee isn't filtered, so the grounds settle in the bottom of the glass. If you want milk added or you don't want sugar, you'll have to ask (see p.516). Nescafé instant coffee is available in tourist restaurants. You'll also find hot lemon or orange juice.

## Alcohol

Locally produced **beer** includes Bali Hai, the most common, fizziest and least pleasant, as well as the two pilsners, Anker and Bintang. Expect to pay from Rp8000 for a 620ml bottle from a supermarket or in an inexpensive losmen or warung, but in a restaurant you'd be lucky to pay Rp10,000, and may be looking at Rp15,000 or more. Draught beer, usually served in a glass of about half a pint, comes in at around Rp8500 at most moderate restaurants.

Many tourist restaurants and bars offer an extensive list of **cocktails** (Rp15,000 upwards). There are reports of some places putting decidedly second-rate liquor into

58

their cocktails, or even no liquor at all – probably difficult to detect unless you're a connoisseur. "Happy Hours" in tourist spots very often last all evening.

Locally produced **wine** is available on Bali, made from grapes grown in the north of the island by Hatten Wines or from imported grape juice by Wine of the Gods. Several different vintages are available in restaurants in the main tourist areas (Rp75,000 upwards per bottle) – the rosé gets the best reports.

Imported spirits are available in major tourist areas, where wines from Australia and New Zealand, California, Europe and South America are also available, mostly Rp30,000 upwards for a glass and Rp190,000 upwards for a bottle. Local brews include *brem*, a type of rice wine, *tuak*, palm beer brewed from palm tree sap, and powerful *arak*, a palm or rice spirit that is often incorporated into highly potent local cocktails.

# Communications

Mail services in Bali and Lombok are reasonably efficient, with at least one post office in every town. The phone network, however, is patchy – oversubscribed in some areas, rudimentary in others – though most major tourist resorts now have plenty of Internet centres.

## Mail

Every town and tourist centre on Bali and Lombok has a **General Post Office** (GPO; *kantor pos*) where you can buy stamps (*perangko*) and aerogrammes (*surat udara*), and can post letters (*surat*) and parcels (*paket*) and, in some cases, collect poste restante, send faxes and use the Internet. All *kantor pos* keep official government office hours (Mon–Thurs 8am–2pm, Fri 8–11am, Sat 8am–1pm; closed on festival days and public holidays), except where otherwise stated in the Guide. In larger towns and resorts, you can also buy stamps and send letters and parcels from **postal agents**, who charge official rates but often open longer hours than the *kantor pos*. Post boxes (*kotak surat*) are square and orangey-red in colour, but they aren't that numerous, so you're usually better off posting letters at GPOs or postal agents. Postage is expensive, with the current rates for **airmail postcards/letters** under 200g as follows: Australia Rp5500/7000, New Zealand Rp5000/7000, Europe Rp6500/10,000, Canada Rp6000/9500 and USA Rp6000/10,500.

Airmail post takes about a week, while a local letter to anywhere in Bali or Lombok takes three to five days.

*Kantor pos* generally don't offer a **parcel-packing service**, but there's normally a stall next door where you pay to have your stuff parcelled up – don't bother packing it yourself as the contents need to be inspected first. Postal rates for parcels are also high: a parcel weighing 250–500g costs $22 to be airmailed to Europe; a 6–10kg parcel sent by sea costs $56 and could take up to three months. A parcel of 1–1.5kg to Australia costs $21 by airmail, and a 6–10kg parcel costs $33 by sea. *Kantor pos* won't handle any parcels over 10kg, but most major galleries and craft shops offer a shipping service.

### Poste restante

Most *kantor pos* in major towns and resort areas offer a **poste restante** service: details are given throughout the Guide. Letters are held for a maximum of one month and should be filed by family name, but mistakes do happen, so check under first-name initials

## Useful numbers and codes

**International operator** ☎101
**International directory enquiries** ☎102
**Domestic operator** ☎100
**Local directory enquiries** ☎108
**Long-distance directory enquiries** ☎106

### Phoning home

Dial ☎001 or ☎008 + IDD country code + area code (minus its initial zero if applicable) + local number. IDD rates shown are for the standard period; there's a twenty-percent surcharge if calling during the weekday peak period, and a 25-percent discount during weekday off-peak periods, at weekends and on national holidays.
**Australia** Country code ☎61. IDD rate: Rp8300/min (peak 9am–noon, off-peak 10pm–6am).
**Ireland** Country code ☎353. IDD rate: Rp7150/min (peak 2–5pm, off-peak 3–11am).
**New Zealand** Country code ☎64. IDD rate: Rp8300/min (peak 9am–noon, off-peak 11pm–7am).
**UK** Country code ☎44. IDD rate: Rp9400/min (peak 2–5pm, off-peak 3–11am).
**US and Canada** Country code ☎1. IDD rate: Rp8300/min (peak 9am–noon, off-peak 11pm–7am).

### Calling Bali and Lombok from abroad

Dial your international access code (☎00 from the UK, Ireland and New Zealand, ☎011 from the US and Canada, ☎0011 from Australia) + **62** for Indonesia + area code minus its initial zero + local number.

### Time difference

Bali and Lombok are on Central Indonesian Time (GMT+8, North American EST+13, Australian EST-2).

---

as well. You're unlikely to have to pay anything for the service.

## Phones

**Phone services** in Bali and Lombok are still in their infancy. Some places, like Amed, Pemuteran and even Ubud, have far too few to cope with demand. Although you'll find public phones in a few major centres (Kuta, Denpasar, Ubud), most phoning is done through the government-run **phone offices** – the main *kantor telkom* and the branch *wartel telkom* – or through the private "telephone shops" known simply as **wartel**. *Kantor telkom* (often open 24hr) and *wartel telkom* (usually 7am–midnight) generally have several coin-operated phones (*telepon umum*) and card phones (*telepon umum kartu*) as well as a few booths for making **IDD** (International Direct Dial) and collect (reverse-charge) calls. Wartel keep similarly long hours, but don't have coin-operated or card phones.

The **rates** at the official *telkom* outlets are standardized throughout Indonesia, but the privately run wartel sometimes charge inflated prices. A ten-percent tax is added to all calls made through *kantor telkom* and wartel. Hotels usually add prohibitive surcharges for calls made from guest rooms.

**Phone cards** (*kartu telepon*) are sold in denominations of Rp5000–100,000 and are available at *kantor telkom* and in some wartel, postal agents and money exchange booths. There are several types of phone card – and two types of card phone – which can make using them very frustrating; if you get stuck with mismatching card and phone, head for the nearest large hotel, which usually have both types of card phone in the lobby. Phonebooks are scarce, but directory enquiries or the operator should be able to help.

You can send domestic and international **faxes** (*fax*) from most *kantor telkom*, *wartel telkom* and wartel, for approximately

Rp15,000 per page (to Europe or the US). Many wartel will also receive faxes for you, for which they charge a small fee.

## Local, long-distance and mobile calls

A **local call** (*panggilan lokal*) is a call to any destination that shares the same area code, and for these you can use a coin-operated phone, a card phone or a wartel phone. Local calls should cost Rp250 for up to three minutes, though hotels often charge up to Rp1000 a minute. In most cases, you put the coins in only after the person you're calling has picked up the phone and started to speak. Card phones work in the same way as they do elsewhere in the world.

**Long-distance calls** (*panggilan inter-lokal*), to any destination within Indonesia that has a different area code, can be made either at a card phone or at any *kantor telkom* or wartel – coin-operated phones don't work for long-distance calls. Bali is divided into several code zones, while Lombok has two codes.

Calls to **mobile phones** are naturally more expensive. Any phone number prefaced by the following code is a mobile: ℡0811, ℡0812, ℡08133, ℡0816, ℡0818, ℡082, ℡0828. Some hotels and other business-es have to rely on **satellite phones** (code ℡086812), which are even costlier to call.

## International calls

You can make **international calls** (*panggilan internasional*) from certain card phones, located in major hotel lobbies and at the airport, and on special **IDD** phones at the *kantor telkom* and wartel, as well as through hotel switchboards. Some *kantor telkom* and wartel will also let you make **reverse-charge calls** for a nominal fee.

To make **IDD calls** you can dial either ℡001 or ℡008: rates for both services are identical (see box opposite), fixed by the government, and use identical time-bands for identical discounts.

**Home Country Direct (HCD)** allows you to reach the operator in your home country, although calls end up being more expensive than dialling direct. It's available on all IDD phones as well as on certain others that have the HCD logo, such as those at Ngurah Rai Airport. You can't use cash for HCD calls (only credit cards) or make reverse-charge calls. On HCD phones, you just press the designated button to reach your home-country operator; on IDD phones, you need to dial ℡001-801 or ℡008-801, and then the special HCD code to reach your home-country operator: Australia ℡61, Canada ℡16, Ireland ℡353, New Zealand ℡64, UK ℡44, USA ℡10.

You can in theory use BT, AT&T, MCI, Tel-stra and other **phone chargecards** (pur-chased at home) to make international calls through the IDD card phones in hotel lob-bies and at the airport. In practice, you may experience some difficulty getting through to the right number.

## Mobile phones

If you want to use your own **mobile phone**, you'll need to check with your phone pro-vider in advance whether it will work in Bali and Lombok (see also ⓦwww.gsmworld .com/roaming/gsminfo/cou_id.shtml). Most **UK**, **Australian** and **New Zealand** mobiles use GSM technology, which works fine in parts of Indonesia, but you'll have to inform your phone provider before leaving home in order to get international access, or "roam-ing", switched on. You're likely to be charged extra to receive calls, but texting usually works as normal. Unless a **US** or **Canadian** phone is a special triband handset it prob-ably won't work in Indonesia; check with your provider.

Buying a **local sim card** can be a use-ful alternative, and a good way of keeping in touch with travelling friends, though you may have to get your phone unblocked first. Savvy staff in the major mobile shops in Bali should be able to do this for you: try Rajawali Cellular, which has outlets at Jl Legian 350 in Kuta (see p.132) and at Jl Teuku Umar 14a in Denpasar, or just ask at your hotel. Mobile-phone-shop staff will advise on the best sim card for your needs, bearing in mind local and international coverage; travellers' forums are also a good source of advice (see p.37). Expect to pay around Rp50,000 for a sim card, which should include around Rp20,000 credit. Top-up cards are sold at phone shops and in minimarkets and department stores.

## Email and Internet access

**Internet access** is becoming increasingly widespread on Bali and Lombok, and there are now hundreds of tourist-friendly Internet centres in the main resorts plus a few in smaller towns: details are given throughout the Guide. Most charge Rp300–500 per minute online; big hotels usually charge very inflated rates.

Before leaving home, check whether your existing **email account** offers a webmail service that enables you to pick up your email from any Internet terminal. Otherwise, you can set yourself up with a **free email account**, either before you leave home or in a cybercafé in Bali or Lombok; the most popular are Hotmail (Ⓦwww.hotmail.com) and Yahoo (Ⓦwww.yahoo.com).

If you plan to email from your **laptop** in Bali and Lombok, be advised that very few losmen have phone sockets in the room. The usual phone plug in Indonesia is the US standard RJ11; see Ⓦwww.kropla.com for detailed advice on how to set up your modem before you go, and how to hardwire phone plugs where necessary. To become a temporary subscriber to a **local ISP**, visit Ⓦwww.baliguide.com/net.html for reviews, prices and links. This site also links to the public ISP Telkom at Ⓦplasa.com/instan/eindex.html, which requires no registration or fee: you simply dial ☎0809/89999 from your laptop, key the username "telkomnet@instan" and the password "telkom", and you're online. This service should cost Rp150 per min, but check with the hotel first as some add surcharges or bar ☎0809 numbers.

# Opening hours, holidays and festivals

Opening hours are not straightforward in Bali and Lombok, with government offices, post offices, businesses and shops setting their own timetables.

Generally speaking, **businesses** such as **airline offices** open at least Monday to Friday 8am to 4pm, Saturday 8am to 1pm, with many open longer, but have variable arrangements at lunchtime. Normal **banking hours** are Monday to Thursday 8am to 2pm, Friday 8am to noon and, in some branches, Saturday 8 to 11.30am, but these do vary and foreign-exchange-counter opening hours are often shorter. Main **post offices** operate roughly Monday to Thursday 8am to 4pm, Friday 8am to 2pm, Saturday 8am to noon, with considerable variations from office to office. Postal agents in tourist areas tend to keep later hours. In tourist areas, **shops** open from around 10am until 8pm or later, but local shops in towns and villages open and shut much earlier. Local **markets** vary; some start soon after dawn with business completed by 10am, others open all day and only close up towards the end of the afternoon.

**Government offices** are open Monday to Thursday 8am to 3pm, Friday 8am to 11.30am, Saturday 8am to 2pm; you'll be most successful if you turn up between 9am and 11.30am. Official government hours shorten during Ramadan; the best advice is to ring offices at that time to check before you make a long journey.

### National public holidays

Most of the **national public holidays** fall on different dates of the Western calendar each year, as they're calculated according to the alternative Muslim and Balinese calendars. For fuller details, see the accounts following.

In addition to national public holidays celebrated throughout Indonesia, there are frequent **religious festivals** occurring

## National public holidays

**Jan 1** – New Year's Day (Tahun Baru).
**Jan** – Muharram, the Muslim New Year.
**March/April** – Good Friday and Easter Sunday.
**March/April** – Maulud Nabi Muhammad, anniversary of the birth of the Prophet.
**May/June** – Waisak Day, anniversary of the birth, death and enlightenment of Buddha.
**Aug 17** – Independence Day (Hari Proklamasi Kemerdekaan).
**Aug/Sept** – Al Miraj, Ascension Day.
**Oct/Nov** – Idul Fitri, celebration of the end of Ramadan.
**Dec 25** – Christmas Day.
**Dec/Jan** – Idul Adha, the Muslim day of sacrifice.

throughout the Muslim, Hindu and Chinese communities. Each of Bali's 20,000 temples also has an anniversary celebration once every *wuku* year, or 210 days (see box below), local communities host elaborate **marriage** and **cremation** celebrations, and both islands have their own particular secular holidays. Your visit is bound to coincide with a festival of one kind or another, and probably several.

All **Muslim festivals**, based on a lunar calendar, move backwards through the seasons, falling earlier according to the Western calendar each year. However, published dates for festivals are approximate since each is based on a local sighting of the new moon.

The ninth Muslim month is **Ramadan**, a month of fasting during daylight hours. It is much more apparent on Muslim Lombok than on Hindu Bali. Followers of the Wetu Telu branch of Islam on Lombok (see p.466) observe their own three-day festival of **Puasa** rather than the full month. Many Muslim restaurants, although not tourist establishments, shut down during the day so it can be hard to get a meal in central and eastern parts of Lombok where you should not eat, drink or smoke in public at this time. However, in all other areas of Lombok you'll find Ramadan much less apparent. **Idul Fitri**, also called Hari Raya or Lebaran, the first day of the tenth month of the Muslim calendar, marks the end of Ramadan and is a national holiday. In fact, many businesses across Indonesia shut for a week and many hotels on Bali and Lombok get booked out with visitors from across the archipelago, most usually Java.

## Balinese festivals

As well as the national public holidays, Bali has its own extra holidays. **Galungan** is an annual event in the wuku calendar, which means it takes place every 210 days. This ten-day festival celebrates the victory of good over evil and all the ancestral gods are

## Traditional calendars

There are two **traditional calendars** in Bali in addition to the Western (or Gregorian) calendar.

The Hindu **saka** calendar operates with years comprising 354–356 days, is divided into twelve months, and runs eighty years behind the Gregorian year: 2005 is 1925 in the *saka* calendar.

Also in use is the magnificently complex **wuku**, *pawukon* or *uku* calendar, based on a 210-day lunar cycle; these cycles are unnumbered. The cycle is divided into weeks that are ten days long, nine days long, eight days long and so on down to weeks that are one day long. All of these weeks run concurrently and have specific names – for example, the three-day week is called Triwara, the five-day week Pancawara – and each day of each week has a specific name. This means that every day has a total of ten names, one from each of the weeks. To add to the complexity, each of the thirty seven-day weeks has its own name. You can buy calendars to keep track of all of this, but the different systems won't affect most visitors: they're used chiefly to determine festival dates and other auspicious days.

thought to come down to earth to take part. Elaborate preparations take place: *penjor* – bamboo poles hung with offerings – arch over the road, offerings are prepared and animals slaughtered for the feasts. Galungan day itself is spent with the family, praying and making offerings. The following day, Manis Galungan, is the day for visiting friends. The final and most important day is **Kuningan**, when families once again get together, pray and make offerings as the souls of the ancestors return to heaven.

The main festival of the saka year is New Year, **Nyepi**, generally in March or April, the major purification ritual of the year. The days before Nyepi are full of activity: religious objects are taken in procession from temples to sacred springs or to the sea for purification. The night before Nyepi is hugely exciting as the spirits are frightened away with drums, gongs, cymbals, firecrackers and huge **papier-mâché monsters** (*ogoh-ogoh*), which are often made to resemble real or fictional villains. On the day itself, everyone sits quietly at home to persuade any remaining evil spirits that Bali is completely deserted. Visitors are expected to stay quietly in their hotels.

Local **temple festivals** may be celebrated according to wuku or saka calendars. Keep an eye on the tourist newspapers, which publish up-to-date lists.

Every temple has its annual **odalan**, an anniversary and purification ceremony. The majority of these are small, local affairs, but the celebrations at the large directional temples draw large crowds (see p.460). There are also local temple festivals related to the moon, some associated with full moon and some with the night of complete darkness.

Another annual event, **Saraswati**, in honour of the goddess of all knowledge (see p.458), takes place on the last day of the wuku year. Books are particularly venerated and the faithful are not supposed to read, while students attend special ceremonies

---

**Galungan** May 3, 2006; Nov 29, 2006; June 27, 2007; Jan 23, 2008; Aug 20, 2008.
**Kuningan** May 13, 2006; Dec 9, 2006; July 7, 2007; Feb 2, 2008; Aug 30, 2008.

---

to pray for academic success. Other annual festivals are **Tumpek Kandang**, when all animals are blessed, and **Tumpek Landep**, a day of devotion to all things made of metal, including tools, motorbikes, cars and buses.

Non-religious anniversaries that are celebrated in Bali include April 21, **Kartini Day**, commemorating the birthday in 1879 of Raden Ajeng Kartini, an early Indonesian nationalist and the first female emancipationist. Parades, lectures and social events are attended by women, while the men and children take over their duties for the day. September 20, the anniversary of the **Badung puputan** in Denpasar in 1906 (see p.449), is commemorated each year by a fair in Alun-alun Puputan. November 20 is **Heroes Day** in Bali, in remembrance of the defeat of the Nationalist forces led by Ngurah Rai at Marga in 1946 (see p.451). The annual **Arts Festival** is a huge celebration of all Balinese arts held at the Taman Budaya Arts Centre in Denpasar (Wwww.baliartsfestival.com; see p.105); it usually takes place in June and July. At around the same time of year, there's also the **Kuta Karnival** (Wwww.kutakarnival.com; see p.116), with parades, watersports competitions and a food festival. Also watch out for **surfing championships** in Kuta: some are annual Balinese events, while others draw competitors from a wider area. The recently established **Ubud Writers and Readers festival** (Wwww.ubudwritersfestival.com) looks like becoming an annual October event, and features talks and workshops from writers about Bali.

## Lombok festivals

In **Lombok**, festivals are a mixture of Hindu, Muslim and local folk festivals. **Ciwaratri** (in Jan) is celebrated by Hindus in West Lombok, where followers meditate without sleeping or eating for 24 hours to redeem their sins. **Nyale** (see p.429) takes place annually

---

**Ramadan begins** Oct 5, 2005; Sept 24, 2006; Sept 13, 2007; Sept 2, 2008.
**Idul Fitri** Nov 4, 2005; Oct 24, 2006; Oct 12, 2007; Oct 2 2008.

in February or March and is celebrated along the south coast when thousands of people flock to witness the first appearance of the sea worms. The **Anniversary of West Lombok**, a formal government event, takes place on April 17. **Harvest festival** is celebrated by Balinese Hindus in March/April at Gunung Pengsong, when they give thanks for the harvest by the ritual slaughter of a buffalo. **Lebaran Topat** occurs seven days after Ramadan, when Sasak people visit family graves and the grave of Loang Baloq at Batu Layar, 10km north of Mataram.

At the end of the year comes **Perang Topat**, celebrated at Pura Lingsar. Offerings are made here from October through to December, at the beginning of the rainy season, by Hindus and adherents of Wetu Teiu to bring rain or give thanks for it. Also at this time, offerings are made at the crater lake of Segara Anak to ask for blessings, known as **Pekelem**, and the **Pujawali** celebration is held at Pura Kalasa temple at Narmada, at Pura Lingsar and at Pura Meru in Cakranegara. December 17 marks the anniversary of the political **founding of West Nusa Tenggara**. Finally, **Chinese New Year** (Imlek) is not an official holiday, but sees many Chinese-run businesses closing for two days in January or February.

# Entertainment and sport

For the Balinese, leisure-time entertainment has traditionally been associated with religious festivals and ceremonies and, despite the relatively recent distractions of discos, cinemas and TV, temple events still take up an enormous amount of time and energy. Such occasions are seen as enjoyable rather than a chore, and tourists are welcome to attend. A major feature of temple ceremonies has always been the performance of sacred dances to the accompaniment of the village gamelan orchestras – entertainments that have in the last few decades transcended the sacred/secular divide and are now also staged for tourists all over the island.

Traditional secular entertainment formerly revolved around gambling, a practice which consumed so many people's fortunes that the Indonesian government banned it in 1981. **Cockfighting** is the one sport to have survived this clampdown, though clandestine betting still continues on other sports, such as cricket fighting. Wagers are also an integral part of the island's **buffalo races**, but this is considered acceptable as they're held only a few times a year: in Negara (see p.358) and in Singaraja. Fortnightly buffalo competitions are held near Negara year-round and more tourist-oriented buffalo races are held regularly during the main tourist season in Lovina (see p.331). Indonesia's national sports are badminton and football.

## Dance and music

If you have any more than a passing interest in the traditional **dance and music** of Bali, you should head for Ubud, where up to five different performances are staged every night of the week for the benefit of tourists (see p.210). This is also the place to take lessons in the performing arts. Ubud and its neighbouring villages have long had a reputation for their superb dance troupes and **gamelan orchestras**, and villagers now supplement their incomes by doing regular shows in the traditional settings of temple courtyards and village compounds. None is exactly authentic, as most comprise a medley of highlights from the more dramatic temple dances, but the quality is generally high and spectators are given English-language synopses. For an introduction to the major themes and styles of Balinese dance and music, see p.468.

Less taxing performances are put on for diners at numerous Sanur, Nusa Dua and Candi Dasa restaurants; there is also a nightly *kecak* show in the temple compound of Pura Luhur Uluwatu. If you go to an Ubud show, expect to **pay** Rp50,000: tours to the same events booked through agents in Kuta and Sanur will cost at least three times as much, including return transport. To see wholly authentic performances you'll need to find out about imminent temple festivals or attend rehearsals, most of which take place in the local *banjar* after sundown; you'll probably be welcome to watch.

## Cockfights

Despite being banned by the Indonesian government in 1981, **cockfights** are still an extremely popular pastime in Bali, where a legal loophole allows the staging of cockfights for religious, but not entertainment, purposes. Because certain Hindu rituals require the shedding of fresh sacrificial blood to placate the most volatile of the evil *bhuta* and *kala* spirits, every temple's purification ceremony is prefaced by a cockfight, but these are far from solemn occasions, attracting massive crowds and even larger bets. Providing you wear suitable temple dress (see p.79) and can stand the gore, tourists are quite welcome to attend; ask at your

hotel or any tourist information service for details.

Prize cocks can earn their owners sizeable sums of money, and a certain status, too, and in Bali you'll see men of all ages and incomes caressing and preening their birds in public. When not being pampered, the birds spend their days in individual bell-shaped bamboo baskets, which are usually placed in quite noisy public places – by the side of the main road for example – so that the bird won't be scared or distracted when it finally reaches the ring.

Fights generally take place in the special cockfighting pavilion or *wantilan* of the appropriate temple. Complicated **rules** written on ancient manuscripts specify the days on which fights may take place, and describe the detailed classification system under which the birds are categorized according to their colour and markings, as well as height and weight.

When a suitable opponent is finally found, the **betting** begins. The owners of each bird both contribute the same amount to a central fund – generally between Rp150,000 and Rp1,000,000 – a sum that comes mainly from the owner's pocket, but is supplemented by friends and other backers. Spectators then set their own bets among themselves.

Before the **fight**, a lethal 11- to 15cm-long blade, or *taji*, is attached to the left ankle of each bird. This is considered a sacred weapon and cockfights are meant to be won and lost by skilful use of the *taji*, not just by brutish pecking. Fights last for a maximum of five rounds, and the winning bird is the cock who remains standing the longest – even if he drops dead soon after. The owner of the winning cock gets the body of the losing bird plus his opponent's share of the central fund.

# Outdoor activities

The sea and the mountains are the two great focuses of outdoor activities in Bali and Lombok. Bali, in particular, is renowned for its world-class surf breaks, and both islands offer some excellent diving off their shores, as well as some spectacular hikes up volcanoes.

## Surfing

Bali's volcanic reef-fringed coastline has made this island one of the great **surfing** meccas of the world, and its reputation for producing an unusually high number of perfect and consistent tubes makes it particularly appealing. The tropical climate means that you rarely need a wetsuit and, although there are two distinct seasons, you can still surf all year round by switching to the other coast. The **best breaks** are concentrated in the south of the island, where the swell from the mighty Indian Ocean gets a chance to build up into massive waves, some of them

### Surf breaks

**Bali**
**Balangan** p.140. A speedy, walling left-hander over a shallow reef; best at high tide.
**Bingin** p.141. Reliable, short left-hand tubes.
**Canggu** p.123. Three decent breaks and fine landward views. Best at mid- to high tide. For fairly experienced surfers.
**Dreamland** p.140. Has a fast left and right peak; can get pretty big.
**Impossibles** p.141. Long and speedy walling left-handers, surfable at all tides.
**Kuta area** p.67. Several breaks offering consistent waves with lots of tubes; most are good for the less confident. **Kuta Beach**, beyond the Jalan Pantai lifeguard station, is best for beginners. **Airport Lefts**, in front of the *Patra Jasa* hotel in Tuban, is another good beginners' wave: a left-hander best surfed at mid- to high tide. **Kuta Reef**, a twenty-minute paddle out from the southern end of Kuta beach, or a short boat ride, is trickier: its ideal left-hand reef breaks are best on mid- to high tides.
**Legian Beach**, off the end of Jalan Padma, is slightly more exposed, with bigger waves – best at high tide. **Airport Rights**, halfway down the Jimbaran side of the airport runway, is accessible by boat from Kuta Reef or from Jimbaran: a high-speed series of right-handers that's best at mid- to high tides and is dangerous at low tide.
**Medewi** p.356. Light current that's nice for beginners.
**Nusa Dua** p.149. Large peaks, long walls and juicy tubes.
**Nusa Lembongan** p.254. Six great breaks, not as crowded as some others.
**Nyang Nyang** p.143. An unpredictable right-hander best surfed between mid- and high tides.
**Padang Padang** p.141. Very challenging, and very famous. One of the classiest and most exciting surf spots in Indonesia. Great left-hander tubes, best at mid- through high tide.
**Pererenan** p.123. Right and left breaks, best at mid- through high tide and in the morning.
**Uluwatu** p.141. Famous set of five left-hand breaks, offering rides from high through to low tide. Gets the most swell of all the breaks along the west coast. The main and most consistent break is the **Peak**, best at mid- through to low tides.

**Lombok**
**Desert Point** p.392. Fabulous, world-famous, fast left-hander.

△ Washing the salt off after swimming, Kuta, Bali

regularly topping five metres. With this kind of challenge, Bali's breaks are a great draw for advanced surfers, but there are also plenty of gentler beach breaks, which are ideal for beginners.

From April through to October, the southeast trade winds blow offshore, fanning the waves off Bali's southwest coast (Uluwatu, Kuta, Legian) and off Nusa Lembongan, and making this both the best time of year for surf, and the pleasantest, as it's also the dry season. Breaks get very crowded during this time, particularly from June to August. From November to March, the winds blow from the northwest, bringing rain to Bali's main beach breaks, though the lesser breaks off eastern Bali (Sanur, Nusa Dua) are still surfable at this time of year. The Balinese have been surfing since the 1930s, and from the 1970s on have become quite serious about the sport: there are now regular **competitions** on the island, and a distinctively fluid Balinese style of surfing has evolved.

As for **Lombok**, readers of Australia's *Tracks* magazine voted Desert Point as their top surf spot in the world. Other breaks in Lombok pale in comparison, but there are a few worth a look along the south coast – in the bays to the west of Kuta; at Awang Bay and Gumbang Bay to the east of Kuta; and off the southeast peninsula.

## Information and contacts

For the best low-down on the **surfing scene** in Bali, head for Kuta (see p.124), where you'll find the biggest choice of surfer-oriented shops, bars and tour agents.

For detailed reviews of surf breaks, see the **book** *Indo Surf and Lingo*, available from ⓦ www.indosurf.com.au for A$29.95 or US$23 plus postage. You can also buy it from surfshops and bookshops in Bali. Good surf **websites** include Bali Waves (ⓦ www .baliwaves.com), Wanna Surf (ⓦ www .wannasurf.com), and Bali Surf Report (ⓦ www.balisurfreport.com).

## Lessons and tours

A number of places in Kuta (Bali) give **surfing lessons** for about $39 per half-day; see p.125 for details. There is also a women-only luxury surf camp, *Surf Goddess Retreats*

(ⓦ www.surfgoddessretreats.com), just north of Seminyak, which offers an all-inclusive week of surfing lessons, yoga, and spa treatments from $1095.

Several companies in Bali organize **surfing tours** to the awesome breaks off Sumbawa, Java, Lombok and West Timor, as well as to the fabulous G-Land off East Java, said to be the world's longest left-hand reef break. See p.124 for details of the Kuta agents, and p.254 for other operators.

## Equipment

There are dozens of surfshops in Kuta (Bali) selling **equipment** from all the top international brands. Brand-new surfboards in Bali cost about US$700 – twice as much as in Australia – but you can also rent boards for about Rp25,000 per day on Kuta beach, and from the Balinese surfers who hang out at the other major breaks. Bring reef shoes for the coral, a helmet for the reef breaks, and an emergency ding-repair kit, though you'll be able to get repairs done in Kuta and at some of the other big surf beaches as well.

Most **airlines** will take boards in the hold for free so long as your total luggage weight doesn't exceed 20kg. Call them in advance to see if they require special insurance. Board bags with straps are a good idea, as a number of the best breaks are accessible by motorbike only. Some **tourist shuttle buses** on Bali and Lombok refuse to carry boards, though Perama buses will take them for an extra Rp10,000 per board. Bemo drivers are similarly unaccommodating, so you're probably best off **renting a car** or a motorbike to get to the breaks. In Kuta, it's fairly easy to rent **motorbikes** with special surfboard clips already attached.

## Health and safety

Bali's shoreline is notorious for its extreme currents and **rip tides**: lifeguards will show you where they are, but if you do get caught in one, stay calm and paddle sideways across the rip to get out of it; never try to paddle straight in or out of it. The beaches at both Kuta and Sanur have several **surfers' lifeguard posts**, but at the other breaks you'll have to rely on help from other surfers.

Be sure to wash your **coral cuts** every

night with a good disinfectant, and to remove sea-urchin spines without breaking them: urinating on the wound is supposed to help alleviate swelling. **Sunburn** and **heatstroke** are very real problems: sunblock is essential, and most surfers wear a rash-vest as well. It's also advisable to bone up on your first-aid knowledge, especially mouth-to-mouth resuscitation techniques, which can be life-saving if someone's been knocked out on a remote break. For general health considerations and details on health care in Bali and Lombok, see p.40.

## Diving and snorkelling

Bali and Lombok are encircled by reefs, which not only make for excellent year-round **diving and snorkelling**, but also mean that you can get a huge variety of dive experiences within even a fortnight's holiday. Staying as close as you can to one of the main diving areas (see box below for a roundup) means that not only will your dive trips or course be a little cheaper, but you won't have to suffer long journeys to the reefs, and you may have the advantage of getting to the dive sites before the day-trippers turn up. In reality, though, relatively few divers stay at the dive sites, most preferring to make excursions from one of the big resorts in the south: Sanur and Tanjung Benoa both have dozens of dive operators and many more hotels, and nearly all tour agents in Kuta can fix you up with a dive operator. One health factor to consider is that you should not go anywhere that's more than **300m above sea level** for eighteen hours following a dive. This means you shouldn't fly, but it also renders certain inland destinations (for example, Kintamani, Wongayagede or Sanda) out of bounds.

Whether you're diving or snorkelling, you should be aware of your effect on the fragile **reef** structures. Any human contact with the

---

## Top dives

### Bali

**Amed** p.286. Huge variety and extent of coral, some of the best in Bali. Plenty of reef fish, too. Wall dives down to about 43m; visibility up to 20m. Gili Selang is at the far eastern tip of Bali where a pristine reef, pelagics and exciting currents are the draw.

**Candi Dasa** p.267. Highlights include an underwater canyon (32m) and steep wall dives. Oceanic sunfish (mola mola) also spotted here sometimes. Currents can be strong.

**Pulau Menjangan (Deer Island)** p.367. Spectacular wall dives, 40–60m drop-offs, plenty of gorgonians and a deep wreck. Visibility up to 50m.

**Nusa Penida and Nusa Lembongan** p.256. Considered among the best dive spots in Bali, but difficult because of strong currents and drifts. It's only suitable for experienced divers. Good chance of spotting oceanic sunfish (mola mola) here from July to September.

**Padang Bai** p.275. The sites are at Blue Lagoon, around the headland to the east of the bay with plenty of corals, which attracts eels, wrasses, turtles, flatheads and lion fish, and where there's a good chance of seeing sharks. There are plenty of species that you won't spot elsewhere in Bali.

**Secret Bay** p.360. The place to go muck-diving (diving on sandy bottoms in search of elusive, hidden marine life): rich in juvenile fish and rare marine species and good for macro-photography.

**Tulamben** p.290. Hugely popular wreck dive (3–29m deep), with visibility from 12–15m. There are plenty of other excellent dives nearby, with a great diversity of coral and marine life. It can get very crowded. Night dives on the wreck are a highlight.

### Lombok

**Gili Islands** p.402. Dives for every level, with plenty of reef fish, but some damage to coral. Whitetip reef sharks and turtles quite frequently spotted.

**South coast** p.405. Rarely dived and only for very experienced, confident divers who can cope with current and surge. Possibility of spotting schools of hammerhead sharks.

microscopic colonies that make up a reef will do some damage, but you can significantly minimize your impact by not stepping on, or supporting yourself on, any part of the reef, and by asking your boatman not to anchor in the middle of one. Don't buy coral souvenirs, as tourist demand only encourages local entrepreneurs to dynamite reefs. See p.368 for more about reefs and reef fish.

Bali's only **recompression chamber** is located inside the efficient Sanglah Public Hospital, Jl Kesehatan Selatan 1, Sanglah, in Denpasar (Mon–Sat 9am–5pm ℡0361/227911–4, ext 123 or 232; outside these hours contact Dr Antonius Natasamudra ℡0361/420842). If your travel insurance does not cover use of recompression chambers, ask your dive operators if their insurance covers you. It's essential for all divers to have travel insurance anyway, in case you need medical evacuation by plane.

See "Books" on p.506 for some recommended diving **books** on Bali and Lombok.

## Diving trips and courses

There are dozens of **dive operators** on Bali and Lombok, so it's always worth checking out several before committing yourself to a trip or a course. If possible, get first-hand recommendations from other divers as well. Always check the dive centre's PADI or equivalent accreditation and check to see if the dive shop is a member of PADI's International Resorts and Retailers Association (IRRA) as this guarantees a certain level of professionalism. You can view a list of IRRAs in Bali and Lombok at ⓦwww.padi.com. Some dive operators in Bali and Lombok do fake their PADI credentials, which is why it's good to get a second opinion. Technical diving using gases other than compressed air is gaining in popularity in Bali and Lombok. The associations specialising in this type of diving are IANTD (ⓦwww.iantd.com) and Technical Diving International (ⓦwww.tdisdi.com). Avoid booking ahead over the Internet without knowing anything else about the dive centre, and be wary of any operation offering extremely cheap courses: maintaining diving equipment is an expensive business in Bali, so any place offering unusually good rates will probably be cutting corners and compromising your safety. Ask to meet your instructor or

dive leader, look at their qualifications, find out how many people there'll be in your group, and look over the equipment, checking the quality of the air in the tanks yourself and also ensuring there's an oxygen cylinder on board.

Many of the dive operators in Bali have a main **office** in Sanur, Tanjung Benoa, Lovina or Candi Dasa and one or two branch offices, for example, in Tulamben or Pemuteran. For a list of some of the main dive operators in south Bali, see pp.158–159; for those in Candi Dasa, see p.268; for Padang Bai, see p.275; for Amed, see p.286; and for Lovina, see p.330. Most dive centres on Lombok are based in Senggigi (see p.399) and/or on the Gili Islands (see p.406). Most charge similar **rates** for dives and courses, though you'll save on transport costs if you're staying locally. One-day **dive trips** usually cost US$70–100 including equipment, and two- to five-day safaris cost US$85–120 per day all-inclusive. Bali International Diving Professionals in Sanur (see p.159) offer dive expeditions for **divers with disabilities**; they have specially adapted equipment available for rent and are a member of the International Association for Handicapped Divers; they also offer **underwater weddings**. Bali Scuba in Sanur (see p.159) is known for its **nitrox** and multi-level dives.

All dive centres offer a range of internationally certified **diving courses**, generally with the first couple of days split between a classroom and a hotel swimming pool, and the next couple of days out on the reef. Sample prices include four-day PADI Open Water courses for US$300–400, and two-day PADI Advanced Open Water courses for around US$240–280. Many dive centres do not include the dive manual and exam papers in the price of the four-day Open Water course. IANTD and TDI courses are available with operators who specialise in technical diving, and most places also cater for beginners with PADI's introductory Discover Scuba course and for rusty divers with PADI's refresher course, Scuba Review.

## Snorkelling

**Snorkellers** are generally welcome on dive excursions, and are usually charged fifty to sixty percent of the diver's fee, which should include the rental of mask, fins and snorkel.

Snorkellers in Padang Bai, Lovina, on the Gili Islands and on Nusa Lembongan can charter their own boat fairly cheaply, as can anyone wanting to explore the spectacular Menjangan reefs (see p.367).

## Bird-watching and hiking

There's just one **national park** in Bali, **Taman Nasional Bali Barat**, which covers about 760 square kilometres of mountain and coast in far western Bali (see p.362). Visitors are prohibited from exploring the park alone, but guides are available for hire at the park headquarters and will accompany you on designated hikes. Bali Barat's landscape is hardly spectacular, but its chief draw are the **birds**, which are well worth packing your binoculars for. This is also the site of a special breeding centre for Bali's only endemic bird, the endangered Bali starling (see p.365).

Other worthwhile bird-watching areas include the forested hills around **Danau Buyan** and **Danau Tamblingan** (p.310) and Bali's second highest mountain, **Gunung Batukau** (p.354). Regular half-day bird-watching excursions are also organized from **Ubud** (p.186). The **Bali Bird Park** (Taman Burung) in nearby Batubulan houses dozens of unusual birds from all over the world.

For reviews of the most useful **guides** to the birds of Bali and Lombok, see p.506.

### Volcano hikes and ricefield walks

Most **hikers** eschew the highlands of Bali Barat and head instead for the islands' grandest mountains. A trek up the active volcano of Lombok's **Gunung Rinjani** (see p.419) usually involves a night spent up on the crater rim or down inside the mountain by the crater lake. But the trip to the summit of what is Indonesia's second highest peak is usually a three- or four-day expedition, with some really hard work to get to the top. Guides are necessary on the routes to the summit. You can rent camping equipment and hire porters at the starting point. Bali's holiest peak, **Gunung Agung** (see p.251), also involves a very strenuous climb – and guides for this walk are essential – but the ascent and descent can be managed in one day. **Gunung Batur** (see p.302), also on Bali, is a much easier proposition and by far the most popular of the volcano walks; don't be put off by this, though, as the sunrise from the top is glorious.

There are several tour companies in Bali running regular **guided hikes** to some of the island's best spots (see p.126 for contact details), including Gunung Batur, Gunung Batukau (see p.352), the Bedugul rainforests (see p.308) and Bali Barat (see p.362). It's also possible to join hikes from Toya Bungkah (see p.303) and Ubud (see p.187). It's easy to organize a Rinjani trek, but if time is very tight a number of Lombok-centred companies will organize the entire trip for you (see p.420).

Walks through rural Bali and its **ricefields** are usually much less tiring than volcano climbs and always offer spectacular views. Ubud is a popular departure point (see p.186), but there are dozens of other possibilities, including around Wongayagede (see p.353), Tirtagangga (see p.280) and Munduk (see p.313).

## Adventure sports

**White-water rafting** is increasingly popular, and as Bali's rivers range from Class 2 to Class 4, there are routes to appeal to first-timers as well as the more experienced; you can book trips in all the major coastal resorts (see p.126) as well as in Ubud. It's also possible to go **kayaking** on the gentler rivers, as well as on Danau Tamblingan; and a little place in Toya Bungkah offers **canoeing** on Danau Batur (see p.303). Lombok lacks the host of adventure companies in Bali, but kayaking, wakeboarding and waterskiing are available from Senggigi (see p.399) and Gili Trawangan (see p.407), where horse-riding is also an option.

## Golf

There are four **golf courses** on Bali: 18-hole courses at the Handara Kosaido Country Club in Bedugul (see p.309), the Bali Golf and Country Club in Nusa Dua (see p.149), and at *Le Meridien Nirwana* in Tanah Lot (see p.347); and a nine-hole course at the *Inna Grand Bali Beach* in Sanur (see p.157). For golf packages, including transfers, green fees and club rental, contact Bali Discount Golf (℡0361/285935, ⊛www.golf-bali.com). Lombok has two 18-hole courses: near Sire Beach on the northwest coast (see p.414), and in the centre of the island (see p.422).

# Spas and traditional beauty treatments

Herbal medicines (*jamu*) and massages using oils and pastes made from locally grown plants have long played an important role in traditional Indonesian health care. In the last few years, this resource has been tapped into and adapted for the tourist market, with dozens of spas and salons now offering traditional beauty treatments to visitors.

The term **"spa"** generally refers to an upmarket massage and beauty parlour, though a Balinese spa complex may well have pools, Jacuzzis and steam baths fed by the waters of a sacred river. You'll find spas and traditional beauty salons in all the main resorts on Bali and Lombok, both inside top-end hotels and at dedicated beauty centres. Most offer a core of fairly similar massages and body rubs, plus a few in-house specialities, but the big attraction is that many use indigenous ingredients and recipes to make their own oils and body pastes, so there's plenty of scope for experiment. Settings are often gorgeous, with spas designed to capitalize on the local penchant for tropical gardens, luxury fabrics and indulgent bathrooms.

## Treatments

The most famous traditional treatment is the Javanese exfoliation rub, **mandi lulur**, in which you're painted and then gently massaged with a paste made chiefly of turmeric but which may also contain ginger, jasmine, rice, ground nuts and aromatic spices. Such is its apparent power to beautify, that Javanese brides are said to have a *lulur* treatment every day for the forty days before their wedding ceremonies. Another popular body wrap is the **Balinese boreh**, a warming blend of cloves, pepper, cardamom and other spices that improves circulation and invigorates muscles. There are dozens of other **body mask treatments**, using ingredients such as seaweed, aloe vera, coconut, salt and even coffee. Most scrub treatments are preceded by a gentle Balinese-style massage and followed by a moisturizing "milk bath" – actually a soothing mask treatment in which you're slathered in yoghurt or condensed milk; the whole package generally takes between an hour and a half and two hours. Prices vary enormously for these scrub packages, from Rp150,000 to US$100, depending on the poshness of the venue.

Most beauty centres can do several different types of **massage**, including Balinese (gentle), Thai (more vigorous), Hawaiian lomi-lomi (therapeutic), Japanese shiatsu (pressure points) and Swedish (very vigorous). Some places offer an assortment of **aromatherapy** massages to treat a range of ailments from coughs to headaches to insomnia. Massage prices range from Rp50,000 (or even less on the beach) to $42 per hour. Every spa and beauty salon does manicures, pedicures, facials, and cream-bath deep-moisturizing hair treatments.

## Practicalities

Spas and beauty salons in Bali and Lombok are very professional and should do their best to minimize awkwardness and embarrassment by giving you precise instructions about how much to undress and which way to lie. All treatment rooms are private but some people prefer to take swimwear with them anyway. Many places are quite happy for couples to have massages and body wraps in the same room. Most masseuses and beauty therapists are women, but some salons use male masseurs for their male customers.

We've listed some of the most famous and most popular spas and beauty salons on p.74, but there are hundreds more. Advance **reservations** are recommended but not always essential, and most hotels welcome non-guests at their spas.

## Top spas

**Bodyworks 2** Seminyak, p.126. Good-value day spa with funky, Moroccan-style decor.

**Damai** Lovina, p.327. Fabulous luxury hotel spa with an open *bale* just above a river in the cool hills above Lovina.

**Ibah** Ubud, p.213. Super-deluxe and enormously expensive hotel spa.

**Matahari Beach Resort** Pemuteran, p.371. Luxuriously classical top-notch hotel spa – with correspondingly high prices.

**Novotel Lombok** Kuta, Lombok, p.434. A brilliant spa overlooking the beach in this luxury hotel.

**Nur Salon** Ubud, p.213. Charmingly traditional and inexpensive day spa that's been offering treatments since the 1970s.

**Nusa Dua Beach Hotel** Nusa Dua, p.149. Famous, long-established hotel spa.

**Puri Bagus Lovina** Lovina p.323. Spa located in fabulous open pavilions surrounded by pools and fountains close to the beach.

**Senggigi Sheraton** Senggigi, p.395. Seafront hotel spa.

**Ubud Sari Health Resort** Ubud, p.214. Serious, expensive centre for aromatherapy, reflexology, shiatsu and reiki.

**Zen Lifestyle Energy Resort** Ume Anyar, p.214. Boutique-hotel spa; treatments include Ayurvedic balancing massage.

# Crime and personal safety

While incidents of crime of all kinds are relatively rare on Bali and Lombok, the importance of tourism to the economy, and the damage that adverse publicity could do, means that the true situation may be kept conveniently obscured. Certainly, the majority of visitors have trouble-free trips, but there have been instances of theft and assault on tourists.

It makes sense to take a few **precautions**. Carry vital documents and money in a concealed moneybelt: bum-bags are too easy to cut off in a crowd. Make sure your luggage is lockable (there are gadgets to lock backpacks) and beware that things can quickly be taken from the back pockets of a rucksack while you're wearing it without you knowing. Beware of pickpockets on crowded buses or bemos and in markets; they usually operate in pairs: one will distract you while another gets what they can either from your pockets or your backpack.

Check the security of a room before accepting it, make sure doors and windows can be secured, and don't forget access via the bathroom. Female travellers should make sure there are no peepholes through into neighbouring rooms. Some guesthouses and hotels have safe-deposit boxes, which neatly solves the problem of what to do with your valuables while you go swimming. A surprising number of tourists do leave their valuables unattended on the beach and are amazed to find them gone when they return.

Keep a separate **photocopy** of your passport so you can prove who you are if you need to get a replacement, and a separate list of travellers' cheque numbers along with the emergency phone number.

It's never sensible to carry **large amounts of cash**, and on Bali it's not necessary. However, on Lombok you may need to carry more than you would like because of the scarcity of moneychangers away from the west-coast resorts. It's wise to keep a few dollars hidden somewhere away from your main stash of cash so that if you get your money stolen you can still get to the police, contact a consulate and pay for phone calls while you sort everything out. There are a number of potential rip-offs when you're changing money; see box on p.47 for more.

Something else to watch out for on Bali is being approached on the street by somebody wanting to ask a few questions about your holiday. These seemingly innocuous questionnaires provide information for **time-share companies**, who have a reputation for hassling visitors once they've divulged their details. Another ruse is for the "researchers" to offer you a prize as a reward for participating – usually a free dinner or tour – which invariably involves a trip to the time-share company's office. Advice on this is to never sign anything unless you've thought about it extremely carefully, examined all the small print – and then thought about it some more. It's also worth being alert to the possibility of spiked drinks and to be aware that **gambling** is illegal in Indonesia and problems can arise from foreigners getting involved in this.

It is foolish to have anything to do with **drugs** in Indonesia. The penalties are very tough, and you won't get any sympathy from consular officials.

If you're arrested, or end up on the wrong side of the law for whatever reason, you should ring the **consular officer** at your embassy immediately (see p.35 for a list).

If you're driving, the chance of entanglement with the police increases; see p.50 for more.

## Women travellers

Bali and Lombok do not present great difficulties for **women travellers**, either travelling alone or with friends of either sex;

basic issues of personal security and safety are essentially the same as they would be at home. However, an image of Western women as promiscuous and on holiday in search of sex is well established on both islands, although attitudes on Bali are a little more open-minded than on Lombok.

Observe how local women **dress** both on the streets and on the beach. While topless sunbathing is popular among tourists – and it's unlikely that local people will say anything directly – it's worth being aware how far outside the local dress code such behaviour is. Whatever you do on the beach, you should cover up when you head inshore, and visits to temples or festivals carry their own obligations regarding dress (see p.79).

There's a large population of **young men** on both Bali and Lombok known variously as Kuta Cowboys, mosquitoes (they flit from person to person) or gigolos, whose aim is to secure a Western girlfriend for the night, week, month or however long it lasts. They vary considerably in subtlety and while the transaction is not overtly financial, the woman will be expected to pay for everything. You'll see these couples all over the islands, and if a Western woman and a local man are seen together, this is the first assumption made about their relationship. Local reaction is variable, from hostility in the more traditional villages through acceptance to amusement. Sex outside marriage is taboo in both the Hindu and Muslim religions, and young girls on both islands – especially in the more traditional villages – are expected to conform to a strict code of morality.

Women involved in relationships abroad, either with local men or other travellers, should be aware of **sexual health** issues; see p.41.

Visitors should take note of the advice about **parties** on Gili Trawangan (see p.409), where there have been reports of attacks on women, and on travelling along the **back roads** of southern Lombok (see p.429).

## Reporting a crime or emergency

If you have anything **lost** or **stolen** you must get a **police report** for insurance purposes, so head for the nearest police station (these are marked on the maps in the Guide). In

In an emergency, call the Integrated Emergency Response Centre (☎112) on **Bali**, or the police (☎110), ambulance (☎118) or fire service (☎113) on **Lombok**.

areas without local police, such as the Gili Islands off the coast of Lombok, ask for the local village headman, *kepala desa* or *kepala kampung* in smaller villages, whose job it is to sort out the problem and take you to the nearest police. The police will usually find somebody who can speak some English, but it's a good idea to take along someone who can speak both Indonesian and English, if you can. Allow plenty of time for any bureaucratic involvement with the police. If you're unfortunate enough to be the victim of violent crime, contact your consulate at once. Government websites are listed on p.37.

# Shopping

Shopping could easily become an all-consuming pastime in Bali and Lombok: the range and quality of artefacts is phenomenal, and although the export trade has dulled the initial impact a little, the bargain prices are irresistible. Bali also has a well-deserved reputation for its elegant modern designs in everything from fashion to tableware, much of it dreamt up by expat designers. The real pleasure on Lombok is visiting the craft villages in the centre of the island where pottery, basketware, woodcarving and textiles are local specialities.

On Bali, you'll get the biggest overall choice in **Kuta–Legian–Seminyak** and in **Ubud**, where the streets are crammed with all manner of outlets. Lombok's shops are fewer but no less enticing: **Senggigi** is a great centre for the crafts of Lombok as well as the islands further east. Traditional covered **markets**, or *pasar*, are also rewarding places to hone your bargaining skills, particularly in the sections known as the *pasar seni*, or **art market**, which sell everything from sarongs and lengths of ceremonial fabric to woodcarvings and T-shirts. The term "art market" has now grown to mean any collection of tourist-oriented stalls or little shops selling inexpensive sarongs and souvenirs.

Remember that touts, guides and drivers often get as much as fifty percent **commission** on any item sold to one of their customers – not only at the customer's expense, but also the vendor's. For information on how to ship purchases home, see p.59.

## Arts and crafts

The best area for buying **paintings, woodcarvings** and **sculpture** is Ubud and its neighbouring villages, where every other family seems to be engaged in some kind of craft. You can buy very cheaply off the shelf, commission your own works and choose picture frames from highly skilled framecarvers. If you have a special interest in the classical *wayang* style of painting, make a trip to Kamasan (see p.244), just south of Klungkung, which is both the historical and modern-day centre for this traditional style of art.

You'll soon realize that original ideas are not all that common, and that certain subjects recur in most commercial galleries. This copying is as much a traditional practice as it is a commercial one, as Balinese culture has always defined a fine artist as one who replicates the work of his or her forbears to perfection. For an overview of the development of styles and techniques in Balinese painting, carving and sculpture, see p.481.

Be particularly careful when choosing **woodcarvings**, which are sometimes sold under false pretences as a more valuable wood, and which don't always travel that well. The easiest wood to fake is **sandalwood**, or *cenana*, an extremely expensive material, mainly imported from East Timor. Sandalwood's pungent aroma is sometimes faked by packing the carvings in real sandalwood sawdust, or by scenting them with sandalwood oil. In either case, the smell doesn't last that long, so either buy from an established outlet or assume that it's faked and reduce your price accordingly. **Ebony**, which comes mainly from Kalimantan and Sulawesi, is another commonly faked wood. Compare its weight with any other wood: ebony is very dense and will sink in water. Most tropical woods **crack** when taken to a climate that's less humid because of the uneven shrinkage that results from escaping moisture. Some carvers add problem by drying the wood in others soak the carvings in a called polyethylene glycol (PEG), whic the cracks before they have a chance to widen out. Always check for cracks before buying.

The traditional village of Tenganan is a famous centre for distinctive, finely woven **basketware** bags, baskets, trays and mats, made from a grass known as *ata*, which originally came from the rivers of central Bali but is now imported to meet demand. The baskets are also sold in the big resorts.

**Pottery** is now big business in Lombok (see p.387), and most of the items you'll see in Bali tourist centres have been shipped across the water. For the best range, check out the shops and the pottery villages of Banyumulek, Penakak and Penujak. Even the most gigantic pots won't set you back much more than Rp150,000 and there are plenty of small items.

## Where to shop

Many villages are famous for a particular craft and have been for many decades.

**Basketware** Tenganan; Ubud.

**Books** Kuta; Ubud.

**Ceramics** Pejaten. Painted ceramic eggs from Negari.

**Fabrics** Traditional *ikat* and *endek* in Tenganan, Sukarara and Gianyar; modern batik on Jalan Arjuna, Seminyak; dress fabrics on Jalan Sulawesi, Denpasar.

**Fashion** Kuta-Legian-Seminyak.

**Furniture** Modern furniture on Jalan Bypass Sanur and in Kerobokan. Repro antique furniture from Batubulan, Mas, Seminyak and Senggigi (both in the resort itself and on the road south).

**Interior decor and homewares** Seminyak; Ubud.

**Jewellery and silver** Celuk is Bali's main silver-producing village; shops in Kuta, Seminyak, Ubud, Lovina and Candi Dasa. Gold shops on Jalan Hasanudin, Denpasar. Gold and silver jewellery in Kamasan, Lombok; pearls in Sekarbela, Lombok.

**Kites** Negari; Sanur.

**Markets and pasar seni** Sukawati; Ubud; Pasar Badung and Pasar Kumbasari in Denpasar; *pasar seni* in Senggigi; general markets in Ampenan, Cakranegara and Sweta next to the bus terminal; Gunung Sari north of Mataram; Lombok Handicraft Centre and Sayang Sayang Art Market north of Cakranegara; tourist art markets along Poppies 1 and Poppies 2, Kuta.

**Paintings** Ubud; Batuan; Kamasan.

**Pottery** Mataram; Senggigi; Banyumulek; Penunjak; Pejangik.

**Puppets** Sukawati.

**Stone sculptures** Batubulan.

**Woodcarvings** Unpainted figurines from Mas, Ubud, Kemenuh and Nyukuning. Painted wooden artefacts from Tegalalang and Ceking.

## Fabric and soft furnishings

The main cloth-producing area on Bali is Gianyar, noted for its distinctive **ikat** or **endek** cloth – a special technique (explained on p.488) that involves dyeing the weft threads into the finished design before weaving begins. This produces a fuzzy edge to the fairly bold designs, and the fabric is popular for cushion covers and bedspreads, as well as for sarongs and other clothes. You can see *ikat* weavers at work in Gianyar, but their produce is sold at outlets all over the island. There's also a highly regarded workshop in Singaraja. The tiny Bali Aga village of Tenganan near Candi Dasa (p.271) is the only place on Bali to produce double *ikat*, or *gringsing*, a painstakingly intricate technique that produces stunning designs – at prices to match. On Lombok, the village of Suka-rara is the place to look if you're interested in weaving.

Although Balinese *ikat* is occasionally used for sarongs, Javanese-style **batik** is currently much more fashionable, and is used for everything from sarongs and shirts, to tablecloths and surfers' board-bags. Some batik is now screen-printed rather than waxed, and the results are generally less good, especially as the dyes on screen-printed fabrics don't penetrate to the reverse side. Many women favour sarongs made from rayon, which is softer, hangs better and doesn't crease so much, but is not a natural fabric and so doesn't breathe so easily. The larger fixed-price tourist shops in Kuta, Nusa Dua, Lovina, Candi Dasa and Senggigi tend to stock the most exhaustive range of batik goods – including exquisite hand-printed and even hand-painted silk sarongs, priced from Rp400,000 – but you'll find cheaper sarongs (Rp50,000–100,000) in the *pasar seni* frequented by the Balinese.

The ceremonial dress worn at temple festivals and other important occasions is usually fashioned from heavier, more luxurious materials such as gold-and-silver brocaded **songket** and gold-stamped **perada** (see pp.488 and 499 for more on all these materials). The best places to buy *songket* and *perada* are the bigger *pasar seni*.

In Kuta, Ubud and Candi Dasa, you'll also find a number of shops specializing in cloth woven to the traditional designs of other Indonesian islands, particularly **Sumba and Flores**. Prices vary enormously, depending not only on the size of the fabric, and whether or not it was hand-woven, but also on how old it is. Shawls and 100x30cm wall-hangings cost from around Rp100,000, but larger and more complicated items, such as Sumbanese *ikat* bedspreads, rarely start at under US$250. A good way to display lengths of cloth at home is on the special carved **wooden hangers** sold in furniture and "antique" shops, and in some *ikat* and souvenir shops; most are made in Lombok and Kalimantan.

In recent years, local and expat designers have really gone to town with **soft furnishings**, making full use of the sumptuous fabrics available and coming up with a stunning array of cushions, bedspreads, curtains, drapes and tablecloths. Legian and Seminyak have dozens of shops specializing in homewares and are probably the best places to begin, but Ubud is a fruitful place to browse, too.

## Clothing and jewellery

Bali also produces some great **clothes**. The island's clothing industry is centred around Kuta–Legian–Seminyak, where you'll find the classiest and most original boutiques, as well as the greatest concentration of stalls selling baggy *ikat* trousers and skimpy batik dresses. Brand-name surfwear and urban sportswear is also good value in Kuta, as is custom-made leatherware, especially shoes, boots and jackets.

There's also a small but thriving **silver** and **gold** industry on Bali, based in the village of Celuk, where silversmiths create filigree pieces and larger items to order, and sell to the public from their workshops. For more unusual jewellery, you're better off scouring the jewellery shops in Kuta, Ubud, Lovina and Candi Dasa, where designs tend to be more innovative and prices similar, if not lower. On Lombok, it's worth taking a trip to the gold and silver workshops in Kamasan, north of Mataram (see p.388); pretty much every house is involved in the business and a lot of their stuff is sold on Bali. For **pearls**, head to Sekarbela (see p.388) south of Mataram, where the products of the pearl farms that dot the Lombok coastline are brought for sale either separately or in jewellery.

## Antiques and reproduction furniture

Several shops in Bali and Lombok advertise, quite ingenuously, "**Antiques** made to order". At least they're honest. The antiques in question generally either come from Java or are reproductions of Javanese items, chiefly **furniture**, screens, carved panels, window shutters and doors. Weather-worn or fashionably distressed, most of the furniture is heavy, made from teak to a Dutch-inspired design, but carved with typical Indonesian grace and whimsy. Bargaining is essential; reasonable sample prices are US$60 for a small table, or US$250 for a cupboard with carved doors. You should check your intended purchase for rot and termite damage (genuine teak is resistant to termites), as well as for shoddy restoration work. See the advice on buying woodcarvings, above, for possible ways of preventing the wood from cracking when transported to a less humid climate.

# Cultural hints

The people of Bali and Lombok are extremely generous about opening up their homes, temples and festivals to the ever-growing crowd of interested tourists but, though they're long-suffering and rarely show obvious displeasure, they do take great offence at certain aspects of Western behaviour. The most sensitive issues on the islands are Westerners' clothing – or lack of it – and the code of practice that's required when visiting holy places.

## Religious etiquette

Anyone entering a **Balinese temple** (*pura*) is required to show **respect** to the gods by treating their shrines with due deference (not climbing on them or placing themselves in a higher position than them) and by **dressing modestly**: skimpy clothing, bare shoulders and shorts are all unacceptable, and in many temples you'll be required to wear a sarong (usually provided at the gate of the most visited temples). In addition, you should wear a **ceremonial sash** around your waist whenever you visit a temple: these can be bought very cheaply at most shops selling sarongs, and can be of any style and pattern (the Balinese sometimes make do with a rolled-up sarong wrapped around their waist or even a towel); they too are provided for visitors to popular temples.

When attending special **temple ceremonies**, cremations and other village festivals, you should make every effort to dress up as formally as possible: sarongs and sashes are obligatory, and shirts with buttons or blouses are preferable to T-shirts. During ceremonies, you shouldn't walk in front of anyone who's praying, or take their photo, and should try not to sit higher than the priest or the table of offerings. Never use a flash.

At temples, you'll be expected to give a **donation** towards upkeep (Rp5000–10,000 is an acceptable amount) and to sign the donation book. There's no need to be prompted into larger sums when you read how much the previous visitor donated – extra noughts are quite easy to add.

Because the shedding of blood is considered to make someone **ritually unclean** (*sebel*) in Balinese Hinduism, women are not

## Balinese caste and names

Balinese society is structured around a hereditary **caste system**, which, while far more relaxed than its Indian counterpart, does nonetheless carry certain restrictions and rules of etiquette, as ordained in the Balinese Hindu scriptures. Of these, the one that travellers are most likely to encounter is the practice of **naming** a person according to their caste.

At the top of the tree is the **Brahman** caste, whose men are honoured with the title **Ida Bagus** and whose women are generally named **Ida Ayu**, sometimes shortened to **Dayu**. Traditionally revered as the most scholarly members of society, only Brahmans are allowed to become high priests (*pedanda*).

**Satriya** (sometimes spelt Ksatriya) form the second strata of Balinese society, and these families are descendants of warriors and rulers. The Balinese rajas were all Satriya and their offspring continue to bear telltale names: **Cokorda, Anak Agung, Ratu** and **Prebagus** for men, and **Anak Agung Isti** or **Dewa Ayu** for women. The merchants or **Wesia** occupy the third most important rank, the men distinguished by the title **I Gusti** or **Pregusti**, the women by the name **I Gusti Ayu.**

At the bottom of the heap comes the **Sudra** caste, the caste of the common people, which accounts for over ninety percent of the population. Sudra children are named according to their position in the family order, with no distinction made between male and female offspring. Thus, a first-born Sudra is always known as **Wayan** (or, less commonly, **Putu** or **Gede**), the second-born is **Made** (or **Kadek**), the third **Nyoman** (or **Komang**) and the fourth **Ketut**. Should a fifth child be born, then the naming system begins all over again with Wayan, and so it goes on. In order to distinguish between the sexes, Sudra caste names are often prefaced by "**I**" for males and "**Ni**" for females, eg I Wayan. Some Wayans and Mades prefer to be known by their second names, and many have distinctive nicknames, but you will come across many more Wayans than any other name in Bali.

Unlike their counterparts in the far more rigid Indian caste system, the Sudra are not looked down upon or denied access to specific professions (except that of *pedanda*), and a high-caste background guarantees neither a high income nor a direct line to political power. There are caste-related **marriage** restrictions, however. Although it's acceptable for a high-caste man to marry a woman from a lower caste, the reverse situation causes the man to "lose caste", and is not considered desirable.

allowed to enter a temple, or to attend any religious ceremonies, during menstruation, and the same applies to anyone bearing a fresh wound. Under the same precepts, new mothers and their babies are also considered to be *sebel* for the first 42 days after the birth (new fathers are unclean for three days), and anyone who has been recently bereaved is *sebel* until three days after burial or cremation. These restrictions apply to non-Balinese as well, and are sometimes detailed on English-language notices outside the temple.

### Mosques

On the whole, the **mosques** of Lombok and Bali don't hold much interest for tourists, but should you have occasion to visit one, it's as well to be aware of certain Islamic practices. Everyone is required to take their shoes off before entering, and to wear long sleeves and long trousers; women should definitely cover their shoulders and may also be asked to cover their heads as well (bring a scarf or shawl, as there probably won't be any provided). Men and women always pray in separate parts of the mosque, though there are unlikely to be signs telling you where to go. Women are forbidden to engage in certain religious activities during menstruation, and this includes entering a mosque. Finally, you should be aware that during the month of **Ramadan** (see p.63 for more), devout Muslims neither eat, drink nor smoke during daylight hours. If visiting Lombok during this time, you should be sensitive to this, although you'll certainly be able to find places to eat. Adherence varies across the island at this time: it is most apparent in the south and the east, but something you might not even notice in Senggigi.

## The body

Despite tolerating skimpy **dress** in the beach resorts, most Indonesians are extremely offended by topless and nude bathing, and by immodest attire in their towns and villages. You'll command a great deal more respect if you recognize this and keep your shortest shorts, vests and bare shoulders for the seaside. This is especially true in central and eastern Lombok, where Sasaks do not subscribe to the relatively relaxed attitudes of their west-coast compatriots in Senggigi and the Gili Islands.

The Balinese and Sasak people themselves regularly expose their own bodies in public when **bathing** in rivers and public bathing pools, but they are always treated as invisible by other bathers and passers-by. As a tourist you should do the same: to photograph a bathing Balinese would be very rude indeed. If you bathe alongside them, do as they do – nearly all Balinese women wash with their sarongs wrapped around them – and take note of the segregated areas: in public pools, the men's and women's sections are usually clearly defined, but in rivers the borders are less tangible. For other bathing practices, see p.52.

According to Hindu beliefs, a person's body is a microcosm of the universe: the **head** is the most sacred part of the body and the feet the most unclean. This means that you should on no account touch a Balinese person's head – not even to pat a small child's head or to ruffle someone's hair in affection; nor should you lean over someone's head or place your body in a higher position than their head without some sort of apology. You should never sit with your **feet** pointed at a sacred image (best to sit with them tucked underneath you) or use them to indicate someone or something. Balinese people will never walk under a **clothes line** (for fear of their head coming into contact with underclothes), so you should try not to hang your washing in public areas, and definitely don't sling wet clothes over a temple wall or other holy building. The **left hand** is used for washing after defecating, so the Balinese will never eat with it or use it to pass or receive things or to shake hands.

## Social conventions

As elsewhere in Asia, the Balinese dislike **confrontational behaviour**, and will rarely show anger or irritation of any kind. Tourists who lose their cool and get visibly rattled tend to be looked down on rather than feared.

A major source of irritation for foreigners is the rather vague notion of **time-keeping** that pervades almost every aspect of Indonesian life, but lack of punctuality is such a national institution that there is even a word for it – *jam karet*, or rubber time – and you'll save yourself a lot of stress if you remember this every time you board a bemo or visit a bank. Public **displays of affection** are also subdued – you're more likely to see affectionate hand-holding and hugging between friends of the same sex than between heterosexual lovers.

Since the downfall of Suharto in 1998, and the subsequent democratic elections, Indonesian people seem to have become much more confident about discussing **political issues** and voicing critical opinions of the state. This is mirrored by a more open press. Religious beliefs, however, are a much more sensitive issue, and it would be bad form to instigate a debate that questions a Balinese person's faith.

You will probably find Balinese and Sasak people only too eager to find out about your **personal life** and habits. It's considered quite normal to ask "Are you married?" and to then express sorrow if you say that you aren't, and the same applies to questions about children: marriage and parenthood are essential stages in the life of most Balinese (see p.494) and Sasaks (see p.496).

# Travellers with disabilities

Indonesia makes few provisions for its disabled citizens, which clearly affects travellers with disabilities, although the situation is definitely improving year on year.

At the physical level, kerbs are usually high (without slopes) and pavements/sidewalks uneven with all sorts of obstacles; access to most public places involves steps (very few have ramps); public transport is inaccessible to wheelchair users (although Perama tourist buses will take them); and the few pedestrian crossings on major roads have no audible signal. On the positive side, many hotels comprise bungalows in extensive grounds and/or have spacious bathrooms, while the more upmarket ones are increasingly making an effort to provide the necessary facilities.

For all of these reasons, it may be worth considering an **organized tour** or holiday – the contacts listed below will help you start researching trips to Bali and Lombok. Arrange **travel insurance**, carefully taking into account any medical difficulties you may have, and use your travel agent to make your journey simpler: airlines cope better if they are expecting you. A medical certificate of your fitness to travel, provided by your doctor, is also extremely useful; some airlines or insurance companies may insist on it. Carry spares of any clothing or equipment that might be hard to find.

Make sure that you take sufficient supplies of any **medications**, and – if they're essential – carry the complete supply with you whenever you travel (including on buses and planes), in case of loss or theft. It's also a good idea to carry a doctor's letter about your drugs prescriptions with you at all times, particularly when passing through customs at Ngurah Rai or Selaparang airports, as this will ensure you don't get hauled up for narcotics transgressions.

Bali International Diving Professionals (ⓦwww.bidp-balidiving.com; see p.159) is the only Balinese member of the International Association for Handicapped Divers (ⓦwww .iahd.org) and has expertise in teaching and guiding both **divers with disabilities** and buddies who will dive with them.

## Contacts for travellers with disabilities

### Online

ⓦ**www.bali-paradise.com/special-needs -traveler/index/cfm** Detailed local information, suggestions and tips.
ⓦ**www.bootsnall.com/guides** An excellent guide to travelling with disabilities.
ⓦ**www.independentliving.org** Dozens of relevant websites are listed in the "Travel and Leisure" links.
ⓦ**thorntree.lonelyplanet.com**. The "Travellers with Disabilities" forum is useful.

### UK and Ireland

**Disability Action** Portside Business Park, 189 Airport Rd W, Belfast BT3 9ED ☏028/9029 7880, ⓦwww.disabilityaction.org. Provides information about access for disabled travellers abroad.
**Holiday Care** 2nd floor, Imperial Building, Victoria Rd, Horley, Surrey RH6 7PZ ☏0845/124 9971 or 020/8760 0072, ⓦwww.holidaycare.org.uk. Provides free lists of accessible accommodation abroad, including long-haul destinations. Information on financial help for holidays is also available.
**Irish Wheelchair Association** Blackheath Drive, Clontarf, Dublin 3 ☏01/818 6400, ⓦwww.iwa.ie. Useful information provided about travelling abroad with a wheelchair.
**RADAR (Royal Association for Disability and Rehabilitation)** 12 City Forum, 250 City Rd, London EC1V 8AF ☏020/7250 3222, minicom ☏020/7250 4119, ⓦwww.radar.org.uk. A good source of advice on all information related to travel, although directed more at the UK.
**Tripscope** Alexandra House, Albany Rd, Brentford, Middlesex TW8 0NE ☏08457/585641, ⓦwww .tripscope.org.uk. Free advice on UK and international transport for those with mobility problems.

### US and Canada

**Access-Able** ⓦwww.access-able.com. Online

resource for travellers with disabilities.

**Directions Unlimited** 123 Green Lane, Bedford Hills, NY 10507 ☏1-800/533-5343 or 914/241-1700. Travel agency specializing in bookings for people with disabilities.

**Mobility International USA** 451 W Broadway, Suite 202, Eugene, OR 97401 ☏541/343-1284, ⓦwww.miusa.org. Information and referral services, access guides, tours and exchange programmes.

**Society for Accessible Travel & Hospitality (SATH)** 347 Fifth Ave, New York, NY 10016 ☏212/447-7284, ⓦwww.sath.org. Nonprofit educational organization that has actively represented travellers with disabilities since 1976. Annual membership $45; $30 for students and seniors.

**Wheels Up!** ☏1-888/389-4335, ⓦwww.

wheelsup.com. Discounted airfare, tour and cruise prices for wheelchair users or those with mobility problems. Also publishes topical online newsletters.

### Australia and New Zealand

**ACROD (Australian Council for Rehabilitation of the Disabled)** PO Box 60, Curtin ACT 2605; ☏02/6282 4333 (also TTY), ⓦwww.acrod.org.au. Provides lists of travel agencies and tour operators for people with disabilities.

**Disabled Persons Assembly** 4/173–175 Victoria St, Wellington, New Zealand ☏04/801 9100 (also TTY), ⓦwww.dpa.org.nz. Resource centre with lists of travel agencies and tour operators for people with disabilities.

# Travelling with children

The Balinese make a great fuss of their own and other people's children, and permit them to go pretty much anywhere.

One peculiar cultural convention you might encounter, though, is that the Balinese abhor young children crawling on the ground – a practice that's considered far too animal-like for young humans – and so kids are **carried** everywhere, either on the hip or in slings made from sarongs, until they're six months old. Don't be surprised if your child gets scooped off the ground for the same reason.

## Activities for kids

There's plenty on Bali and Lombok to appeal to children – especially the beach, the swimming pools and the water-based activities in the more developed resorts. Active children also enjoy many of the walks on the islands as well as **mountain biking** and **white-water rafting** (see box on p.126). Many **dive centres** will teach the PADI children's scuba courses on request: their Bubblemaker programme is open to 8-year-olds and the Junior Open Water course is designed for anyone over 10. The colour and dynamism of

the **dance and music shows** could almost be tailor-made for children – from the beauty and grace of *legong* to the drama of the *barong*. Special **theme attractions** such as Waterbom Park in Kuta, the Elephant Safari Park at Taro, and the Bird and Reptile parks in Batubulan are also ideal. The enormous *Hard Rock Café* swimming pool in Kuta has a "beach", volleyball and a water chute and is open to non-residents (see p.125); Nusa Dua's *Bali Club Med* also welcomes non-guests to buy a day pass for use of all its sporting facilities (see p.149). Nearly all the upmarket hotels in the main Bali resorts and in Senggigi on Lombok have a kids' club for guests, and many also offer **babysitting** services. Older, more fashion-conscious children will relish the varieties of brand-name **clothing** on offer and the endless offers to "plait your hair", while parents will appreciate the bargains to be had in the children's sections of department stores in Kuta and Denpasar and the specialist children's clothing stores. **Ubud** is especially child-friendly, with a huge amount on offer that they will love (see box, p.216), including chances to try their hand at batik, gamelan and dancing, and a multilingual kids' library.

## Practicalities

Many upmarket **hotels** offer extra beds for one or two under-12s sharing a room with their parents. The Tuban area of south Kuta is particularly strong on family-oriented hotels, many of which have grounds that run right down to the sea: the *Bali Dynasty Resort* runs an especially well-regarded programme of kids' activities (see p.120). In Sanur, the mid-range *Swastika* is one of several family-friendly options, complete with children's swimming pool (see p.156). Up near Ubud, in the village of Mas, the characterful and mid-priced *Taman Harum Cottages* also gets rave reviews from families, not least because of all the activities it organizes (see p.178); *Klub Kokos*, also near Ubud, has a kids' playroom and special family unit (see p.191). An increasing number of **losmen**, particularly in Kuta and Ubud, have a family bungalow available for rent, usually with at least two bedrooms and possibly a kitchenette as well. Others offer adjoining rooms. **Villas** are the obvious top-whack alternative. On the whole, children who occupy their own seat on **buses** and **bemos** are expected to pay full fare. Most **domestic flight** operators charge two-thirds of the adult fare for children under 14, and ten percent for infants.

Although you can buy **disposable nappies** (diapers) in the supermarkets of Kuta, Sanur, Denpasar and Ubud, the Balinese don't use them, so prices are inflated; you might want to bring your own. Bring a **changing mat**, as there are precious few public toilets in Bali and Lombok, let alone ones with special baby facilities (though posh hotels are always a useful option). For touring, child-carrier **backpacks** are ideal. Opinions are divided on whether or not it's worth bringing a **buggy** or three-wheeled **stroller** – pavements are bumpy at best, and there's an almost total absence of ramps; sand is especially difficult for buggies, though less so for three-wheelers. Buggies and strollers do, however, come in handy for feeding and even bedding small children, as highchairs and cots are only provided in the most upmarket hotels. Taxis and car-rental companies never provide baby seats, but you can rent **baby car seats**, backpacks and cots through Bali Family Holidays (W www .balifamilyholidays.com). A child-sized **mosquito net** might be useful. **Powdered milk** is available in every major tourist centre, but sterilizing bottles is a far more laborious process in Indonesian hotels and restaurants than it is back home.

**Food** on Bali and Lombok is generally quite palatable to children – not much spice and hardly any unfamiliar textures – but, as with adults, you should be careful about unwashed fruit and salads and about dishes that have been left uncovered for a long time. The other main hazards are thundering traffic, huge waves and strong currents, and the **sun** – not least because the islands' main beaches offer almost no shade at all. Sun hats, sunblock and waterproof suntan lotions are essential, and can be bought in the major resorts. You should also make sure, if possible, that your child is aware of the dangers of rabies (see p.41); keep children away from animals, especially dogs and monkeys, and ask your medical advisor about rabies jabs.

## Information and advice

The Bali for Families **website** W www.balifor-families.com is extremely useful, created by parents who have lots of first-hand experience of travelling in Bali; as well as child-friendly recommendations, there's also a travellers' forum. The more commercial Bali Family Holidays website (W www.balifamily-holidays.com) is another good resource. You might also want to canvas other travellers' opinions on the "Kids To Go" bulletin board at W thorntree.lonelyplanet.com. The logistics of travelling with kids in Asia are addressed in the **book** *Your Child's Health Abroad* by Dr Jane Wilson-Howarth and Dr Matthew Ellis (Bradt Publications). For specific advice about kids' health issues, either contact your doctor, or consult one of the travellers' medical services listed on p.43 or, in the UK, the Nomad Medical Centre (T 020/8889 7014, W www .nomadtravel.co.uk) produces an information sheet on keeping kids healthy when abroad.

# Gay Bali and Lombok

As members of a society that places so much emphasis on marriage and parenthood, the Balinese are generally intolerant of homosexuality within their own culture, to the point where gay Balinese men will often introduce themselves to prospective lovers as hailing from Java, so as not to cause embarrassment to their own people. It's by no means uncommon for men to lead a gay lifestyle for ten or fifteen years before succumbing to extreme social pressure around the age of thirty, getting married and becoming fathers. Lesbians are even less visible, but subject to similar expectations.

On the positive side, it's much more common in Bali and Lombok to show a modest amount of physical affection to friends of the same sex than to friends or lovers of the opposite sex, which means that Indonesian and foreign **gay couples** generally encounter less hassle about being seen together in public than they might in the West. Indonesian law is relatively liberal: the legal **age of consent** for both gay and heterosexual sex is 16.

Despite the indigenous aversion to gay culture, Bali's tourist industry has helped establish the island as one of the two main gay centres of Indonesia (the other being Jakarta). Young gay men from islands as far afield as Borneo gravitate to Bali in search of a foreign partner, and most end up in the Kuta area, where sophisticated Seminyak has become the focus of the island's small but enduring **scene**. Here, Jalan Dhyana Pura has a burgeoning number of dinky boutique gay bays and larger more exuberant clubs (with drag shows, theme nights and the like). A mixed gay crowd of Indonesians and foreigners congregates in certain other Kuta venues, where they're welcomed without a problem; see p.130 for details of all these places. There are also established **cruising** areas in north Petitenget at the far northern end of Kuta beach, and on Alun-alun Puputan in Denpasar. Everything is a lot quieter on Lombok, and you won't find anything resembling a gay scene in any of the resorts.

A lot of gay visitors and expatriates do have **affairs** with Indonesian men, and these liaisons tend to fall somewhere between holiday romances and paid sex. Few Indonesians would classify themselves as rent boys – they wouldn't sleep with someone they didn't like and most don't have sex for money – but they usually expect to be financially cared for by the richer man (food, drinks and entertainment expenses, for example), and some do make their living this way. As a result, there's no visible gay prostitution on Bali, except for the bevy of transvestites known as the "sucky-sucky girls" who hang out in central Kuta.

The Utopia website ⓦwww.utopia-asia.com is an excellent **resource** for gay travellers in Bali and the rest of Indonesia. The Bali-based tour agency Gay Bali Tours (ⓦwww.bali-rainbows.com/links.html) can recommend gay-friendly hotels and organize package tours. The umbrella organization for gays and lesbians in Bali and Lombok is Gaya Dewata, at Jalan Belimbing, Gang Y 4, Denpasar 80231 (daily 9.30am–3.30pm; ☎0361/222620, ⓔycui@denpasar.wasantara.net.id).

# Directory

**Addresses** Because the government has outlawed the use of English-language names, demanding that Indonesian names be used instead, a number of street names in resort areas such as Kuta (Bali) are known by two names: where relevant, we have included both.

**Airline offices** See p.115.

**Airport departure taxes** International: Rp100,000 from Bali, Rp75,000 from Lombok. Domestic: Rp30,000 from Bali, Rp15,000 from Lombok.

**Contraceptives** Condoms (*kondom*) are available from pharmacists on both islands, but don't rely on local suppliers for other contraceptives.

**Cookery and cultural classes** Short courses in Balinese cookery are held regularly at several venues in Ubud (see p.215), Tanjung Benoa (see p.151) and Lovina (see p.333), at Munduk (see p.313) and at the *Alila* and *Puri Bagus* hotels near Candi Dasa (see p.266). Ubud is the most popular place to take workshops in art, dance, music, carving and other Balinese arts and crafts (see p.214 for details). You can learn batik painting in Kuta (see p.134).

**Electricity** Usually 220–240 volts AC, but outlying areas may still use 110 volts. Most outlets take plugs with two rounded pins. See ⓦ www.kropla.com for more.

**Language lessons** Indonesian language lessons are available in Denpasar (see p.108), Kuta (see p.134), Ubud (see p.215) and Munduk (see p.313).

**Laundry services** Most hotels and losmen have a laundry service, and tourist centres have plenty of services outside the hotels as well.

**Left luggage** Informal services are offered by most losmen and all hotels. Bali's Ngurah Rai Airport also has a left-luggage facility (see p.114) and many Perama offices have a left-luggage/locker service for their customers.

**Newspapers and magazines** Most Balinese newspaper readers buy the daily *Bali Post*, while non-Indonesian speakers read the English-language daily *The Jakarta Post* (Rp5000, or more from hawkers and some shops). There's more incisive domestic and international news coverage in the weekly magazine *Tempo*, published in both Indonesian and English versions, but not widely distributed on Bali or Lombok. For tourist-oriented magazines, see p.36. Major international newspapers are available in Kuta (Bali).

**Radio** Radio Republik Indonesia (RRI) broadcasts music, chat and news programmes 24 hours a day on 88.5 FM and 95 FM, with occasional English-language bulletins. Kuta-based Top FM (89.7 FM) is mostly talk shows and easy-listening music, with some English-language programmes. Paradise FM (100.9 FM; daily 8am to 7pm) is a Bali-based English-language station aimed at tourists, with news bulletins at 8am and 9am.

**Time** Bali and Lombok are on Central Indonesian Time, which is eight hours ahead of GMT, thirteen hours ahead of US Eastern Standard Time, and two hours behind Australian Eastern Standard Time. There's no daylight saving.

**Tipping** It's becoming increasingly usual to tip on Bali or Lombok, generally about ten percent to waiters (if no service charge is added to the bill), drivers and tour guides; a few thousand rupiah to bellboys and chambermaids in mid-range and upmarket hotels; and a round-up to the nearest Rp1000 for metered-taxi drivers.

**TV** The government-operated TV station Televisi Republik Indonesia (TVRI) is dominated by soaps and melodramas, but carries headline news and weather reports in English every afternoon. Bali's local station is TVRI Bali. Most hotels also have satellite TV, which includes CNN, TV Australia and sometimes BBC World.

**Work** A few tourists manage to set themselves up as English- or Japanese-language teachers in Kuta and Ubud. Otherwise, the most common money-making ploy is the exporting of Indonesian goods (fabric, clothes, jewellery and other artefacts). The fortnightly *Bali Advertiser* (ⓦwww.baliadvertiser.biz), available free from some hotels and tourist offices, carries a "situations vacant" column.

**Yoga and holistic therapies** Sessions and courses for all levels in Ubud (see p.213), Lovina (see p.332), Lalang Linggah (p.356), Wongayagede (see p.353), Ume Anyar (see p.373), Sidemen (see p.283) and Bondalem (see p.321). Ubud-based Bali Spirit (ⓦwww.balispirit.com; see p.213) is an excellent resource for all things holistic in Bali, and the website carries a detailed programme of all upcoming yoga retreats.

# Guide

# Guide

# 1

# South Bali

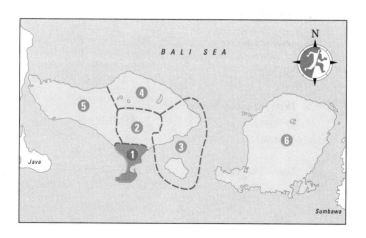

CHAPTER ONE # Highlights

✳ **Bali Museum, Denpasar**
A tantalizing introduction to the island's cultural and religious heritage.
See p.101

✳ **Denpasar markets**
South Bali's most authentic, and chaotic, shopping experience.
See p.104

✳ **Seminyak** Some of the finest dining on the island, at very reasonable prices. See p.129

✳ **Kuta nightlife** Scores of easy-going bars, trendy clubs and packed dance-floors make Kuta a great place to party. See p.130

✳ **Jimbaran beach bar-becues** Fresh fish grilled over coconut husks and served at candlelit tables on the sand. See p.138

✳ **The surf** Awesome, world-famous breaks at Uluwatu and Padang Padang. See p.140

✳ **Sanur** A green, and relatively peaceful, resort that makes an appealing alternative to Kuta. See p.151

△ Match of the day, Kuta beach

# 1

# South Bali

T he triangle of mainly flat land that makes up **the south** is some of the most fertile in Bali, and also the most densely populated, with more than a thousand people resident on every square kilometre. Bali's administrative capital, Denpasar, is here and so, too, are the island's major tourist resorts, which have sprung up along the white-sand beaches: at Kuta in the west, and Sanur and Nusa Dua in the east. Furthermore, the combination of large offshore reefs and a peculiarly shaped coastline have made this region a genuine **surfers' paradise**, with some of the most sought-after breaks in the world.

Most tourists regard **Denpasar** as little more than a transit point for cross-island journeys, but it holds the island's best museum and makes an interesting contrast to the more westernized beach enclaves. Travellers tend to treat the sprawling **Kuta–Legian–Seminyak** resort on the southwest coast as the focal point for booking onward journeys, storing luggage, and stocking up on essentials and souvenirs. Much of it is brash and commercial – despised and adored in equal parts but not easily ignored, not least because of its proximity to Bali's airport, just 3km south of Kuta's southern fringes.

Directly east from Kuta, on the southeast coast, **Sanur** is a quieter, less youthful but more appealing alternative, with abundant greenery and decent watersports facilities. Further south, the finely manicured five-star resort of **Nusa Dua** creams off the wealthier package tourists, protecting them from all that is unnerving about Bali – as well as a lot of what is most attractive. Neighbouring **Tanjung Benoa** is known for its watersports, and its slightly less exclusive accommodation, though not for its beaches. Beyond Nusa Dua, the barren **Bukit** limestone plateau is beginning to attract more overnight visitors to its peaceful, upmarket hotels, particularly at **Jimbaran**, a few kilometres south of the airport, while day-trippers continue to flock to the dramatically sited clifftop temple at **Uluwatu**, perched above the very best surf in Bali.

Aside from Denpasar, which, together with Sanur, is a municipality in its own right, all the towns and villages covered in this chapter come under the administrative region known as **Badung**, a regency that was forged towards the end of the eighteenth century by the Raja of Pemecutan. By 1891, Badung had expanded to include much of the land controlled by the neighbouring kingdom of Mengwi as well, but supremacy was soon wrested from the newly powerful Raja of Badung by the insatiably expansionist Dutch, whose invasion of Badung in 1906 resulted in the ritual suicide of hundreds of Badung citizens, and the subsequent end to raja autocracy on the island. These days, Badung – which covers under eight percent of the island's total land mass – is by far the richest of Bali's eight regencies, incorporating as it does nearly all its most lucrative tourist resorts.

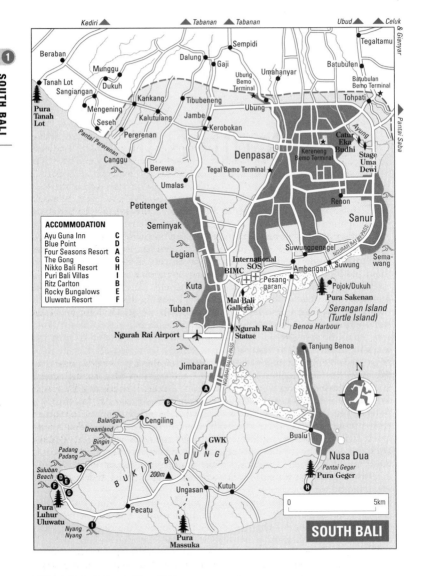

ACCOMMODATION
| | |
|---|---|
| Ayu Guna Inn | C |
| Blue Point | D |
| Four Seasons Resort | A |
| The Gong | G |
| Nikko Bali Resort | H |
| Puri Bali Villas | I |
| Ritz Carlton | B |
| Rocky Bungalows | E |
| Uluwatu Resort | F |

SOUTH BALI

## Transport practicalities

Getting around the region on **public transport** is pretty trouble-free: distances between the main centres are short, and bemo services regular and frequent. All south Bali resorts offer plenty of **cars** and **motorbikes** for rent, though traffic is tiresomely heavy throughout the day and late into the night. **Tourist shuttle buses** operate out of Kuta and Sanur to major destinations in Bali (Ubud, Candi Dasa, Lovina, Padang Bai and so on) and further afield (Nusa Lembongan, the Gili Islands and Lombok). Alternatively, you can use the cheaper but slower **bemo** system: nearly all bemo journeys between places in the south and other parts of the island go via Denpasar.

# Denpasar

Despite roaring motorbikes and round-the-clock traffic congestion, Bali's capital **DENPASAR** (meaning "next to the market") remains a pleasant city at heart, centred on a grassy square, with just a few major shopping streets criss-crossing the core. Department stores and malls do feature but the older neigh-bourhoods are still dominated by family compounds grouped into traditional *banjar* (village association) districts, where time-honoured community events, such as gamelan and dance rehearsals, take place as frequently as in the island's rural villages. The difference in Denpasar is in the marked influence of the size-able immigrant communities, notably Javanese Muslims, Sasaks from Lombok, and Chinese-Indonesians, who together constitute around thirty percent of the city's population of 400,000.

Most tourists whiz into Denpasar as part of a day-trip from one of the south-ern resorts, lingering just long enough to tour the wide-ranging **Bali Museum** and browse the outstanding traditional **markets**. Hardly any visitors stay over-night and the choice of lodgings is correspondingly poor. But the lack of tourist facilities is an attraction in itself, offering travellers a rare chance to experience unadulterated urban Bali, not to mention cheaper food and accommodation; the city also makes a feasible base for trips by public transport to local attractions such as Tanah Lot, Mengwi, Sangeh and Batubulan.

### Some history
Before the Dutch arrived in 1906, control of the city – then known as **Badung**, like the regency it governed – had been divided among several rajas, most notably those at the courts of Pemecutan (southwest Denpasar) and Kesiman (east Denpasar). These districts survive to this day, but the royal families have lost their political power and have either dispersed or turned their ancestral palaces into tourist facilities. After Bali won independence from the Dutch in 1949, the island's administrative capital was moved to Badung from the north-coast town of Singaraja and the city was renamed Denpasar. Almost fifty years later Denpasar's status was upgraded again when, in 1992, it became a self-governing municipality, no longer under the auspices of Badung regency.

---

### Moving on from Denpasar

Denpasar's four main bemo terminals serve towns, villages and beach resorts right across the island; see the plan on p.98 for an overview. **Tegal** bemo terminal serves most destinations south of Denpasar; **Kereneng** terminal serves Sanur; **Batubulan** terminal in the nearby village of Batubulan (see p.172) serves the Ubud area, east Bali, parts of north Bali, and Nusa Dua via Sanur (dropping passengers on the out-skirts at the *Sanur Paradise Plaza* hotel and the eastern outskirts of Kuta (see p.116); and **Ubung** terminal (see p.342) runs bemos to north and west Bali, as well as buses to Padang Bai (for Lombok) and to Java.

There are smaller bemo terminals on Jalan **Gunung Agung**, for transport to Canggu and Kerobokan; near the **Sanglah** hospital, for Benoa Harbour and Suwung; at **Wangaya** for Sangeh and Pelaga; and at **Suci** for Pulau Serangan. For airport departure details, see p.115.

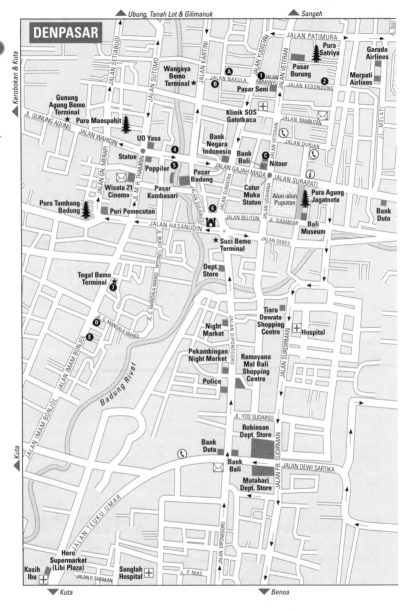

# Arrival, information and city transport

If you're arriving in Bali by air, you'll land at **Ngurah Rai Airport**, which is not in Denpasar as sometimes implied, but just beyond the southern outskirts of Kuta. For full airport arrival and departure information, see the box on p.114.

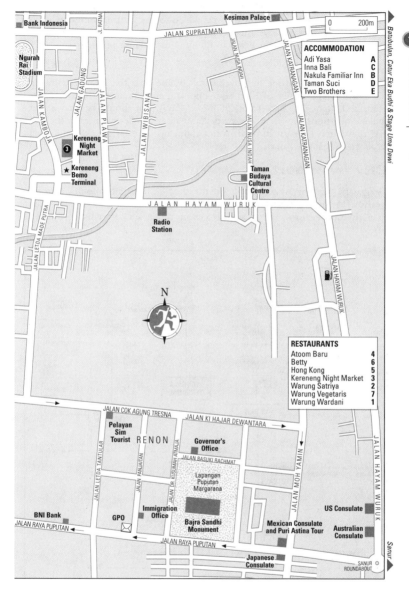

**ACCOMMODATION**

| | |
|---|---|
| Adi Yasa | A |
| Inna Bali | C |
| Nakula Familiar Inn | B |
| Taman Suci | D |
| Two Brothers | E |

**RESTAURANTS**

| | |
|---|---|
| Atoom Baru | 4 |
| Betty | 6 |
| Hong Kong | 5 |
| Kereneng Night Market | 3 |
| Warung Satriya | 2 |
| Warung Vegetaris | 7 |
| Warung Wardani | 1 |

Arriving by bemo or public bus from other parts of the island, you'll almost certainly be dropped at one of the four main **bemo terminals**, which lie on the edges of town: **Tegal**, on Jalan Imam Bonjol, in the southwest corner; **Kereneng**, off Jalan Hayam Wuruk, in east central Denpasar; **Ubung**, way off to the northwest on the main road to Tabanan and effectively in its own suburb (see p.342); and, even further out, **Batubulan** in the northeast (see p.172). The plan below shows which terminal covers which routes. Getting from one bemo terminal to another is fairly easy, but connections can be quite time-consuming, as you have to wait for your bemo to fill up at each transit point.

## Information

Denpasar's **tourist office** is conveniently located near the Bali Museum on the northern perimeter of Alun-alun Puputan, at Jl Surapati 7 (Mon–Thurs 7.30am–3.30pm, Fri 8am–1pm; ☏0361/234569). You should be able to get specific questions answered here, particularly about public transport in the city, and they often have useful information about upcoming festivals – but don't expect much more than that.

## City transport

Denpasar's transport system relies on the fleet of different coloured **public bemos** that shuttle between the city's bemo terminals. However, it isn't a particularly user-friendly network as only certain routes are covered; the complex

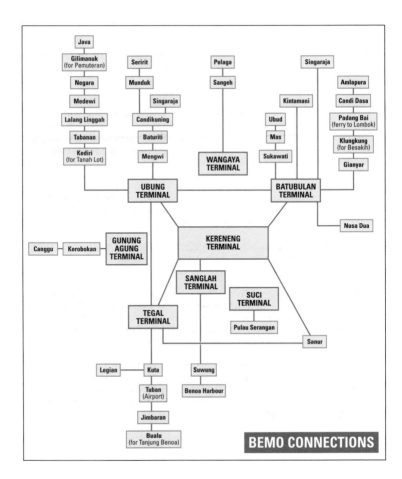

BEMO CONNECTIONS

## City bemo routes

Below is an outline of the major cross-city routes between Denpasar's main bemo terminals. Some routes alter slightly in reverse because of the extensive one-way system, but unless otherwise stated, all routes are identical in reverse.

### Yellow

**Kereneng** – Jl Plawa – Jl Supratman – Jl Gianyar – cnr Jl Waribang (for *barong* dance) – Kesiman – Tohpati – **Batubulan**.

*The return Batubulan–Kereneng route is identical except that bemos go down Jl Kamboja instead of Jl Plawa just before reaching Kereneng.*

### Grey-blue

**Ubung** – Jl Cokroaminoto – Jl Gatot Subroto – Jl Gianyar – cnr Jl Waribang (for *barong* dance) – Tohpati – **Batubulan**.

### Dark green

**Kereneng** – Jl Hayam Wuruk – cnr Nusa Indah (for Taman Budaya Cultural Centre) – Sanur roundabout (for Renon consulates) – Jl Raya Sanur – **Sanur**.

### Turquoise

**Kereneng** – Jl Surapati (for tourist office, Bali Museum and Pura Agung Jagatnata) – Jl Veteran (alight at the cnr of Jl Abimanyu for short walk to Jl Nakula losmen) – Jl Cokroaminoto – **Ubung**.

### Yellow or turquoise

**Tegal** – Jl Gn Merapi – Jl Setiabudi – **Ubung** – Jl Cokroaminoto – Jl Subroto – Jl Yani – Jl Nakula (for budget hotels) – Jl Veteran – Jl Patimura–Jl Melati – **Kereneng** – Jl Hayam Wuruk – Jl Surapati – Jl Kapten Agung – Jl Sudirman – Tiara Dewata Shopping Centre – Jl Yos Sudarso – Jl Diponegoro (for Ramayana Mal Bali shopping centre) – Jl Hasanudin – Jl Bukit Tunggal – **Tegal**.

### Beige

**Kereneng** – Jl Raya Puputan (for GPO) – Jl Dewi Sartika (for Matahari and Robinson department stores) – Jl Teuku Umar – Hero Supermarket – junction with Jl Imam Bonjol (alight to change onto Kuta bemos) – **Tegal**.

*Because of the one-way system, the return Tegal–Kereneng route runs along Jl Cok Agung Tresna instead of Jl Raya Puputan.*

### Dark blue

**Tegal** – Jl Imam Bonjol – Jl Teuku Umar – Hero Supermarket – junction with Jl Diponegoro (for Matahari and Robinson department stores) – Jl Yos Sudarso (for Ramayana Mal Bali shopping centre) – Jl Sudirman – Jl Cok Agung Tresna – junction with Jl Panjaitan (alight for the 500m walk to Immigration Office and GPO) – Jl Hajar Dewantara – Jl Moh Yamin – Sanur roundabout – **Sanur**.

*The return Sanur–Tegal route goes all the way along Jl Raya Puputan after the roundabout, passing the entrance gates of the Immigration Office and the GPO, then straight along Jl Teuku Umar, past Hero Supermarket to the junction with Jl Imam Bonjol (where you should alight to pick up Kuta-bound bemos) before heading north up Jl Imam Bonjol to Tegal.*

one-way system often means that the bemos take slightly different routes on each leg of their journey, and there are no published city-transport maps. The list of city bemo routes on p.99 should help, and we've detailed the most convenient routes in the text. Nearly all Denpasar bemos have at least their first and last stop printed on the back or side of the vehicle (for example, Tegal–Ubung–Kereneng–Tegal), and most are colour coded. Wave to hail one, but be sure to state your exact destination before getting in. **Prices** are supposed to be fixed, but tourists are often obliged to pay more – generally Rp2500 for a cross-city ride. For impartial advice on bemo routes and prices, ask at the controller's office rather than in the bemos themselves. If you can't face the bemo system, metered **taxis** also circulate around the city, as do **dokar**, the horse-drawn carts used by locals for short journeys within town.

# Accommodation

**Accommodation** in Denpasar caters more for the quick-stop Indonesian business traveller than the fussier tourist trade, but there is one particularly inviting budget hotel.

**Adi Yasa** Jl Nakula 23 ☎0361/222679. This long-running losmen, less than ten minutes' walk north of the museum, is most backpackers' first choice. Rooms are exceptionally cheap and all come with fan and bathroom, but they're fairly run-down and not all that secure. From Kereneng, take an Ubung-bound bemo and walk 300m west from the Pasar Seni art market at the Jl Abimanyu junction with Jl Veteran. The weirdly routed Tegal–Kereneng bemos also pass the front door. ❶

**Inna Bali** Jl Veteran 3 ☎0361/225681, ✉ntrbali@denpasar.wasantara.net.id. Central Denpasar's oldest hotel used to be the establishment of choice for the cruise passengers of the 1930s and still has a certain quaint appeal in its colonial architecture, though the rooms – all of which have air-con and a veranda – are now rather faded. There's a pool and a restaurant, and it's a short stroll from the museum. ❻

**Nakula Familiar Inn** Jl Nakula 4 ☎0361/226446, ✉nakula_familiar_inn@yahoo.com. Welcoming little place whose purpose-built guest rooms, adjacent to the family home, are very spruce and modern, and all have their own balcony, fan and bathroom. Not as cheap as *Adi Yasa* across the road (see above for bemo access), but much more comfortable. ❷

**Taman Suci** Jl Imam Bonjol 45 ☎0361/485254, ⓦwww.tamansuci.com. Modern, decently furnished mid-range hotel, just 50m south of Tegal bemo terminal. Good value and well equipped with air-con and TVs in every room, but not terribly convenient for Denpasar's big sights. ❺

**Two Brothers (Dua Saudara)** Jl Imam Bonjol Gang VII 5 ☎0361/484704. Tiny losmen with just three spartan but spotless rooms in a family compound down a residential *gang* off the main street, 300m walk southeast of Tegal bemo terminal. Bathrooms are shared. ❶

# The City

Denpasar's central landmark is *Alun-alun* **Puputan**, the verdant square that marks the heart of the downtown area, the core of the major sights, and the crossover point of the city's major north–south and east–west arteries. On the traffic island here stands a huge stone **statue of Catur Muka**, the four-faced, eight-armed Hindu guardian of the cardinal points, indicating the exact location of the city centre. The main road that runs west from the statue is **Jalan Gajah Mada** (named after the fourteenth-century Javanese prime minister), lined with shop-houses and restaurants and, just beside the Badung River, a huge covered market, **Pasar Badung**. A couple of blocks further west stands the historic **Pura Maospahit** temple, but the more visited attractions dominate the eastern fringes of Alun-alun Puputan itself – the rewarding **Bali Museum** and the state temple, **Pura Agung Jagatnata**.

Denpasar's eastern districts are less enticing, but the art gallery at the **Taman Budaya Cultural Centre** is worth a look, while the suburb of **Renon** is the location of consulates and government offices.

## Alun-alun Puputan

Right in the heart of Denpasar, the grassy public park known as **Alun-alun Puputan** or Taman Puputan (Puputan Square) makes a pleasant retreat from the busy roads that encircle it. The square commemorates the events of September 20, 1906, when the Raja of Badung marched out of his palace gates, followed by hundreds of his subjects, and faced the invading Dutch head on (see p.449 for the full story). Dressed all in holy white, each man, woman and child clasping a golden kris (dagger), the people of Badung had psyched themselves up for a **puputan**, or ritual fight to the death, rather than submit to the Dutch colonialists' demands. Historical accounts vary a little, but it's thought that the mass suicide took place on this square and was incited by Badung's chief priest who, on a signal from the raja, stabbed his king with the royal kris. Hundreds of citizens followed suit, and those that didn't were shot down by Dutch bullets; the final death toll was reported to be somewhere between six hundred and two thousand. The palace itself, just across Jalan Surapati on the north edge of the modern square, was razed to the ground and has now been rebuilt as the imposing official residence of the governor of Bali. The huge **bronze statue** on the northern edge of the park is a memorial to the Badung citizens who fought and died in the 1906 *puputan*, the figures bearing sharpened bamboo staves and kris – an image that you'll see repeated on town and village roadside statues across the island.

The square hosts a commemorative **fair**, with food stalls and *wayang kulit* shows, every year on September 20.

## The Bali Museum

Overlooking the eastern edge of Alun-alun Puputan on pedestrianized Jalan Mayor Wisnu, the **Bali Museum** (Sun–Thurs 8am–3pm, Fri 8am–1pm; Rp2000, children Rp1000; on the turquoise Kereneng–Ubung bemo route) is Denpasar's most significant attraction and makes a worthwhile introduction to the island's culture, past and present. Even if the exhibits hold little interest for you, the museum compound itself is charming, divided into traditional courtyards complete with *candi bentar*, *kulkul* tower, shrines and flower gardens. Work on the museum began in 1910 under the direction of the Dutch Resident, whose idea it was to construct the museum in the traditional *puri-pura* style, mixing elements from traditional palace (*puri*) architecture with temple (*pura*) features. But the project was beset with problems, and it wasn't until the 1930s and the involvement of the expatriate German artist Walter Spies (see p.198), among others, that the collection of ethnographic materials was really taken seriously.

The collection is housed in four separate buildings, each designed in a specific regional and historical style; the most rewarding is the Gedung Karangasem, the second building to the left of the entrance courtyard.

### Gedung Timur

The two-storey **Gedung Timur**, which stands at the back of the entrance courtyard, is the least informative of the collections. Its downstairs hall makes a desultory attempt at introducing key events and places in the island's **history**: cases of stone axes and bronze jewellery are displayed alongside a massive **stone sarcophagus** that was hewn from soft volcanic rock in around the second century BC, plus there are photos of Bali's most important archeological sites – at Gunung Kawi, Goa Gajah and Yeh Pulu – as well as scale models of the major Javanese monuments, Borobodur and Prambanan. The black-and-white **photographs of the 1906 puputan** are unfortunately rather murky but show the landing of the Dutch troops at Sanur and gruesome scenes of massacred bodies heaped up in what is now known as Alun-alun Puputan. The upstairs gallery is given over to a few traditional **paintings and woodcarvings** representing the evolution of artistic styles over the last century, though the display is not a patch on those at the Ubud museums.

## Gedung Buleleng

Passing through the traditional gateway that leads left off the entrance courtyard, you'll come to the compact **Gedung Buleleng**, designed in Buleleng (or Singaraja) style, and holding some fine examples of Balinese **textiles**. The plainest and most common of the styles displayed here is **endek**, sometimes referred to as *ikat*, in which the weft threads are dyed to the finished pattern before being woven – hence the distinctive fuzzy-edged look (see p.488 for more on this and other traditional textiles). **Gringsing**, or double-*ikat*, is a far rarer material that involves a complex dyeing and weaving technique practised only by the villagers of Tenganan.

## Gedung Karangasem

Built to resemble the long, low structure of an eighteenth-century Karangasem-style palace, the **Gedung Karangasem** introduces the **spiritual and ceremonial life** of the Balinese – the cornerstone of the average islander's day-to-day existence – and is the most fascinating section of the museum. Each of its displays focuses on one of the five main religious ceremonies of Balinese Hinduism, the *panca yadnya*, beginning at the far left-hand wall with a presentation on the *dewa yadnya* (ceremonies dedicated to the Hindu gods), and continuing with exhibits on the rituals for ancestors, humans, saints and priests, and finally for the neutralising of evil spirits.

In the *dewa yadnya* display, the bronze image of **Sanghyang Widi Wasa** (the supreme god or being, who is also known as Acintya) is immediately recognizable because of his peculiar stance – the right leg drawn up so that his flame-shaped right foot rests against his left knee. In the same section, look out for the two statuettes constructed out of a thousand ancient **Chinese coins** strung together, meant to invoke the god of wealth. Although these coins, or *kepeng*, are no longer legal tender, they have a special religious significance and are hoarded by Balinese to use as offerings.

Along the back wall, in the *manusa yadnya* display about rituals for humans, the birth-rites exhibit contains a curious bell-shaped **bamboo cage** still used by some villagers to mark the first cycle of a baby's life (210 days). Babies are never allowed to crawl on the ground, as the Balinese eschew any behaviour that appears animal-like, and until their 210th day they are continually carried around. On completion of its first cycle, the baby is placed in the cage and ceremonially lowered to the ground, after which it is expected to totter on two legs.

The Balinese **calendars** on the right-hand wall are immensely complex compositions arrived at through mathematical, astrological and religious permutations. The painted one here is in traditional Kamasan style (see p.481), using muted natural colours on a white cotton background, while the carved wooden calendar is much rarer. Though these particular examples are quite old, the calendar system that they depict is still widely used to determine all sorts of events from temple festivals to the starting day for the construction of a new house. For an explanation of the workings of the Balinese calendar, see p.63.

### Gedung Tabanan

The theme of the **Gedung Tabanan**, designed to replicate a palace from the Tabanan regency, is **music and dance**, and the exhibits include masks, costumes and puppets. Most impressive are the *barong* costumes, representing legendary creatures that feature in nearly every Balinese dance performance. The shaggy-haired **Barong Ket**, representing the forces of good, is probably the most popular character, and is something like a cross between a lion, a pantomime horse and a Chinese dragon. One dancer takes the part of the beast's head and front legs, the other his hindquarters. The witch-like figure of **Rangda** who stands next to him is the embodiment of all that is evil, with her pointed fangs, unkempt hair, snarling mouth and huge lolling tongue (the box on p.235 tells Rangda's story). Less commonly seen on tourist stages, as they play a more vital role in village life, are the two towering **Barong Landung**, huge humanoid male and female puppets. At certain times of the ceremonial year, holy men will don these enormous bamboo skeletons and use them to chase away evil spirits. See p.475 for more on these ritual performances.

## Pura Agung Jagatnata

Just over the north wall of the Bali Museum stands the modern state temple of **Pura Agung Jagatnata**, set in a fragrant garden of pomegranate, hibiscus and frangipani trees. The temple, built in 1953, is dedicated to the supreme god, Sanghyang Widi Wasa, who is here worshipped in his role as "Lord of the World", or Jagatnata.

As with nearly every temple in Bali, Pura Agung Jagatnata is designed as three courtyards, though in this case the middle courtyard is so compressed as to be little more than a gallery encircled by a moat. **Carvings** of lotus flowers and frogs adorn the tiny stone bridge that spans the moat (access at festival times only) and there are reliefs illustrating scenes from the *Ramayana* and *Mahabharata* carved into the gallery's outer wall. If you walk round to the gallery's east wall, you'll see probably the most famous episode in the whole *Ramayana* story – the shooting of the golden deer by Rama, which resulted in Sita's kidnap and the subsequent bookful of battles between Rama and Rawana (see box, p.473).

The temple's focal point is the looming five-tiered **padmasana**, beneath the customary empty throne and balanced on top of a huge cosmic turtle. Built entirely from blocks of white coral, the tower is carved with demons' heads and, on the bottom level, with the face and hands of Bhoma, the son of the earth, whose job it is to repel evil spirits from the temple. The lotus throne at its summit is left empty for Sanghyang Widi Wasa to fill when descending to earth at festival times – the god is represented in a gold relief embossed on the back. Worshippers lay their offerings at the foot of this shrine, heaped up around the heads of the turtle and the two attendant *naga*, which are all swathed in lengths of holy saffron and black-and-white cloth. In the southeast corner of the outer compound stands the **kulkul** (bell) tower, with its split wooden bell hung high up from the rafters. The *kulkul* is still used to summon villagers to festivals, meetings and temple-cleaning duties.

As a state temple, Pura Agung Jagatnata is effectively open to all devotees (village temples are not). Twice a month, on the occasion of the full moon and of the new or "dark" moon, **festivals** are held here and citizens file into the temple compound to lay down their offerings and pray. On the festival evenings, *wayang kulit* shows are sometimes performed at the temple, held from around 9pm to 11pm in the outer courtyard; ask at the nearby tourist office (see p.98) for details.

## Pasar Badung and Pasar Kumbasari

The Chinese shop-houses and glossy department stores of modern Denpasar are nowhere near as interesting as the city's old-fashioned Balinese **markets**. The biggest and best of these is the chaotic **Pasar Badung**, which is housed in a traditional three-storey covered stone-and-brick *pasar* beside the Badung River at the heart of the downtown area, set slightly back off Jalan Gajah Mada. As you approach the market building, you may find yourself landed with a **guide**: local women hang out around the Jalan Sulawesi entrance – some even wait for their prey way up on Gajah Mada – offering to accompany you around the stalls. You'll be steered very persuasively towards certain outlets, and anything you buy will include a commission for your guide. Trading at Pasar Badung takes place 24 hours a day, with buyers and sellers pouring in from all over the island. Fresh fruit and veg occupy the basement, and spices and other groceries are on the ground floor, but the most browsable section is the art market upstairs, where you could easily spend a whole morning bargaining your way through the hundreds of stalls selling very well-priced sarongs, handicrafts, Balinese and western clothes, ceremonial parasols and more.

The one place that can rival Pasar Badung on price and variety is the dedicated four-storey traditional art market **Pasar Kumbasari**, which overflows with clothes, souvenirs, textiles, woodcarvings, paintings and sarongs. It's just west across the narrow Badung River from Pasar Badung, a few metres south of Jalan Gajah Mada.

The much smaller, open-air **Pasar Burung**, north of Alun-alun Puputan on Jalan Veteran, specializes in a quite different sort of produce: live birds and animals sold as pets. As with similar places the world over, a visit here can be extremely depressing, both for the appalling conditions in which the creatures are kept, and for the knowledge that, behind the shuttered doors and temporary walls, there's almost certain to be a caged menagerie of more valuable, endangered birds and animals, captured and sold in secret.

## Pura Maospahit

In contrast with the other major Denpasar sights, **Pura Maospahit** on Jalan Sutomo, just north of Pasar Badung, has a long and significant history that begins with the ancient fourteenth-century Javanese kingdom of Majapahit. It's thought that the oldest part of the temple may actually have been brought over to Bali from East Java, either in the fourteenth century, following the 1343 conquest of the island by the Majapahit empire, or in the sixteenth century by the Hindu aristocracy forced to flee the Islamic invasion of East Java. Certainly, the architectural style is very typically Majapahit: the temple is constructed entirely from brick, and is remarkable for its total absence of superfluous ornamentation. Much of what you see today, however, is reconstruction, as the temple suffered badly in the 1917 earthquake, and has been reassembled from original and replacement brickwork.

Pura Maospahit is rarely visited by tourists, and can feel a bit forgotten – though a temple attendant is almost sure to emerge to greet you with visitors' book, donation bowl and sash. The temple rooftops are visible from Jalan Sutomo, but **access** to the outer courtyard is via a doorway down the narrow *gang* that runs along the compound's southern wall. Once inside the compound, look up at the tree to your immediate right, in whose branches you'll see a most unusual *kulkul* tower, built into its own little treehouse. Beyond this, the massive red-brick *candi bentar* connects the outer and middle courtyards, protected by two huge figures representing a giant and a *garuda*.

Through the towering, impressively chunky and unadorned *padu raksa* gateway, the **inner courtyard** is packed with a dozen or more thatched brick shrines. The central, and most important, structure here is the squat red-brick *candi raras* Maospahit, guarded by two ancient terracotta figurines. It's thought that both this shrine and the almost identical one that stands a short distance to the north were constructed in honour of the Majapahit ancestors of the Balinese people.

## Taman Budaya Cultural Centre

In the eastern part of town, on Jalan Nusa Indah, fifteen minutes' walk from the Kereneng bemo terminal, or direct on a Sanur-bound bemo, the **Taman Budaya Cultural Centre** (daily 8am–3pm; Rp250), designed by one of Indonesia's most renowned architects, Ida Bagus Tugur, does its best to fill in the gaps left by the Bali Museum – namely the history of Balinese painting and a celebration of the island's contemporary artistic life. It's a tall order, which the purpose-built cultural centre doesn't meet, but if you don't have time to visit the far superior Neka Art Museum in Ubud, this will at least give you a taste. And, if you're in Denpasar during the annual **Arts Festival** (usually staged between mid-June and mid-July; see ⓦwww.baliartsfestival.com for details), it's worth dropping by the centre for the huge programme of special exhibitions and dance shows.

The main **exhibition hall** is housed in the long, two-storey building towards the back of the compound, and begins with an overview of Balinese **painting**, with a few examples in the classical *wayang* style, followed by works from several different schools, taking in the so-called Ubud, Batuan and Young Artists styles (see p.481 for an explanation of these). Unfortunately, the presentation and labelling is less than helpful. A selection of religious and secular **woodcarvings** fills the next room, together with an assortment of *Ramayana* and *topeng* **masks**. There are more ambitious carvings downstairs along with a collection of **modern nontraditional paintings**, spanning a range of styles from batik through to works influenced by Cubism and Post-Impressionism.

## Renon

Denpasar's administrative district, **Renon**, is down on the southeastern edge of the city, very close to the resort of Sanur and served by Sanur-bound bemos. Several square kilometres have been landscaped into a leafy green suburb, with wide tree-lined boulevards, shaded pavements and imposing buildings housing government offices, including the governor of Bali's headquarters and the Immigration Office.

Renon is also the location of the huge **Bajra Sandhi** ("Balinese People's Struggle") **monument**, which was designed by the architect Ida Bagus Tugur to resemble a priest's bell, with dimensions – comprising 8 entrances, 17 corners and 45m in height – that represent the date of Indonesia's Declaration of Independence: August 17, 1945. The monument dominates the Lapangan Puputan Margarana and is the focus of rallies and other public events; exhibitions are occasionally staged in its basement gallery.

# Eating and drinking

There are hardly any tourist-oriented **restaurants** in Denpasar, so this is a good chance to sample Bali's cheap, authentic neighbourhood eateries. Smaller restaurants generally shut by 9pm, but hawkers continue to ply the streets with their soup and noodle carts. **Nightlife** in the city centres around Jalan Teuku Umar's karaoke bars and pick-up joints.

**Atoom Baru** Jl Gajah Mada 106. Popular, mid-priced city-centre Chinese restaurant serving lots of seafood. Worth visiting in a group to share the family-sized dishes.

**Betty** Jl Sumatra 56. Cheap, unpretentious café with an extensive English-language menu of Indonesian food that includes *rujak petis* (vegetable and fruit in spicy peanut and shrimp sauce), *botok daging sapi* (spicy minced beef with tofu and coconut milk), *pepes ikan laut* (steamed fish), and a tasty vegetarian selection as well. Closes at 9pm.

**Hong Kong** Jl Gajah Mada 99. Classy, air-con, moderately priced Chinese restaurant offering a huge variety of set meals and à la carte choices, including seafood and some Western dishes. Popular with middle-class Indonesian families. Karaoke at night.

**Kereneng Night Market** Just off Jl Hayam Wuruk, adjacent to Kereneng bemo terminal. Over fifty vendors convene here from dusk to dawn every night, dishing out super-cheap soups, noodle and rice dishes, *babi guling*, fresh fruit juices and cold beers for consumption at the trestle tables set around the marketplace.

**Warung Satriya** Jl Kedondong. Neighbourhood warung serving very cheap nasi campur, nasi goreng, *nasi soto ayam* and lots of noodle dishes. Convenient for the Jl Nakula losmen and stays open till 10pm.

**Warung Vegetaris** Tegal bemo terminal, Jl Imam Bonjol. Tiny, cheap vegetarian food-stall inside the Tegal bemo-terminal compound.

**Warung Wardani** Jl Yudistira 2. The locals' favourite for good, filling plates of nasi campur, *nasi soto ayam*, *soto babat* (meat soup) and gado-gado, most of them costing just Rp10,000. Shuts about 4pm.

# Entertainment

The city's main **cinema** complex is the five-screen Wisata 21 at Jl Thamrin 29 (☏0361/424023). Films are usually shown in the original language with Indonesian subtitles; programmes are listed in the free tourist publications *What's Up Bali* and *Bali Travel News*, and in the *Bali Post* newspaper. Seats cost Rp12,500. Tourist-oriented performances of traditional **Balinese dance** are staged daily at several venues within easy reach of Denpasar. Tickets bought through tour agents generally cost US$10–15 per person including return transport, while tickets bought at the door are Rp50,000 and are available right up until the show starts. For background information on all the dances, see p.471. The **barong**, featuring the battle between the lion-like Barong Ket and the witch Rangda, takes place at the Catur Eka Budhi on Jalan Waribang, in Denpasar's eastern Kesiman district (daily 9.30–10.30am). Batubulan-bound bemos from Ubung and Kereneng pass the corner of Jalan Waribang, from where the stage is a short signposted walk. (If you miss the stop and end up in Batubulan instead, you can also catch a *barong* show there, at the Pura Puseh; see p.174 for details). The spectacular "monkey dance", or **kecak**, is performed nightly at the Stage Uma Dewi, which is also on Jalan Waribang in Kesiman, about 300m south of the *barong* dance stage (daily 6.30–7.30pm). Bemo access is as above, but you'll probably have to get a taxi back.

# Shopping

For **crafts and souvenirs**, the most rewarding places to browse, and bargain, are Pasar Kumbasari and Pasar Badung, described on p.104. For more unusual local souvenirs, the tiny UD Yasa, Jl Gajah Mada 148, is a specialist supplier of religious and ceremonial paraphernalia. The best place for lengths of **fabric**, including rolls of batik, is Jalan Sulawesi, whose entire course from Jalan Hasanudin in the south to Jalan Gajah Mada in the north is devoted to cloth of all descriptions, including *songket* brocades and saree silks. Fabric shops also spill out east along Jalan Gajah Mada as far as Jalan Sumatra. About 100m west along Jalan Gajah Mada from the Sulawesi intersection, Poppiler, at no. 117, specializes in traditional batik prints, selling ready-made shirts and sarongs as well as some designs by the metre. You'll find a dozen outlets for **gold jewellery** on the stretch of Jalan Hasanudin that runs west from Jalan Diponegoro to the river.

The Ramayana Mal Bali shopping centre, Jalan Diponegoro 103 (daily 9.30am–9.30pm; Kereneng–Tegal and Tegal–Sanur bemos), the Matahari department store at Jalan Dewi Sartika 4 (daily 9.30am–9pm; Tegal–Sanur bemo), and the Tiara Dewata shopping centre at Jalan Sutoyo 55 (daily 9am–9pm; Kereneng–Tegal bemo) all carry high-street **fashions** and a few handicrafts. Matahari stocks some English-language novels and **books** about Bali in its basement Gramedia bookstore and also has a **children's department** upstairs, with everything from baby clothes to bottles and mosquito nets (nappies and baby food are sold in the supermarket on the ground floor).

Hero Supermarket in the Libi Plaza shopping complex at Jalan Teuku Umar 104–110 (daily 9.30am–9pm; Tegal–Sanur and Kereneng–Tegal bemos) and Tiara Dewata are good places to buy your own **food and drink** – the Bali *kopi*, gado-gado sauces, clove cigarettes, *arak* and *brem* spirits are all much cheaper here than in the minimarts of Kuta and Sanur.

# Listings

**Airline offices** Garuda has a city check-in at Jl Melati 61 (Mon–Fri 7.30am–4.30pm, Sat & Sun 9am–1pm; ☏0361/254747), where you can get your boarding pass 4–24 hours in advance. For international airline offices, see p.115; for domestic airlines, see p.33.

**Banks and exchange** Most central Denpasar banks have exchange counters. There are ATMs for Visa, MasterCard and Cirrus Maestro every few hundred metres on the main shopping streets.

**Dentist** Dr Indra Guizot, Jl Patimura 19, Denpasar ☏0361/222445.

**Embassies and consulates** See p.35.

**Hospitals and clinics** Sanglah Public Hospital (Rumah Sakit Umum Propinsi Sanglah) at Jl Kesehatan Selatan 1, Sanglah (five lines ☏0361/227911–227915; Kereneng–Tegal bemo and Tegal–Sanur bemo) is the main provincial public hospital, with an emergency ward and some English-speaking staff. It also has Bali's only divers' recompression chamber (ext 123). Kasih Ibu, next to Hero Supermarket at Jl Teuku Umar 120 ☏0361/223036, is a 24hr private hospital that is fine for minor ailments, but not equipped for emergencies; most expats use BIMC or International SOS, both near Kuta, instead (see p.134).

**Immigration Office** At cnr Jl Panjaitan and Jl Raya Puputan, Renon (Mon–Thurs 8am–3pm, Fri 8–11am, Sat 8am–2pm; ☏0361/227828). The Sanur–Tegal and Kereneng–Tegal bemos pass the front door; otherwise, take the Tegal–Sanur bemo, alight where the road splits into the one-way system on Jl Raya Puputan, and walk 750m.

**Internet access** At Hello Internet on the top floor of the Ramayana Mal Bali on Jl Diponegoro.

**Language lessons** Courses in Indonesian language at Indonesia Australia Language Foundation (IALF), Jl Raya Sesetan 90 ☏ 0361/225243, ⓦ www.ialf.edu.

**Pharmacies** Inside Tiara Dewata shopping centre on Jl Sutoyo; Matahari department store on Jl Dewi Sartika; Ramayana Mal Bali on Jl Diponegoro; and Hero Supermarket on Jl Teuku Umar. Also, Apotik Kimia Farma, Jl Diponegoro 125.

**Phone offices** There are Telkom offices at Jl Teuku Umar 6, and on Jl Durian. IDD phones are also available in the Tiara Dewata shopping centre on Jl Sutoyo, and there are dozens of wartels all over the city. There's a Home Country Direct phone at the Bali Museum.

**Police** There are police stations on Jl Patimura and Jl Diponegoro; the main police station is in the far west of the city on Jl Gunung Sanghiang (☏ 0361/424346).

**Post offices** Denpasar's poste restante (Mon–Fri 8am–7pm, Sat 8am–6pm) is at the GPO, located on Jl Raya Puputan in Renon. The Sanur–Tegal and Kereneng–Tegal bemos pass the front door; otherwise, take the Tegal–Sanur bemo, get out at the Jl Cok Agung Tresna/Jl Panjaitan junction and walk 500m south. There's a more central post office on Jl Rambutan, north of Alun-alun Puputan.

**Swimming pools** Tiara Dewata shopping centre has a public pool, or you can use the one at *Inna Bali* hotel for a small fee.

**Travel agents** Domestic airline tickets can be bought from Nitour next to the *Inna Bali* hotel, Jl Veteran 5 ☏ 0361/234742, ⓔ nitourbali@denpasar .wasantara.net.id, and international and domestic airline tickets from Puri Astina Tour, Jl Moh Yamin 1a, Renon ☏ 0361/223552, ⓔ astina@denpasar .wasantara.net.id. Get Pelni boat tickets from Jl Diponegoro 165 ☏ 0361/234680, and train tickets (for Java) from Jl Diponegoro 150 Blok B4 ☏ 0361/227131.

# Kuta–Legian–Seminyak

The biggest, brashest, most untraditional resort in Bali, the **KUTA–LEGIAN–SEMINYAK** conurbation continues to expand from its epicentre on the southwest coast, 10km southwest of Denpasar. Packed with hundreds of losmen, hotels, restaurants, bars, clubs, souvenir shops, fashion boutiques and tour agencies, the eight-kilometre strip plays host to several hundred thousand visitors a year, many of them regular visitors from Australia and all of them here to party, shop or surf. It's a hectic place: noisy, full of hassling touts, traffic jams and constant building work. The narrow main drag, **Jalan Legian**, is often so packed that traffic just crawls along it, every inch of road jammed with taxis and tourist buses, minibuses, bemos, dokar and motorbikes. And yet, for all the hustle, it's a good-humoured resort, almost completely unsleazy, with no strip bars and no high-rises (nothing over the height of a tall coconut tree, in fact).

For many travellers, it's not only the crowds and the assault on the senses that are off-putting, it's that the place seems so un-Balinese: *McDonald's, Billabong* and *Hard Rock* are all here; *Time, Newsweek* and *The Sydney Morning Herald* are sold on every street corner; Hollywood blockbusters show regularly at the dozens of video-bars; and almost every bartender, waiter and losmen employee engages effortlessly in slang-ridden English or Japanese banter. But the resort is, in truth, distinctly Balinese: villagers still live and work here, making religious offerings, attending *banjar* meetings and holding temple festivals. Every morning and afternoon, the women of Kuta–Legian–Seminyak don their temple sashes and place **offerings** in nooks and crannies, in doorways and under tables; you're more than likely to find a tiny palm-leaf basket filled with flowers and rice on the steps of your veranda first thing in the morning. All three former villages have their own **temples**, but none is outstanding and nearly all lock their gates to tourists except at festival times, when you're usually welcome to attend so long as you're suitably attired (see p.79).

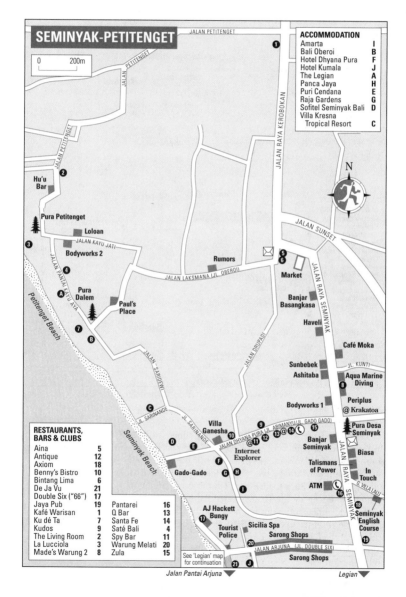

SEMINYAK-PETITENGET

JALAN PETITENGET

0   200m

JALAN PETITENGET

JALAN PETITENGET

JALAN RAYA KEROBOKAN

**ACCOMMODATION**

| | |
|---|---|
| Amarta | I |
| Bali Oberoi | B |
| Hotel Dhyana Pura | F |
| Hotel Kumala | J |
| The Legian | A |
| Panca Jaya | H |
| Puri Cendana | E |
| Raja Gardens | G |
| Sofitel Seminyak Bali | D |
| Villa Kresna | |
| Tropical Resort | C |

N

Hu'u Bar

Pura Petitenget

Loloan

JALAN KAYU JATI

Bodyworks 2

JALAN PANTAI KAYU AYA

Petitenget Beach

Pura Dalem

Paul's Place

JALAN SARIDEWI

JALAN SUNSET

Rumors

JALAN LAKSMANA (JL OBEROI)

Market

Banjar Basangkasa

Haveli

JALAN RAYA SEMINYAK

JALAN DRUPADI

Café Moka

JL. KUNTI

Sunbebek

Ashitaba

Aqua Marine Diving

Periplus @ Krakatoa

Bodyworks 1

Villa Ganesha

JL. SARINANDE

JL. SARINANDE

Seminyak Beach

Gado-Gado

Internet Explorer

JALAN DHYANA PURA (JL. ABIMANYU/JL. GADO GADO)

Pura Desa Seminyak

Banjar Seminyak

Biasa

Talismans of Power

In Touch

ATM

JALAN RAYA SEMINYAK

G. VILLA LALU

Seminyak English Course

AJ Hackett Bungy

Tourist Police

Sicilia Spa

Sarong Shops

JALAN ARJUNA (JL. DOUBLE SIX)

Sarong Shops

See 'Legian' map for continuation

**RESTAURANTS, BARS & CLUBS**

| | | | |
|---|---|---|---|
| Aina | 5 | | |
| Antique | 12 | | |
| Axiom | 18 | | |
| Benny's Bistro | 10 | | |
| Bintang Lima | 6 | | |
| De Ja Vu | 21 | | |
| Double Six ("66") | 17 | | |
| Jaya Pub | 19 | Pantarei | 16 |
| Kafé Warisan | 1 | Q Bar | 13 |
| Ku dé Ta | 7 | Santa Fe | 14 |
| Kudos | 9 | Saté Bali | 4 |
| The Living Room | 2 | Spy Bar | 11 |
| La Lucciola | 3 | Warung Melati | 20 |
| Made's Warung 2 | 8 | Zula | 15 |

Jalan Pantai Arjuna ▼          Legian ▼

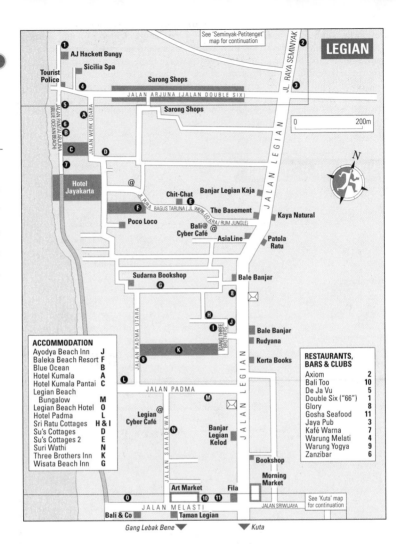

See 'Seminyak–Petitenget' map for continuation

**LEGIAN**

AJ Hackett Bungy

Sicilia Spa

Tourist Police

Sarong Shops

JL. RAYA SEMINYAK

JALAN ARJUNA (JALAN DOUBLE SIX)

Sarong Shops

0        200m

JALAN WERK UDARA

JALAN LEGIAN

Hotel Jayakarta

Banjar Legian Kaja

Chit-Chat

JL. PIRA

BAGUS TARUNA (JL. WERK UDARA / RUM JUNGLE)

The Basement

Kaya Natural

Poco Loco

Bali@ Cyber Café

AsiaLine

Patola Ratu

Sudarna Bookshop

Bale Banjar

JALAN PADMA UTARA

GANG THREE BROTHERS

Bale Banjar

Rudyana

Kerta Books

JALAN LEGIAN

Three Brothers Inn

JALAN PADMA

Legian@ Cyber Café

Banjar Legian Kelod

JALAN SAHADEWA

Bookshop

Morning Market

Art Market

Fila

JALAN MELASTI

JALAN SRIWIJAYA

See 'Kuta' map for continuation

Bali & Co

Taman Legian

Gang Lebak Bene ▼        ▼ Kuta

**ACCOMMODATION**

| | |
|---|---|
| Ayodya Beach Inn | J |
| Baleka Beach Resort | F |
| Blue Ocean | B |
| Hotel Kumala | A |
| Hotel Kumala Pantai | C |
| Legian Beach Bungalow | M |
| Legian Beach Hotel | O |
| Hotel Padma | L |
| Sri Ratu Cottages | H & I |
| Su's Cottages | D |
| Su's Cottages 2 | E |
| Suri Wathi | N |
| Three Brothers Inn | K |
| Wisata Beach Inn | G |

**RESTAURANTS, BARS & CLUBS**

| | |
|---|---|
| Axiom | 2 |
| Bali Too | 10 |
| De Ja Vu | 5 |
| Double Six ("66") | 1 |
| Glory | 8 |
| Gosha Seafood | 11 |
| Jaya Pub | 3 |
| Kafé Warna | 7 |
| Warung Melati | 4 |
| Warung Yogya | 9 |
| Zanzibar | 6 |

## Some history

For centuries, Kuta was considered by the Balinese to be little more than a wasteland, an infertile stretch of coast haunted by malevolent spirits, and a dumping ground for the lepers and criminals cast out from their own villages. Compounding this unpleasant image was Kuta's history as a **slave port** in the seventeenth and eighteenth centuries, during which period hundreds of thousands of men and women were sold by the Balinese rajas to their counterparts in Java and beyond. By the mid-nineteenth century, however, life had become a little less inhumane and a little more prosperous – thanks in no small part to the energetic business acumen of the Dane **Mads Lange**, who set up home here in 1839 and established a flourishing trade in produce from all over Bali. (Lange's tomb stands on the site of his house, 50m east of the modern-day night market, on Jalan Tuan Langa, the road

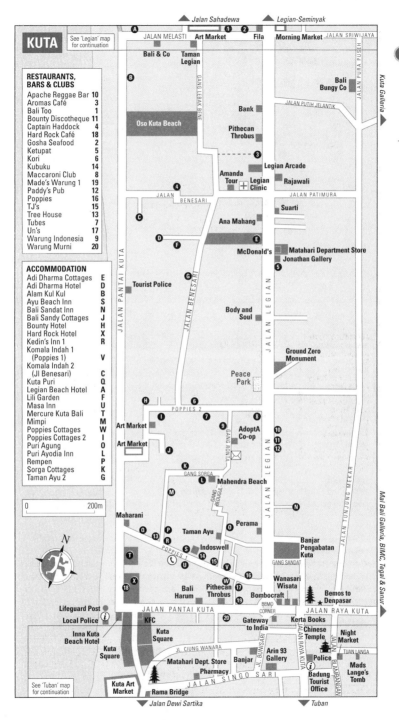

# KUTA

See 'Legian' map for continuation

Jalan Sahadewa   Legian-Seminyak

JALAN MELASTI   Art Market   Fila   Morning Market   JALAN SRIWIJAYA

## RESTAURANTS, BARS & CLUBS

| | |
|---|---|
| Apache Reggae Bar | 10 |
| Aromas Café | 3 |
| Bali Too | 1 |
| Bounty Discotheque | 11 |
| Captain Haddock | 4 |
| Hard Rock Café | 18 |
| Gosha Seafood | 2 |
| Ketupat | 5 |
| Kori | 6 |
| Kubuku | 14 |
| Maccaroni Club | 8 |
| Made's Warung 1 | 19 |
| Paddy's Pub | 12 |
| Poppies | 16 |
| TJ's | 15 |
| Tree House | 13 |
| Tubes | 7 |
| Un's | 17 |
| Warung Indonesia | 9 |
| Warung Murni | 20 |

## ACCOMMODATION

| | |
|---|---|
| Adi Dharma Cottages | E |
| Adi Dharma Hotel | D |
| Alam Kul Kul | B |
| Ayu Beach Inn | S |
| Bali Sandat Inn | N |
| Bali Sandy Cottages | J |
| Bounty Hotel | H |
| Hard Rock Hotel | X |
| Kedin's Inn 1 | R |
| Komala Indah 1 (Poppies 1) | V |
| Komala Indah 2 (Jl Benesari) | C |
| Kuta Puri | Q |
| Legian Beach Hotel | A |
| Lili Garden | F |
| Masa Inn | U |
| Mercure Kuta Bali | T |
| Mimpi | M |
| Poppies Cottages | W |
| Poppies Cottages 2 | I |
| Puri Agung | O |
| Puri Ayodia Inn | L |
| Rempen | P |
| Sorga Cottages | K |
| Taman Ayu 2 | G |

Bali & Co   Taman Legian

GANG LEBAK BENE

Oso Kuta Beach

Bank

Pithecan Throbus

Amanda Tour   Legian Clinic   Rajawali

Legian Arcade

JALAN   BENESARI

JALAN PANTAI KUTA

Ana Mahang

McDonald's

Bali Bungy Co

JALAN PUTIH JELANTIK

JALAN PATIMURA

Suarti

Matahari Department Store

Jonathan Gallery

Kuta Galleria

JALAN PURA PUSEH

Tourist Police

JALAN BENESARI

Body and Soul

Ground Zero Monument

Peace Park

JALAN LEGIAN

0   200m

N

Art Market

Art Market

POPPIES 2

AdoptA Co-op

GANG RONJA

GANG SORGA

Mahendra Beach

GANG BEDUGUL

JALAN LEGIAN

Maharani

Taman Ayu

Perama

JALAN TUNJUNG MEKAR

POPPIES 1

Indoswell

Banjar Pengabatan Kuta

Mal Bali Galleria, BIMC, Tegal & Sanur

Bali Harum

Pithecan Throbus

Bombocraft

Wanasari Wisata

Bemos to Denpasar

BEMO CORNER

Lifeguard Post

Local Police

JALAN PANTAI KUTA

JALAN RAYA KUTA

KFC

Gateway to India

Kerta Books

Inna Kuta Beach Hotel

Kuta Square

Kuta Square

JL. CIUNG WANARA

Matahari Dept. Store

Banjar

Pharmacy

Chinese Temple

Arin 93 Gallery

JALAN RAYA KUTA

Police

Night Market

TUAN LANGA

JALAN BLAMBANGAN

Mads Lange's Tomb

JL. BUNISARI

See 'Tuban' map for continuation

Kuta Art Market

Rama Bridge

JALAN SINGO SARI

Badung Tourist Office

Jalan Dewi Sartika   Tuban

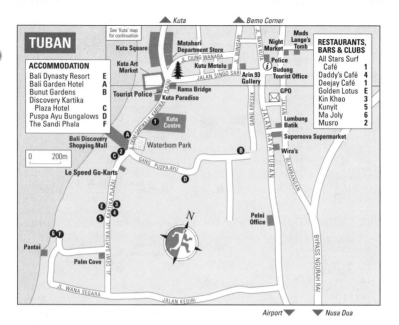

## Alternative road names

In recent years, many roads in the resort have been renamed, though local residents, taxi drivers and some maps often stick to the original names, and streetsigns are rarely consistent. **Alternative road names** are given in brackets on our maps. The following list covers the most confusing examples.

### Petitenget

**Petitenget area** – also known as the Oberoi area, after the hotel.

**Jl Laksmana** – often referred to as Jl Oberoi, after the hotel; along the beachfront, Jl Laksmana is more correctly known as Jl Pantai Kayu Aya.

### Seminyak

**Jl Dhyana Pura** – officially known as Jl Abimanyu (along with its southern offshoot), and also as Jl Gado-Gado after the restaurant at its western end.

### Legian

**Jl Arjuna** – also known as Jl Double Six after the famous nightclub located on the nearby beach.

**Jl Bagus Taruna** – also referred to as Jl Werk Udara (though this is actually the road running north off it). Nicknamed Jl Rum Jungle after a restaurant and hotel on that road.

### Tuban

**Jl Dewi Sartika** – used to be called Jl Kartika Plaza (after one of the big hotels).

named in his honour, in south Kuta.) Lange's political influence was also significant and it was thanks to his diplomatic skills that south Bali avoided falling under the first phase of Dutch control when the north succumbed in 1849.

Kuta's image received a drastic revision in 1936 when an American couple spotted its potential as soon as they saw the beach. Within months, **Bob and Louise Koke** had built a small hotel on Kuta's beachfront: they named it the *Kuta Beach Hotel* (now succeeded by the *Inna Kuta Beach*) and, until the **Japanese invasion** of 1942, the place flourished with a constant stream of guests from Europe and America.

World War II and its aftermath stemmed the tourist flow until the 1960s, when young travellers established Kuta as a highlight on the **hippie trail**. Homestays mushroomed and were eventually joined by smarter international outfits, and Kuta quickly evolved into Bali's most sought-after real estate. Kuta–Legian–Seminyak is now the most prosperous region of the island; wages here are relatively good, and career prospects improve with every English and Japanese phrase learnt, but housing is prohibitively expensive. Many of the shopkeepers, transport touts and waiters rent grotty rooms on the edge of the resort and only return to their village homes for festivals and temple ceremonies – a development that is starting to eat away at the traditional **social fabric**, leaving young people to establish themselves without the support of their families and *banjar* members. Some villages now have so many members in the Kuta area that they've established their own expat *banjar*, enabling villagers to fulfil their community duties even though they're living away from home.

The flood of fortune-seekers from other parts of Indonesia has raised the ugly spectre of racism and religious tension, but no one could have anticipated the viciousness of the **October 12 bomb** attack in 2002, in which Muslim extremists from Java detonated two bombs almost simultaneously at Kuta's most popular nightspots, *Paddy's Pub* and the *Sari Club*. A **Monument of Human Tragedy** dedicated to the 202 people from 22 countries known to have been killed in the attack now occupies the "Ground Zero" site of the original *Paddy's*, across from the Poppies 2 junction on Jalan Legian, and a peace park is slated for the *Sari Club* plot across the way. For more background on the bombing, see Contexts, p.454.

# Orientation and arrival

Although Kuta, Legian and Seminyak all started out as separate villages, they've now merged together so completely that it's impossible for the casual visitor to recognize the demarcation lines. We've used the most common perception of the Kuta–Legian–Seminyak borders: **Kuta** stretches north from the Matahari department store in Kuta Square to Jalan Melasti; **Legian** runs from Jalan

---

### One-way systems

The streets of Kuta-Legian-Seminyak are far too narrow for the volume of traffic that uses them, so a **one-way system** has long been in operation in the resort. However, as this book went to press, the local government had just started trying out a completely new one-way system, reversing the direction of traffic flow in nearly all cases. It was billed as an experiment so, in order not to confuse things even further, we have left off all one-way markers on the map. The change in the one-way system also affects **bemo routes**. Depending on which one-way version wins out, **Tegal–Kuta–Legian bemos** will either travel clockwise: Bemo Corner–Jalan Pantai Kuta–Jalan Melasti north up Jalan Legian as far as Jalan Padma, then do a U-turn to travel back south down Jalan Legian–Bemo Corner; or they will do it anti-clockwise: Bemo Corner north up Jalan Legian as far as Jalan Padma, then do a U-turn to travel back south down Jalan Legian–Jalan Melasti–Jalan Pantai Kuta–Bemo Corner.

Melasti as far north as Jalan Arjuna; and **Seminyak** extends from Jalan Arjuna to the *Bali Oberoi* hotel, where **Petitenget** begins. A few kilometres further up the coast from Petitenget, and accessible via the back road to Tabanan, are the surfing beaches of **Canggu**, **Berewa** and **Pererenan**, isolated spots with just a handful of places to stay. Kuta's increasingly built-up southern fringes, extending south from Matahari to the airport, are defined as **Tuban**.

The resort's main road, which begins as **Jalan Legian** and becomes Jalan Raya Seminyak, runs north–south through all three main districts, a total

## Ngurah Rai Airport

All Bali's international and domestic flights come into the busy **Ngurah Rai Airport**, in the district of Tuban, 3km south of Kuta. For all arrival and departure **enquiries**, call ☏0361/751011 ext 1454.

### Arrival

Queues can be lengthy at **immigration**, where citizens of most countries have to buy a **visa on arrival**: the fee of US$25 (for a thirty-day visa) or US$10 (for a seven-day visa) is payable in any currency (see Basics, p.34, for more info). Once through immigration and customs, you'll find several 24-hour **currency exchange** booths (with fairly disadvantageous rates), and a couple of **hotel reservations desks** that open for all incoming flights and can book hotel rooms costing anything from $8. There are several Visa, Cirrus and MasterCard **ATMs** inside the baggage-claims hall and outside the Arrivals building, along with half a dozen car rental outlets, including Thrifty (☏0361/756485) and Hertz (☏50361/7683750). The **left-luggage** office (Rp10,000–15,000 per day per item) is located outside, midway between International Arrivals and Departures. The **domestic terminal** is in the adjacent building, where you'll find offices of all the dozen or so domestic airlines serving Bali (see p.33).

For **onward transport**, most mid-priced and upmarket hotels will pick you up at the airport if asked in advance. Otherwise, the easiest but most expensive mode of transport to anywhere on the island is **pre-paid taxi**, for which you'll find a counter in the Arrivals area beyond the customs exit doors; you pay at the booth before being shown to the taxi. **Fares** are fixed: currently Rp20,000 to Tuban or south Kuta; Rp25,000 to central Kuta (Poppies 1 and 2); Rp30,000 to Legian (as far as Jalan Arjuna); Rp35,000 to Seminyak; Rp40,000 to outer Seminyak/Petitenget. Further afield, you'll pay Rp25,000 to Jimbaran; Rp40,000 to Denpasar; Rp55,000 to Sanur or Nusa Dua; Rp115,000 to Ubud; or Rp200,000 to Candi Dasa.

Bear these prices in mind before you start bargaining with any of the transport **touts** who gather round both the International and Domestic Arrivals areas. If you opt to go with one, make sure that the agreed price has been clearly decided on and be very firm about which hotel you're heading for, or you could easily end up at the driver's friend's losmen, miles from anywhere. **Metered taxis** ply the road immediately in front of the airport gates (turn right outside Arrivals and walk about 500m – they're not licensed to pick up inside the compound); their rates for rides into Kuta–Legian–Seminyak are around thirty percent lower than the pre-paid taxi equivalents.

Cheaper still are the dark blue **public bemos** whose route (daylight hours only) takes in the big main road, Jalan Raya Tuban, about 700m beyond the airport gates. Note, though, that it's difficult to stash large backpacks in bemos, especially crowded ones. The northbound bemos (heading left up Jalan Raya Tuban) go via Kuta's Bemo Corner, Jalan Pantai Kuta, Jalan Melasti and Jalan Legian (see box on p.113 for details), before continuing to Denpasar's Tegal terminal. You should pay around Rp2500 to Kuta or Legian, Rp3500 to Denpasar, more if you've got sizeable luggage.

If you want to go straight from the airport to **Ubud**, **Candi Dasa** or **Lovina**, the cheapest way (only feasible during daylight hours) is to take a bemo to Tegal terminal distance of 6km. The bulk of the resort facilities is packed into the kilometre-wide strip between Jalan Legian in the east and the coast to the west, an area crisscrossed by tiny *gang* (alleyways) and larger one-way roads.

The other main landmark is **Bemo Corner**, a minuscule roundabout at the southern end of Kuta that stands at the Jalan Legian–Jalan Pantai Kuta intersection. The name's a bit misleading as the Denpasar bemos don't actually depart from this very spot, but it's a useful point of reference.

For information on **airport arrivals**, see the box below.

in Denpasar and continue your journey by bemo from there; see the plan on p.98 for route outlines. A trip by bemo to Ubud will involve three different bemos and cost around Rp13,000 in total. More convenient, but a little more expensive, is to take a bemo or pre-paid taxi from the airport to Kuta's Bemo Corner, then walk 100m north up Jalan Legian to Perama's shuttle bus office, where you can book yourself on to the next tourist shuttle bus, most of which run every two or three hours (see p.117). The priciest way is by pre-paid taxi direct from the airport (see above).

### Departure

For a small fee, any tour agent in Bali will **reconfirm** your air ticket for you, and most can also change the dates of your ticket. Domestic airline information is given in Basics on p.33.

Most hotels in Kuta, Sanur, Nusa Dua and Jimbaran will provide **transport to the airport** for about Rp20,000 (or occasionally for free if you've stayed a week or longer). **Metered taxis** are cheaper: around Rp14,000 from Kuta, Rp18,000 from Seminyak. All tour agents offer **shuttle buses** to the airport from major tourist destinations all over Bali: shop around for the most convenient schedule (journey times also vary), and reckon on paying about Rp10,000 from Sanur, Rp20,000 from Ubud, Rp30,000 from Candi Dasa or Rp50,000 from Lovina. During daylight hours, you can also take the dark blue Tegal (Denpasar)–Kuta–Tuban **bemo** from Denpasar, Kuta or Jimbaran, which will drop you just beyond the airport gates for about Rp3000.

Airport **departure tax** is Rp100,000 for international departures and Rp30,000 for domestic flights. **Excess baggage** is charged between US$7 and US$8.5 per kg for flights to Australian cities and around US$17 per kg to European cities. Airside in the departures area, there's an **Internet centre**, international card **phones**, a couple of snack bars, and dozens of souvenir **shops**; all prices here are inflated.

### International airline offices in Bali

Most airline offices are open Mon–Fri 8.30am–5pm, Sat 8.30am–noon; some close for an hour's lunch at noon or 12.30pm.

**Garuda** has offices and city check-ins (4–24 hours before departure; Mon–Fri 7.30am–4.30pm, Sat & Sun 9am–1pm) inside the *Hotel Sanur Beach* in southern Sanur (℡0361/288011), at the *Kuta Paradiso* hotel in Tuban (℡0361/761414), and at Jl Melati 61 in Denpasar (℡0361/254747).

**Air Asia** Ngurah Rai Airport ℡0361/760116; **Air Paradise** Pertokoan Kuta Megah Blok I–J, Jl Bypass Ngurah Rai, Tuban ℡0361/756666; **Cathay Pacific** Ngurah Rai Airport ℡0361/766931; **China Airlines** Ngurah Rai Airport ℡0361/754856; **Continental Airlines** Ngurah Rai Airport ℡0361/768358; **Eva Air** Ngurah Rai Airport ℡0361/759773; **JAL** Jl Raya Kuta 100x ℡0361/764733; **Lauda Air** Jl Bypass Ngurah Rai 12, Tuban ℡0361/758686; **Malaysia Air** Ngurah Rai Airport ℡0361/757294; **Northwest** *Inna Grand Bali Beach Hotel*, Sanur ℡0361/287841; **Qantas** *Inna Grand Bali Beach Hotel*, Sanur ℡0361/288331; **Royal Brunei** Ngurah Rai Airport ℡0361/757292; **Singapore Airlines/Silk Air** Ngurah Rai Airport ℡0361/768388; **Thai International** *Inna Grand Bali Beach Hotel*, Sanur ℡0361/288141.

### Arrival by bemo

**Public bemos** have a number of routes through the Kuta area. Coming from Denpasar's Tegal terminal, the most convenient option is the dark blue **Tegal–Kuta–Legian bemo** that goes via Bemo Corner and runs as far north as Jalan Padma; the box on the one-way system has more details (see p.113). For destinations a long way north of Jalan Padma, you're probably better off getting a taxi.

The dark blue **Tegal–Kuta–Tuban (airport)–Bualu** route is fine if you're staying in the southern part of Kuta as drivers generally drop passengers on the eastern edge of Jalan Singo Sari – a five-minute walk from Bemo Corner – before they turn south along Jalan Raya Tuban. Coming by bemo **from Jimbaran**, you'll probably be dropped off at the same place.

If you're making the journey **from Sanur** to Kuta by bemo, take the dark blue Sanur–Tegal bemo as far as Denpasar's Jalan Teuku Umar/Jalan Imam Bonjol junction, beside the bridge, then walk left (south) down Jalan Imam Bonjol for about 30m and you'll find Kuta-bound bemos waiting for passengers. If you miss this junction, stay on the bemo until Tegal and pick up the next Kuta-bound bemo at the start of its journey (this adds an extra 10–20min to the trip).

### Arrival by shuttle bus

If arriving in Kuta by **shuttle bus**, you could be dropped almost anywhere, depending on your operator. Drivers for the biggest shuttle-bus operator, Perama, drop passengers at their office on Jalan Legian, about 100m north of Bemo Corner, but will sometimes stop at spots en route if asked.

### Arrival by car or motorbike

Along with the new one-way systems (see box on p.113), new **parking** restrictions are also being tested and are likely to prohibit parking on several of the main thoroughfares. Where it is legal to park, parking attendants charge around Rp1000 to wave you in and out and keep an eye on your vehicle; if there's an attendant there, it's almost obligatory to pay them. Otherwise, you can use the public underground car parks at the Matahari department stores on Jalan Legian and in Kuta Square.

# Information and local transport

All sorts of people in Kuta will be only too willing to offer you information, but the official, and pretty unhelpful, **Badung tourist office** is at Jl Raya Kuta 2 (Mon–Thurs 8am–3pm, Fri 8am–noon; ℡0361/756175), with a counter beside the lifeguard post on the beach off Jalan Pantai Kuta (Mon–Fri 9am–noon; ℡0361/755660).

You'll get a lot more tourist information and details about forthcoming events from the bevy of **tourist newspapers and magazines** available at hotels and some shops and restaurants; see Basics, p.36, for details.

The **Kuta Karnival** (ⓦ www.kutakarnival.com) was inaugurated in 2003 in response to the 2002 bombing and now seems set to become an annual event. Highlights of the week-long carnival, held at the end of June, include parades, surfing and beach-sport competitions, and an outdoor food festival.

### Bemos

The dark blue public **bemos** originate in Denpasar at the Tegal terminal and cover only a very limited route around the resort – basically, doing a loop around Kuta (see box on p.113 for details), leaving out most of Legian and all

## Moving on from Kuta

### Bemos

To get from Kuta to most other destinations in Bali by **bemo** will almost always entail going via Denpasar, where you'll probably have to make at least one cross-city connection.

Dark blue bemos to **Denpasar**'s Tegal terminal (Rp3500; 25min) run regularly throughout the day; the easiest place to catch them is at the Jl Pantai Kuta/Jl Raya Kuta intersection, about 15m east of Bemo Corner, where they wait to collect passengers, although you can also get on anywhere on their loop around Kuta (see p.113 for details). From Tegal, other bemos run to **Sanur** and to Denpasar's other bus terminals for onward connections; full details are on p.99 and on the map on p.98. Note that, to get to Batubulan terminal (departure point for **Ubud**), the white Damri bus service from Nusa Dua is quicker than taking a bemo to Tegal and another to Batubulan; you can pick it up at the Kuta fuel station on the intersection of Jl Imam Bonjol and Jl Setia Budi, about ten minutes' walk northeast of Bemo Corner. Dark blue bemos from Tegal to Bualu (for **Nusa Dua** and **Tanjung Benoa**) also pass this intersection, and will pick you up on Jl Setia Budi if you signal. Some Tegal–Bualu bemos serve **Jimbaran** on the way, and there's also a dark blue Tegal–Jimbaran bemo.

### Shuttle buses

If you're going anywhere beyond Denpasar, the quickest – and priciest – public transport option from Kuta is to take a tourist **shuttle bus**. Every one of the hundred or more tour agencies in Kuta–Legian–Seminyak offers "shuttle bus services": some are little more than one man and his minivan, others are big buses run by professional operators. Prices are always competitive; most travellers choose according to convenience of timetable and pick-up points. Drop-offs are unknown on the smaller operations, most of which will drop you only at their offices in your destination.

Bali's biggest and best-known shuttle-bus operator is **Perama**, whose unobtrusive head office is located 100m north of Bemo Corner at Jl Legian 39 (daily 7am–10pm; ☎0361/751551, ⊛www.peramatour.com). This is the departure point for all Perama buses, although you can pay an extra Rp5000 to be picked up from your hotel (and another Rp5000 for a precise hotel drop-off) and can buy tickets on the phone and through other agents. Perama buses are non-air-con and run between Kuta and all the obvious tourist destinations on Bali as well as to some major spots on Lombok and the Gili Islands (prices include the boat transfer); see "Travel details", p.166, for a full list. Prices are reasonable: examples are Rp20,000 to Ubud, Rp50,000 to Lovina, Rp130,000 to Senggigi on Lombok, and Rp180,000 to the Gilis. Some Perama routes are quite convoluted: for example, their buses from Kuta to Padang Bai/Candi Dasa go via both Sanur and Ubud, which adds an extra hour to a journey that should only take 2hr. In this case, it can make more sense, and be less time-consuming, to split a transport-tout's fare between a group of you.

### Transport to other islands

Many Kuta travel agents (see p.135 for a list) sell **boat tickets** to Lombok, Nusa Lembongan and other Indonesian islands. Details of the local Pelni office (for long-distance ferries to other parts of Indonesia) are on p.135. For Perama shuttle-bus and boat tickets, see above.

All Kuta travel agents sell **domestic air tickets**. Sample one-way fares are Rp237,000 to Mataram on Lombok, Rp473,000 to Yogyakarta, and Rp529,000 to Jakarta. Full airport information is on p.114.

---

of Seminyak – before returning to Denpasar after pausing near Bemo Corner at the Jalan Pantai Kuta–Jalan Raya Kuta intersection to fill up with Denpasar-bound passengers. You can flag them down at any point along the route; the standard fare for any distance within this area is Rp2250, but tourists are some-times obliged to pay more. During the day, bemos usually circulate at five- or ten-minute intervals, but very few bemos run after nightfall and none at all after about 8.30pm.

## Taxis, touts and dokar

Dozens of **metered taxis** circulate throughout the resort, all with a "Taxi" sign on the roof. There are several companies, the most common being the light-blue Blue Bird Taxis (☎0361/701111) and the white Ngurah Rai Airport Taxis (☎0361/724724); North Seminyak and Petitenget are covered by the Liberty Group (☎0361/7455229). All charge Rp4000 flagfall and then Rp2000 per kilometre day or night; always double-check that the meter is turned on when you get in the car. A longish ride, say from the west end of Poppies 1 in Kuta to *Made's Warung 2* in Seminyak, should cost around Rp10,000. You can often save yourself both time and money by walking a short distance to pick up a taxi on its way out of Kuta's long-winded one-way system; some drivers refuse to go along the narrow lanes of Poppies 1 and Poppies 2 anyway, forcing you to walk out to the main street.

Another option is the informal taxi service offered by the "transport, trans-port" **touts** who hang around on every corner. For brief journeys it's usually more hassle than it's worth even to start bargaining with a transport tout, and many won't do short rides anyway, but they can be worthwhile for longer journeys or trips with several stops.

A few **dokar** (horsecarts) congregate at the Jalan Singo Sari–Jalan Dewi Sar-tika intersection in Tuban and can be fun for short hops to Tuban hotels; again, always bargain before the journey begins.

## Cars, bikes and motorbikes

Every major road in the resort is packed with tour agents offering **car rental**: see Basics, p.50, for price guidelines and advice. Most places will also provide a **driver** for the day, which is a good way of organizing a private tour of outlying sights: the island is so small that you can pack in quite a lot in eight hours. A recommended freelance English-speaking guide and driver is Wayan Artana (☎0812/396 1296, ⓔiartana@hotmail.com), who charges Rp250,000 per day inclusive; for other personal recommendations, check the archives of the online travellers' forums listed on p.37. You can also rent **motorbikes** from many car rental outlets, as well as from Chitchat on Legian's Jalan Bagus Taruna; see p.51 for information on costs and insurance. Whether you're in a car or on a bike, bear in mind that signposting is not always as helpful as it might be, and that traffic congestion is a fact of life in southern Bali and on the main westbound highway.

The heavy main-road traffic and the irritating one-way systems can make **cycling** around Kuta rather trying, though if you stick to the back lanes it's not a bad way of getting about. Notices on the central stretch of Kuta beach forbid all vehicles, including bicycles, though once you get north of Jalan Melasti, cycling along the sand seems to be acceptable. Ask about rental at your losmen or at the motorbike rental places.

# Accommodation

Of south Bali's main beach resorts, Kuta–Legian–Seminyak has by far the great-est amount of **accommodation**, and also the biggest range of cheap and mod-erately priced rooms. Many mid-range and expensive hotels are pictured on the

Bali accommodation websites listed on p.54 and these always offer **discounts**; most hotels offer discounts on their own websites, too.

The inexpensive losmen are mainly concentrated in **Kuta**, though **Legian** has some, too, along with a decent share of good-value mid-range places. **Tuban**, **Seminyak** and **Petitenget** are dominated by expensive, and often very stylish accommodation, a lot of it right on the beach. The scene is much quieter in **Berewa**, **Canggu** and **Pererenan**, some 10km north of Seminyak, where just a handful of mid-range and upmarket hotels occupy the shorefront.

# Kuta

**Kuta** is the most congested and frantic part of the resort, where you'll find bars, restaurants, clubs and shops squashed into every available square inch of land. The beach gets crowded, but it's a long stretch of clean, fine sand and deservedly popular. It's also the surfing centre of the resort, with most of the board rental and repair shops, surfwear outlets and surfer-oriented bars clustered on and around Poppies 2.

## Inexpensive

**Ayu Beach Inn** Poppies 1 ☎0361/752091, ⒻI752948. Well-located budget option with fairly shabby losmen-style rooms that are decent enough if not exactly spotless, plus a good-sized pool. Rooms with fan ❷ With air-con ❸

**Bali Sandat Inn** Jl Legian 120 ☎0361/753491. Clean and well-maintained terraced rooms right in the heart of the action, just a few metres from the main nightspots and shopping area. Rooms with fan ❷ With air-con ❸

**Kedin's Inn** Poppies 1 ☎0361/756771. Twenty-four large, fairly basic, fan-cooled losmen rooms, crammed into a small compound in the heart of Poppies 1. ❷

**Komala Indah 1 (Poppies 1)** Poppies 1, #20 ☎0361/751422. Handily located compact square of seven terraced bungalows set around a courtyard garden. Rooms are clean and good value. ❷

**Komala Indah 2 (Jl Benesari)** Jl Benesari ☎0361/754258. Good, simple rooms in a pleasant garden on a quiet part of Jl Benesari, just a couple of minutes' walk from the beach. Prices vary a little according to size. ❷

**Lili Garden** Jl Benesari ☎0361/750557, Ⓔduarsa@dps.centrin.net.id. Small, friendly, family-run losmen offering a dozen clean, unadorned rooms set around a garden between Jl Legian and the beach. Fan rooms ❷ Family house with kitchen ❺

**Masa Inn** Poppies 1, #27 ☎0361/758507, Ⓦwww.masainn.com. Well-priced hotel that's efficiently run, has a good pool and sociable garden area, and serves decent breakfasts. Rooms in the two-storey blocks are plain but fine and all come with air-con. Popular with surfers and rowdy groups of revellers. ❹

🏃 **Mimpi** Gang Sorga, off Poppies 1 ☎0361/751848, Ⓔkumimpi@yahoo.com.

sg. Just seven unusually characterful, thatched, fan-cooled Balinese cottages dotted round an attractive, shady garden with a reasonable-sized pool. Also has a couple of huge villa-style options with separate living areas. Reservations advisable. ❸–❺

🏃 **Puri Agung** Gang Bedugul, off Poppies 1 ☎0361/750054. Welcoming little losmen with just twelve sprucely kept and very good-value rooms packed into two storeys around a minuscule courtyard. ❶

**Puri Ayodia Inn** Gang Sorga ☎0361/754245. Exceptionally cheap, quite funky little pastel-painted place in a convenient but quiet location between Poppies 1 and Poppies 2. Has nine terraced rooms and bungalows, all of them pretty primitive. Fills up fast. ❶

**Rempen** Gang Sorga, off Poppies 1 ☎0361/758320. Cheap, reasonable enough rooms, some in a three-storey tower affording rooftop views of Kuta from the veranda, others in terraced garden bungalows. ❶

**Sorga Cottages** Gang Sorga, off Poppies 1 ☎0361/751897, Ⓕ752417, Ⓦwww.angelfire.com/ nb/sorgacott. Good-value rooms in a three-storey block set round a small pool and a restaurant. Lacks local character but is comfortably furnished and efficiently run. Also offers Internet access. Rooms with fan ❷ With air-con ❹

**Taman Ayu 2** Jl Benesari ☎0361/754376, Ⓕ754640. A small block of very reasonably priced and notably well-maintained bamboo-walled rooms, some with nice garden bathrooms, plus a handful of bungalows. With fan ❶ With air-con ❷

## Moderate

**Adi Dharma Hotel and Cottages** Access from both Jl Legian 155 and Jl Benesari: hotel ☎0361/754280, cottages ☎751527, both www.adhidharmahotel.com. A surprisingly appealing package-tourist-oriented operation with 37 pleasantly furnished "cottage" rooms in a terraced block just off Jl Legian, and 86 more upmarket, contemporary-styled hotel rooms in a separate building off Jl Benesari. Two pools, a spa, a restaurant and a games room. ⑥

**Bali Sandy Cottages** Off Poppies 2 ⊕0361/753344, www.balisandy.com. Attractive, pleasantly secluded hotel offering fifty sizeable, comfortably furnished and well-priced air-con rooms in two- and three-storey wings set around a large pool and lawn. Just three minutes from the beach and about 100m from the shops and restaurants on Poppies 2. ⑤–⑥

**Bounty Hotel** Poppies 2 ⊕0361/753030, www.boun-tyhotel.com. Large, very good-value operation – mainly patronized by young Australians – with 165 exceptionally well-maintained terraced bungalows set in a garden, plus two pools and a games room. Each room is equipped with air-con, TV and fridge. Guests can choose whether to stay in the "lively" area of the complex, near the 24-hour pool. ⑥

🏃 **Kuta Puri** Poppies 1 ⊕0361/751903, Ⓔkuta_puri@hotmail.com. Occupying an ideal location less than a minute from the beach and just a few minutes' walk from Kuta Square, this set of bungalows enjoys an unexpectedly spacious and green setting, with a charming garden, large pool, and on-site massage service and restaurant. The terraced air-con rooms and more luxurious bungalows are in Balinese style and attractively furnished, and some have appealing garden bathrooms. Deservedly popular, so booking is advisable. ⑥

**Poppies Cottages 2 (Old Poppies)** Poppies 2 ⊕0361/751059, www.poppiesbali.com. Pleasantly old-fashioned if slightly faded set of Bali-style cottages with carved wooden doors, fridges and air-con. Pretty garden, and use of the pool at the sister operation, *Poppies Cottages*. Lots more character than most other places in this price bracket. ⑥

### Expensive

**Alam Kul Kul** Jl Pantai Kuta ⊕0361/752520, www.alamkulkul.com. Sophisticated, award-winning boutique-style hotel with 80 rooms and 23 villas packed village-style into a long narrow compound across the road from the beach. Decor is modish but welcoming, and though there's no real garden, each room has a terrace, plus there are two pools and a spa. ⑧–⑨

**Hard Rock Hotel** Jl Pantai Kuta ⊕0361/761869, www.hardrockhotelbali.com. Aimed at the well-heeled, mainstream rock fan, with sleek, contemporary rooms and rock hall-of-fame iconography and memorabilia all over the place (choose whether you want to stay in the "blues" block, for example, or the "psychedelic" wing). Occupies a prime location across from the beach, and boasts a fantastic series of swimming pools, a spa and a kids' club. ⑨

**Mercure Kuta Bali** Jl Pantai Kuta ⊕0361/767411, www.accorhotels-asia.com. Impressive urban-chic styling and an awesome rooftop infinity pool offering unrivalled views over Kuta beach makes this hotel stand out. The rooms are tastefully modern, but balconies are disappointingly poky in the cheaper ones, so it's worth splashing out on a junior suite. Thirty percent discounts available online. ⑧–⑨

**Poppies Cottages** Poppies 1 ⊕0361/751059, www.poppiesbali.com. Elegant, extremely popular traditional-style air-con cottages secluded within a tranquil tropical garden of arbours, miniature bridges and a bougainvillea-shaded swimming pool. Reservations essential. Call for free airport pick-up. ⑦

# Tuban

A few hundred metres south of Jalan Pantai Kuta, beyond Kuta Square's Matahari department store, Kuta beach officially becomes **Tuban** beach and things quieten down a great deal. Nearly all the hotels here enjoy direct access to the beach and are deservedly popular with families. No bemos run down the main drag, Jalan Dewi Sartika, so you're likely to end up forking out for taxis to Kuta's shops and entertainments as the local offerings are not exciting.

**Bali Dynasty Resort** Jl Dewi Sartika ⊕0361/752403, www.balidynasty.com. Big, package-tourist-oriented hotel that's lacking in local character but nicely set in landscaped gardens that run down to the beach. Its busy programme of organized activities makes it a good choice for families, plus there are two swimming pools, a playground and a kids' club. ⑧

**Bali Garden Hotel** Jl Dewi Sartika ⊕0361/752725, www.baligardenhotel.com. Large, attractively designed low-rise hotel complex, with good-value rooms, a pool, spa and garden-view restaurant. The pretty garden stretches right down to the beach; the rooms overlooking it are nicer and quieter than those on the street side. Two children free if sharing with adults; and free airport pick-up. **7**

**Bunut Gardens** Gang Puspa Ayu ☏0361/752971, ✉bunutgarden@yahoo.com. Just thirteen rooms set round a small yard down a quiet, residential lane, about 800m from the beach and the shops. Rooms are a good standard and all have fans and nice bamboo furniture. **3**

**Discovery Kartika Plaza Hotel** Jl Dewi Sartika ☏0361/751067, ⓦwww.discoverykartikaplaza. com. Large, upmarket beachfront outfit where rooms are set in a lush tropical garden, with a huge freeform pool right on the shore. Fitness club, kids' activities, and three restaurants. **9**

**Puspa Ayu Bungalows** Gang Puspa Ayu ☏0361/756721. The cheapest and most popular accommodation on this refreshingly peaceful residential street occupies a quiet and pleasant spot with sixteen typical Bali-style rooms and bungalows (fan and air-con) set round a garden 200m off the main road. **3**

**The Sandi Phala** Jl Wana Segara ☏0361/753780, ⓦwww.the-sandiphala.com. Pricey boutique hotel with eleven elegantly furnished rooms, a beautiful swimming pool and the stunning *Ma Joly* restaurant – all right on the beach. Rates from $250. **9**

# Legian

Slightly calmer than Kuta, **Legian** to the north has just as many shops and restaurants, fewer backpackers and more Australian families and package tourists. The beach is less crowded, and many of the smaller hotels are better value than their Kuta equivalents. If you've got your eye on a beachfront hotel in Legian, note that the beachfront road between Jalan Melasti and Jalan Arjuna is open only to local toll-paying drivers and is therefore very quiet; tourist vehicles have to go the long way round.

## Inexpensive

**Ayodya Beach Inn** Gang Three Brothers ☏0361/752169, ✉ayodyabeachinn@yahoo.com. Cheap and friendly, if rather dilapidated, losmen with fifteen terraced fan rooms, set in a garden just a 75m walk from Jalan Legian. **1**

**Blue Ocean** Jl Pantai Arjuna (Jl Blue Ocean Beach) ☏0361/730289, ℻730590. A five-star location at one-star prices, this place occupies a prime spot on the beachfront road within a few seconds' walk of a fine stretch of shore and several shore-view restaurants. Rooms are simply furnished and fan-cooled and many have kitchen facilities. The School of Surf (see p.125) has its headquarters here, so this is also a great spot for aspiring surfers. **3**

**Hotel Kumala** Jl Werk Udara ☏0361/732186, ⓦwww.hotelkumala.com. Lots of appealingly furnished rooms and more comfortable cottages, all with air-con. With two pools and a good location just 250m from the beach and 100m from Jalan Arjuna, this is excellent value. **4–5**

**Legian Beach Bungalow** Jl Padma ☏0361/751087, ✉gadinglbb@yahoo.com. A small, inviting place with simple but pleasant rooms and bungalows set in a spacious garden close to the shops but not far from the beach. Well priced considering its location and its swimming pool. Rooms with fan **2** With air-con **4**

**Sri Ratu Cottages** Gang Three Brothers ☏0361/751722, ⓦwww.users.bigpond.com/rhi-norok. Two compounds on either side of a quiet but conveniently located *gang*, comprising seven huge if rather spartan bungalows with kitchens, living areas and two double beds, and nineteen very clean air-con rooms built around a pool across the way. The cheapest rooms are a bit dark, but well priced for the area, while the better upstairs ones overlook the garden terrace. Rooms **3–4** Bungalows **5**

**Suri Wathi** Jl Sahadewa 12 ☏0361/753162, ✉suriwati@yahoo.com. Friendly, family-run losmen with 46 well-maintained rooms and bungalows, a decent pool and a garden. Quiet but convenient, and excellent value. Rooms with fan **2** With air-con **3–5**

**Su's Cottages** Jl Werk Udara 532 ☏0361/730324, ℻762202. Spotless, nicely furnished rooms in a small, friendly, family-run losmen, with a tiny plunge-pool. Rooms with fan **4** With air-con **4**

**Su's Cottages 2** Jl Pura Bagus Taruna ☏0361/752127, ℻750372. The sister operation to *Su's Cottages* is located on a livelier road, in amongst the bars and restaurants. Rooms here are just as immaculate and the pool's larger. With fan **3** With air-con **4**

**Wisata Beach Inn** Off Jl Padma Utara ☏0361/755987. Quiet little place at the back of a beauty parlour, with just four bungalows in a small garden, each offering split-level accommodation with beds for up to four people and balconies on both floors. **2**

## Moderate and expensive

**Baleka Beach Resort** Jl Pura Bagus Taruna ℡0361/756205, ⓦwww.balekabeachresort.com. Popular, laid-back place with 45 air-con rooms in two-storey blocks scattered over a large garden area that stretches from Jl Pura Bagus Taruna to Jl Werk Udara. Has a pool and restaurant. ❻

**Hotel Kumala Pantai** Jl Werk Udara ℡0361/755500, ⓔkumalapt@indosat.net.id. Very popular, good-value beachfront hotel comprising ninety smart, comfortable air-con rooms, each with a balcony, bathtub and cable TV. Rooms are in a series of three-storey buildings set in grounds that run down to the sea. Has a good-sized pool and two restaurants. Large discounts usually available but reservations are essential. ❼

**Hotel Padma** Jl Padma 1 ℡0361/752111, ⓦwww.hotelpadma.com. Smart, top-notch place with classy service and thoughtful touches. Offers rooms in a hotel wing as well as more attractive deluxe bungalow accommodation set around a spacious tropical sculpture garden that extends down to the beachfront road. Two pools and a complimentary kids' club and nursery. ❽

**Legian Beach Hotel** Jl Melasti ℡0361/751711, ⓦwww.legianbeachbali.com. Huge collection of large, comfortable four-star bungalows, conveniently located on Legian's southern boundary and set in an attractive garden that runs down to the shorefront road. Has two decent-sized pools and a spa. All bungalows have air-con and TV, but the slightly cheaper rooms in the hotel wing overlook a car park. ❽

**Three Brothers Inn** Gang Three Brothers ℡0361/751566, ⓕ756082. One of the most characterful places in the resort, this lush, rambling garden complex stretches all the way from Jl Padma Utara to Gang Three Brothers and holds dozens of large, attractive bungalows and a pool. There are numerous different types of room, but the best are the upstairs fan-cooled ones with open (barred) windows, mosquito nets and four-poster beds. The air-con rooms are the least interesting options. ❺/❻

# Seminyak and Petitenget

Upmarket **Seminyak**, north of Legian, is quiet and pleasant, attracting return visitors seeking extra peace and seclusion second time around, many of whom choose to rent villas up here (see Basics, p.54, for villa contacts). The further north you go the classier the hotels, with a particularly exclusive enclave occupying the fine stretch of shore near **Pura Petitenget**, off Jalan Laksmana. Seminyak is also home to many expats, so the shops, restaurants and bars tend to cater for these more discerning tastes. Jalan Dhyana Pura, in particular, has a glamorous concentration of fashion-conscious DJ-bars and gay bars, while posh restaurants are two-a-penny on Jalan Laksmana.

**Amarta** Jl Abimanyu 2000x ℡0361/734793, ⓦwww.amartabali.com. Boutique hotel comprising a series of beautifully outfitted two-storey villas, each set in its own walled compound and with a fully equipped kitchen, two bedrooms and bathrooms, a living room (with TV and CD player) and a small patio. The high walls can make you feel rather enclosed, but there's an attractive hotel pool area. ❽

**Bali Oberoi** Jl Laksmana ℡0361/730361, ⓦwww.oberoibali.com. One of the most elegant and discreet hotels on Bali, offering fabulously appointed rooms and villas set in gorgeous beachfront grounds in peaceful Petitenget. Numerous awards and celebrity guests testify to its superb service and tranquil luxury. There's an on-site Banyan Tree Spa. Published rates from US$255. ❾

**Hotel Dhyana Pura** Jl Abimanyu ℡0361/730442, ⓦwww.hoteldhyanapura.com. Good-value hotel, with pleasantly furnished if rather old-fashioned air-con rooms, some in a two-storey terraced block, others in garden cottages. There's a pool, and the garden runs down to the sea. Run by the Protestant Christian Church of Bali and located next door to Seminyak's impressive church. ❼

**The Legian** Jl Pantai Kayu Aya ℡0361/730622, ⓦwww.ghmhotels.com. *The* choice of weekending Asian sophisticates, who love the muted minimalist style and staggering size of the deluxe apartment-style rooms here (the bathrooms have to be the biggest in Bali). Enormous private verandas make the most of the unparalleled ocean views, and there's a shorefront pool and a spa. Published rates from US$250. ❾

**Panca Jaya** Jl Abimanyu ℡ & ⓕ0361/737373. Surprisingly inexpensive for the area, offering simple fan-cooled accommodation in two-storey bungalows a couple of minutes' walk from the beach. ❷

**Puri Cendana** Jl Dhyana Pura ℡0361/730869, ⓦwww.puricendana.com. The air-con Balinese-style two-storey suites here are good value and have huge bathrooms as well as downstairs living areas. The single-storey rooms are less interesting and overpriced. There's a pool, and the hotel is just 30m from the beach. ⑥

🏃 **Raja Gardens** Jl Abimanyu
ⓣ0361/730494, ⓔjdw@eksadata.com. Six unusual, nicely furnished fan-cooled bungalows in a spacious garden one minute's walk from the beach. Bungalows have garden bathrooms, four-poster beds and mosquito nets, plus there's a two-person cottage and a four-person house (with air-con). Peaceful, family run and good value, with a big pool. Bungalows ⑤ Cottage ⑥ House ⑥
**Sofitel Seminyak Bali** Jl Dhyana Pura
ⓣ0361/730730, ⓦwww.sofitelbali.com. Plush, classy hotel rooms and villas (some with private

pools) set in a tropical beachfront garden that affords fine views at sunset. Two swimming pools, a spa and several tennis courts. ⑨

🏃 **Villa Kresna Tropical Resort** Jl Sarinande 19 ⓣ0361/730317, ⓦwww.villa-kresna. com. A tiny compound of colonial-style suites, villas and rooms set around a small bougainvil-lea-shaded saltwater pool and restaurant, just one minute's walk from the beach and five minutes from the bars and restaurants of Jl Dhyana Pura. The six air-con "Lotus Suites" are charming: stylish but homely, most with separate living areas and all with a kitchenette and a balcony or terrace. Rooms ⑦ Suites ⑦ Villas ⑨

## Canggu, Berewa and Pantai Pererenan

Beyond the Jalan Laksmana turn-off in northern Seminyak, the road contin-ues to the crossroads at Kerobokan where the left-hand fork leads west past ricefields, villages and a burgeoning number of luxurious expat villas to the **Canggu** stretch of coast – a road distance of 10km in all. The **Berewa** (or Brawa) beach area of Canggu is renowned for its surfing (see p.67) and long stretch of good sand, and is fronted by a few fairly upmarket hotels. The current is notoriously strong up here, and all the hotels advise their guests – confident surfers excepted – against swimming in the sea (they all have pools). There are a few warung on the road down to Berewa beach, as well as some transport rental outlets, but most people who stay in Canggu rent their own transport and use the Kuta area for entertainment and other necessities. A couple of kilometres further up the coast, **Pantai Pererenan** is another highly rated if less well known surf beach, with one surfers' homestay and café on the shore plus a growing string of rental villas along the as yet still pleasingly rural three-kilometre-long access road.

**Bolare Beach Hotel** Berewa beach
ⓣ0361/730258, ⓔbolare@indosat.net.id. Com-fortably equipped air-con cottages, though the standard ones are rather cramped so it's worth upgrading. The garden runs down to the beach, and there's a pool and a restaurant. ⑥
**Pondok Wisata Nyoman** Pantai Pererenan
ⓣ0812/394 5967. Just a few steps from the sea – and the Pererenan surf break – this losmen caters mainly to wave riders with its large, simply furnished fan-cooled rooms and adjacent, shore-front *Surfwatch Café*. ③
**Tugu** Batu Bolong beach ⓣ0361/731701, ⓦwww .tuguhotels.com. One of the loveliest hotels in the whole of Bali, set a little further up the coast from

Berewa on Batu Bolong beach (just as unswim-mable as Berewa). Comprising a series of traditional polished-teak houses that are all built to different designs and furnished with exquisite antiques, the hotel is full of character: each of the 25 elegant suites (published rates US$300–450) has a living room, bedroom and garden bathroom, and some have private plunge-pools. There's a hotel pool, restaurant, spa and library, and free transport to Kuta. ⑨
**Wanna Villas** Berewa beach ⓣ0361/730263, ⓦwww.wanavillas.com. Posh adobe-walled private villa compounds, each with two storeys of living accommodation, a sleek modern interior, VCD players, a private pool and courtyard garden. Free transport to Kuta. ⑨

# The resort

There's nothing much to see in Kuta–Legian–Seminyak, but there's plenty to do, both in the resort and on day-trips out. The **beach** is one of the most beautiful in Bali, with its gentle curve of golden sand stretching for 8km, its huge breakers, which lure amateur and experienced surfers alike, and the much-lauded Kuta sunsets – at their blood-red best in April, but streaky-pink at any time of year. Though crowded with tourists from dawn to dusk every day of the year, the beach remains amazingly clean, and also refreshingly clear of hawkers, thanks to a couple of local bylaws. The most congested swathe is Kuta beach itself, along Jalan Pantai Kuta; the most peaceful is at Petitenget, north of *La Lucciola* restaurant. The sands around Jalan Pantai Arjuna in north Legian make a pleasant alternative, fronted by a barely used road and graced with sunloungers and several restaurants where you can laze away the sweltering midday hours while admiring the local surfing talent.

The waves that make Kuta such a great beach for surfers make it less pleasant for **swimming**, with a strong undertow as well as the breakers to contend with. You should always swim between the red and yellow striped flags, and take notice of the warning signs that dot the beach (fourteen people drowned off Kuta beach in 2004, and another 309 were rescued). **Lifeguards** are stationed in special towers all along the Kuta–Legian stretch; the central lifeguard post is on the beach at the corner of Jalan Pantai Kuta.

## Surfing

Kuta is the perfect **surfers' base**, with dozens of surfwear and board-repair shops, plenty of off-water entertainment facilities and some pretty good surf breaking daily on the doorstep. Because the beach is sandy and there's no coral or rocks to wipe out on, it's the best place in Bali to learn to surf. The breaks offer consistent, almost uniform waves, with lots of tubes, and the one known as **Kuta Beach** (beyond the Jalan Pantai Kuta lifeguard station) is particularly appealing for beginners – it's fun but not too daunting. It was off this stretch of shore in 1936 that surfing was supposedly introduced to Bali by American hotel-owner Bob Koke. The first pro-am competition was organized here in 1980, and local and international surf championships have since become annual events, usually held between March and July. For general surfing info, see p.67.

### Equipment, information and lessons

Poppies 2, Poppies 1 and Jalan Benesari form the heart of Kuta's surf scene, and these are the best areas to buy **boards** or get them repaired; you can also rent them here or on the beach: Rp25,000 will get you a decent two-metre board for the day. Boogie boards go for around Rp25,000, including fins.

The best **time of year** for surfing off Kuta is during the dry season (April–Oct), when the southeast trade winds blow offshore – at their strongest in July and August. From November to March, the wind arrives from the northwest,

---

### Surfaris

Several outfits in Kuta organize "**surfari**" surfing tours to the mega-waves off Sumbawa, East Java (including the awesome G-Land; March–Oct only), West Java, Lombok and West Timor. Prices usually include boat transport, shared accommodation and food and start from US$140 for a four-night budget package at G-Land, or $279 for a six-day Sumbawa package. **Operators** include: Wanasari Wisata, Jl Pantai Kuta 8b ☎0361/755588, ⊛www.grajagan.com; Indoswell.com on Poppies 1 ☎0361/763892, ⊛www.indoswell.com; *Tubes* bar on Poppies 2 ☎0361/751620, ⊛www.g-land.com; and Bali Surfing in Seminyak ☎0361/730184, ⊛www.bali-surfing.com.

bringing rain and blowing onshore, sending most surfers across to Sanur and Nusa Dua on the east coast. Monthly **tide charts** are compiled by the helpful folk at *Tubes* bar on Poppies 2 and are available there as well as at most surfwear shops in the resort; many surf shops also keep copies of the five-day **swell forecast**.

Surfing **lessons** are offered by the Rip Curl School of Surf, based at the *Blue Ocean* hotel on Jalan Pantai Arjuna in Legian (☎0361/735858, ⓦwww .schoolofsurf.com); Bali Adventure Tours, bookable through most tour agents (☎0361/721480, ⓦwww.baliadventuretours.com); Odyssey's Surf School at the *Mercure Kuta Bali* on Jalan Pantai Kuta and opposite *Tree House* restaurant on Poppies 1 (☎0361/742 0763, ⓦwww.odysseysurfschool.com); and *Tubes* surfers' bar on Poppies 2 (☎0361/751620). Prices average $39 for a half-day introduction, or $185 for a three-day course.

## Diving and other watersports

Surfing aside, Kuta is not a great centre for watersports. However, all tour agencies in the resort can organize **diving** trips and courses with one of south Bali's major dive centres, most of which are based in Sanur or Tanjung Benoa (see p.159 for details), a notable exception being the UK-run AquaMarine Diving, Jl Raya Seminyak 2a (☎0361/730107, ⓦwww.aquamarinediving.com).

Many of the Sanur and Tanjung Benoa dive centres also offer other **watersports**, including snorkelling, sea-kayaking and fishing trips, as well as parasailing, jet-skiing, windsurfing and water-skiing. All these can also be booked through Kuta tour agencies, but it's usually cheaper to make a day-trip and organize it yourself: ask to be dropped at places that rent out equipment, such as Yos Marine Adventures in Tanjung Benoa (see p.148), or near one of the small offices on the beaches in front of the *Inna Grand Bali Beach* or *Sanur Beach* hotels in Sanur (see p.157).

### Water parks

Kuta's **Waterbom Park** on Jalan Dewi Sartika, Tuban (daily 9am–6pm; adults US$18.50, 3- to 12-year-olds $9.50, family tickets $50; children under 12 must be accompanied by an adult) is a large and very popular aquatic adventure park, with water slides, chutes and helter-skelters, a lazy river to paddle inner-tubes down and a special playground for 2- to 10-year-olds. It also features a set of trampolines and a climbing wall. Another good watery option is to spend the day at the **Hard Rock swimming pool** (daylight hours; adults Rp100,000, kids Rp50,000), inside the *Hard Rock Hotel* complex on Jalan Pantai Kuta. It's a huge, fantastic construction, hundreds of metres long, with several sections plus water chutes, a sandy beach area and volleyball net. For an extra Rp125,000 (or Rp75,000 after 3pm) you can even rent a little waterside "cabana" for the day, complete with day bed and room service. Non-guests can use the charming little bougainvillea-shaded swimming pool at *Poppies Cottages* on Poppies 1 for Rp18,000.

## Adventure sports

The craze for **bungee jumping** has subsided, but there are still a couple of jumps in the resort – both of them from towers that dangle you over a swimming pool. Each place sells you videos of your jump and, at around Rp700,000 a go, prices are a lot cheaper than in the West. Bali Bungy Co (daily 9am–8pm; phone ☎0361/755425 for free pick-up) is on Jalan Pura Puseh in north Kuta. A.J. Hackett Bungy (daily noon–8pm and Fri & Sat

## Active days out

All the following activities can be booked through travel agents, but the bigger adventure-tour operators offer discounts for direct online booking. All operators do free picks-up from hotels in Kuta, Sanur, Nusa Dua and Ubud, and some will pick up from Candi Dasa.

**White-water rafting** is a big thing in Bali, and dozens of companies now offer two-hour trips for around US$70 (kids $45), including lunch and showering facilities. Safety standards vary, so it's worth grilling your chosen operator before you sign up. Two of the most reputable long-established outfits are **Bali Adventure Tours** (BAT; ☎0361/721480, ⓦwww.baliadventuretours.com) and **Sobek** (☎0361/287059, ⓦwww.99bali.com/adventure/sobek), which both offer rafting on the Class 2 and 3 rapids of the Ayung River, just west of Ubud; Sobek also run the Class 4 rapids of Telaga Waja River in central Bali. BAT also offer **kayaking** on the Ayung River for $66.

On land, Sobek run guided **mountain-bike** trips down the side of Gunung Batur (as does BAT) and down Gunung Batukau for $55, and BAT do bike rides in Sangeh Monkey Forest and neighbouring villages ($54, kids $37). Both outfits lead **jungle treks** in the rainforest and **rice-paddy walks** (around $50). Rice-paddy activities are the speciality of **Paddy Venture** (☎0361/289748), which do guided walks ($40), cycling trips ($45) and jaunts on All-Terrain Vehicles (ATVs) and Land Rovers ($69) through the spectacular scenery around Jatiluwih. Waka Tangga (☎0361/482064, ⓦwww.wakaexperience.com) offer more cultural **guided hikes** to the temples dotted along the slopes of the sacred mountain Puncak Tedung in central Bali ($57). Alternatively, you could go **camel riding** (☎0361/776755) on the sand at Nusa Dua, or **elephant trekking** with BAT through the forests around the village of Taro near Ubud (see p.223).

night 2–5am) is further north, in the grounds of the *Double Six* nightclub on Jalan Arjuna; their **2am jumps** on Friday and Saturday nights are popular with tripped-out clubbers from next door. At **Bali Slingshot** in the Kuta Centre on Jalan Dewi Sartika in Tuban (daily noon until late; $25), you can get catapulted 52m into the air in just over one second – and have it all captured on video. There's also a Le Speed **go-kart** track (daily 10am–10pm) further south down Jalan Dewi Sartika.

## Spas and beauty treatments

Massages and **beauty treatments** are very popular in Bali: many of Kuta's upper-bracket hotels have built their own spa centres to cater for this appetite, and there are plenty of smaller **day spas** offering good-value massages, facials and manicures, as well as the ever-popular Javanese *mandi lulur* body scrub (there's a description of this on p.73). Many places make their own products so there's plenty of scope for experimenting. Advance reservations are recommended but not essential.

One long-running outfit that gets good reviews is Bodyworks, which has two centres – the more central Bodyworks 1, at Jl Raya Seminyak 63 (☎0361/730454), and Bodyworks 2, in a quieter location at Jl Kayu Jati 2 in Petitenget (☎0361/733317). Designed in earthy, Moroccan-influenced style around a courtyard, they both offer a long menu of massages (from Rp150,000) including Balinese, Javanese (*mandi lulur*), Thai, shiatsu and aromatherapy, plus hair, facial, waxing and manicure treatments. In north Legian, the popular Sicilia Spa on Jalan Arjuna (☎0361/736292, ⓦwww.siciliaspa.com) offers a similar range of massages and treatments (*mandi lulur* from Rp115,000) in its cute, airy little rooms. Putri Bali beauty salon, next to *Wisata Beach Inn* on Jalan Padma Utara in Legian (℡0361/755987) offers exceptionally inexpensive treatments, including hour-long *mandi lulur*, Balinese *boreh* (blood-circulation), and coconut (after-sun) scrubs for Rp75,000 each.

# Eating

There are hundreds of **places to eat** in Kuta–Legian–Seminyak, and the range is phenomenal, from tiny neighbourhood warung to design-obsessed dining experiences. Unless otherwise stated, all places listed below are open daily from breakfast-time through to at least 10pm. In general, the most sophisticated, interesting – and expensive – restaurants are located in Seminyak and Petitenget, while Kuta and Legian are dominated by low-grade but decent enough tourist restaurants and international fast-food joints.

For a cheap but authentic change, try one of the numerous Sumatran **Masakan Padang** restaurants dotted along Jalan Legian between Jalan Melasti and Jalan Bagus Taruna; they're easily spotted by their pyramid window display of available dishes (see p.57 for more details). Kuta's main **night market** (*pasar senggol*) on Jalan Blambangan at the southern edge of Kuta is another enjoyable culinary event, with hawkers gathering to cook everything from noodle soup to barbecued corn, and the adjacent warung offering very cheap barbecued fresh fish. Elsewhere in the resort, **itinerant vendors** keep going right through the night, usually staking their pitch in the lay-bys of beachfront Jalan Pantai Kuta and anywhere along Jalan Legian; there's also a permanent knot of food carts stationed on Gang Bedugul, off Poppies 1.

## Kuta

**Aromas Café** Jl Legian. Delicious, moderately priced vegetarian food served in large portions in a garden dining room out of sight of the street. The menu includes Lebanese, Italian, Indian and Indonesian dishes (the Rp25,000 nasi campur sounds pricey but will keep you going all day), mostly made with organically grown ingredients. Also does cheesecakes, chocolate mousse, good Italian coffee and lots of vegetable juices.

**Captain Haddock** Jl Benesari. Tiny little warung with cushion-seating upstairs and a well-priced travellers' menu that covers all the standards, but specializes in fish dishes such as marlin cooked to a French recipe (Rp25,000).

**Ketupat** Behind the Jonathan Gallery jewellery shop at Jl Legian 109. Superb, moderately expensive menu of exquisite Indonesian dishes based around fish, goat and chicken, plus vegetarian options using interesting combinations of banana flowers, jackfruit and aubergine. Deep-fried squid with pickles and rainbow sauce (*chumi chin chin*) is recommended, as are the curried vegetables (*sayur tiga warna*). Tables are set around a swimming pool away from the road.

**Kori** Poppies 2. Refined dining in a cool, sophisticated setting, where the menu features delicious swordfish plus unusual grill-your-own "stone cuisine" dishes such as pork medallions, lobster mornay, red fish curry and roasted-vegetable lasagna. Also home-made ice-cream and sticky-toffee pudding. Not great for vegetarians, but otherwise worth the fairly expensive price tag, especially if you order before 7pm, when you're entitled to a ten percent discount.

**Kubuku** Poppies 1. Surprisingly flash for such a big, rowdy and unfailingly popular restaurant – and the wide-ranging, well-priced menu doesn't disappoint, especially the fried fish with basil and the beef fillet in Bali spices.

**Maccaroni Club** Jl Legian 52. Mixing Seminyak chic with Kuta populism, this place exudes a relaxing loungey vibe with its mellow DJ sounds, comfy armchair seating and extensive list of twenty Absolut cocktails and a hundred Australian wines (from Rp190,000 a bottle). The predominantly Italian food is variable – great gnocchi with four cheeses, less inspiring woodfired pizzas (Rp60,000), tempting eggs Benedict breakfasts – and there's free Internet access and wi-fi compatibility for diners.

**Made's Warung 1** Jl Pantai Kuta. Long-standing if rather overpriced Kuta landmark whose table-sharing policy encourages sociability. Serves Indonesian and Balinese fare (chicken rice-porridge, nasi campur), seafood such as fresh snapper in garlic sauce, multi-dish *rijsttafels* at Rp80,000 per person (24hr notice required), plus cappuccinos, black-rice ice-cream and cakes.

**Poppies** Poppies 1 ☎0361/751059. Another Kuta institution that doesn't really deserve to be so popular – or so expensive. Disappointingly small menu that accents Western meat dishes and lacks unusual choices, but it all tastes fine. Covered garden setting, though the tables are squashed together. It's advisable to reserve a table a few hours in advance.

🏃 **TJ's** Poppies 1. Popular, long-running Californian/Mexican restaurant with tables set around a water-garden. The mid-priced menu covers the full gamut of tortillas, fajitas, buffalo wings and enchiladas (around Rp40,000), and includes mango cheesecake, Mexican coffees (spiced up with Kahlua) and those all-important margaritas and strawberry daiquiris.

🏃 **Tree House** Poppies 1. Cheap and tasty travellers' fare served in large, well-prepared portions, including good fruit salads with yoghurt, filling *tempeh* burgers, great juices and plenty of cocktails. Though it no longer resembles a treehouse, it's a relaxed spot for watching the Poppies 1 parade of surfers and shoppers.

**Un's** Poppies 1. Small but perfectly executed menu dominated by pasta, steak and seafood. The "four-in-one combo" of two raviolis, gnocchi and tortellini is delicious but quite pricey at Rp45,000. Pleasant ambience, with in-house serenading musicians in the evenings.

**Warung Indonesia** Gang Ronta. Welcoming, surfer-friendly warung (you can book G-Land tours here) where you can either fill up on your own assortment of veg and non-veg nasi campur dishes for an unbeatable Rp5000 or splash out on *bihun kuah* (rice-noodle soup) or *soto ayam*.

**Warung Murni** Jl Pantai Kuta. Exceptionally cheap, old-style travellers' warung with just half-a-dozen formica tables, where the nasi goreng costs a bargain Rp7500.

## Tuban

🏃 **Daddy's Café** Jl Dewi Sartika. Reasonably priced Greek restaurant with an unrivalled selection of mezze, including aubergine *imam*, cheese *saganaki*, and delicious potatoes stuffed with spinach, feta and aromatic herbs. Good-value mixed seafood platters, plus genuine kebabs, *souvlaki* and *moussaka*.

**Golden Lotus** Inside the *Bali Dynasty Resort* on Jl Dewi Sartika. Upmarket but medium-priced *dim sum* and à la carte Chinese restaurant that's very popular with local Chinese and Indonesian families,

especially for the all-you-can eat buffets on Sundays (10am–2.30pm; Rp50,000, kids Rp25,000). On other days, *dim sum* is served from noon to 2.30pm.

**Kin Khao** Jl Dewi Sartika 170. This Tuban branch of the reliable, mid-priced chain of Thai restaurants does great deep-fried chicken wings with chilli sauce, aromatic *tom yam kung* soup (Rp28,000), and a range of red, green and yellow curries.

**Kunyit** Jl Dewi Sartika. Breezy, fairly elegant pavilion restaurant serving mostly classy, moderately expensive Balinese food. Its specialities are its seven-course Indonesian and Balinese *rijsttafels* (Rp118,000 for two) and its roast duck.

**Ma Joly** Jl Wana Segara ☎0361/753708. Tuban's most sophisticated fine-dining restaurant occupies a glorious spot right on the sand, with the sea view artfully framed, and serves expensive, top-notch French cuisine, with an emphasis on seafood. Predictably popular at sunset but also great for lunch.

## Legian

**Bali Too** Jl Melasti. Popular cheapie that's famous for its good-value breakfast buffets: all you can eat for Rp15,000 (daily 7.30–11.30am).

**Glory** Jl Legian 445, 200m north of Jl Padma. Long-running mid-priced tourists' favourite that's known for its huge Rp27,500 "outback breakfasts", its creamy chicken pancakes, barbecued spare ribs and reliably good fresh seafood.

**Gosha Seafood** Jl Melasti 7. For years this has been the most popular seafood restaurant in Legian, with its mid-priced menu that specializes in lobster cooked any number of ways – lobster thermidor or lobster mornay, for example – crab, prawns and squid, supplemented by steaks, frogs legs and rice dishes.

**Kafé Warna** Jl Pantai Arjuna (Blue Ocean beach). Mid-priced home-made tortillas, enchiladas and other Mexican favourites, plus California-style burgers and salads, served in a funky crows' nest of a building overlooking the waves.

🏃 **Warung Melati** Jl Arjuna. A favourite of economy-minded expats, this Masakan Padang–style place is a bargain, with a good range of ready-cooked foods from which to assemble your very cheap meal, including deep-fried *tahu*, curried eggs, *tempeh* chips, corn fritters and chilli-spiked water spinach.

**Warung Yogya** Jl Padma Utara 79. Another deservedly popular, unpretentious and cheap Indonesian eatery, where nasi campur (veg or non-veg) costs Rp11,000, juices start at Rp4000, plus there's *nasi pecel* and fried chicken.

**Zanzibar** Jl Pantai Arjuna (Blue Ocean beach). Good sandwiches and cakes, plus fifteen different pizzas and calzones (about Rp40,000), all served with uninterrupted sea views.

## Seminyak, Petitenget and beyond

**Antique** Jl Dhyana Pura. Dinner only; closed Mon. Creative Asian cuisine with strong Thai, Japanese and Indonesian influences: try the *nasi jingo Antique*, a tasty chicken, prawn and *urap* combo steamed and served in a banana leaf (Rp28,000), or the "prawn delight" (prawn samosas, skinny spring rolls and fritters). Cosy, unpretentious and good value.

**Axiom** Jl Raya Seminyak 18a ☏0361/738820. Open for dinner only. Disregard the off-puttingly stark concrete-box interior and make the most of the outstanding Asia–Pacific menu: the beef tenderloin is perfect (Rp120,000), or try a bit of everything with the Rp290,000 degustation set. Expensive and rather self-conscious (and not great for veggies), but worth it.

**Benny's Bistro** Jl Dhyana Pura. Good, standard, mid-priced tourist restaurant with indoor/outdoor dining areas and lots of fresh seafood cooked any style (from Rp25,000), plus grilled chicken, nasi campur and the like.

**Bintang Lima** Jl Laksmana 5a ☏0361/733038. Closed Sat. Unpretentious, unusual Indonesian restaurant that serves food from all over the archipelago, including grilled tuna with lemongrass, and fish in spicy green curry, and brews a huge range of herbal teas and *arak* cocktails. There are only eight tables, so it's worth phoning ahead to reserve.

**Kafé Warisan** Jl Raya Kerobokan 38, about 1km north of the Jl Laksmana turn-off ☏0361/731175. Mon–Sat lunch and dinner, Sun closed for lunch; reservations strongly advised. Delicious, beautifully cooked and very pricey gourmet French food – grilled rosemary lamb rack, duck confit, raspberry soufflé – is the hallmark of this long-running expats' favourite overlooking the ricefields. Also has an extensive wine list from all over the world. A genuine fine-dining experience.

**Ku dé Ta** Jl Laksmana ☏0361/736969. Opinions are divided on this, the most talked-about restaurant in south Bali. The look – a dramatic, mostly open-roofed beachfront piazza embraced by a cloister that frames a stunning sea-view – is as breathtaking as the prices (Rp135,000 for a plate of gnocchi, Rp210,000 for Australian pork ribs) and the modern-European food is variable. Many people prefer to soak up the setting over a long, lazy breakfast.

**La Lucciola** Jl Petitenget, accessed only by a footpath from the Pura Petitenget car park, or from the beach ☏0361/730838; reservations advisable, especially for a sea-view table. Built right on the edge of the shore, this open-sided pavilion is a popular spot for sunset cocktails and romantic dinners under the glow of flaming torches. The expensive Mediterranean-inspired menu doesn't always live up to the setting, but includes Moroccan duck pie, swordfish steak with aubergine salsa, and an array of tropical fruit sorbets.

**The Living Room** Jl Petitenget ☏0361/735735. Nightly from 7pm; reservations advisable. Elaborate presentation is central to this delightful, colonial-style eating experience, where every dish on the outstanding, and expensive, pan-Asian menu is a detailed work of art: red-on-red swordfish with red capsicum coulis, baby squid marinated in lemongrass, duo-chocolate mousse laced with five different fruit coulis.

**Made's Warung 2** Jl Raya Seminyak. More stylish offshoot of the long-running Kuta eatery, with a lively plaza setting and a moderately expensive Indo-European menu that looks unadventurous but tastes extremely good.

**Pantarei** Jl Raya Seminyak 17. Stylish, moderately expensive place with a contemporary Mediterranean ambience and outdoor tables that are illuminated by garden candles. The menu is predominantly Greek and includes perfect mixed-meat kebabs, unusually good multicoloured salads, grilled swordfish, some mezze dishes and the famous (and famously expensive) spaghetti lobster.

**Saté Bali** Jl Pantai Kayu Aya ☏0361/736734. Tiny, inviting place specializing in classy, authentic and reasonably priced Balinese cuisine, especially satés, meat and seafood *rijsttafels* (Rp140,000 for two). Also, some very unusual options: *ayam betutu* (spicy chicken that's slow-cooked overnight), and minced duck in spiced coconut milk. Phone for details of their cooking classes.

**Zula** Jl Dhyana Pura 5. Good, mid-priced organic vegetarian fare, with macrobiotic nasi campur (Rp38,000), daily grain specials, booster juices, raw soup of the day, and more.

# Nightlife and entertainment

Kuta–Legian–Seminyak boasts the liveliest and most diverse **nightlife** on the island, with dozens of clubs and bars, many featuring live bands. Most places stay open until at least 1am, with several clubs continuing to churn out the sounds until 6am. As much of the action is concentrated in Kuta, it's quite possible to walk from bar to bar and then home again: the main streets are well-lit and usually pretty lively until at least 3am (although be aware that muggings do occur). There are always plenty of metered taxis running down the main drag.

Women are unlikely to get serious hassle, although you will get seriously chatted up by the resident gaggle of **gigolos** who haunt the dancefloors and bars. Female prostitution is on the increase in Kuta, but is mainly confined to a few well-known pick-up joints. There's also quite a public **transvestite** scene, which includes a group known as the "sucky sucky girls" who tout for custom on Jalan Legian after the nightclubs close.

## Bars and clubs

**Kuta**'s nightlife is loud, laddish and good-humoured. It's the home of the jam jar (large, lethal *arak* cocktails) and countless happy hours, and the province of crowds of drunken Australians and partying backpackers; just start at *Paddy's Pub* and follow the crowds. Up in **Legian–Seminyak** the scene is more self-consciously sophisticated, and more expensive. Seminyak's Jalan Dhyana Pura is the place to begin, with upwards of a dozen trendy little dance- and lounge-bars competing to be the most fashionable spot of the week; this is also the heart of the resort's **gay scene**, too. For listings of special gigs, club events and parties, check the free fortnightly **magazine** *the beat*, or the weekly freebie *What's Up? Bali* (Ⓦ www.whatsupbali.com), both available at various restaurants and nightlife venues.

### Kuta and Tuban

**All Stars Surf Café** Kuta Centre, Jl Dewi Sartika 8x, Tuban. Popular, long-running Tuban surf bar where bands and DJs play Top 40 hits nightly (8pm–midnight), surfing videos are screened back-to-back, and autographed boards and other surfing hall-of-fame memorabilia cover the walls and ceiling. Also has pool tables, and stages regular sumo competitions in which customers don protective suits and hurl themselves at each other.

**Apache Reggae Bar** Jl Legian 146. Mellow place with a dark, sunken dancefloor, where bands and DJs play exclusively reggae music. Upstairs, the *Apache Surfers' Bar* sticks to more mainstream pop. Nightly from 11pm.

**Bagus Pub** Poppies 2. Large and loud tourist restaurant and video bar, popular with Australians and surfers.

**Bounty Discotheque** behind *Paddy's* on Jl Legian, just south of Poppies 2 intersection. Infamous hub of Australian excess, housed in a novelty building built to resemble Captain Bligh's eighteenth-century galleon. The rigging, gangplanks and moat are prettily illuminated at night and the several differ-ent bars and dancefloors are always packed: there are videoscreens and R&B on the top deck, pool tables and hard-house below deck, plus an open-air courtyard bar and stage out front. *Arak*-attack jam jars are the signature drink (get wasted for Rp30,0000); happy hour runs from 9pm–midnight, and the place stays open 24hr.

**Deejay Café** Behind the *All Stars Surf Café* in the Kuta Centre, Jl Dewi Sartika 8x, Tuban. Early-hours club that's part open-air and part air-con, where the resident and guest DJs spin mainly trance and tribal underground. Nightly midnight–6am; Rp30,000 including one drink.

**Hard Rock Café** Jl Pantai. Despite being part of the international chain, this place has a good reputation with local youth and attracts a huge crowd from around 11pm when the nightly band comes on stage. Expect slick performances of cover songs, with some audience participation, plus the occasional big-name appearance. Drinks are expensive. Closes 2am (weekends 3am).

**Musro** in the *Discovery Hotel* complex, Jl Dewi Sartika, Tuban. A nightlife-entertainments venue that's geared towards domestic and Taiwanese punters who come for the glitzy cabaret and laser show, and the karaoke room. Top 40 sounds from DJs and live bands. Rp60,000 including one drink. From 8pm.

**Paddy's Pub** Jl Legian 66, just south of Poppies 2 intersection. Part of the *Bounty* complex and just as popular, this open-walled place gets crammed with Australian drinkers who need little encourage-ment to enter the frequent drinking competitions and foam parties. Regular live music and reason-ably priced beer (happy hour 9–11pm). Daily 11am–4am.

**Tubes** Poppies 2. Enter Kuta's number-one surfers' hangout via the huge blue wave-wall and immerse yourself in surfing videos, surf info, surfari tour desks – and of course surf talk. Serves cheap food and drink (happy hour daily 3–6pm) in its mainly open-plan, open-air space. Closes around 2am.

## Legian, Seminyak and Petitenget

**Aina** Jl Laksmana 41, Petitenget. A low-key, arty kind of place, very much part of the Seminyak scene. It serves a good selection of wines, beers and cocktails, and plays decent music. Mon–Sat 8pm–2am.

**De Ja Vu** Jl Pantai Arjuna 7 (Blue Ocean beach), Legian. Sleek and slender beach-view lounge-bar where you can work your way through the cocktail list as you savour the waves from sunset through sunrise. Daily from 4pm.

**Double Six ("66")** Off the beachfront end of Jl Arjuna, Legian. Huge, lively, very popular club that's long been a Legian institution and is more sophisticated than *Paddy's* and the *Bounty* but not as narcissistic as the Jalan Dhyana Pura DJ-bars. The airy, open-fronted dancefloor heaves to current club sounds from around the world, often spun by European DJs (check flyers for one-off nights from visiting UK clubs). On Saturday nights, you can do a bungee jump in the club grounds (see p.125). Nightly 11pm–6am; free before midnight, after which it's Rp30,000 including one free drink. Free transport from *Paddy's* every Wed & Sat at 2am.

**Jaya Pub** Jl Raya Seminyak 2. Fairly sedate live music venue and watering-hole for older tourists and expats.

**Kudos** Jl Dhyana Pura, Seminyak. Capacious DJ-lounge and dance-bar that's popular with gay sophisticates, though mixed crowds are welcome, and stages regular drag, cabaret and go-go shows. Nightly from 10pm.

**Q Bar** Jl Dhyana Pura, Seminyak. Seminyak's main gay venue stages different events every night, including drag shows, cabarets and retro theme nights. Most of the action is downstairs around the lilac-and-mango-coloured bar and diminutive dancefloor, while upstairs is the chill-out zone and restaurant. Nightly 6pm till 1.30am.

**Santa Fe** Jl Dhyana Pura, Seminyak. Very popular bar and restaurant, less trendy than many on this road, that pulls in big crowds quite soon after dark and has live music from cover bands several nights a week. Open 24hr.

**Spy Bar** Jl Dhyana Pura, Seminyak. Long, slinky streetfront chrome-and-leather-clad lounge-bar that's perfect for street-watching and is popular with Seminyak fashionistas. From 6pm.

# Entertainment

Kuta's not exactly renowned for its wealth of cultural entertainment, but most tour agencies organize trips to see **Balinese dancing** at venues outside the resort – only worth considering if you're not planning to visit Ubud (where there are dance performances every night). *Kecak* and *barong* dances are per-formed every day in Denpasar (see p.106) and Batubulan (see p.174), both well worth seeing and within easy reach of Kuta. Tour agencies charge a lot more than you'd expect to pay on the door at these places – US$10–15 per person, including return transport, for a show that costs Rp50,000.

The nearest **cinema** is the Galleria 21 Cineplex at the Mal Bali Galleria/Planet Hollywood Complex on Jl Bypass Ngurah Rai, near the road to Sanur (℡0361/767021). Most mainstream blockbusters are shown in their original language with subtitles; tickets cost Rp20,000. The weekly freebie *What's Up? Bali* publishes the programme. Or there's the Wisata 21 complex in Denpasar, not far from Tegal bemo terminal (see p.106).

Matahari department store on Jalan Legian no longer operates as a shop, but its ground floor is jammed with **arcade games** and usually packed out with kids.

# Shopping

Kuta–Legian–Seminyak has the best and most diverse shopping in Bali, especially for clothes, kids' wear, surfing gear, homewares and souvenirs. And there's nowhere better to start than on Jalan Legian, whose six kilometres of shops begin at the southern end with an emphasis on cheap, mass-market stuff and gain in style and price as you reach Seminyak. For basic necessities, cosmetics, groceries and mass-produced clothes, head for the **Matahari department store** in Kuta Square (daily 10am–10pm); its kids' department stocks child-sized mosquito nets, baby bottles and dummies, and the fashion department sells traditional Balinese formal wear such as women's lacy *kebaya* tops and men's batik shirts. You can also get **mobile phones** and local sim cards at Matahari, though the best outlet is Rajawali, opposite *Mama's Restaurant* and the Legian Arcade at Jalan Legian 350, Kuta. Most stores stay open until at least 9pm.

## Books, DVDs and music

There are second-hand **bookstores** along Poppies 1, Poppies 2, Jalan Benesari and Jalan Padma Utara, but prices are not as competitive as in Ubud or Candi Dasa. The resort is full of shops selling recent-release DVDs for Rp10,000.

**Bombocraft** Jl Pantai Kuta 8c, Kuta. Hand-made musical instruments, mainly African-inspired *jimbeh* drums carved from teak and mahogany, and bamboo didgeridoos.

**Bookshop** Jl Legian, just north of Jl Melasti intersection. Keeps a range of new books in English, particularly hardbacks on Bali and the other islands of Indonesia. It also stocks some recent paperback fiction, and a few American and Australian newspapers.

**Kerta Books** Four branches: two on Jalan Legian, plus one each on Jalan Pantai Kuta and Jalan Padma Utara. Good stocks of second-hand books in English, German, Swedish, Italian and Japanese.

**Periplus** Three branches: inside Matahari department store, Kuta Square; inside Mal Bali Galleria, Jl Bypass Ngurah Rai (eastern outskirts of Kuta); in the *Made's Warung 2* complex, Jl Raya Seminyak. Outstanding chain bookshop specializing in English-language books about Bali and the rest of Southeast Asia, but also good for contemporary fiction and some international newspapers.

## Clothes and jewellery

Bali's **clothing** industry is based in the resort, and the shops here stock some superb one-off designs, a lot of them designed with cooler climes in mind – unquestionably Kuta's best bargain. On the whole, you'll find the most stylish and exclusive boutiques quite far north up Jalan Legian and along its continuation, Jalan Raya Seminyak; Kuta Square has several international designer outlets, including Versace, Polo and Armani, though these clothes (mostly jeans and T-shirts) are locally produced and not "export quality".

**AdoptA Co-op** Gang Ronta, off Poppies 2. Tiny outlet for the co-operative run by and for women who were widowed by the 2002 Kuta bomb (see Basics, p.44, for more info). Mostly very cheap T-shirts, bags, earrings etc.

**Animale** Kuta Square, and several outlets along Jl Legian. One of Bali's most popular womenswear chains, with a good line in stylish, loose-fitting, unstructured trousers, dresses and tops.

**Fila** Jl Melasti, Legian. Big stock of brand-name sportswear.

**Biasa** Jl Raya Seminyak, Seminyak. Specializes in elegant chiffon, cotton and silk creations for women and men.

**Body and Soul** Kuta Square and Jl Legian 162, Kuta. Young street and beach fashions.

**Jonathan Gallery** Jl Legian 109, Kuta. Stunning, idiosyncratic silver and semi-precious jewellery, plus a fair collection of antique trinkets brought in from other parts of Indonesia. Expensive.

**Kuta "Art Market"** Beach end of Jl Singo Sari, Tuban. Collection of small shops and stalls selling racks of inexpensive clothing, such as baggy cotton trousers, strappy tie-dyed beach dresses, shorts and T-shirts.

**Kuta Kids** Jl Pantai (Bemo Corner) and Jl Legian. Bright fabrics and cute designs for under-12s.

**Rascals** Kuta Square, and two branches on Jl Legian. Sophisticated and tasteful good-quality batik-print swimwear and beachwear.

**Suarti** Jl Legian, near *Mastapa Garden* hotel. Eye-catching window displays which use huge lumps of rock to set off their distinctive silver necklaces, bracelets and earrings.

**Surfwear shops** Dozens of outlets including Jungle Surf, Mambo, Quicksilver, Stussy and Surfer Girl – along Jalan Legian and every other shopping street in the resort. All stock brand-name surf- and skate-wear, plus some surfing equipment.

**Talismans of Power** Jl Raya Seminyak 30, Seminyak. Dramatic silver jewellery in highly individual designs, generally set with semi-precious stones. Especially interesting necklaces, pendants and rings. Also sells sumptuous silk cushions and scarves in vibrant shades.

**Uluwatu** Jl Pantai Kuta and several branches on Jl Legian. The original Balinese chain specializing in white, hand-made Balinese lace and cotton clothes (it's spawned several imitators).

## Handicrafts, souvenirs and homewares

The shops and stalls that line Poppies 1 and the Kuta end of Jalan Legian are the place to start looking for **artefacts**, **antiques** and other **souvenirs** from all over Indonesia. As with fashions, the most interesting and well-made **handicrafts** and **homewares** are found in the shops of Legian and Seminyak.

**Arin 93 Gallery** Jl Singo Sari 20, Tuban. Batik paintings in traditional, surrealist and modern styles by master batik artist Heru, plus cheaper pictures by his students, and works on canvas. You can also study batik painting with Heru (see "Listings" p.134) and buy batik dyes and waxes from him. Batik paintings cost from Rp50,000.

**Ashitaba** Jl Raya Legian 358, Legian and Jl Raya Seminyak 6, Seminyak. Intricate *ata*-grass basketware from Tenganan, fashioned into everything from mats to bowls.

**Asialine** Jl Legian 457, Legian. Stunning hand-painted batik-print masks, picture frames and boxes from Java, plus other tasteful artefacts from across Indonesia.

**Bali & Co** Jl Melasti 18, Legian. Inlaid and laminate coconut-wood artefacts, including boxes, bowls, trays and photo frames.

**Bali Harum** Jl Pantai Kuta 28a, Kuta, and Jl Legian 419, Legian. Small, local chain specializing in prettily packaged aromatherapy toiletries, soaps, oils

and incense.

**Haveli** Jl Raya Seminyak 15, Seminyak. Classy and pricey homewares, especially hand-woven cotton drapes, tablecloths and cushions.

**Kaya Natural** Jl Legian 466, Legian, opposite the Jl Bagus Taruna junction. Inexpensive but tasteful cushion covers, soapdishes and other homewares.

**Kuta Metelu** Jl Singo Sari 14, Tuban, cnr of Jl Bunisari. In among the usual woodcarvings and souvenirs are some interesting traditional temple artefacts, including gaily painted square offering-baskets, gold-printed *perada* temple parasols, and painted wooden pedestals for fruit offerings.

**Pithecan Throbus** Jl Pantai Kuta, Kuta, and Jl Legian, Kuta. Traditional sarongs, attractive batik-print sarongs, shirts and skirts, and unusual, classy handicrafts.

**Sunbebek** Jl Raya Seminyak 6, Seminyak. Arresting geometric hand-woven cotton designs made into cushion covers, drapes, bedspreads, handbags and wallets.

## Sarongs and traditional textiles

The cheapest places to buy everyday **sarongs** are the street stalls and art markets of Kuta, where you'll find piles of rayon and cotton wraps in traditional Javanese designs as well as *ikats* and modern patterns, plus the occasional much more expensive silk version. Several shops in Kuta and southern Legian also specialize in **traditional textiles** from other parts of the archipelago, chiefly the distinctive, mass-produced *ikat* wall hangings, scarves, bags and jackets from Sumba and Flores.

**Ana Mahang** Jl Legian 159, Kuta. A large selection of *ikat* textiles and weavings from Sumba and Flores, including scarves, bedspreads and hangings.

**Sarongs** Jl Arjuna, Legian. This road is almost entirely given over to shops selling all kinds of bright, modern-style sarongs (tie-dyed, beach-look,

lurid), retail and wholesale.

**Lumbung Batik** East of Supernova Supermarket on Jl Kahuripan, Tuban (between Jl Raya Tuban and Jl Blambangan). Useful fixed-price one-stop shop for traditional batik sarongs, Sumbanese hangings and *ikat* bedspreads. Also some basketware and

Lombok pottery.

**Patola Ratu** Jl Legian 456, Legian. Recommended outlet for traditional woven *ikat* hangings from the island of Sumba. Run by an effervescent Sumbanese woman who will happily fill you in on the meanings of the motifs. Also stocks all sizes of

carved wooden textile hangers.

**Wira's** 50m south of Supernova Supermarket, Jl Raya Tuban. Enormous emporium stuffed full of fabrics sold by the metre, with everything from plain linen to thick cotton weaves and brightly printed rayons.

# Listings

**Airline offices** Garuda has a sales office and city check-in (4 to 24 hours before departure) inside the *Kuta Paradiso* hotel in Tuban (Mon–Fri 7.30am–4.30pm, Sat & Sun 9am–1pm; ☎0361/761414). For international airline offices, see p.115; for domestic airlines, see p.33.

**Banks and exchange** There are Visa, MasterCard and Cirrus ATMs every few hundred metres throughout the resort. There's a Moneygram agent at Bank BII in Kuta Square. Be very careful about being ripped-off at exchange counters in Kuta: many places short-change tourists by using several well-known rip-offs (see p.47 for details). One chain of recommended money-changers is PT Central Kuta, which has several branches on Jl Legian plus one on Jl Melasti, many of them inside Kodak film shops. There's another reputable money changer just a few metres north up Jl Legian from Bemo Corner, on the east side of the road. If you do get caught in a money-changing scam, contact the community police (see below).

**Batik-painting classes** Batik artist Heru gives workshops for beginners and experienced artists at his Arin 93 Gallery at Jl Singo Sari 20, Tuban ☎0361/763091, ✉arin93batik@hotmail.com. Three-day workshops cost Rp400,000 including materials and artwork. He also sells batik-painting materials and comprehensive starter kits.

**Cookery classes** At *Saté Bali* restaurant, Jl Pantai Kayu Aya, Petitenget, where the former chef of Jimbaran's *Hotel InterContinental* teaches Balinese cooking for Rp250,000 including lunch; phone ☎0361/736734 to reserve.

**Email and Internet access** You're rarely more than 500m away from an Internet centre in the resort. Prices are competitive, with most places charging Rp200–300/minute. Some of the longest-established cybercafés will download digital photos, scan graphics and print out emails: Bali@*Cyber Café*, Jl Pura Bagus Taruna 4 in Legian; Legian Cyber C@fé, Jl Sahadewa 21, Legian; and Internet Explorer, Jl Dhyana Pura in Seminyak.

**Embassies and consulates** See p.35.

**Hospitals and clinics** The nearest hospitals are in Denpasar; see p.107. In the Kuta area, most expats

go to one of two very reputable places on the outskirts of Kuta, both of which have English-speaking staff, A&E facilities, ambulance and medivac services: Bali International Medical Centre (BIMC) at Jl Bypass Ngurah Rai 100x, near the Simpang Siur roundabout on the road to Sanur ☎0361/761263, ⊛www.bimcbali.com; and International SOS just a few hundred metres further east at Jl Bypass Ngurah Rai 505 ☎0361/710505, ⊛www.sos-bali .com. Alternatively, there's Legian Clinic 1, part of an efficient chain of tourist-oriented clinics, on Jl Benesari, Kuta ☎0361/758503, which offers 24hr consultation and dental services. Nearly all the large, upmarket hotels have an in-house doctor.

**House rental** There are fruitful noticeboards full of adverts offering long- and short-term house rentals in Legian and Seminyak at: Krakatoa business centre, Jl Raya Seminyak 56; Bali@*Cyber Café*, Jl Bagus Taruna 4; and *Café Moka*, Jl Raya Seminyak. Alternatively, contact the nearby property agent In Touch, Jl Raya Seminyak 22 ☎0361/731047, ⊛www.intouchbali.com. See p.55 for useful websites.

**Language lessons** Indonesian language classes at Seminyak English Course, Gang Villa Lalu, off Jl Raya Seminyak, Seminyak (☎0361/733342); Rp750,000 for five hours.

**Left luggage** All hotels and losmen will store your luggage if you reserve a room for your return; some charge a nominal fee. There's also left luggage at Amanda Tour, La Walon Plaza complex, Jl Benesari 7, Kuta (daily 9am–6pm; Rp3000/day) and at the airport (see p.114).

**Pharmacies** You'll find a pharmacy on every major shopping street, as well as next to Legian Clinic 1 on Jl Benesari, Kuta; next to Bemo Corner on Jl Legian, Kuta; inside the Matahari department store in Kuta Square; and on Jl Singo Sari, Tuban.

**Phones** The government wartel is inconveniently sited down at the airport, but there are dozens of private wartels in the resort, most of them open from 8am–midnight.

**Police** The helpful and energetic local community police, Satgas Pantai Desa Adat Kuta, are English-speaking and in 24hr attendance at their office on the beach in front of *Inna Kuta Beach Hotel* (☎0361/762871). The government police station is at the intersection of Jl Raya Tuban and Jl Singo Sari (☎0361/752110).

**Post offices** Kuta's GPO is on indistinct, unsign-posted Gang Selamat, between Jl Raya Tuban and Jl Blambangan in Tuban (Mon–Thurs 8am–2pm, Fri 8am–11, Sat 8am–1pm); services include parcel-packing and poste restante. There are many small postal agents elsewhere in the resort, including: on the ground floor of the Matahari department store in Kuta Square; on Gang Ronta off Poppies 2, Kuta; opposite *Glory* restaurant on Jl Legian, Legian; and on Jl Laksmana, Seminyak.

**Travel agents** Domestic and international airline tickets are available from the following agents, some of which also sell express boat tickets: Lila Tours, inside *Inna Kuta Beach* hotel, Jl Pantai Kuta, Kuta ☎0361/761827; Perama, Jl Legian 39, Kuta ☎0361/751551, ⓦwww.peramatour.com; KCB Tours, Jl Raya Kuta 127 (the main road to Den-pasar, on the eastern outskirts) ☎0361/751517, ⓦwww.kcbtours.com; and Amanda Tour, La Walon Plaza complex, Jl Benesari 7 ☎0361/754090. Pelni boat tickets from the Pelni office, about 500m south of Supernova Supermarket at Jl Raya Tuban 299 ☎0361/763963.

# The Bukit and Nusa Dua

Some 4km south of Kuta, Bali narrows into a sliver of land before bulging out again into the **Bukit**, a harsh, scrubby limestone plateau that dangles like a foot-ball from a thread off the far southern end of the island. Officially called Bukit Badung (*bukit* means "hill" in Bahasa Indonesia), this part of the south has more in common with the infertile scrub of Nusa Penida across the water than with the generously lush paddies of the rest of Bali. Farming is almost impossible here, but it's the dramatic, craggy coastline that fuels the local economy: surfers flock to the Bukit's famously challenging breaks – the best on Bali – particularly those at Uluwatu and Padang Padang, while everyone else simply enjoys the glorious clifftop views from the burgeoning number of coastal hotels.

This account follows an anti-clockwise route around the plateau, beginning at the fishing village of **Jimbaran**, which lies just a couple of kilometres south of the airport on the isthmus, and has a fine beach and several luxury hotels. Con-tinuing southwest, the road passes a number of good surf spots before reaching **Uluwatu**, location not only of some internationally renowned surf, but also of one of Bali's major clifftop temples, perched right on the island's far southwest-ern tip. The road then sweeps round southeast to **Nusa Dua**, a purpose-built deluxe resort offering superb facilities but distinctly lacking in character, and its adjacent alter-ego **Tanjung Benoa**, a centre for watersports and the location of some cheaper accommodation.

Public **transport** in the Bukit is sporadic at best, and there are many parts that bemos just don't penetrate; more details are given in the relevant sections below. It's easy enough to join a tour to Uluwatu from any of the resorts, but the best option is to **rent your own transport** and explore by yourself. Motorbikes are often more practical than Jeeps for negotiating the potholed tracks down to the surfing beaches.

# Jimbaran

With its safe, crescent-shaped bay of soft, golden sand fronted by a string of well-spaced, peaceful, mostly upmarket, hotel developments, the tiny fishing village of **JIMBARAN** makes a quieter, more interesting alternative to purpose-built Nusa Dua, and yet is just a few kilometres' drive from the temptations of Kuta.

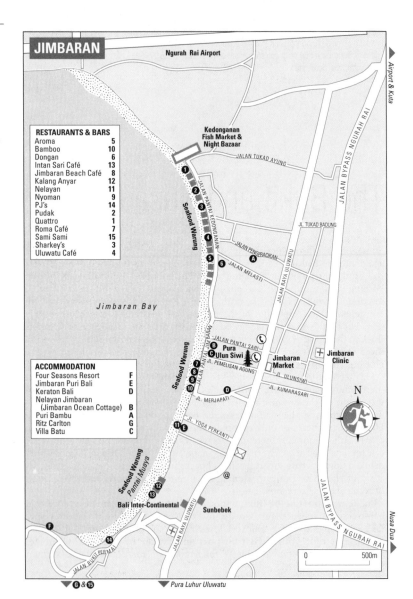

JIMBARAN

Ngurah Rai Airport

Airport & Kuta

Kedonganan
Fish Market &
Night Bazaar

JALAN TUKAD AYUNG

JALAN BYPASS NGURAH RAI

JL. TUKAD BADUNG

JALAN PANTAI KEDONGANAN

Seafood Warung

JALAN PENGRACIKAN

JALAN MELASTI

JALAN RAYA ULUWATU

**RESTAURANTS & BARS**
| | |
|---|---|
| Aroma | 5 |
| Bamboo | 10 |
| Dongan | 6 |
| Intan Sari Café | 13 |
| Jimbaran Beach Café | 8 |
| Kalang Anyar | 12 |
| Nelayan | 11 |
| Nyoman | 9 |
| PJ's | 14 |
| Pudak | 2 |
| Quattro | 1 |
| Roma Café | 7 |
| Sami Sami | 15 |
| Sharkey's | 3 |
| Uluwatu Café | 4 |

Jimbaran Bay

JALAN PANTAI SARI

Pura
Ulun Siwi

JL. PEMELISAN AGUNG

Seafood Warung

Jimbaran
Market

Jimbaran
Clinic

JL. ULUNSIWI

JL. KUMARASARI

JL. MERJAPATI

**ACCOMMODATION**
| | |
|---|---|
| Four Seasons Resort | F |
| Jimbaran Puri Bali | E |
| Keraton Bali | D |
| Nelayan Jimbaran | |
| (Jimbaran Ocean Cottage) | B |
| Puri Bambu | A |
| Ritz Carlton | G |
| Villa Batu | C |

JL. YOGA PERKANTI

N

Seafood Warung
Pantai Muaya

Bali Inter-Continental     Sunbebek

JALAN RAYA ULUWATU

JALAN BYPASS NGURAH RAI

Nusa Dua

JALAN BUKIT PERMAI

0     500m

G & 15          Pura Luhur Uluwatu

Jimbaran is famous throughout Bali for its **fish**, and every morning at dawn the fishermen return with hundreds of kilos of sardines, tuna, mackerel, snapper and baby sharks. Most of the trading goes on between about 5am and 7am, at the fish market at the far northern end of the beach in the *banjar* of Kedonganan, close by the airport runway. In the evening, the day's catch is served up on the seafront at the dozens of beach warung that specialize in barbecued fish and seafood. The Balinese **cooking schools** in Nusa Dua begin their lessons with a tour of Jimbaran fish market, so if you're staying in Jimbaran and want to join them, you can arrange to be picked up from your hotel: see p.151 for details.

Most of Jimbaran's villagers live away from the beach, down the *gang* that run off the busy main Kuta–Jimbaran–Uluwatu road that cuts a swathe through the heart of the village. The fruit and vegetable market thrives at the crossroads in the centre of the village and, just across from here, under a huge holy tree, stands **Pura Ulun Siwi**. Closed to all casual visitors except at festival time, this temple dates back at least to the eleventh century and is dedicated to the spirits that inhabit the ricefields of the island.

## Practicalities

You can get to Jimbaran on the dark-blue **bemo** service that runs throughout the day from the Tegal terminal in Denpasar to Jimbaran, via Kuta's eastern fringes (see p.117). Fares are about Rp2500 from Kuta and Rp3500–4500 from Denpasar. A **taxi** ride from Kuta will set you back about Rp20,000; the prepaid taxi service from the airport costs Rp25,000. No tourist shuttle buses run to Jimbaran, but all the mid-range and upmarket Jimbaran hotels run transport to Kuta and occasionally to Nusa Dua as well. Metered taxis also circulate around Jimbaran day and night.

The beachfront Waterworld **watersports** booth (℡0361/701888) just north of the *Keraton Bali* offers all manner of activities and equipment, from jet skis ($25/15min) and kayaks ($12/hour), to parasailing ($15/round) and windsurfing lessons ($60 for 3hr), though they bus most of their customers across to Tanjung Benoa. They also run PADI dive courses ($375 for the four-day Open Water) and expeditions (from $60 for one local dive). The **surf** break known as Airport Rights is off the coast here, located halfway down the Jimbaran side of the airport runway and best reached by chartering a prahu from an off-duty fisherman (about Rp15,000 one way).

The **post office** is at Jl Raya Uluwatu 35; the public **telephone office** is also on Jalan Raya Uluwatu, just north of the market; and the main **clinic** for minor ailments is the 24-hour Jimbaran Clinic at Jl Bypass Ngurah Rai 95xx (℡0361/701467), though more serious medical cases will be transferred to one of the hospitals in Denpasar (see p.107).

## Accommodation

Most **hotels** are upmarket and have grounds that lead down to the beach. There are a couple of mid- and bottom-range options, and some of the independently run places offer great discounts during low season.

**Four Seasons Resort** South Jimbaran ℡0361/701010, ℗www.fourseasons.com. One of the finest, and most expensive, hotels in Bali, and consistently voted as one of the top ten hotels in the world. Each villa here is built inside its own little traditional Balinese compound, comprising a series of three thatched pavilions – a living area, a sleeping area and a garden bathroom; published rates start at US$575 ($675 for a sea view). The resort is situated high up on a hillside overlooking the far southern end of Jimbaran Bay and facilities include infinity-edge swimming pools, a spa and tennis courts. ❾

**Jimbaran Puri Bali** Jl Yoga Perkanti

ⓣ0361/701605, ⓦwww.pansea.com. Forty-one gorgeously designed individual cottage compounds, each with elegantly minimalist furnishings in the bedrooms, plus a walled garden, a terrace and a garden bathroom. Adult and kids' swimming pools, children's play area and babysitting service. ❾ **Keraton Bali** Jl Merajapati ⓣ0361/701961, ⓦwww.keratonjimbaranresort.com. Smart rooms in a series of tasteful, attractively designed cottage-style buildings dotted around a peaceful tropical garden that stretches right down to the beach. All rooms have air-con, TV and fridge. Swimming pool, tennis court, table tennis and watersports. One child under 12 goes free if sharing with parents. ❾

**Nelayan Jimbaran (Jimbaran Ocean Cottage)** Jl Pantai Jimbaran 3 ⓣ0361/702253, ⓦwww.bali-foryou.com/jimbaranocean. Jimbaran's cheapest beachfront place offers a good range of well-maintained rooms, friendly service and a restaurant. Its losmen-style accommodation has fans and cold-water showers, and there are more appealing bamboo-walled rooms with air-con, as well as a four-person suite with a kitchen. Rooms with fan ❸ With air-con ❺ Suite ❺

🏃 **Puri Bambu** Jl Pengeracikan, Kedonganan, north Jimbaran ⓣ0361/701468, ⓦwww.puribambu.com. This comfortable and deservedly popular place keeps its prices reasonable because

there's no beachfront access. However, the beach is about three minutes' walk away and the 48 very large, inviting rooms are quite stylish and all have air-con; there's a nice big pool, pretty gardens and Internet access on the premises. A free shuttle bus service runs into Kuta and you can call ahead for free airport pick-up. ❻–❼

**Ritz Carlton** Jl Karang Mas Sejahtera, south of Jimbaran ⓣ0361/702222, ⓦwww.ritzcarlton.com. Renowned for its excellent service and a frequent contender for one of Asia's top ten hotels, this deluxe outfit enjoys a very impressive location on a cliffside several kilometres south of the Jimbaran beachfront. Most of the 375 luxuriously furnished rooms are in a central block, with ocean or garden views. There's a spa, several swimming pools and tennis courts, plus an 18-hole putting green, but the nearest swimmable beach is a couple of kilometres away. ❾

**Villa Batu** Jl Pemelisan Agung 21a ⓣ & ⓕ0361/703186, ⓦwww.business-bali.com. A dozen unusual losmen-style rooms (some rather dark) with adobe-look walls, funky bathrooms and the option of connecting rooms and a living area, all set in a compound across the road from the beach. Also here are two appealing villas, sleeping two to four, both with kitchen/living area and sharing a small pool. Rooms with fan ❸ With air-con ❺ Villas ❻–❼

# Eating

Jimbaran has an island-wide reputation for its fresh seafood served at the countless tiny warung strung along the beachfront. But there are other **places to eat**, too, most notably the restaurants inside the more exclusive Jimbaran hotels, where you can expect a classy meal – and a top-of-the-range bill.

## The seafood warung

The **fresh fish barbecues** served up by Jimbaran's beachfront warung are so good that people travel here from Kuta, Nusa Dua and Sanur just to sample them, and restaurants across the island try to re-create the taste in their "Jimbaran-style fish barbecues". There are over fifty of these beach-shack warung, grouped in three distinct areas along the shorefront between Kedonganan in the north and Jalan Bukit Permai in the south. Some warung look a little more polished than others, but the setup is similar in every one, with chairs and tables set out on the sand, and a menu that sells the day's catch (priced per 100g), grilled in front of you over smoky fires of coconut husks. You can almost guarantee having the choice of lobster, prawns, red snapper, squid, mussels and clams at the very least. Though food is served during the day, the warung are at their liveliest from around 7pm. It's always a good idea to eat at the busier places, to be sure that the fish really is that morning's catch; some of the warung chefs stage quite a show with the coconut embers, so you may get a performance thrown in with your dinner. They all serve beer and soft drinks, and fish prices usually include various marinades and sauces plus a generous spread of rice and vegetable dishes, so accompanying vegetarians will not starve.

Broadly speaking, the knot of warung up near the fish market in **Kedonga-nan** offer the cheapest food and the least refined ambience (plastic chairs and no-frills table settings). Competition is extremely fierce up here and several of the most crowded places attract customers by offering commission, and even lottery tickets, to taxi drivers. As margins have tightened some places have started to **rig their scales** so that diners unwittingly get less than what they paid for: if doubtful, the easiest way to check this is to place a full one-litre bottle of water on the scales first and see if they read "1kg" (which they should). The most popular warung here include *Aroma, Uluwatu Café, Sharkey's* (phone ☎081/2381 8701 for free transport) and *Pudak*.

The warung that occupy the shorefront between Jalan Pemelisan Agung and the *Keraton Bali* hotel in **central Jimbaran** are not quite as basic as those up at Kedonganan and are popular with domestic tourists; prices are very reasonable and the atmosphere is good. Reputable options include *Bamboo, Nyoman, Jimbaran Beach Café* and *Roma Café*.

Some distance further south, at the foot of the road up to the *Four Seasons* on the very attractive stretch of beach sometimes referred to as **Pantai Muayu**, you'll find the most upmarket of the Jimbaran warung, with more salubrious setups (comfortable chairs, tiled kitchens and customer toilets) and slightly more expensive price lists. Here, *Kalang Anyar* gets good reviews, and *Intan Sari Café* is usually pretty busy.

### Restaurants

**Dongan** Jl Pantai Kedonganan, Kedonganan, north Jimbaran. Less formal and much less expensive than the restaurants attached to the five-star hotels, this mid-priced independent eatery serves a tasty and good-value menu of Western and Indonesian dishes as well as competitively priced fish and seafood, barbecued in the same style as at the beach warung.

**Nelayan** At the *Jimbaran Puri Bali*, Jl Uluwatu. Occupies a perfect spot right on the sand and serves elegant, expensive (Rp60,000–180,000) Asian-Pacific cuisine, such as pan-fried tiger prawns with tamarind sauce, and seared tuna with sesame.

**PJ's** Jl Bukit Permai, south Jimbaran. This *Four Seasons* restaurant has an island-wide reputation for exquisite, and pricey, Mediterranean and South-east Asian food (Rp100,000–190,000), as well as for wood-fired pizzas with innovative toppings. It also occupies a fantastic position in a couple of gazebos perched right over the sand.

**Quattro** Jl Pantai Kedonganan, Kedonganan, north Jimbaran. Posh *trattoria* on the beach serving moderately expensive Mediterranean food and especially good seafood.

**Sami Sami** Inside the *Ritz Carlton*, Jl Karang Mas Sejahtera, south of Jimbaran. This restaurant occupies a particularly awesome spot on a cliff ledge right over the waves, and its expensive Mediterranean-inspired menu includes paella, mezze, couscous, seafood barbecues and pasta.

# Around the Bukit

Just a couple of kilometres south of Jimbaran, the road climbs up on to the limestone plateau, with views back across southern Bali. Once up on the plateau, past a massive limestone quarry, the typical **Bukit** landscape of cracked earth and leafless trees begins. Bukit people do grow a few crops here, mainly cassava, a root tuber vegetable used to make tapioca flour, and grass-like sorghum, whose seeds are also pounded into flour. You'll see plenty of **kapok trees**, too, instantly recognizable from the fluffy white fibre that bursts out of the long brown pods. This fibre is water resistant and extremely soft, and is the stuff that fills cushions, cuddly toys and even life-jackets the world over. Every mature tree produces about 20kg of fibre a year, and the kapok seeds are pulped for oil.

# Garuda Wisnu Kencana (GWK)

About 2km south of the *Four Seasons* junction, a huge sign points you east off the main Uluwatu road to **Garuda Wisnu Kencana**, or **GWK** (daily 8am–10pm; Rp15,000, cars Rp5000, motorbikes Rp1000). This massive project, which is still being carved out of the hillside, is set to be a cultural park and events centre, centred around a towering 146-metre **statue** of the Hindu god Vishnu astride his sacred vehicle, the half-man, half-bird Garuda. When completed, the statue (said to be the world's largest) will stand on top of an eleven-storey **entertainments complex**, the intention being to make the whole monument so high (230m above sea level) that it will serve as a Welcome-to-Bali landmark for passengers arriving at Ngurah Rai Airport, 9km to the north. The project was due to be completed by 2003, but at the moment all that's open is the partially constructed statue (currently comprising Vishnu's head and torso plus the head of the gigantic Garuda, which you can climb), a **restaurant** offering a commanding view of southern Bali's coastlines, and an **art gallery**, which hosts temporary exhibitions by contemporary Balinese artists.

GWK is privately funded and is intended to attract more tourists to the area. The respected artist and sculptor who conceived the idea, Nyoman Nuarta, sees it as a celebration of Bali's past as well as its future, though some critics have deplored the commercial rather than religious motivation of the project and accused GWK's supporters of trying to turn Bali into a Hindu theme park (see p.500 for more on the "touristification" of Balinese culture).

# Surfing beaches

About 1km south of the GWK turn-off, the road forks, veering left for Nusa Dua and right for Uluwatu and the **surfing beaches**. The Bukit surf breaks are the most thrilling and the most popular in Bali, especially those at Padang Padang and Uluwatu, which, though consistent, are tantalizingly difficult, even for competent surfers. They're at their best from April to October when the southeast winds blow offshore.

### Dreamland and Balangan

Follow the Uluwatu road southwest for a few kilometres to reach the turn-off to Dreamland and Balangan surf beaches. This access road runs through a condo project (one of several unpopular development schemes on Bali that were associated with Tommy Suharto, the notorious son of the former president) and vehicles are sometimes subject to a small toll. About 4km after leaving the main road, a couple of short dirt tracks veer off to **DREAMLAND** beach, a long stretch of stunning coast with great surf, wide, gloriously white sands, and breathtakingly aquamarine waters. Accessible via a long flight of steep steps, it's a popular spot both with day-trippers from Kuta and with surfers who come for the fast left and right peak and the chance of grabbing some unusually long rides. There are several **warung** down on the sands: some have sunloungers for rent and a couple, including *Warung Wayan*, also offer basic overnight **accommodation** (❷). The set-up at **BALANGAN**, accessed via a dirt track running north from Dreamland, is similar, and the attraction here is the speedy left-hander over the shallow reef; you might be lucky enough to spot the white-collared kingfisher here, too.

## Bingin, Impossibles and Padang Padang

Back on the main Bukit road, a couple of kilometres south of the Dreamland turn-off, there's a right fork signed to Bingin, Impossibles and Padang Padang: take this road for the surf spots and the longer, more scenic route to Pura Luhur Uluwatu, or the left fork for the more direct road to the temple. Bingin and Impossibles are accessible only via a potholed dirt track that takes you a couple of kilometres off the road, while Padang Padang is visible from the road.

**BINGIN** offers short left-hand tubes, while, breaking over the reefs beyond, **IMPOSSIBLES** provides long and peeling left-handers, surfable at all tides. Both breaks are popular and often busy, and Bingin offers plenty of accommodation (new arrivals are greeted by touts competing for custom) and charges a Rp3000 parking fee. There is also a track from the car park to Dreamland but it's four-wheel-drive only and best on a motorbike. Even if you don't surf, Bingin is worth visiting for its magnificent rocky views, but the beach is unsuitable for swimming because of the tricky currents and large expanses of shallow reef that lie just offshore. The cheapest **places to stay** at Bingin are the warung that almost literally tumble down the cliff-face, many of them built hard against the rock: at the top of the steps, *Mama and Ketut* (❷) offers a dozen simple, thin-walled rooms with sea views from the veranda and shared bathrooms. Up on the clifftop itself, about five minutes' walk from the car park, *Pondok Indah Gung and Lynie* (☎081/855 3756, ✉made_linie@yahoo.com; ❸–❹) has eight pretty, rather tasteful, fan-cooled coconut-wood-and-thatch bungalows set round a garden a way back from the cliff edge. At the edge of the cliff, *Mick's Place* (☎0812/391 3337, ✉micksplacebali@yahoo.com.au; ❼) enjoys fine sea views and offers just four exceptionally elegant, contemporary-styled circular huts, their open design making the most of the location; it's rather pricey considering there's no electricity, though there is a tiny infinity pool in the garden.

Back on the road, **PADANG PADANG**'s accommodation begins almost immediately, lining the roadside, with most of it within a short walk from the famous Padang Padang **break**, considered to be one of the classiest and most exciting surf spots in Indonesia, not least because of a twist in the final section. **Accommodation** is cheap and fairly basic: *Sunny* (❷) has simple, woven-bamboo huts, or try either *Padang Sari* (❷) or nearby *Kongsi Inn* (❷). There are more comfortable *lumbung*-style bungalows at *Ayu Guna Inn*, Jl Melasti 39x (☎0815/575 6294, ✉ayugunabali@yahoo.com; ❷), where you get a mattress, fan, balcony and private outside bathroom. Within the Padang Padang accommodation cluster you'll also find several **restaurants** and an Internet centre.

### Suluban

**SULUBAN**, location of the famous **Uluwatu surf breaks**, is signed off the Uluwatu road about 2km south of Padang Padang. The views here are gorgeous – the golden curves of Kuta and Legian in the distance, and the turquoise water, crashing white surf and olive-green seaweed of Suluban in the foreground. But for surfers, the Uluwatu breaks (named after the nearby temple) are something of a mecca, with five separate left-handers, all of them consistent and surfable at anything from two to fifteen feet. Access to the breaks is either down the steep steps beside the ultra-posh *Blue Point* villas (parking near here costs Rp2000 per car or Rp1000 per motorbike) or from close by *Uluwatu Resort*. There's plenty of **accommodation** on the clifftop above the breaks and along the roadside nearby: *Uluwatu Resort* (☎0361/742 2689, ☷www.uluwaturesort .com; ❽) occupies a prime spot along the cliff's edge and offers, as well as a pool and Internet access, the most attractive rooms on this entire stretch of coast – sixteen of them, stylishly furnished with four-poster beds and linen drapes, each enjoying an uninterrupted sea view from enormous windows and balcony. Their *Top Rock Café* shares the view and makes a perfect lunch spot. The more affordable accommodation is set further back from the sea: the twelve comfortable fan rooms at *Rocky Bungalows* (☎081/734 6209; ❷) are a short bike-ride from the surf, down a side-road off the main Uluwatu road, but still enjoy long-range views of the surf from their verandas. Heading south about one kilometre, towards Pura Luhur Uluwatu, there's a cluster of cheap surfer-oriented places near *The Gong* surf shop and café. *The Gong* itself (☎0815/578 4754, ✉thegongacc@yahoo.com; ❷), behind the shop, has six fan-cooled losmen rooms, runs surf tours, rents bikes and changes money. Next door, *Mama Inn* (❷) has similar rooms and an effervescent manager, while tiny *Fortune Inn* (❷) across the road offers the most characterful accommodation, with nice beds and garden bathrooms in bamboo-walled bungalows.

# Pura Luhur Uluwatu

One of Bali's holiest and most important temples, **Pura Luhur Uluwatu** commands a superb position on the tip of a sheer rocky promontory jutting out over the Indian Ocean, 70m above the foaming surf, at the far southwestern tip of Bali – 18km south of Kuta and 16km west of Nusa Dua. Views over the serrated coastline to left and right are stunning, and, not surprisingly, this is a favourite spot at sunset, when tour buses pour in to admire the added drama of a pink and orange horizon. The temple structure itself, though, lacks magnificence, being relatively small and for the most part unadorned.

Accounts of Uluwatu's early **history** are vague and shrouded in myth, but it's fairly certain that two of Bali's most influential holy men played significant roles in its evolution. The first was a Hindu priest from Java called Empu Kuturan (sometimes known as Empu Rajakerta) who arrived in the tenth century and constructed *meru* (multi-tiered thatched shrines) all across southern Bali – including one at Uluwatu. Six hundred years later, another Hindu priest from Java, Nirartha, landed in west Bali and set about founding some of the island's most awesome sea temples: one at Rambut Siwi (p.357) and another at Tanah Lot (p.344), as well as adding to the cliffside shrine at Uluwatu.

Pura Luhur Uluwatu is now sanctified as one of Bali's sacred **directional temples**, or *kayangan jagat* – state temples having influence over all the people of Bali, not just the local villagers or ancestors. It is the guardian of the southwest and is dedicated to the spirits of the sea. Its festivals are open to all, and during the holy week-long period of Galungan, for example, Balinese from all over the island come here to pay their respects.

## The temple complex

The access roads lead right into the **car park** in front of Pura Luhur Uluwatu, usually overflowing with tour buses and souvenir stalls (parking fee Rp1000). At the booth at the base of the temple steps, you'll need to borrow a sarong and sash if you haven't brought your own, and pay the Rp3000 admission fee.

Climbing the frangipani-lined stairway to the temple's **outer courtyard**, you'll get your first brush with Uluwatu's resident troupe of monkeys, who have a reputation for stealing earrings, sunglasses and cameras. The outer courtyard is dominated by the elegant **candi bentar** that connects this area with the middle courtyard, built of greyish-white coral blocks to a very unusual winged design. Images of the elephant god Ganesh flank the entrance.

If you peer through the gate into the middle courtyard (casual visitors are not allowed to enter), you'll see the **paduraksa**, the archway that divides the middle from the inner courtyard, which is made of coral blocks, studded with mythological images and crowned by an unusual three-pronged tower. The **inner sanctum** extends right to the cliff edge and over its low walls you can see the three thatched *meru* and the stone *padmasana*, set off to their best advantage by the deep blue sea beyond. A tiny courtyard leading from the temple's outer courtyard contains a locked shrine housing an ancient statue, thought by some to depict the sixteenth-century priest Nirartha. The statue is kept here in his honour as it is thought that the priest achieved his own spiritual liberation, or *moksa*, on this very spot.

You'll get some of the best **views** of Pura Luhur Uluwatu's astonishingly dramatic position if you follow the pathway that heads off to the right as you stand with your back to the temple stairway. This track winds its way along the cliff-edge for a few hundred metres, affording fine, silhouetted vistas of the three-tiered *meru* perched daintily atop the massive sheer wall of limestone.

### Practicalities

If you don't have your own **transport**, the easiest way to visit the temple is by joining a "Sunset Uluwatu" **tour** arranged through any south Bali tour operator for around $15, which should include a *kecak* performance (see below). You'd be lucky to find a **bemo** from Denpasar or Kuta going all the way to Uluwatu, so your cheapest option is to get a dark blue Tegal (Denpasar)–Kuta–Jimbaran bemo to its Jimbaran terminus and then flag down a metered taxi for the last leg. Coming back from Uluwatu is more of a problem as you're very unlikely to find a taxi here, though you could try and hitch a ride from the temple car park, or take an unofficial motorcycle taxi ride with one of the lads who hang around the temple complex. The **kecak and fire dance** (*sanghyang jaran*) are performed at Uluwatu every evening (6–7pm; Rp35,000).

## The Bukit's south coast

Returning from Uluwatu along the main Jimbaran road you'll soon pass *Puri Bali Villas* (T0361/744 8300, Wwww.puribalivillas.com; ○), whose dramatically located restaurant enjoys a fine outlook over the unpredictable **Nyang Nyang** surf breaks, and where you can rent one of five spacious villas set around English-style parkland, with pool. Access to the sea is via a long, steep path.

Continuing almost as far as the turn-off for Nusa Dua, a sign for **Pura Massuka** diverts a tiny trickle of traffic off to the right, down to the southern coast of the Bukit. No bemos cover this area, so you'll need **private transport** to visit anything east of the Jimbaran–Uluwatu road, except Nusa Dua. The road to Pura Massuka winds its way for 12km right down to the coast, through an almost uninhabited landscape of parched red earth, dotted with the occasional kapok tree. At the end of the road, the minuscule Pura Massuka hardly seems to merit the title of temple, but the **views** most definitely make up for it. This is the southernmost point of Bali that is accessible, offering an uninterrupted panorama out over the clear blue ocean. The backdrop adds to the drama of the setting, with coarse thorny bushes interspersed with the bright orange flower clusters of lantana shrubs.

# Nusa Dua and Tanjung Benoa

Some 11km southeast of Kuta, Bali's most artfully designed high-class beach resort luxuriates along a coastal stretch of reclaimed mangrove swamp. This is

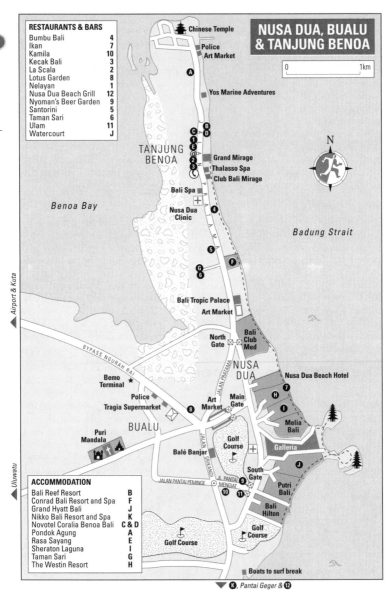

**RESTAURANTS & BARS**

| | |
|---|---|
| Bumbu Bali | 4 |
| Ikan | 7 |
| Kamila | 10 |
| Kecak Bali | 3 |
| La Scala | 2 |
| Lotus Garden | 8 |
| Nelayan | 1 |
| Nusa Dua Beach Grill | 12 |
| Nyoman's Beer Garden | 9 |
| Santorini | 5 |
| Taman Sari | 6 |
| Ulam | 11 |
| Watercourt | J |

**NUSA DUA, BUALU & TANJUNG BENOA**

0     1km

Chinese Temple
Police
Art Market
Yos Marine Adventures

TANJUNG BENOA

Grand Mirage
Thalasso Spa
Club Bali Mirage

Bali Spa

Nusa Dua Clinic

*Benoa Bay*

*Badung Strait*

Bali Tropic Palace
Art Market

North Gate

Bali Club Med

NUSA DUA

Nusa Dua Beach Hotel

BYPASS NGURAH RAI

Bemo Terminal

Police
Tragia Supermarket

BUALU

Puri Mandala

Main Gate

Art Market

Melia Bali

Galleria

Balé Banjar

Golf Course

South Gate

Putri Bali

JALAN PANTAI PEMINGE

JL. PANTAI MENGIAT

Bali Hilton

Golf Course

Golf Course

Boats to surf break

Pantai Geger &

N

**ACCOMMODATION**

| | |
|---|---|
| Bali Reef Resort | B |
| Conrad Bali Resort and Spa | F |
| Grand Hyatt Bali | J |
| Nikko Bali Resort and Spa | K |
| Novotel Coralia Benoa Bali | C & D |
| Pondok Agung | A |
| Rasa Sayang | E |
| Sheraton Laguna | I |
| Taman Sari | G |
| The Westin Resort | H |

*Airport & Kuta*

*Uluwatu*

**NUSA DUA**, a sparklingly pristine enclave that was purpose-built to indulge the whims and smooth away the grievances of upmarket tourists, while simultaneously protecting the Balinese from too many negative touristic influences (see p.498 for the full story). The dozen or so five-star hotels all boast expansive grounds running down to a white-sand beach, and each one offers huge swimming pools, tennis courts, and several bars and restaurants. But there's nothing

Don't confuse Tanjung Benoa with **Benoa Harbour** (Pelabuhan Benoa; described on p.166), which lies about a kilometre north across the water from Tanjung Benoa's northern tip, but is only accessible to the public by a circuitous land route. Fast boats to Lombok, Pelni boats to other parts of the Indonesian archipelago, sea planes, and most excursion boats depart from Benoa Harbour, not Tanjung Benoa.

else in Nusa Dua: no losmen or mid-range hotels and no markets, *banjar* or noodle stalls. There used to be a central shopping and entertainments centre, the Galleria, but Nusa Dua was so badly affected by the downturn in tourism following the 2002 bomb that the Galleria is currently closed with major renovations pending.

There are a few more signs of real life along the narrow sandbar that extends north from Nusa Dua. **Tanjung Benoa**, as this finger-like projection is known, still just about functions as a fishing village, with a few homes and neighbourhood warung left standing, but it is fast developing as a more mid-market offshoot of Nusa Dua, with a wider spread of accommodation and a heap of watersports facilities as well. The main drawback is the beach: the northern stretch is scruffy and unappealing, and though the smarter, more southerly, hotels have trucked in sand to line the front of their establishments, these areas still suffer from the continual revving of the jet skis hired from nearby watersports centres. Nor is there an inland heart to the Tanjung Benoa resort: the few decent restaurants and shops are strung out over three kilometres of road, with numerous abandoned and overgrown lots in between. In addition, Tanjung Benoa has the dubious distinction of being the centre of Bali's turtle trade (see box, p.146).

Sandwiched between Nusa Dua and Tanjung Benoa, the village of **BUALU** is where you'll find the *banjar*, temples, warung, family homes and non-tourist-oriented business common to any small Balinese town, particularly along Jalan Srikandi. The cluster of tourist restaurants on the Bualu side of Nusa Dua's South Gate, and to a lesser extent the stalls around the Main Gate, are a useful enticement to explore beyond the too-perfect confines of Nusa Dua itself.

## Arrival

If you're arriving straight from the **airport** (see p.114) and staying in one of the more expensive hotels, you'll almost certainly be picked up by a hotel limousine. The official taxi rate from the airport is Rp55,000 to Nusa Dua and Rp60,000 to Tanjung Benoa, a journey of around twenty minutes. A **metered taxi** from Kuta costs about Rp40,000.

The only means of **public transport** to Nusa Dua and Tanjung Benoa are the Damri **buses** from Denpasar's Batubulan bemo terminal (see p.172) and the dark blue Tegal–Kuta–Bualu **bemos** that depart Denpasar's Tegal bemo terminal (see p.95). The bemos (about every 30min; 45min) go via the eastern edge of Kuta (picking up passengers from the Jalan Imam Bonjol/Jalan Setia Budi intersection) and then via Jimbaran before racing down the highway to terminate just west of Bualu's Tragia supermarket. From here, you'll either have to walk to your hotel (1–2km to Nusa Dua, further to most Tanjung Benoa hotels) or hail a taxi. If you're returning by bemo to Kuta, the driver should drop you close to Kuta's Badung tourist office on Jalan Raya Kuta; however, getting bemos back from Bualu to Kuta or Denpasar is a very unreliable business after about 3pm, and you may be forced to charter one.

## The turtles of Bali

**Turtle meat** is a popular luxury in Bali, and also plays a part in certain religious ritu-als: the flippers are made into sate, and the flesh ground down into the ceremonial *lawar* served at weddings, tooth-filing ceremonies and cremations. Weighing up to 180kg as adults, **green turtles** are the most sought-after source of meat (they are, in fact, mottled brown in colour, but get their name from the colour of the soup made from their flesh) but over-hunting has resulted in the near-extinction of these turtles in Balinese waters. Bali also used to have a number of turtle **hatching grounds** on its shores – female turtles will only lay their eggs on the beach on which they themselves were born, each pregnant female swimming thousands of miles to return to her original birthplace – including at Sanur, Nusa Dua, Tanjung Benoa, Pulau Serangan, Jimbaran and Pemuteran. But nearly all have become unsafe or unusable, either as a result of tourist development or because they are well-known to **hunters** and poach-ers eager to get their hands on turtle eggs and flesh. Over the last four decades, this plunder has been so extensive that turtle sightings off the coast have become quite rare and many hatching grounds have been abandoned. As only one in a thousand eggs produces a turtle that survives thirty years to adulthood, Bali's turtle population is in crisis. Local fishermen now trawl the seas much further afield, bringing back thousands of live green turtles to Bali every year for sale and slaughter.

The situation has become so dire, and attracted so much adverse international publicity, that in 1999 a local law was passed banning the sale, possession and consumption of all green turtles except those destined for ceremonial feasts – and fishermen are supposed to apply for special licences for these. Pressure groups even persuaded an important Hindu priest to declare that turtle meat was not an essential part of Hindu rituals and that substitutes could be used. However, with a single turtle fetching up to a million rupiah, poaching can seem a risk worth running, and every year hundreds of turtles still reportedly pass through the half-dozen clandestine hold-ing pens and slaughterhouses in Tanjung Benoa and nearby Pulau Serangan (see p.165). The police have been slow to crack down on the most notorious traders (who have responded violently to intervention by police and conservationists), but mount-ing public pressure led to a high-profile arrest in 2004 and promises of further action. **Hawksbill turtles** are also much prized, captured for their beautiful shells rather than their meat, but since 1992 international trade in tortoiseshell has been banned under the Convention of International Trade in Endangered Species (CITES), which effec-tively means that tourists now have tortoiseshell souvenirs impounded.

### Campaign organizations and hatcheries

Greenpeace **campaigns** against the unnecessary slaughter of all turtles, and travel-lers can support this by avoiding all products made from turtle flesh or tortoiseshell, and by boycotting restaurants that serve turtle meat, informing the managers exactly why. Many organizations in Indonesia are dedicated to **conserving** local turtle populations, including ProFauna Indonesia in Denpasar (℡0361/424731, ⊛www .ksbk.or.id), PPLH in Sanur (℡0361/281648, ⊛www.pplhbali.or.id), and the Denpasar branch of the World Wide Fund for Nature (℡0361/247125, ⊛www.wwf.or.id). Sev-eral people have established small turtle **hatcheries** on Bali and Lombok, including at *Bumbu Bali* restaurant in Tanjung Benoa (see p.150) and at Reef Seen Aquatics in Pemuteran (see p.373).

## Transport and tours

As the resorts, restaurants and shops are strung over a distance of some 6km from the northern tip of Tanjung Benoa to southern Nusa Dua, getting around can be a hot and time-consuming business. The shortest route between hotels is nearly always via the paved beachfront **walkway**, which begins in front of the *Bali Hilton* at the far southern end of Nusa Dua and runs north to Tanjung Benoa's *Grand Mirage*; it takes about thirty minutes to walk from the *Bali Hilton* to the *Bali Club Med*, or around an hour to the *Grand Mirage*.

Alternatively, nearly all the big hotels in both resorts offer free transport around Nusa Dua and Tanjung Benoa, and there's always the fleet of pale brown Kowinu Bali **metered taxis** (T0361/773030; Rp4000 flagfall, then Rp2000 per km) that circulate around both resorts.

Or you could capitalize on the flat terrain and fairly traffic-free roads by **renting a bicycle** from your hotel (around Rp30,000 per day). **Car rental**, with or without driver, can also be arranged through Nusa Dua hotels (around $30 per day) or from Tanjung Benoa rental outlets on Jalan Pratama. All the big hotels in Nusa Dua offer **organized tours** to major sights on and around Bali.

## Accommodation

In Nusa Dua, four- and five-star **accommodation** is the norm, with most hotels offering smart if slightly bland rooms set around enormous pools in luscious seafront grounds. Rates for rooms booked via hotel websites or through travel and online agents (see p.54) start at around US$100, excluding tax and a possible high-season supplement, which makes them very good value.

Tanjung Benoa caters for a wider span of budgets, with some lower- and mid-range hotels at the north end of the peninsula and a burgeoning number of four- and five-star operations on the beachfront further south.

### Nusa Dua

**Grand Hyatt Bali** T0361/771234, W www.hyatt .com. Terraced rooms and cottages grouped into "villages" surrounded by sumptuous grounds filled with ponds, fountains and tropical flowers. Has an amazing series of free-form swimming pools complete with water chutes, bridges and sunken bars, plus tennis and squash courts, and a kids' club. Free shuttle bus to the sister operation, the *Bali Hyatt*, in Sanur. ❽

**Nikko Bali Resort and Spa** Pantai Sawangan T0361/773377, W www.nikkobali.com. Occupies a spectacular cliffside position above Pantai Sawangan, about 3km south of the *Bali Hilton*, with one block of rooms built right on the shorefront in what is effectively a private golden-sand bay. Other rooms have back doors that open right on to small swimming pools. Facilities include a spa, a lagoon swimming pool, and a kids' club. ❾

**Sheraton Laguna** T0361/771327, W www.starwood.com/bali. A super-deluxe hotel whose 270 rooms are set around a series of seven awesomely turquoise lagoon-like swimming pools, complete with little sandy beaches, islands and waterfalls. The most expensive rooms have terraces that give direct access to the lagoons. Also offers free 24hr butler service, six restaurants, a spa, and beachfront cabanas with wi-fi access. ❽

**The Westin Resort** T0361/771906, W www .westin.com/bali. A typical *Westin* hotel, with a central block of 355 contemporary-styled rooms done out in neutral tones and centred round the trademark, ultra-luxurious "heavenly" bed, plus a spa, gym and kids' club as well as some enticing beachfront lounging pavilions. Also has freshwater, salt-water and kids' pools, plus broadband and wi-fi access in every room. ❽

### Tanjung Benoa

**Bali Reef Resort** Jl Pratama T0361/776291, W www.balireef-resort.com. Small, rather elegant beachfront hotel with 28 smart bungalows, all furnished with air-con and TV, lining a long, narrow garden that runs down to the sea. Rooms are quite compact but comfortable and there's a pool and spa, Internet access in the lobby, and a shorefront restaurant and bar. ❽

**Conrad Bali Resort and Spa** Jl Pratama 168 T0361/778788, W www.conradhotels.com. Strong, uncluttered lines, pale cream stone and dark wood give this chain hotel a modish air, and the stylish rooms are surprisingly pretty. A 33-metre-long lagoon pool snakes its way right round the resort and all rooms have some sort of sea view, though the beach itself is not great here. There's a spa and kids' club, and some rooms are wheelchair-accessible. ❽–❾

**Novotel Coralia Benoa Bali** Jl Pratama T0361/772239, W www.novotelbali.com. Chic and contemporary but comfortable low-rise hotel where every spaciously designed room has its own balcony or small garden and is furnished in Balinese style. The grounds run down to a decent stretch of beach and are spread over both sides of the road.

Facilities include three pools, a children's club, a games room and tennis courts. Has a good baby-sitting service and is child-friendly. ❽–❾

🏃 **Pondok Agung** Jl Pratama 99
⊤0361/771143, €roland@eksadata.com. Homely, stylish place with just eleven comfortably furnished rooms and a nice veranda overlooking the attractive garden. The best-value accommodation, though not the cheapest, in Tanjung Benoa. Rooms with fan ❷ With air-con ❸–❺

**Rasa Sayang** Jl Pratama 88x ⊤0361/771643, €rsbind@yahoo.com. Small hotel in central Tanjung Benoa offering twenty perfectly decent if rather soulless rooms in a terraced block; upstairs

rooms are lighter. Rooms with fan ❷ With air-con ❸

🏃 **Taman Sari** Jl Pratama 61b
⊤0361/773953, ⓦwww.tamansarisuite-bali.com. The mellowest place in Tanjung Benoa, comprising just ten nicely designed Balinese-Japanese-style air-con bungalows, each with a garden bathroom, plus a good-value four-person villa with its own pool. Aside from a spacious garden, there's a large lagoon-pool, a charmingly traditional spa (see opposite) and a good restaurant. As there's no beach access, the hotel runs free transport to its Taman Sari Beach Club on Pantai Geger (see p.below). Phone for free airport pick-up. ❼–❾

# The resorts

**Nusa Dua beach** is long, white and sandy, and reasonably wide even at high tide, though at low tide the reef is exposed and you're better off beachcombing than swimming. The areas in front of each Nusa Dua hotel are dotted with sunloungers, but it's quite easy to wander from one to another via the walkway and there's no law against outsiders on the sand (although non-guests have to pay to use the sunloungers). Halfway down the shoreline, the land blossoms out into two little clumps, or "islands" (Nusa Dua means "Two Islands"), on which stand two of the area's original temples: the shorefront here is shaded with trees, and at weekends it's a popular picnicking spot, with the inevitable food carts in attendance.

Few people swim or sunbathe on the northern part of **Tanjung Benoa beach** as it's strewn with debris and dominated by watersports facilities and the constant whine of jet skis. Things are more appealing further south, from the *Bali Reef Resort* onwards, though still not as inviting as at Nusa Dua.

For a different, more local beach experience, head south of Bali Golf and Country Club, towards the *Nikko Bali Resort & Spa*, and follow signs for **Pantai Geger** (about a one-kilometre drive from the golf course). The broad, white-sand beach here is quite pleasant and rarely busy: there's seaweed farming (see p.262) at the southern end, below the clifftop temple, Pura Geger (which is also accessible via a more southerly road), plus sunloungers for rent, a decent surf break and a couple of shoreside restaurants, one of which is the recommended *Nusa Dua Beach Grill* (see p.150). An informal taxi service operates from the beach; if you bring your own vehicle you'll be charged Rp2000 parking fee.

### Sports and activities

Tanjung Benoa is well known for **watersports** and one of its best-known operators is Yos Marine Adventures, Jl Pratama 106 (⊤0361/773774, ⓦwww.yosdive.com). In Nusa Dua, Surya Segara has a booth on the beach in front of the *Grand Hyatt Bali* (⊤0361/771234, €suryasegaradive@yahoo.com) and Waterworld has one beach-side of the *Sheraton Laguna* (⊤0361/771801). Activities and prices at all outfits are competitive and include **parasailing** ($15 per round), **water-skiing** ($20 for 10min), **jet-skiing** ($20 for 15min), kayaking ($10 per hour) and **wakeboarding** ($25 for 15min), as well as morning boat rides to see **dolphins** off the south Bukit coast, apparently with a ninety-per-cent chance of actually seeing some ($59), plus a range of **fishing** expeditions ($65–180 per person). They all organize **snorkelling trips** ($8–50 depending on destination), and **diving** expeditions ($50–90) and courses ($350 for the

PADI Open Water) and, while the courses tend to take place in and around Nusa Dua, most diving tours head off to the reefs and wrecks elsewhere; see the box on p.158 for full information. Prices in Nusa Dua tend to be higher than the same deals offered in Kuta.

Nusa Dua's **surf breaks** catch the most swell of all the breaks in Bali, though currents can get pretty vicious. The main Nusa Dua break (accessible by boat from a signposted point south of the *Bali Hilton* and the golf course), is a right-hander about 1km offshore, while further north, a brief paddle beyond the *Bali Club Med*, Sri Lanka is a short speedy right-hander.

Nusa Dua has a world-class, 18-hole championship **golf** course within the resort boundaries: the Bali Golf and Country Club (℡0361/771791, Ⓦwww.baligolfandcountryclub.com), spread across three areas of the resort, the main part dominating the southern end of Nusa Dua. Green fees are $156 including cart and caddy, and you can rent clubs for $27. The *Bali Club Med* resort (daily 10am–6pm; ℡0361/771521), just inside Nusa Dua's North Gate, issues a good-value **day pass** to non-guests (Rp340,000, kids Rp170,000), which buys use of all sports facilities except the trapeze, including windsurfing equipment, archery gear, tennis courts and swimming pools, as well as a buffet lunch.

For **bird-watchers**, the mangrove swamp and sewage works to the west of Nusa Dua's North Gate, at the far southern end of Tanjung Benoa, is a reward-ing place to spend an hour or two in the early morning; you're likely to see several species of kingfisher here, as well as lots of wading birds. *Nikko Bali Resort* (℡0361/773377 ext 215) do one-hour **camel safaris** along the beach (4 daily; $29, or $15 for under-12s).

### Spa treatments

Many of the top-notch hotels have **spas** on their premises, offering a full menu of traditional Balinese, Thai, Swedish and aromatherapy massages, as well as the popular Javanese *mandi lulur* (see p.73). Non-guests are usually welcome to use the facilities, though it's always advisable to phone ahead for a reservation. One of the best-known and longest-established spas in Bali is the award-winning spa at *Nusa Dua Beach* (℡0361/771210), which enjoys a beautiful tropical watergarden setting and where the treatments include a jet-lag massage. At the *Grand Mirage* in Tanjung Benoa, the Thalasso Bali spa (℡0361/773883, Ⓦwww.thalassobali.com) specializes in therapies using heated sea water and seaweed, while the well-respected chain of Mandara spas have spa centres at *Nikko Bali Resort* (℡0361/773337), which features beachfront spa villas and a cave Jacuzzi, and at *Club Med* (℡0361/771521). Treatments at all these spas start from US$75. More low-key is the charmingly traditional spa at *Taman Sari* in Tanjung Benoa (℡0361/773953; treatments from US$35), with its partially open-air treatment rooms, while Bali Spa (℡0361/777997; treatments from Rp210,000) at Jl Pratama 87 is less atmospheric but much cheaper.

## Eating and drinking

You'll find the cheapest and most authentic Balinese **food** at the warung along Jalan Srikandi in **Bualu** village, some of which have English-language menus. At the pricier tourist restaurants on the Bualu side of Nusa Dua's South Gate the atmosphere is livelier and less stilted than in Nusa Dua, though prices are still pretty high. **Tanjung Benoa** has a few notable places to eat among its many unexciting identikit options, but they're quite spread out. **Nusa Dua** offers the most upmarket selection, most within the compounds of the big hotels: recommendations include the Balinese food at the *Grand Hyatt Bali*'s *Watercourt* and the beachfront *Ikan* seafood restaurant at *The Westin Resort*. For details of packages featuring buffet dinners and a Balinese dance performance, see p.151.

Many restaurants in Tanjung Benoa and Bualu offer **free transport** from local hotels: where this service is available, we have included the phone number in the review.

**Bumbu Bali** Jl Pratama, Tanjung Benoa ☏0361/771256. Founded and managed by renowned expat chef and food writer Heinz von Holzen, this is the most famous restaurant in the area. It serves classy, if variable, fairly expensive Balinese cuisine, including duck roasted in banana leaves, seven-course *rijsttafels* (vegetarian and meat options, from Rp85,000–155,000), seafood platters and saté set meals. Diners have an open-plan view of the chefs at work, and you can also take Balinese cooking lessons here (see opposite).

**Kamila** Jl Pantai Mengiat 2, Bualu. Tiny warung serving the cheapest food in the area: assemble your own nasi campur for as little as Rp3000.

**Kecak Bali** Jl Pratama, Tanjung Benoa ☏0361/775533. Formerly a sister restaurant to *Bumbu Bali*, and still offering a similar if slightly cheaper menu, specializing in fine Balinese food. The menu includes duck saté (Rp22,500), a multi-course seafood dinner (Rp105,000); and a meat- or fish-based *rijsttafel* (Rp105,000), and the setting, in a series of pavilions, is pleasant.

**La Scala** Jl Pratama 93, Tanjung Benoa ☏0361/775605. One of at least a dozen places on this road serving an almost identical menu that ranges from seafood (large platters for Rp155,000) to Indonesian classics like gado-gado and mixed saté (Rp29,500) to pizzas and Mexican favourites. Sit upstairs under a canopy of sails or downstairs beside the kitsch waterfall feature.

**Lotus Garden** Just outside the Main Gate on Jl Bypass Ngurah Rai in Bualu ☏0361/773378. The Bualu branch of this prolific Bali-wide chain serves a lot of moderately priced Italian dishes, including its trademark wood-fired pizzas, plus Mediterranean cuisine ranging from mezzes to *moules* and *tabbouleh* (Rp35,000–100,000).

**Nelayan** Jl Pratama 101, Tanjung Benoa ☏0361/776868. Deservedly popular mid-priced place that serves great Balinese curries and a good range of fresh fish and seafood dishes, mostly at around Rp30,000. Delicious rum-and-raisin ice-cream, too.

**Nusa Dua Beach Grill** Pantai Geger ☏0361/743 4779. Breezy, boho-chic café on the low-key beach at Pantai Geger (see p.148), where you can watch the waves – and the seaweed harvesters – while scoffing the special fisherman's basket (Rp35,000) or any number of fish dishes and salads, and rebooting with a power smoothie. Easiest road access is via the rough track just south of *The Balé* villas. Phone for free pick-up in the Nusa Dua area.

**Nyoman's Beer Garden** Just outside the South Gate on Jl Pantai Mengiat, Bualu ☏0361/775746; daily 3–11pm. Cheap draught beer, pool tables, well-priced Chinese, Balinese and vegetarian dishes (Rp35,000–45,000), and a lively atmosphere.

**Santorini** opposite the *Conrad Bali Resort and Spa* on Jl Pratama, Tanjung Benoa ☏0361/777942. Good, authentic Greek food from the same team behind the *Mykonos* restaurant in Seminyak, served up in a kitsch Neoclassical building, complete with doric columns. Everything from *souvlaki* (Rp32,000) and *dolmades* to *patzaria* (sweet potato and beetroot salad) and lamb medallions (Rp67,000), plus a wine list that features a few Greek labels.

**Taman Sari** Beside *Taman Sari* bungalows, Jl Pratama 61b, Tanjung Benoa ☏0361/773953. Known for its pricey Thai cuisine, including a recommended dish of fried chicken with cashew nuts, and spicy squid salad. Also features quality fish meals, such as slow-grilled marinated snapper, and lobster and asparagus salad.

**Ulam** Just outside the South Gate at Jl Pantai Mengiat 14, Bualu ☏0361/771590. Locally famous Balinese seafood restaurant whose menu includes grilled lobster with garlic butter (Rp39,000), steamed crab, and seafood baskets (Rp80,000).

## Shopping and entertainment

When Nusa Dua's central **Galleria** shopping plaza reopens (possibly in late 2005) it is likely to be the most rewarding place to shop, with all sorts of outlets from fashion boutiques to souvenir stalls, sportswear shops to supermarkets. In the meantime, the Bualu road just outside the Main Gate is lined with several dozen **art market** stalls selling cheap, standard Balinese souvenirs, T-shirts and arts and crafts, and there's a smaller, similar cluster just outside the North Gate. There are also little knots of souvenir and handicraft shops on Bualu's Jalan

Pantai Mengiat and across from the *Grand Mirage* on Jalan Pratama in Tanjung Benoa; these are also the two best areas to look for **tailors' shops**, with half a dozen places vying for business in each location.

All the hotels stage regular **Balinese dance** shows for $25–30 including dinner: *The Westin Resort's* (T0361/771906) weekly *kecak* show is performed on the beach, while the *Nikko Bali Resort and Spa's* (T0361/773377) "Desa Bali Night" includes fire-blowing, cock-fighting, Balinese dance, and village food stalls (Wed 7–9.30pm; Rp297,000, kids Rp150,000).

## Listings

**Airline offices** For international airline offices, see p.115; for domestic airlines, see p.33.
**Banks and exchange** There is an ATM for Visa, MasterCard and Cirrus inside the Circle K minimart opposite the *Grand Mirage* in Tanjung Benoa. You can change money in Tanjung Benoa at several shops on the nearby stretch of Jl Pratama, and at all Nusa Dua hotels. See p.47 for advice on moneychangers' scams.
**Cooking lessons** In Balinese cuisine from chef and food writer Heinz von Holzen at his *Bumbu Bali* restaurant in Tanjung Benoa (Mon–Fri; T0361/771256, W www.balifoods.com; US$65, book two days ahead, individuals accepted). Lessons are also available from the chefs at

*Kecak* restaurant in Tanjung Benoa ($40–50; T0361/775533, W www.kecakbali.com). Lessons at both schools begin with a trip to Jimbaran fish market and the local fruit and veg market.
**Email and Internet** At all major hotels and some minor ones; also at email centres opposite the *Club Bali Mirage* hotel in Tanjung Benoa and on Jl Srikandi in Bualu.
**Hospitals and clinics** Nusa Dua Clinic, Jl Pratama 81a, Tanjung Benoa (daily 24hr; T0361/771324), staffed by English-speaking medics. All Nusa Dua hotels provide 24hr medical service. See also p.134 for expat-oriented clinics near Kuta and p.107 for Denpasar hospitals.

# Sanur and around

Stretching down the southeast coast 18km from Ngurah Rai Airport, **SANUR** is an appealing, more peaceful alternative to Kuta, and not as manufactured as Nusa Dua, with a long, fairly decent white-sand beach, plenty of attractive accommodation in all price brackets and a distinct village atmosphere. Because it lacks the clubs and all-night party venues of Kuta, Sanur can seem a bit tame to younger travellers, but there are plenty of restaurants to keep most visitors entertained, and nearly everyone appreciates the calmer ambience. It's also a good place to bring the kids, is one of Bali's main centres for watersports, and works well as a base for exploring other parts of the island, particularly Ubud, which is about forty minutes' drive north, and the craft villages in between.

The written history of Sanur dates back to 913 AD, as inscribed on the ancient stone pillar **Prasasti Blanjong**, which is enshrined in a glass case at the back of Pura Blanjong on Jalan Danau Poso in southern Sanur. You can't actually see the inscriptions, as the two-metre-high pillar is wrapped in cloth, but they tell of a Javanese king who arrived in Sanur to set up a Mahayana Buddhist government.

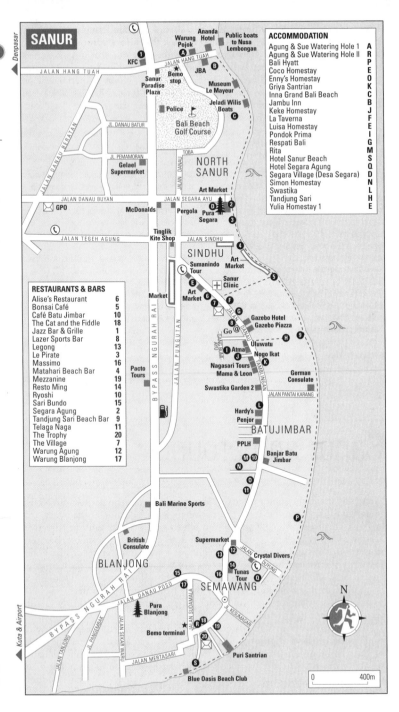

# SANUR

**ACCOMMODATION**

| | |
|---|---|
| Agung & Sue Watering Hole 1 | A |
| Agung & Sue Watering Hole ll | R |
| Bali Hyatt | P |
| Coco Homestay | E |
| Enny's Homestay | O |
| Griya Santrian | K |
| Inna Grand Bali Beach | C |
| Jambu Inn | B |
| Keke Homestay | J |
| La Taverna | F |
| Luisa Homestay | E |
| Pondok Prima | I |
| Respati Bali | G |
| Rita | M |
| Hotel Sanur Beach | S |
| Hotel Segara Agung | Q |
| Segara Village (Desa Segara) | D |
| Simon Homestay | N |
| Swastika | L |
| Tandjung Sari | H |
| Yulia Homestay 1 | E |

**RESTAURANTS & BARS**

| | |
|---|---|
| Alise's Restaurant | 6 |
| Bonsai Café | 5 |
| Café Batu Jimbar | 10 |
| The Cat and the Fiddle | 18 |
| Jazz Bar & Grille | 1 |
| Lazer Sports Bar | 8 |
| Legong | 13 |
| Le Pirate | 3 |
| Massimo | 16 |
| Matahari Beach Bar | 4 |
| Mezzanine | 19 |
| Resto Ming | 14 |
| Ryoshi | 10 |
| Sari Bundo | 15 |
| Segara Agung | 2 |
| Tandjung Sari Beach Bar | 9 |
| Telaga Naga | 11 |
| The Trophy | 20 |
| The Village | 7 |
| Warung Agung | 12 |
| Warung Blanjong | 17 |

Labels on map: Warung Pojok, Ananda Hotel, Public boats to Nusa Lembongan, KFC, JALAN HANG TUAH, Bemo stop, Sanur Paradise Plaza, JBA, Museum Le Mayeur, Police, Jeladi Wilis Boats, Bali Beach Golf Course, JL. DANAU BATUR, JL. PEMAMORAN, Gelael Supermarket, TOBA, NORTH SANUR, JALAN DANAU BERATAN, JALAN DANAU BUYAN, GPO, McDonalds, Art Market, JALAN SEGARA AYU, Pergola, Pura Segara, JALAN TEGEH AGUNG, Tinglik Kite Shop, JALAN SINDHU, SINDHU, Art Market, Market, Sumanindo Tour, Sanur Clinic, Art Market, JALAN DANAU TOBA, Gazebo Hotel, Gazebo Piazza, Go, GANG BUMI SARI, Uluwatu, Atma, Nogo Ikat, JALAN PUNGUTAN, BYPASS NGURAH RAI, Nagasari Tours, Mama & Leon, German Consulate, Swastika Garden 2, JALAN PANTAI KARANG, Pacto Tours, Hardy's, Penjor, BATUJIMBAR, JALAN TANJUNG, PPLH, Banjar Batu Jimbar, Bali Marine Sports, British Consulate, BLANJONG, Supermarket, Crystal Divers, JALAN SUDAMALA, Tunas Tour, SEMAWANG, JALAN DANAU POSO, Pura Blanjong, Bemo terminal, JL. PANGERMBAH, JL. SEKAR WARU, JL. KESUMASARI, Puri Santrian, JALAN MERTASARI, Blue Oasis Beach Club, N

0    400m

Ten centuries later, Sanur began to attract significant numbers of foreigners to its shores, many of whom chose to build homes here. Of these, the house of the Belgian artist **Le Mayeur** (now a museum) is the only one that still stands, but his more influential contemporaries included the American dancer Katharane Mershon and her husband Jack, Vicki Baum (author of *A Tale from Bali*), and art collectors Hans and Rolf Neuhaus. After World War II, Australian artist Donald Friend also made his home here. In the 1960s, during the Sukarno era, Sanur was chosen as the site of Bali's first major beach hotel, the *Grand Bali Beach*, an ugly high-rise. It has been rebuilt after suffering severe fire damage in 1992 and remains a blot (it's currently part of the *Inna* hotel group) – but, amazingly, is the only such disfigurement in the resort.

Sanur is famous across the island as the source of some of Bali's most powerful **black magic** and home of the most feared sorcerers and most respected healers or *balian*. It's not uncommon, for example, to hear stories of police enquiries that use the black-magic practitioners of Sanur to help them track down and capture criminals.

# Orientation, arrival and information

Sanur is comprised of several districts, though they are not very distinct to outsiders. Beginning in the north, Jalan Hang Tuah, which has just a few small hotels, and the area around the nearby *Inna Grand Bali Beach* are in **north Sanur**; south of Jalan Segara Ayu as far as Jalan Pantai Karang is **Sindhu**, location of many guesthouses, hotels, shops and restaurants; less congested, **Batujimbar** runs from Jalan Pantai Karang as far as the *Bali Hyatt*. **Semawang** is the southern coastal strip from the *Bali Hyatt* to *Hotel Sanur Beach* and beyond, and is home to an increasing number of tourist-oriented shops, hotels and businesses; the more residential inland area covering Jalan Danau Poso and Bypass Ngurah Rai is **Blanjong**.

Sanur is Rp55,000 by pre-paid taxi from the **airport** (see box, p.114), or about Rp30,000 by metered taxi from central Kuta. The fastest and most direct way of getting to Sanur from most other places on Bali is by tourist **shuttle bus**. The biggest operator, Perama, has several ticket agents in Sanur: the main one, which is the official drop-off point, is Warung Pojok minimarket, Jl Hang Tuah 31 in north Sanur (☏0361/285592); the bus driver may agree to drop you off elsewhere along Jalan Danau Tamblingan, otherwise you'll need to take a bemo or taxi to your hotel from opposite Warung Pojok.

The slightly cheaper but more long-winded way of getting to Sanur is by **bemo**, though this will entail travelling via Denpasar and changing at least once. Dark green bemos from Denpasar's **Kereneng terminal** run to north Sanur (15min; Rp3500), where they drop off outside the *Inna Grand Bali Beach* compound at the Bypass Ngurah Rai/Jalan Hang Tuah junction only if asked; otherwise, they usually head down Jalan Danau Beratan and Jalan Danau Buyan, before continuing down Jalan Danau Tamblingan to *The Trophy* pub in Semawang. Dark blue bemos from Denpasar's **Tegal terminal** run direct via Jalan Teuku Umar and Renon (30min; Rp3500) and then follow the same route as the green Kereneng ones, depending on passenger requests.

**From Kuta**, you'll need to change at Tegal in Denpasar, though you can save time if you get off the Kuta bemo at the bridge where Jalan Imam Bonjol intersects with Jalan Teuku Umar and hop onto a blue Sanur-bound bemo instead. Coming **from Nusa Dua**, you can take the white, Batubulan-bound Damri

Most hotels and losmen will arrange transport to the **airport** from around Rp40,000, or you can hail a metered taxi for slightly less.

The most painless way of moving on to most other tourist destinations is by **tourist shuttle bus**. The majority of tour agents advertise shuttle-bus services; the largest operator is Perama (ⓦwww.peramatour.com). Perama's main ticket agent and pick-up point is Warung Pojok minimarket, Jl Hang Tuah 31 in north Sanur (ⓣ0361/285592); other Perama ticket outlets, where you may also be able to be picked up, include the more central Nagasari Tours (ⓣ0361/288096), opposite *Griya Santrian* hotel, at Jl Danau Tamblingan 102 in Sindhu, and Tunas Tour, further south at Jl Danau Tamblingan 105, Semawang (ⓣ0361/288581), next to *Resto Ming*. Perama buses are not air-con; sample fares include Rp10,000 to Kuta or Ngurah Rai Airport, Rp15,000 to Ubud, Rp30,000 to Candi Dasa, and Rp130,000 to Senggigi on Lombok. See "Travel details", p.166, for more.

Moving on by **bemo** to anywhere on Bali entails going via Denpasar – either the green bemo to Kereneng, or the blue bemo to Tegal. For **Kuta** and **Jimbaran**, it's easiest to go via Tegal (see "Orientation, arrival and information", p.153, for a handy short-cut); for most other destinations, the Kereneng service is more efficient, though you'll have to make another cross-city bemo connection from Kereneng in order to get to the Batubulan terminal (for **Ubud and the east**) or the Ubung terminal (for **the west and the north**).

Sanur is the main departure point for **boats** to **Nusa Lembongan**, which leave from a jetty at the eastern end of Jalan Hang Tuah in north Sanur. There are currently two public services a day, for which tickets are sold from the beachfront office near the *Ananda Hotel*; these depart daily at 8am (Rp33,000) and 10.30am (Rp43,000), and take 1hr 30min. There is also one Perama shuttle boat, which should be booked the day before (daily 10.30am; 1hr 30min; Rp50,000); see p.254 for full details. It's also possible to charter a private boat for a Lembongan day-trip from the Jeladi Wilis Boat Cooperative (ⓣ0361/284206), whose booth is on the beachfront in front of the *Inna Grand Bali Beach*; they charge $35 per person (minimum six people).

bus, which drops passengers on Bypass Ngurah Rai, near the *Sanur Paradise Plaza* hotel in north Sanur; you can also use this service if coming **from Ubud**, changing on to the Damri bus at Denpasar's **Batubulan** terminus.

There are no official tourist offices in Sanur, but plenty of tour agents are only too happy to provide **information** about potential day-trips.

# Transport and tours

Sanur stretches 5km from its northernmost tip to the far southern end. The green and blue public **bemos** to and from Denpasar's two terminals (see "Orientation, arrival and information", p.153) are quite useful if you're sticking to the main streets; the standard tourist price is Rp2500 for any journey within Sanur. Otherwise, flag down one of the numerous **metered taxis**. The main company is the light blue Blue Bird Taxis (ⓣ0361/701111); all metered taxis charge Rp4000 flagfall, then Rp2000 per km thereafter, day and night. If you're planning a long trip, it may be worth negotiating a fee with one of the roadside **transport touts**, but they rarely offer competitive prices for short transfers.

The transport touts also **rent cars** and **motorbikes** by the day and the week, as will most of Sanur's tour agencies. JBA are one of the few Sanur outlets to sell car insurance, and they will also supply a **car with driver**; they are located inside the compound of the *Diwangkara Hotel*, Jl Hang Tuah 54 in north Sanur (☏0361/286501, @jbadwkbl@denpasar.wasantara.net.id). See Basics, p.50, for vehicle rental advice and price guidelines, and for first-hand recommendations of Sanur drivers check the archives of the online travellers' forums listed on p.37. Sanur is an ideal place for **bicycles**, as it's almost completely flat and traffic is pretty light, so long as you keep off the thundering Bypass Ngurah Rai on the western perimeter. Most hotels will be able to get hold of a bike for you to rent, or try *Segara Village* hotel on Jalan Segara Ayu in Sindhu (see p.156), who also run guided bicycle tours (Rp40,000).

Most tourist businesses in Sanur offer a range of **sightseeing tours** around Bali as well as further afield to neighbouring islands. See "Listings", p.164, for some recommended travel agents.

# Accommodation

There's a surprisingly decent amount of low-key, low-budget homestay **accommodation** in Sanur, none of it more than ten minutes' walk from the beach, and many of the mid-range and expensive hotels are also small, personable places, set in lovely gardens, the best of which run down to the shore. For the mid-priced and expensive hotels, you'll always find the most competitive rates on the hotels' own **websites** and on the Bali accommodation websites detailed on p.54.

## Inexpensive

**Agung & Sue Watering Hole** Jl Hang Tuah 37, north Sanur ☏0361/288289, @wateringhole_sanurbali@yahoo.com. Long-established, family-run place offering the cheapest rooms in this part of Sanur, only 250m from the beach. Set in two-storey blocks around a small courtyard, all rooms are of a high standard, clean and comfortable, and the larger ones have air-con and a streetside balcony. Also has Internet access and a good restaurant. Very handy for boats to Nusa Lembongan, and there's luggage storage, too (Rp10,000 per day). Rooms with fan or air-con ❷

**Agung & Sue Watering Hole II** Jl Danau Tamblingan 36, Semawang ☏0361/270545, @wateringhole_sanurbali@yahoo.com. Run by *Agung and Sue I*'s daughter, the fourteen rooms here are just as clean, and though the compound is smaller and feels rather hemmed in, it has a tiny pool. It's also close to the quietest stretch of the beach. Rooms with fan ❷ With air-con ❸ Family rooms ❹–❺

**Coco Homestay** Jl Danau Tamblingan 42, Sindhu ☏0361/287391, @ketutcoco@hotmail.com. Archetypal homestay offering just eight budget rooms behind the family art shop. Some of the cheapest accommodation in Sanur. ❶

**Enny's Homestay** Jl Danau Tamblingan 172, Semawang ☏0361/287363. The seven rooms behind the family shop are spotless, immaculately tiled and attractively furnished in modern losmen style. The cheapest have fans and cold water, the

most expensive have air-con and hot water. There's a tiny upstairs roof-garden balcony and you're just across the road from a path down to the beach. ❷

**Jambu Inn** Jl Hang Tuah 57, north Sanur ☏0361/286501, @jbadwkbl@denpasar.wasantara.net.id. Tiny, quiet place next to JBA tour agent on the edge of the *Diwangkara Hotel* compound, with just seven bungalows set round a cute little shady garden complete with pool and gazebo. Rooms are a good size and most have a living area as well as a spacious veranda. Rooms with fan ❸ With air-con ❹

**Keke Homestay** Gang Keke 3, off Jl Danau Tamblingan 96, Sindhu ☏0361/287282. Tiny losmen that's basic but good and offers five simple fan rooms with cold-water mandi. ❷

**Luisa Homestay** Jl Danau Tamblingan 40, Sindhu ☏0361/289673. One of three very similar losmen clustered together in family compounds behind streetside businesses. Elementary but cheerful accommodation in thirteen rooms, some with hot water, which are among the cheapest in Sanur. ❶–❷

**Pondok Prima** Gang Bumi Ayu 23, Sindhu ☏0361/286369, @primacottage@telkom.net. Quiet, good-value place that's well off the main road and offers a range of rooms, including some in very spacious bungalows in secluded spots around a tropical garden. The rooms in the main two-storey block are less interesting. There's a pool and a restaurant, and you can choose to pay extra for use of the air-con. Rooms with fan ❸ With air-con ❹–❺

**Simon Homestay** Down a tiny *gang* at Jl Danau Tamblingan 164d, Batujimbar ☏ 0361/289158. Small losmen with six decent rooms in the family compound, set back off the main road. Rooms with fan ❷ With air-con ❸

🏃 **Yulia Homestay 1** Jl Danau Tamblingan 38, Sindhu ☏ 0361/288089. This friendly, family-run losmen is the largest, longest-running and best of the three similar outfits in this cluster; accommodation is in 23 nice, terraced, fan-cooled bungalows, some of which have hot water. ❷

## Moderate

**Respati Bali** Jl Danau Tamblingan 33, Sindhu ☏ 0361/288427, ✉ brespati@indo.net.id. A pristine collection of sixteen large, well-kept, good-value air-con bungalows in a narrow but pretty compound that runs down to the sea. Also has a pool and restaurant. ❻

**Rita** Jl Danau Tamblingan 152, Batujimbar ☏ 0361/282630, 🖷 287969. Just a handful of exceptionally good-value concrete bungalows in a garden that's set well off the main road. All bungalows have air-con, kitchenette, TV and a large bedroom. Popular with expats. ❺

🏃 **Hotel Segara Agung** Jl Duyung 43, Semawang ☏ 0361/288446, 🖳 www.sega-raagung.com. Occupying a very quiet spot down a beautifully floral residential *gang* just a couple of minutes' walk from the beach, this is an attractive place of sixteen brick bungalows set in a soothingly spacious garden compound with a swimming pool. Rooms are clean and well furnished; the cheapest ones have fans and unusually big windows, the most expensive have air-con, and there are family options, too. Rooms with fan ❺ With air-con ❻

🏃 **Swastika** Jl Danau Tamblingan 128, Batujimbar ☏ 0361/288693, 🖳 www.swastika-bungalows.com. Deservedly popular mid-range place, with 78 comfortable rooms in variously styled bungalows set around a delightful garden with two sizeable swimming pools and a kids' pool. Most of the fan-cooled rooms have pretty garden bathrooms and shrubbery-enclosed verandas, and many of the air-con ones have private garden-view gazebos. Named after the ancient Buddhist symbol, not the Nazi emblem. Rooms with fan or with air-con ❻

## Expensive

**Bali Hyatt** Jl Danau Tamblingan, Semawang ☏ 0361/281234, 🖳 www.bali.hyatt.com. Enormous, appealingly plush establishment, offering a range of top-notch rooms, many with direct ocean views, and 36 acres of gorgeous, award-winning tropical gardens stretching down to the beach. Watersports facilities, tennis courts, several swimming pools and a spa.

One child under-12 can stay free if sharing parents' room, and there are regular organized kids' activities. Free shuttle bus to sister hotel in Nusa Dua. ❽

**Griya Santrian** Jl Danau Tamblingan 47, Sindhu ☏ 0361/288181, 🖳 www.santrian.com. Popular series of 96 smart, roomy, detached and semi-detached air-con bungalows scattered around an attractive garden compound that runs down to the beach. There are two swimming pools, one right by the shore, a kids' pool, and four restaurants. ❽

**Inna Grand Bali Beach** Off Jl Hang Tuah, north Sanur ☏ 0361/288511, 🖳 www.grand-balibeach.com/english. Huge establishment covering a long stretch of the northern end of the Sanur coast. Most rooms are in the central tower block, but there are also a fair number of cottages in the extensive grounds. The hotel fronts a good beach and offers lots of watersports, as well as three swimming pools, tennis courts and table tennis. Two kids under-12 go free if sharing with parents. ❼

**La Taverna** Jl Danau Tamblingan 29, Sindhu ☏ 0361/288497, 🖳 www.latavernahotel.co. Small, seafront hotel offering characterful and cosy if not always pristine bungalows, including some stylish split-level ones attractively furnished with antique doors; most have verandas overlooking the garden, and the grounds, with pool, run down to the beach. ❼–❽

**Hotel Sanur Beach** Jl Danau Tamblingan, Semawang ☏ 0361/288011, 🖳 sanurbeach.aerowisata.com. Sprawling complex of 425 rooms in landscaped gardens that give direct access to a fine stretch of sandy, tree-shaded beach in the quietest part of the resort. Luxury-grade rooms in the central block plus swimming pools, tennis courts, a delightful Mandara spa complex and a well-equipped watersports centre. ❾

**Segara Village (Desa Segara)** Jl Segara Ayu, Sindhu ☏ 0361/288407, 🖳 www.segaravillage.com. Offers various styles of smart air-con accommodation in small blocks set around an extensive seafront garden featuring ponds, fountains, two swimming pools, a kids' club and playground, and tennis courts. The nicest rooms are the new-style upstairs garden-view bungalows, which all enjoy large terraces. ❼

🏃 **Tandjung Sari** Jl Danau Tamblingan 41, Sindhu ☏ 0361/288441, 🖳 www.tandjung-sari.com. Elegant, beautifully appointed collection of 28 traditional-style personal cottage compounds each with its own living area, courtyard garden, shaded gazebo and garden shower. Many retain original antique Chinese floor tiles and they all have refined Javanese batik furnishings. There's a swimming pool, and the garden runs down to the shore. ❾

# The resort

The entire length of Sanur's five-kilometre **shoreline** is fronted by a partially shaded paved esplanade, so it's easy to wander down the coast in search of the perfect spot. There are busy patches of beach around the *Inna Grand Bali Beach* in the north – where non-guests can rent sunloungers and thick hotel towels for a few dollars a day (which also includes use of the hotel pool), though there's nothing to stop you from just laying out your sarong on the fine coral sand here – and, further south, in Sindhu, between *Segara Agung* restaurant and the *Gazebo Hotel*. The southern stretch of shore, in Semawang, is much quieter: the area around Jalan Kesumasari is mainly the province of fishermen and their brightly painted wooden *jukung*, while the bit in front of the *Hotel Sanur Beach* is a pleasant stretch of fairly peaceful sand.

A huge expanse of Sanur's shore gets exposed at low tide and the reef lies only about 1km offshore at high tide; the **currents** beyond it are dangerously strong. This makes it almost impossible to swim here at low tide (though it's okay for paddling kids), but at other times of day swimming is fine and watersports are popular.

## Sports and activities

You can rent **watersports** equipment at several outlets along the beachfront, including, in north Sanur, Jeladi Wilis Boat Co-operative (☏0361/284206), in front of the *Inna Grand Bali Beach*, and, in Semawang, at the Blue Oasis Beach Club (☏0361/288011) in front of *Hotel Sanur Beach*. Many of the dive centres listed in the box on p.158 also rent out watersports equipment, including **kayaks** ($6 per hour), **windsurfers** ($10–15 per hour,) and **jet skis** ($20 for 15min). Most also offer **parasailing** ($10 a round) and **water-skiing** ($16 for 15min). Blue Oasis offers a range of different watersports **courses**, including half-day windsurfing and sailing courses ($80), kite-surfing instruction ($22 per hour), and PADI **dive** courses and dive excursions.

Sanur is a popular base for **divers**: see the box on p.158 for details of local reefs, dive operators and courses. **Snorkellers** can usually join organized dive excursions, as well as specialist snorkelling trips; or you can charter glass-bottomed boats or prahu to take you out to the Sanur reef ($10–15 per hr).

The main departure point for **fishing** expeditions off southern Bali is Tanjung Benoa (see p.148), though some boats do leave from Sanur: ask at any Sanur tour agent or watersports outlet, or try the *Inna Grand Bali Beach*. A four-hour trip will generally cost $50–75 per person for coral fishing, including tackle and bait, and $75–100 per person for trolling; for a full day's game fishing, expect to pay $485 for a four-person boat.

From September to March, when the northwest winds blow offshore, there are several decent **surf breaks** off Sanur, including the Sanur break directly in front of the *Inna Grand Bali Beach*, the Tandjung Sari Reef break in front of *Tandjung Sari* hotel, and the Hyatt Reef break, 1.5km offshore from the front of the *Bali Hyatt*. You can rent surfboards ($10 per day) and boogie boards ($6) at the Blue Oasis Beach Club (see above), where you can also organize a fishing *jukung* to take you out to the breaks, or you can negotiate direct with the boat owners yourself.

Sanur has its own nine-hole **golf course** in the grounds of the *Inna Grand Bali Beach*, whose guests get a fifty percent reduction on the $50 green fees. Clubs and shoes can be rented at the club house (☏0361/288511 ext 1388).

## Spa treatments

Many of the more expensive hotels have built luxury **spa** treatment centres where you can receive a range of massages, including aromatherapy, traditional Balinese, and the Javanese *mandi lulur* exfoliation scrub (see p.73), as well as facials and hair treatments. Two of the best known are the beautifully designed Mandara spa complex in the grounds of *Hotel Sanur Beach* (℡0361/288011), and the traditional village-style spa complex at the *Bali Hyatt* (℡0361/281234). There are several other smaller and much cheaper day spas, too, including Atma, Jl Danau Tamblingan 94 in Sindhu (℡0361/283850), which charges Rp190,000 for a two-hour *mandi lulur*. Or there's always the massage-and-manicure ladies who hang out on the beach and charge around Rp30,000 for a half-hour massage.

## Museum Le Mayeur

One of Sanur's earliest expatriate residents was the Belgian artist Adrien Jean Le Mayeur de Merpres (1880–1958), whose home has remained standing for more than seventy years and is now open to the public as **Museum Le Mayeur** (Mon–Thurs & Sun 8am–3pm, Fri 8am–12.30pm; Rp2000, kids Rp1000); access is via the beachfront just south of Jalan Hang Tuah in north Sanur. Le

---

### Diving in south Bali

Many of the outfits that sell **dive** excursions from shops in Kuta and Nusa Dua have their headquarters in Sanur. It's a good place to learn to dive, or to refresh your memory after a long break, as the local dive sites are close by. More experienced divers usually prefer the dives off the east and north coasts of Bali, either arranging them as day or overnight trips from the south, or basing themselves in accommodation nearer those places. For **general advice** on diving in Bali and Lombok, see p.70.

There is one **divers' recompression chamber** on Bali, located at Sanglah Public Hospital, Jl Kesehatan Selatan 1 in Denpasar (℡0361/227911–4 ext 123).

#### Dive courses and excursions

All the centres listed below run internationally **certificated diving courses**, including four-day PADI Open Water **courses** (US$300–380) and two-day PADI Advanced Open Water courses ($240–280); most also offer introductory dives for non-certificated divers ($60–85, depending on dive site). Prices are competitive, but be sure to check whether equipment rental, insurance and course materials are included. Be wary of any operation offering extremely cheap courses: maintaining diving equipment is an expensive business in Bali so any place offering unusually good rates will probably be cutting corners and compromising your safety.

Despite the proliferation of dive shops, **Sanur's own dive sites**, which lie just a short distance off the coast along the east-facing edge of the reef, are a bit of a disappointment. The coral is not that spectacular here, and visibility is only around 6–10m, with dives ranging from 2–12m, but the area does teem with polychromatic fish, especially parrot fish, angel fish, butterfly fish, groupers and fusiliers. Even though the reef is only about five to ten minutes' boat ride from the beach, most boats can't get to and from the reef at low tide, so check with operators how long you're likely to have for diving. The average cost of a single dive off Sanur is about $50, including guide and full equipment. Accompanying snorkellers pay $12 each, including equipment.

Rates for **one-day dive excursions** to the more interesting reefs elsewhere in Bali (including two tanks but not necessarily all equipment) include: the east-coast reefs and wrecks of Tulamben (see p.290) or Amed (see p.286) for $70; Pulau Menjangan

Mayeur arrived in Bali at the age of 52, and after travelling down from the north of the island chose to settle for a while in the village of Klandis on the outskirts of Denpasar. The teenage Ni Pollok was at this time the chief *legong* dancer of Klandis and considered by many to be the best dancer in the whole of Bali. An outstandingly beautiful young woman, she began to pose regularly for the middle-aged Le Mayeur. Romance blossomed, and by 1935 the two were married. The couple subsequently moved to this house on Sanur beach where he painted and she posed.

When World War II hit Bali, many foreign residents were interned, but Le Mayeur somehow avoided this indignity and stayed put in Sanur, though the couple's house was looted by the Balinese, apparently acting under Japanese orders. Most of the paintings survived the looting, but wartime shortages meant that Le Mayeur had to switch from canvas to sackcloth, and several of these raw-looking works are now on show in the museum. When Le Mayeur died, he left his house and his work to his wife, with the proviso that his paintings and his home would eventually be donated to the Indonesian government. On Ni Pollok's death in 1985, the marital home became the Museum Le Mayeur.

**Le Mayeur's house** dates back to around 1935 and is idyllically located right on the shore, with a compound gate that still opens directly on to the sand.

(Deer Island; p.367) for $95; and the east-coast islands of Nusa Lembongan (p.256) and Nusa Penida (p.260) for $85. **Diving safaris** to Tulamben, Amed, Nusa Penida or Menjangan cost $85–120 per person per day including equipment, accommodation and food.

### Dive centres

All tour agents in south Bali sell diving trips organized by Bali's major **diving operators**, but for specific queries, especially about the difficulty of the dives, you should try to speak directly to one of the dive leaders; in addition, some dive operators only sell direct, not through agents. Some of the most established PADI-certified operators include:

**AquaMarine Diving** Jl Raya Seminyak 2a, Kuta ☏0361/730107, ⓦwww.aquamarine-diving.com. UK-run.

**Bali International Diving Professionals** Jl Danau Poso 26, Blanjong, Sanur ☏0361/285065, ⓦwww.bidp-balidiving.com. Also offers underwater weddings and special dives for disabled divers. UK/Balinese-run.

**Bali Marine Sports** (aka **Bali Pesona Bahari**), Jl Bypass Ngurah Rai, Blanjong, Sanur ☏0361/289308, ⓦwww.bmsdivebali.com.

**Bali Scuba** Jl Danau Poso 40, Blanjong, Sanur ☏0361/288610, ⓦwww.baliscuba.com. Known for its use of nitrox diving, and multi-level dives and courses.

**Crystal Divers** Jl Duyung 25, Semawang, Sanur ☏0361/286737, ⓦwww.crystal-divers.com. One of only a few PADI five-star IDC dive centres in Bali. UK/Danish-run.

**ENA Dive Center** Jl Tirta Ening 1, Blanjong, Sanur ☏0361/288829, ⓦwww.enadive.co.id.

**Tauch Terminal** Jl Danau Tamblingan X / 40-42, Jimbaran☏0361/774504, ⓦwww.tulamben.com. One of only a few PADI five-star IDC dive centres in Bali. Also do dive & sail safaris around Bali and liveaboards to Flores, Sumbawa and Komodo.

**Yos Marine Adventures** Jl Pratama 106, Tanjung Benoa ☏0361/773774, ⓦwww.yosdive.com.

△ Traditional *jukung*, Sanur

Much more interesting than the tattered paintings it contains, the single-storey house is a typical low-roofed wooden building, sumptuously carved with red and gold painted doors, lintels and pediments, and partitioned into rooms by walls that reach only two-thirds of the way up to the ceiling. Le Mayeur did most of his painting in the courtyard garden – a compact tropical wilderness ornamented with stonecarvings, shrines, and tiny *bale*, which features in many of his paintings and photographs. Inside the house, dozens of the artist's **paintings** and charcoal and crayon sketches are displayed, though they are mostly in such bad condition that it's hard to get excited about them, and the relentless gallery of Balinese beauties with dreamy expressions and ridiculous pouts soon gets wearying.

# Eating

Sanur has dozens of inexpensive, almost indistinguishable little tourist-oriented **restaurants** but, surprisingly, lacks the choice of fine-dining experiences found in Kuta and Ubud. You'll find the most authentic Indonesian food at restaurants beyond the main drag, particularly along predominantly residential Jalan Danau Poso in Blanjong. The **night market** that sets up at the Jalan Danau Tamblingan/Jalan Sindhu intersection is another good place for cheap Indonesian dishes, or there's always the takeaway noodles, rice and soups from the handcarts that set up along Jalan Danau Tamblingan after sundown. Many restaurants offer **free pick-ups** for diners within the Sanur area: for these places we've listed the telephone number.

**Alise's Restaurant** part of the *Tamukami Hotel*, Jl Tamblingan 64, Sindhu ☎0361/282510. The genial Belgian proprietor is likely to be on hand to explain the extensive and inventive menu at this thoughtfully run place, which offers both Indonesian and European cuisine and includes several daily specials and set menus. The snapper stuffed with spinach is good (Rp47,500), and there's Balinese champagne plus some well-priced Australian and Balinese wines (from Rp31,000 a glass). Live crooners nightly.

**Bonsai Café** Beachfront walkway just north of *La Taverna* hotel, access off Jl Danau Tamblingan, Sindhu. Breezy seafront café, restaurant and bar (open till late) that serves the usual range of unexceptional nasi goreng, pizza, pasta and seafood (Rp25,000–45,000), plus good-value cocktails. The beach part of the restaurant is dotted with bonsai, and there's a huge nursery of these artfully pruned little trees round the back.

**Café Batu Jimbar** Jl Danau Tamblingan 152, Batujimbar. Best for mid-priced (Rp25,000–35,000) salads, home-baked cakes, breads and herbal teas.

**Le Pirate** Seafront restaurant belonging to the *Segara Village* hotel, Sindhu. The extensive, fairly pricey menu (Rp30,000–65,000) lists lots of wholesome dishes, including plenty of pizzas plus seafood, pasta, and some Indian and Thai specialities.

Occupies a very pleasant seaside location.

**Massimo** Jl Danau Tamblingan 206, Semawang. The home-made *gelato* ice-cream (Rp16,500) at this genuinely South Italian restaurant is outstanding, and there's a very long list of classic and original pizzas (around Rp35,000) plus pasta (Rp27,000–37,000) to tickle your savoury palate beforehand.

**Mezzanine** Part of *Puri Santrian* hotel, beside its gateway at Jl Danau Tamblingan, Semawang. The impressively chic barn-like dining hall, complete with comfy chairs for aperitifs and coffee, adds a touch of class to an unexceptional but decent enough menu of fairly pricey Asian classics (Rp45,000–75,000) that runs to Sumatran beef *rendang* curry, Thai seafood platter with lemongrass, and Manado pan-fried snapper. Live music from around 9.30pm.

**Resto Ming** Jl Danau Tamblingan 105, Semawang ☎0361/281948. Deservedly popular, moderately priced place that's known for its French cuisine (most dishes Rp30,000–65,000). Seafood is a speciality here, particularly lobster thermidor and king prawns, and the restaurant is filled with an outstanding collection of Balinese artefacts, paintings and statues.

**Ryoshi** Jl Danau Tamblingan 150, Batujimbar. As well as a decent selection of sushi, the Sanur branch of Bali's ever-reliable chain of Japanese restaurants has an admirable menu of appetizers that includes spinach and sesame salad, deep-fried tofu, barbecued chicken, and baked aubergine (Rp30,000–65,000).

**Sari Bundo** Jl Danau Poso, Blanjong. Typical, very cheap Masakan Padang place (see p.57 for details) serving spicy Sumatran dishes 24 hours a day.

**Segara Agung** Beachfront next to *Segara Village*, Sindhu ☎0361/288574. With its tables set out on the sand under two sprawling trees, this makes a great spot for a long lunch, though it's fun in the evening, too, and on Saturday nights there's a kids' *legong* dance performance. Offers a huge choice of moderately priced dishes (Rp20,000–45,000) from lobster and *babi guling* to less flashy seafood and Chinese standards. It's run as a cooperative with all profits going to local schools and clinics.

**Telaga Naga** Opposite the *Bali Hyatt* on Jl Danau Tamblingan, Semawang. Atmospheric, very upmarket *Hyatt* restaurant comprising a series of traditional, torchlit pavilions set amidst lotus ponds in gardens across the road from the hotel compound. Specializes in Cantonese and Sichuan

dishes (Rp25,000–110,000) and is famous for its smoked duck, and scallops in blackbean sauce. Nightly 6–11pm.

**The Village** Opposite *La Taverna* hotel, Jl Danau Tamblingan 66, Sindhu. Classy menu of unusual, mid-priced dishes (Rp25,000–45,000) including spicy chicken, cinnamon and pumpkin bisque, delicious European breads, plenty of seafood, and mouthwatering macadamia-nut ice-cream.

**Warung Agung** Jl Danau Tamblingan 97, Sema-wang ☎0361/288029. Cheerful little place serving well-priced tourist fare (Rp14,000–37,000), includ-ing Balinese grilled chicken, plenty of seafood, a *rijsttafel*-style Balinese platter, Indonesian and Swedish specialities (meatballs, pancakes etc), plus special kids' dishes.

**Warung Blanjong** Jl Danau Poso 78, Blanjong. Serves only Balinese dishes, all of them cheap (Rp15,000–30,000), including excep-tionally good veggie delights such as *tipat* (fried vegetables with sticky rice cakes and peanut sauce), veggie nasi campur, and non-veg specialities like *pepes pe pasih* (grilled fish in banana leaves).

# Nightlife and entertainment

There are several **bar-restaurants** along Sanur's beachfront, particularly between *La Taverna* and Jalan Sindhu (in the Sindhu district) and between Jalan Kesumasari and Jalan Duyung (in the Semawang district), some of which stage live music. For **clubs**, however, you'll need to head for Kuta. If you're carousing in Sanur after 10pm you might find it difficult to find a taxi, so ask bar staff to phone Blue Bird Taxis (☎0361/701111) for you.

## Bars and live music

**The Cat and the Fiddle** Opposite the entrance to *Hotel Sanur Beach*, Jl Danau Tamblingan, Sema-wang. Inviting, expat-oriented bar-restaurant serv-ing such hearty classics as Irish bangers and mash (Rp36,000), draught Guinness (from Rp12,000), and even Guinness pie. Holds popular live Irish-music nights every Tuesday from 8pm.

**Jazz Bar & Grille** Komplek Pertokoan Sanur Raya 15, next to *KFC* at the Jl Bypass Ngurah Rai/Jl Hang Tuah crossroads, north Sanur. In the downstairs bar, some of Bali's best jazz, blues and pop bands play live sets every night from about 9.30pm (8pm on Sun, when it's more of a jam session); the atmosphere is mellow but lively and the place attracts a friendly mix of locals, expats and the occasional tourist. The upstairs restaurant serves quality food including a whole range of fish and seafood barbecued over coconut husks – the

grilled tuna is delicious – and a bizarre but tasty banana pizza concoction. There's a pool table, too. Daily 8am–1am.

**Lazer Sports Bar** opposite *Gazebo Hotel* at Jl Danau Tamblingan 68, Sindhu. Rowdy place domi-nated by big-screen TV sports coverage and live music from local MOR bands to fill in the gaps.

**Matahari Beach Bar** Beachfront end of Jl Sindhu, Sindhu. Breezy beachfront bar and restaurant attached to the *Inna Sindhu* hotel, with a pool table and a well-stocked bar. Stages live music and occasional dance performances from 7pm. Closes around 1am.

**Tandjung Sari Beach Bar** Inside the *Tandjung Sari Hotel* compound, Jl Danau Tamblingan 41, Sindhu. Elegant shorefront bar, known for its fiery local brew, the *arak bumbu*, in which rice liquor is spiced up with honey, lime, ginger, garlic and pepper.

**The Trophy** In the *Trophy Pub Centre*, Jl Danau Tamblingan 49, Semawang. Typical expat pub with darts board, pool table and satellite TV. Live music (Wed, Fri & Sat) and Western bar food.

## Entertainment

You can see **Balinese dancing** in or around Sanur on any day of the week, either at one of the restaurants, or by making a trip to dance stages in nearby Denpasar. Check the free weekly pamphlet *What's Up? Bali* (Ⓦ www.whatsup-bali.com), available from hotels and restaurants, for current times and schedules.

To see two of Bali's most spectacular dances, you'll need to venture out. The exuberant shaggy-haired lion dance, the **barong**, and the spectacular "monkey dance", or **kecak**, are performed daily in the Kesiman district on Denpasar's eastern fringes, just 3km by taxi from Sanur's Jalan Hang Tuah (see p.106 for details). All Sanur tour agencies offer trips to these for as much as $25 including return transport, so it's usually cheaper to make your own way there and buy the fixed-price Rp50,000 tickets at the door.

Balinese dance performances are staged free for diners at some **restaurants** on Jalan Danau Tamblingan, with times and details advertised on boards outside: *Penjor* stages nightly shows from 7.30pm, with different dances on three successive nights; or try either *Legong* in Semawang or *Swastika Garden 2* in Batujimbar. Beachfront *Segara Agung* stages a children's *legong* performance every Saturday evening, while on Thursday evenings *Agung and Sue Watering Hole I* hotel and restaurant at Jl Hang Tuah 37 puts on a *legong* show with buffet dinner (Rp60,000; 8pm).

Films are shown daily at the home **cinema** upstairs at the Gazebo Piazza on Jalan Danau Tamblingan (5pm; Rp20,000 includes free popcorn).

# Shopping

Compared to Kuta there are far fewer **shops** to browse in Sanur, though the cheaper souvenir shops and art-market stalls sell much the same range of sarongs, paintings, woodcarvings, wind chimes and the like. Designer boutiques and trendy homeware outlets do feature in moderation but most lack the panache of the better Seminyak shops. There are currently no dedicated **bookstores** in the resort, but you'll find small selections of new books inside the arcades at the *Inna Grand Bali Beach* and the *Hotel Sanur Beach*, at the Gazebo Piazza's Internet centre and in Hardy's supermarket.

**Animale** Next to *Swastika* bungalows on Jl Danau Tamblingan, Batujimbar. One of Bali's most popular womenswear chains, with a good line in well-made, loose-fitting trousers, dresses and tops in both plain cottons and bold prints.

**Art markets** Sanur has three main clusters of "art market" stalls selling cheap cotton clothes, beachwear, sarongs, woodcarvings and bamboo wind chimes: on the northern stretch of Jalan Danau Tamblingan in Sindhu, near *Yulia*, *Luisa* and *Coco* homestays; on the beachfront between Jalan Sindhu and the *Bonsai Café*; and at the beach end of Jalan Segara Ayu in Sindhu.

**Ashitaba** Jl Danau Tamblingan 39, south of the Gazebo Piazza, Sindhu. Part of a small chain of good-quality Balinese basketware shops selling placemats, containers, handbags and more, all made from *ata* grass in Tenganan.

**Bali Harum** Jl Danau Tamblingan 97, Semawang. Balinese chain selling aromatherapy products and attractively presented toiletries, soaps, oils and incense.

**Bé** Opposite *Tandjung Sari* hotel, Jl Danau Tamblingan 80, Sindhu. Beautifully made, quality handicrafts, including palm-leaf photo albums and notebooks of hand-made paper, coconut-shell spoons, bowls and tablemats, and batik wallets.

**The Hanging Tree** Jl Danau Tamblingan 210, Semawang. Phenomenal choice of leather and woven rattan handbags and baskets.

**Hardy's** Jl Danau Tamblingan, Batujimbar. The entire first floor of Sanur's main supermarket is devoted to local handicrafts, with a large, if uninvitingly displayed, range of reasonably priced, fixed-rate souvenirs, from baskets to woodcarvings. Among other things, the ground-floor supermarket sells groceries, pharmacy items, sandals and motorbike helmets. Daily 9am–11pm.

**Mama & Leon** Opposite *Griya Santrian*, at Jl Danau Tamblingan 99a, Sindhu. Elegantly understated mid-priced women's fashions in plain-coloured natural fabrics.

**Nogo Ikat** Jl Danau Tamblingan 100, Sindhu. Pricey but high-quality fabric shop that specializes in *ikat* cloth (also known as *endek*; see p.488) that's sold by the metre as well as being made up

into bedspreads, tablecloths, cushion covers and clothes. They will also tailor-make almost anything on request.

**Pisces** Two branches on Jl Danau Tamblingan, one beside *Alise's Restaurant* inside the *Tamukami Hotel* complex in Sindhu, the other just south of *Resto Ming*, Semawang. Womenswear shop whose trademark clothes are all black and white, in innovative modern batik-style prints.

**Tingklik Kite Shop** Jl Sindhu, Sindhu. Sanur is famous for its fantastic, creative, and often enormous kites, and for its annual inter-village kite festival, which is held on the beach every July. This is one of several places where you can buy charismatic ready-made papier-mâché kite-creatures, and you can get them custom-made here, too.

**Uluwatu** Jl Danau Tamblingan, Sindhu. Balinese chain specializing in hand-made Balinese lace and good-quality womenswear made in white and cream cotton and linen.

# Listings

**Airline offices** Garuda has a sales office and city check-in inside the *Hotel Sanur Beach*, Semawang (Mon–Fri 7.30am–4.30pm, Sat & Sun 9am–1pm; ☎0361/288011), where you can get your boarding pass 4–24 hours in advance. For international airline offices, see p.115; for domestic airlines, see p.33.

**Banks and currency exchange** There are ATMs for Visa, MasterCard and Cirrus dotted all over Sanur. The best rates are from the exchange counters and booths across the resort; see p.47 for advice on how to avoid scams.

**Cultural classes** At *Segara Village* on Jl Segara Ayu, Sindhu ☎0361/288407: woodcarving, flower arranging, batik and Balinese dance courses by arrangement.

**Email and Internet** At Go, opposite *Besakih* hotel at Jl Danau Tamblingan 84; and in the nearby Gazebo Piazza.

**Embassies and consulates** See p.35.

**Hospitals and clinics** The tourist-oriented Sanur Clinic at Jl Danau Tamblingan 27, Sindhu ☎0361/282678 is open 24hr, has English-speaking staff and a dental service and will respond to emergency call-outs. All the major hotels provide 24hr medical service; if yours doesn't, try the doctor at the *Inna Grand Bali Beach* ☎0361/288511, or the *Bali Hyatt* ☎0361/288271. Expats tend to use the two international clinics on the edge of Kuta (see p.134); the nearest hospitals are all in Denpasar (see p.107).

**Library** You can find information on Balinese environmental issues from the resource library at PPLH in

the lobby of *Hotel Santai* at Jl Danau Tamblingan 148, Batujimbar ☎0361/281648, ⊛www.pplhbali.or.id.

**Pharmacies** Several on Jl Danau Tamblingan, as well as one inside Hardy's Supermarket on central Jl Danau Tamblingan.

**Phones** There are plenty of private wartels in central Sanur, and Direct Dial public phones in the basement shopping arcade of the *Inna Grand Bali Beach*.

**Police** The police station is on the Bypass Ngurah Rai in north Sanur, just south of the *Paradise Plaza* hotel ☎0361/288597.

**Post office** Sanur's main post office is on Jl Danau Buyan, Sindhu. There are several small postal agents throughout the resort, including opposite *Respati Bali* hotel at Jl Danau Tamblingan 66, Sindhu, and inside the *Trophy Pub Centre* in Semawang. Most major hotels also offer general postal facilities. You can receive poste restante c/o Agen Pos, Jl Danau Tamblingan 66, Sanur 80228 (Mon–Fri 8.30am–5.30pm, Sat 8.30am–1pm).

**Travel agents** International and domestic flights, plus day-trips and organized tours, from Sumanindo Tour, Jl Danau Tamblingan 22, Sindhu ☎0361/288570; JBA, inside the compound of the *Diwangkara Hotel*, Jl Hang Tuah 54, north Sanur ☎0361/286501, ⓔjbadwkbl@denpasar.wasantara .net.id; Nagasari Tours, Jl Danau Tamblingan 102, Sindhu ☎0361/288096, ⓔnagasari@mega.net .id; and Tunas Tour, next to *Resto Ming*, Jl Danau Tamblingan 107, Semawang ☎0361/288581, ⓔtunas@denpasar.wasantara.net.id.

# Serangan (Turtle) Island

A few hundred metres off southern Sanur's coastline, almost blocking the entrance to Benoa Harbour, lies the sandbar settlement of Pulau Serangan, more commonly referred to as **Serangan Island** or **Turtle Island**. The reefs around Serangan Island used to be popular with local snorkelling tours – and tourists used to visit the turtle-breeding pens on the island, too – but all this changed in the mid-1990s when big chunks of Serangan Island were bought up for a huge real-estate development project, **Bali Turtle Island Development** (BTID). Phase One of this project, which originally centred around a huge hotel resort complex, involved connecting the island to the mainland by a kilometre-long causeway and tripling the size of the island by encircling it with "reclaimed" land made up of dredged sand and limestone. By the summer of 1997, this phase had been successfully completed and Pulau Serangan was no longer an island.

As with several other tourist-oriented mega-projects on Bali (including *Hotel Nirvana* at Tanah Lot), the Serangan development caused a lot of local resentment, partly because it was associated with Tommy Suharto, the unpopular son of the former president, and partly because the land reclamation and destruction of mangrove forest around the island has caused a significant change in local tidal patterns – resulting in much faster **erosion** of Sanur's beaches (whose missing sand has recently been restored, at vast expense). Worse still, however, is the fact that Serangan is the site of an important temple, Pura Sakenan, whose outlook is now dominated by the new causeway. With the downfall of the whole Suharto family, the hotel project came to a standstill halfway through construction and the latest twist in the saga is the plan to build a **casino** on the island. Casinos are illegal in Muslim Indonesia, and gambling is an illegal (though still popular) activity on Bali, but this "island" off the archipelago's only Hindu enclave could be considered a special case – much to the continuing irritation of local groups. At the time of writing, the pro- and anti-development lobbies were still at stalemate, seven years on.

As for Serangan's former tourist attractions, the surrounding **reefs** have all been pulverized into sand or buried beneath landfill, and the **turtles** – which were always a sorry sight anyway – have been moved to a tiny island nearby, though this hasn't stopped south Bali tour operators advertising trips to see the reefs and turtles of Turtle Island.

## Pura Sakenan

On the northwest coast of this small, beleaguered island stands **Pura Sakenan**, which is thought to have been founded in the sixteenth century by the Javanese priest Nirartha (the same man associated with the coastal temples at Tanah Lot, Uluwatu and Rambut Siwi). It figures very importantly in the spiritual life of the people of south Bali, for whom it's a public temple – as opposed to an ancestral or village temple. The **annual festival** held here at Kuningan (see p.64) is a huge event that lasts for several days and attracts throngs of worshippers in full ceremonial gear. At low tide when boats are unable to make the crossing, devotees have traditionally waded across the exposed mud flats from Tanjung Benoa, sarongs hoisted up around their knees and piles of offerings balanced on their heads. It is a scene that recurs in numerous traditional Balinese paintings but is fast being consigned to the history books now that cars, bemos and bikes can drive on to the island.

# Benoa Harbour (Pelabuhan Benoa)

**BENOA HARBOUR** (Pelabuhan Benoa) is located off the end of a long causeway 5km southwest of southern Sanur, and is the arrival and departure point for many sailing trips and tourist **boat services**, including luxury trips to Nusa Lembongan (see p.254), as well as for all Pelni ships from elsewhere in Indonesia, plus cruise liners.

Despite the shared name, there's just over a kilometre of sea between the harbour and the northern tip of the Tanjung Benoa peninsula, and the journey between the two has to be done the long way round, by land. The easiest way to reach Benoa Harbour is by **metered taxi**; it's a short ride of about Rp20,000 from Sanur, or about Rp25,000 from Kuta, plus the Rp1000 causeway toll. Occasional public **bemos** also run here from near Denpasar's Sanglah hospital, and there is also a sporadic return service.

Tickets for **Pelni** boats to other islands must be bought in advance (booking opens three days before departure), either through travel agents or at the Pelni offices in Benoa Harbour (Mon–Fri 8am–4pm, Sat 8am–12.30pm; ☏0361/723689) or Kuta (see p.135); for more on Pelni, see p.32. **Tickets** for tourist boats to Nusa Lembongan and sailing trips can be booked through any tour agent and include transfers to the harbour.

# Travel details

## Bemos and public buses

It's almost impossible to give the frequency with which bemos and public buses run: see Basics, p.49, for details. Journey times given are the minimum you can expect. Only the direct bemo and bus routes are listed; for longer journeys you'll have to go via one of Denpasar's four main bemo terminals (full details on p.95).

**Bualu** to: Denpasar (Tegal terminal; 35min); Denpasar (Batubulan terminal; 1hr); Kuta (20min); Ngurah Rai Airport (20min).

**Denpasar (Batubulan terminal)** to: Amlapura (2hr 30min); Bualu (for Nusa Dua; 1hr); Candi Dasa (1hr); Gianyar (1hr); Klungkung (1hr 20min); Mas (35min); Padang Bai (for Lombok; 1hr 40min); Sukawati (20min); Ubud (50min).

**Denpasar (Kereneng terminal)** to: Sanur (15–25min).

**Denpasar (Tegal terminal)** to: Jimbaran (40min); Kuta (25min); Ngurah Rai Airport (35min); Bualu (for Nusa Dua; 35min); Sanur (25min).

**Denpasar (Ubung terminal)** to: Bedugul (1hr 30min); Gilimanuk (3hr 15min); Jakarta (Java; 24hr); Kediri (for Tanah Lot; 30min); Lalang Linggah (for Balian Beach; 1hr 15min); Medewi (1hr 30min); Mengwi (30min); Singaraja (Sukasada terminal; 3hr); Solo (Java; 15hr); Surabaya (Java; 10hr); Tabanan (35min); Yogyakarta (Java; 15hr).

**Denpasar (Wangaya terminal)** to: Sangeh Monkey Forest (45min).

**Jimbaran** to: Denpasar (Tegal terminal; 40min); Kuta (15min); Ngurah Rai Airport (10min).

**Kuta** to: Bualu (for Nusa Dua; 20min); Denpasar (Tegal terminal; 25min); Jimbaran (15min); Ngurah Rai Airport (10min).

**Ngurah Rai Airport** to: Bualu (for Nusa Dua; 20min); Denpasar (Tegal terminal; 35min); Kuta (10min); Jimbaran (10min).

**Sanur** to: Denpasar (Kereneng terminal; 15–25min); Denpasar (Tegal terminal; 25min).

## Perama shuttle buses

*STO = overnight stopover is sometimes needed*

**Kuta** to: Bedugul (daily; 2hr 30min–3hr); Candi Dasa (3 daily; 3hr); Gili Islands (daily; 9hr 30min); Kuta, Lombok (daily; STO); Lovina (daily; 4hr); Mataram (Lombok; 2 daily; 8hr 30min); Ngurah Rai Airport (3 daily; 30min): Nusa Lembongan (daily; 2hr 30min); Padang Bai (3 daily; 2hr 30min); Sanur (4 daily; 30min); Senggigi (Lombok; 2 daily; 9hr); Ubud (4 daily; 1hr–1hr 30min).

**Sanur** to: Bedugul (daily; 2hr–2hr 30min); Candi Dasa (3 daily; 2hr–2hr 30min); Gili Islands (daily; 9hr); Kuta/Ngurah Rai Airport (5 daily; 30min–1hr); Kuta, Lombok (2 daily; STO); Lovina (daily; 2hr 30min–3hr); Mataram (Lombok; 2 daily; 8hr);

Padang Bai (3 daily; 1hr 30min–2hr); Senggigi (Lombok; 2 daily; 8hr 30min); Ubud (4 daily; 30min–1hr).

## Boats

### Pelni

For more on Pelni, see p.32.

**Denpasar (Benoa Harbour)** Except where indicated, fortnightly services to: Bima (Sumbawa; 3 times a fortnight; 21–31hr); Bitung (Sulawesi; twice a fortnight; 5 days); Ende (Flores; 2 days); Kupang (West Timor; 3 times a month; 26hr); Labuanbajo (Flores; 30hr); Makassar (Sulawesi; 3 times a fortnight; 2–4 days); Maumere (Flores; 3 times a month; 3 days); Surabaya (Java; monthly; 23hr); Waingapu (Sumba; 26hr).

### Others

**Sanur** to: Jungutbatu (Nusa Lembongan; 3 daily; 1hr 30min).

## Domestic flights

**Denpasar (Ngurah Rai Airport)** to: Bima (Sumbawa; 1–2 daily; 1hr 15min); Ende (Flores; daily; 2hr); Jakarta (Java; 15 daily; 1hr 40min); Jayapura (West Papua; 4 weekly; 5hr 10min); Kupang (West Timor; 3–4 daily; 1hr 35min); Labuanbajo (Flores; 4 weekly; 2hr 20min); Makassar (Sulawesi; daily; 1hr 10min); Mataram (Lombok; 8 daily; 30min); Maumere (Flores; 6 weekly; 2hr 20min); Medan (Sumatra; 5 daily; 4hr 30min); Surabaya (Java; 3 daily; 45min); Waingapu (Sumba; 4 weekly; 1hr 50min); Yogyakarta (Java; 3 daily; 1hr 10min).

# ② Ubud and around

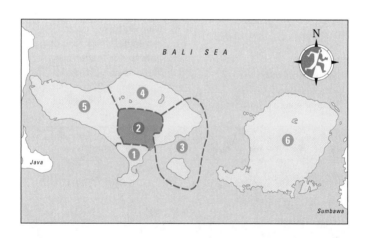

CHAPTER TWO # Highlights

* **Bali Bird Park** A vast and beautifully landscaped aviary, with elusive Bali starlings in residence. See p.174

* **Sukawati Art Market** A great place for bargain-priced baskets, sarongs, paintings, fabrics, woodcarvings, parasols and wind chimes. See p.176

* **Neka Art Museum, Ubud** The finest collection of Balinese paintings on the island. See p.198

* **A walk through the rice-paddies** Classic vistas of emerald terraces and coconut groves, framed by distant volcanoes. See p.196

* **Traditional dance performances** Gods and demons flirt and fight by torchlight. See p.210

* **Cultural classes** Return home with a new skill in batik painting, gamelan, traditional dance or Balinese cookery. See p.214

* **Gunung Kawi** Impressive eleventh-century rock-cut royal tombs in the valley of the sacred Pakrisan River. See p.224

△ Rock-cut "tombs" at Gunung Kawi

# Ubud and around

The inland village of **Ubud** and its surrounding area form Bali's cultural heartland, home to a huge proliferation of temples, museums and art galleries, where Balinese dance shows are staged nightly and a wealth of arts and crafts studios provide the most absorbing shopping on the island. It's also surrounded by a stunning physical environment – a lush landscape watered by hundreds of streams (including Bali's longest waterway, the Ayung River), with archetypal terraced paddy vistas at every turn – all of which gives plenty of scope for leisurely hikes and bicycle rides. The route to Ubud **north of Denpasar** takes you through a string of craft villages dubbed the "tourist corridor", a great shopping experience where you can also watch craftspeople at work. You'll need to venture out to the villages around Ubud, however, for a sense of old-fashioned Bali – to the classic adobe-walled settlements of **Penestanan** and **Peliatan**, for example, or to **Pejeng,** which still boasts relics from its Bronze Age inhabitants.

**Ubud** and all the other villages described in this chapter lie within the boundaries of **Gianyar district**, formerly an ancient kingdom. (Gianyar itself, 10km east of Ubud, lies on the main route into east Bali and is described in Chapter 3, as are all the villages east of the T-junction at Sakah.) Roads within the Ubud region tend to run north–south down river valleys, making it very difficult in places to travel east–west; this chapter reflects that restriction, and follows the main bemo routes.

Ubud has always played second fiddle to the royal and political centre of Gianyar, and it has only been with the advent of mass tourism in the last few decades that it has assumed such a dominant role. Ubud's development is closely bound to the fortunes of the **Sukawati family**, who for centuries ruled over much of Gianyar regency from their court, 10km south of Ubud. The Sukawati royal household was established in the early eighteenth century by **Dewa Agung Anom**, who called in musicians, dancers, puppeteers, artists and sculptors from all over the island to live and work at his court. This was the foundation of the strong **artistic** heritage of the area, and over the next two hundred years, Dewa Agung Anom's like-thinking descendants established satellite courts in Peliatan, Ubud and Singapadu, among others. Gianyar was one of only two kingdoms to remain intact after the **Dutch** takeover in 1908, and it became the island's centre for royal patronage of the arts, with Ubud, in particular, flourishing under the rule of Cokorda Gede Agung Sukawati. The 1930s saw the arrival of a bevy of expat artists in Ubud, injecting a new vigour into the region's **arts and crafts**, which have thrived ever since.

# North of Denpasar

The stretch of road running 13km **north of Denpasar** to Ubud has become something of a sightseeing attraction in itself due to the almost unbroken string of **arts- and crafts-producing villages** that line its course. Over the last decade, these villages have mushroomed so dramatically that they now merge into each other, coalescing into one extended shopping experience; but despite the obvious commercialization, these villages all have genuine histories as centres of refined artistic activity. Most were renowned as specialists of a certain craft, and this trend continues today: **Mas**, for example, is the place for woodcarvings, **Celuk** for silverwork, and **Batubulan** for stone sculptures.

Nearly all the craft villages described below lie on the main bemo route between Denpasar's Batubulan terminal and Ubud. With private transport they are easily visited on a day-trip from Ubud or the southern resorts; access from Sanur is particularly easy, with Batubulan less than 10km north of its northern outskirts.

## Batubulan

Barely distinguishable from the northeastern suburbs of Denpasar, **BATUBU-LAN** acts as the capital's public-transport interchange for all bemos heading east and northeast, but it's also an important village in its own right, home of the most famous *barong* **dance troupes**, and respected across the island for its superb stonecarvers. There's also a **bird park** and a **reptile park** here.

The village is strung out over 2.5km along the main road, defined by the bemo station in the south and the huge **Barong statue** at the Singapadu/Celuk junction in the north. Beyond the Barong statue, along the minor road to Singapadu, the northern stretch of the village – known as **Tegaltamu** – is the most interesting bit, and it's here that you'll find the shops selling Batubulan's finest **stonecarvings**, displayed to their best advantage in disorderly ranks along the roadside. Local sculptors specialize in free-standing images and use three main **stone types**. The distinctive rough grey lava stone, *paras*, is good quality, quite hard, and quite expensive: it's popular for outdoor pieces, as its texture gains character from exposure to the elements. The smooth, friable, grey, yellow

---

### Batubulan bemo terminal

Batubulan's **bemo station** is at the far southern end of the village and has clearly signed bays for each destination. Bemos across **Denpasar** to the Kereneng or Ubung terminals (see plan on p.98) cost Rp3500. Chocolate-brown bemos to **Ubud** (50min; Rp7000; last departure 6pm) travel via Celuk, Sukawati and Mas. Destinations east of Batubulan are served by both dark-blue bemos and (cheaper) buses, which run through Gianyar, Klungkung, **Padang Bai** (bemos Rp20,00; last departure 5.15pm) and **Candi Dasa** (buses Rp10,000; last departure 6.10pm), most on their way to **Amlapura** (buses Rp12,000; last departure 5.15pm). Buses also run to **Kintamani** (Rp10,000; last departure 4pm) via Tegalalang, and to **Singaraja** (Rp10,000; last departure 3pm). Hourly white Damri buses serve **Nusa Dua**, via the western edge of Sanur, the eastern outskirts of Kuta and the airport (Rp4000 flat fee).

The bemo terminal is transformed into a **night market** every evening, with a good selection of street food and food carts.

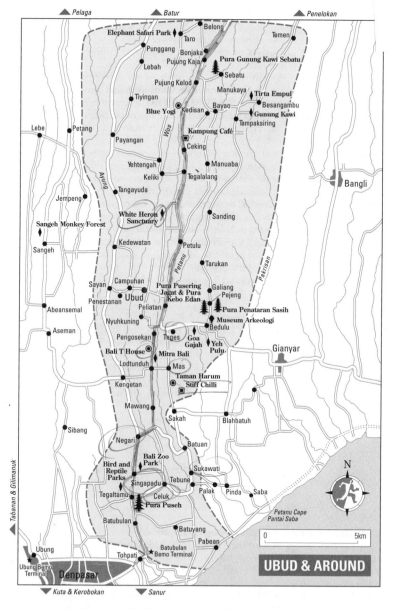

Belong
Elephant Safari Park
Taro
Punggang
Bonjaka          Temen
Lebah          Pujung Kaja          Pura Gunung Kawi Sebatu
Pujung Kelod          Sebatu
Tiyingan          Manukaya          Tirta Empul
Blue Yogi          Kedisan          Bayao          Besangambu
          Gunung Kawi
Payangan          Tampaksiring
Lebe     Petang
          Kampung Café
          Ceking
Yehtengah          Manuaba
Keliki          Tegalalang
Tangayuda
Jempeng          Bangli
          White Heron          Sanding
Sangeh Monkey Forest     Sanctuary
Sangeh     Kedewatan          Petulu
          Tarukan
Sayan     Campuhan     Galiang
          Pura Pusering     Pejeng
Abeansemal     Penestanan     Jagat & Pura
          Kebo Edan          Pura Penataran Sasih
     Peliatan          Museum Arkeologi
Aseman     Nyuhkuning          Bedulu
     Pengosekan     Teges     Goa     Yeh
Bali T House          Gajah     Pulu
     Lodtunduh     Mitra Bali          Gianyar
          Mas
Kengetan          Taman Harum
          Stiff Chilli
     Mawang
Sibang          Sakah     Blahbatuh

     Negari          Batuan
          Bali Zoo
Bird and     Park
Reptile          Sukawati
Parks     Singapadu
Tegaltamu     Celuk     Tebune
     Pura Puseh     Palak     Pinda     Saba
Batubulan
          Batuyang     Petanu Cape
               Pantai Saba
          Batubulan     Pabean
Ubung     Tohpati     Bemo Terminal
Ubung Bemo
Terminal     **Denpasar**          0          5km

          **UBUD & AROUND**

Wos     Ayung     Petanu     Pakrisan

N

◀ Tabanan & Gilimanuk

and pink sandstones, including the attractively stripey ones from Lombok, also age well and work fine for both outdoor and indoor sculptures, though they are quite fragile. Slinky white Javanese limestone can look stunning, but only if kept inside, as it turns black outdoors. As with all other artistic disciplines in Bali, you'll find that the stonecarvers of Batubulan tend to copy each others' ideas a lot, and the same pieces recur in most workshops. Top subjects include demons, deities, mythological and religious figures, as well as animals, people, and an increasing number of primitive and abstract works.

There are plenty of **outlets** to browse and it's hard to distinguish between them, but if you need a focal point, start opposite the entrance to the Bali Bird Park (see below) and work south. A number of places will organize shipping, but be prepared for a huge bill; the minimum container size is one cubic metre, which will set you back at least US$200, even to Australia. In among the stonecarving outlets, you'll also come across a number of **woodcarving** places specializing in elegant antique-style furniture, doors and window frames.

### Pura Puseh

As you'd expect in a village so renowned for its fine carvings, the main temple, **Pura Puseh**, 200m east off the main road in the north of the village (follow the signs for the *barong* dance held next door), is exuberantly decorated. It's built to an unusual design that includes a five-tiered gateway tower inspired by Indian religious architecture, and a number of Buddha images not normally associated with Bali's Hindu temples. The rest of the icons and decorations, however, are characteristically and flamboyantly Balinese: a grimacing Bhoma head overlooks the main gateway and, to his right, the god Wisnu poses proudly astride a bull; to the right of him, Siwa stands ankle-deep in skulls and wears a string of them around his neck, while majestic elephant torsos protrude from the central stairway balustrade.

### Traditional dance shows

The plot adjacent to Pura Puseh is occupied by a purpose-built **barong dance** stage, where, every morning of the year (9.30–10.30am; Rp50,000), the local dance troupes perform the spectacular drama of the fight between good and evil, as represented by the shaggy-haired lion-like creature, the Barong Ket, and the macabre widow-witch Rangda. It's quite feasible (and certainly cheaper) to get here by public bemo (see below), but most spectators come on tours arranged through agents in Kuta, Sanur or Ubud.

If you come under your own steam, consider attending the well-regarded show at the Denjulan Barong and Kris stage instead (daily 9.30–10.30am; Rp50,000), whose dancers are said to be the best in the region. The Denjulan stage is 300m south down the main Denpasar road from the Pura Puseh junction.

Batubulan dancers also put on nightly performances of the **kecak dance** in a double bill with the **fire dance** (daily 6.30–7.30pm; Rp50,000) at the Barong Sahadewa stage on Jalan SMKI, signed off the main Denpasar road about 500m south of the Pura Puseh junction.

### Bali Bird Park and Bali Reptile Park

Both the Bali Bird Park and the Bali Reptile Park (not to be confused with the vastly inferior reptile park in Mengwi) are fun places for children and fairly interesting for adults, too. The parks are right next door to each other, about 500m north of the Barong statue at the Singapadu/Celuk intersection, then west about 400m, or about 3.5km northwest of Batubulan bemo terminal. All bemos between Batubulan and Ubud or Gianyar can drop you at the intersection. There's a good but expensive **restaurant** inside the Bird Park, or you can get cheap food at a tiny warung about 30m outside the car park.

The **Bali Bird Park** (**Taman Burung**; daily 8am–6pm; $9.50, kids $4.50, family ticket $23.50) is beautifully laid out with ponds, waterfalls, pavilions, flowers and an impressive array of birds, all identified with English-language labels. Highlights include various birds of paradise (most of them from Irian

Jaya), bright scarlet egrets, the weird-looking rhino hornbill, a massive pair of cassowaries and iridescent blue Javanese kingfishers. You shouldn't miss this rare chance to see the fluffy white Bali starling, Bali's only endemic bird and a severely endangered species (it's thought there may be as few as four left in the wild); see the box on p.365 for more. There are also a couple of non-avian attractions in the shape of a pair of two-metre-long Komodo dragons.

All the creatures at the **Bali Reptile Park** (**Rimba Reptil**; daily 9am–6pm; $8, kids $4) are informatively labelled: look out for the green tree pit viper, which is very common in Bali, and very dangerous, as well as for the astonishing eight-metre-long reticulated python, thought to be the largest python in captivity in the world. There are Komodo dragons here too, and visitors are invited to pick up and cuddle one of the park's scaly green iguanas.

## Singapadu and the back road to Ubud

The main road from Denpasar divides at Batubulan's Barong statue roundabout, the principal artery and bemo routes veering right (east) to Celuk (see below), and the left-hand (north) prong narrowing into a scenic **back road**. This runs past the Bali Bird Park and on through very traditional villages as far as Sayan, a few kilometres west of Ubud, before continuing to Payangan and eventually to Kintamani.

Just over 1km north of the T-junction, you'll pass through the charming village of **SINGAPADU**, a classic central Bali settlement of house and temple compounds that hide behind low adobe walls and effusive roadside shrubbery. Some of Bali's most expert mask-carvers come from this village, but as most of them work only on commissions from temples and dance troupes, there's no obvious commercial face to the local industry. Singapadu is also the site of the **Bali Zoo Park** (daily 8am–6pm; $8.50, kids $4.25), which is home to a walk-in aviary as well as a range of creatures – including crocodiles, cassowaries, lions, tigers and Komodo dragons – mostly housed in depressingly bare enclosures.

Some 13km north of Singapadu the road runs through the village of **SAYAN**, located in the spectacular Ayung River valley, site of several superb hotels (see Ubud accommodation, p.192) and a couple of **white-water rafting** centres (see p.126). To reach Ubud from Sayan, follow the narrow right-hand turning off the main road, which will take you 3km down a winding route via Penestanan to Campuhan, where you turn right for Ubud.

For a more direct, quieter and even more scenic route to Ubud, turn east off the Sayan road a couple of kilometres north of Singapadu, in the heart of the kite-making and ceramic-egg-painting village of **NEGARI**. This route soon takes you over the wide Wos River and on through beautiful countryside via the art galleries and mask-making workshops of **LODTUNDUH**, before arriving in Pengosekan near the Agung Rai Museum of Art on the southern edge of Ubud. The Mitra Bali **fair-trade arts and crafts** NGO has its headquarters in Lodtunduh, on Jalan Gunung Abang in *banjar* Lodsema (Mon–Fri 8am–5pm; ☎0361/295010, ⓦwww.mitrabali.com), and encourages visitors to learn more about its work, meet some of its members, and visit its small on-site shop (see Basics, p.45, for more info). There's some appealingly affordable little *Bali T House* **villas** for rent on the northern edge of the village (☎0812/365 9398, ⓦwww.tonysthouse.com/balit; ❻), which have been ecologically designed for second-homers by the American architect Tony Gwilliam and are quite simple wood-and-thatch constructions, peaceful and cosy, with kitchen facilities, living areas, pretty views and use of a pool; they're about 3km south of Ubud.

# Celuk

Strung out along the main road, Jalan Raya, just east of Batubulan, is **CELUK**, known as the "silver village" because it's a major centre for **jewellery** production. Local silversmiths have extended their homes to include workshops and salerooms and welcome both retail and wholesale customers, though designs are often less innovative than in Kuta's shops. The best-priced Celuk outlets are along Jalan Jagaraga (a back road to Singapadu), which runs north from the western end of Jalan Raya; among dozens of possibilities, you could try Ketut Sunak at no. 28, which has a workshop at the back. The more upmarket Ana's ll, signed off the eastern end of Jalan Raya, also has a good reputation. Batubulan–Ubud **bemos** pass through Celuk, but be warned that the shops and workshops are spread out over a three-kilometre stretch.

## Sukawati and around

The lively market town of **SUKAWATI**, 4km east of Celuk, is an important commercial centre for local villagers and a chief stop on the tourist arts and crafts shopping circuit, especially convenient for anyone reliant on public transport: Batubulan–Ubud **bemos** stop right in front of the central market.

Sukawati's chief draw is its **art market** (Pasar Seni), at the heart of the village, which trades every day from dawn till dusk inside a traditional covered two-storey building on the main road, Jalan Raya Sukawati. Here you'll find a tantalizing array of artefacts, paintings, fabrics, clothing and basketware, piled high on stalls that are crammed together so tightly you can barely walk between them. Sarongs and lengths of *ikat* cloth are excellent buys, as are ceremonial temple parasols and huge decorative fans made from gold-stamped *perada* cloth. If you can't face the scrum, there are several good basket shops outside, on Jalan Raya, just to the north.

Sukawati is also famous for its *wayang kulit* **shadow puppet makers and performers**. *Wayang kulit* shows are still very popular across the island, and puppet masters (*dalang*) are often commissioned to entertain villagers at temple festivals with performances of Hindu legends such as the *Mahabharata* that run right through the night. The puppets (*wayang*) they use are made out of very thin animal hide, perforated to let the light shine through in intricate patterns, and designed to traditional profiles that are instantly recognizable to a Balinese audience (for more, see p.478). Several of Sukawati's *dalang* make, and perform with, both *wayang kulit* puppets and the wooden *wayang golek* puppets, selling their creations from workshops inside their homes: **I Wayan Nartha** (☏0361/299080) has a shop on Jalan Padma (the road that runs east off Jalan Raya, one block south of the Pasar Seni); and **I Wayan Mardika** (☏0361/299646) sells from inside his home on Jalan Yudisthira, the road that runs parallel to the east of Jalan Raya, reached by walking east down Jalan Ciung Wanara (opposite the Pasar Seni) and then walking left for about 100m. Both workshops are in the *banjar* of Babakan and are signed off Jalan Raya Sukawati.

There are several cheap **warung** on Jalan Raya Sukawati, including the tiny *Warung Vegetarian Karuna Vittala*, about 1km north of the Pasar Seni on the east side of the road, which is run by a follower of the famous Indian guru Sai Baba and serves only vegetarian food, including nasi campur made with soya products instead of meat, and various fruit and vegetable juices.

### Batuan

Northern Sukawati merges into southern **BATUAN**, another ribbon-like roadside development, which was the original home of the **Batuan style of**

**painting** and is now a commercial centre for all the main Balinese styles. The Batuan style first evolved in the 1930s when a group of young villagers, notably Ida Bagus Made Togog and Ida Bagus Made Wija, started experimenting with ink-washed paintings on black backgrounds, peopling their visions with dozens of figures cowering beneath ominously dense forests. Later, the artists changed to gouache, and then acrylics, but the atmosphere remained just as forbidding and the canvases just as congested and full of minute detail, creating a sense of frenetic activity.

The public face of modern Batuan is now dominated by **galleries**: huge emporia line the main road, while smaller studios hide within those houses in the traditional core of the village, west of the main road, that hang "painter" signboards above their gateways. One of the larger, quality galleries is the **I Wayan Bendi Gallery**, on the west side of the main road, named after a contemporary artist whose Batuan-style pictures have been exhibited all over the world as well as in Ubud's Neka Art Museum. A few examples of his work hang in the gallery (not for sale) along with a sizeable collection by other artists. Another worthwhile if undeniably commercial gallery is the sprawling **Dewa Putu Toris**, 250m west off the southern end of the main Batuan–Ubud road in the *banjar* of Tengah: turn west at the *raksasa* (demon-giant) statue and follow the signs. Just before the gallery you'll pass Batuan's main temple, the **Pura Desa–Pura Puseh** (dawn to dusk; donation), which serves as both the ancestral and village temple; you can tell from the elaborate gold-painted woodwork that this is both an artistic village and a wealthy one.

At the northern limit of Batuan, a plump stone **statue** of a well-fed baby Brahma (officially known as Brahma Rare and unofficially as the Fat Baby statue) marks the Sakah turn-off to Blahbatuh and points east (see p.236), while the main road continues north.

## Mas and Teges

Long established as a major **woodcarving** centre, **MAS** is a rewarding place both to browse and to buy, but be warned that it stretches 5km from end to end.

The woodcarvers of Mas gained great inspiration from the Pita Maha arts movement during the 1930s (see p.193), which encouraged the carving of secular subjects as well as the more traditional masks and religious images. Today, the range of carvings on display in the Mas shops is enormous; you'll find superbly imaginative portraits of legendary creatures and erotic human figures, alongside tacky cats, dogs and fish. Some of the woodcarving outlets in Mas are managed by the carvers and their families, while others buy their pieces in from less commercially minded villagers.

A good place to start is the studio of one of Bali's most famous woodcarving families, the **Nyana Tilem Gallery**, located approximately halfway along the Mas–Ubud road, about 2km north of the baby Brahma statue. Born in 1912, Ida Bagus Nyana (also spelt Njana) was one of the most prolific and innovative craftsmen of the 1930s and 1940s, closely associated with the Pita Maha arts movement, and credited with introducing the sleek, simple and slightly surreal style of elongated figures that's now so popular across the island (for more, see p.486). The Mas gallery was founded by Ida Bagus Nyana's son, Ida Bagus Tilem, who has continued the quest for new forms and is especially renowned for highly expressive pieces using gnarled and twisted wood. It has plenty of works by father and son on show, alongside a huge range of other carvings, including valuable collectors' items from the 1930s and 1940s, plus plenty of more affordable pieces created by contemporary woodcarvers working for the gallery.

The large and impressive **Tantra Gallery**, housed in two buildings on either side of the main road, about 500m south of Nyana Tilem (1.5km north of the baby Brahma statue), is run by Ida Bagus Tilem's younger brother, Tantra. All the works sold here are contemporary, mostly high-quality interpretations of fairly standard subjects, such as elegantly tapered hands, masks, chess sets and weeping Buddhas; prices are on the high side, but everything is finely crafted. The Tantra compound on the east side of the road also contains a delightful small hotel (see below).

### Practicalities

All Batubulan–Ubud **bemos** zip through Mas. At its northern end, Mas runs into the village of Teges, which is about 2.5km from Peliatan on the outskirts of Ubud. The charming *Taman Harum Cottages* (☎0361/975567, ⓦwww.taman-nharumcottages.com; ❼) is the only **place to stay** in Mas, located in the compound of Tantra Gallery, at the southern end of the village. The standard rooms in its small two-storey block are pleasant if unexceptional, but the two-storey villas and suites are delightful and great value, affording fine ricefield views from upstairs; they're especially recommended for families with children. All rooms are air-conditioned, there's a pool and a restaurant, free transport to Ubud, and a popular programme of **cultural classes**, including cooking, woodcarving, batik painting and making temple offerings. Five hundred metres south along the main road from *Taman Harum*, a three-hundred-metre side-road leads to the *Stiff Chilli* **restaurant** (daily 8am–6pm), which overlooks a glorious ricefield panorama, serves wood-fired pizzas, and offers free use of the swimming pool to anyone who spends Rp20,000 or more on food and drink.

### Museum Rudana, Teges

Sandwiched between Mas to the south and Peliatan to the north, the main attraction in the woodcarving village of **TEGES** is the **Museum Rudana** (daily 9am–5pm; Rp20,000), 800m north of the Nyana Tilem gallery in Mas and about 1.5km south of the junction with Jalan Peliatan, a ten-minute bemo ride from central Ubud (Rp2000) or an hour's walk. The museum focuses on an overview of **Balinese painting**, from Kamasan-style traditional calendars through Batuan-style and Ubud-style pictures to contemporary works. Many of the artists represented here also feature in the Neka Art Museum (see p.198) and the Agung Rai Museum of Art (see p.206); there's more information on the history of Balinese art on p.481. The best thing about this collection – apart from the inspiring rice-paddy views out of the picture windows – is its unusual approach to captions, each of which discusses the subject of the painting (eg the Balinese attitude to the sea) rather than the artistic style. The collection of contemporary work is especially good, and includes paintings by Nyoman Gunarsa (see p.243), Made Budhiana and Nyoman Erawan, all of whom are associated with the influential Sanggar Dewata Indonesia style, best described as Balinese Hindu abstract expressionism, which has been the dominant form of modern Balinese painting since the 1970s.

# Ubud

Ever since the German artist Walter Spies arrived here in 1928, **UBUD** has been a magnet for any tourist with the slightest curiosity about Balinese arts. It is now a fully fledged resort, visited by nearly every holidaymaker on the island, even if only as part of a day-trip to the much-publicized Monkey Forest.

Although it's fashionable to characterize Ubud as the "real" Bali, especially in contrast with Kuta, it bears little resemblance to a typical Balinese village. Cappuccino cafés, riverside bungalows and craft shops crowd its central marketplace, chic expat homes occupy some of the most panoramic locations, and sidestreets are dotted with spas and alternative treatment centres. It even hosts an annual literary festival, the Ubud Writers and Readers festival (Wwww .ubudwritersfestival.com), held in October. There is major development along the central **Jalan Monkey Forest** (officially known as **Jalan Wanara Wana**), a kilometre-long strip of hotels, restaurants, tour agencies and souvenir shops, and the village has expanded to take in the neighbouring hamlets of **Campuhan**, **Penestanan**, **Sanggingan**, **Nyuhkuning**, **Padang Tegal**, **Pengosekan** and **Peliatan**. Yet the traditional village of dancers and craftspeople is still apparent, and the atmosphere remains undeniably seductive – an appealing blend of ethnic integrity and tourist-friendly comforts. The people of Ubud and adjacent villages really do still paint, carve, dance and make music, and religious practices here are so rigorously observed that hardly a day goes by without there being some kind of festival celebrated in the area. The surrounding countryside and traditional hamlets give ample opportunity for exploration on foot or by bike, and **shopping** tends to become a major pastime, too, with Balinese carvers and painters selling their wares at every corner and a proliferation of outlets run by expat fashion designers and artists. But, above all, it's the **restaurants** and **accommodation** that set Ubud apart from Bali's other tourist centres: mouthwateringly imaginative menus are the norm here, and most hotels and homestays make full use of their charming locations. An increasing number of travellers are now choosing to stay in Ubud for the duration of their holiday, using it as a convenient base from which to explore nearby attractions (such as Goa Gajah, Pejeng and Gunung Kawi), as well as sights a little further afield: the volcanic peak of Gunung Batur and its crater lake are just 40km north of Ubud; local tour operators offer sunrise treks up Gunung Agung; and it takes less than two hours on a tourist shuttle bus or bemo to reach the east-coast beach of Candi Dasa.

## Some history

Ubud became a royal seat only towards the end of the nineteenth century, when a member of the royal household in Sukawati, **Cokorda Gede Sukawati**, distinguished himself in battle and was made a *punggawa* (ruling nobleman), choosing to establish his court at Ubud. When the Gianyar kingdom disintegrated a few years later, Cokorda Gede Sukawati was powerful enough to fight off encroaching armies and Ubud became one of only three former districts of Gianyar (along with Peliatan and Tegalalang) to assert their independence, under the protection of the raja of Karangasem. Cokorda Gede Sukawati grew in power, continuing to extend his lands, and in 1893 helped the Gianyar royal family wrest back much of their former territory. Ubud's allegiances were once again firmly tied to those of Gianyar. In 1900, when Gianyar finally acknowl-

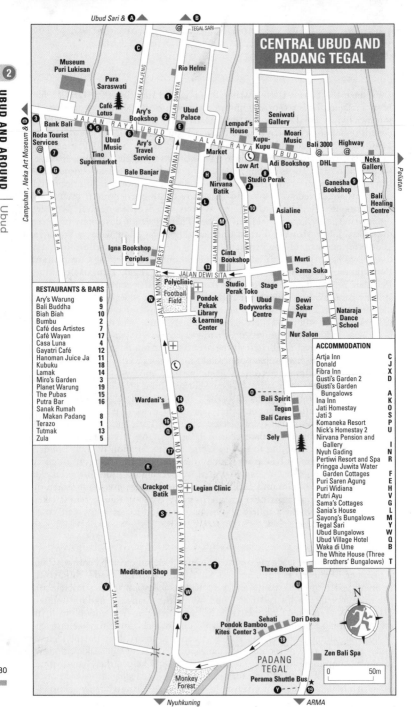

edged that it could no longer hold out against the constant incursions from neighbouring kingdoms, and asked for Dutch protection, Ubud too came under the protectorate of the Netherlands Indies government.

With no more wars to worry about, the Sukawati family and the people of Ubud were able to get on with the business of making carvings and paintings and refining their dancing and gamelan skills. Cokorda Gede's son, **Cokorda Gede Agung Sukawati** (1910–78) focused his energy on the cultivation of the arts, and began actively to encourage foreign artists to live in his district. The most significant of these early visitors was a German artist called **Walter Spies**, who established himself in the hamlet of Campuhan on the western border of Ubud in 1928 (see p.198). Over the next nine years, Spies introduced influential new ideas to Ubud's already vibrant artistic community and

## Moving on from Ubud

Numerous **shuttle buses** run out of Ubud every day to destinations all over Bali, and there's a cheaper but more time-consuming network of public **bemos**, too.

### By shuttle bus

Bali's ubiquitous **shuttle bus** operator, Perama, has pretty much cornered the market from Ubud and most tour operators in town only sell tickets for Perama buses. The only alternative is the transfer service offered by transport touts and some losmen and hotels, though this generally works out more expensive unless you have a full car-load. **Perama**'s head office is inconveniently located in Padang Tegal at the far southern end of Jalan Hanoman (☎0361/973316, ⊛www.peramatour.com), but the buses do pick-ups from their tour operator agents in the centre, including from Ary's Business and Travel Service just west of the market on Jalan Raya Ubud (☎0361/973130). Perama buses are non-air-con and run to most of the major tourist destinations on Bali, as well as to Lombok, including **Kuta** and the **airport** (Rp20,000), **Padang Bai** and **Candi Dasa** (Rp30,000), **Lovina** (Rp50,000), and the **Gili Islands** (Rp180,000); see "Travel details" on p.224 for a full list. For Pemuteran, Gilimanuk and other parts of **northwest Bali**, take a shuttle bus to Lovina and then change on to a westbound bemo for the last coastal stretch.

### By bemo

All **bemos** depart at least half-hourly from about 6am until around 2pm, then at least hourly until about 5pm. They all leave from near the central crossroads on Jalan Raya Ubud; the east- and southbound bemos leave from the central market, and the north- and westbound ones from in front of the tourist information office. The **Ubud–Tegalalang–Pujung–Kintamani** route is usually served by brown bemos, while the **Ubud–Campuhan–Kedewatan–Payangan–Kintamani** bemos are generally either brown or bright blue. Frequent turquoise or orange bemos go to **Gianyar** (via Goa Gajah), where you can make connections to **Padang Bai** (for Lombok), **Candi Dasa**, **Singaraja** and **Lovina**. Any journey south, to Kuta or Sanur, involves an initial bemo ride to Denpasar's **Batubulan** station, plus at least one cross-city connection unless you take the Batubulan–Nusa Dua bus, which makes drops on the western fringe of Sanur and at the eastern edge of Kuta. To reach western Bali and Java by bemo, you'll need to take an equally convoluted route via Batubulan as well.

### Boat and airline tickets

Many Ubud travel agents sell Perama **bus and boat tickets** for the Gili Islands and Lombok, as well as international and domestic **airline tickets**. The easiest way to get **to the airport** from Ubud is by shuttle bus (Rp20,000 per person); transport touts charge about Rp100,000 per car. Airport information is on p.114.

**ACCOMMODATION**

| | |
|---|---|
| Alam Jiwa | bb |
| Alam Sari | A |
| Amandari | C |
| Ananda Cottages | E |
| Artja Inn | T |
| Family Guest House | W |
| Four Seasons Resort Bali | N |
| Garden View Cottages | Y |
| Gusti's Garden 2 | M |
| Gusti's Garden Bungalows | P |
| Hotel Tjampuhan | O |
| Klub Kokos | B |
| Kori Agung Bungalow | I |
| Londo 2 | H |
| Londo Ricefield Bungalows | S |
| Melati Cottages | R |
| Penestanan Bungalows | Q |
| Rona | V |
| Sari Bungalows | aa |
| Sayan Terrace | K |
| Sri Sunari | U |
| Sunrise Villas | D |
| Swasti 2 Hideaway | |
| Nyuhkuning | Z |
| Taman Bebek | J |
| Taman Indrakila | F |
| Taman Rahasia | L |
| Tegal Sari | X |
| Waka di Ume | G |

White Heron Sanctuary

Bangkiang Sidem, Keliki &

Payogan

Payangan and Gunung Batur

*Petanu*

JALAN ANDONG

Mitra Bali Fair Trade

Police

KUTUH

JALAN SUWETA

SAMBAHAN

see "Central Ubud" map for detail

Threads of Life

Ubud Sari

JALAN KAJENG

Ubud Palace

Museum Puri Lukisan

JALAN RAYA UBUD

UBUD

*Wos Timor*

Neka Art Museum

SANGGINGAN

Pura Dalem

Ibah Spa

CAMPUHAN

Ubud Clinic

*Wos Barat*

JALAN RAYA SANGGINGAN

Bali Sunrise 2001

LUNGSIAKAN

Design Unit

JALAN RAYA CAMPUHAN

Symon's Studio

Pura Gunung Lebah

Museum Blanco

Dewa Bharata Bungalows

*Blangsuh*

Sobek

PENESTANAN

KEDEWATAN

Bali Adventure Tours

*Ayung*

SAYAN

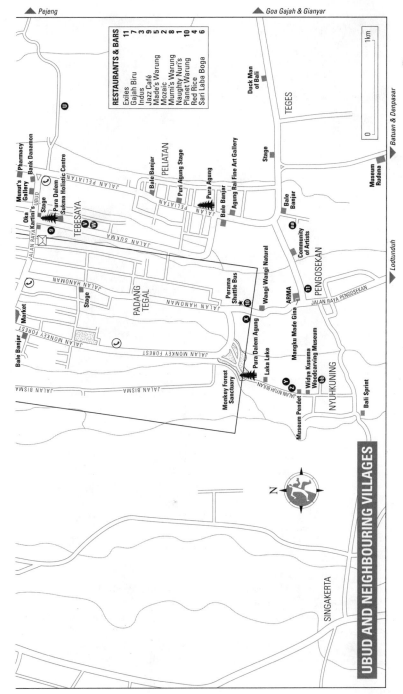

UBUD AND NEIGHBOURING VILLAGES

N

SINGAKERTA

NYUHKUNING

Bali Sprint
Widya Kusuma Woodcarving Museum
Museum Pendet
Mangku Made Gina
Laka Leke
Pura Dalem Agung

Monkey Forest Sanctuary

JALAN BISMA
JALAN MONKEY FOREST
JALAN HANOMAN

Market
Bale Banjar
Stage
Padang Tegal
Perama Shuttle Bus
Wangi Wangi Natural
ARMA
JALAN RAYA PENGOSEKAN
Pengosekan
Community of Artists
Lodtunduh
Batuan & Denpasar

Oka Kartini's
Munut's Gallery
Pharmacy
Bank Danamon
Pura Dalem Sukma Holistic Centre
Tebesaya
Stage

JALAN RAYA UBUD
JALAN SUKMA

Bale Banjar
Peliatan
Puri Agung Stage
Puri Agung
Bale Banjar
Agung Rai Fine Art Gallery
JALAN PELIATAN

Teges
Stage
Bale Banjar
Museum Rudana
Duck Man of Bali

Pejeng
Goa Gajah & Gianyar

**RESTAURANTS & BARS**

| | |
|---|---|
| Exiles | 11 |
| Gajah Biru | 7 |
| Indus | 3 |
| Jazz Café | 9 |
| Made's Warung | 5 |
| Mozaic | 2 |
| Murni's Warung | 8 |
| Naughty Nuri's | 1 |
| Planet Warung | 10 |
| Red Rice | 4 |
| Sari Laba Boga | 6 |

0        1km

△ Museum Puri Lukisan, Ubud

helped secure foreign patronage. In his wake came a whole crowd of other Western artists and intellectuals, some of whom, including the Dutch artist Rudolph Bonnet, the American musician Colin McPhee, and the American anthropologist Jane Belo, were inspired to set up home in the Ubud area.

# Arrival and information

From the **airport**, a fixed-fare taxi to Ubud costs Rp115,000 and takes about an hour; see p.114 for details.

Perama runs several daily **shuttle bus** services to Ubud from all the major tourist centres on Bali and Lombok. Unfortunately, their Ubud terminus is inconveniently located at the southern end of Jalan Hanoman in Padang Tegal, about 750m from the southern end of Jalan Monkey Forest, and 2.5km from the central market. As there's no local bemo or taxi service from here, you can either choose to pay an extra Rp5000 for the Perama drop-off service (which entails a change of van at the terminus) or you can take your chances with touts offering free transport to whichever losmen they are promoting. Alternatively, there are several places to stay within reasonable walking distance of the Perama terminus. Other shuttle-bus operators are more likely to make drops either on Jalan Monkey Forest or near the market on Jalan Raya Ubud (some even offer a door-to-door service), but be sure to find this out before booking.

Arriving by public **bemo**, you'll be dropped right in the centre, in front of the marketplace, at the junction of Jalan Raya Ubud (the main road) and Jalan Monkey Forest (signed as Jalan Wanara Wana, but rarely referred to as such). Any bemo coming from Batubulan (Denpasar) or Kintamani can drop you off in Peliatan on the eastern fringe of Ubud before terminating at the central market. If you're heading for the losmen around the western edge of Ubud, in Campuhan, Sanggingan, Penestanan or Sayan, for example, you might want to take another bemo from the market (see below) rather than make the sweaty thirty-minute walk. For Nyuhkuning, you'll either have to walk from the market (about 30min) or negotiate a ride with a transport tout.

## Information

Ubud's **tourist office** (daily 8am–8pm; ☎0361/973285) is located just west of the Jalan Raya Ubud/Jalan Monkey Forest intersection, right at the heart of central Ubud. It's run by a village organization and has useful outdoor noticeboards giving weekly dance performance schedules and details of upcoming festivals. The staff sell tickets for dance shows in the area, organize free transport to the less accessible venues and run their own inexpensive day-trips to local sights (see p.186).

The tourist office doesn't stock **maps**, so if you're planning to do any serious walking or cycling around the Ubud area, you should buy the excellent *Bali Pathfinder* map, which is reissued annually and is available in all the Ubud bookstores. Another good investment, though less widely available, is the slim, offbeat volume of **guided walks**, *Bali Bird Walks*, written by the local expatriate ornithologist Victor Mason.

# Transport, tours and activities

The most enjoyable way of seeing Ubud and its immediate environs is **on foot**, making your way via the tracks through the rice-paddies and the narrow *gang* that weave through the more traditional *banjar*. **Bicycles** make a pleasant alternative, and can be rented from many streetside outlets along Jalan Monkey Forest (from Rp20,000).

There are no metered taxis in Ubud, so you have to bargain for rides with the **transport touts** who hang around on nearly every corner; typically, you can expect to pay around Rp8000 for a ride from the central market to the Neka Art Museum, or about the same from the Perama office to Jalan Bisma. If you're staying outside central Ubud, this can make getting around a real headache, so it's worth renting your own transport. Some of the outlying losmen and most of the larger mid-range and expensive hotels provide free transport in and out of central Ubud.

It's also possible to use the public **bemos** for certain short hops: to get to the Neka Art Museum, for example, flag down any bemo heading west (such as the turquoise ones going to Payangan) or ask at the terminal in front of the central market; tourists are generally charged about Rp2000 for the ten-minute ride from the market. You can get to Pengosekan or Peliatan on bemos heading for Batubulan, or to Petulu on the orange bemos to Pujung or the brown bemos to Tegalalang and Kintamani. These local rides should cost about Rp2000, and they all go via Ubud's central market and/or tourist office.

## Vehicle rental and tours

The transport touts and rental agencies along Jalan Monkey Forest all rent out **motorbikes**; see Basics, p.51, for price guidelines and advice, but note that if you're driving up to the Kintamani volcanoes or to the north coast from here, it's worth getting a more powerful Kijang rather than opting for the cheaper Jimny. Two reputable car-rental places, both of which offer optional third-party insurance, are the very efficient Ary's Business and Travel Service (℡0361/973130), next to Ary's Bookshop on Jalan Raya Ubud, and Three Brothers (℡0361/973240), which has two outlets on Jalan Monkey Forest and another on Jalan Hanoman (℡0361/975525).

Many car-rental outlets can also provide you with a **driver**, which is often the best way of doing a tailor-made tour. A day-trip to Kintamani, for example, could cost you just Rp200,000 all-in. One recommended freelance driver is Putu Purnawan (℡0816/4716857, ⓔputu09@yahoo.com); for other drivers recommended by recent travellers to Ubud, browse the archives of the online travellers' forums listed on p.37.

The Ubud tourist office and all Ubud travel agencies offer programmes of standard **tours**, usually available for a minimum of two people (Rp75,000–125,000 per person). Most also advertise inclusive trips to local **festivals** and **cremations**, though prices for these tend to be a bit high, especially when the celebrations are happening within walking distance of Ubud; forthcoming events are posted weekly on the board outside the tourist office. If possible, ask at your losmen instead and make your own way there. Note that whether you go to a temple ceremony with a group or on your own, formal dress (sashes and sarongs) is required.

## Walks, treks and other activities

One of Ubud's more unusual attractions is its regular **Bali bird walks**, organized by local expat author Victor Mason (℡0361/975009 from 8am–4pm,

T0812/391 3801 after 4pm, @su_birdwalk@yahoo.com). The walks (Tues, Fri, Sat & Sun 9am) cost US$33, including lunch and the use of shared binoculars. Routes vary according to the season, but are all based around the Campuhan hinterland; guides guarantee sightings of several dozen species of indigenous and visiting birds.

Keep Walking Tours, alongside Tegun Galeri, Jl Hanoman 44 (T0361/970992, @www.balispirit.com/tours/bali_tour_keep_walking.html), has an interesting programme of guided **cultural and ecological walks** (minimum two people), where the emphasis is on learning about rural traditions and meeting village craftspeople (from Rp75,000). They also offer **sunrise treks** up Gunung Batur ($49; see p.302) and Gunung Agung ($99; see p.251). The reputable and long-running Bali Sunrise 2001, Jl Raya Sanggingan 88, Campuhan/Sanggingan (T0818/552669, @www.balisunrise2001.com), with another office in Toya Bungkah (see p.303), also do sunrise treks up Gunung Batur (from $45) and Gunung Agung ($100). The stretch of the Ayung River just west of Ubud is the island's centre for **white-water rafting** and **kayaking**; several companies based on the south coast run white-water excursions along its course – you can either contact Bali Adventure Tours (T0361/721480, @www.baliadventuretours .com) or Sobek (T0361/287059, @www.99bali.com/adventure/sobek) direct, or book the trips through any Ubud tour agent. The two-hour courses stretch about 8km along the Ayung River, cross Class 2 and 3 rapids, and pass through gorges and alongside cliffs and waterfalls en route. Prices are around $70 per person ($45 for under-12s where appropriate; discounts sometimes available online), and include all equipment, hotel transfers and food.

Sobek and Bali Adventure Tours also do guided **hikes** in the area (see p.126). Bali's only **elephant treks** are organized out of the Elephant Safari Park in the village of Taro, 13km north of Ubud (see p.223). Most Ubud tour agents also sell **diving packages** run by the dive operators of south Bali, picking up from Ubud and covering transport to major dive sites (see box, p.158).

### Bike rides

There are countless possibilities for good **bike rides** in the Ubud area and the *Bali Pathfinder* map is the best planning tool. The Campuhan ridge walk described on p.203 is a good route for mountain bikes, or you might consider cycling up to Tegalalang (see p.222), about 13km north of Ubud, via Jalan Suweta in central Ubud, a back road that's both calm and fairly traffic-free, if a little hilly.

You can also join a **guided mountain-bike ride** (Rp360,000 including lunch): Bali Budaya Tours on Jalan Raya Pengosekan (T0361/975557) and Ary's Business and Travel Service on Jalan Raya Ubud, central Ubud (T0361/973130, @ary_s2000@yahoo.com), both run full-day cycling trips that drive you up to Kintamani and Gunung Batur and then let you cycle back down on minor village roads. Sobek and Bali Adventure Tours (see p.126) do guided cycle trips around Gunung Batukau, Gunung Batur and Sangeh Monkey Forest.

# Accommodation

Anywhere in Ubud, you're almost certain to find that your **accommodation** is set in lush surroundings and that there are plenty of terraces or balconies from which to appreciate them. Light sleepers might want to bring earplugs as Ubud's frog population is ubiquitous, loud, and stays up late. Rooms in all price brackets in Ubud are subject to a local **tax** of 10–21 percent; some places include this in their published rates, but most do not. For the best rates at mid-range and expensive hotels, check the hotel websites and the online booking agents detailed on p.54.

Few places on Jalan Monkey Forest have a road number but all listed accommodation is marked on a **map** – either the Central Ubud and Padang Tegal map (p.180) or the Ubud and neighbouring villages map (p.182). For accommodation in Mas, see p.178; for Lodtunduh, see p.175.

## Central Ubud and Padang Tegal

The kilometre-long **Jalan Monkey Forest** is the most central, but also the most congested and commercial, part of town. It has few genuine homestays, with the emphasis instead on small mid-range or upmarket hotels comprising just a dozen bungalows and a pool. The tiny roads that run off Jalan Monkey Forest or parallel to it have a very different feel and, amazingly, still retain a peaceful village atmosphere. Much of the accommodation on these conveniently central lanes – Jalan Karna, Jalan Maruti, Jalan Gautama, Jalan Kajeng and Jalan Bisma, for example – is in small, archetypal homestays, where just a handful of rooms have been built in the family compound; they're usually very friendly places, though some people find the compounds too enclosed.

The village of **Padang Tegal** merges with the eastern borders of central Ubud, so staying here means you're rarely more than a fifteen-minute walk from Jalan Monkey Forest, though you may be quite a hike from the marketplace. It's quieter than Jalan Monkey Forest but has plenty of shops and restaurants.

### Inexpensive

**Artja Inn** Jl Kajeng 9 ☎0361/974425. Set away from the road at the back of a typical family compound in a garden with a stream and wooded surrounds, this classic losmen offers six simple but pleasant bamboo-walled cottages with open-roofed, cold-water mandi. **❶**

**Donald** Jl Gautama 9 ☎0361/977156. Tiny but well-run and friendly homestay offering four exceptionally cheap, sparsely furnished bungalows (two with hot water) in a secluded garden compound. **❶–❷**

**Gusti's Garden 2** Jl Abangan, about 600m walk north along a path from the aqueduct on western Jl Raya Ubud (see map on p.182): follow signs from *Abangan Bungalows* ☎0361/971474, ✉gustigarden@yahoo.com. Occupying a quiet spot overlooking the paddies on the far western fringes of central Ubud, this little cluster of seven nicely designed, contemporary rooms (the upstairs ones have the best views) is deservedly popular, so reservations are advisable. Also has a grotto-like swimming pool. Phone for pick-up within the Ubud area and for help carrying luggage from the road. **❸**

**Gusti's Garden Bungalows** Jl Kajeng 27 ☎0361/973311, ✉gustigarden@yahoo.com. Fifteen pleasant, better-than-average losmen rooms, all with hot water, set around a swimming pool in an attractive, stepped garden, and a peaceful location. **❸**

**Ina Inn** Off Jl Bisma ☎0361/973317, ✉inainn@eudoramail.com. Located in a panoramic spot on a small *gang* surrounded by ricefields, these twelve attractively furnished cottages all have four-poster beds, bathtubs and hot water (but no air-con). The most expensive penthouse rooms have a spacious living area and huge windows affording wide views, and there's a rooftop swimming pool. Good value. **❸–❹**

**Jati Homestay** Jl Hanoman, Padang Tegal ☎0361/977701, ✉asa_dewa2000@yahoo.com. Ten nicely finished bungalows built in a two-storey block facing the rice-paddies (upstairs rooms cost a little extra) and well away from the road. All have hot water and peaceful views. Run by a family of painters. **❷–❸**

**Jati 3** Off Jl Monkey Forest ☎ & ☏0361/973249. Located at the end of a quiet *gang* (if arriving by car, access is via the *Lotus Lane* car park next door), this place offers five good-quality losmen-style bungalows in a courtyard, all with hot water. But the real attractions are the four split-level bungalows in an adjacent plot that slopes down to the river. Each of these has huge glass windows and can accommodate up to four people. Losmen bungalows ❷ Riverside bungalows ❸

**Nick's Homestay 2** Jl Hanoman 57, Padang Tegal ☎0361/975526, 📧nicksp@indosat.net.id. Seven clean, very good-value rooms with bamboo beds and hot showers in a tidy, losmen-style garden compound. Guests can use the pool at *Nick's 1* (some way away on Jl Monkey Forest). ❷

🏃 **Nirvana Pension and Gallery** Jl Gautama 10 ☎0361/975415, 📧rodanet@denpasar.wasantara.net.id. Six inviting, artistically designed and comfortably furnished rooms in the traditional house compound of painter and batik teacher Nyoman Suradnya (see p.214). ❹

**Nyuh Gading** Jl Monkey Forest ☎0361/973410. Seven standard bungalows set in a pretty garden behind a restaurant, plus one family house with kitchen. Very central and family run. Bungalows ❷ Family house ❹

**Puri Widiana** Jl Karna 5 ☎0361/973406. Just four very inexpensive rooms, with fans, cold-water showers and mosquito nets, in a small, central family compound. ❶

🏃 **Sama's Cottages** Jl Bisma ☎0361/973481, 🌐www.balilife.com/sama's. Neither the cheapest nor the most pristine of its kind, this place is nonetheless a lovely, ultra-typical Ubud hideaway. The eight fan-cooled, brick-and-thatch cottages are built on steep tiers that drop into the river gully and each has a sizeable terrace screened by profuse tropical shrubbery. Also has a couple of slightly cheaper rooms. Breakfasts are large, and there's a tiny pool. ❹ •

**Sania's House** Jl Karna 7 ☎0361/975535. Everything about this place is well done: bungalow rooms are clean and well furnished, breakfasts are enormous, and there's even a small swimming pool. The drawback is that with twenty bungalows (some in three-storey towers) crammed into the smallish compound it can feel lacking in privacy. Rooms with cold water ❷ With hot water ❸ With air-con ❺

**Sayong's Bungalows** Jl Maruti ☎0361/973305. Seven simply furnished bungalow rooms in a variety of sizes but all with hot water, set around a typical losmen garden at the end of a very quiet residential *gang*. Swimming pool across the lane. ❷

**The White House (Three Brothers' Bungalows)** Off Jl Monkey Forest ☎0361/974855. One of the few places on Jalan Monkey Forest still to offer (partial) ricefield views from some of its upstairs rooms, this is central and has a pool. Its ten sizeable rooms are attractively decorated and all have hot water and a veranda. ❸

## Moderate and expensive

**Fibra Inn** Jl Monkey Forest ☎0361/975451, 🌐www.fibrainn.com. A tiny hotel whose ten rooms are stylishly furnished with antiques and set in an elegant little tropical sculpture garden. There's also a pool, a pretty spa and a restaurant. ❻–❼

🏃 **Komaneka Resort** Jl Monkey Forest ☎0361/976090, 🌐www.komaneka.com. Sophisticated boutique hotel comprising twenty large, light, air-con bungalows, stylishly appointed with sleek furnishings, huge beds, and verandas overlooking the paddy-fields. There's a beautiful pool, a spa, and an expensive art shop on the premises. ❾

**Pertiwi Resort and Spa** Jl Monkey Forest, ☎0361/975236, 🌐www.pertiwiresort.com. An extensive, nicely landscaped compound of high-standard accommodation that spans the river and runs all the way back to peaceful Jl Bisma. There's a choice of 38 air-con bungalows as well as a dozen plush villa compounds, two pools and a spa. Rooms ❼–❽ Villas ❾

**Pringga Juwita Water Garden Cottages** Jl Bisma ☎0361/978274, 🌐www.fibrainn.com. Prettily designed, characterful bungalows, including some attractive two-storey deluxe ones, all featuring traditional rooms in dark wood with antique furniture and garden bathrooms. Surrounded by lotus ponds, this is a peaceful hideaway, and there's a swimming pool too. Only a few rooms have air-con. ❻–❼

**Puri Saren Agung** Jl Raya Ubud ☎0361/975057, 📠975137. This fine collection of eight pavilions occupies part of the palace belonging to Ubud's influential Sukawati family (see p.194), which means you've daily dance performances literally on your doorstep. Accommodation is styled on traditional palace lines so most rooms have four-poster beds, carved doors, sculpted wall panels, and elegant outdoor sitting rooms (plus air-con). ❼

🏃 **Putri Ayu** Far southern end of Jl Bisma, access on foot also from southern end of Jl Monkey Forest and via the *Pertiwi* compound ☎0361/972590, 🌐www.bali-travelnet.com/hotels/putri_ayu. Occupying a stunning position surrounded on three sides by unadulterated (for the moment at least) ricefields and coconut groves, this place has just eight enormous rooms in two buildings, with those in the upper storeys well worth the few extra dollars. Wall-to-wall windows, huge verandas (which connect, so they're good for families), big bamboo beds, a swimming pool and great breakfasts. Just five minutes' walk from Jl Monkey Forest. ❻

🏃 **Tegal Sari** Jl Hanoman, Padang Tegal ☎0361/973318, 🌐www.tegalsari-ubud.com. Exceptionally appealing set of fifteen tasteful-

ly furnished rooms, all with both fan and air-con, in two-storey blocks strung out alongside the paddy-fields (the upstairs rooms are best). With fine sunset views, thoughtful service, massage facilities and a pool, this is a deservedly popular spot. Also runs a cooking school and does day treks. Located just across the road from the Perama shuttle-bus office (free local transport is provided). **⑤**–**⑦**
**Ubud Bungalows** Jl Monkey Forest ☏0361/971298, ✉w_widnyana@hotmail.com. Good-value, comfortable, detached fan-cooled bungalows set in a pretty garden with an attractive pool at the bottom. Also some very smart versions with air-con and bathtubs. Rooms with fan **⑤** With air-con **⑥**
**Ubud Village Hotel** Jl Monkey Forest ☏0361/975571, ⊛www.ubudvillagehotel.com.

Good-value hotel where each room occupies its own small compound, complete with chic furnishings, air-con, a courtyard garden and a sunken bath. The most expensive rooms have spacious terraces overlooking the river. There's a large pool, a restaurant and an attractive lounge-pavilion. **⑧**–**⑨**
**Waka di Ume** About 1.8km north along Jl Suweta from Ubud market, in the hamlet of Sambahan ☏0361/973178, ⊛www.wakaexperience.com. Delightful set of sixteen thatched bungalows designed in the *Waka* group's distinctive natural-chic style, with an antique flavour to the soft furnishings. Each bungalow has a picture-perfect rice-paddy view (best from the upstairs rooms), and the hotel has two stunningly sited pools (one for kids), a spa and a restaurant. Regular shuttle buses into central Ubud. **⑨**

# Tebesaya, Peliatan and Nyuhkuning

To the east of Padang Tegal, **Tebesaya** is a very appealing, almost entirely residential, area centred on Jalan Sukma, around fifteen minutes' walk from Ubud market; while east again, **Peliatan** is dominated by the main road, but harbours a couple of nice places to stay.

Stretching south from the Monkey Forest, **Nyuhkuning** is peaceful and still fairly rural, offering lots of uninterrupted paddy-field views while still being just a pleasant ten-minute walk from the shops and restaurants at the southern end of Jalan Monkey Forest. The one drawback is that you need to walk or cycle through the eerie Monkey Forest after dark if you're going into central Ubud in the evening.

**Alam Jiwa** 100m east off the Nyuhkuning road, Nyuhkuning ☏0361/977463, ⊛www.alamindahbali.com. Ten large, stunningly sited bungalows, secluded alongside a small river, each one enjoying dramatic views of ricefields and Gunung Agung from the bathtub as well as the balcony. There's a pool and free transport into Ubud. **⑦**–**⑧**
**Family Guest House** Jl Sukma 39, Tebesaya ☏0361/974054, ✉familyhouse@telkom.net. Exceptionally friendly place offering ten well-designed bungalows with stylish furniture and garden verandas (the suites are enormous and undeniably luxurious). Famous for its excellent breakfasts. Bungalows **②** Suites **⑤**
**Garden View Cottages** Nyuhkuning ☏0361/974055, ✉gardenviewubud@yahoo.com. Plush, pleasantly furnished downstairs rooms and two-storey, two-room bungalows, all with rice-paddy views. Swimming pool in the garden. Rooms with fan **⑤** With air-con **⑥** Bungalows **⑥**
**Rona** Jl Sukma 23, Tebesaya ☏0361/973229, ✉rona_chicken@yahoo.com. Welcoming place offering good-value terraced bungalows, furnished with comfortable bamboo beds and armchairs. There's a second-hand bookstore, library, kids'

playroom and big bar-restaurant on the premises, and a babysitting service is available. Free pick-up from Ubud area. Rooms with cold water **②** With bathtub and hot water **②**–**③**
**Sari Bungalows** Off the southern end of Jl Peliatan, Br Kalah, Peliatan ☏0361/975541, ✉ironkic@hotmail.com. The fifteen simple bungalows here are some of the cheapest in Ubud and many of them are fronted by verandas affording views out over the paddies beyond. Great value. **①**
**Sri Sunari** 700m east off Jl Peliatan on Jl Gunung Sari, Peliatan (follow signs for neighbouring *Maya Ubud* hotel) ☏0361/970542, ✉sunari@dps.centrin .net.id. This is a good place to come if you want to be away from the commercial heart of Ubud, whose market is around 2km away. Overlooking an inspiring expanse of paddy-fields just off a quiet village road, the guesthouse comprises just four large, well-furnished rooms (with fine views) and a pool. **⑥**
**Swasti 2 Hideaway Nyuhkuning** Nyuhkuning ☏0361/974079, ✉swasti2@hotmail.com. Six large, spacious and comfortably furnished rooms, all with hot water, and ricefield views from the balconies. There's a pool in the garden. Rooms with fan **⑤** With air-con **⑥**

# Campuhan, Sanggingan, Bangkiang Sidem and Keliki

West of central Ubud, **Campuhan** and **Sanggingan** hotels can only be reached via Jalan Raya, the busy main road, which is not a particularly pleasant walk, but public bemos run this way, and some hotels offer free transfers. Rural **Bangkiang Sidem**, on the other hand, is accessible via a delightful path from the edge of Campuhan. If you're staying in the remote but charming village of **Keliki**, you'll need your own transport.

**Alam Sari** Keliki ☎0361/240308, ⓦwww.alam-sari.com. Prettily located set of twelve attractively furnished air-con bungalows on a slope overlooking the terraced ricefields and coconut groves of Keliki village, about 10km north of Ubud. Also has a spa, swimming pool and babysitting service. The design is environmentally aware and the hotel tries hard to be a positive addition to the village. Ubud is about two hours' walk away, though the hotel has bikes for rent and runs a free shuttle. ❼

🏃 **Ananda Cottages** Jl Raya Sanggingan, Sanggingan/Campuhan ☎0361/975376, ⓦwww.anandaubud.com. Atmospheric collection of one- and two-storey bungalows set in attractive gardens that include miniature rice-paddies, ornamental ponds (with resident frog chorus), a pretty swimming pool, and paths lit by flaming torches at night. Most rooms are characterfully furnished with carved doors, antique furniture and garden bathrooms: the upper-level fan ones are the nicest and enjoy paddy views, though the stylishly contemporary air-con bungalows are also tempting. A half-hour walk, or five-minute bemo ride, from central Ubud; bicycles, motorbikes and cars are available for rent. Rooms with fan ❻ With air-con ❼

**Klub Kokos** Bangkiang Sidem ☎0361/978270, ⓦwww.klubkokos.com. Located on the edge of the remote ridge-top village of Bangkiang Sidem, midway along the Campuhan ridge walk (see p.203), this is an ideal spot from which to soak up traditional village life. The seven one- and two-storey bungalows are comfortably furnished and set in a garden; there are family units as well as a pool, restaurant, library, Internet access and kids' games room. A lovely twenty-five-minute walk from the

Campuhan bridge, following signs from the *Ibah* hotel (or 45min from Ubud market); also accessible by car via Payogan. ❻–❼

**Sunrise Villas** Jl Raya Sanggingan, Sanggingan/Campuhan ☎0361/979360, ⓦwww.indopac.com. Three large, sumptuously well-appointed, three-tiered thatched houses, each with two bedrooms, tons of space, hardwood floors, breezy verandas (with daybeds) and a basement kitchen – plus glorious views of the Campuhan ridge right ahead. The villas share a pool. One bedroom ❽ Both bedrooms ❾

**Taman Indrakila** Jl Raya Sanggingan, Sanggingan/Campuhan ☎0361/975017. Offering a five-star view at two-star prices, this is a low-key operation with half a dozen cottage rooms and two enormous apartments ranged along the hillside, all affording spectacular views over the Campuhan ridge. Rooms are unimaginatively furnished but fine, and all have fans. Also has a pool. Rooms ❹ Apartments ❺

**Hotel Tjampuhan** Jl Raya Campuhan, Campuhan ☎0361/975368, ⓦwww.tjampuhan.com. Built on the site of the 1920s' home of influential expat German artist and musician Walter Spies (see p.198), the cottages here are stunningly positioned on terraces that drop right down to the Wos Barat river. The large and elegantly designed fan and air-con rooms are secluded amid the stepped tropical gardens, which also contain tennis courts, two swimming pools and an unusual grotto-like spa complex (see p.213). Not ideal for guests with mobility problems. Fifteen minutes' walk from Ubud market. Rooms with fan ❼ With air-con ❽ Walter Spies's house ❾

# Penestanan

Occupying a ridgetop and a river valley between Campuhan and Sayan, **Penestanan** offers some very affordable hilltop bungalows that enjoy a lordly position overlooking Sanggingan to the east or across ricefields to the west, plus some appealing mid-range options down in the peaceful village. Access can be a bit tortuous: some village accommodation is quite a trek from Ubud without your own transport, and all ridgetop places are inaccessible to cars, so you've either got to get transport to the nearest drop-off point (bungalow staff are usually in attendance to help carry luggage if necessary) or slog up the steep steps from the main Campuhan road, Jalan Raya Campuhan.

**Kori Agung Bungalow** Northern ridgetop ☎0361/973100. A little bit more luxurious than nearby *Londo 2*, and correspondingly more expensive, with six well-furnished rooms, each with a large terrace and some with nice westerly paddy views. Accessible only on foot, via the Campuhan steps on Jl Raya Campuhan. ❷–❸

**Londo Ricefield Bungalows** Southern ridgetop ☎0361/976548, ⊛www.londobungalows.bigstep .com. Friendly little place up on the ridge offering four large two-storey west-facing cottages, fairly basic but furnished with two double beds and a kitchenette. Guests can use the swimming pool at *Melati Cottages* next door (see below). Car access to *Dewa Bharata Bungalows* on Jl Raya Penestanan, then 75m walk. ❷–❹

🏃 **Londo 2** Northern ridgetop; contact details as *Londo Ricefield* above, but specify *Londo 2* ☎0361/976548, ⊛www.londobungalows .bigstep.com. Located towards the end of the track that runs north from the top of the Campuhan steps on Jl Raya Campuhan, the three two-storey bungalows here offer spectacular west-facing views of the surrounding ricefields and palm groves. The bungalows are simply furnished but sleep four, have spacious balconies and kitchen facilities and are amazingly good value. Run by one of the original Young Artists, I Nyoman Londo, whose studio is

here, too. Accessible only on foot, via the Campuhan steps on Jl Raya Campuhan. ❶

**Melati Cottages** Jl Raya Penestanan ☎0361/974650, ⊛www.bali-hotels.co.uk/melati .html. Small hotel offering 22 large, attractive, traditional-style fan and air-con rooms with huge picture windows and a lovely rice-paddy setting. There's a pool, too, and direct car access. ❺

**Penestanan Bungalows** Southern ridgetop ☎0361/975604, ℻288341. Comfortable bamboo-walled bungalow rooms, pleasingly furnished and with hot water and large, east-facing balconies overlooking Sanggingan far below. Also has a pool. Car access to *Dewa Bharata Bungalows* on Jl Raya Penestanan, then a 100m walk. ❸–❹

**Taman Rahasia** Penestanan Kaja ☎0361/979395, ⊛www.balisecretgarden.com. A classy little American-run boutique hideaway deep in the heart of the village, about ten minutes' walk from Campuhan via the Campuhan steps or 1.5km by road via the Museum Blanco. The eight large fan-cooled rooms are pleasingly furnished with four-poster beds, tasteful artworks and local fabrics and there's a small pool, a spa, and a charming lounging and dining area in the profuse little garden. Also has a cooking school (see p.215). Not recommended for under-12s. Direct car access. ❼–❽

## Sayan and Kedewatan

Overlooking the spectacular Ayung River valley to the west of central Ubud, **Sayan** and **Kedewatan** are famous for their luxurious five-star resorts, all of which capitalize on the stunning panoramas, though the views are losing impact now because of all the new developments.

**Amandari** Kedewatan ☎0361/975333, ⊛www .amanresorts.com. Exclusive thirty-room hotel (part of the *Aman* chain) that is repeatedly voted one of the best in the world. Each guest lives in their own traditional thatched compound, enclosing a garden bathroom and minimalist-chic accommodation; some also have private plunge-pools. Glorious views out over the Ayung River, a stunning cliff-edge pool, and a lotus-pond spa. Published rates from $650. ❾

**Four Seasons Resort Bali at Sayan** Sayan/Kedewatan ☎0361/977577, ⊛www.fourseasons .com. Innovatively designed, ultra-modern five-star deluxe hotel built on several levels in the spectacular Ayung River valley. The style is unadorned chic, and the suites and villas are beautifully appointed, each with a huge living area and private garden; villas also have plunge pools. There's a large pool and a spa, but because of the location it's not ideal

for children. Considered to be one of the world's top hotels. Published rates from $450. ❾

**Sayan Terrace** Sayan ☎0361/974384, ⊛www .sayanterraceresort.com. Just eight enormous fan and air-con rooms (some of them designed for families), all with wooden floors and huge windows that make the most of the Ayung River views. Has a pool and a restaurant. A 10min drive from central Ubud. ❽

🏃 **Taman Bebek** Sayan ☎0361/975385, ⊛www.baliwww.com/tamanbebek. Top choice here are the three delightful self-contained valley-view villas, built in airy colonial style (no air-con) with verandas, sliding screens, carved doors and furniture, and views over the Ayung River terraces. Each villa has a separate living area and kitchen facilities, and there's a pool and restaurant. A 10min drive from central Ubud. ❾

# Central Ubud

Covering the area between Jalan Raya Ubud in the north and the Monkey Forest in the south, and between the Campuhan bridge in the west and the GPO in the east, **Central Ubud**'s chief attractions are its restaurants and shops. However, it does hold a few notable sights, including the atmospheric lotus-garden temple, **Pura Saraswati**, Ubud's oldest art museum, **Puri Lukisan**, and the much more modern **Seniwati Gallery of Art by Women**.

## Museum Puri Lukisan

Although billed as central Ubud's major art museum, the **Museum Puri Lukisan** on Jalan Raya Ubud (daily 9am–5pm; Rp20,000; ⊛ www.mpl-ubud.com) suffers from poor labelling and inadequate background information and should be visited only as an adjunct to the far superior Neka Art Museum, 2km west in neighbouring Sanggingan (see p.198).

Set in attractive gardens, complete with lotus-filled ponds and shady arbours, Puri Lukisan ("Palace of Paintings") was founded in 1956 by the Ubud *punggawa* Cokorda Gede Agung Sukawati (whose descendants are still involved with the museum) and the Dutch artist Rudolf Bonnet. Both men had amassed a significant collection of work by local artists through their involvement with the Pita Maha group (see box, below), and almost the whole of the **First Pavilion**, located at the top of the garden, is still given over to these works (identifiable by the words "donated by Rudolf Bonnet" on the label). Some of these are **wayang-style** canvases, but most are black-and-white **Batuan-style** and early

---

### The Pita Maha arts movement

By the early 1930s, Bali was firmly established on the cruise-liner circuit and the island was playing host to a stream of well-heeled visitors from Europe and America who began buying significant numbers of paintings and woodcarvings. Artists churned them out in ever increasing numbers and the result was a dramatic drop in standards, with patrons and collectors bemoaning the lowering in quality and the mushrooming of shoddy imitations. To combat this decline, Ubud's patrician prince, **Cokorda Gede Agung Sukawati**, joined forces with his architect and chief carver, **I Gusti Nyoman Lempad**, and enrolled the help of his expatriate painter friends **Walter Spies** and **Rudolf Bonnet**. Together, the four men founded the **Pita Maha arts movement** in Ubud in 1936.

The main aim of the movement was to preserve high artistic standards and to steer artists away from the temptation to mass-produce their works. Weekly meetings were held to discuss work brought in by Pita Maha members, and the artists were encouraged to explore new themes and subjects in their work, particularly secular ones, and to give full expression to their individual interpretations. The best pieces were exhibited and put up for sale. Over its six-year existence, the group's membership grew to include about 150 painters, carvers and sculptors, most of them from the neighbouring villages of Nyuhkuning, Padang Tegal and Pengosekan.

The movement ground to a halt with Spies's death in 1942; the only legacy of works from that era are the paintings and carvings bought from Pita Maha members by Bonnet and Sukawati and then donated to the **Museum Puri Lukisan** in central Ubud. With hindsight, some anthropologists and art historians have criticized Pita Maha for imposing Western artistic ideals and techniques on an already sophisticated artistic heritage, but others have appreciated the way it breathed new life into a native art that was in danger of stagnating or even dying out.

**Ubud-style**, depicting local scenes, with great attention paid to the detail of the foliage, the temple carvings and the villagers' attire (see p.481 for more). There are also plenty of works that don't fit into the recognized Balinese "schools", including a good selection of distinctive ink drawings by the multitalented I Gusti Nyoman Lempad (see opposite).

The Pita Maha group also promoted the art of **woodcarving**, and a handful of these finely crafted pieces from the 1930s, 1940s and 1950s are scattered about the First Pavilion gallery. Especially notable are the elegantly surreal figure of the earth goddess, *Dewi Pertiwi*, by Ida Bagus Nyana, the charming hibiscus wood *Buffalo Bathing in a River* by I Mangku Tama, and the sinuous portrait of the rice goddess *Dewi Sri* by I Ketut Djedeng. I Nyoman Cokot's energetic figures of weird animals and terrifying human forms were so innovative that he spawned a now much-emulated Cokot style; his *Garuda Eating Snake* is a typical example.

The **Second Pavilion**, to the left of the First Pavilion, contains a pretty extensive showcase of works in the **Young Artists** style, though the gallery is unfortunately poorly lit. Many of these pictures were donated to the museum by the painter Arie Smit, who was closely associated with the early years of this naive expressionist school of local art in the 1960s. Most were produced by the young people of nearby Penestanan (see p.204), who drew their inspiration from daily village life. I Nyoman Mundik is an especially prolific painter in this style, and several of his canvases displayed here were painted in his teenage years. Also in this pavilion you'll find a few paintings in the Ubud style, including one by Anak Agung Gede Sobrat, as well as works in the so-called **modern traditional** style, such as Ida Bagus Nadera's *Story of Rajapala*.

The **Third Pavilion**, to the right of the First Pavilion, houses temporary exhibitions.

## Pura Saraswati

At the end of the nineteenth century, I Gusti Nyoman Lempad arrived in Ubud from service at the court of Blahbatuh and was employed as chief stonecarver and architect to the Sukawati royal family; **Pura Saraswati** was one of his many commissions. He set the whole temple complex in a delightful water garden, landscaped around a huge lotus pond, and dedicated it to Saraswati, a sacred Hindu river and the goddess of water and learning. A **restaurant**, *Café Lotus*, now capitalizes on the garden view.

To get to the temple, you can either take the gateway that opens onto Jalan Raya Ubud, or go through the restaurant. A forest of metre-high lotus plants leads you right up to the red-brick *paduraksa* whose main entrance is blocked by a very unusual **aling-aling** (the wall device built into nearly every temple to disorient evil spirits), which is in fact the back of a rotund statue of a *raksasa* demon guardian. Inside the **courtyard** on the right, you'll find a *bale* housing the two huge *barong* costumes used by local villagers for exorcizing rituals: the lion-like Barong Ket and the wild boar Barong Bangkal. Nearby, the main lotus-throne **shrine** is covered with a riot of *paras* carvings, with the requisite cosmic turtle and *naga* forming the base, while the tower is a swirling mass of curlicues and floral motifs. The walk-in shrine occupying the northeast corner of the complex displays some more distinguished Lempad carvings, the central wall-panel describing a farewell scene.

## Puri Saren Agung (Ubud Palace)

A few hundred metres east of Pura Saraswati, **Puri Saren Agung** – generally known as **Ubud Palace** – stands at the heart of Ubud, opposite the main market and junction of Jalan Raya Ubud and Jalan Monkey Forest. From the late nineteenth century until the 1940s, Ubud and its catchment area was ruled from this palace complex by the resident Sukawati clan and, despite its modern incarnation as a hotel and dance stage, Puri Saren Agung has retained much of its original style and elegance. Casual visitors are welcome to walk around the compact central courtyards, and every night the outer courtyard is transformed into a spectacular backdrop for traditional dance performances (see p.211).

Built to a classic design that is really just a grander version of the traditional family compound, the palace was divided into a series of **pavilions**, each serving a particular purpose. The centrepiece was the open-sided reception *bale*, its imposing wooden pillars, sculpted stone panels and huge guardian statues of elephants, lions and *raksasa* still much as they were in the Sukawatis' heyday. The veranda is still furnished with Dutch-style carved wooden armchairs, and piles of old photograph albums lie heaped on the floor, full of early pictures of the Ubud gentry. The small thatched *bale* nearby is decorated with stonecarvings and painted wooden reliefs ascribed to I Gusti Nyoman Lempad. Most of the **hotel rooms** have been adapted or purpose-built, but retain authentic features (see p.189).

## Lempad's house

Ubud's most versatile and accomplished artist, **I Gusti Nyoman Lempad**, lived on Ubud's main street for most of his life in a **house** that still belongs to his family but is now also open to the public (daily 8am–6pm; free). Lempad was said to be quite a traditionalist in certain matters and would only work on propitious days; significantly, he is said to have chosen the day of his death – the auspicious *Kajeng Kliwon* day of the Balinese calendar, April 25, 1978. He was approximately 116 years old. His friends Rudolf Bonnet and Cokorda Gede Agung Sukawati both died within a few months of Lempad, and the three men were cremated together at a spectacular ceremony held in Ubud in January 1979.

Disappointingly, there's little evidence of the great man on show in his former residence, as the place now functions chiefly as a gallery and showroom for a group of artists working under the "Puri Lempad" by-line. Some of them are descendants of I Gusti Nyoman and much of their work takes inspiration from his impressive canon of paintings and drawings. Only a handful of Lempad's original ink drawings are exhibited here: for the best collection of his work, you'll need to visit the Neka Art Museum (see p.201), though the Museum Puri Lukisan (see p.194) also owns a few examples. The *bale* at the back of the Lempad compound does, however, house a small exhibition of Lempad **memorabilia**, including a couple of stone busts and photos of the artist, plus the Piagam Anugerah Seni certificate – government recognition of his lifetime's contribution to the island's cultural heritage – and a magazine article on the biographical film, *Lempad of Bali*, made by local expats John Darling and Lorne Blair in 1980.

## Seniwati Gallery of Art by Women

Balinese women feature prominently in the paintings displayed in both the Neka Art Museum and the Museum Puri Lukisan, but there is barely a handful of works by women artists in either collection. To redress this imbalance, British-born artist Mary Northmore set up the Association of Women Artists in Bali, out of which was born the **Seniwati Gallery of Art by Women** at Jl Sriwedari 2b (Tues–Sun 9am–5pm; free; ⓦwww.seniwatigallery.com).

Committed to the promotion, display and sale of work by women artists, the Seniwati organization currently represents about seventy local and foreign women resident in Bali, many of whom have pictures on show in the gallery's permanent collection. Another element of the project is the regular art classes held at the gallery, and there's a small shop selling cards as well as their famous *Women Artists of Bali* calendar.

The Seniwati Gallery's small but charming permanent collection covers the range of mainstream Balinese art styles, and the works are supported by excellent information sheets on each of the artists and by a staff of highly informed gallery attendants. A few of the most notable exhibits include a classical Kamasan-style depiction of the *Vindication of Sita* by **Ni Made Suciarmi**, whose childhood was spent helping with the 1930s' renovations on the Kerta Gosa painted ceilings in Klungkung (see p.244). Batuan-born **Ni Wayan Warti** continues the traditional style of her village, producing dark and highly detailed scenes, while the already well-known young painter **I Gusti Agung Galuh** works chiefly in the popular Ubud style, her landscapes of watery paddies showing distinct Walter Spies influences. Pengosekan resident **Gusti Ayu Suartini** also reflects her roots, concentrating on the pastel bird and flower compositions characteristic of the Pengosekan Community of Artists. **Tjok Istri Mas Astiti**, on the other hand, strikes out on her own to record the daily lives and activities of local women, tackling less aesthetic aspects, such as fading *legong* dancers

---

## A rice-paddy walk through Ubud Kaja

Running east of, and almost parallel to, the Campuhan ridge walk (see p.203) is a track defining an almost circular **rice-paddy walk** that begins and ends in the northern part of Ubud known as Ubud Kaja (*kaja* literally means "upstream, towards the mountains"); the walk – also detailed on the *Bali Pathfinder* map – takes two and a half hours round trip and is flat and not at all strenuous. There's no shade for the first hour, though, so you'll need a hat, sunblock and some water.

The walk begins from the western end of **Jalan Raya Ubud**, between the Casa Lina shop and the overhead aqueduct, where a track leads up to the *Abangan Hotel* on the north side of the road. Head up the slope and, at the top, follow the track which bends to the left before straightening out, passing *Gusti's 2* and heading north. From here the route is straightforward, following the dirt track for about 3km as it slices through gently **terraced ricefields** fringed with coconut palms on either edge – you'll probably see scores of beautifully coloured dragonflies zooming around, and plenty of birdlife, including, possibly, iridescent blue Javanese kingfishers.

After about 1hr 10min, the track comes to an end at a sealed road. Turn right here to cross the river, then look for the **southbound track** that starts almost immediately after the bridge and runs east of the river. The southbound track becomes indistinct in places and for the next ten minutes you should try to follow the narrow paths along the top of the ricefield dykes and stick to a southerly direction by keeping the river in view on your right. Get back on the proper track as soon as you see it emerging from the woods alongside the river; don't forget to look back at the amazing **views of Gunung Agung** (cloud cover permitting): with the mountain in the background and the conical-hatted farmers working in the glittering ricefields, these views are perfect real-life versions of the Walter Spies–style paintings you see in the museums and galleries of Ubud. This track will take you back down to Ubud Kaja again, finishing at the far northern end of Ubud's **Jalan Kajeng**, the little road paved with graffitied stones that runs all the way down to Jalan Raya Ubud. The stones are inscribed with the names, messages and doodlings of the Ubud residents and businesses who helped finance the paving of the lane.

and obvious poverty. Tabanan-born **Gusti Ayu Kadek Murni** is even bolder: disregarding sexual and social taboos, she is famous for her witty, provocative and uninhibited style, which has made her one of Bali's most famous modern artists.

## Threads of Life Textile Arts Center

The **Threads of Life Textile Arts Center and Gallery** (Mon–Sat 10am–6pm; Ⓦ www.threadsoflife.com), next to *Rumah Roda* restaurant at Jl Kajeng 24, aims to introduce visitors to the complex and highly skilled art of traditional weaving in Bali, Sumba, Flores, Lembata and Sulawesi, on all of which certain weaving designs and techniques are in danger of being lost forever. The Threads of Life foundation was established to try and halt the decline by commissioning modern-day weavers to re-create the ritual textiles of their grandmothers, using natural dyes and traditional methods. Many of these commissioned pieces, which can take two years to complete, are on display in the Arts Center, alongside information on the origin and meaning of the most important motifs, plus exhibitions on the ritual use for the textiles, their cultural context, and the specialized weaving and dyeing implements and techniques. The centre also sells exquisite, if pricey, **textiles** and runs regular **classes** on traditional textile appreciation (see p.215).

# Campuhan, Sanggingan and Penestanan

Sited at the confluence of the rivers Wos Barat and Wos Timor, the hamlet of **CAMPUHAN** (pronounced *cham-poo-han*) officially extends west from Ubud only as far as the *Hotel Tjampuhan*, and is famous as the home of several of Bali's most charismatic expatriate painters, including the late **Antonio Blanco**, whose house/gallery has been turned into a museum; the late **Walter Spies**, whose delightful early twentieth-century villa has become the centrepiece of the *Hotel Tjampuhan*; and **Symon**, who still paints and presides at his enticing studio-gallery across the road from the hotel.

North up the Campuhan hill from this knot of artistic abodes, Campuhan turns into **SANGGINGAN** (though few people bother to distinguish it from its neighbour), and it's here that you'll find Bali's best art gallery, the **Neka Art Museum**.

Otherwise, Campuhan and Sanggingan comprise little more than a sprinkling of residences sandwiched between the road and the rivers, some notable restaurants and an increasing number of prettily sited hotels, plus a few commercial galleries. Campuhan/Sanggingan also makes a good starting point for **walks** around Ubud, including the picturesque route to the neighbouring and still quite traditional hamlet of Penestanan. If you don't fancy walking or cycling along the busy main road that tears through its heart, you can take any westbound **bemo** from in front of the tourist information office on Jalan Raya Ubud.

In the 1960s, Campuhan's westerly neighbour **PENESTANAN** became famous for its home-grown, so-called **Young Artists**, who forged a naive style of painting that's since been named after them. Some are still painting, but Penestanan's new niche is **beadmaking**, and the village now has several little shops selling intricately strung belts, bags, bracelets and other accessories.

## Walter Spies in Campuhan

The son of a German diplomat, **Walter Spies** (1895–1942) left Europe for Java in 1923, and relocated to Bali four years later. He set up home in Campuhan and began devoting himself to the study and practice of Balinese art and music. He sponsored two local gamelan orchestras and was the first Westerner to attempt to record **Balinese music**. Together with the American composer Colin McPhee, he set about transposing gamelan music for Western instruments, and with another associate, Katharane Mershon, encouraged Bedulu dancer I Wayan Limbak to create the enduringly popular **kecak dance** (see p.475).

Spies was an avid collector of Balinese **art**, and became one of the founding members of the Pita Maha arts movement in 1936 (see p.193), holding the weekly meetings in his Campuhan house. He is said to have inspired, if not taught, a number of talented young Ubud artists, among them the painter Anak Agung Gede Sobrat, and the woodcarver I Tegelan. Characteristic of Spies's own Balinese works are dense landscapes of waterlogged paddies set within double or triple horizons, and peopled with elongated silhouettes of conical-hatted farmers, often accompanied by water buffaloes – a distinctive style that continues to be imitated by contemporary painters. There's currently only one Walter Spies painting on show in Ubud, at the Agung Rai Museum of Art in Pengosekan (see p.206).

In 1937, Spies retired from his increasingly hectic social life in Ubud to the tranquil hillside village of Iseh in the Karangasem district. He turned his Campuhan home into a **guesthouse**, the first of its kind in the Ubud area, and employed a couple of Germans to manage it. He died in 1942, and the guesthouse became *Hotel Tjampuhan* (see p.191).

# The Neka Art Museum

Boasting the most comprehensive collection of traditional and modern Balinese paintings on the island, the well-curated **Neka Art Museum** (daily 9am–5pm; Rp20,000; ⊛www.museumneka.com) is housed in a series of pavilions set high on a hill overlooking the Wos Barat river valley, alongside the main Campuhan/Sanggingan road, about 2.5km from Ubud market.

The museum was founded in 1982 by the Ubud collector and art patron, **Wayan Suteja Neka**, a former teacher and son of the award-winning woodcarver I Wayan Neka, who was a member of the influential 1930s' art movement, Pita Maha. In establishing this private collection, Suteja Neka's stated intention was "to document the history of paintings inspired by the Balinese environment", a brief that neatly encompasses traditional works as well as those by expatriate and visiting artists. Highly informative English-language labels are posted alongside every one of the museum's several hundred paintings, but you might also consider splashing out on one of the **books** about the Neka collection: both *Perceptions of Paradise: Images of Bali in the Arts* by Garrett Kam, and *The Development of Painting in Bali: Selections from the Neka Art Museum* by Suteja Neka and Garrett Kam, are on sale at the museum as well as in several Ubud bookstores. For more on styles of art on display, see pp.481–485.

### First Pavilion: Balinese Painting Hall

Divided into fairly distinct sections, the first pavilion attempts to give an overview of the three major schools of **Balinese painting** from the seventeenth century to the present day. The collection opens with an introduction to the earliest-known "school", the two-dimensional narratives inspired by *wayang kulit* shadow puppets (also displayed here), which earned the label **Kamasan style** after the east Bali town where most of them were produced. The Kamasan style dates back to the seventeenth century, but the nineteenth-century pictures displayed here show all the hallmarks, notably the use of distinctive, naturally produced ochre, brown and red pigments, and the stylized figures drawn in three-quarter profile. Kamasan paintings traditionally depict episodes from popular *wayang* stories, in particular the *Ramayana* and *Mahabharata* epics, and these tales continue to be the inspiration for contemporary artists, such as the late **Ketut Kobot**. A former puppet-maker himself, Kobot adapted the stark outlines of the *wayang* style, introducing softer pastel shades and filling out the canvases with more modern decorative motifs, as you can see from *Rajapala Steals Sulasih's Clothes*. Similarly, *The Pendawa Brothers Disguised as Common Beings*, painted in black and white by **Ida Bagus Rai**, fuses classical elements with a more modern sensuality.

The other galleries in the first pavilion are given over to those schools of painting that evolved from the *wayang* style and took some inspiration from foreign artists as well. In the 1930s, Ubud artists began to paint scenes from everyday life and to experiment with perspective and the use of light and shadow. These works have retrospectively been given the umbrella label **Ubud style**, and many contemporary artists still work with the same techniques and subject matters today. One of the finest Ubud-style paintings in the museum is *The Bumblebee Dance* by **Anak Agung Gede Sobrat**, a prolific member of the Pita Maha group who was said to have been much influenced by his sometime teacher, the German artist Walter Spies; the scene shows a traditional flirtation dance (*oleg tambulilingan*), which is still regularly performed on local Ubud stages.

Of all the four major Balinese art styles, the dark and densely packed canvases that characterize the **Batuan style** lend themselves most to humour, political observation and social commentary. Originally the province of a group of young 1930s' painters from the nearby village of Batuan, these works are often very small and depict multiple scenes featuring demons and legendary figures as well as villagers engaged in everyday activities. The most dramatic Batuan-style pictures in this pavilion, however, tackle major themes: **I Wayan Bendi**'s depiction of the 1949–1950 *Indonesian War of Independence* and his wry, two-metre-long portrait of the effect of tourism on the island, *Busy Bali*, both use the traditional juxtaposition of disparate characters and activities to fine effect. **I Made Budi**'s very detailed 1987 work, *President Suharto and His Wife Visit Bali*, is a similarly humorous take.

### Second Pavilion: Arie Smit Pavilion

The second pavilion is devoted to the hugely influential Dutch expatriate artist **Arie Smit**, a Campuhan resident who has been based in Bali since 1956, and to works by the group of painters with which he was associated, who came to be known as the Young Artists. You enter the pavilion via the upstairs gallery, which is filled with pictures by Smit – instantly recognizable from their bold, expressionist tone; many feature imaginative landscapes inspired by Ubud scenes, generally depicted in vibrant oils and often either pierced by fractured light or splintered into blocks of broken colour rimmed in black, like stained glass. The collection includes some breathtakingly beautiful recent works, including *A Tropical Garden By the Sea*, which has a Cézanne-like quality, and the intriguing *Rhythms of Life*.

The ground-floor hall exhibits works in the **Young Artists style**, a term coined by Arie Smit to describe the naive, expressionistic pictures created by a group of teenagers living in Penestanan in the 1960s (see p.204 for more. **I Wayan Pugur**'s *In the Village* is a typical example. The downstairs gallery also exhibits works by other Balinese artists who don't fit so neatly into the more traditional schools of Balinese art. These include 1960s' ink paintings by renowned Sanur artist **Ida Bagus Nyoman Rai**, as well as an energetic abstract, *Water of Life*, by **I Made Sumadiyasa**.

### Third Pavilion: Photography Archive Center

The third pavilion houses a very interesting archive of black-and-white **photographs** from Bali in the 1930s and 1940s, all of them taken by the remarkable American expatriate **Robert Koke**. He and his wife, Louise, founded the first hotel in Kuta in 1936 (see p.113) and spent the next six years entertaining guests there as well as getting involved with artists, dancers and musicians from all corners of Bali. His photographic record includes some stunning shots of village scenes, temple festivals and cremations, but its highlights are the pictures of the *legong* and *kecak* performances and the portraits of the charismatic dancer Mario (see p.347), who invented the *oleg tambulilingan* (bumblebee dance) and of the *kecak* choreographer I Wayan Limbak. The photos are labelled with extracts from Louise Koke's enjoyable book *Our Hotel in Bali* (reviewed on p.502).

## The tale of Men and Pan Brayut

**Men and Pan Brayut** ("Mother and Father Brayut") are the protagonists of a popular Balinese folk tale about a poverty-stricken couple who have an unruly brood of eighteen children to care for. Men Brayut has become the archetypal symbol of any poor woman with lots of kids and, together with her huge family, is the subject of numerous paintings showing episodes from their lives. The most famous illustrator of the Brayut story is the Ubud artist **I Gusti Nyoman Lempad**, who did a series of ink drawings featuring the family that serve as close-up illustrations of typical Balinese activities. Scenes from the Brayut story are also depicted in the classical *wayang*-style murals that cover the walls and ceilings of Klungkung's Bale Kambang hall (see p.242), and in the earthy stonecarved reliefs at Pura Dalem Jagaraga, near Singaraja (see p.319). The fullest account is to be found in an epic poem called *Gaguritan Brayut*, housed in Singaraja's Gedong Kirtya library.

According to one version of the **story**, the reason that Men Brayut has so many children is her enormous and uncontrollable appetite. When hungry, she gets irritable and rows with her husband, Pan Brayut. After fighting, the couple always make up in the time-honoured fashion – hence, the constantly expanding brood. Another version puts the size of the family down to Pan Brayut's insatiable desire for his wife, which he acts upon regardless of place or circumstance. The family name, Brayut, is thought to have come from an old Javanese word that translates as "burdened with many children".

Men Brayut is both full-time mother and part-time weaver, and so her husband does the bulk of the domestic chores. Lempad shows him cleaning the yard and cooking ceremonial dishes, and in his spare time he studies religious practice. One of the highlights of their story is the **wedding ceremony** of their amorous son I Ketut Sabaya (an episode pictured in the Bale Kambang murals). Eventually, after all their hard parenting, Men and Pan Brayut renounce the material world and enter a retreat (still common practice, especially among elderly Balinese men), leaving their home and its contents to be divided among the children.

Although the Brayut story is always illustrated to accent its strong **Hindu** overtones with lots of scenes showing temple offerings, ceremonies and blessings, Men Brayut is also associated with **Buddhist** lore. In this mythology she is said to have evolved from an evil ogress named Hariti who spent her time devouring children until she converted to Buddhism and became not only a protector of children, but also a fertility goddess. Statues of Men Brayut in her Hariti manifestation can be found at Goa Gajah, near Ubud (p.218), and at the temple in Candi Dasa (p.266).

## Fourth Pavilion: Lempad Pavilion

The small fourth pavilion is dedicated to the works of local Renaissance man **I Gusti Nyoman Lempad** (see p.195) and holds the largest collection of his pictures in Bali. Lempad took up painting fairly late in his long and varied artistic career, using deceptively simplistic, almost cartoon-like line drawings in black Chinese ink to describe scenes from religious mythology and secular folklore. Some of his best-known works are from a series on **Men and Pan Brayut** (see box, opposite), a humorous reworking of the well-known folk story about a poor couple who have a family of eighteen children to bring up. Lempad shows the family in various states of harmony and discord, either engaged in typical domestic activities, as in *Scene 3: Making Pork Saté*, or in wryly observed comical situations as in *Scene 5: Mother Brayut Eats the Offerings* (she is reduced to doing this, apparently, because looking after her huge brood leaves her too tired to cook).

## Fifth Pavilion: Contemporary Indonesian Art Hall

The fifth pavilion focuses on works by Indonesian artists whose style is sometimes labelled "**Academic**" because the painters were academically trained, mostly at the Yogyakarta Academy of Fine Arts on Java. Many of the Academic artists displayed here are associated with the Sanggar Dewata Indonesia art movement, whose abstract expressionist style has dominated modern Balinese art since the 1970s; see Contexts, p.484, for more on this. Outstanding works displayed here include a couple of large oils by Javanese-born **Anton H** (Anton Kustia Widjaja), who moved to Ubud in 1969: *Three Masked Dancers*, which ponders the role of traditional *topeng* dancers, and *Divine Union*, which shows the symbolic fusion of the male and female aspects of the Hindu deity Siwa, which resulted in the creation of the world. Also displayed in this pavilion is **Abdul Aziz**'s cute and much-reproduced diptych entitled *Mutual Attraction*.

## Sixth Pavilion: East–West Art Annex

The sixth pavilion opens with a roomful of portraits of members of the Neka family by various famous contemporary Indonesian and expatriate artists, including *Suteja Neka Waking Up on a Cold Morning* and *Portrait of Mrs Suteja Neka*, both painted by the Javanese artist **Jeihan**. On this floor you'll also find some striking works by Javanese expressionist **Affandi**, notably his portrait of fighting cocks, *Fight to the Finish*, and his depiction of a *barong* and *rangda* dance.

The upstairs galleries feature the paintings of **foreign artists in Bali**, many of whom lived and worked here in Ubud, such as the Dutch painter **Rudolf Bonnet**, whose *Temptation of Arjuna* is a sensual portrait of the *Mahabharata* hero. Bonnet's style is said to have been very influential in creating what became known as the Ubud style. Although Bonnet's friend **Walter Spies** also influenced many artists with his distinctive use of light and dark in landscapes peopled by elongated silhouettes of farmers, Spies is only represented in the Neka collection by a photographic reproduction of his *The Death of Arya Penringsang*.

The bright Gauguin-esque oils of Swiss-born **Theo Meier** draw on the lurid light and tropical emotions of Bali, in strong contrast to the Dutchman **Willem Gerard Hofker**'s minutely observed crayon studies of temples, such as *Temple at Campuhan, Ubud*, and his romanticized soft-focus portraits of local women. More recent expatriate artists are also represented here, including some erotically charged portraits by the Catalan-born **Antonio Blanco**, whose nearby studio-gallery is open to the public (see p.202); the Australian **Donald Friend** with his charmingly fanciful Chagall-esque evocation of his Sanur home, *Batujimbar Village*; and the Dutchman **Han Snel**, whose striking *Girls Carrying Offerings* is characteristic of this versatile painter's work.

## Symon's Studio

Across the road from the *Hotel Tjampuhan* complex, it's hard to ignore the ebullient studio-gallery of American-born artist **Symon**, with its eye-catching assortment of vivacious paintings and weird artefacts suspended around the steps leading up to the entrance. Inside, the multi-levelled **gallery** (daily until about 9pm; free; ⓦwww.symonbali.com) houses unconventional displays of Symon's paintings, sculptures and other creations, as well as a working atelier for the artist and his assistants. Symon has lived in Bali since 1978 and is best known for his bold portraits of sensual young Balinese men, done in vivid tropical colours and often to an exaggerated scale, as in his series of Big Heads. Symon has a second gallery and workshop, the Art Zoo, in AlasSari on the northeast coast (see p.320). An insightful book about Symon and his work, *Property of the Artist* by Philip Cornwel-Smith, is available at the Ubud studio, as well as at some local bookshops.

## Museum Blanco

A few hundred metres down the main road into Ubud from Symon's Studio and *Hotel Tjampuhan*, beside the Penestanan turn-off, the ostentatious gateway announcing in huge curly letters "Antonio Blanco", and then in a slightly smaller script "The Blanco Dynasty", sets the tone for the Blanco experience beyond. This is the entrance to the former home of the flamboyant Catalan expatriate artist – complete with gilded pillars and sweeping Spanish balustrades – now open to the public as the enjoyably camp **Museum Blanco** (daily 9am–5pm; Rp20,000).

Blanco, who died in 1999 at the age of 88, specialized in **erotic paintings** and drawings, particularly portraits of Balinese women in varying states of undress and abandon. As with countless other Western male artists before and since, Blanco fell for a local girl, Ni Ronji, soon after arriving in Ubud in 1952, singling her out as his top model and later marrying her. Aside from his erotica, Blanco's collection also includes lots of his multimedia pieces, many of them surreal and mischievous flights of poetic fancy, and many idiosyncratic picture frames created from unorthodox materials.

## Pura Gunung Lebah and around

Just across the road from Museum Blanco, **Pura Gunung Lebah** (sometimes known simply as Pura Campuhan) stands on the tip of a grassy spur at the confluence of the Wos Barat and Wos Timor rivers, a site occupied by holy buildings since the eighth century. These days, it makes a pleasant vantage point for views up- and downstream and across to the Campuhan ridge. The temple itself is hardly spectacular, though its shrines and *bale* boast impressive red and gold paintwork on their woodcarved lintels and doors, and immaculate wiry thick thatch made from layers and layers of the elephant grass that carpets the hilly ridge beyond.

The healthy gurgling of the two rivers all but drowns out the thunderous roar of the road traffic and the temple compound gives access to both waterways and to several enticing **bathing spots** nearby. A hibiscus-lined path leads down from the west (Campuhan-side) temple steps and along the river bank facing the *Hotel Tjampuhan* (though the river is fast-flowing, it's

## The Campuhan ridge walk

The track that extends north along the grassy spine behind Pura Gunung Lebah forms part of a very pleasant ninety-minute circular **walk** around the outskirts of Campuhan, bringing you back to the main road about 1.5km northwest of the Neka Art Museum. Alternatively, if you continue the complete length of the ridge, you'll eventually reach the tiny village of **Keliki** (7km), renowned for its intricate miniature paintings of *barong* dances, beyond which the track, asphalted in some sections, proceeds to **Taro** (13km) before eventually joining the main Sayan road to **Kintamani** (32km). All routes are good for **mountain bikes**, too: see the *Bali Pathfinder* map for details. If you have an umbrella and reasonable shoes, the shorter, circular walk also makes a pleasant outing in the rain: you don't get hot and the scenery looks even more lush when everything is glistening.

If you're starting the walk **from central Ubud**, walk (or take a bemo) west from Ubud market almost as far as the Campuhan bridge, turning north (right) off the main road about 100m before the bridge, into the entrance of the *Ibah* hotel, where an immediate left fork, signed for *Klub Kokos* hotel, takes you down some steps to the back of Pura Gunung Lebah. From here, the **track** (which is paved for the first 1500m) ascends a fairly gentle slope before quickly levelling out along the flattened ridgetop between the two river valleys. The perspective from this elevated route is breathtaking: to the left, you'll see the steep, increasingly developed westerly banks of the Wos Barat valley, and some way off, the distinctive orange rooftops of the Neka Art Museum. To the right, the eastern panorama across the Wos Timor valley remains unadulterated – nothing but savannah, coconut grove and rocky river gorge. There are few trees to speak of along this first stretch of the ridge walk, and therefore no shade, just a seemingly endless long-haired carpet of **elephant grass** (*alang-alang*) swaying in the breeze. The grass is a valuable resource for local villagers who harvest it regularly and dry the sheaves for thatch for houses and shrines across the island. Down below, the rocky river beds also provide a good source of income: the Wos valleys harbour a rich supply of **volcanic sandstone**, or *paras*, swept down from the mountains, which is quarried out in blocks for carving.

About twenty minutes from Pura Gunung Lebah, the track passes through the first little ridgetop settlement, site of the *Klub Kokos* hotel (see p.191) and restaurant. Nearly all the grassland beyond has been sculpted into ricefields (*sawah*), irrigated by a complex system of water channels that draw on the Wos Barat below. About 1500m further on, the track enters **Bangkiang Sidem**, whose main street extends just a few hundred metres from end to end, skirting a row of family compounds built mainly from adobe bricks and elephant-grass thatch, a warung, a *bale banjar* and a temple. Just beyond the temple, the route **forks**: left for the round trip back to the Campuhan road, straight on for Keliki. On a clear day you get a superb view of **Gunung Agung** from this junction.

The left-hand branch of the track is now a sealed all-weather road, but it's only used for local access so is still a pleasant walk. It cuts through an ocean of water-logged ricefields – which attract several **bird** species, in particular the iridescent blue Javan kingfisher and the chubby, brown cisticola warbler – before dropping down quite steeply towards the Wos Barat. Fifteen minutes after crossing the river, you pass through the adjacent, still fairly traditional hamlets of **Payogan** and **Lung-siakan**, before reaching **Jalan Raya Sanggingan**, from where you can either hop on to any bemo heading east (left) for a ten-minute ride into Ubud, or continue walking for twenty minutes east down to the Neka Art Museum, or twenty minutes west (right) to Kedewatan and the main Kintamani road.

fairly easy to wade across), while over to the east you just follow the signs for *Klub Kokos* that lead you off the roadside forecourt of the *Ibah* hotel and down some steps to the back of the temple complex, above the rocky pools of the Wos Timor, from where you can veer off up the track that runs along the Campuhan ridge (see box).

## Penestanan

Just west of the Campuhan bridge, but invisible from the main road, the hamlet of **PENESTANAN** is more old-fashioned than its neighbour and makes a good focus for a pleasant two-hour circular walk. It's accessible from a side-road that turns off beside Museum Blanco, but the most dramatic approach is via the steep flight of steps a few hundred metres further north along Jalan Raya Campuhan, just south of Symon's Studio. The steps climb the hillside to a narrow west-bound track, which passes several arterial north–south paths leading to panoramic and inexpensive hilltop accommodation (see p.191), then drops down through ricefields into the next valley, across a river and through a small wooded area, before coming to a crossroads with Penestanan's main street; for restaurants in this area, see p.209. Go straight across (west) if you're heading for Sayan (600m away), right for *Taman Rahasia* hotel (200m), or left for the walk through the village to Museum Blanco in Campuhan (1.5km).

Penestanan's main claim to fame is as the original home of the **Young Artists**. When the Dutch painter Arie Smit settled here in the 1960s he began encouraging village children to experiment with Western paints and techniques and to disregard the conventional styles and themes passed down by their fathers. The resulting works were bold and naive, distinguished by their use of unrealistic colour, an absence of perspective, and their largely expressionless, even featureless, figures. The paintings were warmly received by collectors, and the style was soon labelled "Young Artists" and adopted by painters in other villages as well. One of the first young artists to come under Smit's influence, albeit briefly, was I Nyoman Londo. Now in his sixties, Londo is still painting in the recognized Young Artists style and has a studio attached to his *Londo 2* bungalow accommodation on the hilltop (see p.192).

You can still find scores of painters and about a dozen browsable **galleries** in Penestanan, though not all the artists stick to their village's home-grown style. The people of Penestanan are also the most skilful **bead** workers on the island, adorning an amazing array of items – from shoes and handbags to baskets, belts, caps, earrings and bracelets – with hundreds of painstakingly strung beads. Their work is on sale in shops in Penestanan and across Bali.

# The Monkey Forest and Nyuhkuning

Ubud's best-known tourist attraction is its **Monkey Forest Sanctuary** (8am–6pm; Rp10,000, kids R5000), which occupies the land between the southern end of Jalan Monkey Forest and the northern edge of the woodcarvers' hamlet of **Nyuhkuning**.

The focus of numerous day-tours because of its resident troupe of over one hundred malevolent but photogenic long-tailed macaques, the forest itself is actually small and disappointing, traversed by a concrete pathway and with little exceptional flora to look at. The only way to visit is on foot: the entrance is fifteen minutes' walk south from Ubud's central market, and a stroll around the forest and its temple combines well with a walk around neighbouring Nyuhkuning.

## Pura Dalem Agung Padang Tegal

Five minutes into the forest, you'll come to **Pura Dalem Agung Padang Tegal**, the temple of the dead for the *banjar* of Padang Tegal (you can borrow the requisite sarong and sash at the temple entrance, for which a small donation is requested). *Pura dalem* are traditionally places of extremely strong magical power and the preserve of *leyak* (evil spirits); in this temple you'll find half a dozen stonecarved images of the witch-widow **Rangda** (see p.235) flanking the main stairway, immediately recognizable from the hideous fanged face, unkempt hair, lolling metre-long tongue and large pendulous breasts. Two of the Rangda statues are depicted in the process of devouring children – a favourite occupation of hers.

Casual visitors are not allowed to enter the inner sanctuary, but in the outer courtyard you can see the ornate *kulkul* **drum tower**, built in red brick and lavishly decorated with *paras* carvings of Bhoma heads and *garuda*. When not being used to summon villagers to a cremation or a festival, the drums themselves sit high up on the red-and-gold-painted platform, swathed in lengths of holy black-and-white-checked *kain poleng*.

You can stop for **refreshments** at the *Laka Leke* café, just south of the temple at the start of the track into Nyuhkuning, or there are several other small restaurants further along the track.

## Nyuhkuning

Continuing south from the Pura Dalem Agung Padang Tegal, the track enters the tiny settlement of **NYUHKUNING**, whose villagers are renowned for their woodcarving skills. Both sides of the track are dotted with shops selling **woodcarvings**, and the whole commercial process is more low-key and workshop-oriented than in Mas, for example. Many of the carvers will give woodcarving lessons to interested tourists – just ask inside the shops.

A number of the best local carvings have been preserved in the **Widya Kusuma Woodcarving Museum**, a tiny makeshift gallery that keeps random hours and is set on its own in a sea of ricefields about ten minutes south of the Pura Dalem. The rather small collection is hardly riveting, though it does include a few lovely carvings of fish and monkeys, some of them made back in the 1960s. There's also a collection of woodcarvings in the small, nearby **Museum Pendet**, which features works by the late I Wayan Pendet as well as a number of the sparse, cartoon-like line-drawings by his son, the prolific *Bali Post* cartoonist and artist I Wayan Gunasta, better known as GunGun; both men are from Nyuhkuning. Scattered in amongst the woodcarving shops are several attractively sited small **hotels** (see p.190).

Just beyond the museums, beside Nyuhkuning football field, the track feeds into a minuscule roundabout; whichever of the two routes you choose will take you on a circular tour of the tiny hamlet. Heading straight on, along the peaceful **main street**, you'll pass walled family compounds where many of the carvers have their workshops. At the southern end of the main street, a six-hunded-metre walk, the left arm of the T-junction leads into the next village of Pengosekan (1km to the east; see below), while the right one completes the circular tour of Nyuhkuning, taking you west past the *Bali Spirit* hotel, overlooking the River Wos, and north again to the football field at the top of the village, from where you can head back to the Monkey Forest and central Ubud.

# Pengosekan, Peliatan and Petulu

The villages of **Pengosekan**, **Peliatan** and **Petulu** lie to the east of central Ubud, and can be reached fairly easily on foot in an hour or less from the main market. For Peliatan accommodation, see p.190.

## Pengosekan

At the southern end of Jalan Hanoman, the road enters **PENGOSEKAN**, known locally as the centre of the Pengosekan Community of Artists, a cooperative that was founded in 1969 by I Dewa Nyoman Batuan and his brother I Dewa Putuh Mokoh, to help villagers share resources, exhibition costs and sales. The cooperative was so successful that most of the original members have since established their own galleries, but the spirit of the collective lives on in the **Pengosekan Community of Artists showroom** (daily 9am–6pm), which stands just east of the river on the Pengosekan–Peliatan road. As with other local communities of artists, the Pengosekan painters developed a distinct style, specializing in large canvases of birds, flowers, insects and frogs, painted in gentle pastels and depicted in magnified detail. Their art also features increasingly on carved picture frames, boxes and small pieces of furniture.

### Agung Rai Museum of Art (ARMA)

Pengosekan's main attraction is the impressive **Agung Rai Museum of Art**, or **ARMA** (daily 9am–6pm; Rp20,000; Ⓦ www.armamuseum.com), whose collection nearly matches that of the Neka Art Museum and also features an excellent public-access **library** and research centre on the premises, as well as a small bookshop and an open-air dance stage. It's run by the same collector behind the commercial gallery on Jalan Peliatan (see below). Access is either via Jalan Hanoman or through the main gateway next to the *Kokokan Club* restaurant on the Pengosekan–Peliatan road.

From the main entrance, pass through the temporary exhibition hall and across the garden to the large pavilion signed as **Bale Daja**. The upstairs **Ruang Pita Maha** gallery gives a brief survey of the development of Balinese art, though the labels aren't that helpful and there's no obvious order to the exhibition. Historically speaking, you should begin with the **wayang style** (also known as Kamasan style) canvases that are hung high up on the walls overlooking the central well. These all depict episodes from the *Mahabharata* and are in typical seventeenth-century style, though they probably date from much later. Ida Bagus Belawa's *Cockfight* probably dates from the 1930s or 1940s and is a good example of how some early twentieth-century painters stuck with the two-dimensional Kamasan style, but chose more modern subject matter.

Most **Batuan–style** artists painted real-life scenes too and there are lots of pictures in this style – instantly recognizable by their sheer volume of detail and activity. The very early examples from the 1930s and 1940s were done in black and white ink, but contemporary Batuan artists, such as the innovative and very popular I Wayan Bendi, use plenty of colour. *Life in Bali* is typical of his work: crammed with archetypal Balinese scenes, including a temple procession, a dance performance, a market scene and a cockfight, it's also laced with satirical comments, notably in the figures of long-nosed tourists who pop up in almost every scene, poking their camera lenses at village events. If you look closely you'll find a surfer in the picture too. Anak A. Sobrat's *Baris Dance* is a typical example of **Ubud–style** art, and look out, too, for the pen and ink cartoons of I Gusti Nyoman Lempad, an important Ubud character whose former house is open to the public (see p.195). The **downstairs** gallery in the Bale Daja houses temporary exhibitions.

Across the garden, the **Balé Dauh** is dedicated to works by expatriate artists who lived in, worked in or were inspired by Bali. The middle gallery, **Ruang Walter Spies**, reads like a directory of Bali's most famous expats, and includes works by Adrien Jean Le Mayeur (see p.158), Rudolf Bonnet (p.201), Antonio Blanco (p.202) and Arie Smit (p.199). The highlight is *Calonarang* (1930) by the influential German artist **Walter Spies** (p.198), a very dark portrait of a demonic apparition being watched by a bunch of petrified villagers; this is the only Spies painting currently on show in Bali. The other major work is the double portrait of the *Regent of Magelan and His Wife* (1837) by the Javanese artist **Raden Saleh**, considered to be the father of Indonesian painting. In the adjacent **Ruang Affandi** gallery, you'll find a classic Affandi (p.201) picture of a cockfight, as well as portraits of ARMA founder Anak Agung Gede Rai and his wife Agung Rai Suartini, both by Srihadi Sudarsono.

## Peliatan

The best way to approach **PELIATAN** from central Ubud is on foot via Jalan Sukma, which runs south from Jalan Raya Ubud through the *banjar* of Tebesaya. The upper part of residential Jalan Sukma is peppered with losmen (see p.190) and a few warung, but the architecture is very traditional and the pace of life still gentle so it's a pleasure to wander through. Peliatan's eastern flank, however, has a completely different character, as the main Denpasar–Ubud–Kintamani road roars right through it. This heavily trafficked route is lined with an almost continuous string of arts and crafts shops.

To the Balinese, Peliatan is best known as the home of one of the island's finest **dance troupes**, and particularly for its highly skilled pre-pubescent *legong* dancers. When a Balinese dance group was invited to perform at the Paris Colonial Exhibition in 1931, it was the Peliatan dancers that made the grade, and contributed to the first serious wave of European interest in Bali and Balinese culture. Peliatan dancers again represented Bali on a 1952 tour of Europe and the United States. There are currently over a dozen different dance and gamelan groups active in the village – including, very unusually, a women's gamelan – most of which perform in Peliatan and Ubud on several nights every week (see p.210).

## Petulu

Every evening at around 6pm, hundreds of thousands of white herons fly in from miles around to roost in certain trees in the village of **PETULU**, immediately northeast of Ubud – a quite astonishing spectacle. To find this so-called **white heron sanctuary**, follow Jalan Andong north from the T-junction at the eastern edge of Ubud for about 1.5km, then take the left-hand (signed) fork for a further 1.5km. You may be asked to give a donation just before reaching the roosting area. Lots of public bemos ply Jalan Andong, but you'll have to walk the section from the fork.

If you happen to have binoculars, you might be able to distinguish between the four different species of wading birds that frequent the heronry. The **Javan pond heron** is easiest to spot during the breeding season, when its usual plumage of grey feathers streaked with white darkens to brown on the breast and black along the back. The three types of egret are harder to differentiate: the **plumed egret** is the largest and has pure white plumage, a long neck, black legs and either a black or a yellow beak; the shorter-necked **little egret** also has white feathers, black legs and a black beak. The smaller, yellow-billed **cattle egret** is at its most distinctive during the breeding season, when its normally white feathers become flecked with reddish brown.

No one knows for certain why the herons and the egrets have chosen to make their home in Petulu, though one local story claims that the birds are reincarnations of the tens of thousands of men and women who died in the civil war that raged through Bali in 1966. Many of the victims were buried near here, and the birds are said to have started coming here only after an elaborate ceremony was held in the village in memory of the dead.

# Eating

Ubud is packed full of **places to eat**, many with a higher proportion of vegetarian and organic dishes than anywhere else on the island. Where phone numbers are given for restaurants outside central Ubud it's worth calling to ask about free transport (generally provided when business is good). A mandatory ten percent local government tax is added to all restaurant bills. Most restaurants shut at about 10pm.

## Central Ubud and Padang Tegal

**Ary's Warung** Jl Raya Ubud. Classic Ubud indulgence at this fashionable local landmark, where the contemporary Asian menu includes veal cutlets with *wasabi* sauce (Rp130,000), slowly roasted duck in Balinese spices, frozen lemongrass parfait and over a hundred imported wines (but not much of a vegetarian selection). Best for dinner, unless you splash out on the three-course lunchtime tasting menu (Rp145,000).

**Bali Buddha** Jl Jembawan 1, opposite the GPO. The perfect place to compose postcards or simply chill out: floor cushions and comfortable chairs, organic juices, reasonably priced filled bagels, chocolate mud pie, and brown-bread sandwiches (from Rp15,000). Plus a noticeboard with details of yoga and language classes, and houses for rent.

**Biah Biah** Jl Gautama 13. Authentic, well-priced Balinese fare that can be ordered in individual servings of *lawar*, *urap* and the like, or as part of a vegetarian or fish nasi campur set (Rp13,000).

**Bumbu** Jl Suweta 1. Delicious Indian and Balinese fare, with plenty of veggie options, served in a pleasant water-garden setting. The menu includes banana and coconut curry, chilli-fried fish, vegetarian *thalis* (from Rp25,000), rose-petal ice-cream, plus a range of unusual *lassis* and excellent iced coffees. Also offers cookery classes (see p.215).

**Café des Artistes** Jl Bisma 9x. Sophisticated but welcoming place with changing exhibitions by local artists and a delicious Belgian-style menu that features steak *au poivre*, grilled tuna kebabs (Rp30,000), home-made pastas, lime and vodka sorbet – plus half a dozen Belgian beers (Rp35,000).

## Be a good tourist...

... and **recycle** your plastic water bottle. Discarded plastic bottles pose a major problem in Bali, as they don't decompose and tend to pile up in nasty heaps at the back of losmen and restaurants; they're also relatively expensive and wasteful to manufacture. To help minimize this problem, you can reuse your plastic water bottle by **refilling** it with the filtered water supplied at certain clued-in outlets in Ubud. These include Pondok Pekak Library and Learning Centre off Jalan Dewi Sita in central Ubud; *Gandra* losmen at Jalan Karna 8; *Rumah Roda* losmen at Jalan Kajeng 24; *Bali Buddha* café opposite the GPO on Jalan Jembawan; Roda Internet Café on Jalan Bisma; *Kubuku* café, off the southeastern end of Jalan Monkey Forest in Padang Tegal; and, on Jalan Hanoman, at *Hanoman Juice Ja* restaurant at no. 12, Tegun Galeri crafts shop at no. 44, and *Tegal Sari* hotel at the far southern end. All will refill your bottles for less than what it would cost to buy a replacement.

**Café Wayan** Jl Monkey Forest. Long-established place that's known for its scrumptious, fairly pricey breads and cakes (eat in and take-away), which include the signature temptation, "Death by Chocolate". Also offers a fairly good, mid-priced menu of Indonesian, Thai and European dishes (from Rp20,000), and does occasional traditional Balinese feasts, served buffet style.

**Casa Luna** Jl Raya Ubud. Another very popular Ubud institution specializing in mid-priced breads and cakes, but also offering great salads, Indonesian and Indian fare (Rp15,000–35,000), plus plenty of veggie dishes, as well as Sunday-brunch specials (served until 2pm). Screens nightly videos in a separate room and runs cookery classes (see p.215).

**Gayatri Café** Jl Monkey Forest 67. Deservedly popular, not least because the prices are some of the cheapest in Ubud (from Rp15,000). The menu is varied, ranging from chilli (vegetarian or meat), red bean soup and pizza to salads and nasi campur.

**Hanoman Juice Ja** Jl Hanoman 12, Padang Tegal. Tiny, mid-priced juice bar and café serving lots of fresh fruit and vegetable juices, many of them available with added wheatgerm, chlorophyll, ginseng or royal jelly. Also bakes its own brownies and apple cake, and sells bagels, organic salads, sandwiches and soups.

**Kubuku** Off south end of Jl Monkey Forest, Padang Tegal. Laid-back café whose partial ricefield view and collection of wind-powered chimes and gongs makes it a good place to chill out for an hour or two. The fairly cheap menu (from Rp20,000) is all vegetarian and features home-baked bread, salads, hummus and tempura.

🏃 **Lamak** Jl Monkey Forest. Outstanding, exceptionally creative food is the hallmark of this large, fashionable restaurant, which is sectioned into several modishly designed dining areas (including an air-con room) and boasts a cocktail bar and wine cellar as well. There is much to recommend on the innovative modern-Asian menu, including medallions of butterfish with risotto (Rp55,000), avocado and radicchio salad with mango dressing, and caramelized apple with chocolate mousse. Also has a special vegetarian menu. Well worth the money.

🏃 **Miro's Garden** Jl Bisma. An especially atmospheric place at night, when the dining *bale* are candlelit and the garden is illuminated by oil lamps. Specializes in Indian and Balinese dishes, including various *dosa*-style filled pancakes (Rp35,000), plus a decent vegetarian selection. Unusually, they also offer *babi guling* without having to order it in advance, but only at lunchtimes.

**Sanak Rumah Makan Padang** Jl Hanoman 7. Authentic, very cheap, Sumatran fare (see p.57), including fried chicken, baked eggs, potato cakes and fish curry. Assemble your own meal from the selection of cold platters in the window display (from Rp6000).

**Terazo** Jl Suweta. Above-average Mediterranean cuisine including delicious gazpacho, very good porcini fettuccine and lots of daily specials (Rp60,000–80,000), served in a split-level dining area with funky orange-and-lime decor.

**Tutmak** Jl Dewi Sita. A favourite place for Ubud's expats to gossip over exceptionally good, mid-priced coffee and cakes; also popular for breakfasts and brown-bread sandwiches (around Rp25,000).

**Zula** Jl Raya Ubud 24. Small, innovative, organic veggie restaurant (sister to the Seminyak branch) that does macrobiotic nasi campur featuring different daily grains, various wholesome platter sets (from Rp28,000), raw soups, and a range of energy, cleansing and anti-oxidant juices. Also sells some organic products.

## Campuhan, Sanggingan, Penestanan and Sayan

**Gajah Biru** Jl Raya Penestanan ☎0361/979085. Although it opens from 11am, you need to come here after dark to appreciate the romance of the candlelit water-garden. The mid-priced food is Indian and, aside from the set vegetarian and non-vegetarian *thalis* (from Rp42,000), the menu changes daily, though it always features half a dozen vegetable dishes as well as a chicken course and a lamb speciality.

🏃 **Indus** Jl Raya Sanggingan ☎0361/977684. Occupying a fine position overlooking the Campuhan ridge and the Wos Barat river valley, this is a good place to come for breakfast (muffins on the menu from 7am), lunch, or at sunset, as you'll miss out on the view after dark. Run by the same team behind *Casa Luna* restaurant in central Ubud, the moderately priced menu here features lots of dishes using local *tenggiri* river fish – cooked in Thai, Vietnamese or Indian style – plus the trademark cakes, home-made breads, vegetable juices and healthy salads. Free shuttle from *Casa Luna* in central Ubud.

**Made's Warung** Penestanan ridge, between the steps and the river. Homely spot that's handy for the ridgetop losmen and serves travellers' favourites, including good nasi campur, pancakes, and (with 24hr notice) Balinese smoked duck (Rp95,000 for two).

**Mozaic** Jl Raya Sanggingan ☎0361/975768; closed Mon. The poshest and most expensive restaurant in Ubud (main courses from Rp100,000) serves a menu inspired by contemporary French and Asian cuisine that includes duck *foie gras* with guava in a *rujak* sauce, honey-soy caramelized suckling pork, and dark chocolate fondant with sour-cherry sauce. Also offers tantalizing six-course tasting menus (Rp240,000). Reservations advisable.

**Murni's Warung** Jl Raya Campuhan. Follow the stairs all the way down to the lowest level of this multi-tiered restaurant and you'll appreciate the setting, for it's built into the wall of the steep-sided Wos River valley. The restaurant is an Ubud institution and serves curries, home-made soups and Indonesian specialities as well as a good line in sweet things, such as strawberry cheesecake, and banana and caramel cake (Rp12,500).

**Naughty Nuri's** Jl Raya Sanggingan. Long-running, fairly cheap warung that's a favourite

expat hangout and is ideally located right opposite the entrance to the Neka Art Museum. Fresh tuna is a speciality – served as steaks, sashimi and saté – and barbecues are a regular event. All sorts of Indonesian standards, too (from Rp20,000), plus great Martinis.

**Red Rice** Opposite *Sayan Terrace*, Jl Raya Sayan ☎0361/974433. Unpretentious mid-priced restaurant that disingenuously calls itself "a warung with wine" but actually serves an eclectic and adventurous menu (from Rp30,000) that fuses Asian and Western cuisines, including Donald Bebek (duck) spring rolls, quiche lorraine, *soto ayam*, and banana soup; some experiments are more successful than others.

**Sari Laba Boga** Jl Raya Penestanan. Cheap and tasty travellers' fare and Indonesian favourites – including good *urap* and *nasi kuning* – plus a long menu of vegetarian options (from Rp12,000).

# Nightlife and entertainment

Ubud is hardly a hotbed of hedonistic **nightlife**: many tourists spend the early part of the evening at one of the numerous Balinese **dance performances**, staged every night in and around central Ubud, before catching last orders at a restaurant at around 9pm. Less traditional entertainment is limited to the live music staged at some of Ubud's **bars**, or the nightly **video showings** at some of the restaurants, including *Casa Luna* on Jalan Raya Ubud.

## Bars and live music venues

**Exiles** Across from the main ARMA entrance on the Pengosekan–Peliatan road. Small restaurant where local jazz, blues and funk musicians meet for weekly jamming sessions on Saturday nights.

**Jazz Café** Jl Sukma 2, Peliatan ☎0361/976594. Lively bar-restaurant that stages quality live jazz from Tuesday to Saturday from about 7.30pm. The atmosphere is usually good, there's just about room to dance in-between the tables, and the per-fectly respectable mid-priced menu of Indonesian and Continental dishes is enlivened by jugs of draught beer and assorted margaritas. Check fly-ers and the board outside for performance details. Phone for free local transport.

**Planet Warung** Southern end of Jl Hanoman. This bar-restaurant is the main nightlife venue in this part of town, with live music twice a week – rock (Wed) and reggae (Sat) – and occasional video shows on other nights.

**The Pubas** Jl Monkey Forest. Bar-lounge that serves wine, beer and cocktails till late and stages occasional special events.

**Putra Bar** Jl Monkey Forest. Very lively bar-restaurant that runs a weekly schedule of different theme nights, including frequent reggae evenings, complete with live band. There's a dancefloor, live international sports on the TV, and a faintly Kuta-ish atmosphere. Check boards outside for upcoming events.

## Dance and drama

When the first wave of expatriates settled here in the 1920s, Ubud was more renowned as a centre of **Balinese dance** and **gamelan** than for its arts and crafts; today, the region still boasts dozens of outstanding dance and music groups, many of which stage regular performances for tourists. The **kecak** (monkey dance) and the **barong** (lion dance) are the most exciting, accessible and visually interesting, with lots of drama and fairly easy plot lines. Both are performed in venues across the island, as is the more refined and understated **legong**, but Ubud also stages some highly unusual shows such as the village exorcism, **calonarang**, in which half the village seems to participate. Here, too, you'll also get a rare chance to see Javanese shadow-puppet dramas, or **wayang kulit**, and to hear the unique **all-female gamelan**.

A lot of the dance groups combine up to eight different dances into a medley show. Sometimes, this is not indicated in the publicity – the show at Ubud Palace by the Sadha Budaya dance group, for example, is advertised as *legong*, but also features the brilliantly eloquent flirtation dance **oleg tambulilingan** (bumblebee dance) and the touching **topeng tua** (old man's mask dance). Similarly, the Tirta Sari group's show in Peliatan includes a superbly melodramatic solo dance, the **kebyar trompong**, performed as a very camp repartee between the dancer and the gamelan players.

### Practicalities

There are up to five different dance shows every night in the Ubud area; the tourist office has copies of the regular weekly schedule and also arranges **free transport** to the more outlying venues. You can also see an online timetable at Ⓦ www.whatsupbali.com/dance.html. Most **tickets** are Rp50,000 and can be bought either at the tourist office, from touts or at the door. Performances generally start between 7pm and 8pm, and it's advisable to arrive at least half an hour early, as there are no seat reservations. For more on Balinese dance, see p.468.

If you have only one evening to catch a show, then consider seeing whatever is playing at **Puri Saren Agung (Ubud Palace)**, opposite the market in the centre of Ubud (see p.194). The setting is breathtaking, with the torchlit courtyard gateways furnishing a memorable backdrop. You can also watch Ubud children doing their dance practice here (Sun 9.30am–noon, Tues 3–5.30pm; free). The *kecak* performance twice a month at the **ARMA** stage in Pengosekan (see p.206) is also worth catching; it's an unusually fiery and humorous version and is staged only on the nights of the full moon and dark moon; see Ⓦ www .armamuseum.com/stage_performance.php for dates.

# Shopping

**Shopping** for arts and crafts is a major pastime in Ubud: there are enjoyably browsable outlets in all its neighbourhoods, but if you're short on time the northern stretch of Jalan Hanoman has the biggest concentration of interesting, quality handicraft shops. You might also want to explore the specialist "craft villages" on the Denpasar–Ubud road (see pp.172–178), and the woodcarving outlets on the way to Tegalalang (see p.222) before making any significant purchases. Many of the more expensive outlets can organize shipping as well. Most Ubud shops open daily, many not closing until 9pm. Tino Supermarket, on Jalan Raya Ubud, stocks all major essentials, from suntan lotion to beer.

### Art

**Agung Rai Fine Art Gallery** Jl Peliatan. High-quality outlet for paintings of all styles, owned by the man behind the ARMA in Pengosekan.
**Duck Man of Bali** Jl Raya Goa Gajah, about 1.5km east along the road to Goa Gajah. Known for its phenomenal gallery of wooden ducks in all sizes

and styles, carved by "the duck man", Ngurah Umum, and his assistants.
**Low Art** Jl Raya Ubud 8. Unmissable gallery and outlet for popular, "street" art, film posters and kitsch from Bali and elsewhere. Especially intriguing are the vinyl picture-mats used in the *kococan* gambling game played at temple festivals, which

feature different casts of popular characters, including cartoon creatures, TV personalities, politicians and mythological figures.

**Munut's Gallery** Far eastern end of Jl Raya Ubud. Recommended dealer in paintings of all styles, with a large selection on display.

**Neka Gallery** Eastern end of Jl Raya Ubud. Huge warren of a showroom owned by the founder of the Neka Art Museum. Specializes in good-quality works, many by well-known artists.

**Rio Helmi** Jl Suweta 5. Small gallery and showroom of prints by the respected eponymous expat photographer.

## Books

**Adi Bookshop** Jl Hanoman 1. Small second-hand bookstore.

**ARMA Bookshop** Inside Agung Rai Museum of Art, Pengosekan. Small range of (mostly art-related) books on Bali and Indonesia.

**Ary's Bookshop** Jl Raya Ubud. Extensive stock of books and maps on Bali and Indonesia. Also sells foreign newspapers and magazines.

**Cinta Bookshop** Jl Dewi Sita. Lots of second-hand books for sale plus some also available for rent.

**Ganesha Bookshop** Jl Raya Ubud, cnr Jl Jembawan ⓦ www.ganeshabooksbali.com. The best bookshop in Bali, with a huge stock of new books on all things Balinese; also sells maps and some second-hand books, and has an online ordering service.

**Igna Bookshop** North end of Jl Monkey Forest. Reasonable number of second-hand books, plus a few new ones.

**Neka Art Museum Bookshop** Jl Raya Sanggingan. Specializes in books on Balinese, Indonesian and expat artists.

**Periplus** North end of Jl Monkey Forest. The Ubud branch of the well-stocked Bali-wide chain carries a good range of local-interest titles, plus novels and general non-fiction.

**Pondok Pekak Library and Learning Centre** Jl Dewi Sita. Plenty of well-priced second-hand books available for sale, rent and part-exchange.

**Rona Bookshop** Jl Sukma 23, Peliatan. Second-hand bookstore and library attached to *Rona Losmen*.

## Clothes, jewellery and accessories

**Animale** Western end of Jl Raya Ubud. Womenswear chain known for floaty outfits and bold prints.

**Kamar Sutra** Jl Monkey Forest. Stunning batik designs on very expensive silk and crêpe scarves, wraps and shawls.

**Pasar Seni** Jl Raya Ubud. Two-storey "art market"

with dozens of stalls selling cheap cotton clothes, sarongs and batik shirts. There are several inexpensive tailors here, too.

**Prama Shop** Jl Hanoman 23. Central Ubud outlet for some of the Penestanan beadworkers, selling beaded belts, bags, bracelets etc.

**Puspita** at Jl Hanoman 53 and at Jl Suweta 5. Tiny boutiques selling cute, creative women's clothes, designed with young Japanese customers in mind.

**Sely** Jl Hanoman. Inexpensive cosmetic bags, purses and shoulder bags, made from brightly coloured Balinese silk.

**Studio Perak Toko** Jl Dewi Sita. Stylish silver jewellery from the people who run Ubud's silver-smithing courses (see p.214).

**Suarti** Jl Monkey Forest. Chain of jewellery shops specializing in original designs.

## Crafts, textiles and homewares

**Asialine** Jl Hanoman 8. Classy handicrafts from across Indonesia, especially wooden frames and bowls painted with intricate batik-print motifs.

**Bali Cares** Jl Hanoman 44b. A cooperative outlet for handicrafts, paintings, toiletries and accessories, proceeds from which are used to fund the work of eleven Balinese charities. Run by the IDEP foundation (see Basics, p.44).

**Dari Desa** Off the far southern end of Jl Monkey Forest, Padang Tegal. Vibrant soft furnishings, including quilts, throws and beanbags, made from Indonesian textiles, much of it commissioned directly from village women.

**Design Unit** Jl Raya Sanggingan, 100m north of *Mozaic* restaurant. Alluring, fashionable modern-Asian homewares, lamps, furniture and the like, at fairly high prices.

**Kites Center** 3 Off the far southern end of Jl Monkey Forest, Padang Tegal. Traditional kites, many in spectacular designs such as butterflies, vampire bats and dragons. Can be made to order.

**Kupu-Kupu** Jl Raya Ubud. Small outlet for inexpensive works produced by disabled woodcarvers, kite-makers, painters, beadworkers and weavers, under the auspices of the Kupu-Kupu foundation (see Basics, p.45, for more info). Staffed by the artists.

**Mangku Made Gina** Near ARMA at the southern end of Jl Hanoman. Unrivalled collection of exquisite palm-leaf baskets made by a family of Pengosekan basket-weavers.

**Murti** Jl Hanoman 19. Outlet for the distinctive ceramics from the kilns at Pejaten in west Bali (see p.347), mostly glazed in mint green and pale blues.

**Pasar Seni** Jl Raya Ubud. The "art market" is stacked full of stalls selling sarongs, bamboo windchimes, tightly woven *ato*-grass baskets and the like.

**Sama Suka** Jl Hanoman. Luxurious sheets and duvet covers made from sumptuous hand-woven cotton.

**Tegun** Jl Hanoman 44. Exceptionally fine Indonesian artefacts, including puppets, jewellery, and exquisite wooden bowls hand-painted with batik motifs.

**Wangi-Wangi Natural** Near ARMA at the southern end of Jl Hanoman. Curtains, blinds and cushions, mostly made from rough-weave cottons and raffias. Also made to order.

**Wardani's** central Jl Monkey Forest. Ubud's best fabric shop, with scores of different cotton *ikats*, silks and cottons sold by the metre, as well as ready-made soft furnishings.

## Musical instruments, CDs and DVDs

**Ganesha Bookshop** Jl Raya Ubud, cnr Jl Jembawan ⓦ www.ganeshabooksbali.com. CDs and tapes of Indonesian and Balinese music; online ordering service also available.

**Moari Music** Jl Raya Ubud. Specializes in traditional Balinese musical instruments, from bamboo flutes to full-sized gamelan.

**Pondok Bamboo** Off the far southern end of Jl Monkey Forest, Padang Tegal. Sells the full range of Balinese instruments made from bamboo, with everything from *genggong* to the component parts of the *gamelan joged bumbung*, the bamboo gamelan.

**Ubud Music** Jl Raya Ubud. Ubud's main outlet for cheap CDs and DVDs.

# Spas, beauty treatments and alternative therapies

Arty, spiritual-minded Ubud is Bali's centre for **holistic practices** and **alternative therapies**, and also offers lots of opportunities to indulge in traditional **spa** and **beauty treatments** (for more on which see Basics, p.73). Except where stated, all listed centres open daily until at least 7pm. For more information on holistic activities and therapies in Ubud and the rest of Bali, visit the website of the Ubud-based **Bali Spirit** network (ⓦ www.balispirit.com).

**Bali Spirit** Jl Hanoman 44b ☏ 0361/970992, ⓦ www.balispirit.com. A spacious yoga studio and holistic information centre that holds regular yoga classes in various disciplines and levels (phone for schedules). Also sells yoga mats.

**Ibah Spa** Jl Raya Campuhan ☏ 0361/974466, ⓦ www.ibahbali.com. The treatment rooms at this luxury boutique hotel are among the most indulgent in Ubud, and the spa menu includes the Mandara massage where each client is massaged by two therapists at the same time, using five different massage styles. Advance booking essential. Reassuringly expensive.

**Meditation Shop** Jl Monkey Forest ☏ 0361/976206. The local Brahma Kumaris meditation group holds free meditation sessions every evening for anyone who's interested, and runs five-day meditation courses.

**Nur Salon** Jl Hanoman 28 ☏ 0361/975352, ⓔ nursalonubud@yahoo.com. Ubud's first massage and beauty salon has been in operation since the 1970s and enjoys a very good reputation; the *mandi lulur* treatments are especially famous, and prices are among the lowest in Ubud. The salon occupies a traditional Balinese compound and treatment rooms are designed in keeping with the surroundings. Uses male masseurs for male customers.

**Sukma Holistic Centre and Tarot Studio** Jl Sukma 1a ☏ 0361/975523; closed Sun. Tiny centre for tarot readings and workshops (call or drop by for an appointment), with an attached café serving juices and organic salads. Also sells tarot cards, metaphysical jewellery, crystals and healing stones.

**Tjampuhan Spa** At *Hotel Tjampuhan*, Jl Raya Campuhan ☏ 0361/975368, ⓦ www.tjampuhan .com. Unusual, rather kitsch, grotto-like spa complex built into the cliffside near the river below the *Hotel Tjampuhan*. Pools, waterfalls and surreal figurines evoke a watery fantasyland, and there are saunas and a steam room as well as a large programme of massages, scrubs and facials. Non-guests can use all the facilities for US$15; or $49 including one treatment ($89 per couple).

**Ubud Bodyworks Centre** Jl Hanoman 25 ☏ 0361/975720, ⓦ www.ubudbodyworkscentre .com. Traditional baths and massages, beauty treatments, acupressure, energy balancing and reflexology. Also organizes yoga sessions and courses, and sells essential oils.

**Ubud Sari Health Resort** Jl Kajeng 35 ☎0361/974393, ⓦwww.ubudsari.com. The most serious, and expensive, of Ubud's health and beauty centres, with an on-site swimming pool and health restaurant. Treatments include massage, aromatherapy, reflexology, shiatsu, reiki, sports massage, yoga, and sessions with a chiropractor.

You can also stay at the resort's tranquil bungalows (ⓖ) or book an all-inclusive healing week for $200 per day.

**Zen Bali Spa** Jl Hanoman ☎0361/970976, ⓦwww.zenbalispa.com. Funky little day-spa with a good reputation, a range of well-priced massages, scrubs and beauty treatments, and cute orange-and-blue treatment rooms.

# Courses and workshops

With so many creative types in residence, Ubud is a great place to get learning: there are tourist-oriented **courses** here in everything from making offerings to creating jewellery, from traditional Balinese dance to textile appreciation. In addition to the more formal venues listed, it's always worth asking advice from the more traditional homestays, whose managers are often dancers, musicians or painters. For yoga courses, see above.

## Arts, crafts, music, dance and traditional culture

**ARMA Cultural Workshops** Jl Raya Pengosekan ☎0361/976659, ⓦwww.armamuseum.com. Museum-endorsed classes in Balinese painting, woodcarving, batik, gamelan, dance and theatre, traditional architecture, Hinduism, astrology and making offerings. Most classes last two hours and cost $22–50 per person, depending on subject and class size.

**Balinese Traditional Healing Centre** Jl Jem-bawan 5 ☎0361/7426189, ⓔbalihealer@hotmail .com. Balinese healer Ni Wayan Nuriasih shows participants how to recognize and gather medicinal plants from the wild, then demonstrates how to use them. Rp250,000 including vegetarian lunch.

**Crackpot Batik** Jl Monkey Forest. Design your own batik fabrics, paintings and T-shirts, to your own timetable. Rates vary but are always reasonable.

**Dewi Sekar Ayu** Jl Hanoman 26 ☎0361/975350. If you have a serious interest in Balinese dance, Ayu will be happy to arrange a tailor-made course for you.

**Museum Puri Lukisan Cultural Workshops** Jl Raya Ubud ☎0361/971159, ⓦwww.mpl-ubud .com. Serious, reputable classes run by and at Ubud's oldest art museum. Courses include batik, woodcarving, beadwork, classical painting, bas-ketry, kite-making, mask-painting, shadow-puppet making, gamelan and Balinese dance. Most last one day and cost Rp350,000.

**Nataraja Dance School** Jl Sugriwa 20 ☎0361/975916, ⓔgauranataraja@yahoo.com. Dancer and musician Wayan Karta gives individual dance and gamelan lessons in the dance of your choice (*legong* or *baris*, for example). Lessons cost Rp50,000 per hr, but to get a good grounding, students are advised to sign up for at least fourteen hours of tuition.

**Nirvana Batik Course** Jl Gautama 10 ☎0361/975415, ⓔrodanet@denpasar.wasantara .net.id. Renowned Ubud painter, village activist and batik artist I Nyoman Suradnya runs one- to five-day courses in batik painting, charging $25–$35 per day, including all materials. His family also runs the *Nirvana Pension* guesthouses (see p.189).

**Nyuhkuning woodcarving shops** Nyuhkuning. There are plenty of opportunities to learn wood-carving in this village of woodcarvers; just ask at any of the shops.

**Pondok Pekak** Jl Dewi Sita ☎0361/976194, ⓔpondok@indo.net.id. "Art of Bali" beginners' classes in dance, gamelan, painting and wood-carving (Rp50,000–200,000), held at the Pondok Pekak Library and Learning Centre.

**Sehati** Off the far southern end of Jl Monkey Forest, Padang Tegal ☎0361/976341, ⓔhanaubud@indo.net.id. Learn to play the game-lan and other Balinese instruments, or to master the rudimentary elements of Balinese dance from a graduate of Denpasar's prestigious school of performing arts. Rp50,000 per hour.

**Studio Perak** Jl Gautama ☎0812/365 1809, ⓔstudioperak@yahoo.ca; closed Sun. Courses in silversmithing, where in half a day you can produce your own ring (Rp100,000 inclusive). In two to five days (Rp120,000 per day excluding materials) you can learn more advanced techniques and design skills.

Threads of Life Jl Kajeng 24 ☏0361/972187, ⓦwww.threadsoflife.com. The Threads of Life Textile Art Center and Gallery (see p.197) holds two scheduled classes a week on Indonesian textile appreciation (from Rp50,000) and a weekly workshop on indigo dyeing and batik-making. Phone for times and reservations.

## Cookery and language

Bumbu restaurant Jl Suweta 1 ☏0361/974217, ⓔbumbu_bali@plasa.com. Half-day workshops in Balinese cooking, which begin with a trip to the local market and culminate in lunch. Rp138,000.
Casa Luna restaurant Jl Raya Ubud ☏0361/973282, ⓦwww.casalunabali.com. Famous, long-running half-day Balinese cooking workshops, some of which feature trips to the market; see website for schedules. Rp200,000.

Secret Garden Cooking School *Taman Rahasia* hotel, Penestanan Kaja ☏0361/979395, ⓦwww. balisecretgarden.com. One- and two-day intensive courses in Balinese cooking at Penestanan's *Taman Rahasia* hotel; see website for schedules. $50/90.
Tegal Sari Southern end of Jl Hanoman ☏0361/973318, ⓦwww.tegalsari-ubud.com. Half-day courses in Balinese and Indonesian cuisine at the *Tegal Sari* hotel in Padang Tegal. Rp175,000 including lunch.
Pondok Pekak Library and Learning Centre Jl Dewi Sita ☏0361/976194, ⓔpondok@indo.net .id. Intensive Indonesian language courses (24hr; Rp600,000), usually spread over four weeks but can be changed to suit; also offers lessons at Rp50,000/hour.

# Listings

Banks and exchange There are plenty of ATMs on Jl Raya Ubud, a couple on Jl Monkey Forest, and one just north of Perama on Jl Hanoman in Padang Tegal; there are currency exchange facilities but no ATMs in Campuhan, Sanggingan, Penestanan and Sayan. Numerous tour agents throughout the Ubud area, and particularly on Jl Raya Ubud and Jl Monkey Forest, offer exchange services, but see p.47 for details of common scams.
Email and Internet Some of the most efficient

## Ubud for kids

Many of the **courses and workshops** listed on p.214 welcome younger participants. In particular, most kids enjoy creating their own **batik** T-shirts and paintings, which they can do on an informal basis at the batik centres, and Studio Perak welcomes all over-8s to make their own silver **jewellery**. Pondok Pekak Library and Learning Centre on Jalan Dewi Sita (☏0361/970194, ⓔpondok@denpasar.wasantara.net.id) runs children's classes in **gamelan** and Balinese **dance**, which are suitable for most over-6s, and holds weekly story-and-singing hours for toddlers. It also has a well-stocked library of **children's books**.

Traditional **dance-drama performances** can also be entertaining for kids, particularly the *kecak* (monkey) dance, which is performed somewhere in the Ubud vicinity almost every night (see p.210), and the *wayang kulit* shadow-puppet shows, which are staged several nights a week at *Oka Kartini's* on Jalan Raya Ubud (check with the tourist office for details). Pondok Pekak also stages weekly dance performances by children.

The three animal parks within 45 minutes' drive of Ubud make fun days out for children of most ages. The **Elephant Park** in Taro (see p.223) gives everyone the chance to feed the elephants and watch them bathe, and you can also join a short elephant safari ride through the surrounding forest. In Batubulan, the **Bali Bird Park** (see p.174) is a pleasure to wander through, with plenty of pretty specimens to admire and an attractively landscaped setting. Next door, the **Bali Reptile Park** has strange, slimy creatures, including huge pythons, chameleons and little Komodo dragons.

Most **white-water rafting** operators (see p.126) also accept children (depending on the course), but river kayaking is unsuitable for children under 14.

Internet centres are: Highway on Jl Raya Ubud (high-speed connection and personal laptop hookups; open 24hr); Bali 3000 on Jl Raya Ubud; Roda Tourist Services, Jl Bisma 3; and Ary's Business and Travel Service on Jl Raya Ubud.

**Embassies and consulates** See p.35.

**Hospitals and clinics** For minor casualties, go to the Legian Clinic, Jl Monkey Forest ☎0361/970805, or to the Ubud Clinic, which also has a dental service, at Jl Raya Campuhan 36 ☎0361/974911. Both are open 24hr, are staffed by English-speakers, and will respond to emergency call-outs. For anything serious, the nearest hospitals are in Denpasar (p.107).

**House rental** Check the noticeboards at *Bali Buddha* café on Jl Jembawan, at *Casa Luna* restaurant on Jl Raya Ubud, and at Bali 3000 Internet café on Jl Raya Ubud. See p.55 for online rental agencies.

**Libraries** The Pondok Pekak Library and Learning Centre off Jl Dewi Sita (Mon–Sat 9am–9pm, Sun noon–5pm) has lots of books about Bali as well as Asia travel guides and English-language novels. You can read them on the spot in the comfortable upstairs reading room or borrow them for a small fee. There is also a children's library and learning centre here, which aims to encourage Ubud children to read Indonesian- and English-language books; donated books and funds are always welcome – see p.45 for more details. The Agung Rai Museum of Art (ARMA) has the island's best library of books about Bali, including famous esoteric works, language books and travelogues.

**Pharmacies** Two on Jl Monkey Forest.

**Phone and fax services** The government Kantor Telcom is inconveniently located at the eastern end of Jl Raya Ubud, but there are IDD direct-dial phones at the GPO on Jl Jembawan as well as at all the above-listed email and Internet centres; the latter also offer fax services.

**Police** The main police station is on the eastern edge of town, on Jl Andong. There's a more central police booth beside the market at the Jl Raya Ubud /Jl Monkey Forest crossroads.

**Post offices** The Ubud GPO on Jl Jembawan (daily 8am–6pm) keeps poste restante, and there's a parcel-packing service next door. There are plenty of postal agents all over Ubud where you can buy stamps and send mail and parcels.

**Safety boxes** For rent at Ary's Business and Travel Service on Jl Raya Ubud (☎0361/973130), and at many mid-range and all expensive hotels.

**Travel agents** Try the reputable Ary's Business and Travel Service just west of the market on Jl Raya Ubud (☎0361/973130, ✉ary_s2000@yahoo.com).

# East of Ubud

Slicing through the region immediately **east of Ubud**, the sacred rivers Petanu and Pakrisan flow down from the Batur crater rim in parallel, framing a narrow strip of land imbued with great spiritual and historical importance. This fifteen-kilometre-long sliver has been settled since the Balinese Bronze Age, around 300 BC, and now boasts the biggest concentration of antiquities on Bali. From the stone sarcophagi and Bronze Age gong of **Pejeng** to the eleventh-century rock-hewn hermitage at **Goa Gajah** and fourteenth-century **Yeh Pulu reliefs**, these relics all lie within 7km of Ubud.

**Access by bemo** is very easy from Ubud – take any Gianyar-bound one – and similarly straightforward by bike or motorbike. This area also combines well with Tirta Empul and Gunung Kawi, 11km further north, and direct bemos connect the two. There are a couple of places to stay near Goa Gajah and at Yeh Pulu.

## The legend of Dalem Bedaulu

Between the tenth and the fourteenth centuries, the sacred land between the Pakrisan and Petanu rivers was the seat of the **Pejeng dynasty**, which ruled the region from a court located a few kilometres south of modern Pejeng, in the village of Bedulu. The most notorious of the Pejeng rulers was also its last, **Dalem Bedaulu**, whose armies were the last on the island to capitulate to the invading forces of East Java's Majapahit empire in 1343. Legend relates how Dalem Bedaulu had enormous supernatural power, which he liked to demonstrate by regularly cutting off his own head and then replacing it. The god **Siwa** became so incensed by this boastful behaviour that, on one occasion, he made Dalem Bedaulu's severed head roll away into a fast-moving river. The king's quick-thinking servant cut off the head of the nearest living creature, a pig, and placed it on the royal neck. After this, the king was so embarrassed about his pig's head that he established himself in a special high tower, passed a law forbidding anyone to look up at his face, and forced everyone to speak to him from ground level, eyes downcast. When East Javanese prime minister **Gajah Mada** heard of this, he plotted to get round the prohibition by asking, in Dalem Bedaulu's presence, to be brought drinking water from a traditional vessel with a very long spout. To drink, he was obliged to tip his head backwards, and so caught a glimpse of Dalem Bedaulu's pig's head. Dalem Bedaulu was so furious at Gajah Mada's cunning that he immediately self-combusted; that was the end of the Pejeng dynasty and the start of Majapahit's complete hegemony over Bali.

# Goa Gajah

Thought to have been a hermitage for eleventh-century Hindu priests, **Goa Gajah** (Elephant Cave; 8am–5.30pm; Rp4100, children Rp2100, including sarong rental) is a major tourist attraction, owing more to its proximity to the main Ubud–Gianyar road than to any remarkable atmosphere or ancient features. Besides the cave itself, there's a traditional bathing pool here, as well as a number of ancient stone relics.

### The pool and the cave

Descending the steep flight of steps from the back of the car park, you get a good view of the rectangular **bathing pool**, whose elegant sunken contours dominate the courtyard below. Such pools were usually built at holy sites, either at the source of a holy spring as at Tirta Empul or, like this one, near a sacred spot so that devotees could cleanse themselves before making offerings or prayers. Local men and women would have bathed here in the segregated male (right-hand) and female (left-hand) sections, under the jets of water from the Petanu tributary channelled through the protruding navels of the full-breasted statues lining its back wall. Although the water still flows, the pool is now maintained for ornamental purposes only.

The carvings that trumpet the entranceway to the hillside cave are impressive, if a little hard to distinguish. The **doorway** is a huge gaping mouth, framed by the upper jaw of a monstrous rock-carved head that's thought to represent either the earth god Bhoma, or the widow–witch Rangda, or a hybrid of the two. It would have served both as a repeller of evil spirits and as a suggestion that on entering you were being swallowed up into another, holier, world. Early visitors interpreted it as an elephant's head, which is how the cave got its modern name. A series of mythical creatures is also said to be carved into the bare rock face to the left and right of the head, but from the ground it's hard to spot them.

Passing into the monster's mouth, you enter the dank and dimly lit T-shaped **cave**, hewn by hand from the rocky hillside to serve as meditation cells, or possibly living quarters, for the priests or ascetics. As with most of Bali's rock-cut monuments, the mythical giant Kebo Iwa is also associated with Goa Gajah, and legends describe how he gouged out the cells and the carvings here with his powerful fingernails, a feat that took him just one night. A statue of the Hindu elephant-headed god Ganesh sits in a niche to the left of the far end, while to the right are three lingga, phallic emblems of the god Siwa.

Outside the cave, in the small pavilion to the left of the gateway, sits a weather-worn **statue** of a woman surrounded by a horde of kids. Carved from a single block of stone, this piece shows the Balinese folk heroine **Men Brayut**, a typical village woman whose resolute struggle against poverty has made her into a saint-like figure in Bali (see box, p.200). Men Brayut is known as the goddess Hariti in Buddhist literature, and this statue – along with a number of other relics found nearby – have led archeologists to believe that the site may have a **Buddhist** as well as a Hindu history. You can see some of the other Buddhist fragments by following the concrete steps that climb down the side of the ravine just beyond the bathing pool. These include the relief of a multi-tiered stupa carved into a huge fragment of rock, and a couple of small, seated stone Buddha images.

### Practicalities

To get to Goa Gajah, either walk, cycle or drive the 3km east from Ubud's Jalan Peliatan, or take one of the numerous (usually orange) Ubud–Gianyar **bemos**, which pass the entrance. The site car park borders the main Ubud–Gianyar road. You can also walk here from the Yeh Pulu rock carvings (see below), along the irrigation channels that zigzag through the ricefields, but you'll need to hire one of the guides who hang around both at Yeh Pulu and Goa Gajah.

There's a pleasant **place to stay** nearby, on the edge of the lively but untouristed village of **BEDULU**. Continue along the main road about 500m east of Goa Gajah and then turn to the south (right), following signs for *Puri Yeh Pulu Bungalows* (T0361/7419677, E agung_inhady@yahoo.com; ❹). The five bungalows here are spacious and comfortable and sit in a garden that enjoys nice views down over the steep Petanu valley.

# Yeh Pulu

In contrast with the overcrowded and overrated carvings at Goa Gajah, the rock-cut panels at **YEH PULU** (daylight hours; Rp4100 including sarong and sash rental, kids Rp2100) are delightfully engaging, and the site is often empty – partly due to its relative inaccessibility.

Chipped away from the sheer rock face, the 25-metre-long series of Yeh Pulu **carvings** are said to date back to the fourteenth or fifteenth century. They are thought by some historians to depict a five-part story and, while the meaning of this story has been lost, it's still possible to make out some recurring characters and to speculate on the connections between them; local people, however, simply describe the carvings as showing daily activities from times past. The name of the site – *yeh* ("holy spring"), *pulu* ("stone vessel") – refers to the holy spring that rises from near the Ganesh statue at the far end of the carved sequence, and it's possible that the jar featured in scene three is for carrying holy water.

The series begins with an **introductory panel** separated from the others, showing a man with his arm raised, thought to be the Hindu god Krishna. In the **first scene**, a man carrying two jars of river water on a shoulder pole follows a woman of higher caste, who is bedecked with jewels. **Scene two** shows a different woman, seated, with her right arm stretched out towards a man carrying a hoe. To his left sits a figure whose distinctive turban-like hat indicates that he is either a priest or an ascetic (modern Balinese priests still wear very similar headdresses). A sarong-clad boy stands alone at the end of this panel, beside a kneeling statue of a Jaga Desa, the mythical village giant whose job it is to protect the village from evil spirits. **Scene three** features a boar-hunting scene, above which two figures kneel either side of a (possibly holy) water jar. **Scene four** shows two men carrying five boars away on a pole. In **scene five**, another hunter looks set to gallop off, and is either aided or hindered by a woman pulling on the animal's tail. Just as the story opened with a religious image, so the **concluding panel** is carved into a niche containing the elephant-headed god Ganesh.

The small **holy spring** after which the site is named rises close by the statue of Ganesh and is sacred – hence the need for all visitors to wear temple dress and, for the same reason, you will probably also be asked by the temple guardian for a donation when you get to this point. The Balinese believe that all water is a gift from the spirits, so on the occasions when the spring fails to rise, this is seen as an indication of troubled or even angry spirits and special ceremonies are required to restore a harmonious flow.

### Practicalities

The prettiest approach to Yeh Pulu is **on foot** along the dykes that skirt the sculpted rice-terraces behind Goa Gajah, but you'll need to hire a guide to lead the way – they wait for customers at both sites and charge Rp50,000 for up to two people, or Rp100,000 for larger groups. Guides can also take you on the two-hour return ricefield **walk** from Yeh Pulu to the rice temple Dukuh Kedongan, with the chance of a dip in the Petanu River (prices as above); or the longer, hotter option (3–5hr), which continues to the Durga Kutri temple, Pura Bukit Dharma Durga Kutri, in the village of Kutri (see p.234), and costs Rp100,000/200,000.

If you're using the Ubud–Gianyar **bemo**, get off at the Yeh Pulu signs just east of Goa Gajah or west of the Bedulu crossroads, then walk the kilometre south through the hamlet of Batulumbang to Yeh Pulu. If driving, follow the same signs through Batulumbang to where the road peters out, a few hundred metres above the stonecarvings. *Made's Café* occupies a pretty position at the end of this road and serves a perfectly respectable menu of **snacks** and rice dishes. There's a small **losmen** next door, *Pondok Wisata Lantur* (☎0361/942399; ②), which offers simple accommodation on the edge of the family compound.

# Pejeng

Inhabited since the Bronze Age, and considered a holy site ever since, the village of **PEJENG** and its immediate environs harbour a wealth of religious antiquities, from carvings and rock-cut *candi* to bronze artefacts and massive stone statues. Some of these have been left in their original location, alongside riverbeds or buried in among the paddy-fields, while others have been housed in local temples; several have also been carted off to museums, here and in Denpasar,

Jakarta and Amsterdam. The remains have rather an esoteric appeal, and the area gets relatively few visitors and rarely features on the tour-bus circuit.

### Practicalities

Pejeng's three main temples all lie within a few hundred metres of each other on the Bedulu–Tampaksiring road and are clearly signposted.

Coming from Ubud, take an orange, Gianyar-bound **bemo** to the Bedulu crossroads and then either wait for a bluey-grey Tampaksiring-bound one, or walk the kilometre to the temples. The alternative route from Ubud – by bike or motorbike – is the quiet, fairly scenic five-kilometre **back road** that heads east from the Jalan Raya Ubud/Jalan Peliatan junction at the eastern edge of Ubud, passes the posh *Maya Ubud* hotel, and then zigzags through paddies and small villages before finally emerging at the market on the main road, just 25m north of Pura Penataran Sasih (turn right for the temple).

Although the major temples are clearly signed, you might want to employ a local **guide** for the more out-of-the-way sites; the best place to find one is at Pura Penataran Sasih. For **food** in Pejeng, try *Warung Pejeng*, between Pura Pusering Jagat and Pura Kebo Edan.

## Pura Penataran Sasih

Balinese people believe **Pura Penataran Sasih** (donation requested during daylight hours; obligatory sarong and sash can be borrowed at the entrance) to be a particularly sacred temple, because this is the home of the so-called Moon of Pejeng – hence the English epithet **Moon Temple.**

The moon in question is a **large bronze gong**, shaped almost like an hourglass, suspended so high up in its special tower at the back of the temple compound that you can hardly see the decorations scratched onto its surface. It probably dates from the Balinese Bronze Age, from sometime during the third century BC, and – at almost two metres long – is thought to be the largest such kettledrum ever cast. Etched into its green patina are a mass of geometric and abstract **designs** and, around the central rim, a chain of striking heart-shaped **faces** with huge round eyes and distended earlobes. Legend tells how the gong fell towards earth one day from its home in heaven, where it had served as the wheel of a chariot that transported the moon through the skies. At that time, the wheel shone just as brightly as the moon itself, and when its fall was broken by a tree in Pejeng, a local thief became so incensed by the incriminating light it gave out that he tried to extinguish it by urinating over it. The wheel exploded with a thunderous echo, killed the thief, and dropped to the ground in its present form. Ever since, the Balinese have treated the Moon of Pejeng as sacred, making offerings to it whenever they need to move it, and always keeping a respectful distance.

Though now faded and rather dilapidated, the **temple** itself was once the most important *pura* of the area, and there's little doubt that, whatever the origins of the gong, it would have been used for much the same purposes as its modern counterpart, the *kulkul* – sounded with a stick to summon the people of Pejeng to religious ceremonies and secular gatherings, to announce war, and also to invite rain to fall.

## Pura Pusering Jagat

**Pura Pusering Jagat**, literally translated as the "Temple of the Navel of the World", stands 100m south down the main road from Pura Penataran Sasih. As elsewhere in Pejeng, a donation is requested at the temple entrance, where you can also borrow a sarong and sash.

The most interesting feature of this temple is its metre-high, elaborately carved vessel for storing holy water, whose exterior is sculpted with a detailed relief thought to depict the Hindu myth "The Churning of the Sea of Milk". There are several versions of this legend, but they all relate the story of the gods and the demons desperately trying to get their hands on the elixir of immortal life. Under Wisnu's guidance, they set about churning the Cosmic Soup (also known as the Sea of Milk) with the aid of a holy mountain as their pestle and serpentine *naga* as the pulleys. Finally, through a combination of trickery and good sense, the gods managed to extract, distil and drink the elixir. The vessel was carved in the fourteenth century from a single block of sandstone, and although the detail has become rather worn, you can still make out several figures, including the undulating *naga* ropes and a number of dancing deities supporting them.

Housed in a nearby pavilion is another significant icon, the metre-high phallic *linggam* and its female receptacle, the *yoni* – an important shrine for newlywed and infertile couples.

## Pura Kebo Edan

Some 200m south of Pura Pusering Jagat, **Pura Kebo Edan** (donation requested) is also considered lucky for childless couples. The attraction here is a massive lifelike phallus, attached to the huge stone body of a man, nicknamed the **Pejeng Giant**. In fact, this giant, nearly four metres tall, is said to possess six penises in all; aside from the one swinging out for all to see, one is supposed to have dropped to the ground during his very vigorous dancing, and four more are said to be hidden inside him, awaiting the correct point of the dance before emerging. His principal penis is pierced from front to back with a huge bolt-like pin, probably a realistic reference to an age-old Southeast Asian practice designed to increase women's sexual pleasure. With his hands on his hips, the giant – his face hidden behind a blank mask – dances on a prone female figure thought to represent the earth. The giant's identity is debatable; some think he's Bhima, one of the chief characters from the *Mahabharata*, while others see him as a manifestation of the Hindu deity Siwa, who harnessed enormous cosmic power whenever he danced.

## Museum Arkeologi

As the main treasure-house of such a historically significant region, Pejeng's **Museum Arkeologi** – the government-run archeological museum – 500m south of Pura Penataran Sasih (Mon–Fri 7.30am–2.30pm; donation requested), makes disappointing viewing. Its four tiny pavilions house a small, eclectic assortment of artefacts found in the area, ranging from Paleolithic chopping tools to bronze bracelets and Chinese plates. Objects are poorly labelled, and the more valuable pieces have all been snapped up by the Bali Museum in Denpasar.

The most interesting exhibits are the dozen **sarcophagi** at the back of the museum compound. These massive coffins, up to three metres long and fashioned from two fitted sections of hollowed-out stone, probably date back to around 300 BC. It's thought that they were all designed to hold adult skeletons (those placed in the smallest vessels would have been flexed at knees, hips and shoulders), as only the more important members of a community would have merited such an elaborate burial. Bronze jewellery, coins and weapons were found in some of the sarcophagi, though most of the tombs are thought to have been robbed at a much earlier date.

# North of Ubud: routes to Gunung Batur

All three major roads **north of Ubud** lead eventually to the towering peak of Gunung Batur and its huge crater. Whether you go via **Payangan** to the west, **Tegalalang** directly to the north, or **Tampaksiring** to the east, the villages and paddy-fields along each route make for a pleasant drive. Distances are comparable, about 40km to Batur whichever way you go, but the most significant tourist sights are located along the most easterly route, around the Tampaksiring area.

The most frequent and reliable **bemo** service running north from Ubud is the brown fleet that covers the **central route** via Tegalalang and Pujung; there are frequent turquoise and brown bemos along the first section of the **westerly route**, as far as Payangan, but only some of them continue as far as Kintamani. For the **easterly route** via Tampaksiring, you'll need to change bemos at the Bedulu crossroads.

Although there's little of specific interest on the westerly route, which takes you via Campuhan and Payangan, this is the quietest, least congested and prettiest of the three routes, and the best one to take if you have **private transport**. The villages on the way are exceptionally picturesque, interspersed with lychee, durian and pineapple plantations, and in Payangan you pass the village's famously huge roadside banyan tree. The road ends up at the impressive Pura Ulun Danu Batur (see p.300) on the Batur–Kintamani road, about 5km west of Penelokan.

## Tegalalang, Sebatu and Taro

The **central route** up to Gunung Batur begins at the eastern edge of Ubud, from the point where Jalan Raya Ubud intersects with Jalan Peliatan; if heading up here on a bicycle, you might prefer the more peaceful route that starts on Ubud's Jalan Suweta.

### Tegalalang, Sebatu and around

The village of **TEGALALANG**, 7km north of Ubud, is known for its brightly **painted woodcarvings**, a craft that has caught on so successfully in the area that almost the entire length of the twelve-kilometre-long Ubud–Tegalalang–Pujung road is now lined with shops selling painted mobiles, animals and figurines, interspersed with outlets specializing in antique or contemporary furniture. With several hundred possibilities, recommendations are almost futile, but you may want to show your support for local craftspeople by stopping at the little shop run by the **Mitra Bali Fair Trade** organization (see p.45 for more on them), which is about 700m north of the Ubud junction, in **ANDONG**, the first village along the main road. Next up is **PETULU**, famous for its nightly heron-roosting spectacle, described on p.207.

The views get increasingly spectacular as you pass through Tegalalang, with Bali's greatest mountains looming majestically ahead – Gunung Batur to the north, and Gunung Agung to the east – and rice terraces providing the classic foreground. In **CEKING,** the village just north of Tegalalang that's famous for its *garuda* woodcarvings, several restaurants make the most of these vistas, including the beautifully situated *Kampung Café,* which is built on two levels overlooking the valley and serves classy *nouvelle cuisine* and Southeast Asian dishes.

A couple of kilometres further north there are more choice views – this time over the steep, densely wooded valley of the Wos River – from the open-sided restaurant and three good-value bungalows at the *Blue Yogi* (T0361/901550, Wwww.theblueyogi.com; ❷), just west off the main road in **PUJUNG KELOD**.

If you continue north along the main road for another 16km, you'll reach the Gunung Batur crater rim. Alternatively, a right turn 2km beyond Pujung Kelod takes you to Tampaksiring via the village of **SEBATU**, site of the exceptionally attractive and refreshingly uncrowded **Pura Gunung Kawi Sebatu** water-temple complex (daylight hours; Rp4100, kids 2100, including sarong rental). Not to be confused with the more-visited Gunung Kawi in nearby Tampaksiring, the Sebatu temple is built on the site of holy springs, whose water is channelled through carved stone spouts into the segregated sections of seven different, traditional walled bathing-pools within the temple complex. Four of these pools are used as regular public-bathing amenities, while the three most sacred, built at the spring itself, are only unlocked for cleansing rituals before certain important ceremonies. Around the pools, shrub-lined paths run through the manicured gardens, past ornamental ponds and pavilions, to the temple's main shrines.

## Taro and the Elephant Safari Park

Turning left off the main Kintamani road a couple of kilometres beyond Pujung Kelod, a signposted little road leads you 6km west to the village of **TARO** and the **Elephant Safari Park**. This area is known for its distinctive grey-and-black-flecked tufa stone, used all over Bali to build temples, houses and hotels, and there are lots of sculpture workshops in the villages here. Taro itself is famous as the home of a small herd of sacred white Brahmin cows. Balinese people come here to pay their respects to the cows, who play an important role in certain temple ceremonies; as you pass into the Elephant Safari Park itself, you may be asked by the local priest to give a donation for their upkeep.

The Elephant Safari Park (daily 9am–5pm; $14, kids $5.75, family discounts available) is a landscaped area of grassy fields, pools and village forest, and is home to a group of elephants brought over from Sumatra, where they had been trained to work in the logging industry but were then abandoned when the industry declined. The park admission fee allows you to feed and stroke the elephants, admire their painting skills – the trunk is apparently as adept with a paintbrush as the human hand, and some of these elephants have exhibited their work internationally – and watch them having their twice-daily baths. There's also an elephant museum. The chief attraction, however, is the rather pricey half-hour elephant safari ride (an additional $39 for adults, $29 for kids), which takes you through a fairly sparse area of forest. Most people visit the park as part of a **tour**, which includes transport, lunch and the elephant ride ($68/47); book at any travel agent or direct with Bali Adventure Tours (T0361/721480, Wwww.baliadventuretours.com).

# Tampaksiring

The most **easterly route** from Ubud to the mountains takes you along the Bedulu–Penelokan road, passing through Pejeng before reaching **TAMPAKSIRING**, 11km further on. A fairly nondescript town that's really only interesting as the access point for nearby **Tirta Empul** and **Gunung Kawi**, Tampaksiring is nonetheless well stocked with craft and souvenir shops: carved wooden chess sets and knick-knacks made from bone are a speciality. The bluey-grey Gianyar–Bedulu–Tampaksiring **bemos** terminate near the market in the centre of the long settlement, close by several warung. The bemo service between Tampaksiring and Penelokan, about 20km north, is patchy and unreliable at best, but you should at least be able to charter a bemo.

## Gunung Kawi

A few hundred metres north of Tampaksiring's bemo terminus, a sign points east off the main road to **Gunung Kawi** (daylight hours; Rp4100, kids Rp2100), the site of a series of eleventh-century royal "tombs" hewn from the rock face. It's a lovely, impressive spot, completely enclosed in the lush valley of the sacred Pakrisan River. To reach it, walk past the souvenir stalls and down the steep flight of three hundred steps, through a massive rock-hewn archway, to the river.

Archeologists have several theories about the **origins** and **function** of the Gunung Kawi "tombs" or *candi*, of which the least contentious is that they were erected as memorials to a king – possibly the eleventh-century Anak Wungsu – and his queens. The four Queens' Tombs are thought to be for Anak Wungsu's minor consorts, while the five Royal Tombs across the river are believed to honour the king himself and his four most favoured wives. There are no signs of bones or ashes in the *candi*, so the structures were not actual tombs, yet over the false door of each were found inscriptions (most of them unreadable) thought to be names or titles. As well as being a lasting testament to these people, the *candi* may also have indicated that the full programme of religious rites had been completed.

Before crossing the river, turn sharp left for the **Queens' Tombs**. Like the larger, more important structures on the other side of the river, these four *candi* are huge square-tiered reliefs, chiselled from the riverside cliff face to resemble temple facades. Originally, the surface would have been decorated with plaster carvings, but now all that's left are the outlines of a single false door on each one. The design of the *candi* is very similar to that of structures in central and east Java, built in three distinct sections to reflect a hell–earth–heaven cosmology, and with a stone-lidded hollow dug at the foot of each.

Crossing the Pakrisan River you enter the Gunung Kawi temple complex, which contains an unusual **cloister**, complete with courtyard, rooms and cells, entirely cut from the ravine rock wall. This was probably built for the holy men who looked after the tombs and carried out all the necessary rituals. The five **Royal Tombs** at the back of the temple complex are in better condition than the Queens' Tombs, their false doors and facades quite distinct. Because the *candi* at the far left end is slightly higher than the others, this is believed to be that of Anak Wungsu.

Returning across the river, follow the exit signs up the track beside the rice-paddies and then veer off along the narrow path, branching left through the fields to reach the so-called **Tenth Tomb**, an often slippery five-minute walk away. Thought to have been erected in memory of an important member of the

_PEJANU/BAKRISAN VALLEYS : GOA GARBA CAVE_

royal household who died after the king and his wives, possibly a prime-ministerial figure, this *candi* stands on its own, framed only by rock-cut cloisters.

## Tirta Empul

_HERMITAGE Del nu 12thC PURA PENGUKUR UKUPAN temple where all thing one measured_

Balinese from every corner of the island make pilgrimages to **Tirta Empul** (daylight hours; Rp4100, kids Rp2100), signposted off the main Tampaksiring–Kintamani road, about 500m north of the turn-off to Gunung Kawi. They come seeking to spiritually cleanse themselves and to cure their physical ailments by bathing in the **holy springs** here. Legend describes how the springs were first tapped by the god Indra during his battle with the evil Mayadanawa, an early ruler of the Pejeng kingdom. Mayadanawa had poisoned the nearby river and made hundreds of Indra's retainers sick, so Indra pierced the earth to release a spring of pure and sacred water – the elixir of immortality – that would revive his flagging troops. The new spring was named Tirta Empul, and has been considered the holiest in Bali ever since the tenth century, if not longer. A temple was built around the springs and special bathing-pools constructed for devotees, and the complex is now an extremely popular destination, both for Balinese and foreign tourists.

The shallow red-brick **bathing pools** are sunk into the ground of the outer courtyard of the temple, fed by water from the springs in the inner sanctuary. Men, women and priests each have their own segregated sections in which to immerse themselves, though most modern devotees just splash their faces and smile for the camera. However, for pregnant women and anyone who's just recovered from a long illness, a visit to Tirta Empul has particular significance as one of three places in which they must bathe for a special ritual called *melukat*. This ceremony requires immersion in the waters of each of the three holiest springs in Bali: the "holy waters of the mountain" at Tirta Bungkah, the "holy springs of the plain" here at Tirta Empul, and the "holy springs of the sea" at Tirta Selukat. In the inner courtyard, you can see the clear slate-blue spring water bubbling up into its own enclosed rectangular pool through a sedimentary layer of black sand.

_guide: Ketut manta Pejeng 2hr 0361 982149 walk_

# Travel details

### Bemos and public buses

It's almost impossible to give the frequency with which bemos and public buses run: see Basics, p.49, for details. Journey times given are the minimum you can expect. Only the direct bemo and bus routes are listed; for longer journeys, you'll have to go via Denpasar's Batubulan terminal (see p.172) or Gianyar (see p.232).
**Batubulan (Denpasar)** to: Amlapura (2hr 30min); Candi Dasa (2hr); Celuk (10min); Gianyar (1hr); Kintamani (1hr 30min); Klungkung (1hr 20min); Mas (35min); Ngurah Rai Airport (40min); Nusa Dua (1hr); Padang Bai (for Lombok; 1hr 40min); Peliatan (45min); Singaraja (Penarukan terminal; 3hr); Sukawati (20min); Tegalalang (1hr 15min); Ubud (50min).

**Ubud** to: Campuhan/Sanggingan (5–10min); Celuk (40min); Denpasar (Batubulan terminal; 50min); Gianyar (20min); Goa Gajah (10min); Kedewatan (10min); Kintamani (1hr); Mas (15min); Peliatan (5min); Pujung (25min); Sukawati (30min).

### Perama shuttle buses

*STO = overnight stopover is sometimes needed*
**Ubud** to: Bedugul (daily; 1hr 30min); Candi Dasa (3 daily; 1hr 30min–2hr); Gili Islands (daily; 8hr); Kuta/Ngurah Rai Airport (5 daily; 1hr–1hr 30min); Kuta, Lombok (2 daily; STO); Lovina (daily; 1hr 30min–2hr); Mataram (Lombok; 2 daily; 7hr); Nusa Lembongan (daily; 2hr 30min); Padang Bai (3 daily; 1hr–1hr 30min); Sanur (5 daily; 30min–1hr); Senggigi (Lombok; 2 daily; 7hr 30min).

# 3

# East Bali

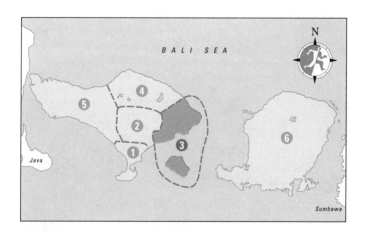

N

BALI SEA

Java

Sumbawa

# CHAPTER THREE Highlights

* **Gunung Agung** Volcano towering majestically over the entire east of the island. See p.251

* **Nusa Lembongan** Islanders, surfers and sun-seekers mingle on the great beaches and in the rural hinterland. See p.254

* **Candi Dasa** This well-established, relaxed resort is an ideal base for exploring the east. See p.263

* **Padang Bai** Laid-back village in a pretty little bay; perfect for chilling out, snorkelling and diving en route to Lombok. See p.272

* **Tirtagangga** Lovely views of the mountains, attractive ricefields, a water palace and cool temperatures. See p.279

* **Iseh and Sidemen** Small villages famed for fabulous rice terraces, among the most picturesque on the island. See p.282

* **Amed** Some 14km of beautiful coast offering get-away-from-it-all peace and quiet. See p.283

△ Lagoon, Candi Dasa

# 3

# East Bali

The **east of Bali** is dominated both physically and spiritually by the towering volcano **Gunung Agung**, and the **Besakih** temple high on its slopes. The landscape ranges from sweeping rice terraces, built on the fertile soil deposited by successive volcanic eruptions, to the dry, rocky expanses of the far east.

Most visitors come to the east for the **coast**, which extends from the black-sand bays south of Gianyar, through the natural harbour of **Amuk Bay**, to the peaceful beaches known collectively as **Amed** that range along the northeast coast. The area offers some of the best diving and snorkelling in Bali: the resorts of **Candi Dasa**, **Padang Bai**, **Tulamben** and **Amed** are the main centres. Off the south coast lie three islands: **Nusa Lembongan**, with its white-sand beaches; tiny **Nusa Ceningan**; and little-visited **Nusa Penida**, whose south coast consists of towering limestone cliffs. Only Lembongan, with easy access from Sanur, has a developed tourist trade, catering for surfers, day visitors and anyone in search of relaxation.

Inland, Gunung Agung and Besakih are the major tourist draws, although the hassles and mist frequently disappoint visitors to the temple. However, there are other peaks and impressive **temples** – especially Pura Kehen in Bangli, Pura Lempuyang Luhur, accessible from Tirtagangga, and Pura Pasar Agung, above Selat – where you can escape the crowds. **Tenganan**, within easy reach of Candi Dasa, is the most welcoming of the traditional Bali Aga villages on the island, home to descendants of the early inhabitants of Bali. This is the place to head for if you're interested in **textiles**, baskets and *lontar* palm drawings, among a host of other craftwork.

Formerly divided into a multitude of kingdoms, the area witnessed vicious internal battles and power struggles, followed later by the incursions of the invading **Dutch**. During the fourteenth century, the first Majapahit capital was in **Samprangan**, now a small village just east of **Gianyar** and, in the following centuries, each of the towns of the area had its own royal dynasty; the now sleepy Klungkung suburb of **Gelgel** once ruled a kingdom stretching from the island of Sumbawa in the east to Java in the west. Evidence of these ancient courts remains in the Taman Gili in **Klungkung**, the Puri Agungin **Amlapura** and the **Puri Gianyar**. Once the focus of the area that they dominated, these small relics of past glory are now surrounded by busy administrative and market towns with traffic pouring past the walls.

## Practicalities

The east is easily accessible by public **transport** from Kuta and Ubud. The new road that is under construction from Tohpati, just north of Sanur, to Kusamba,

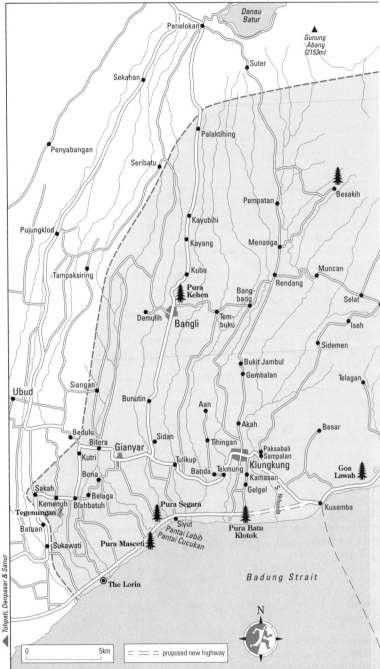

▲ *Kintamani*    ▲ *Toya Bungkah*

*Danau Batur*

Penelokan

▲ *Gunung Abang (2153m)*

Suter

Sekahan

Palaktihing

Penyabangan

Seribatu

Besakih

Pempatan

Kayubihi

Menanga

Pujungklod

Kayang

Muncan

Tampaksiring

Kubu

Rendang

Selat

**Pura Kehen**

Bang-bang

Iseh

Demulih

**Bangli**

Tem-buku

Sidemen

Bukit Jambul

Gembalan

Telagan

Siangan

Bunutin

Aan

Akah

Besar

**Ubud**

Bedulu

Sidan

Tihingan

Paksabali

Bitera

**Gianyar**

Tulikup

Sampalan

Kutri

Banda    Takmung

**Klungkung**

**Goa Lawah**

Bona

Belaga

Kamasan

Sakah

Blahbatuh

Gelgel

Kemenuh

Kusamba

**Tegenungan**

**Pura Segara**

Batuan

Siyut

**Pura Batu Klotok**

Sukawati

*Pantai Lebih*

**Pura Masceti**

*Pantai Cucukan*

◉ **The Lorin**

*S. Yehunda*

*Badung Strait*

N

◀ *Tohpati, Denpasar & Sanur*

230

0        5km    = = = proposed new highway

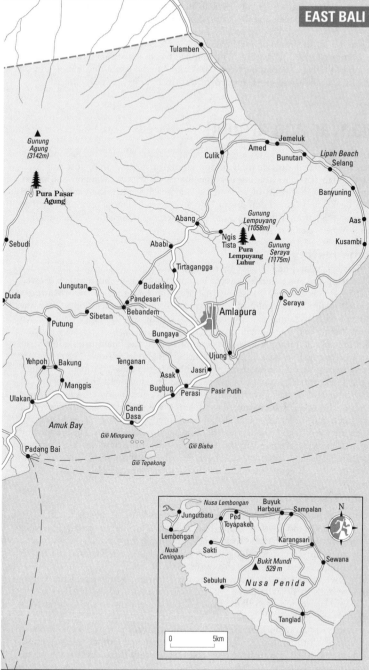

**EAST BALI**

Kubu & Singaraja

Tulamben

Gunung
Agung
(3142m)

Pura Pasar
Agung

Culik

Amed

Jemeluk

Bunutan

Lipah Beach
Selang

Banyuning

Aas

Sebudi

Abang

Ababi

Ngis
Tista

Gunung
Lempuyang
(1058m)

Pura
Lempuyang
Luhur

Gunung
Seraya
(1175m)

Kusambi

Tirtagangga

Jungutan

Budakling

Pandesari

Duda

Sibetan

Bebandem

Amlapura

Seraya

Putung

Bungaya

Yehpoh

Bakung

Tenganan

Asak

Jasri

Ujung

Manggis

Bugbug

Perasi

Pasir Putih

Ulakan

Candi
Dasa

Amuk Bay

Gili Mimpang

Gili Biaha

Padang Bai

Gili Tepekong

Boats to Senggigi (Lombok) ▶

Boats to Lembar (Lombok) ▶

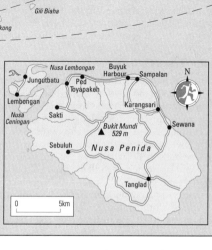

Nusa Lembongan

Buyuk
Harbour

Sampalan

N

Jungutbatu

Ped
Toyapakeh

Lembongan

Karangsari

Nusa
Ceningan

Sakti

Bukit Mundi
529 m

Sewana

Sebuluh

Nusa Penida

Tanglad

0          5km

Boats to Nusa Penida & Nusa Lembongan

west of Padang Bai, has already, even in its unfinished state, made travel to the east pleasant and speedy, and the traffic thins dramatically the further east you go. This is a relaxed and relaxing part of the country, and the best way to enjoy it is to give it a bit of time. The ideal bases are Candi Dasa, Padang Bai (the port for the Lombok ferries), Tirtagangga, surrounded by attractive rice terraces, and the section of the far east coast between Culik and Aas, the fastest developing area of the east. Outside these spots, **accommodation** options are more limited.

# Gianyar and around

**GIANYAR** is the administrative capital of Gianyar district, the second most densely populated district in Bali. Something of a travel hub, you may well pass through if you're heading east, but there's no reason to linger. The **coast** south of Gianyar consists of wide black-sand beaches with fine views across to Nusa Penida and Nusa Lembongan. This area is gradually opening up now that the new road from Tohpati to Kusamba is nearing completion, but there are currently few facilities.

## Some history

Gianyar was established as a separate **kingdom** in the late seventeenth century and during the next hundred years became enormously powerful. However, in 1883, it was annexed to Klungkung after the ruling raja, **Dewa Manggis VII**, fell victim to the political machinations of his wilier neighbours. He was interned with his family and eventually died, leaving two sons: the crown prince Dewa Pahang and his younger brother, Dewa Gde Raka. In 1893, they escaped from prison and, raising a local army, re-established the Gianyar kingdom over much of its previous area. The neighbouring kingdoms, however, were out for blood, and to save Gianyar from its neighbours, the new raja made a request to the Dutch for Gianyar to be placed under the authority and protection of the Netherlands Indies government. They agreed, and in March 1900 Gianyar became a **Dutch Protectorate**. Thus, Gianyar was spared the fighting between the Dutch and the other southern Balinese kingdoms during the early years of the century – instead it thrived and became a centre for the arts. The aristocratic line and lifestyle continued; in the 1930s, the raja of the time drove a Fiat with a solid gold *garuda* radiator cap. These days the royal family still live in Puri Gianyar, but have ceremonial and religious rather than political duties.

## The Town

Gianyar has little to detain you other than its specialities of spit-roasted suckling pig (*babi guling*) and *endek* weaving, plus an exuberant line in statuary; there's a massive white **statue** on the main road in from the west, which shows Arjuna in his three-horsed chariot along with his godly charioteer, Krishna, and there's another huge Arjuna statue on the eastern side of town.

The town centres on the main road just west of the royal palace, **Puri Gianyar**, first built in 1771 by Dewa Manggis IV, but destroyed by the 1917 earthquake and largely rebuilt. Still the home of the descendants of the Gianyar royal family, it's not open to the public.

A short walk away on Jalan Berata, Gianyar's **market** comprises two modern buildings, each three storeys high, with food in one and clothes and household goods in the other. The main market takes place every three days, but there are always some stalls here.

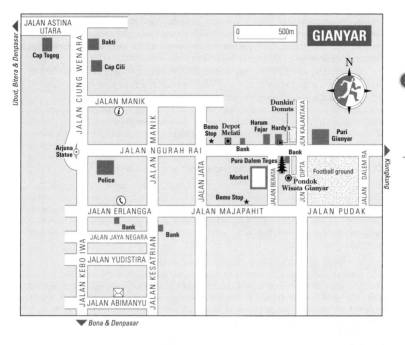

Gianyar is well known for **endek weaving** (see p.488 for more), produced in the factories on the western outskirts of town, just over 1km from the centre. Two of the most established are Cap Cili and Bakti (both daily 8am–5pm) close together on Jalan Ciung Wenara, which are good starting points, especially as Cap Cili's goods carry price labels. Cap Togog (daily 8am–5pm), slightly further west from the centre, on Jalan Astina Utara, is another big concern. These operations cater largely for the tour-bus market but are happy for you to wander around and watch the process. *Endek* cloth starts at Rp40,000 a metre for cotton up to a stratospheric Rp400,000 a metre for pure silk. Sarongs cost upwards of Rp100,000, bedspreads from Rp300,000 and cushion covers from Rp60,000 depending on the thread used. You'll also find clothing and small gift items, although there's a depressingly large amount of imported cloth from Java and the thread for *endek* weaving is now imported from India, as Balinese production is insufficient to meet demand.

## Practicalities

Heading east **from Denpasar** (Batubulan terminal), most public transport follows the route to Gianyar via Sakah, Kemenuh, Blahbatuh, Kutri and Bitera, although there are also local bemos from Blahbatuh that ply the alternative road through Bona and Jasri. Coming **from Ubud**, your best bet is to get a bemo down to the large junction at Sakah and pick up Gianyar transport there.

At the Gianyar government **tourist office**, Jl Manik 12b (Mon–Thurs 7am–3pm, Fri 7am–noon; ☎0361/943401), staff appear rather startled to see visitors. The main **telephone office** is on Jalan Erlangga (daily 24hr), just to the east of which **Internet access** is available at several small shops. The **post office** (a Western Union agent) is at Jl Abimanyu 4. Bank Rakyat Indonesia is on the corner of Jalan Ngurah Rai and Jalan Anom Sandat and BNI is further south on Jalan Kesatrian; there are ATMs with Visa, MasterCard and Cirrus links at BCA on Jalan Erlangga and at the BNI ATM near the Harum Fajar shopping centre.

With Ubud so close, there's no reason to stay overnight and the **accommodation** in town is merely functional. The best choice is *Pondok Wisata Gianyar*, Jl Anom Sandat 10x (℡0361/942165; ●), just off Jalan Ngurah Rai, with very basic rooms in a small compound. About 5km northwest of Gianyar, in the small village of **SIANGAN**, the excellent *Siangan Bungalows* (℡0361/954832, ⓔdewaparwata@hotmail.com; ●) are located in a gorgeous garden with swimming pools on the edge of paddy-fields. There are nine well-furnished rooms with hot water, and a choice of air-con or fan, plus deep verandas and *bale* in the garden. They offer free transport to Ubud, 8km west. This is a delightful spot although difficult to find. To get there, turn north in Bitera, just by Bitera Palace, about 500m west of Gianyar. After 800m, take the first significant turning on the left – there's a small sign to Pura Dalem Penataran Agung. Follow the road as it dips across a river and then climbs through fields for almost 3km. Turn right in the village of Siangan between the volleyball court/football field and the somewhat derelict Siangan Palace, then turn right again along the far side of the volleyball court. *Siangan Bungalows* are at the end of this track.

For **food**, Gianyar is famous for its *babi guling* (spit-roasted suckling pig), a Balinese speciality of roast pork stuffed with chillies, rice and spices, served with rice and usually *lawar* (chopped meat, vegetables and coconut mixed with pig's blood). Several shops in the main street sell it; try *Depot Melati*, Jl Ngurah Rai 37, but get there before 2pm as they shut up early. Western fast food takes the form of a *Dunkin Donuts* counter at the front of the Harum Fajar shopping centre in the middle of town.

## West of Gianyar

A number of interesting **villages** lie to the west and southwest of Gianyar. From Gianyar, there are bemos to Blahbatuh, via Bona and Belaga. Buses and minibuses to Denpasar follow the main road via Kutri, Blahbatuh and Kemenuh. **KUTRI**, some 4km west of Gianyar, is home to the **Pura Bukit Dharma Durga Kutri**. Well established on the tour-bus circuit, this temple has some fine carvings, although the most interesting feature is the statue of the goddess **Durga**; head up the staircase from the back of the inner courtyard to the top of the hill, where you'll find the statue shrouded in holy white cloths and shaded by parasols. The figure is eroded, but a many-armed Durga slaughtering a bull, with her weapons of conch, flames, bow and arrow, javelin and shield is discernible. Many people believe, however, that the carving depicts **Mahendratta**, the source of the legendary Rangda (see box opposite), and that this is her burial place. It's also possible to walk to Kutri from the Yeh Pulu rock carvings east of Ubud, but you'll need to hire a guide to show you the way (see p.219).

At the village of **BLAHBATUH**, 5km south of Kutri, the main road, lined with bamboo-furniture workshops, meets an alternative road from Gianyar through Bona and Belaga. A few hundred metres along the Bona road, the splendid entrances of **Pura Gaduh**, guarded by stone elephants outside and mounted horsemen inside, lead into a maze of courtyards, which were rebuilt following an earthquake in 1917. Of particular interest is a gigantic carved head with bulging eyes, supposedly the legendary **Kebo Iwa**, who is said to have created this and many other temples in the area. **BONA** and neighbouring **BELAGA** have a huge number of shops selling wooden and bamboo furniture

## Rangda

The image of **Rangda**, Queen of the Witches, is everywhere in Bali: you'll see her in dance-dramas and on masks, temple carvings, paintings and batiks. Several features are standard in her portrayal and contribute to her grotesque and terrifying appearance. She has a long mane of hair with flames protruding from her head. Her face is hideous with bulging eyes, a gaping mouth, huge teeth or tusks, and a long tongue often reaching to her knees. Her fingernails are long and curled, and she has enormous, pendulous breasts. She wears a striped shirt and pants, with a white cloth around her waist, an important instrument of her evil magic.

Several versions of the Rangda story are enacted across the island, the most common being the **barong** and **calonarang** (see p.474 for more details of these dramas), but she always speaks in the ancient Javanese Kawi language and alternates between high whining tones, loud grunts and cackles. To the Balinese, Rangda represents the forces of evil, death and destruction, and she's associated with the Hindu goddess Durga.

It's possible that Rangda is based on a real woman, **Mahendratta**, a Javanese princess who married the Balinese Prince Udayana and bore him a son, Erlangga, in 1001 AD. According to legend, the king later banished Mahendratta to the forest for practising witchcraft. When Udayana died, Mahendratta, now a *rangda* (widow), continued to build up grudges against her unrelenting son. Eventually, she used her powers to call down a plague upon Erlangga's kingdom, nearly destroying it. Erlangga, learning the source of the pestilence, despatched a troop of soldiers who stabbed Rangda in the heart; she survived, however, and killed the soldiers. In desperation, the king sent for a holy man, **Empu Bharadah**, whose assistant stole Rangda's book of magic, with which he was able to restore Rangda's victims to life, and destroy the witch by turning her own magic on herself.

Even in performances of the story, the figure of Rangda is believed to have remarkable powers, and offerings and prayers precede each show to protect the actors from the evil forces they are invoking. Village performances of the drama are often a means of pacifying Rangda's anger and averting her destructive forces.

plus plenty of smaller items made from bamboo and the fronds of the sugar palm, including baskets, bags, purses and boxes in all shapes and sizes.

### Kemenuh and Sakah

At **KEMENUH**, 7km southwest of Gianyar, **Tegenungan waterfall**, also known as **Srog Srogan**, drops a sheer 30m. Access is via a side-road, 1.5km west of the market in Blahbatuh, signed to the now-defunct *Waterfall Restaurant*. After a few hundred metres, a left turn just opposite a drinks stall brings you to a good look-out spot across from the falls. A path leads to the riverside from here – it's a long climb down, the area isn't especially pristine and the strong current is a deterrent to swimming. A few small warung perched on the edge of the gorge offer the best views.

About 400m south of the main road, on the left as you head towards the falls, a narrow avenue of coconut palms marks the path to the **Pura Dalem** of Kemenuh, a large and dramatic temple notable for its intricate carvings hidden among a stand of trees in the middle of the fields. On the *kulkul* tower is a carving of Pan Brayut, the legendary character with numerous children (see box on p.200), who according to local belief has the power to help infertile couples.

Heading back north to the main road, the turning directly opposite leads past a concentration of **woodcarving** shops; a good range of subject, style and wood is on show and, as much of the carving is done in sheds outside the shops, you can watch the work as well. Some of the shops are on the tour-bus circuit, but groups don't stay long, and you can usually have the place to yourself, especially if you explore all the way through to the northern end of this twisting road at Goa Gajah, a distance of about 5km.

An innovative tourist development is located on the northern side of Kemenuh, near the hamlet of Medahan. *Sua Bali* (ⓣ0361/941050, ⓔsuabali@indosat.net.id; ❼) offers simple accommodation in attractive bungalows set on the banks of the Petang River. It is committed to sustainable village tourism, and cultural courses can be arranged; contact them directly for details.

Some 3km west of Kemenuh, at the junction of the road and bemo route north to Ubud, sits the small village of **SAKAH**, with its giant Buddha statue resembling a podgy baby. There are a few woodcarving and art shops to pass the time in if you're waiting for a connection, but they're nothing out of the ordinary.

## The coast south of Gianyar

The coast **south of Gianyar** is an attractive but little-visited part of Bali, best accessed by private transport, with long beaches of pure black sand and some fine views. Bear in mind, that, aside from a couple of spots that are opening up for experienced surfers, this is an area for beach walks rather than for swimming, as the Badung Strait – the patch of ocean between the mainland and Nusa Lembongan – is one of the deepest and most treacherous stretches of water off Bali. There are plenty of temples to base your explorations around – all are fabulous during festivals and ceremonies but pretty deserted otherwise.

The **new road** eastwards, Jalan Prof Dr Ida Bagus, starts at **Tohpati**, 4km north of Sanur, a small village where the road is lined with plant and flower nurseries and stone-carving workshops. It's hard to miss the beginning of the road as it passes through a giant arch on which its name is emblazoned in huge letters. At the time of writing, the final 6km needed to reach Kusamba was still under construction. However, the completed section has already opened up the whole coast south of Gianyar and chopped a great deal of time and anguish off travel to the east. It's worth noting that the road winds behind the coast, sometimes a few hundred metres inland and sometimes several kilometres. The scenery is picturesque, with increasingly fine views of Gunung Agung as you travel east, but you'll need to explore the multitude of side-roads that head to the beaches to enjoy the coastal views.

Eight kilometres from Tohpati, *The Lorin* (ⓣ0361/297070, ⓦwww.lorinresortsababai.com, ❾) offers comfortable accommodation in a serene garden with a glorious swimming pool just behind the beach. The most expensive pool villas are better value than the "cheaper" rooms as they have private plunge pools and upstairs sitting areas; but published prices are high, starting at $250.

Another four kilometres to the east, Pantai Masceti is signed to the right. It's a kilometre to the beach where an apparent jumble of buildings off to the right is **Pura Masceti**, one of Bali's directional temples, or *kahyangan jagat* (see p.460), serving the south of the island. It's an extremely important temple with highly ornate carvings and statues, and is especially busy on the day before Nyepi (usually March or April), when religious objects are brought to the temple for purification.

Experienced surfers are discovering the breaks off the coast at **Pantai Cucukan**, signed off the main road another kilometre to the east. Accommodation is likely to develop here, but in the meantime it's a quiet, attractive sweep of sand.

At a set of traffic lights another kilometre further along the coast, **Pantai Lebih** is signed off to the right. This is a great beach lined with hundreds of local fishing boats and dozens of tiny warung cooking and selling the day's catch. *Sate languan, ikan bakar, ikan pepes, ikan goreng* and *nasi sela* are the specialities. Some of the warung are open from midday but most get going at 4–5pm and stay open until midnight – it's an extremely popular spot with Balinese people in the evening and is heaving during national holidays. Back across the main road (it's a left turn if coming from the west) the entrance of **Pura Segara** (Sea Temple) is imposing, but there's no real hint of the importance of this site. Magical forces are believed to be focused on the temple, and an annual ceremony is held here to placate the demon I Macaling, who is thought to bring disease and ill fortune to the mainland from Nusa Penida (see box on p.260).

One of the most picturesque stretches of the south coast is at **SIYUT** where the bay stretches in a wide sweep for several kilometres, with the rice terraces inland forming a fabulous foreground to the bulk of Gunung Agung. It is signed seawards two kilometres to the east from the Pantai Lebih turning. You'll share the beach – another one popular with locals come holiday time – with line fishermen, and there are several small drinks stalls.

Moving eastwards the scenery becomes more picturesque, greener and more fertile. Another 3km on, **Pantai Batu Klotok**, or Watu Klotok, is signed to the right. It's a kilometre to the beach along a small ridge with terraced fields sloping away on either side. **Pura Batu Klotok**, one of the four state temples of Klungkung, stands in a beachside position. The temple is particularly revered: the sacred statues from the "Mother Temple" Besakih, are brought here during the annual cleansing ritual of *malasti*. During the 1963 and 1979 Eka Dasa Rudra ceremonies at Besakih (see box on p.250), the procession to the sea was over a mile long, and tens of thousands gathered on the beach for the rituals, which included the sacrificial drowning of a buffalo. An imposing statue of Dewa Baruna, the god of the sea, stands beside the temple, carrying a container of holy water. It was built following the appearance in 2001 of an unusual turtle bearing sacred markings, which died on the local beach and was cremated in the temple. The turtle was believed by local people to be a manifestation of Dewa Baruna, who was bestowing good fortune and honour on the village.

At the time of writing, the new road ended at the junction to Pantai Batu Klotok, 19km from Tohpati, and all traffic had to turn left and head north towards Klungkung. The road to Kusamba is scheduled for completion by the end of 2005.

## Northeast of Gianyar

Essential viewing for anyone interested in Balinese temples is the **Pura Dalem** at **SIDAN**, 1km north of the main Gianyar–Klungkung road, on a sharp bend with parking spaces opposite. The turning leaves the main road about 2km east of Gianyar. This temple of the dead, dating from the seventeenth century, drips with gruesome carvings and statues of the terrible Rangda squashing babies, while the *kulkul* tower graphically depicts the punishments that await evildoers in the afterlife – which include having your head sawn off or being boiled up in a vat. The small shrine in front of the temple is dedicated to Merajapati, the caretaker of the dead, and is a common feature of *pura dalem*. There are occasional performances of the **barong** including the **kris** dance (see p.474 for more), generally during full-moon ceremonies; consult the sources of information on p.36 for details.

At **BUNUTIN**, 3km north of Sidan and 7km south of Bangli, **Pura Penataran Agung** (also known as Pura Langgar), is signed east off the main road. It's an attractive temple, set about 100m down the small track, overlooking a lake, with two small shrines built on artificial islands. The **red-brick shrine** with the two-tiered red roof is the main point of interest, having four unusual doors, one in each side. A local story tells of a seventeenth-century Hindu prince whose brother became very sick; seeking advice from a traditional healer, a *dukun*, the prince was told about a Muslim ancestor, originally from Java, who had settled in the Bunutin area and was instructed to build a temple to honour this man. The prince designed one that partly incorporated Muslim principles, with four doorways corresponding to the directions of the four winds. The sick brother recovered, and the descendants of his family are said to still abstain from eating pork in honour of their ancestor.

# Bangli and around

Situated between Gianyar and the volcanoes of Batur, **BANGLI** is a cool and spacious market town and the administrative capital of Bangli district. It fits in well on any itinerary to or from Batur, but don't be fooled by its proximity to Besakih: there are no public bemos on the Bangli–Rendang road.

## Some history

While it was never one of the major Balinese kingdoms, Bangli played a crucial role at pivotal points in Balinese history. Originally set up under the rule of the **Majapahit** dynasty based in Gelgel, Bangli, along with the other small kingdoms, gradually asserted its **independence**. By the nineteenth century, all the kingdoms were involved in a complex dance of attempted expansion during which **Gusti Ngurah Made Karangasem**, ruler of Buleleng in the north, annexed the entire Batur area from Bangli. Between 1841 and 1843, the princes of Bali signed "friendship agreements" with the Dutch government. The disparity between the Dutch and Balinese interpretation of these eventually led to a crisis in which it became clear that the Dutch would use force against Buleleng. Gaining his revenge for the loss of Batur, the Bangli raja, **Dewa Gde Tangkeban**, announced his support for the Dutch, refusing help to Buleleng, and reoccupied the Batur area. Following a **Dutch victory** in 1849, Dewa Gde Tangkeban reclaimed his former lands and also annexed Gianyar and Mengwi. Fighting between the kingdoms, including a long-running war between Bangli and Gianyar, dominated the second half of the nineteenth century, until the common threat from the Dutch diverted attention. Following the defeat of Badung regency and the *puputan* in Denpasar in 1906, the Dutch forced Dewa Gde Tangkeban to sign away his powers in return for permission to remain as a figurehead. However, he became convinced that the Dutch would eventually overrun his kingdom, and requested the same status as Gianyar and Karangasem. In January 1909, Bangli became a **Dutch Protectorate**, and the whole of Bali came under outside control.

## The Town

Most visitors come to Bangli for the ancient **Pura Kehen** (daily 6am–6.30pm; Rp3500 including a car or motorbike), 1.5km north of the town. Rising up steeply in **terraces** lined with religious statues, Pura Kehen is large and imposing – one of the gems among East Bali's temples. Sporting several remarkably fierce Bhoma leering above fabulously carved doors, the great entrance leads into the **outer courtyard** containing a massive banyan with a *kulkul* tower built among the branches. A small compound, guarded by *naga* under a frangipani tree, contains a stone that is supposed to have glowed with fire when the site of the temple was decided. Steps lead up to the middle courtyard, from where you can look into the **inner courtyard**, with its eleven-roofed *meru*, dedicated to Siwa, and other shrines dedicated to mountain gods.

Just across the road from the main temple, the lavishly restored **Pura Peny-impenan** (Temple for Keeping Things) contains three ancient bronze inscriptions (*prasasti*) dating from the ninth to the thirteenth centuries. This suggests Kehen was a site of ancient worship even before the generally accepted founding of the temple around 1206.

A short walk southeast from Pura Kehen, the rather grand **Sasana Budaya Arts Centre**, one of the largest arts complexes in Bali, hosts occasional exhibitions and dance and drama performances; enquire locally for details.

At the opposite end of town, the temple of the dead, **Pura Dalem Pengungekan**, is a pleasant stroll away from the town centre. The outside walls depict the fate of souls in hell and heaven as witnessed by Bhima, one of the Pandawa brothers, while trying to retrieve the souls of his parents from hell (see box on p.472). The carvings are a riot of knives, pleading victims, flames and decapitated bodies. You'll also see plenty of images of the evil witch Rangda. The central shrine is especially fine and details stories of Siwa, Ganesh, Uma and Rakshasha.

## Practicalities

The turning to Bangli leaves the main Gianyar–Klungkung road 2km east of Gianyar. Blue bemos wait at the junction, but you can also pick up a bemo in Gianyar, on Jalan Berata, just outside the market entrance. Buses plying the route between Denpasar (Batubulan terminal) and Singaraja (Penarukan terminal) pass through Bangli.

The Bangli government **tourist office** is in the grounds of the Sasana Budaya Arts Centre at Jl Sriwijaya 23 (℡0366/91537) but is pretty deserted. There are **exchange** facilities at Bank Rakyat Indonesia at the junction of Jalan Kusumayudha and Jalan Merdeka in the town centre, where there is an ATM linked to the Visa, MasterCard and Cirrus networks, or at BNI slightly further north on Jalan Nusantara. The **wartel** (daily 24hr) is on Jalan Ngurah Rai and the **post office** is at Jl Kusumayudha 18. Bangli's **market** bursts into activity every three days.

There are a couple of places **to stay** in town. The *Artha Sastra Inn*, Jl Merdeka 5 (℡0366/91179; ❶–❸), is just opposite the bemo terminal and close to the market. Guests can enjoy the kudos of staying in an old palace (the building was once the royal palace of Bangli), though the grandeur is very faded indeed. The nine rooms vary enormously, so look at a few. All have attached cold-water bathrooms. The more conventional *Bangli Inn*, Jl Rambutan 1 (℡0366/91518; ❷–❸), has clean rooms with attached cold-water bathrooms built around a small courtyard.

For **food** during the day, the bus terminal has several stalls while the road beside the terminal transforms into a small **night market** with the full range of sates, soups, rice and noodle dishes. *Depot Murni*, Jl Merdeka 18, just south of the town centre, is a typical local warung with the usual rice and noodle offerings at inexpensive prices.

# Klungkung and around

Just 16km from Gianyar, **KLUNGKUNG**, also known by its older name of **Semarapura**, is a bustling town, with plenty of sights. Its highlights are the remains of the royal palace, collectively known as the **Taman Gili**, which include the ancient **Kerta Gosa painted ceiling**. These murals are the only surviving examples of classical *wayang* painting *in situ* on the island (see p.481 for more on the *wayang* style). They underwent major restorations in the 1930s, and in 1960 and 1982, and although the pictures are decidedly grubby, located on the corner of the main Klungkung crossroads, they remain required viewing. The centre of modern classical-style Balinese painting is at **Kamasan**, a few kilometres south of town, while the **Gunarsa Museum of Modern and Classical Art** to the west of Klungkung houses a moderately diverting collection. South

On several **bemo routes**, most notably from Padang Bai, the name **Semarapura** is used instead of Klungkung.

of Klungkung, the sleepy village of **Gelgel** is these days a shadowy remnant of the thriving royal capital that ruled Bali for three hundred years.

### Some history

Following the **Majapahit conquest** of Bali under the leadership of Gajah Mada in 1343, the conquerors set up a court in Samprangan, moving in 1400 to **Gelgel**, just south of modern Klungkung. From this base, Bali was ruled by a dynasty appointed by Gajah Mada, each ruler taking the title **Dewa Agung** (Great God). When the Majapahit empire in Java collapsed in 1515, large numbers of Javanese royalty in exile swelled the community in Bali. In 1550, when **Batu Renggong** became *dewa agung*, his area of influence increased and the Gelgel court flourished, becoming a centre for art, literature and culture. However, decline set in gradually, and under the rule of Batu Renggong's grandson, Dewa Agung Di Made, control of the empire was gradually lost. Towards the end of the seventeenth century, Di Made's son, Gusti Sideman, moved the palace and the court to **Klungkung**, believing that the decline of the kingdom was due to a curse upon the Gelgel palace. But it was downhill from then on: Gianyar was established as a separate kingdom in 1667, and the *dewa agung* of Klungkung never again reached such influential heights.

The Dutch attacked southern Bali in 1906, and by 1908 had subdued all the kingdoms except Klungkung and Bangli. Gelgel was destroyed, and when the Dutch set up their weapons outside the Semarapura palace in Klungkung on April 28, 1908, the *dewa agung* led two hundred members of his family and court in the traditional **puputan**. When he marched into the guns and was killed, six of his wives surrounded his body and stabbed themselves with their kris. The rest of the entourage were either shot or killed themselves. The monument opposite the Taman Gili in Klungkung commemorates the *puputan*. Surviving members of the Klungkung royal family were then exiled to Lombok and didn't return until the 1920s.

## The Town

Klungkung centres on a crossroads, marked by the dramatic white **Kanda Pat Sari statue**, which guards the four cardinal directions. Beside it is the Taman

Gili, with the Puputan Monument opposite, the central market tucked away just to the east, behind the main street, and the bus and bemo terminal about a kilometre south.

## The Taman Gili and Museum Daerah Semarapura

The **Taman Gili** (daily 7am–6pm; Rp5000), meaning "Island Gardens", has its entrance on Jalan Puputan. It's the only surviving part of the original Semarapura palace. Built around 1710, and largely destroyed by fighting in 1908, the only remains of the palace are the Kerta Gosa (Consultation Pavilion for Peace and Prosperity), the Bale Kambung (Floating Pavilion), a *kulkul* tower, and a massive red-brick **gateway**, which marked the entrance to the inner courtyard of the palace. Legend tells how the gateway was created by two craftsmen who, while sleeping in separate temples, each dreamt about half of a massive and wonderful doorway. When they met and compared their dreams they realized that their visions fitted together perfectly, and they brought their dream to life. Legend also claims that at the time of the *puputan* in Klungkung in 1908, the wooden doors sealed themselves shut and nobody has been able to open them since.

Perched on one corner of the main crossroads, the **Kerta Gosa** is a raised open *bale*. It's sometimes described as a criminal court, which adds poignancy to the pictures of gruesome punishments on the ceiling, but it's more likely that it was the pavilion where the king and his ministers met to debate. The **painted ceiling** is a superb example of the Kamasan style of classical painting, often referred to as the *wayang* style, as the characters are the same as those in the *wayang* puppet theatre.

There are nine levels of paintings. **Level one**, nearest the floor, shows scenes from the Tantri stories, an Indonesian version of the *Thousand and One Nights*, in which the girl, Tantri, weaves tales night after night. **Levels two and three** illustrate the Bhima Swarga story (part of the *Mahabharata* epic; see p.472), and the suffering of souls in the afterlife as their sins are atoned for by cruel punishments: you can be sawn in half for disobedience to your parents, have your tongue pulled out for witchcraft or have your intestines extracted through your anus for farting in public. Bhima is the aristocratic-looking chap with moustache, tidy hair, a big club and a long nail on his right thumb. **Level four** shows the Sang Garuda, the story of the Garuda's search for *amerta*, the water of life, so that he can free his mother, Winita, and himself from eternal slavery to the thousand *naga*. **Level five** is the *palalindon*, predicting the effects of earthquakes on life and agriculture, while **levels six and seven** are a continuation of the Bhima Swarga story. **Level eight** is the Swarga Roh, which shows the rewards that the godly will receive in heaven; unfortunately, it's so far above your head that it's hard to see whether good behaviour is worth it. **Level nine**, the *lokapala*, right at the top of the ceiling where the four sides meet, shows a lotus surrounded by four doves symbolizing good luck, enlightenment and salvation.

The **Bale Kambung**, almost beside the Kerta Gosa, was the venue for royal tooth-filing ceremonies (see p.494). Its ceiling is less famous than its neighbour's but equally interesting; six levels of paintings cover Balinese astrology, the tales of Pan Brayut (see box on p.200) and, closest to the top, the adventures of Satusoma, a legendary Buddhist saint.

The **Museum Daerah Semarapura** in the Taman Gili grounds is worth a quick look. It contains a motley collection including kris, textiles, and stones from the ancient monuments of Gelgel. Only a few labels are in English and descriptions are rather scant.

### Pura Taman Sari

Just under 1km northeast from the town centre, **Pura Taman Sari** (Flower Garden) is a pleasant place to relax. The eleven-roofed *meru* stands in the middle of a moat resting upon a stone turtle, who looks rather squashed and beady-eyed, while just one massive *naga* curves around the base. During the reign of the *dewa agung* in Bali, this temple was the site of an annual ceremony in which offerings were made to the kris and other weapons belonging to the royal family of Klungkung.

## Practicalities

The main **bus and bemo terminal**, Terminal Kelod, also known as Terminal Galiron after the market that bustles around it, is about 1km south of the town centre; most public transport stops or passes through here. In addition, a few bemos pass along Jalan Gunung Rinjani just north of the main crossroads, where you can pick up bemos for Rendang and Besakih.

The Klungkung government **tourist office** is in the same building as the Museum Daerah Semarapura, Jl Untung Surapati 2 (Mon–Thurs 7.30am–3.30pm, Fri 7am–1.15pm; ☎0366/21448). Across the road from the Kerta Gosa is the **wartel** (daily 24hr), while the **post office** is just west of the museum on Jalan Untung Surapati. Several banks along Jalan Diponegoro to the east of the main crossroads **change money**, and there's a BNI ATM in the main street with links to the Visa, MasterCard and Cirrus networks.

Most people visit Klungkung as a day-trip from Candi Dasa but if you want to stay, the best **accommodation** is at *Loji Ramayana* in the eastern part of town (☎0366/21044; ●), which has simple rooms with attached bathrooms set back from the road in a courtyard with a small restaurant. Klungkung has plenty of cheap **places to eat**: on Jalan Nakula, *Bali Indah* at no. 1 and *Sumba Rasa* at no. 5 both have small menus written in English and are used to foreign diners. Local people eat at the inexpensive warung gathered on Jalan Gunung Rinjani. There's a **supermarket**, Cahaya Melati, on Jalan Puputan opposite the entrance to the Taman Gili, next to the wartel.

## Around Klungkung

There are several places worth a trip **around Klungkung**, especially if you're interested in arts and crafts, and all are accessible by public transport.

### Gunarsa Museum of Classical and Modern Art, and Tihingan

Some 5km west of Klungkung, just beyond the village of Takmung on the main road to Gianyar, the **Gunarsa Museum of Classical and Modern Art** (daily 9am–5pm; Rp10,000), formerly known as Museum Seni Lukis Klasik Bali, is reached on any westbound transport from Klungkung. Get out when you see the massive Trimurti statue with mock policemen at the base.

There is a vast collection of historical objects and traditional art, including painting, embroidery, stone sculptures, masks and ancient furniture. Scenes from the *Mahabharata*, the *Ramayana* and the *Karmapala* feature extensively. It's a fascinating hoard to wander through, and the guides will do their best to answer questions. A guidebook in English (Rp60,000) is descriptive rather than explanatory.

The museum also contains a collection of works by **Nyoman Gunarsa**, the founder of the museum. Born in nearby Banda village, he is one of the foremost modern Balinese painters. Initially his work appears quite abstract, but resolves o the forms of dancers and musicians, the artist's constant theme. His studio :hin the museum is also sometimes open to visitors.

From the Gunarsa Museum a side-road leads 3km to **TIHINGAN**; bemos ply this route through the villages of Banda and Penasan. Tihingan is home to a number of **gong-makers**, and there are several showrooms on the main street (7am–3pm); if you come early, you may be able to see the craftsmen creating bronze gongs ranging in size from tiny tourist models no bigger than a hand-span, to giants, 1m in diameter and costing several million rupiah.

## Kamasan

South of Klungkung, 500m beyond the Kelod bemo terminal, is the turning to **KAMASAN**, a tiny village packed with artists' studios and renowned in Bali as the centre of **classical wayang painting** (see p.481). *Wayang* style depicts religious subjects, astrological charts and calendars, in muted reds, ochres, blues, greens and blacks. Many of the artists here work in family concerns where one member of the family sketches out the work, while and others make and mix the colours and fill in the outlines.

After visiting a few studios you'll find it easy to pick out the better-drawn, more carefully coloured pictures. While the artists obviously want to make sales, the atmosphere is pleasant and relaxed – although you should shop around and still bargain hard. **I Nyoman Mandra** has a fine reputation and his work will give you a basis for comparison. Notice the fine but solid outlines, the absence of large unfilled spaces on the canvas and the careful, detailed colouring and shading. He also organizes a school (Mon–Sat 2–4.30pm) where local children learn classical painting and visitors are welcome to see their efforts. Donations are appreciated and it's a heartening attempt to keep the skills of classical art alive. **Ni Made Suciarmi** is one of very few **women artists** working in Kamasan in what is very much a male preserve; many women mix colours and fill in the outlines, but she does the drawing, too. She comes from a family of artists and was involved in the 1930s renovation of the Kerta Gosa ceiling in Klungkung when she was a very young girl. Her work is represented in the Seniwati Women's Art Gallery in Ubud (see p.196).

There's **accommodation** at Yayasan Gunung Merta Art Centre (☎0361/462611, ✉g_legong@hotmail.com; ❸ full board), in small, neat bungalows around a courtyard. They can arrange programmes involving local walks, gamelan lessons and visits to artists' studios.

## Gelgel and beyond

The ancient court centre of **GELGEL**, 4km south of Klungkung, is a quiet little village with nothing but its history to offer visitors; large numbers of its

---

### Why Bali has remained Hindu

Gelgel is home to a **Muslim** community, one of the three communities established on Bali at the time of the **Majapahit** rule over the island. It's believed that Muslim missionaries who came to Bali to convert the people failed, and were too ashamed to go home, so the *dewa agung* allowed them to stay. Legend tells that the *dewa agung*'s main objection to Islam was circumcision. The missionaries explained that the bamboo knife used was very sharp. The *dewa agung* demanded to see the knife, tried to cut his fingernail and failed. He then tried to cut the hairs on his arm and failed. Refusing to allow the knife near any other parts of his anatomy, he gave it back and declared that he and Bali would remain Hindu.

ancient stones have been removed to museums elsewhere. There are bemos from Terminal Kelod in Klungkung.

**Pura Dasar** on the main street is the most imposing temple, with massive courtyards, *bale*, and nine- and eleven-roofed *meru* in the inner courtyard. Each year this temple is the site of the **Pewintenan ceremony**, held on the fourth full moon of the Balinese calendar (check the sources of information on p.36 for dates), which attracts pilgrims from all over Bali. The purpose of the ceremony is to purify those ready to become *pemangku* (village priests). The ritual lasts all day and at midnight culminates with the new *pemangku* walking over the skin and sometimes the head of a dead buffalo.

# Besakih and Gunung Agung

The major draw in the east of Bali, with around a quarter of a million tourists a year, is undoubtedly the **Besakih** temple complex, the most venerated site in Bali, situated on the slopes of **Gunung Agung**, the holiest and highest mountain on the island. The sheer volume of people can be overwhelming: it's worth **arriving early** in the morning or **late** in the afternoon to get the best of the atmosphere.

Besakih is totally schizophrenic. On the one hand it is the most sacred spot on Bali for Balinese Hindus, who believe that the gods occasionally descend to earth and reside in the temple, during which times the worshippers don their finery and bring them elaborate offerings. The complex's sheer scale is impressive, and on a clear day, with ceremonies in full swing, it is a wonderful place. On the other hand, Besakih is a jumble of buildings, unremarkable in many ways, around which has evolved the habit of separating foreign tourists from as much money as possible. Even the stark grandeur of Besakih's location is often shrouded in mist, leaving Gunung Agung towering behind in all-enveloping cloud and the splendid panorama back south to the coast an imaginary delight. You can well end up wondering why you bothered.

## Arrival and information

Without your own transport, the easiest way of getting to Besakih is to take an **organized tour**, which also has the advantage of protecting you to some extent from the attentions of the local guides. If you decide to do this, check how much time you'll have to look around; anything less than an hour is hardly worth it.

By **public transport**, one way is to approach from Klungkung: bemos pass through Jalan Gunung Rinjani just north of the main road in the town centre, although you may have to change at Rendang or Menanga, the turn-off for Besakih. Green bemos also run from Amlapura via Selat and Muncan to Rendang, with some going on to Menanga and Besakih. Plenty of bemos run in the morning, but they dry up in the afternoon. There are no public bemos north of Menanga to Penelokan, or between Rendang and Bangli.

The **tourist office** (daily 8am–7pm) is on the right as you head through the main gate beyond the car park, and appears to be staffed by guides who are eager for you to engage their services. In the car park you'll also find a wartel and a small post office. Moneychangers – offering poor rates – line the road up to the temple.

# Besakih

The **Besakih complex** (daily 8am–5pm; Rp7500, camera Rp1000, video camera Rp2500, parking Rp1000) consists of more than twenty separate **temples**, each with its own name, spread over a site stretching for more than 3km. The central temple – the largest on the island – is **Pura Penataran Agung**, with the other temples ranged around it. There's as yet no written guide available at the site, but a **map** is mounted on a noticeboard situated just at the top of the road leading from the car park to the temples.

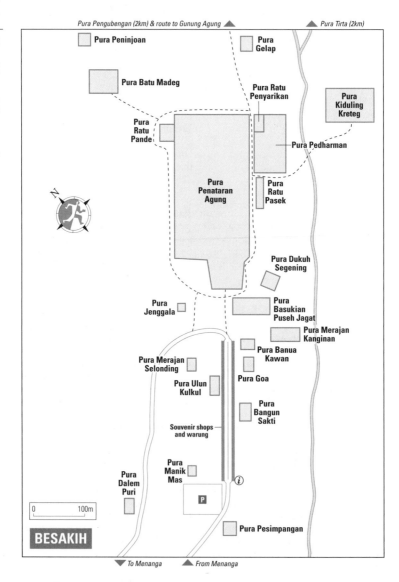

Pura Pengubengan (2km) & route to Gunung Agung ▲       ▲ Pura Tirta (2km)

Pura Peninjoan

Pura Gelap

Pura Batu Madeg

Pura Ratu Penyarikan

Pura Kiduling Kreteg

Pura Ratu Pande

Pura Pedharman

Pura Penataran Agung

Pura Ratu Pasek

N

Pura Dukuh Segening

Pura Jenggala

Pura Basukian Puseh Jagat

Pura Merajan Kanginan

Pura Merajan Selonding

Pura Banua Kawan

Pura Ulun Kulkul

Pura Goa

Pura Bangun Sakti

Souvenir shops and warung

Pura Manik Mas

Pura Dalem Puri

*i*

P

0        100m

**BESAKIH**

Pura Pesimpangan

▼ To Menanga       ▲ From Menanga

## Guides at Besakih

In recent years, Besakih has developed an appalling reputation among visitors as a place of aggravation and non-stop hassle, leaving many feeling angry and insulted. The problem stemmed from the hundreds of local men who styled themselves as **guides**, **guardians** or **keepers** of the temple, insistently attached themselves to tourists and then demanded large sums in payment for their "services". The authorities now claim to have addressed this problem, and the official advice to visitors is only to engage a guide who has an official guide badge and is wearing a traditionally woven, geometrically patterned *endek* shirt as uniform. They hang around the tourist office, so you're unlikely to miss them. There's no reason why you need a guide at all, though; stick to the paths running along the walls outside the temples shown on the map opposite, wear a sarong and sash, and you'll be in no danger of causing any religious offence. If you do engage a guide, establish the **fee** beforehand; Rp20,000 is reasonable and you can always add extra if you feel you've received a good service. Be aware that if you're escorted by a guide into one of the temples to receive a blessing from a priest you'll be expected to make a "donation" to the priest, the amount negotiable through your guide.

If you're including Besakih in your own tour using a Balinese driver, you may find they're reluctant to bring visitors to Besakih because of problems their guests have encountered in the past. They can all suggest other temples as alternatives and will warn you of the problems if you insist on coming to Besakih, although they'll be unable to intervene on your behalf.

Unless you're praying or making offerings, you're **forbidden to enter** any of the temples in the complex, and most temples remain locked unless there's a ceremony in progress. However, a lot is visible through the gateways and over walls. The rule about wearing a sarong and sash appears to be inconsistently applied but you'll definitely need them if you're in skimpy clothing; **sarong rental** is available, with negotiable prices from Rp2000. It's much easier to take your own.

### Some history

It's likely that Besakih was a religious site long before the start of recorded history; Pura Batu Madeg (Temple of the Standing Stone), in the north of the complex, suggests megalithic connections through its ancient terraced structure based around a central stone. However, Besakih's founder is generally believed to be **Sri Markandeya**, a priest who came from eastern Java at the end of the eighth century with a party of settlers. Markandeya's son became the first high priest of the temple, attracting priests and successive rulers of the island, many of whom built shrines or temples here. An important ceremony was staged here in 1007, widely thought to be the cremation rites of Queen Mahendratta, origin of the Rangda legend (see box, p.235). **Empu Bharadah**, the holy man attributed with subduing Rangda, took part and there are shrines dedicated to him throughout the complex.

By the time the **Majapahit dynasty** conquered Bali in 1343, Besakih was very important. It became, in turn, the state temple of the powerful Gelgel and Klungkung courts, and its pre-eminent position on the island was confirmed. An **earthquake** severely damaged the buildings in 1917 but it was repaired by the Dutch, and in 1932 the road to the temple was completed. Further damage occurred in 1963 during the eruption of Gunung Agung (see box, p.250), and Besakih again underwent restoration. As a result, the temples in the complex are a vibrant mix of old and new, and fresh building and restoration work continues.

## Besakih festivals

Every temple in the Besakih complex has its timetable of **festivals**. There are more than fifty annual festivals in all; exact dates are published in the sources of information in Basics on p.36. The most important annual festival is the **Bhatar Turun Kabeh** (The Gods Descend Together), which takes place in March or April and lasts a month, with the high point on the full moon of the tenth lunar month. At this time, the gods of all the shrines are believed to come and dwell in Besakih; worshippers converge here from all over the island for the ceremonies. Besakih's most revered festival is **Eka Dasa Rudra** (see box, p.250), held every hundred years, but which took place in 1963 and then again in 1979. More frequently, the **Panca Wali Krama** festival occurs every ten years and involves a forty-two-kilometre, three-day procession from the coast to the temple.

## The temples

To get the best out of Besakih, it's a good idea to see **Pura Penataran Agung** first, and then wander; most of the tourist crowds stick to the area around the central temple. The *meru* of **Pura Batu Madeg**, rising among the trees in the north of the complex, are particularly enticing, while **Pura Pengubengan**, the most far-flung of the temples, is a good 2km through the forest.

While it's possible to consider each of the temples as a single entity, they do fall into various groups. The **Trimurti**, the "three shapes" of the supreme God, consists of three temples: Pura Kiduling Kreteg (Temple South of the Bridge), dedicated to Brahma, the creator; Pura Batu Madeg (Temple of the Standing Stone), dedicated to Wisnu, the preserver; and Pura Penataran Agung, dedicated to Siwa, the destroyer. Each of the gods has an associated colour, and on festival days the respective temples are decked with flags and banners: black for Wisnu, red for Brahma and a multicoloured array for Siwa at the centre. Five of the temples are considered to represent the **panca dewata**, the five gods of the four directions and the centre – Pura Ulun Kulkul the west, Pura Gelap the east, Pura Batu Madeg the north, Pura Kiduling Kreteg the south and Pura Penataran Agung the centre. **Pura Dalem Puri**, the Temple of the Dead, is especially significant for the Balinese and, during the seventh lunar month, pilgrims come to pray for the souls of the dead.

### Pura Penataran Agung

The Great Temple of State, or **Pura Penataran Agung**, is the central and most dramatic building in the complex. It is built on **six ascending terraces**, and there are more than fifty *bale*, shrines and stone thrones inside; about half are dedicated to specific gods, while the others have ceremonial functions, such as receiving offerings, providing seating for the priests or the gamelan orchestra, or as residences for the gods during temple festivals.

A giant stairway, lined by seven levels of **carved figures**, leads to the first courtyard; the figures to the left are from the *Mahabharata* and the ones to the right from the *Ramayana*. You can look into the courtyard, although views are obstructed by the *bale* just inside the gate. This pavilion is in two parts with a small walkway between. As worshippers process through here they symbolically sever their connection with the everyday world, before proceeding through the *kori agung* into the second courtyard – the most important in the temple. A path skirts the perimeter wall of Pura Penataran Agung, from which you can see most of the temple's terraces. If you're hoping to see religious ceremonies, the second courtyard is the one to watch (the best views are from the west

## LEVEL I
**1. Candi bentar** An earlier entrance was toppled in the earthquake following the 1963 eruption.
**2–3. Bale kulkul** Contains the wooden kulkul (slit gongs).
**4. Bale pegat** Two-part *bale* to symbolize pilgrims passing from the material to the spiritual world.
**5–6. bale palegongan** and **bale pagambuhan** Used for dance performances during festivals.
**7–8. Bale ongkara** Represent the sacred syllable *om*.

## LEVEL II
**9. Kori agung** Gateway into next courtyard.
**10. Bale gong** For the gamelan orchestra.
**11. Bale pawedan** Where high priests prepare holy water.
**12. Bale kembangsirang** For conducting rituals.
**13. Panggungan** Place for offerings.
**14. Bale agung** For meetings.
**15. Bale kawas** Dedicated to Ida Bhatara Ider Buwana.
**16. Padma capah** Throne dedicated to Ida Ratu Sula Majemuh, lord of the weather.
**17. Bale paruman alit** Containing a stone *lingge*.
**18. Nine-roofed meru** Dedicated to Sanghyang Kubakal, god of instruments used in ceremonies.
**19. Eleven-roofed meru** Dedicated to Ratu Manik Maketel.
**20. Bale pepelik** For offerings.
**21. Bale tegeh** Dedicated to Empu Bharadah.
**22. Padmatiga** Triple lotus throne and centrepiece of the temple, where homage is paid to the supreme god Sanghyang Widhi Wasa in his three manifestations.
**23. Bale pasamuhan agung** Home of the gods at festival time.
**24. Bale pepelik** For offerings.

## LEVEL III
**25–30. Meru and shrines** Dedicated to spirits
**31–32. Shrines** To the ancestors of a clan from the Besakih area.
**33. Bale pepelik** For offerings.
**34–35. Shrines** To the ancestors of another local clan.
**36. Panggungan** For offerings during ceremonies at the shrines.
**37. Seven-roofed meru** Dedicated to Saraswati, Hindu goddess of learning.
**38. Panggungan** For offerings during ceremonies at the shrines.
**39. Bale pepelik** For offerings.
**40. Eleven-roofed meru** Dedicated to Ida Ratu Maspahit.
**41. Three-roofed kehen** Temple store for sacred objects.

## LEVEL IV
**42. Bale** Containing ancient statues.
**43. Gedong** Dedicated to Ida Ratu Ulang Alu, god of wandering salesmen.
**44. Gedong** Dedicated to Ida Ratu Ayu Subandar, god of merchants.
**45. Bale pepelik** For offerings.
**46. Bebaturan** Dedicated to Ida Ratu Sedahan Panginte.
**47. Bale pepelik** For offerings.
**48. Eleven-roofed meru** Dedicated to Ida Ratu Sunaring Jagat, god of the light of the world.
**49–51. Bale tegeh** Dedicated to the courtiers and nymphs of heaven (*widadara* and *widadari*).

# PURA PENATARAN AGUNG

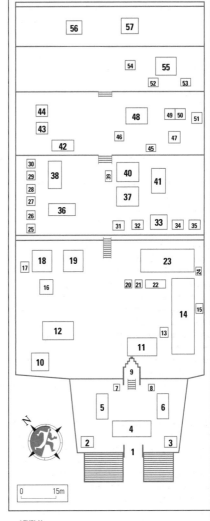

## LEVEL V
**52–53. Bale pepelik** For offerings.
**54. Three-roofed meru** Dedicated to Ida Ratu Ayu Mas Magelung, goddess of performing arts.
**55. Eleven-roofed meru** Dedicated to Sanghyang Widi Wasa.

## LEVEL VI
**56. Gedong** Dedicated to Ida Ratu Bukit Kiwa, god of the left mountain.
**57. Gedong** Dedicated to Ida Ratu Bukit Tengen, god of the right mountain.

side). It's the largest courtyard in the temple and contains the **padmatiga**, the three-seated lotus throne dedicated to Brahma, Siwa and Wisnu, where all pilgrims pray.

## Practicalities

The shops that line the road up from the car park, and the stalls dotted throughout the complex, offer a range of **souvenirs** including bedspreads, clothes, woodcarvings, baskets and paintings in all styles. **Accommodation** near Besakih is limited. The *Lembah Arca* hotel (☎0366/23076; ❷–❸) on the road between Menanga and Besakih, a couple of kilometres before the temple complex, has very basic rooms with attached cold-water bathrooms if you get stranded. There are also some unauthorized lodgings (❷–❸) behind the road from the car park up to the temple; ask at the tourist office for details. These places are simple, with few private bathrooms, but are useful if you get stuck, are climbing Gunung Agung, or want to explore the site early or late. Several

---

### 1963

The year **1963** is recalled in Bali as a time when the gods were displeased and took their revenge on the island. Ancient texts prescribe that an immense ceremony, **Eka Dasa Rudra** – the greatest ritual in Balinese Hinduism – should be held every hundred years for the spiritual purification of the island and to bring future good fortune. Before 1963, it had only been held a couple of times since the sixteenth century. In the early 1960s, religious leaders believed that the trials of World War II and the ensuing fight for independence were indicators that the ritual was once again needed, and these beliefs were confirmed by a **plague of rats** that overran the entire island in 1962. Preparations began on October 10, 1962, with ceremonies inviting and welcoming the gods from Gunung Semeru in Java and Gunung Rinjani in Lombok, and the purification of sacrificial animals.

The climax of the festival was set for March 8, 1963, but on February 18, **Gunung Agung**, which had been dormant for centuries, started rumbling; the glow of the fire became visible within the crater and ash began to coat the area. Initially, this was interpreted as a good omen sent by the gods to purify Besakih, but soon doubts crept in. Some argued that the wrong date had been chosen for the event and wanted to call it off. However, by this time it was too late to cancel: President Sukarno was due to attend, together with a group of international travel representatives.

By March 8, black smoke, rocks and ash were billowing from the mountain, but the ceremony went ahead, albeit in a decidedly tense atmosphere. Eventually, on March 17, Agung **erupted** with such force that the top hundred metres of the mountain was ripped apart. The whole of eastern Bali was threatened by the poisonous gas and molten lava that poured from the volcano, villages were engulfed, and between 1000 and 2000 people are thought to have died, while the homes of another 100,000 were destroyed. Roads were wiped out, some towns were isolated for weeks, and the ash ruined vast amounts of crops, causing serious food shortages. The east of Bali took many years to recover; hundreds of homeless people joined Indonesia's *transmigrasi* programme (see p.453) and moved to the outer islands.

Despite the force of the eruption and the position of Besakih high on the mountain, a surprisingly small amount of damage occurred within the temples themselves, and the **closing rites** of Eka Dasa Rudra took place on April 20. Subsequently, many Balinese felt that the mountain's eruption at the time of such a momentous ceremony was an omen of the civil strife that engulfed Bali in 1965 (see p.452).

In 1979, the year specified by the ancient texts, Eka Dasa Rudra was held again, this time passing off without incident.

restaurants in the area cater for the tour-bus trade, though you'll find more reasonably priced food at the *Lembah Arca* hotel (see above) and at the *Warung Mawar* in Menanga, just on the left as you turn off to Besakih. There are a few warung on the walk up to Besakih from the car park.

# Gunung Agung

According to legend, **Gunung Agung** was created by the god Pasupati when he split Mount Meru (the centre of the Hindu universe), forming both Gunung Agung and Gunung Batur. At 3142m, superb conical-shaped Agung is the highest Balinese peak and an impressive sight from anywhere in East Bali. The spiritual centre of Bali, it is believed that the spirits of the ancestors of the Balinese people dwell on Gunung Agung. Villages and house compounds are laid out in relation to the mountain, and many Balinese people prefer to sleep with their heads towards it (see p.491).

### Climbing the mountain

Two main **routes** lead up Gunung Agung, both involving a long hard climb. One path leaves from Besakih and the other from Pura Pasar Agung on the southern slope of the mountain, near Selat (described on p.282). You'll need to set out very early in the morning if you want to be at the top in time to see the spectacular **sunrise** (around 7am). It's essential to take a **guide** with you, as it's easy to get lost. You'll also need strong footwear, a good flashlight that you can attach to some part of yourself – leaving both hands free for climbing – and water and snacks to keep you going; for the descent, a stout stick is handy.

This is an extremely sacred peak for the Balinese, and is not permitted at many times of the year because of **religious festivals**: March and April are generally impossible from the Besakih side because of ceremonies. You'll also have to make **offerings** at temples at the start and on the way. **Weather**-wise, the dry season (April–mid-Oct) is the best time to climb Gunung Agung; you may get a few dry days during the rainy season but don't even contemplate it during January and February, the wettest months.

**From Pura Pasar Agung**, it's at least a three-hour climb with an ascent of almost 2000m, so you'll need to set out at 3am or earlier, depending on how fit you are. You'll also have to either sleep at the temple or get up even earlier to get to the start of the climb. The track initially passes through forest, ascending onto bare, steep rock. It doesn't go to the actual summit, but ends at a point on the rim that is about 100m lower. From here, the summit masks views of part of the island and, between April and September, the sunrise on the horizon, but you'll be able to see Gunung Rinjani, the south of Bali and Gunung Batukau and look down into the five-hundred-metre crater.

**From Besakih**, the climb is longer (5–7hr) and much more challenging; you'll need to leave between 10pm and midnight. This path starts from Pura Pengubengan, the most distant of the Besakih temples, and leads to the summit of Agung with views in all directions. As with the other route, you climb initially through forest, but the path gets very steep, very quickly, even before it gets out onto the bare rock, and you'll soon need your hands to help haul yourself upwards. The descent is particularly taxing from this side and feels very precarious when you're already exhausted; allow at least five hours to get down.

A route from the north side, **from Dukuh Bujangga Sakti**, is offered by just one company, M & G Trekking (see below). Dukuh is inland from Kubu on the north coast, and you start out at 300m altitude, so the climb is greater but not as steep as the other routes. This is also less painful as you start climbing in the afternoon, camp on the mountain at 1750m and complete the three hours to the summit pre-dawn. The north of Bali is generally drier so it is less often shrouded in cloud. You can walk round the rim to the absolute summit if you climb from this side, and you can see the sunrise on the horizon all year round from this approach.

## Practicalities

There are many established **guiding** operations leading climbs up Agung from bases throughout Bali and new ones are appearing all the time. Bear in mind that this is a serious trek: talk to potential guides and satisfy yourself that they have the necessary experience and knowledge.

Closest to **Pura Pasar Agung**, you'll find guides at Muncan, 4km east of Rendang, at Selat (see p.282 for more on the road east of Rendang) and up at the temple. In Muncan, I Ketut Uriada (☎0812/364 6426), a part-time teacher and guide, is one of the most experienced guides and has climbed Agung over two hundred times in recent years. These days, he rarely climbs himself but has trained several local guides. His house is marked by a sign advertising his services, on the left as you enter Muncan from the east. Expect to pay around US$30 for a guide for one person, $40 for two, $50 for three. Larger groups may need more than one guide. Ketut Uriada will help you arrange a bemo charter between Muncan and Pura Pasar Agung (about $10) and will also quote for climbs from Besakih. If you go directly to Pura Pasar Agung, you'll be looking at $35 for a guide who will take up to four people, but you'll need to negotiate and take all your own food and water. There's **accommodation** at *Pondok Wisata Puri Agung* (☎ & ℻0366/23037; ❸) in Selat, 4km east of Muncan on the Amlapura road, who can also provide a guide for the climb, quoting $35 for two people. This doesn't include accommodation or transport to and from Pura Pasar Agung. In Selat, Gung Bawa, Jl Sri Jaya Pangus 33 (☎0366/24379 or 0812/384 0752, ✉gbtrekk@yahoo.com), offers packages from $40 for two people climbing from Pura Pasar Agung and from $60 for two people climbing from Besakih; both prices include resting time in a local guesthouse, transport to and from the start of the climb, and snacks and mineral water on the way. Transport to and from Selat can also be arranged; check the price at the time of booking. They also offer a longer package leaving Selat at midday and climbing to a camping spot at 2560m, leaving a climb of one to two hours the next morning to see the sunrise ($100 including all equipment, meals and transport from Selat).

If you're at **Besakih**, guides can be arranged at the tourist office in the temple complex; they can also help with nearby lodgings. The going rate from this side is Rp700,000 per guide, for two people.

Inevitably, prices are higher if you arrange the trek **from further afield**. One established guide in Tirtagangga is Komang Gede Sutama (☎081/338 770 893 or contact him through *Good Karma* restaurant), who charges Rp500,000 per person, including transport and breakfast, to climb from Pura Pasar Agung (Rp750,000 for two people, Rp900,000 for three people) with prices from Rp650,000 per person from Besakih. The *Pondok Lembah Dukuh* and *Geria Semalung* losmen in the nearby village of Ababi also arrange Agung climbs. M & G Trekking (☎0363/41464 or 0812/361 9625, ✉mgtrekking@hotmail.com) has an office in Balina, Candi Dasa (see p.263). They quote Rp890,000 per person for a minimum of two people for the longer, but potentially more rewarding, climb from Dukuh including all transport, equipment and food. Bali Sunrise 2001 in **Ubud** (☎0361/980470 or 0818/552669, 🌐www.balisunrise2001.com) will arrange pick-ups for the trek from pretty much anywhere on Bali, charging from $100 per person depending on where you start from. The guiding operations in **Toya Bungkah** charge from $80 per person (minimum numbers apply); in the same area Made Senter at *Losmen Miranda* in Kintamani (see p.301) charges $100 for a group of four people. Perama will also help you organise the climb – they use Roijaya Wisata at Toyah Bungkah and charge $100 per person; contact any of their offices.

# Nusa Lembongan, Nusa Ceningan and Nusa Penida

Southeast of Bali, across the treacherous Badung Strait, the islands of Nusa Lembongan, Nusa Ceningan and Nusa Penida rise alluringly out of the ocean swell, although relatively few visitors make the short crossing. The nearest island to the mainland is **Nusa Lembongan**, encircled by a mixture of white-sand **beaches** and mangrove. Seaweed farming is the major occupation, while the island's other main source of income is the tourist facilities scattered around the west and south coasts. Visitors include surfers, day-trippers, and anybody seeking attractive beaches, a bit of gentle exploring and an addictively somnolent atmosphere. Generally, Jungutbatu is the place for budget accommodation, Chelegimbai and the surrounding bays feature moderately priced options, while Mushroom Bay hosts the luxury end of the market.

Only a few hundred metres separates Nusa Lembongan from tiny **Nusa Ceningan**. The island is 4km long by 1km wide, essentially a hill sticking out

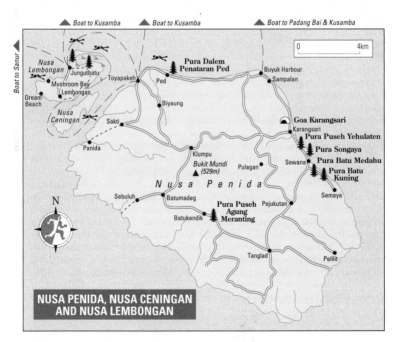

NUSA PENIDA, NUSA CENINGAN AND NUSA LEMBONGAN

## Boats and trips to the islands

**From Benoa** to Nusa Lembongan. It's possible to use the daily Bounty Cruise (see opposite) to get to or from the island for $15 one way, departing Benoa at 9am, returning 4pm. This is a faster and more comfortable crossing in rough seas than the small Sanur boats.

**From Kusamba** to Nusa Penida (Buyuk Harbour, Toyapakeh and Sampalan) and Nusa Lembongan (Jungutbatu). Rp20,000–30,000; takes 1–2hr. Local boats leave when (very) full, most heading out early in the morning. A charter is possible (Rp400,000–500,000 per boat), though this isn't for the faint-hearted. For return times, enquire in the villages.

**From Padang Bai** to Nusa Penida (Buyuk Harbour). Rp25,000; takes 1hr. Boats leave when full, starting around 7am. You can charter a boat to take you to Nusa Lembongan from Padang Bai (also available **from Candi Dasa**): it'll cost about Rp300,000 one way, but many of these boats seem too small for the big swell.

**From Sanur** to Nusa Lembongan (Jungutbatu). Takes 1hr 30min–2hr. Boats leave at 8am (Rp33,000) and 10am (Rp43,000), returning at 8am (Rp35,000) from Jungutbatu and 7am (Rp35,000) from Mushroom Bay. Buy tickets from the office at the beach end of Jalan Hang Tuah near the *Ananda Hotel* and from the beachfront office in Jungutbatu. Perama operate a daily tourist shuttle boat (Rp50,000) at 10.30am from Sanur to Nusa Lembongan (Jungutbatu), returning at 8.30am; book one day in advance. It's also possible to charter a private boat for a Lembongan day-trip from the Jeladi Wilis Boat Cooperative booth on the beachfront in front of the *Grand Bali Beach* (℡0361/284206); they charge $35 per person (minimum six people).

### Luxury trips

A day-trip out to the **luxury resorts** on the islands or to a watersports pontoon moored just offshore is a pleasant, if pricey, way to visit Nusa Lembongan or Nusa Penida. Most include free snorkelling, many of the resorts have pools and there are plenty of activities laid on. All trips include transfers between your hotel and the boat, and lunch; some also throw in an island tour. Prices vary quite considerably so it pays to shop around. See p.259 for more on the accommodation add-ons on offer.

---

of the water. With around four hundred inhabitants, it's a sleepy place with only a small section of tarmac road and no tourist facilities at present.

Beyond is **Nusa Penida**, roughly 20km long, dominated by a high, limestone plateau with a harsh, dry landscape reminiscent of the Bukit, the far southern tip of the mainland. The island is crisscrossed by miles of small lanes ripe for exploring, and its south coast has some of the most spectacular scenery in Bali.

The best **surfing** here is from June to September, although full moons during other months are worth a try. The breaks are mostly offshore from Jungutbatu (including Shipwreck, which breaks off the remains of a vessel on the reef), although there are also breaks off Mushroom Bay and in the channel between Nusa Lembongan and Nusa Ceningan.

If you're interested in **surf safaris** that incorporate Nusa Lembongan, try Purnama Indah (℡0811/398553, in Sanur ℡0361/289213, ⓦwww.indosurftour .com) and Dreamweaver (℡0812/380 8607, ⓦwww.dreamweaver-surf.com), which also take in the main surf breaks along the southern coast of Lombok and Sumbawa; prices depend on the length of trip and the destination.

## Nusa Lembongan

A small island, 4km long and less than 3km at its widest part, **Nusa Lembongan** is sheltered by offshore coral reefs that provide excellent snorkelling and

**Bali Hai** ⓣ0361/720331, ⓦwww.balihaicruises.com. The biggest operator offers a choice of vessels. Trips (from $75) include watersports based on the pontoon moored in Mushroom Bay or relaxing at the Lembongan Island Beach Club on the coast at Mushroom Bay, where there's an excellent pool. Parasailing and diving are available for an extra charge. A high-speed ocean-rafting trip is also possible ($69), taking in the incredible scenery of the south coast of Nusa Penida and snorkelling at Crystal Bay. Cruise and dive packages and overnight stays at *Hai Tide Huts* are also available.

**Bounty** ⓣ0361/726666, ⓦwww.balibountycruises.com. Organizes water activities off the coast at Mushroom Bay, including banana-boat rides, snorkelling, canoeing, glass-bottomed boat trips and a forty-four-metre waterslide. From $85.

**Island Explorer** ⓣ0361/728088, ⓦwww.bali-cruise.com. With a choice of sailing, motor yacht or fast catamaran, full-day trips (from $69, but discounts heavily advertised in quiet seasons) are available to the *Coconuts Beach Resort* where staying overnight is a possible add-on. There's a pool at the resort, from where it's a short walk to the beach. Fishing, diving and a village tour are optional extras.

**Lembongan Island Cruise** ⓣ0361/271212, ⓔvillawayan@dps.centrin.net.id. Visitors use *Villa Wayan* and Chelegimbai beach for the day's relaxation ($45); there's no pool, but the beach is attractive and peaceful. It's possible to arrange overnight stays at *Villa Wayan*, and diving packages are also available.

**Quicksilver** ⓣ0361/729564, ⓦwww.quicksilver-bali.com. Transport is by catamaran to Toyapakeh on Nusa Penida where watersports from the pontoon are the speciality and there are also beachside facilities ($89).

**Sail Sensations** ⓣ0361/725864, ⓦwww.bali-sailsensations.com. Visitors use the facilities at the *Anchorage* resort on the coast at Mushroom Bay. Day-cruises are available onboard a luxurious sailing catamaran ($89). Overnight stays are possible at the super-luxury *Nusa Lembongan Resort*.

**Waka Louka** ⓣ0361/723629, ⓦwww.wakaexperience.com. Day-cruise to the *Waka Nusa* resort on the beach at Mushroom Bay using a sailing catamaran ($86). Diving or fishing are optional extras. Overnight accommodation at *Waka Nusa* can be arranged.

create the perfect conditions for seaweed farming (see box on p.262). You can **walk** around the whole island in three to four hours, and there are **bicycles** (from Rp20,000 per day) and **motorbikes** (Rp25,000–30,000 per hour) for rent in Jungutbatu; ask at your losmen or check out the places advertising on the beach. A bridge, sturdy enough for motorbikes, spans the narrow strait that separates Nusa Lembongan and Nusa Ceningan.

Accommodation is in **Jungutbatu** on the west coast and to the south in **Coconut Beach**, **Chelegimbai** and **Mushroom Bay** (Tanjung Sanghyang), informally named after the mushroom coral in the offshore reef, to the south-west of this, where most of the upmarket places are situated, and further south at **Dream Beach**. There's no post office, and electricity is produced by a generator from 3pm to 8am and all day on Sunday, which some hotels supplement with their own generators.

## Jungutbatu

Spread out along the west coast for well over 1km, the attractive village of **JUNGUTBATU** is a low-key place, with losmen and restaurants, a bank, moneychanger, wartels, and a few shops selling textiles and crafts. Arriving by public boat, you'll be dropped off according to the tide; this could be anything up to 1km along the beach from the majority of the accommodation. With

## Diving and snorkelling

The area around the islands is popular for **diving**, although the sea can be cold with currents over four knots. For **dive sites**, Toyapakeh, SD Point and Mangrove are the most reliable, predictable and frequently dived, and can get busy. **Toyapakeh** offers huge coral boulders and pillars, which protect an inland area of gorgonians and soft coral bushes, and where it's possible to see *mola mola* from June to October and other pelagics such as manta rays and hammerhead sharks. At **SD Point** there are large coral heads, a diverse collection of corals and sponges, and the possibility of spotting green and hawksbill turtles, manta rays, sea snakes, octopus and white-tipped reef sharks. **Mangrove** is an easy site, used a lot for training dives. It has a forty-five-degree sloping reef with excellent coral coverage off the northeast corner of Nusa Lembongan.

The most established **dive operator** on the islands is the highly professional World Diving Lembongan (℡0812/390 0686, ⊛www.world-diving.com), based next to *Pondok Baruna* in Jungutbatu. They offer dives for certified divers ($30 each for the first two dives, less for more, including equipment), PADI courses up to Dive-master level, a Scuba Review ($35), and Discover Scuba ($60). They dive the more frequented sites less often, and have explored and opened up eighteen rarely dived local sites where the coral is in better condition and the larger ocean life more likely to appear.

You can charter boats from Nusa Lembongan to take you **snorkelling** (ask at your losmen); one of the best spots is off **Mushroom Bay** with others at **Mangrove Corner** (also known as **Jet Point**) to the north, and **Sunfish** nearby. Boats will also take you to Nusa Penida where **Crystal Bay** is renowned for its clear waters; **Gamat**, off the coast near Sakti, and the reef off the coast at **Ped** are also popular. Prices depend on distance; start negotiating at around Rp100,000 per hour for a boat holding up to four people, including equipment. World Diving also take snorkellers along on day-trips for Rp60,000 per person, including equipment, for about four hours.

Perama, you'll come in as close to the office as they can get. The places to stay are not that obvious from the sea, but there'll be plenty of people to point you in the right direction.

You can **change money** at the moneychangers along the beach or at Bank Pembangunan Daerah Bali (Mon–Fri 10am–1pm). There's a **wartel**, which also has **Internet access**, at *Mainski Inn* and Internet access further down the beach at *Bunga Bungalows* – both are open during the hours of electricity. The Perama office (daily 7.30am–6pm) is situated between *Pondok Baruna* and *Nusa Indah* bungalows, and you can book tickets here to tourist destinations on Bali and Lombok. There's one departure daily (8.30am), but many destinations require a stopover on the way.

The ticket office for **public boats** is towards the southern end of the beach; boats leave at 8am. You can also **charter** a local boat to take you back to the mainland: it'll cost about Rp300,000 to Padang Bai, but many of these boats seem too small for the crossing. *Playgrounds* and *Villa Aman* have their own boat and will arrange transfers to and from the mainland (Sanur, Padang Bai, Candi Dasa); prices depend on the number of people but start at Rp400,000 (with discounts for guests).

### Accommodation

Most of the **accommodation** is just behind the beach in the north of Jungutbatu, with a couple of places a few hundred metres to the south.

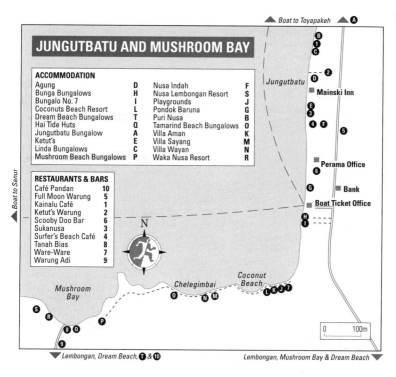

# JUNGUTBATU AND MUSHROOM BAY

**ACCOMMODATION**

| | | | |
|---|---|---|---|
| Agung | D | Nusa Indah | F |
| Bunga Bungalows | H | Nusa Lembongan Resort | S |
| Bungalo No. 7 | I | Playgrounds | J |
| Coconuts Beach Resort | L | Pondok Baruna | G |
| Dream Beach Bungalows | T | Puri Nusa | B |
| Hai Tide Huts | Q | Tamarind Beach Bungalows | O |
| Jungutbatu Bungalow | A | Villa Aman | K |
| Ketut's | E | Villa Sayang | M |
| Linda Bungalows | C | Villa Wayan | N |
| Mushroom Beach Bungalows | P | Waka Nusa Resort | R |

**RESTAURANTS & BARS**

| | |
|---|---|
| Café Pandan | 10 |
| Full Moon Warung | 5 |
| Kainalu Café | 1 |
| Ketut's Warung | 2 |
| Scooby Doo Bar | 6 |
| Sukanusa | 3 |
| Surfer's Beach Café | 4 |
| Tanah Bias | 8 |
| Ware-Ware | 7 |
| Warung Adi | 9 |

*Boat to Toyapakeh*

*Jungutbatu*

Mainski Inn

Perama Office

Bank

Boat Ticket Office

*Boat to Sanur*

N

*Mushroom Bay*

*Chelegimbai*

*Coconut Beach*

0    100m

*Lembongan, Dream Beach, ① & ⑩*

*Lembongan, Mushroom Bay & Dream Beach*

Buildings are mostly concrete and tile, although some bamboo and thatch places do remain. Rooms at the front with sea views are more expensive than those behind. All the places below offer en suite cold-water bathrooms and fans but, unless otherwise stated, no breakfast. Although included in the reviews below, it's worth noting that *Villa Aman* and *Playgrounds* are just a few minutes' walk along the footpath that leads around the coast from the southern end of Jungutbatu beach, and are easily accessible from here.

**Agung** ☏0366/24483. Some rooms in a concrete building, but the two-storey thatched places have most character; ones at the front have the best views, and there's a good sunbathing area just above the beach. ❶–❷

**Bunga Bungalows** ☏0366/24529. At the southern end of the beach, about 400m south of *Pondok Baruna*, with several standards of rooms in two-storey buildings. ❷–❸

**Bungalo No. 7** ☏0366/24497. Popular, good-value rooms at the far southern end of the beach, all with balconies or verandas. There's a sunbathing area overlooking the beach. ❶–❷

**Jungutbatu Bungalow** ☏0817/734 3138. The most northerly accommodation, about 200m beyond *Puri Nusa*. Rooms are in two-storey buildings widely spaced in an attractive garden set slightly back from the beach with a sunbathing

area out on the sand. It's a busy local beach up here, set a little apart from the main tourist area. Price includes breakfast. ❹

**Ketut's** ☏0366/24487. Well-built, attractive accommodation, some of it with excellent sea views, set in pleasant grounds. Air-con and hot water available. ❷–❻

**Linda Bungalows** ☏0812/360 0867. Rooms are in well-built two-storey buildings with good-quality furnishings. The owners pride themselves on Aussie cleanliness. ❷

**Nusa Indah** ☏0366/24480. Set back slightly from the beach behind the *Surfer's Beach Café*, there's a choice of older, cheaper rooms or better-quality, newer ones at the front. ❶–❷

**Pondok Baruna** ☏0812/390 0686, ⓦwww .world-diving.com. A few hundred metres south of the main accommodation area, this small place has clean, tiled rooms looking straight onto the beach and a small attached restaurant. The operator World Diving Lembongan is based here. ❷

**Puri Nusa** ☏ & ℱ 0361/298613. Reasonable rooms in one-, two- and three-storey buildings with good verandas or balconies in an attractive garden. One of the most northerly places. ❶–❷

## Eating

All the places to stay have **restaurants** attached, most of them right on the beachfront with pleasant views of the sea and a cooling breeze. They all offer a good range of international and Indo-Chinese favourites and local seafood, plus the usual travellers' fare, all at inexpensive to moderate prices. *Kainalu Café* and *Agung* both have great daytime views from their upper storeys, *Surfer's Beach Café* shows surfing videos, *Scooby Doo Bar* has satellite TV, and there are fish barbecues at *Linda's* in the high season. *Sukanusa* 🍴 offers some more imaginative choices, impressively cooked and presented, with good vegetarian options. *Ketut's Warung* 🍴, tucked away behind the beach and accessed via the plot of land to the north of *Agung*, is well worth searching out for excellent, cheap local food and a variety of Thai dishes. *Full Moon Warung* on the road through the village has a purely Indonesian menu with fresh, well-cooked food in a peaceful setting. Slightly further afield, *Ware-Ware* is a short walk along the footpath that heads towards Chelegimbai beach from the southern end of the beach at Jungutbatu and serves a mixture of local and Western dishes, while *Café Pandan* at Dream Beach offers free transport (see opposite).

### Around the coast

Around the coast southwest of Jungutbatu, the glorious white-sand bays of **Coconut Beach** (Pantai Songlambung), **Chelegimbai** (also known as Selegimpak) and **Mushroom Bay**, and the footpaths linking them, offer a wide range of attractive moderate and top-end accommodation. This area is the destination for day-trips from the mainland, which can disturb the peace in the middle of the day but can't detract from the idyllic white sand and turquoise waters. Slightly further afield, **Dream Beach**, around on the south coast of the island, has just one accommodation option.

You can **charter a boat** to Mushroom Bay from Jungutbatu. **On foot**, the most attractive route is to walk around the coast. Climb the steps that lead up from the extreme southern end of the beach at Jungutbatu to a path that leads along the hillside past *Playgrounds*, *Villa Aman* and *Coconuts Beach Resort* to Coconut Beach, then up the far side of the bay to Chelegimbai beach. Another path leads up from the far southern end of Chelegimbai past *Tamarind Beach Bungalows* and passes above a couple of tiny bays before descending to the Mushroom Bay accommodation. To reach Dream Beach, follow the signs off the road between Lembongan village and Mushroom Bay. A daily (7am) public boat heads direct from Mushroom Bay back to Sanur. Most of the accommodation in these areas will take you to and from the public and Perama boat drop-off points.

### Accommodation

The **accommodation** around this part of the coast is more upmarket than in Jungutbatu, although some are rather over-priced for the facilities on offer. It's worth repeating that several of the luxury places are best booked as an add-on to the day cruises that operate to the island (see p.254). Doing this will get you the best rates as well as a luxurious trip to and from the mainland.

**Coconuts Beach Resort** ☎0361/728088, ⓦwww.bali-cruise.com. Book as an add-on to an Island Explorer Cruise. Accommodation is in circular, thatched bungalows (with fans or air-con) ranged up the hillside. The bungalows higher up have glorious views. There are two pools, and it's a short walk to the nearest beach. ❼–❽

**Dream Beach Bungalows** ☎0812/367 1123. In a secluded setting in the far south of the island above a fantastic white-sand beach. Accommodation is in large, well-kept rooms with fans and cold-water bathrooms. They will collect guests from Jungutbatu if you let them know which boat you're arriving on. ❸–❹

**Hai Tide Huts** ☎0366/24541, ⓦwww.balihaicruises.com. A large set-up with accommodation in attractive, two-storey brick and thatch huts with great lounging platforms underneath; the ones on the beachfront have fine views. Bathrooms are not attached to each hut. The pool even has a small island in the middle. Book as part of a package with a Bali Hai cruise. ❼

**Mushroom Beach Bungalows/Tanjung Sanghyang Bungalows** ☎0823/612161. Simple rooms with attached cold-water bathrooms, on a small headland at the eastern end of Mushroom Bay. You're paying for the brilliant location. ❹–❺

**Nusa Lembongan Resort** ☎0361/725864, ⓦwww.nusa-lembongan.com. The most expensive resort on the island, with accommodation in twelve superbly appointed air-con villas positioned in an excellent garden with an infinity pool, at the far western end of Mushroom Bay. Prices start at $200 for a garden view. Can be arranged as an add-on to a Sail Sensations cruise but day visitors do not disturb the peace, as they use another location. ❾

**Playgrounds** ☎0366/24524, ⓦwww.playgroundslembongan.com. Five rooms in a large house perched on the cliff at the southern end of Jungutbatu beach. There are fans or air-con, cold-water bathrooms and cable television, but the real highlight are the balconies of the rooms on the top storey, which offer one of the most spectacular views on Lembongan, along the whole of the coast at Jungutbatu. There's also one large family room. ❺

**Tamarind Beach Bungalows** ☎0812/398 4234. Huge, high-ceilinged bungalows with fans and attached cold-water bathrooms, plus great views along Chelegimbai beach from their location at the far eastern end, near an excellent sunset-viewing spot. They'll meet you from the boat. ❹

**Villa Aman** ☎0366/24524, ⓔbillysmith53@hotmail.com. Two very comfortable rooms, each with a fan and attached cold-water bathroom, and one of the best views on the island across the whole of Jungutbatu from the communal balcony. A housemaid is included and will cook from a small menu on request. Next door to *Playgrounds*, a few metres along the footpath at the southern end of Jungutbatu beach. ❺

**Villa Sayang** ☎0815/574 9656, ⓔpurniasa@yahoo.com. Perched on the cliff high above the eastern end of Chelegimbai beach and offering great views. ❺

**Villa Wayan** ☎0361/271212, ⓔvillawayan@dps.centrin.net.id. Rooms are simple, with fan and attached cold-water bathroom in and near a large house just behind the beach, with a great lounge area on the upper storey. Book as an add-on to the Lembongan Island cruise. ❻

**Waka Nusa Resort** ☎0361/723629, ⓦwww.wakaexperience.com. Accommodation is in comfortable air-con or fan-cooled, hot-water, thatched bungalows with plenty of natural fabrics – the hallmark of the *Waka* group – although this one lacks the "wow" factor enjoyed by many of the others. Located just behind the beach, there's a small pool. Book as an add-on to a Waka Louka cruise. ❽

## Eating

Most of the places to stay have attached **restaurants**, with ambience, decor and price in direct relation to the luxury and cost of the accommodation. The cheapest place to eat in this part of the island is *Warung Adi* a few hundred metres up the road towards Lembongan village from Mushroom Bay, offering a small, inexpensive menu. A moderately priced alternative is *Tanah Bias* in a prime spot on the beach next to *Hai Tide Huts*, with good views and a large menu of Indonesian and international food. For views with your food, the restaurants at *Mushroom Beach Bungalows* and *Villa Sayang* are two of the best, also moderately priced. Another place with great views but further afield is *Café Pandan* at *Dream Beach Bungalows* (☎0812/367 1123 or 0812/398 3772), which offers free transport, a huge list of cocktails and a wide-ranging menu also at moderate prices.

## Around Nusa Lembongan

For a trip **around Nusa Lembongan**, it's best to walk or cycle in a clockwise direction, avoiding a lengthy climb up out of Jungutbatu to the south. The road is tarmac most of the way, although a bit rough in places. Allow three to four hours to walk around the island, two hours to cycle, or less than an hour by motorbike. Add on more if you want to explore Nusa Ceningan.

Heading north on the tarmac road that runs parallel to the coast about 200m behind the beach, the road splits a couple of kilometres north of Jungutbatu. The left-hand fork follows the coast and a few hundred metres later passes **Pura Sakenan**, recognizable by its highly decorated central shrine. This road leads a couple of kilometres to the northernmost tip of the island, but the mangrove is high here and there are no views. Taking the right fork leads to **Pura Empuaji**, with its highly carved doorway, the most venerated temple on the island (take a sarong if you want to visit). The road continues south from here for four almost uninhabited kilometres with mangroves on the left, and scrub and cacti on the right. You may notice a few derelict salt-makers' huts here (see box on p.432) but production has now been replaced by more lucrative **seaweed farming**. Gradually the mangrove clears and there are views of Nusa Ceningan just across the water with Nusa Penida rising up dramatically behind. At the point where the channel between Nusa Lembongan and Nusa Ceningan is narrowest, matching temples face each other across the water and a **bridge** links the islands: you can walk, cycle or ride a motorbike across. The waters here are crystal clear over white sand almost completely filled with frames for seaweed farming.

Further round the island, a steep hill climbs up from the coast into **LEMBONGAN**, the largest town on the island, 3km south of Jungutbatu. It's a crisscross of streets and alleyways and is much busier than Jungutbatu. The island's only "sight" is here, the **Underground House** (open on request; Rp10,000), dug by a traditional healer or *dukun* named Made Biasa. One night in 1965 he supposedly dreamt that he lost a fight with a spirit and, taking this to mean he would soon die, decided to dig an underground house as his memorial. Hale and hearty, he dug every night from 7pm to midnight with the energy of a young man and, having dug for over fifteen years, eventually died in the 1980s, never having completed his work. There's a bedroom, kitchen, dining room, bathroom and meditation room, but it's all dank and enclosed.

All roads heading uphill through the village eventually join to become the main road up past the school and over the hill to Jungutbatu, with some fine coastal views on the way. A left turn on the climb up through the village is well signed with the names of the accommodation at Mushroom Bay, and it is about a kilometre down to the coast if you want a side-trip. A turning to the left on the way down to Mushroom Bay, also signed, leads to the south coast and Dream Beach.

# Nusa Penida

Tell a Balinese person you're heading to **Nusa Penida** and you won't get a positive reaction. The island is renowned as the home of the legendary evil figure **I Macaling**, also known as Jero Gede Macaling, who is believed to be responsible for disease and floods, which he brings across to the mainland from Nusa Penida, landing at Lebih, south of Gianyar. The island is regarded as *angker*, a place of evil spirits and ill fortune, and many Balinese make the pilgrimage to the Nusa Penida to ward off bad luck by making offerings at Pura Dalem Penataran Ped, home of I Macaling. I Macaling and his wife, Jero Luh, appear regularly in the drama **barong landung** (for more details, see p.475), portrayed respectively as a gigantic black creature and a white-faced woman. The drama is performed throughout Bali to protect villages from illness and evil spirits.

Nusa Penida is too dry to cultivate rice, and while you'll see maize, cassava, beans and tobacco in the fields during the rainy season, there's nothing at all in the dry season. The island can only sustain a small population and many local people leave to work on the mainland or as part of the government's *transmigrasi* programme (see p.453). There are no dive operators based on Nusa Penida, but mainland and Nusa Lembongan operators offer trips to sites near the island; see p.256 for more.

### Sampalan

**SAMPALAN**, on the northeast coast of the island, is Nusa Penida's largest town, and has a shady street of shops, a bemo terminal, a market, and the only post office, hospital and phone office on the island. The town is spread out along the **beach**, and its highlight, the **Pura Dalem**, close to the cemetery near the football field, has a six-metre-tall gateway adorned with five leering Bhoma and a pendulous-breasted Rangda.

There are several **warung** in the main street, serving rice and noodles, and the town has a couple of **places to stay**. *Losmen Made* (☎0818/345204; ❷), on Jalan Segara, 100m west of the bemo terminal, is small and friendly and has four rooms with attached mandi and squat toilet, 200m from the beach and 100m from the main road. At the other end of town, next to the beach, the government-run *Bungalows Pemda* (☎0366/21448; ❶–❷) has standard rooms with mandi and squat toilets and more expensive, better-quality rooms with Western-style toilets, showers and bathtubs – ring to check they're still open before travelling out here.

### Toyapakeh and around

Some 9km from Sampalan, the village of **TOYAPAKEH** is separated from Nusa Ceningan by a channel less than 1km wide but over 100m deep in places. With its lovely white **beach** and peaceful atmosphere, it's the best place to stay on Nusa Penida. There's a small daily **market** and a tiny mosque serving the town's Muslim population. There's **accommodation** at *Losmen Trang* (☎0823/614868; ❶), which has five basic rooms right next to the beach, with attached mandi and squat toilet, and also serves simple meals. There are plans for a new set of bungalows just behind the beach in Toyapakeh; check out Ⓦwww .penida.com for progress.

**Pura Dalem Penataran Ped**, dedicated to I Macaling and built from volcanic sandstone and local limestone, lies 5km east of Toyapakeh on the Sampalan road. The size of the courtyards and the grand entrances emphasize the prestige of the temple. There are three **courtyards**, the inner one containing a three-storey-high shrine with intricately carved doors, used to store the sacred statues of the temple. The small red-and-white-tiled compound to the west contains the shrine of I Macaling. The *odalan* festival here is well attended by pilgrims hoping to stave off sickness and ill fortune; every three years a larger *usaba* festival draws enormous crowds.

### Around Nusa Penida

By far the best way to see Nusa Penida is by **motorbike** – ask at your guesthouse for rental details – although you'll need to be confident on very steep terrain. The island is a maze of country lanes, and signposts are few, so make sure you start early and have plenty of fuel. A full circuit is only about 70km, but

## Seaweed farming

Areas of Nusa Penida, Nusa Lembongan and Nusa Ceningan, the Geger beach in south Bali and some areas of Lombok are big producers of **seaweed**, source of two lucrative substances: **agar**, a vegetable gel used in cooking, and **carrageenan**, used in cosmetics and foodstuffs. It is cultivated in areas protected by a reef, so it doesn't get battered by strong currents but has a flow of water through it. The temperature must not get too high, the salinity needs to be constant and, at low tide, the seaweed must remain covered by water. To "**farm**" seaweed a bamboo frame is made with lengths of twine tied across it. Farmers tie small pieces of seaweed – both green *cotoni* and red *spinosum* varieties (*cotoni* produces better-quality carrageenan and fetches at least twice the price) – to the twine, harvesting the long offshoots after 45 days. The seaweed is then dried and compressed into bales; 8kg of wet seaweed reduces to 1kg when dry.

Seaweed is responsible for the vast improvement in prosperity experienced in these areas over the last few decades from the time when salt production was the major occupation. Current prices for dried *cotoni* are around Rp3500 per kilogramme and for *spinosum* Rp1500 per kilogramme. Families can now measure their monthly income in millions of rupiah in a reasonable month, though drying anything in the rainy season is distinctly tricky and, like all producers of raw materials that sell on a world market, they remain subject to price fluctuations and market forces way beyond their control.

allowing time to visit the major attractions and to get lost a few times, it takes most of a day. The road between Toyapakeh and Sampalan is the busiest on the island and roughly follows the coast; traffic elsewhere is much lighter.

About 10km south of Sampalan, you reach the limestone cave of **Goa Karangsari**. The tiny entrance is about 100m above the road and is quite tight, but opens up into a large, impressive cavern. Children lurk around the entrance as "guides"; you might like to choose the one with the best flashlight or pressure lantern. The cave emerges after 300m onto a ledge with fine views looking out across a quiet mango grove, surrounded by hills on all sides. The annual festival of Galungan (see p.63) is celebrated here with a procession and ceremony inside the cave.

On the way to **SEWANA** (or Suana), you'll pass **Pura Puseh Yehulaten**, with its seven-roofed *meru*, perched on a cliff edge offering great views back along the coast. Look out for the attractive **Pura Songaya** at the southern end of Sewana village, whose two *meru* are backed by a sheer cliff. Just beyond, a side-road to the left leads 2km further down the coast to **SEMAYA**. A couple more impressive temples can be found along here: first is the large **Pura Batu Medahu** on the coast side of the road and, further down, with grand views back to the north, **Pura Batu Kuning**, with some fabulous carvings. Semaya itself is a small fishing village around a long bay lined with frames for seaweed farming.

Returning to the main road, you climb dramatically and steeply up to the plateau that forms the centre of the island. Approaching the village of **PEJUKUTAN**, 6km from Sewana, the land is dotted with giant concrete dishes for catching rainwater, which is then stored in massive underground tanks. Some 2km further on, a right fork heads to **TANGLAD**, a cool, upland village, with an ancient throne to the sun god, Surya, on the village green. Nestling among hills 9km from Tanglad is the village of **BATUKANDIK**, whose **Pura Puseh Agung Meranting** houses a remarkable – though much eroded – carving of a woman supporting the top of a stone altar. Supposedly prehistoric, the figure is swathed in holy clothes. **BATUMADEG**, 6km beyond Batukandik, is the island's second-largest village.

Turn left at Batumadeg to **SEBULUH**, where the road ends a couple of hundred metres beyond the village green. From here, a path leads to the left between high stone walls and heads out to the coast, a walk of about 45 minutes. There are numerous paths through the outskirts of the village to the cliffs and you may be lucky enough to find an English-speaking guide. The coast here consists of dramatic limestone cliffs rising sheer out of the ocean and views that are utterly spellbinding. There are also two **temples**, one out on a promontory linked to the mainland by an exposed ridge, and the other at the bottom of a narrow, exposed path that winds down the face of the cliff to a freshwater spring at the bottom. This type of scenery is typical of the whole southern coast of the island; there are waterfalls in places and several spots where hairy descents to the sea are possible – ask locally.

Returning to Batumadeg, the road turns inland and skirts close to the summit of **Bukit Mundi**, at 529m the highest point on the island, where the goddess Dewi Rohini, a female manifestation of Siwa, is said to dwell. The road reaches the edge of the plateau, dropping down through the small, red-roofed village of **KLUMPU**, shortly after which the left fork continues to **SAKTI**, from where you can walk the 4km to the freshwater spring on the coast at **PANIDA** or continue straight back to Toyapakeh.

# Candi Dasa and Amuk Bay

**CANDI DASA** is a relaxed and pleasant resort at the eastern end of **Amuk Bay**. There's a wide choice of accommodation and restaurants, and it's a good centre for snorkelling and diving as well as a convenient base from which to explore the east of Bali.

Originally centred on the lagoon, tourist developments now spread west around the bay, through the villages of **Senkidu**, **Mendira**, **Buitan** and **Manggis**. Further west, just around the headland, the tiny cove of **Padang Bai** is the access port for Lombok and has a small tourist infrastructure.

Following the destruction of the offshore reef in the 1980s (to produce lime for cement to fuel the building boom for tourist facilities), the beach in the centre of Candi Dasa was left so exposed that it simply washed away. Large sea walls now protect the land and jetties protrude into the sea to enable the beach to build up behind them. There are many pockets of white sand nestling here and there, while the beaches to the west and east of the centre are a respectable size. From throughout the resort excellent views take in a clutch of tiny offshore islands with Nusa Lembongan and Nusa Penida rising mistily in the distance.

The entire coastal area is well served by **public transport**, both buses and minibuses from Denpasar (Batubulan terminal) to Amlapura, and local bemos on shorter runs.

## Arrival and information

Hotel development in the Candi Dasa area extends for about 8km along the main Denpasar–Amlapura road with much of the accommodation located on small lanes leading down to the sea; it's easy to get **bemo** drivers to drop you off where you want. **Shuttle buses** from the main tourist destinations serve Candi Dasa, and Perama has an office with daily arrivals from destinations on Bali and Lombok (see "Travel details" on p.291). Fixed-price taxis serve Candi Dasa from Ngurah Rai Airport (Rp199,000; 2hr). The centrally located **tourist**

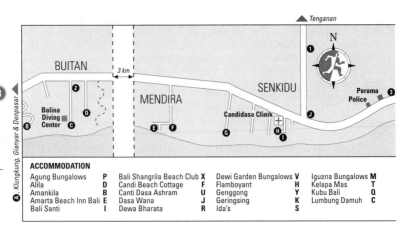

**ACCOMMODATION**

| | | | | | | | |
|---|---|---|---|---|---|---|---|
| Agung Bungalows | **P** | Bali Shangrila Beach Club | **X** | Dewi Garden Bungalows | **V** | Iguana Bungalows | **M** |
| Alila | **D** | Candi Beach Cottage | **F** | Flamboyant | **H** | Kelapa Mas | **T** |
| Amankila | **B** | Canti Dasa Ashram | **U** | Genggong | **Y** | Kubu Bali | **Q** |
| Amarta Beach Inn Bali | **E** | Dasa Wana | **J** | Geringsing | **K** | Lumbung Damuh | **C** |
| Bali Santi | **I** | Dewa Bharata | **R** | Ida's | **S** | | |

**office**, in the main street close to the lagoon, has somewhat erratic opening hours and staffing.

## Accommodation

Plenty of **accommodation** to suit every taste and pocket is available in the area. Most of the places listed below do not have street addresses but all are keyed on the map.

### Candi Dasa

Accommodation is spread about 1km along the main road running just behind the beach in central **Candi Dasa**. Beware of rooms that are too close to the road and therefore noisy.

**Agung Bungalows** ☏ & ℱ 0363/41535. Well-finished seafront bungalows with good-sized verandas, fans, and hot and cold water, located in a lush garden complete with ponds. **❸**

**Canti Dasa Ashram** ☏ & ℱ 0363/41108, contact in Denpasar ☏ 0361/225145, ✉ gandhiashram@telkom.net. This Ghandian ashram gets some of its income from renting out bungalows set in one of the best sites in Candi, with the lagoon on one side and the ocean on the other. Guests are free to take as much or as little part in the daily round of puja, yoga, meditation and lectures as they wish, but are asked not to smoke, drink or sunbathe nude; only married couples may share rooms. Charges include three vegetarian meals a day. Booking is essential. **❻**

**Dasa Wana** ☏ 0363/41444, ℱ 0361/462611. Air-con rooms and villas with hot water and tea- and coffee-making facilities, in landscaped grounds across the road from the sea. A small restaurant overlooks an attractive pool. Good value in this price bracket. **❺–❻**

**Dewa Bharata** ☏ 0363/41090, ℱ 41091. Attractive,

good-value bungalows, all with hot water, plus a good pool and seafront restaurant set in well-maintained gardens. Top-end rooms have air-con and sea views. **❺–❻**

**Dewi Garden Bungalows** ☏ 0363/41166, ℱ 41177. Tile, brick and bamboo bungalows set in a spacious garden close to the lagoon and the sea. Hot water is available in more expensive ones. **❷**

**Geringsing** ☏ 0363/41084. Smart, new stone and tile bungalows all with air-con and hot water. The ones at the front have brilliant sea views. **❻**

**Ida's** ☏ 0363/41096, ✉ jsidas1@aol.com. Six large, wood and thatch cottages all with fan, attached cold-water bathrooms and huge verandas in the centre of Candi, set in a coconut grove stretching down to the sea. Don't confuse this with a place with a similar name on Forest Road. **❸–❺**

**Iguana Bungalows** ☏ 0363/41973, ✉ .iguana_café_bali@yahoo.com. Clean, comfortable bungalows with a choice of fan or air-con and cold or hot water, set on the seafront in central Candi. There's a pool just above the beach. **❹–❺**

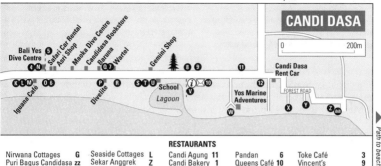

▲ *Amlapura*

**CANDI DASA**

0                        200m

3

EAST BALI | Candi Dasa and Amuk Bay

*Path to beach*

▶ *Path to beach*

Bali Yes Dive Centre

Safari Car Rental
Asri Shop
Maoka Dive Centre
Candidasa Bookstore
Baruna
Wartel
Gemini Shop
Candi Dasa Rent Car
FOREST ROAD

Iguana Café
Divelite
School
Lagoon
Yos Marine Adventures

| Nirwana Cottages | **G** | Seaside Cottages | **L** | **RESTAURANTS** | | Pandan | **6** | Toke Café | **3** |
|---|---|---|---|---|---|---|---|---|---|
| Puri Bagus Candidasa | **zz** | Sekar Anggrek | **Z** | Candi Agung | **11** | Queens Café | **10** | Vincent's | **9** |
| Puri Bagus Manggis | **A** | Sindhu Brata | **W** | Candi Bakery | **1** | Raja's | **8** | Warung Taman Sari | **2** |
| Puri Pandan | **O** | The Watergarden | **N** | Ciao e basta | **5** | Seasalt | | Watergarden Kafé | **4** |
| | | | | Kubu Bali | **7** | Restaurant | **D** | | |
| | | | | Legenda | **12** | | | | |

**Kelapa Mas** ☎0363/41369, ⓦwww
.kelapamas.com. Justifiably popular and
centrally located, offering a range of clean bungalows
set in a lovely garden on the seafront. The most
expensive options have hot water and air-con. ❸–❺

**Kubu Bali** ☎0363/41532, ⓦwww.kububali
.com. Excellent, well-furnished bungalows
with deep verandas. All have fan and air-con and hot
water, and are widely spaced in a glorious garden
ranging high up the hillside, dotted with statues and
*bale* for relaxing. There's a great swimming pool at
the top of the garden and a nearby coffee shop with
brilliant views. Service is friendly yet efficient. ❼

**Puri Pandan** ☎ & ⒻO363/41541. Attractive
brick, thatch and bamboo bungalows in central
Candi Dasa in a nice garden but without a
sea-frontage or a pool. All have hot water and
spacious verandas, and the most expensive have
air-con. ❸–❺

**Seaside Cottages** ☎0363/41629, ⓦwww
.bali-seafront-bungalows.com. Small, central place
that offers several standards of clean, fan-cooled
accommodation in a pretty garden, from basic
bungalows to ones on the seafront with picture
windows and hot water. There's also a family
room. ❶–❺

**Sindhu Brata** ☎0363/41825, Ⓕ41954. Tiled,
well-kept bungalows set in a neat garden which
fronts onto the sea and located in a quiet spot near
the lagoon. Hot water and air-con is available in the
more expensive rooms. ❷–❹

**The Watergarden** ☎0363/41540, ⓦwww
.watergardenhotel.com. Superb, characterful, centrally located hotel. Accommodation is
in excellently furnished bungalows with deep
verandas, each overlooking a lotus pond, set in an
atmospheric, lush garden. All have air-con and hot
water. There's a pretty, secluded swimming pool.
Service is excellent. ❽

## Forest Road

East of the central section of Candi Dasa accommodation, **Forest Road**
offers a number of quiet guesthouses and hotels dotted among coconut
palms.

**Bali Shangrila Beach Club** ☎0363/41829,
ⓦwww.balishangrila.com. Small, seafront place
built in warm, cream stone. All accommodation
has hot water and air-con, and the most expensive
have a small kitchen. ❻–❼

**Genggong** ☎0363/41105. Bungalows plus rooms
in a two-storey block with big balconies and
verandas. There's a choice of fan or air-con and
hot water is available. The big plus, though, is the
large garden and picturesque stretch of white-sand
beach just over the wall. ❷–❸

**Puri Bagus Candidasa** ☎0363/41131,
ⓦwww.bagus-discovery.com. In an excellent location at the far eastern end of Forest Road, behind
a white-sand beach with fine views of the offshore
islands, this hotel offers well-furnished tiled
accommodation with a glorious pool, flourishing
garden and lovely spa surrounded by fountains and
pools. The ten deluxe rooms with sea views are the
ones to go for – well worth the additional cost. For
a more rural location, consider the sister operation,
*Puri Bagus Manggis* (see below). ❽–❾

**Sekar Anggrek** ☏ 0363/41086, ⊛ www
.sekar-orchid.com. Great little place offering
excellent value on Forest Road, with seven clean,
good-quality bungalows, all with fan, hot water,
and mosquito screens at the windows, in a quiet
seafront garden. The website is in German but the
photographs are useful. ❸

## Senkidu and Mendira

The village of **Senkidu** is about 1km to the west of Candi Dasa, slightly detached
and quiet, but still convenient for the resort's main facilities. The adjacent village
of **Mendira** is located on the coast a short walk from the main road.

**Amarta Beach Inn** ☏ 0363/41230. Large, tiled
bungalows, all with fans, set in a pretty garden
facing the ocean at Mendira. The more expensive
ones have hot water. There's a beachside restaurant and plenty of space for sunbathing. ❷–❸

**Bali Santi** ☏ 0363/41611, ⊛ www.balisanti.
com. Good-quality accommodation in a
lovely garden with fine views along the coast and
a beachside bar and restaurant. One room has air-
con, all others have fan and cold water. *Flamboyant*
is just next door. ❷–❹

**Candi Beach Cottage** ☏ 0363/41234, ⊛ www
.candibeachbali.com. Top-price accommodation
in rooms or bungalows in an attractive compound
with beachside pools and tennis courts. The beach
is good here. Plenty of activities are on offer,
including trekking and village visits, and there's a
Pineapple Divers desk. ❽

**Flamboyant** ☏ 0363/41886, ✉ flamboy-
ant_bali@tiscali.co.uk. Spotless bungalows in
a gorgeous, quiet garden beside the sea at Senkidu
with great coastal scenery. There's a restaurant, a
*lesehan* in the garden above the fish ponds, and you
can refill mineral-water bottles here. ❷–❸

**Nirwana Cottages** ☏ 0363/41136, ✉ nirwana-
cottages@telkom.net. A small establishment with
rooms and bungalows in a lush garden with an
excellent beachside pool and restaurant. The four
bungalows facing seawards across the pool with
air-con and hot water are the ones to go for. Booking is recommended. ❻–❼

## Buitan and Manggis

If you decide to stay any further west towards **Buitan** you'll need your own transport to enjoy Candi's nightlife, as public transport stops at dusk. Further west again,
most of **Manggis** village is spread inland, but it does offer two luxury hotels.

**Alila** Buitan ☏ 0363/41011, ⊛ www
.alilahotels.com. One of the most impressive
hotels in eastern Bali is situated in a picturesque
coconut grove beside the sea, rooms ranged around
a gorgeous pool. Stylish, modern minimalist chic
characterizes the decor, service is excellent and
there's a Mandara Spa attached to the hotel. The
hotel has an international reputation for its cooking
school; from half-day to five-day programmes are
available. Plenty of activities are on offer with regular
tai chi and yoga, and shuttles to Tenganan and Candi
Dasa. Prices start at $180. ❾

**Amankila** Manggis ☏ 0363/41333, ⊛ www
.amanresorts.com. This jetset hideaway (rumour
has it that Mick Jagger and Jerry Hall honeymooned
here) offers fabulous accommodation and facilities
ranged up the hillside with a beach at the bottom and
excellent coastal views at the top. For Rp100,000
a day, at the manager's discretion, non-residents
can use the Beach Club facilities (which include a
45m pool), although you won't be allowed in the
much-photographed three-tiered main pool up above.
Published prices from US$660. ❾

**Lumbung Damuh** ☏ 0363/41553, ⊛ www
.damuhbali.com. Three *lumbung*-style cottages in
a lush garden right on the coast at Balina Beach,
bedrooms are upstairs and bathroom and sitting areas
are down. Look out for the sign to *Royal Bali Beach
Club* to identify the turning from the main road. ❹–❻

**Puri Bagus Manggis** ☏ 0363/41304, ⊛ www
.bagus-discovery.com. Part of the small *Puri Bagus*
stable, with beautifully furnished rooms in a rural
setting in Manggis – the only accommodation in
the village itself. There's a small swimming pool
and orchid garden in the paddy-fields just across
the road. Cooking and trekking can be arranged,
and there's free transport to the sister hotel at the
beachside in Candi Dasa. ❽–❾

## The resort

Candi Dasa is an ancient settlement, and its **temple**, just opposite the lagoon, is
believed to have been founded in the eleventh century. The statue of the fertility

goddess Hariti in the lower section of the temple, surrounded by numerous children, is still a popular focus for pilgrims (the name Candi Dasa originally derives from "Cilidasa", meaning ten children). Having washed away in the 1980s, the **beach** at Candi Dasa is now returning behind concrete jetties, and there are plenty of areas along the coast where it is more than respectable. Throughout the resort the attractive coastal views more than make up for deficiencies in the foreground. A large, deserted beach lies just to the east of the resort. Go straight on at the crossroads at the end of Forest Road; don't make the right turn down to *Puri Bagus Candidasa*, but take the road up onto the headland where it follows the top of the cliffs for a few hundred metres before eventually descending onto a glistening black-sand beach on the other side. There's good **walking** in the hills behind Candi Dasa, which are crossed by various footpaths. The path from the upper temple compound opposite the lagoon in Candi Dasa will take you up into the hills, where you can pick up a path to Tenganan, 4km to the north. Some of the paths aren't that easy to follow, so if you want to head to a particular destination, it's a good idea to find a guide; ask at your accommodation. It's possible to arrange **fishing trips** with local boats, either pre-dawn or after sunrise, with prices similar to snorkelling.

### Diving and snorkelling

Just off the coast, a group of Candi Dasa's small islands offers excellent **diving**, although it's not suitable for beginners as the water can be cold and the currents strong. **Gili Tepekong** (also known as Gili Kambing or Goat Island) is the biggest island, although only 100m by 50m; **Gili Biaha** (also known as Gili Likman) is only marginally bigger than **Gili Mimpang**, just three rocks sticking out of the ocean. The area offers several walls, a pinnacle just off Mimpang and the dramatic scenery of Tepekong Canyon, lined with massive boulders. The current is too strong for the growth of big coral, but the variety of fish is excellent, including barracuda, tuna, white-tipped reef sharks, sunfish and manta rays.

The reef along the coastline in Candi Dasa is gradually rejuvenating and there is now **snorkelling** just offshore, stretching for about a kilometre westwards from just in front of *Puri Bagus Candidasa*. Don't venture too far out and stay aware of your position – the currents can be hazardous. Not all of the dive spots offer great snorkelling: the best places are off Gili Mimpang and Blue Lagoon on the western side of Amuk Bay, closer to Padang Bai (see p.275). Local boat-owners will approach you to arrange snorkelling trips; with negotiation, the going rate is around Rp100,000–150,000 for a couple of hours for a boat taking up to three people including equipment. Many dive shops take snorkellers along on dive trips; prices vary from $25 to $39 so shop around; always be clear whether or not equipment is included in the price.

As well as the local sites, Candi Dasa is an ideal base from which to arrange **diving trips** to Padang Bai, Nusa Penida, Nusa Lembongan, Amed and Tulamben. It's also feasible to arrange dive trips from here to Gili Selang, the most easterly point in Bali; it has a reputation as an exciting diving spot and has yet to be fully explored. Candi Dasa is a good place to take a course, as hotel swimming pools are available for initial tuition; PADI Open Water ($300–380), Advanced Open Water ($250–300) and Divemaster (contact them directly for prices) courses can all be arranged. On trips for experienced divers, prices vary but are about $50–70 for the Candi Dasa, Padang Bai, Tulamben and Amed areas, $75–85 for Nusa Lembongan and Nusa Penida, and $70 for Pulau Menjangan. See p.71 for general advice on choosing a dive operator. Most places in Candi Dasa quote equipment rental on top of this (approx $15 per set per day) so check at the time of booking.

## Candi Dasa dive operators

**Bali Yes Dive Centre** ☎0363/41604, ✉bali_yesdive@hotmail.com. Offers PADI courses from Open Water to Advanced Open Water; their counter is in the middle of Candi Dasa, opposite *Iguana Café*.

**Balina Diving Center** ☎0363/41725, ☻www.balinadivingcenter.com. Located at Balina Beach near *Lumbung Damuh*, they offer PADI courses from Open Water to Advanced Open Water, and diving trips for the experienced.

**Baruna** Has a counter in town (☎0363/41185), and one at *Puri Bagus Candidasa* hotel (☎0363/41217). These are the Candi Dasa offices for this large Bali-wide operator, offering the full range of trips and courses.

**Divelite** ☎0363/41660, ☻www.divelite.com. A full range of PADI (up to Divemaster) and SSI (to Instructor) courses plus trips for experienced divers. They offer tuition in Japanese, Indonesian and English.

**Maoka Dive Centre** ☎0363/41563. Offers PADI courses up to Advanced Open Water plus the usual destinations for experienced divers.

**Pineapple Divers** At *Candi Beach Cottage* ☎0363/41760, ☻www.bali-pineapple-divers.com. The usual dives and courses plus two- and three-day package tours of the dive sites around the island, including accommodation.

**Yos Marine Adventures** At *Asmara* hotel ☎0363/41929, ☻www.yosdive.com. This well-respected southern Bali operator has branched out into Candi Dasa, offering a range of dives and courses.

# Eating, drinking and nightlife

Candi Dasa offers a great variety of **places to eat**, and the quality of the food, especially seafood, is excellent. Several places have set menus for Rp20,000 upwards, and others feature Balinese dancing to accompany your meal – look out for local adverts.

Unless otherwise stated, all the places listed below offer inexpensive to moderately priced food and are on or near the main road through the resort, which can, unfortunately, be rather noisy.

**Candi Agung** This long-standing Candi place has a big food and drink menu with well-cooked main courses and set menus from Rp29,000 for three courses. There are nightly *legong* dances.

**Candi Bakery** About 300m up the road to Tenganan from the main road, producing an appetizing selection of bread and cakes plus lunches and dinners.

**Ciao e basta** Slightly hidden away off the main street, this two-storey place has an extensive menu of pasta, pizza, salads, home-made ice-cream and desserts plus a good selection of drinks and coffees. Pizzas are recommended.

**Kubu Bali** The large, dramatic kitchen in the restaurant at the front of the hotel in central Candi Dasa specializes in seafood, but also offers moderately and expensively priced Western, Chinese and Indonesian food in attractive, relaxed surroundings. Better tables are at the back near the fish ponds. There's a big list of drinks, too.

**Legenda** Situated close to the junction of Forest Road and the main road, this is a venue for live music. They also have a wide-ranging menu with plenty of Western dishes, including spaghetti, pizza and steak, alongside Indonesian food.

**Pandan** Ignore the breakwater in the foreground and this is a fair spot for a sunset drink in central Candi Dasa. There's a big menu including some good seafood.

**Queens Café** There's a good buzz here. Diners get a free welcome drink and set menus are Rp18,000–22,000; although the choices aren't vast, the food is cheap and cheerful.

**Raja's** Almost opposite the lagoon in central Candi Dasa and popular for the nightly videos, but there's also a vast drinks list and plenty of Indonesian and Western dishes, including sausage and mash. Pizzas are worth the 30min wait: they're thin and crispy with a generous topping.

**Seasalt Restaurant** at the *Alila* ☎0363/41011. The premier dining experience in eastern Bali, this restaurant is an open-sided *bale* designed in modern, minimalist Asian style and full of natural materials. The huge, expensive gourmet menu changes daily but includes sections of Balinese, seafood, Cuisine Naturelle and Pan Asian-Pacific fusion dishes. There's an emphasis on produce from the hotel's organic garden, with the cooking intricate but beautifully executed.

**Toke Café** This long-term local favourite is set back from the main road at the western end of central Candi Dasa. There's gamelan music three times a week, diners get a free welcome drink, and there's a vast menu of seafood, pasta, pizza,

Indian, Indo-Chinese and International dishes. Set menus at Rp35,000–55,000 are feasts, and the more expensive ones include a glass of wine. **Vincent's** ☎0363/41368. Lazy jazz on the music system and original artwork on the walls give this unique spot not far from the lagoon a laid-back feeling. The menu is enormous, with Balinese, Indonesian and International food extremely well presented in the moderate to expensive range, and there's a huge wine list. Free transport in the Candi Dasa area. **Watergarden Kafé** The moderate to expensive

menu is an eclectic assortment of Indonesian, International and seafood dishes, with daily specials adding to the choice. There are twice-weekly barbecues, a *rijsttafel* dinner for two is available with 24 hours' notice, and there are also iced coffees, diet-busting desserts, a huge drinks list and the best croissants in eastern Bali. **Warung Taman Sari** A small, inexpensive, friendly place in Buitan with breakfasts and a selection of Indonesian and Western favourites for lunch and dinner, including plenty of local seafood.

### Nightlife

**Nightlife** is low-key in Candi Dasa: apart from a few late-opening restaurants, things are pretty quiet by 11pm. There's no club scene, and live music currently alternates between *Legenda* and *Iguana Café*. Videos are the main entertainment at *Raja's* and *Ciao e basta* and are advertised with flyers around town.

## Shopping

While nobody would head to Candi Dasa just for the **shopping**, there's a good range of stores selling a variety of crafts and textiles. Asri Shop and Gemini Shop (daily 8am–10pm) are both central supermarkets, selling everything for everyday as well as souvenir needs and have fixed prices that serve as a good guide for your bargaining elsewhere. There's a dense stretch of **clothing** shops along the main road just east of the Perama office that sell tourist sarongs, pants, skirts, shirts and T-shirts. Gogos, near the Perama office, does a good range of **silver** items.

Moving eastwards, Geringsing Shop, near the hotel of the same name, is a treasure-trove of the old and not-so-old, including an extensive selection of **textiles** and **wooden carvings** from across Indonesia. Check out Lenia for great baskets, textiles and statues from throughout Indonesia, and the shop at *The Watergarden* for some of the most desirable and tasteful items in town, including clothes, textiles, jewellery, wood and paper crafts to suit all budgets. The shop in the wartel next to *Kubu Bali* boasts a selection of small pottery, wooden and bone items plus **jewellery** and some textiles including a few rolls of cloth sold by the metre. Nusantara Archipelago, just east of the lagoon, has an excellent selection of **paper**, **wood** and **metal** items, all well crafted and tasteful and, slightly further east again, Surya Gana sells lovely cotton and silk **batik** – from small bags and purses through to hand-painted pure-silk sarongs at more than half a million rupiah.

If you're looking to really splash out, *Kedai*, the shop attached to the restaurant next to *Toke Café*, sells gorgeous stuff, both decorative and useful. Everything is natural including superbly crafted wood, stone, silk, shell, leather and cow-hide, although there's not much under Rp60,000. Equally enticing, and in the same price range, the shop at the *Alila* hotel in Buitan has a fabulous selection including the natural toiletries that they use in the hotel.

There's also a great choice of textiles and other crafts up the hill in the village of Tenganan, but if you can't make it to the village the Ata Shop is about 200m along the Tenganan turning from the main road; they have a reasonable selection of baskets and textiles for sale.

# Listings

**Bike rental** Enquire at your losmen or at the places in the main street; Rp20,000–25,000 a day. Beware the busy traffic on the main road.

**Books** Several bookstores in Candi sell new and second-hand books; the Candidasa Bookstore has the largest selection.

**Car and motorbike rental** You'll be offered transport every few yards along the main road, or else enquire at your accommodation. There are also plenty of rental companies around the resort, with prices comparable to Kuta/Sanur (Rp80,000–100,000 for a Suzuki Jimney for one day, Rp150,000 for a Kijang). A motorbike costs Rp30,000–50,000. Well-established companies are Safari (☎0363/41707) in the centre of town; and Candidasa Rent Car (☎0363/41225), just at the start of Forest Rd. The insurance included varies considerably.

**Charter transport** To put together your own day-trip, you'll be looking at Rp250,000–300,000 per day for vehicle, driver and petrol, depending on your itinerary. Negotiate with the touts along the main street, ask at your accommodation or approach the car rental companies. One-way drops to destinations throughout Bali are a convenient and – if you're in a group – a reasonable way of moving on: Rp50,000 to Padang Bai, Rp125,000 to the Amed or Ubud areas, Rp150,000 to the Kuta area (including the airport), Rp250,000 to Lovina. If you want to charter transport, Ketut Lagun (☎0812/362 2076) and I Nengah Parni (☎0812/399 4975) are both recommended drivers.

**Doctor** Contact staff at your hotel initially if you need medical attention. Alternatively, Dr I Wayan Artana (☎0363/41321 or 0812/390 0447) offers a 24hr service at Candidasa Clinik on the track from the main road to *Flamboyant* and *Bali Santi* in Sengkidu. The nearest hospitals are at Amlapura, Klungkung or Denpasar (see p.107).

**Exchange** You'll find moneychangers every few metres along the main street. There's an ATM linked to the Visa, MasterCard and Cirrus networks at the BNI Bank opposite Asri Shop.

**Internet access** Available at several spots on the main street (Rp300/min), though access can be unreliable.

**Massage** You'll be approached throughout the resort and on the beach. The going rate is Rp30,000/hr – more if you arrange it through your hotel.

**Phones** There's a wartel (daily 7am–10.30pm) next to the *Kubu Bali* restaurant.

**Police** The police post is just west of the Perama office in central Candi Dasa.

**Post office** Near the lagoon (Mon–Thurs & Sat 8am–noon, Fri 8–11am). They provide a poste restante service: mail should be addressed to you, c/o Post Restan, Kantor Pos, Candi Dasa, Amlapura, Bali 80851.

**Tourist shuttle buses** Plenty of places offer shuttle buses from Candi Dasa to destinations throughout Bali and Lombok. Perama ☎0363/41114 (daily 8am–9pm) is the most established operator, but note that in the tourist downturn from 2002–2004 they drastically cut back services and at the time of writing buses no longer served Tirtagangga, Amed and Tulamben (though charter transport was available between Candi Dasa and these destinations for Rp50,000 per person for a minimum of two people). Check ⊛www.peramatour.com for the current situation. See "Travel details" on p.291 for destinations and frequencies.

**Tours** Available at Perama, the tourist booths on the main road, or through hotels and car rental companies. Alternatively, talk to the transport touts who linger on the main road. Prices range from Rp250,000 per vehicle for a full day, but shop around and be clear whether prices quoted are per person or per vehicle. It may be preferable to put together your own tour chartering a car and driver for the day (see above). The standard tours are: Amlapura (the palace, Tirtagangga and Tenganan), Besakih (Putung, Muncan, Besakih, Klungkung), Kintamani (Bangli, Kintamani, Penelokan, Tampaksiring, Gunung Kawi), Kuta (Kuta, Nusa Dua, Sanur, Uluwatu, sometimes including the sunset), Sangeh (Sangeh, Mengwi, Bedugul and Danau Bratan, Tanah Lot), Singaraja (Tirtagangga, Tulamben, Air Sanih, Lovina, Singaraja) and Ubud (Goa Gajah, Monkey Forest, Mas, Celuk, Ubud).

## Around Candi Dasa

It's worth making the trip out to **Pura Gomang** for good views of the area around Candi Dasa. Take an Amlapura-bound bemo for a couple of kilometres east, up the hill to the pass marked by a small shrine on the road. Concrete steps followed by a steep path head seawards from here to the temple at the top of the hill. Every two years, around October, four of the local villages – Bugbug, Bebandem, Jasi and Ngis – participate in a ritual battle near the top of Gomang Hill to settle an ancient dispute.

Some 6km northeast of Candi, the cove of **Pasir Putih** has a five-hundred-metre pure-white beach sheltered by rocky headlands with good views of Gili Biaha. Take a bemo as far as Perasi, from where a small road called Jalan Pasir Putih leads past paddy-fields to the coast. Two or three kilometres along the track, you reach a small temple where the path forks. The left fork leads to two black-sand beaches; the right descends through coconut groves to Pasir Putih. There are no facilities here at present but the beach is rumoured to be earmarked for a big resort development.

From Manggis, 6km west of Candi, a glorious road – check the condition before setting off in a vehicle – heads up into the hills with fabulous views of the area. If you're on foot, get an ojek from the junction of the Manggis road with the main road (Rp10,000) for the steep 8km up to *Pondok Bukit Putung* near Pesangkan (see p.281) on the Amlapura–Rendang road. You can have a drink or lunch here and then walk back down.

### Tenganan

The village of **TENGANAN** (admission by donation) is one of the Bali Aga communities of the island and adheres to traditional ways. Rejecting the Javanization of their land, the caste system and the religious reforms that followed the Majapahit conquest of the island in 1343, the **Bali Aga** or Bali Mula, meaning "original Balinese", withdrew to their village enclaves to live a life based around ritual and ceremony. Today, Tenganan is an extremely wealthy village and the only place in Indonesia that produces the celebrated **gringsing** cloth.

Laid out on either side of broad cobbled avenues that run north–south, Tenganan rises in a series of terraces up the hill. The *bale agung* is the most imposing building and the meeting place for the *krama desa* (village council). All the house compounds are identical, with small *bale* in courtyards behind high stone walls. Despite the emphasis on tradition, however, you'll still see noisy motorbikes scurrying around the village and television aerials and satellite dishes crowding the skyline.

The road up to Tenganan is a pleasant **walk** from the centre of Candi Dasa but **ojek** (Rp5000) wait at the bottom to transport you the 3km up to the village. It's a major stop on the tour-bus circuit: avoid the 11am to 2pm rush if you can.

#### Rituals, ceremonies and festivals

Tenganan's inhabitants pursue a complex round of **rituals and ceremonies**. The rituals are laid down in ancient texts and their observance is believed to prevent the wrath of the gods destroying the village. Most of the daily rituals

---

### The founding of Tenganan

A famous legend details the **founding of Tenganan**. In the days before the Majapahit invasion of Bali, **King Bedaulu** ruled the island. One day his favourite horse went missing, and the king offered a large reward for anybody who found it. The horse was eventually discovered dead near Tenganan and the king decided that he would give the local people the land near where the horse was found; in fact, he would donate the area within which the stench of the rotting animal could be smelled. One of the king's ministers was sent to the village to adjudicate, and he and the village headman set out to decide the boundaries. Incredibly, the smell of the horse could be detected over a huge area. The lines were duly drawn and the minister departed. At this point, the devious village headman took out from under his clothes the piece of rotting horse meat with which he had fooled the minister. The limits of the village lands are still the ones set at that time, and cover more than ten square kilometres.

observed by the villagers are not open to the public, but there are many **festival** days where visitors are welcome (for details of these, check the sources of information on p.36). During the month-long Usaba Sambah festival, generally in May and June, a massive wooden swing, like a giant Ferris wheel, is set up by the young men of the village for the young girls to swing on. You may also see the *perang padan* or *mekare-kare*, a fight between combatants armed with shields of woven bamboo and weapons made of the thorny pandanus leaves.

### Tenganan crafts and skills

The most famous product of Tenganan is **gringsing** or double *ikat* (see p.489), a highly valued brown, deep-red, blue-black and tan cloth, which Bhatara Indra, the god of creation, supposedly taught the women of Tenganan to weave. It can take many years to make one piece, and it is prized throughout Bali, as protection against evil. Many religious ceremonies require the use of the cloth; for example, during the tooth-filing ceremony (see p.494) a piece of it is placed beneath the head, and during part of cremations it is wrapped around the coffin.

In recent years, **basketwork** from *ata* grass has become another distinctive product of the village. This is an ancient skill, but since the 1980s it has become more commercial, and supplies of grass are now imported from Flores, Kalimantan, Sulawesi and East Java. Depending on the complexity, it can take a month to produce a basket: the grass is first split and woven, then boiled to tighten the weave, dried for up to a week and smoked over a coconut wood or husk or *cempaka* wood fire for three days, turning every three hours, to give its glossy, golden finish. You can see all the stages of production at I Nyoman Uking's Ata Shop (☎0363/41121) towards the top of the village over in the right-hand section, the *banjar pande*. There's a small sign outside, you're welcome to take photographs, and Nyoman speaks English. Baskets are sent from here to outlets in Nusa Dua and other southern resorts, and you can buy them for Rp55,000–200,000. He also has a shop in the car park outside the village, as do many other village producers, and he owns the Ata Shop close to the junction of the Tenganan road with the main road.

**Traditional calligraphy** is another attractive product of the village. Calendars and pictorial representations of traditional stories are incised on narrow lengths of *lontar* palm, which are then strung together to create a small hanging. Compare several before you buy: it soon becomes easy to spot the more skilful examples. The work of Wayan Tumben, whose stall is on the left beyond the main cluster inside the main entrance to the village, is especially fine. Ask to see his astonishing pictures of the buildings in the village.

Tenganan is also famous for its unusual gamelan **selonding** music, using instruments that are believed to have considerable religious power. Musicians in the village make and play the *genggong*, a bamboo jew's-harp, and it's possible to arrange lessons here; make enquiries in the village if you're interested.

# Padang Bai

Deriving from two languages – *padang* is Balinese for grass and *bai* is Dutch for bay – **PADANG BAI**, the port for Lombok, nestles in a small cove with a white-sand beach lined with fishing boats. Ferries and tourist boats run regularly to **Lombok**; the jetty, Perama office, ferry office and car park are all at the western end of the bay, from where everything is within easy walking distance.

**PADANG BAI**

Diving Groove

Water Worxx — Geko Dive

Purnama

Ticket Office for Nusa Penida

Pura Dalem

Pura Segara

Celagi

*Beachside Warung*

Market

Pura Telagamas

Pura Silayukti

Bank

Boats to Nusa Penida

Pura Tanjunsari

Perama

Blue Lagoon

Police

Ticket Office for Lombok

Footpath to Biastugal

Boats to Lombok

| ACCOMMODATION | |
|---|---|
| Bagus Inn | C |
| Darma | I |
| Kembar Inn | J |
| Kerti Beach Inn | E |
| Made Homestay | G |
| Padang Bai Beach Homestay | D |
| Pantai Ayu | B |
| Parta | H |
| Puri Rai | F |
| Serangan Homestay I | K |
| Serangan Inn II | A |

| RESTAURANTS & BARS | |
|---|---|
| Babylon Reggae Bar | 3 |
| Café Kerti | E |
| Café Papa John | 7 |
| Dewi Café | 2 |
| Dharma | 5 |
| Marina | 4 |
| Omang Omang | 1 |
| Ozone | 6 |

Increasingly, visitors are choosing to stay a night or two, and Padang Bai has developed into a small, laid-back resort. The pace of life only speeds up when a cruise ship comes to town: there are several a month in the peak cruising season (Nov–Feb), when you can watch the hundreds of visitors being decanted ashore and whisked off for trips around the island.

### Arrival and transport

**Bemos and minibuses** arrive at, and depart from, the port entrance, orange bemos from Amlapura via Candi Dasa, blue or white bemos from Klungkung (also known as Semarapura) and pale-brown minibuses from Amlapura or Batubulan. Plenty of counters along the seafront offer tourist information, but these are commercial set-ups; the nearest government tourist office is in Candi Dasa (see p.263). The ticket office for **Nusa Penida** is a little way east

### Moving on to Lombok

The following operate from Padang Bai to **Lombok**. See p.382 for information on other routes to Lombok.

**Ferry** Every 90min; takes 4hr–4hr 30min. Tickets cost Rp15,000. There's an extra charge for bicycles (Rp17,600), motorbikes (Rp36,400) and cars (from Rp225,000). See p.50 for information on taking rental vehicles between the islands.

**Tourist boat** Perama offer a daily boat at 1.30pm direct to Senggigi (3–4hr; Rp100,000) and on to the Gili islands (5–6hr; Rp150,000).

**Tourist buses** Perama and other operators advertise throughout the resort and use the public ferry to Lembar, then tourist bus from there.

of the port; from 7am onwards, boats leave from the beach, when they're full, for Buyuk Harbour (Rp25,000).

Perama **tourist shuttle buses** operate from their office (daily 7am–7pm; ℡0363/41419) near the jetty (see "Travel details" on p.291 for more). If you're heading to the far east of Bali it's worth noting that, at the time of writing, the Perama bus to Tirtagangga and Tulamben was suspended but the company were offering charter services from Padang Bai and Candi Dasa to Tirtagangga, Amed and Tulamben for Rp50,000 per person (minimum two people). There are plenty of other shuttle services advertised throughout the resort. There's a **post office** near the port entrance and **wartels** on the seafront (daily 7am–10pm). **Internet** services are available throughout the resort (Rp300 per min) but connection can be slow. Many seafront restaurants **change money**, and there's a BRI bank with an ATM linked to the Visa, MasterCard and Cirrus networks. **Car rental** (Rp125,000 per day for a Suzuki Jimney, Rp200,000 for a Kijang) and **motorbike rental** (Rp40,000 daily) are easy to arrange; ask at your accommodation or any of the seafront tourist counters. The **police** post is just by the port entrance.

## Accommodation

A wide choice of **accommodation** is available both in the village and strung out along the road behind the beach. A lot of the accommodation towards the eastern end of the beach is poor, but watch out for renovations and new places as the locations are glorious. Upstairs rooms in the village accommodation, especially up on the hill, catch the breeze and have fine views.

**Bagus Inn** ℡0363/41398. A good budget choice with small rooms with attached bathroom in a friendly family compound. ➊

**Darma** ℡0363/41394. A clean family set-up in the village; upstairs rooms are bigger and have good sitting areas outside. ➊–➋

**Kembar Inn** ℡ & ℻0363/41364. Pleasant tiled place in the village. There are many options: air-con and hot water at the top end, fan and cold water at the bottom end. There's also a pleasant sitting area upstairs. ➊–➌

**Kerti Beach Inn** ℡0363/41391. Near the beach; some accommodation is in bungalows, some in two-storey *lumbung*-style bamboo and thatch barns. ➊–➋

**Made Homestay** ℡0363/41441, ✉mades_padangbai@hotmail.com. Clean, tiled rooms with fan and attached cold-water bathrooms in a two-storey block in a small compound, convenient for both the beach and the village. ➊–➋

**Padang Bai Beach Homestay** ℡0812/360 7946. In an attractive location on the seafront in a garden complete with ponds. Newer rooms are worth considering. ➋–➌

**Pantai Ayu** ℡0363/41396. Lots of rooms ranged over several floors – worth a look if the *Serangan Inn II*, next door, is full. ➊

**Parta** ℡0363/41475. Pleasant, clean village place with rooms upstairs and down, some with hot water and air-con. The real gem is the room perched way up on the top floor, where there's a great sitting area. ➊–➌

**Puri Rai** ℡0363/41385, ✉purirai_hotel@yahoo.com. Large, tiled rooms with hot water and fan or air-con. Best rooms overlook one of the two swimming pools. ➍–➎

**Serangan Homestay I** ℡0363/41425. Simple, clean, good-value place in the village – the same owners as the *Serangan Inn II*. ➊–➋

**Serangan Inn II** Spotless place built high up with some great views. Catches the breeze and boasts good rooms, all with fan and attached cold-water bathroom. ➊–➋

## The beaches

If you find the main beach too busy, head for the smaller, quieter bay of **Biastugal** (also known as Pantai Kecil), to the west, with just a few tiny warung. Follow the road past the post office and, just as it begins to climb, take the track to the left. Alternatively, head over the headland in the other direction and take the path from Pura Silayukti to another small, white cove named **Blue Lagoon** after the snorkelling and diving site located just offshore here.

## Snorkelling and diving at Padang Bai

Several places in Padang Bai rent **snorkelling** equipment (Rp20,000 per day); the water in the bay is surprisingly clear, although the best snorkelling is at Blue Lagoon (see below). You can snorkel off the beach there or charter a boat (about Rp100,000–150,000 for 2hr per boat) but be sure to check whether equipment is included; you'll be approached on the beach about this, or ask at *Celagi* restaurant or your guesthouse.

There are now many **dive** operations in Padang Bai. The most established is Geko Dive (☎0363/41516, ⓦwww.gekodive.com), a large set-up on the seafront with a lot of experience diving in the area. Other established operators are Water Worxx (☎0363/41220, ⓦwww.waterworxbali.com), just along the seafront, and Diving Groove (☎0812/398 9746, ⓦwww.divinggroove.com), up the hill; they all offer the full range of PADI courses (in several languages), dives for experienced divers and the Discover Scuba introductory day. Expect to pay about US$45 for two dives in the Padang Bai area (including equipment rental), $55 for two dives in Amed, Tulamben or Candi Dasa, and $60 for two dives at Nusa Lembongan, Nusa Penida, Pulau Menjangan or Gili Selang. The Discover Scuba day is $55–65, the PADI Open Water course $280 and the PADI Advanced Open Water course $200. Some operators use Candi Dasa hotel swimming pools for early training. All these companies welcome approaches by email and can arrange airport transfers and offer advice on accommodation; combined accommodation packages are also available. See p.71 for general advice on selecting a dive operator.

The local dive sites are at **Blue Lagoon**, around and beyond the headland to the east of the bay. There are several different dive sites on the reef here and lots of hard and soft coral, including elephant and table corals – which attract eels, wrasses, turtles, flatheads and lion fish – plus a good chance of spotting sharks. There are plenty of species that you won't see elsewhere in Bali. This is a feasible area for night diving, when Spanish Dancers are frequently spotted. The operators in Padang Bai are also adept at knowing when and where there's the best chance of spotting *mola mola*.

It's possible to arrange **fishing** trips from Padang Bai; you'll be approached on the beach about this, or ask at *Celagi* restaurant or your guesthouse. **Massages** are on offer every few yards along the beach; Rp30,000 per hour seems to be the going rate. **Shopping** isn't a reason to come to Padang Bai but the beach hawkers have a good range of sarongs, clothes, jewellery and paintings. Purnama, on Jalan Silayukti just opposite the market, sells a selection of art and crafts. A row of small shops along the beach road just east of the parking area supplies everyday needs.

### Temples

To the east of Padang Bai, the paved road around the bay climbs up to the headland, which is topped with three temples. The largest and most important is **Pura Silayukti**, where the priest Empu Kuturan supposedly lived and meditated in the eleventh century; the three-roofed *meru* is dedicated to him. Just behind the main temple is the smaller **Pura Telagamas**. A path from the back of Pura Silayukti leads down the cliff face to a tiny shrine in a rock crevice above the pounding waves. Although surrounded by a modern wall and *candi bentar*, the ancient stones shrouded in holy cloths and a tiny turtle sarcophagus looking out across the vast ocean conjure a feeling of absolute timelessness. About 100m along the headland you'll see **Pura Tanjunsari**, dedicated to Empu Bharadah, the brother of Kuturan, who came to Bali about two years after Kuturan and was connected with the early history of Besakih (see p.247) and the defeat of the evil witch, Rangda (see box on p.235).

## Eating and drinking

Seafood is the speciality in Padang Bai **restaurants**, with marlin, barracuda, snapper and prawns on offer, depending on the catch, alongside the usual traveller's fare. All are in the inexpensive to moderate price range and have happy hours, but tend to stop serving early. The small places on the beach side of the road are unbeatable value, offering the perfect setting for that first cool drink of the evening. They are in two clusters: the main one starts with *Dharma* to the west through to *Marina*; then there's a break, after which there's a row of reggae cafés and bars from *Babylon Reggae Bar* through to *Dewi Café*. Away from here, it's worth checking out *Café Kerti* at *Kerti Beach Inn*, where the restaurant is upstairs near the beach so has a breeze; *Café Papa John*, with a relaxed atmosphere; and *Ozone* in the village, offering good food in slightly wacky surroundings. The classiest dining experience in Padang Bai is at *Omang Omang* ⚵, which has a small menu of extremely well-cooked food including splendid cakes and desserts, and excellent coffee.

## Nightlife

Padang Bai is a laid-back place without an established **nightlife**. The reggae bars towards the eastern end of the beach have live music most evenings, getting going around 10pm and open while there are customers. They don't operate when there are large local ceremonies. *Omang Omang* also has regular live music and is hugely popular.

## Goa Lawah and Kusamba

Positioned near the coast, **Goa Lawah** (Bat Cave; daily 8am–6pm; Rp2000, sarong rental Rp2000, parking Rp1000), 7km west of Padang Bai, is a major tourist draw. The **temple**, probably founded by Empu Kuturan in 1007, is small but much revered by the Balinese, being one of the island's nine directional temples (see p.460); this one is dedicated to the southeast. The focus is the **cave** at the base of the cliff, which heaves with thousands of fruit bats; you'll hear and smell them long before you spot them. The cave is supposedly the start of a tunnel that stretches 30km inland to Pura Goa in Besakih and is said to contain the cosmic *naga* Basuki. If you engage a local guide to show you round the temple, establish the fee beforehand; Rp20,000 is reasonable.

Some 3km further west, the farming, fishing and salt-producing village of **KUSAMBA** spreads about 2km along the beach (see box, p.432, for more on salt production in Bali). **Boats** run daily from here to Nusa Penida and Nusa Lembongan, but they're small and get loaded above the gunwales – the alternative routes are less hairy (see p.254). From Kusamba, it's 6km west to Klungkung along the old road. On completion, the new road along the south coast from Tohpati will join the old road a couple of kilometres west of Kusamba.

# East of Candi Dasa

The area **east of Candi Dasa** offers lush rice terraces just a few kilometres from parched landscapes. The central volcanic mass of the island, most apparent in the awesome bulk of Gunung Agung, extends down to the gentler slopes of Gunung Lempuyang and Seraya at the far eastern end of the island, with settlements and road systems clinging to the coast or the mountain foothills.

The main road beyond Candi Dasa cuts inland, passing close to sleepy **Amlapura**, before crossing the hills to the north coast and continuing on the long coastal strip right round to Singaraja, via Tulamben, the main diving mecca on Bali. You can follow this route by public transport, but to explore the **Amed** area or the countryside around **Iseh** and **Sidemen**, you'll need your own transport.

## Amlapura

Formerly known as Karangasem, **AMLAPURA**, 40km east of Klungkung, was renamed after the 1963 eruption of Gunung Agung, when much of the outskirts of the town were flattened by the lava flow. (Balinese people sometimes change their names after serious illness, believing that a name-change will bring about a change of fortune.) A remote district capital, its relaxed atmosphere makes it a pleasant place to spend a few hours, but the only sight, **Puri Agung**, won't detain you for long.

### Some history

For much of its history, the far eastern **regency of Karangasem** was involved with Lombok, only 35km across the Lombok Strait. Initially under the authority of the *dewa agung* of Klungkung, Karangasem gradually developed its independence and, during the late seventeenth century, wrested control of Lombok from Muslim Sulawesi. Four Hindu rajas were installed to rule over the Sasak population, but ended up fighting among themselves. In 1849, the

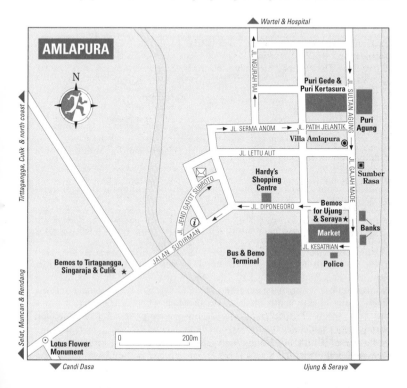

raja of Lombok, seeking to even old scores, provided four thousand troops to help the Dutch in their attack against Karangasem (see p.447). The Lombok troops ambushed and killed **Jelantik**, the hero of the Buleleng military, and the raja of Karangasem and his family committed *puputan*. The raja of Lombok was rewarded with the Karangasem regency, which he ruled from 1849 to 1893. Following a series of adventures in Bali and Lombok, the colourful **Gusti Gede Jelantik** was appointed as Dutch regent in 1894 and ruled until 1902, succeeded by his son, Anak Agung Gede Jelantik. Today, his descendants occupy the other palaces in Amlapura.

### Puri Agung

Built around a hundred years ago by Anak Agung Gede Jelantik, **Puri Agung**, also known as Puri Kaningan, is the only one of the Amlapura royal palaces ever open to the public. Puri Gede and Puri Kartasura across the road to the west are occupied and can only be seen from the outside.

The palace compound was under renovation at the time of writing. The main buildings are the **Maskerdam building**, a corruption of the name "Amsterdam", as a tribute to the Dutch; the **Bale Kambang**, formerly used for meetings, dancing and dining, which rises from the middle of a pond; the **Bale Pemandesan**, scene of royal tooth-filing ceremonies; and the **Bale Lunjuk**, used for religious ceremonies. Prior to its renovation it had become extremely faded, so it will be interesting to see if any hint of its former grandeur is restored.

### Practicalities

Public transport coming into Amlapura terminal completes a circle around the top of town, passing the **wartel** (open 24hr) and **hospital** on the way up Jalan Ngurah Rai and Puri Agung on the way down to the terminal. The **post office** is at Jalan Jend Gatot Subroto 25. **Exchange** facilities are at Bank Danamon and BRI on Jalan Gajah Made and both have ATMs linked to the Visa, MasterCard and Cirrus networks.

In the afternoon, Amlapura seems to die quickly so it's best to travel early. **Bemos** from the terminal serve Candi Dasa and Padang Bai (orange); some of those to Selat and Muncan (green) go on to Besakih. Bemos for Ujung and Seraya (blue) leave from the southern end of Jalan Gajah Made not far from the terminal. There are also **buses** north to Singaraja, with some on to Gilimanuk (not after 3.30pm) and around the south to Batubulan (final departure 4pm). On both these routes minibuses may make runs later than this, but don't count on it. Bemos to Culik and Tianyar via Tirtagangga leave from the turn-off on the outskirts of town, as do dark red minibuses to Singaraja. This turning is marked by a huge black and white pinnacle, a monument to the fight for independence, which is adorned with a *garuda*.

The **tourist office** is on Jalan Diponegoro (Mon–Thurs 7am–3pm, Fri 7am–noon; ☎0363/21196), but they get very few callers. The **police** post is in the market on Jalan Kesatrian.

Most people stop off in Amlapura for a couple of hours on their way elsewhere, and both Tirtagangga or Candi Dasa offer more **accommodation**. However, *Villa Amlapura* on Jalan Gajah Made (☎0363/23246; ❸–❹) has neat rooms, with hot water, in a small compound just south of Puri Agung. For **food**, *Sumber Rasa* further south on Jalan Gajah Made offers a selection of soups, sate, steak, spaghetti, noodles and rice at inexpensive prices, and there are also warung near the market and the bus and bemo terminal. Should the market not meet all your **shopping** requirements, the gleaming Hardy's shopping centre is on Jalan Diponegoro.

# Tirtagangga and around

Some 6km northwest of Amlapura, **TIRTAGANGGA**'s main draw is its attractive Water Palace. The altitude and location amidst beautiful paddy-fields mean cool, pleasant walks are possible with glorious views of Gunung Agung and Gunung Lempuyang as a bonus. Tirtagangga is served by **mini-buses** and **buses** plying between Amlapura and Singaraja, and by Perama charters from Candi Dasa. See "Travel details", p.291, for frequency and journey durations.

There's a **moneychanger** and **wartel** next to *Rijasa* on the main road and a postal agent on the track to the Water Palace from the main road.

## Accommodation

All the **accommodation** listed below is in or near Tirtagangga and accessed by road from the village or from Temega, slightly to the south. It's also worth considering the accommodation around the village of **Ababi** (see below): most is around 2km from Tirtagangga by road, but there are short footpaths that lead down to Tirtagangga in thirty minutes or less.

**Cabé Bali\*** ☎ 0363/22045, ⓦ www .cabebali.com. The most luxurious accommodation in the area, offering superb, tasteful bungalows, all with hot water, in lovely gardens surrounded by ricefields with excellent views of Gunung Agung and Gunung Lempuyang. There's a relaxed atmosphere, excellent, friendly service and a swimming pool. Accessed from Temega – about 1.5km south of Tirtagangga look out for the sign opposite the market; it's 500m along a rough road into the paddy-fields. ❻

**Dhangin Taman Inn** ☎ 0363/22059. Close to the Water Palace with a good sitting area overlooking the pools, this place has some reasonable rooms, but the compound is very crowded. ❶–❷

**Good Karma** ☎ 0363/22445. Tiled, clean, simple rooms set in a small garden in the paddy-fields. Enquire at the restaurant of the same name close to the main parking area. ❶–❷

**Kusumajaya Inn** ☎ 0363/21250. About 300m north of the centre of Tirtagangga, on a hill; it's a climb of about 100 steps to reach them from the road. All have verandas that make the most of the splendid views. ❶–❷

**Puri Prima** ☎ 0363/21316. About 500m north of the *Kusumajaya Inn*, with quite basic rooms with cold-water bathrooms, offering great views of Gunung Lempuyang. Road noise can be a bit intrusive as trucks labour up the road below. ❷

**Puri Sawah** ☎ 0363/21847. Just 100m beyond the Water Palace, on a track heading left from a sharp turn in the main road. There are four rooms with verandas in a small, peaceful garden. One room has hot water. The attached *Rice Terrace Coffee Shop* serves good food in a lovely location among the fields. ❸–❹

**Rijasa** ☎ 0363/21873. Across the main road from the track leading to the Water Palace, this is a good-value, centrally located place with a neat row of straightforward bungalows in an attractive garden. ❶–❷

**Tirta Ayu** ☎ 0363/21697, ⓕ 21383. Set on the hill in the grounds of the Water Palace, there are four large bungalows all with hot water and dramatically adorned bathrooms. ❺

**Villa Tirta Mas** ☎ & ⓕ 0363/21383. Next door to *Tirta Ayu* and overlooking the Water Palace, with three comfortably furnished two-storey villas with hot water. ❼–❽

## Ababi

Heading north from Tirtagangga, the road climbs through the small village of **ABABI**, a cool, rural spot. It has a number of **accommodation** options, all of which are reached along a left-hand turn signed from the main road just over 1km from Tirtagangga. About 600m along this side-road, another left onto a track leads 200m to the hidden *Geria Semalung* (☎ & ⓕ 0363/22116; ❸–❹), with four clean, tiled bungalows with hot water in a pretty garden with stunning views. There's a small vegetarian restaurant attached. Staff here can arrange a **guide** for local treks and climbs (Rp35,000 per person per hour) and for Gunung Agung climbs ($60 for one person; negotiable for more). From here, it's about thirty minutes' walk along local footpaths to Tirtagangga.

Another 200m further along the road, another track to the left leads to two more places. Taking the left fork when the track divides brings you to *Pondok Batur Indah* (☏0363/22342; ❸), which offers four clean, tiled rooms with hot water in a small family compound with fine views. It's about fifteen minutes' or so walk down to Tirtagangga. The right fork in the track brings you to *Pondok Lembah Dukuh* (❷), with five simple rooms with cold-water bathrooms and equally lovely views, just five minutes' walk from Tirtagangga. Staff can arrange trekking both locally (Rp20,000 per person per hour) or further afield to Gunung Agung (Rp700,000 for two people including transport).

### The Water Palace

Tirtagangga's **Water Palace** (daily 7am–6pm; Rp3100, Rp1000 for camera, Rp2500 for video camera; ⓦwww.tirtagangga.com) was built in 1946 by Anak Agung Anglurah, the last raja of Karangasem, as one of the three testaments to his obsession with pools, moats and fountains. The others are Taman Sukasada at Ujung (see p.289) and the less accessible Tirta Telaga Tista at Jungutan (see opposite). It is an impressive terraced garden featuring well-maintained pools, water channels and fountains. Check the website for historic photographs and information, plus details of the restoration efforts. You can **swim** in an upper, deeper pool (Rp6000) or a lower, shallower pool (Rp4000).

### Walking and trekking

It seems that every person you meet in Tirtagangga is now a **trekking** guide. Go by personal recommendation or ask at your accommodation. One established guide is Komang Gede Sutama (☏0813/3877 0893 or contact him through *Good Karma* restaurant; see "Eating"), who offers short two-hour local programmes, longer four- to five-hour programmes (Rp20,000 per person per hour) as well as treks from Tirtagangga to Tenganan, to Amed via Pura Lempuyang and Gunung Seraya, and up Gunung Agung. It's also worth checking out Nyoman Budiarsa's small shop (☏0363/22436), next to *Genta Bali Warung* on the main road. He sells a printed **map** of local walks and can also arrange **guides** for local walking trips plus climbs up Gunung Agung.

### Eating

Tirtagangga caters primarily for passing tourists; the **warung** on the track to the palace offer the usual rice and noodle options. The **restaurants** below all serve inexpensive to moderately priced food. The *Rice Terrace Coffee Shop* attached to *Puri Sawah* is one of the quietest spots in the village and has excellent baguettes, crumble, crêpes, salads, stuffed baked potatoes and soups, plenty of vegetarian choices and a children's menu. Above the car park, the *Good Karma* restaurant offers comfortable seating, a relaxed atmosphere and a big tourist menu. The location of the restaurant at *Tirta Ayu*, within the Water Palace grounds and looking down across the gardens and pools, is excellent as is *Ryoshi* Japanese restaurant (part of the small Balinese chain), which is below the road between *Kusumajaya Inn* and *Puri Prima*.

### Pura Lempuyang Luhur

From Ababi, the road climbs to the village of **ABANG**, where a large sign points to the temple of **Pura Lempuyang Luhur**, on the slopes of Gunung Lempuyang, 8km off the main road, gleaming white against the verdant greens of the surrounding forest. One of the *kahyangan jagat* or directional temples of Bali (see p.460), giving protection from the east, it's among the most sacred temples on the island and offers some of the best views in Bali. Festival days are the best time to visit (see "Basics", p.36, for sources of information on festival dates), when the 1700 steps up to the temple swarm with worshippers, and extra public **bemos** run almost all the way to the temple. On other days, bemos only run from Abang to **NGIS TISTA**, about 2km off the main road.

Pura Telaga Mas marks the bottom of the staircase, where two fierce *naga* greet visitors. It's a two-hour climb up the staircase to the temple. Pura Lempuyang Luhur, believed to be the dwelling place of the god Genijaya (Victorious Fire) has recently been renovated – but it's the view of Gunung Agung, perfectly framed in the *candi bentar*, that makes it all worthwhile. The **courtyard** contains a stand of bamboo, and on festival days the priest makes a cut in the bamboo to release holy water. From the temple, a ninety-minute climb up another staircase brings you to the **summit** of Gunung Lempuyang, where there's another small temple and even more spectacular views (the coast around Amed is clearly visible). The day after Galungan (see p.63) is the most popular day for local people to make a pilgrimage up here.

# The Amlapura–Rendang road

From Amlapura, a **picturesque road** heads about 32km west through Sibetan and Muncan, joining the main Klungkung–Penelokan road 14km north of Klungkung at Rendang. Public **bemos** ply the Amlapura–Rendang route, but without **private transport** the highlights of this area – Pura Pasar Agung above Selat and the rice-paddies around Iseh and Sidemen – are difficult to get to. Heading west from Amlapura, the city soon gives way to fields and, on clear days, the towering bulk of Gunung Agung appears startlingly close. About 9km west of Amlapura, the village of **BEBANDEM** holds a large cattle market every three days.

### Tirta Telaga Tista and westwards

Two kilometres west of Bebandem there's a sign off the main road to Desa Jungutan; an excursion along here will bring you to **Tirta Telaga Tista** at **JUNGUTAN**, one of the water palaces built by the last raja of Karangasem. After 1km, head left at the family monument and then left again 500m further on, at the *padmasana* in the village. Tirta Telaga Tista is an artificial lake fed by a freshwater spring. It was never as grand as Tirtagangga or Ujung, but it's an attractive and quiet spot surrounded by ricefields, with hills rising up behind.

Continuing west on the main road, with excellent views of Gunung Agung along the way, the road heads through **SIBETAN**, the *salak* centre of Bali. *Salak*, or snakeskin fruit, has a brown scaly skin hiding a crisp flesh with a totally unique flavour. It grows on an aggressively prickly palm about 3m high, usually planted among coconuts for shade; the main season is January to February, but fruit is available for a couple of months either side of this.

At the small village of **PESANGKAN**, 9km west of Sibetan, *Pondok Bukit Putung*, signed from the main road, has brilliant views from its **restaurant** terrace, where moderately priced food and drinks are available; the countryside down to the coast forms an amazing panorama before you. A glorious road winds 8km down to the main Candi Dasa–Klungkung road through the villages of Bakung and Manggis with gorgeous views of the entire area. If you've got your own transport, check the condition of the road locally before setting off, as it's sometimes impassable. There are no bemos along here, but if the road is open to motorbikes it makes a good trip walking down to the junction of the Manggis road with the main Candi Dasa road and getting an *ojek* back up to Putung (Rp10,000).

## Selat and around

A further 4km west is the small village of **SELAT**, with accommodation in reasonable rooms at *Pondok Wisata Puri Agung* (T & F 0366/23037; ❸), on the east side of the village just after the post office. The rooms are a bit close to the road, but there's a pleasant sitting area in the garden behind. They also offer rice-field **trekking** (Rp50,000–75,000 per person for two to three hours) and **climbing** up Gunung Agung (Rp350,000 for two people, not including transport).

Selat also marks the turn-off to **Pura Pasar Agung** (Temple of Agung Market), one of the nine directional temples of Bali, which is signposted from the village. The temple was destroyed by the 1963 eruption of Gunung Agung and has been rebuilt. The road to the temple climbs steeply 10km through bamboo stands and a few *salak* and acacia forests, set in countryside scored by deep lava-carved gorges. From the car park, five hundred concrete steps lead up to the temple. Rising in three terraces to the inner courtyard, it's an impressive and dramatic place, perched at about 1200m on the slopes of Gunung Agung, and is the starting-point for one of the routes up the mountain (see p.251). Even if you're not climbing Agung, this is a lovely spot with fabulous views.

### Iseh and Sidemen

From **DUDA**, just east of Selat, a beautiful route leaves the Amlapura–Rendang road, heading south through Iseh and Sidemen to Klungkung. The views of the ricefields along this road are among the loveliest in Bali.

Artists Walter Spies (see p.198) and Theo Meier (see p.201) both lived in **ISEH** for some time, and Anna Mathews wrote her evocative *Night of Purnama* about her life in the village before and during the 1963 eruption of Gunung Agung. Just south of Iseh, a small sign on the left points to *Pondok Wisata Patal Kikian* (T & F 0366/23005; ❻–❼; full board available), with three gorgeous bungalows sitting in mature grounds with fabulous views straight towards Gunung Agung. All bungalows have hot water. Reservations are essential.

Just over a kilometre south, **SIDEMEN** is an attractive base to experience rural Bali, with extensive footpaths through the surrounding countryside. You can watch *endek*-weaving on foot looms at the roadside Pelangi workshop in the centre of the village. If you want **to stay** in the village, *Pondok Wisata Sidemen* (T 0366/23009; ❻ full board) has a pleasant garden, startling views across the valley, and four huge, tiled rooms. They can arrange cooking, language and gamelan classes as well as trekking. Reservations are recommended. In the middle of the village, a signed turning leads to accommodation out in the rice-fields. The road forks after a few hundred metres; 100m along the right-hand turn is *Pondok Wisata Lihat Sawah* (T 0366/24183; ❸–❹), which has clean, tiled bungalows with fine ricefield views – hot water is available. The same owner has a nearby house, *Pondok Soria Moria* (❹), about 500m away, where all rooms have hot water and there's a kitchen for guests' use. Just under a kilometre further along this road out into the countryside, *Sacred Mountain Sanctuary* (T 0366/24330, F 23456; ❽–❾) offers several standards of accommodation in wood, bamboo and thatch bungalows in lush gardens with a huge swimming pool. The most expensive have river views.

Taking the left fork in the road from Sidemen brings you after 700m to *Tanto Villa* (T 0812/395 0271; ❻). The four rooms in the house are well furnished and bright and have hot water and private balconies. A pool is planned. The attached *Kafé Ketut* offers a small Indo-Chinese menu at moderate prices. Another 600m along the road brings you to the *Nirarta Centre for Living Awareness* (T0366/24122, W www.awareness--bali.com; 6–7), set up by psychologist Peter Wrycza. The accommodation is used by groups for courses and seminars, but guided individual retreats are also available. Visit the website to read more about "The Way of Unfolding", the philosophical and spiritual base of the centre. The attached **restaurant** is semi-vegetarian (serving chicken and fish) and guests may join in the twice-daily Awareness Meditation sessions if they wish. From Sidemen the road drops down another 9km before reaching the main Klungkung–Kusamba road at Paksabali.

### Muncan and Rendang

About 4km west of Selat along the Amlapura–Rendang road, **MUNCAN** is a quiet little village and another possible base for climbing Gunung Agung (see p.251). West of Muncan, the valleys become narrower and deeper; the River Telaga Waja here is used by Sobek rafting company (see W www.99bali.com/adventure/sobek for more information). A further 4km west at **RENDANG**, an attractive village with colourful gardens lining the street, the route joins the main Klungkung–Penelokan road, and there are bemos to Besakih.

# Amed

The stretch of coast in the **far east of Bali** from Culik to Aas is known as "**Amed**" in traveller-speak, although Amed is just one village in an area of peaceful bays, clear waters and stunning coastal views. Accommodation is spaced out along an eleven-kilometre stretch of coast from Amed to Aas and, although it's developing fast, it's an ideal spot for a quiet few days of sunbathing, snorkelling and diving. An increasing number of accommodation options cater for all tastes and budgets with Lipah and Bunutan the most developed areas, though even these remain quiet and low-key. Many hotels rent out snorkelling gear and there are several dive companies in the area; see p.71 for advice on choosing a dive company. The **beaches** vary from black to white sand, via a mix of the two, and you'll share them with plenty of local boats (*jukung*). There's no post office but there are several moneychangers.

Access to Amed is from **CULIK**, just over 9km northeast of Tirtagangga. All public transport between Amlapura and Singaraja – and minibuses heading north through Tirtangangga – pass through Culik. **Transport** along the coast, though, is slim. From Culik, **bemos** run via Amed to Aas in the morning; hard bargaining should get a fare of around Rp5000 to Lipah beach or use an ojek (Rp10,000 to Lipah Beach). Later in the day you'll need to use an ojek or charter a bemo. You can also use a Perama charter service from Candi Dasa (Rp50,000 per person, minimum two people). Staff at your accommodation will help arrange transport for your return. For the section from Aas south to Seraya you'll need your own vehicle. The entire coastal route from Culik around to Amlapura is only 44km, but allow yourself the best part of a day to negotiate it and enjoy the scenery. It's a lovely trip, winding in and out of the hills, but isn't something to try at night; motorcyclists lacking in experience or confidence may find some of the drops beside the road rather unnerving. Check the condition of the road before setting off from either direction.

### Amed, Congkang and Jemeluk

From Culik, it's 3km east to the picturesque, sleepy fishing village of **AMED** with a black-sand beach, much of it lined with salt manufacturing (see p.432), although

△ Amed coastline

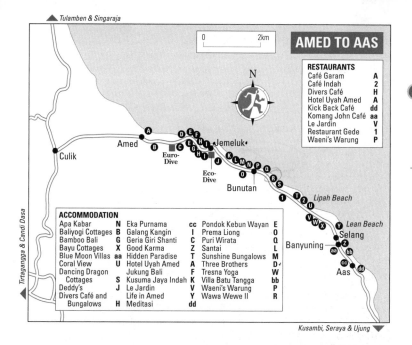

Kusambi, Seraya & Ujung ▼

you'll only see activity in the dry season. The following **accommodation** and **eating** options are described in order, as you come across them heading east.

Just beyond Amed village, *Hotel Uyah Amed* (☎0363/23462, ⓦwww .naturebali.com/amed_eco_hotel_bali.htm; ❺–❻) has eight bungalows nestling between the road and the beach. They're well furnished, with fan and solar-powered hot water, clustered around the pool. The attached *Café Garam* is an attractive, open *bale* with displays detailing the salt-making process. It has a large menu of moderately priced Western, Thai and Indonesian food and a wood-burning pizza oven, and has regular live music. Two hundred metres further east, the new *Baliyogi Cottages* (☎0363/23459, ⓔGedenyeneng@yahoo.com; ❷–❸) has eight tiled cottages with fan and cold water around a small pool; four of the cottages are big enough for families.

## Congkang

Another kilometre further east, almost next door to Euro-Dive, in the area known as **CONGKANG**, *Geria Giri Shanti* (❷) has five large, tiled, good-value bungalows just above the road, all with fine verandas. Almost opposite, *Three Brothers* (☎0363/23472; ❸) offers clean, tiled bungalows right beside the beach facing seawards in a garden with excellent views west as far as Gunung Agung. A hundred metres further east, *Pondok Kebun Wayan* 🏃 (☎0363/23473, ⓦwww .amedcafe.com; ❸–❻) is a big set-up offering several standards of room with most near a small pool, across the road from the beach. There's air-con and hot water at the top end and Internet access, a supermarket and dive shop here as well. Just next door on the beach side of the road, *Jukung Bali* (☎0363/23479; ❷–❸) is a smashing little place with two tiled bungalows with cold-water garden bathrooms, fans and deep verandas, just a few feet from the beach in a pretty garden.

## Diving at Amed and Jemeluk

There are several **dive operators** around the coast. Transport difficulties make it tempting to go with the one that is closest to where you're staying. However, see our general notes (p.71) on choosing an operator. The main **diving area** is around the rocky headland to the east of the parking area at Jemeluk: a massive sloping terrace of coral, both hard and soft, leads to a wall dropping to a depth of more than 40m. Gorgonians, fans, basket sponges and table coral are especially good, there's a high density of fish (including schools of red-tooth trigger fish and sergeant majors) with sharks, wrasses and parrotfish spotted in the outer parts, and the current is generally slow.

All operators offer trips for certified divers – expect to pay US$40–50 for two dives in Jemeluk, $40–65 in the Tulamben area (Batu Kelebit is most expensive) and $55–65 in the Selang area. Introductory dives range from $50 to $90, while the PADI Open Water course costs $290–320 and the Advanced Open Water course $240–250.

**Amed Café Divers** ☎0363/23473, ⓦwww.amedcafe.com. Attached to *Amed Café* at *Pondok Kebun Wayan*.

**Amed Dive Centre** ☎0363/23462, ⓦwww.ameddivecenter.com. Based at *Hotel Uyah Amed*.

**Eco-Dive** ☎0363/23482, ⓦwww.ecodivebali.com. Well established in the area, with tremendous local knowledge. Offers dives for experienced divers and PADI courses. Advanced divers can explore Gili Selang, the easternmost tip of Bali, where a pristine reef, pelagics and exciting currents are the draw.

**Euro-Dive** ☎0363/23469, ⓦwww.eurodivebali.com. A smart Dutch-owned dive operation in Congkang offering all PADI courses up to Divemaster level.

**Stingray** ☎0363/23479, ⓦwww.balidiverscafe.com. At the *Divers' Café and Bungalows* just before Jemeluk.

**Wirata Dive School** ☎/0363/23523, ⓦwww.diveamed.com. Attached to *Puri Wirata* in Bunutan.

### Jemeluk

Some 200m further east, at the beginning of **JEMELUK**, *Bamboo Bali* (☎0363/23478; ❶–❷) is a good budget choice, across the road from the beach, with clean, tiled, fan-cooled bungalows in a pretty garden on the hillside to catch the breeze and enjoy good views. A couple of hundred metres further on, just before the centre of the village, *Divers' Café and Bungalows* (☎0363/23479, ⓦwww.balidiverscafe.com; ❷–❸) has ten bungalows, with hot water and air-con in the more expensive ones, across the road from the beach, and a beachside café. A hundred metres further east, the rooms in *Galang Kangin* 🏕 (☎0363/23480; ❷–❸) are in a two-storey block on the beach side of the road, all with good sea views, and the cottages are in a garden across the road. Another hundred metres or so brings you to the beach at Jemeluk, the diving focus of the area, with a big car park. Just behind Eco-Dive (☎0363/23482, ⓦwww.ecodivebali.com; ❶) there are very basic bamboo and thatch rooms with attached bathroom. Hardened backpackers will relish the bamboo doors, lack of windows and limited comfort.

### Bunutan

Over a headland and in the next bay along, the next village to the east is **BUNUTAN**, about 8km from Culik and location of some of the most luxurious accommodation in the area.

About 600m from the centre of Jemeluk, *Deddy's* (☎0363/23510, ⓔwarung_deddys@hotmail.com; ❷) has three bungalows set on the hillside; it's a walk across some scrubland to reach the beach. Hot water is available, but there's no air-con. Another 500m along, *Kusuma Jaya Indah* (☎0363/23488, ➎) has clean, tiled, spacious bungalows with a choice of fan or air-con set in a lush garden ranging down the hillside from the road to the beach. There's a good beachside pool and restaurant. Next door, the delightful *Santai* ♨ (previously *Gubuk Kita*; ☎0363/23487, ⓦwww.santaibali.com; ➑) offers accommodation in lovely Sulawesi-style wood, bamboo and thatch bungalows with comfortable verandas, the more expensive ones with ocean views. All have air-con and hot water, and the pool is terrific. Some 300m further around the coast, *Sunshine Bungalows* (☎0363/23491, ⓦwww.geocities.com/sunshineamed; ➎–➏) features bungalows with hot water and air-con clustered around a small pool beside the beach. Next door, *Apa Kabar* (☎0363/23492, ⓦwww.apakabarvillas.com; ➒) is another good luxury choice and is a small, friendly place with a great garden and cute pool just behind the beach. All bungalows have air-con and hot water, and two-bedroom villas are available. The beachside restaurant here, adorned with statues and ponds, offers moderately priced Western (lots of pizzas) and Indo-Chinese favourites. Across the road, *Prema Liong* ♨ (☎0363/23486, ⓦwww .bali-amed.com; ➌–➍) comprises two-storey bungalows topped by thatch way up on the hillside with stunning views, fans and cold-water bathrooms. There's an eccentric bell system to call the staff up to collect refreshment orders.

On the climb up out of the village look out for tiny *Waeni's Warung* (☎0363/23515; ➋) on the headland with fabulous views west to Gunung Agung and beyond. Their three tiled bungalows have attached cold-water bathrooms.

Down the other side of the headland, about 300m further on, *Puri Wirata* (☎0363/23523, ⓦwww.diveamed.com; ➏–➐) has seven large tiled rooms in a two-storey building all with air-con and hot water, and verandas with lovely sea views. There are also a couple of detached cottages and a good, deep pool just above the beach. Tucked away down a track 400m east of *Puri Wirata*, *Wawa Wewe II* (☎0363/23522, ⓔwawawewevillas@yahoo.com; ➍–➎) has straightforward bungalows set down from the road in a lush garden overlooking the coast with a choice of fan or air-con, hot or cold water. A pool is under construction so prices may rise. Almost next door, *Dancing Dragon Cottages* (☎ 0363/23521, ⓦwww.dancingdragoncottages.com; ➑) is designed using Balinese and feng shui principles. All cottages have hot water and air-con, with a choice of smaller ones on the seafront or larger ones in the garden behind. There's a pretty swimming pool and excellent beachside restaurant with fine views and a vast, moderately priced Italian, Indonesian, Chinese and Japanese menu including lots of cocktails, plus apple crumble and chocolate brownies.

## Lipah Beach

**LIPAH BEACH**, located around 10km from Culik, is the most developed beach in the area, although it's still very peaceful. There's reasonable **snorkelling** just off the coast and, for **divers**, Lipah Bay is the site of the wreck of a small freighter (6–12m depth), which is now covered with coral, gorgonians and sponges. The reef nearby is rich and diverse. The road is lined with enough restaurants for you to eat at a different place each day for a fortnight. *Restaurant Gede* has a fine view up on the headland at the western end, *Café Indah* has a nice location on the beach (it's signed to the west of *Coral View*), and there are good-value set menus at *Le Jardin*. There's also plenty of **accommodation** in all price brackets. Operated by the same company, *Hidden Paradise* (☎0363/23514, ⓦwww.hiddenparadise-bali.com; ➏–➒) and, slightly beyond this, *Coral View* (☎0363/23493, same web site; ➐–➑), both offer large, well-furnished bungalows in lush gardens with lovely pools. *Coral View* is slightly more comfortable, but in both places the fan rooms at the bottom end are poor value. Two hundred metres beyond *Coral View* at *Le Jardin* (℡0363/23507, ✉lejardin@indo.net; ⑤) there are four simple bungalows in a lovely garden with the beach just a one-hundred-metre walk away. There's a choice of fan or air-con but only cold water. Another 200m on, two good-value places lie across the road from the beach: *Tresna Yoga* (℡0818/0556 2960, ✉igedejiwa@yahoo.com; ②) has clean, tiled rooms in two-storey buildings, while next door, *Bayu Cottages* (℡0363/23495, ⓦwww .bayucottages.com; ④–⑥) has six rooms all with hot water and a choice of fan or air-con, and a small pool. There are lovely views to Gunung Agung and beyond from up here. The beach is a short walk across the road from both places.

## Lean Beach, Selang, Banyuning and Ibus

Another 800m, past the next headland, is **LEAN BEACH**, 11km from Culik. *Life in Amed* (℡0813/3864 5037, ⓦwww.lifebali.com; ⑦–⑧) is a new place offering cottages and two-storey villas. All are well furnished, have air-con and hot water and are set in a small garden with a pool.

Over the next headland in the bay at **SELANG**, almost 12km from Culik, the long-standing, ever-popular *Good Karma* (℡0817/471 3352; ③–⑤) is located right on the black-sand beach, with two standards of accommodation in wood, bamboo and thatch bungalows, all with fan and cold water. About 500m further on, *Blue Moon Villas* ⚑ (℡0812/362 2597, ⓦwww.bluemoon-villa.com; ⑦) is set in a lush garden up on the headland. They have excellent rooms with air-con and hot water, there's a great little pool and some superb views. The attached *Komang John Café* has an extensive menu of moderately priced local and travellers' food served in a relaxed atmosphere. Trekking can be arranged from here, and there is excellent snorkelling off the local beach, a short walk away. *Villa Batu Tangga* (℡0813/3858 9809, ✉leepc12@wxs.nl; ⑦) is 400m further along the coast and offers four large rooms in the main house and guesthouses nearby. All have hot water and air-con, the location is fabulous, almost perched in the air above the cliffside, and there's a lovely pool.

The road then descends to **IBUS**, where the beach is lined with local *jukung*, and climbs up again out of the bay before descending again to the long bay of **BANYUNING**, where the beach is lined with colourful *jukung* and the inland hills slope steeply and impressively upwards. On the way down, *Eka Purnama* (℡0868/1212 1685, ⓦwww.eka-purnama.com; ③), 700m beyond *Villa Batu Tangga*, has four bamboo bungalows with tiled roofs perched on the hillside above the road. All have large verandas looking seawards, fan and attached cold-water bathroom. There's a Japanese wreck not far off the coast here, which is visible to snorkellers.

## Aas

The village of **AAS** is 1.5km beyond *Eka Purnama*, almost 15km from Culik. *Meditasi* (③) is situated just behind the beach in a lovely garden, offering three bamboo bungalows with garden bathrooms and entire walls that open to reveal a fine seaward view for the sunrise. The attached *Kick Back Café* offers cheap travellers' fare. Accommodation doesn't come much more isolated than this in modern Bali.

## Kusambi, Seraya and Ujung

Continuing around the coast from Aas, the country east and south of the mountains is arid and barren. It's too dry to grow rice and the only crops are peanuts, soya beans and corn, grown in the wet season. The scenery is dramatic, with hills sweeping up for hundreds of metres from the coast and the road twists and turns into and out of the folds of the hills. It's 18km from Aas to the centre of Seraya and another 6km on to Taman Sukasada but allow at least 1hr 30min for the trip. Take local advice before setting off – the road has been improved radically in recent years but it's wise to make sure it remains passable, especially in the rainy season. There's no public transport between Aas and Seraya.

The road leaves the coast at **KUSAMBI**, about 5km from Aas and marked by a massive beacon. This is the most easterly point on Bali – on clear days you'll be able to see Lombok, 35km across the strait.

Another 13km further on, the small market town of **SERAYA** features a grand temple, dominated by the looming Gunung Seraya. From here the road heads down to the coast, where rows of colourful boats line the beach. Five kilometres southwest of Seraya, *Seraya Shores* ⚲ (☎0813/3874 9108, Ⓔserayashores@hotmail.com; ❻) is a hidden gem. There are five rooms in wood and thatch buildings in a lush garden with deep verandas and lovely views. A pool is under construction, and the moderately priced restaurant is perched just above the beach. Just 300m further west, *Kebun Impian* (☎0813/3872 1842, Ⓔjoway_bali@ yahoo.com; ❺) has three large, clean, tiled fan rooms set around a pool just above the beach. Both these places can arrange transport from Amlapura or Candi Dasa or there are bemos between Amlapura and Seraya in the mornings (Rp5000), and ojek at all times (Rp10,000).

It's just over a kilometre on to **UJUNG**, 5km south of Amlapura, and **Taman Sukasada** (8am–5pm; admission by donation), the largest, if not the most picturesque, of the three water palaces built by the last raja of Karangasem, Anak Agung Anglurah, in 1921. Recent renovations have re-created lakes, pavilions and statues in extensive grounds. From here the road passes through attractive rice terraces with views across to Gunung Lempuyang and Gunung Seraya, before reaching the southern side of Amlapura.

## Tulamben and around

Heading north from Culik, the landscape changes from lush ricefields to parched boulder-strewn folds and channels, relics of the lava flow from the 1963 eruption of Gunuing Agung (see p.250).

The small village of **TULAMBEN**, about 10km northwest of Culik, has little to draw you unless you're into **diving** or **snorkelling**. This is the site of the most popular dive in Bali, the **Liberty wreck**, attracting thousands of visitors every year. Built in 1915 in the US as a cargo steamship, the 120-metre-long *Liberty* was carrying a cargo of rubber and rail parts when she was torpedoed on January 11, 1942, 15km southwest of Lombok. Attempts to tow her to port at Singaraja failed and she filled up with water and was beached at Tulamben. In 1963, earth tremors accompanying the eruption of Gunung Agung shifted the hull off the beach into deep water. Up to a hundred divers a day now visit the site, so it's worth avoiding the rush hours (11.30am–4pm). Night dives here are especially exciting.

### Practicalities

Tulamben is easily **accessible** from either Singaraja or Amlapura by public minibus or bus. At the time of writing, there were no tourist shuttle buses serving Tulamben but charters were available from Perama in Candi Dasa (Rp50,000 per person for a minimum of two people). One-way drops are widely available to Amed (Rp80,000 per car), Candi Dasa (Rp100,000), Padang Bai (Rp150,000), Lovina (Rp150,000), Ubud (Rp200,000) and Kuta

## Diving and snorkelling at Tulamben

Most divers come to Tulamben on day-trips from elsewhere. However, there are many **dive operations** in Tulamben, which all arrange local dives for certified divers and run courses; see p.71 for general notes about choosing a dive operator. Tauch Terminal (☏0363/22911, or contact in Kuta ☏0361/774504, ⓦwww.tulamben.com) and Tulamben Wreck Divers (☏0363/23400, ⓦwww.tulambenwreckdivers.com) are among the most respected. Operators also arrange dives at sites throughout Bali. Expect to pay around $55 for two dives at Tulamben or Amed, $55–60 at Padang Bai or Candi Dasa, $60–75 at Pulau Menjangan and $70–85 at Nusa Lembongan or Nusa Penida, and $300 for a PADI Open Water course. Snorkelling gear is also available for rent. Several places offer **dive and accommodation packages**, including *Tauch Terminal*, which also offers **dive safaris**; check their websites for details.

Many places offer a variety of **languages** in addition to English, including several European languages and Japanese; at the time of writing, Deep Blue Studio (☏0363/22919, ⓦwww.subaqua.cz) was offering Czech, Slovak, Polish and Russian.

### Dive sites

The **Liberty wreck** lies almost parallel to the beach, on a sandy slope about 30m offshore, and is encrusted with soft **coral**, gorgonians and hydrozoans plus a few hard corals, providing a wonderful habitat for around three hundred species of reef fish that live on the wreck and over a hundred species that visit from deeper water. A lot of the fish are very tame. The wreck is now pretty broken up and there are plenty of entrances letting you explore inside. Parts of the wreck are in shallow water, making this a good snorkelling site, too.

Although most divers come to Tulamben for the wreck, there are plenty of other excellent sites in the area – enough, in fact, to keep most divers happy for a week or more. The **Tulamben Drop-off**, sometimes called "The Wall", off the eastern end of the beach, comprises several underwater fingers of volcanic rock, which drop to 60m and are home to an enormous variety of fish, including unusual species such as comets, though it's also a good place for black coral bushes. Many divers rate this area at least as highly as the wreck itself – if not higher – although there can be more of a current to contend with. **Batu Kelebit** lies further east again and consists of two huge boulders with underwater coral-covered ridges nurturing a somewhat different but equally rewarding sea-life; it's possibly the best local site for the bigger creatures such as sharks, barracuda, jacks, mantas, molas and tuna. There are several other sites accessible from the beach in Tulamben; the site known as **The River** or **The Slope** is actually a bowl lined with sand and rocks and is possibly the best place in the whole of Bali to see rare, although perhaps not large or dramatic, species. **Tulamben Coral Garden** and **Shark Point** are pretty self-descriptive. Drift dives are possible along the coast here. Tulamben Wreck Divers dive a site called **Batu Ringgit**, excellent for coraks, nudibranches, barrell sponges, rays and sometimes sharks. They also dive **Kubu Reef**, along the coast from Tulamben.

(Rp300,000). Several **restaurants** offer the usual range of rice, noodles and pasta. The restaurants at *Tauch Terminal Resort* and *Matahari Resort* have pretty locations near the sea; *Sandyha* (currently on the main road but soon to move to the track down to *Puri Madha*) offers moderately priced travellers' fare; while *Wayan Restaurant* on the main road offers inexpensive to moderate food with lots of vegetarian options in simple surroundings. There's a **wartel** at the eastern end of the village, and **Internet access** is available at Tulamben Wreck Divers (Rp500 per min), but there's no post office – don't trust the post box on the main road – and it isn't easy to **change money** here.

**Bali Coral Bungalows** ☎ & ⓕ 0363/22909. On the track leading to *Tauch Terminal Resort*. Set in a small area, all rooms face seawards but only a few have sea views. Hot water and air-con are available in the top-end ones. Thirty percent discount is available if you dive with the attached dive centre. **②–③**

**Matahari Resort** ☎ 0363/22907, ⓔ matahari .tulamben@hotmail.com. Signed off the main road towards the sea at the eastern end of the village. There are two standards of rooms, fan and cold-water or air-con and hot water, and there's a pretty little pool just behind the beachside restaurant. **②–④**

**Paradise Palm Beach Bungalows** ☎ 0363/22910, ⓔ dive@bali.net. Long-established bungalows signed off the main road in the village, offering several standards of accommodation in the cosy compound – the most expensive having air-con and hot water – and with a small restaurant overlooking the sea. **②–⑤**

**Puri Aries** ☎ 0363/23402. Eight budget bungalows set above the main road in a small compound. All have fan, cold-water bathrooms and verandas, and are fine if you don't need to be next to the sea. **①**

**Puri Madha** ☎ 0363/22921. The most westerly place, about 400m beyond the village and very near the *Liberty* wreck, although there is wasteland between the beach and the bungalows. Rooms have fan and cold-water bathrooms, and there's a beachside restaurant. **②**

**Scuba Seraya Resort** ☎ 0812/383 7514, ⓔ scubaseraya@eksadata.com. Eight appealing bungalows all with hot water and air-con in an attractive garden next to the beach 3km east of Tulamben. There's a lovely pool, and a dive centre attached. **⑥–⑦**

**Tauch Terminal Resort*** ☎ 0363/22911 or contact in Kuta ☎ 0361/774504, ⓦ www.tulamben.com. Large, gleaming, lively establishment that fronts a long section of the coast. Features landscaped gardens, an attractive pool and a busy dive centre. All rooms, the best in the area, have air-con and hot water, with good furnishings and balconies. Accommodation and diving packages are available. **⑥**

**Tulamben Wreck Divers** ☎ 0363/23400, ⓦ www .tulambenwreckdivers.com. Just above the main road, with three standards of rooms. All have air-con and are tiled and spacious. At the bottom end, bathrooms, although with hot water, are not en suite. There's a good pool. Dive/accommodation packages are available. **⑤–⑥**

### North of Tulamben

From Tulamben, it's a long haul along the parched north coast to Singaraja, featuring few villages and very limited coastal views. However, there are fine views of the mountains inland initially to Gunung Agung, which appears very close and much more stark than in views from the south, and then to the mountains of the Batur area. Cashew orchards are the most apparent vegetation. Heading on from Tulamben, the villages of **Tembok**, **Sembirenteng** and **Bondalem** offer accommodation. From Bondalem, a pretty – although very steep – back road leads to Kintamani.

# Travel details

### Bemos and public buses

It's almost impossible to give the frequency with which bemos and public buses run: see Basics, p.49, for details. Journey times given are the minimum you can expect. Only the direct bemo and bus routes are listed.

**Amlapura** to: Air Sanih (2hr); Candi Dasa (20min); Culik (45min); Denpasar (Batubulan terminal; 2hr); Gianyar (1hr 20min); Gilimanuk (4–5hr); Klungkung (1hr); Lovina (3hr 30min); Padang Bai (45min); Seraya (40min); Singaraja (Penarukan terminal; 3hr); Tirtagangga (20min); Tulamben (1hr); Ujung (20min).

**Bangli** to: Denpasar (Batubulan terminal; 1hr 30min); Gianyar (20min); Singaraja (Penarukan terminal; 2hr 15min).

**Candi Dasa** to: Amlapura (20min); Denpasar (Batubulan terminal; 2hr); Gianyar (1hr); Klungkung (40min); Padang Bai (20min).

**Culik** to: Aas (1hr 30min); Air Sanih (1hr 30min); Amed (20min); Amlapura (45min); Bunutan (45min); Jemeluk (30min); Lipah Beach (1hr); Lovina (2hr 30min); Selang (1hr 15min); Singaraja (Penarukan terminal; 2hr 30min); Tirtagangga (30min); Tulamben (1hr).

**Gianyar** to: Amlapura (1hr 20min); Bangli (20min);

Batur (40min); Blahbatuh (30min); Candi Dasa (1hr); Denpasar (Batubulan terminal; 1hr); Klung-kung (20min); Ubud (20min).

**Klungkung** to: Amlapura (1hr); Besakih (45min); Candi Dasa (40min); Denpasar (Batubulan terminal; 1hr 20min); Gianyar (20min); Padang Bai (30min); Rendang (30min).

**Padang Bai** to: Amlapura (45min); Candi Dasa (20min); Gilimanuk (3–4hr); Klungkung (30min).

**Tirtagangga** to: Air Sanih (2hr); Amlapura (20min); Culik (30min); Lovina (3hr); Singaraja (2hr 30min); Tulamben (1hr).

**Tulamben** to: Air Sanih (1hr); Amlapura (1hr); Culik (30min); Lovina (2hr 30min); Singaraja (2hr); Tirtagangga (1hr).

## Perama shuttle buses

*STO = overnight stopover is needed*

**Candi Dasa** to: Bedugul (daily; 2hr–2hr 30min); Gili Islands (daily; 7–8hr); Kuta/Ngurah Rai Airport (3 daily; 3hr); Lovina (2 daily; 3hr–3hr 30min); Mataram (Lombok; 2 daily; 5hr–5hr 30min); Padang Bai (3 daily; 30min); Sanur (3 daily; 2hr–2hr 30min); Sengiggi (Lombok; daily; 5hr–6hr); Ubud (3 daily; 1hr 30min–2hr).

**Nusa Lembongan** to: Bedugul (daily; STO); Candi Dasa (3hr); Gili Islands (daily; STO); Kuta/ Ngurah Rai Airport (daily; 2hr 30min–3hr); Lovina (daily; 5hr); Mataram (Lombok; daily; 9hr); Padang

Bai (daily; 3hr 30min); Senggigi (Lombok; daily; 9hr); Ubud (daily; 3hr).

**Padang Bai** to: Candi Dasa (3 daily; 30min); Gili Islands (daily; 7–8hr); Kuta/Ngurah Rai Airport (3 daily; 2hr 30min); Lovina (daily; 2hr 30min–3hr); Mataram (Lombok; 2 daily; 4hr 30min–5hr); Nusa Lembongan (3 daily; STO); Sanur (3 daily; 1hr 30min–2hr); Sengiggi (Lombok; 2 daily; 5hr–5hr 30min); Ubud (daily 2hr–2hr 30min).

## Boats

**Buyuk Harbour** (Nusa Penida) to: Kusamba (daily; 1–2hr); Padang Bai (daily; 1hr).

**Jungutbatu** (Nusa Lembongan) to: Kusamba (daily; 1–2hr); Sanur (daily; 1–2hr); Toyapakeh (Nusa Penida; daily; 45min).

**Kusamba** to: Buyuk Harbour (Nusa Penida; daily; 1–2hr); Jungutbatu (Nusa Lembongan; daily; 1–2hr); Sampalan (Nusa Penida; daily; 1–2hr); Toyapakeh (Nusa Penida; daily; 1–2hr).

**Padang Bai** to: Gili Islands (Perama; daily; 6–7hr); Lembar, Lombok (every 1hr 30min; 4–5hr); Buyuk Harbour (Nusa Penida; daily; 1hr); Senggigi (Lombok; Perama; daily; 4hr–4hr30min).

**Sampalan** (Nusa Penida) to: Kusamba (daily; 1–2hr); Padang Bai (daily; 1hr).

**Toyapakeh** (Nusa Penida) to: Jungutbatu (Nusa Lembongan; daily; 45min); Kusamba (daily; 1–2hr).

# North Bali and the central volcanoes

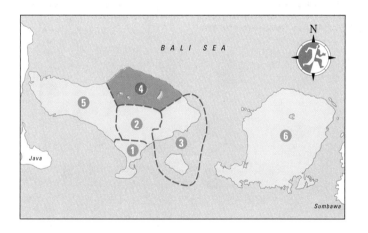

CHAPTER FOUR # Highlights

* **Gunung Batur** Volcano set amidst dramatic scenery: wonderful views as part of the panorama from Penelokan or from the summit at sunrise. See p.297

* **Danau Tamblingan** The quietest, smallest and most picturesque of the lakes in the Bedugul area. See p.312

* **Munduk** Cool temperatures, fine scenery and easy access make this an ideal base for exploration. See p.313

* **Singaraja** Bali's second city offers wide boulevards, a stimulating ethnic mix and bustling street life. See p.314

* **Pura Meduwe Karang** The best example of the exuberant carving typical of northern temples. See p.319

* **Lovina** Laid-back beach resort offering something for everyone. See p.322

* **Damai Lovina Villas dinner** The most exquisite food in northern Bali, worth every rupiah. See p.331

△ Canoes line the shore of Danau Batur

# North Bali and the central volcanoes

Heading into **north Bali** from the crowded southern plains, you initially enter another world, with a slower pace, cooler climate and hugely varied countryside. The centre of the island is occupied by the volcanic masses of the **Batur** and **Bedugul** areas, where dramatic mountains shelter crater lakes, and small, peaceful villages line their shores. The **mountains** don't rival Gunung Agung in stature, but their accessibility and beauty are unbeatable. Most people come to the Batur area to gaze at the crater panorama or to trek up **Gunung Batur**, the most climbed peak in Bali, which still sends up occasional puffs of smoke. The Bedugul area offers more lakes, mountains and forests, but on a smaller scale. The **central lakes** are the sites of several important temples dedicated to Ida Batara Dewi Ulun Danu, the goddess of the lake, and they are the focus of pilgrimages by Balinese worshippers and day-trips by foreign visitors, especially to the stunning lakeside temple of **Pura Ulun Danu Batur**. (The third of Bali's central mountain areas, Batukau, is described on p.352, as access is via routes covered in Chapter 5.)

Beyond the mountains, the northern **coast** is arid and rugged as the mountains drop steeply to the coastal plain with villages and roads squeezed between shore and mountain, although there are some areas of gentler hillsides and glorious rice terraces. Many visitors head straight for the resort of **Lovina**, which is the largest outside the Kuta–Legian–Seminyak conurbation but somehow manages to retain a laid-back air: it's a great place to relax or to use as a base for exploring the surrounding region.

For hundreds of years, the north of Bali was the part of the island most open to foreign influence, as Chinese and Muslim traders plied their wares through the port of **Singaraja**. The north was the first area subdued by the Dutch, almost half a century before the south, and Singaraja was their administrative capital right up until World War II. After 1924 and the start of the weekly KPM steamship service from Java, a steady stream of tourists and longer-term visitors began to arrive through Singaraja. When the first commercial hotels opened in Kuta in the 1930s, and Ngurah Rai Airport was completed in 1969, the pendulum swung away from the north in tourist terms, though today, Singaraja,

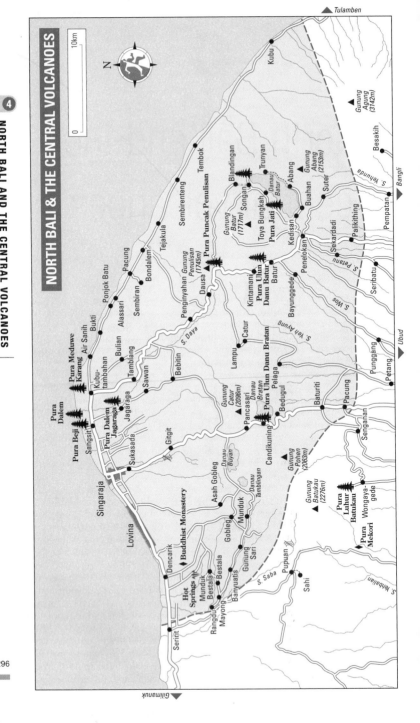

# NORTH BALI & THE CENTRAL VOLCANOES

administrative capital of Buleleng district and a bustling, modern city, still retains its function as a transport hub; indeed, it's impossible to avoid.

The exuberant and distinctive **temple carvings** of the north depict bicycle-riding, car-driving Dutch invaders and ordinary Balinese folk alongside religious figures. The best-known temples of the area – **Kubutambahan**, **Jagaraga** and **Sangsit** – offer an accessible and light-hearted interlude, in pleasant contrast to the more solemn temple experiences further south. Close to Lovina, the sole **Buddhist** temple on the island is at Banjar. In Singaraja, the **Gedong Kirtya** is the only *lontar* manuscript library in the world and, although pretty esoteric, is a good way to while away an hour or so in the city.

### Transport practicalities

The Singaraja–Gilimanuk road threads along the north coast, taking in Lovina, and public transport plies the three main southbound roads through the mountains – from Seririt via Pupuan, Singaraja via Bedugul, and Kubutambahan via Kintamani. With good **bus** links from Java, Denpasar and Amlapura and **bemo** connections within the area, most of the sights in the north are easy to get to on public transport, although with your own vehicle you'll be able to explore less accessible areas such as Danau Tamblingan. A good range of accommodation throughout the region makes this an ideal touring area.

# Batur and Bedugul

The lakes within the volcanic craters of the **Batur** and **Bedugul** areas are the source of water for a vast area of agricultural land and, as home to Ida Batara Dewi Ulun Danu, the goddess of the lake, are pivotal to religious belief on the island. The cool mountain air, trekking opportunities and the good transport services have long made this region a favourite with local and foreign visitors.

## Gunung Batur and Danau Batur

The **Batur** area was formed thirty thousand years ago by the eruption of a gigantic volcano. Confusingly, the entire area is sometimes referred to as **Kintamani**, although this is the name of just one of several villages dotted along the rim of the ancient crater. Another group of villages is situated around **Danau Batur** at the bottom of the crater: **Toya Bungkah** is the start of the main route up Gunung Batur, and is the chief accommodation centre, although **Kedisan** offers a few options, and is the access point for boat trips across the lake to the Bali Aga village of **Trunyan**. South of Kedisan, **Buahan** is the quietest spot of all, and **Songan**, at the northern end of the lake, is the start of walks up to the crater rim.

The highest points on the rim are **Gunung Abang** (2153m) on the eastern side, the third highest mountain in Bali, and **Gunung Penulisan** (1745m) on the northwest corner, with Pura Puncak Penulisan perched on its summit.

Rising from the floor of the main crater, **Gunung Batur** (1717m) is an active volcano with four craters of its own. Every morning, trekkers set off before dawn to climb the peak and admire the sunrise from the top.

Sadly, the Batur area has developed a reputation among travellers for hassles. However, the dramatic landscape makes it worth taking a deep breath, keeping a hold on your patience and heading upwards for at least a glimpse of its remarkable scenery.

## The crater rim

Spread out along the road that follows the rim of the crater for 11km, the villages of **Penelokan**, **Batur** and **Kintamani** almost merge with each other. The road is one of the main routes between the north and south coasts, so, while public transport is frequent and the views spectacular, a quiet stroll isn't an option. If you're planning to stay up here, be aware that cloud often rolls in in late afternoon and the nights are extremely chilly; at the very least, you'll need a sweater.

There's an **admission charge** to the crater area, of Rp3100 per person (Rp2000 for a car, Rp1000 for a motorbike). The ticket offices are just south of Penelokan on the road from Bangli and at the junction of the road from Ubud and the rim road. In practice, collection appears haphazard, with rental cars and tour buses the main targets.

### Practicalities

The crater rim is included in many **day-trips** from the major resorts, although this usually means a quick stop to admire the panorama from Penelokan amid serious hassle from hawkers, and lunch with a view. However, getting to the rim independently is straightforward, with **buses** running about every half-hour until mid-afternoon between Singaraja (Penarukan) and Denpasar (Batubulan), via Gianyar and Bangli. Coming from Air Sanih on the north coast, you can pick up the bus from Singaraja at the junction at Kubutambahan, from where Kintamani is 40km away. The route from Ubud is served by brown (Kintamani) **bemos**, and the roads via Suter, Tampaksiring and Payangan are easy to drive. At the time of writing, Kintamani was not on Perama's **tourist shuttle bus** schedule but charters (Rp50,000 per person, minimum two people) were available from Ubud; check their website (Ⓦwww.peramatour.com) or enquire at

---

### Eruptions at Gunung Batur

Gunung Batur has **erupted** more than twenty times since 1800. In 1917, a major eruption killed over a thousand people, but the lava stopped just outside the temple of Batur village, which was at that time situated in the crater beside the lake. Considering this a good omen, the population remained in the village until August 3, 1926, when another eruption completely engulfed the village and the temple, and the people of Batur were evacuated up onto the crater rim. The longest-lasting eruption took place in September 1963, a few months after the massive explosion of Gunung Agung (see p.250), and continued until May 1964. At Yehmampeh, on the road around the base of the mountain, you'll see lava flows from an eruption in March 1974. The newest crater, Batur IV, was formed during the eruption that started on August 7, 1994, and that continues periodically. It's startling to see the volcano still smoking, but local belief is that it's better if Batur lets off a little steam regularly rather than saving it all up for a major blow.

Check Ⓦwww.vsi.esdm.go.id for the current level of volcanic activity.

**GUNUNG BATUR AND DANAU BATUR**

any of their offices for the current situation. Once in the area, there are plenty of bemos zipping to and fro along the rim (Rp2000).

The **post office** and **phone office** are close together just off the main road 2km north of Penelokan. It is difficult to **change money** so bring plenty of cash.

### Penelokan

Literally meaning "Place to Look", the views from **PENELOKAN** (1450m) are majestic: Danau Batur lies far below, with Gunung Batur and Gunung Abang towering on either side. Thousands of tourists pass through Penelokan every day, attracting **hawkers** selling everything from fruit, chess sets and wooden carvings to T-shirts and sarongs. It's a pain but the only way to really avoid the circus is to come early or late, or stay overnight.

Yayasan Bintang Danu, a local organization, runs the **tourist office** (℡0366/51730; daily 9am–3pm), almost opposite the turning down to Kedisan.

Most people who **stay** in the area head down to the lake but, if your budget will run to it, go for the *Lakeview Hotel* 🏊 (℡0366/51394, 🌐www.indo.com/hotels/lakeview; ❻–❼), located right on the edge of the crater rim. It's totally without frills but has hot water, thick quilts and stunning views. They arrange sunrise treks up Gunung Batur. A couple of hundred feet below, on the road down to Kedisan, *Windu Sari* (℡0366/52467, 🖷52468; ❻) is a smaller set-up but has equally fine views and similar facilities.

The crater rim is packed with **restaurants** offering expensive buffet lunches to day-trippers. For something cheaper, try *Ramana*, on the crater rim about

## Climbing Gunung Abang

Thickly forested and lacking sweeping views, climbing **Gunung Abang** (Red Mountain), is less popular and rewarding than tackling Batur. Allow a couple of hours to get to the top from the start of the footpath and take enough food and water. You don't really need a guide on this route but you should tell somebody responsible where you're going. If you do want a **guide**, enquire at the trekking agencies in Toya Bungkah (see p.303), Yayasan Bintang Danu in Penelokan, losmen *Miranda* in Kintamani or the Association of Mount Batur Trekking Guides in Toya Bungkah. Shop around; the Association is currently quoting Rp750,000 per guide for a party of up to four people, the trekking companies about $55 per person, transport included.

The route starts on the Suter road, which heads east around the rim from Penelokan, from just below the *Lakeview Hotel* (there are no public bemos going here). Approximately 4km from Penelokan, the road turns abruptly south away from the crater rim, but a rough track continues along the edge. Follow this track for a further 2km, passing **Pura Munggu** in the middle of the forest. The track eventually turns away from the crater rim; at this point, take the footpath straight in front of you that heads up the mountain. You'll pass the small forest temple, **Pura Manu Kaya**, about halfway, reaching **Pura Puncak Tuluk Biyu**, enclosed by trees, at the summit.

A track continues down the other side of Gunung Abang to the far side of the crater above Songan. However, this path is long and little used; you definitely need a guide to attempt it.

300m towards Kintamani from Penelokan. Closer to Penelokan, on the opposite side of the road, *Wibisana* is also good value.

### Pura Ulun Danu Batur

About 4km north of Penelokan, four temples stand in a row along the crater's rim. The most northerly – and most imposing – is **Pura Ulun Danu Batur** (admission by donation; sarong and scarf rental available) the second most important temple on the island after Besakih and one of the highly venerated *kayangan jagat* (directional temples): this one protects Bali from the north. It's fascinating at any time but the eleven-day *odalan* festival (see p.464) is particularly spectacular.

The original temple was located down in the crater until the 1926 eruption of Gunung Batur, when the village and temple were rebuilt on the rim. The temple honours **Ida Batara Dewi Ulun Danu**, the goddess of the lake, who controls the water for the irrigation systems throughout the island and shares dominion of Bali with the god of Gunung Agung. A manuscript in the temple proclaims, "Because the Goddess makes the waters flow, those who do not follow her laws may not possess her rice terraces." A virgin priestess selects 24 boys who will serve the goddess as **priests** in the temple for life. The high priest, Jero Gde or Sanglingan, is selected by the virgin priestess, and is believed to be the earthly representative of the goddess of the lake. His days are spent making offerings to her on behalf of visiting pilgrims, and at night he dreams under her guidance. Farmers or *subak* with plans for, or conflicts about, irrigation systems come to confer with the Jero Gde, whose word is accepted as final. The sheer number of shrines is overwhelming for many visitors, but the most significant is the **eleven-roofed meru** in the inner courtyard, dedicated to both the goddess of the lake and the god of Gunung Agung. The *kulkul* tower in the outer courtyard houses a drum that is beaten 45 times each morning to honour the 45 deities worshipped in the temple.

## Kintamani

Two kilometres north of Pura Ulun Danu Batur, **KINTAMANI** isn't particularly attractive and is too far north along the rim of the crater for the best views. It's famous for its breed of furry dogs and the huge market held every three days. It's better **to stay** at the lakeside, where there are more accommodation options, or in Penelokan, where the views are better, although Kintamani has the only budget accommodation on the rim – *Miranda* (☎0366/52022; ❶), and 100m north of the market; all public transport along the rim passes the door. The rooms are very basic but have attached mandi and squat toilet. The lounge cheers up when there are a few people staying and the open fire is lit. The owner, Made Senter, also works as a **tour guide**; he charges Rp400,000, including transport, for up to four people to climb Gunung Batur, leaving at 3am for the sunrise. The price is the same for treks up Gunung Abang, rising to $100 for a group of up to four people to climb Gunung Agung (see p.251).

### Pura Puncak Penulisan

About 5km north of Kintamani on the road towards Singaraja, in the village of Sukawana, **Pura Puncak Penulisan**, also known as Pura Tegeh Koripan (admission by donation), built on the summit of Gunung Penulisan, is the highest temple on Bali and one of the most ancient, being referred to in ninth-century inscriptions. There are 333 steps from the road to the top temple, **Pura Panarajon**, dedicated to Sanghyang Grinatha, a manifestation of Siwa and god of the mountains. On this top terrace, *bale* shelter an array of ancient lingga and statues from the eleventh to thirteenth centuries, which predate the Majapahit invasion of the island. These include a wedding portrait widely believed to portray the marriage of King Udayana and Queen Mahendratta, the source of the Rangda myth (see box, p.235).

## Danau Batur

Home to **Ida Batara Dewi Ulun Danu** (or Dewi Danu for short), the goddess of the lake, **Danau Batur** is especially sacred to the Balinese. The waters from the lake, generated by eleven springs, are believed to percolate through the earth and reappear as springs in other parts of the island. Situated 500m below the crater rim, this is the largest lake in Bali, 8km long and 3km wide, and one of the most glorious: the villages dotted around its shores are referred to as *bintang danu* (stars of the lake). See p.299 for a **map** of the area.

The road to the lakeside, served by **public bemos**, leaves the crater rim at Penelokan. Bemos go as far as Songan on the western side of the lake and Abang on the eastern side; the tourist fare from Penelokan to any of the accommodation around the lake is about Rp5000. Be aware that the peace by the lake can sometimes be shattered by trucks ferrying stone from the quarry on the western side of Gunung Batur, although most of them use an alternative road that avoids the tourist developments. In addition, many visitors have negative experiences from being hassled and overcharged, and there have been incidents of intimidation. Most people stay the minimum amount of time needed to complete their trek.

If you **arrive by car**, there's pressure on you to pay someone to "look after" your vehicle while you climb. The best advice is to leave vehicles in the care of staff at a hotel you've stayed at or restaurant where you've eaten, or to take a driver with the car and ask him to stay with it while you trek.

Bear in mind that Batur remains **active** so treks depend on the mountain remaining safe. Periodically, certain parts are closed; in late 2004, for example, Batur II was declared off-limits for a few weeks.

With four main craters and several access points, there's a choice of **routes up Gunung Batur**. If you have your own wheels, the easiest way to get to the top is to drive to **Serongga**, up a signed turning off the Yehmampeh road, west of Songan. From the car park, it's a climb of thirty minutes to an hour to the highest peak and largest crater, **Batur I**. Steam holes just below the crater rim confirm that this volcano is far from extinct, although the crater itself is grassed over.

The most common walking **routes** up to Batur I are from Toya Bungkah and Pura Jati. The path from Pura Jati is shadeless and largely across old lava fields, while about half of the ascent from Toya Bungkah is in forest. From Toya Bungkah, numerous paths head up through the forest (one starts just south of the car park near *Arlina's*); after about an hour you'll come out onto the bare slope of the mountain, from where you can follow the paths that head up to the tiny warung perched along the crater rim way up on the skyline. This is the steep bit, slippery with black volcanic sand. Allow two to three hours to get to the top from Toya Bungkah or Pura Jati, and about half that time to get back down.

A **medium-length trek** involves climbing to Batur I, walking around the rim and then descending by another route. The **long-trek** option, sometimes called the **Exploration** (about 8hr in total) involves climbing up to Batur I, walking around the rim to the western side, descending to the rim of Batur II and then to the rim of Batur III. From here, the descent is to Toya Bungkah or Yehmampeh.

### Practicalities

Climbing Batur is best done in the **dry season** (April–Oct). The path becomes unpleasant in the wet and clouds often engulf the summit. However, the wet season isn't unrelenting, and you might hit a few dry days – more likely at the beginning and end of the rains than in the middle.

In **daylight**, you don't need a guide to find the way if you're just intending to climb up to Batur I from Toya Bungkah or Pura Jati and you've a reasonable sense of direction. However, it's unwise to climb alone and you should let somebody responsible know where you are going. For the longer treks or the less well-trodden paths, you do need a guide: routes are trickier and it's important to stay away from the most active parts of the volcano. However, most people climb **in the dark** to reach the top

### Kedisan

At the bottom of the steep descent, 3km from Penelokan, the road splits in the lakeside village of **KEDISAN**: the right fork leads to the jetty for boats to Trunyan and continues on to the villages of Buahan and Abang; the left fork leads to Toya Bungkah and Songan.

A few hundred metres from the junction, towards Toya Bungkah, *Hotel Segara* (☎0366/51136, ✉hotelsegara@plasa.com; ❷–❹) has three standards of **accommodation**, with hot water and TV in the most expensive rooms and cold-water bathrooms attached to the cheaper ones – all have small sitting areas outside, although they overlook a car park. The hotel offers pick-ups from Penelokan (Rp40,000 per car), Kuta (Rp150,000 per car), Lovina or Ubud (Rp125,000 per car), although it's advisable to check the cost when you phone to arrange it. Next door, *Hotel Surya* (☎0366/51139; ❷–❸) also has decent rooms, some with hot water. Many of the balconies here have lovely views. They offer a free pick-up service from local areas plus Ubud, Bangli, Besakih, Gianyar and Klungkung, and discounted pick-ups from Kuta, Sanur, Air Sanih for dawn: the view over the lake as the sun rises behind Gunung Abang and Gunung Rinjani on Lombok is definitely worth the effort. You'll need to leave around 4–5am and a guide is a good idea, as it's easy to get lost in the dark.

Anyone who climbs Batur is under intense pressure to engage a local guide. These are now organized into the **Association of Mount Batur Trekking Guides** (⊤0366/52362, ⒺVolcanotrekk@hotmail.com), known locally as "the Organization", which has two offices where prices are displayed: one in Toya Bungkah and another at Pura Jati. The published price for the short climb to see the sunrise is "fixed" at Rp300,000 per guide for a maximum of four people, Rp450,000 for a five- to six-hour trek around the main crater and Rp600,000 for the seven-hour exploration trek, though chances are you'll be offered (or be able to negotiate) a price significantly below these.

### Trekking agencies

Aside from the Association of Mount Batur Trekking Guides, you can get **information** about the Gunung Batur area from staff at your hotel and from the three **organized trekking services** in Toya Bungkah: Roijaya Wisata (⊤0366/51249, ⒺJero_Wijaya@hotmail.com), which has an office at *Lakeside Cottages*; Bali Sunrise 2001, at the *Volcano Breeze Café* (⊤0366/51824, mobile ⊤0818/552669, Ⓦwww.balisunrise2001.com); and *Arlina's* (⊤0366/51165). They use guides from the Association of Mount Batur Trekking Guides, but are more used to working with tourists. The agencies charge US$20 per person for the short climb to see the sunrise, $25 for the medium trek and $30–38 for the long trek. There are minimum numbers required – sometimes two people, sometimes four. Bali Sunrise 2001 can also arrange pickups for Batur treks in Nusa Dua, Kuta, Sanur, Ubud, Candi Dasa or Lovina, but transport costs are high: you'll pay $45–70 for the sunrise trek, depending on where you're picked up.

In addition, all can arrange other treks in the area; prices vary, so it pays to shop around. There are climbs up **Gunung Abang** ($50 per person) and **Gunung Agung** ($75–95 per person), and it's also possible to climb to the outer caldera above Songan for the sunrise and then continue around the ridge to approach Trunyan from above ($15–25, depending on the length of the trek). Longer caldera treks cost around $60.

Treks in the Bedugul area are also available (see p.308).

*Arlina's* has **canoes** for rental ($1 per hr or $30 per day with "driver", $10 or $25 per day without), and they rent out **fishing** gear at Rp20,000 per day. Enquire at any of the trekking agencies about **shuttle bus** tickets and charter transport.

and Lovina (all Rp100,000 per car); check the details when you phone ahead. A couple of hundred metres further on, *Hotel Astra Dana* (⊤0366/52091, Ⓔdizzymade@yahoo.com; ❶–❷) has a dozen rooms by the lakeside; the most expensive have hot water and fabulous lake views.

Turning right at the bottom of the road from Penelokan brings you to the quietest part of the lake and the jetty for boats to Trunyan. See p.305 for accommodation options further round this side of the lake.

### Toya Bungkah and around

**TOYA BUNGKAH**, 8km from Penelokan, is the accommodation centre of the lakeside area and the main starting-point for climbs up Gunung Batur.

About 4km before Toya Bungkah, **Pura Jati**, dedicated to the god Wisnu, has some fine carvings, and it's near here that Magening, one of the eleven springs within the lake, rises. Every five years, the festival of Bakti Pekelem takes place here, involving considerable sacrifice of animals to Dewi Danu through ritual drowning in the lake.

Pura Jati, Kedisan & Penelokan

Toya Bungkah's **natural hot springs** (daily 8am–5pm, $5) are clean and attractive, with a cold-water swimming pool and smaller hot-water pools, but are pricey. Traditionally, the springs here, known as Tirta Bungkah (the Holy Waters of the Mountain), form a trinity along with Tirta Empul (the Holy Waters of the Plains) at Tampaksiring and Tirta Selukat (the Holy Waters of the Sea) at Medahan in Gianyar. Pilgrims, especially women in early pregnancy and anyone who has recovered from a long illness, bathe in each of the three waters in turn.

**Changing money** can be difficult, so it's best to bring cash. There's a 24-hour **wartel** at the start of Toya Bungkah with **Internet** access.

## Accommodation, eating and drinking

There is plenty of **accommodation** in Toya Bungkah, both near the road and lakeside. Several losmen have inexpensive **restaurants** serving a good range of Western and Indo-Chinese options, and fish from the lake.

**Arlina's** ☎0366/51165. A friendly, popular set-up at the southern end of town, with clean rooms (some with hot water) and small verandas. ④–⑤

**Awangga** A newer place on the road down to the lake with simple accommodation, all with good verandas. ①

**Lakeside Cottages** ☎0366/51249, ℗51250. Aptly named place, with large cottages with good verandas, lake views, hot water and TV, down to cheaper, cold-water rooms further from the lake. There's also a swimming pool. ③–⑥

**Nyoman Mawar** *(Under the Volcano)* ☎0366/51166. Located in the village, with clean, good-value rooms. Cold-water bathrooms only. ①

**Nyoman Mawar III** *(Under the Volcano III)* ☎0366/51166. Bungalows set in a great location close to the lake with fabulous views; all are simple and clean, with cold water only. ①

**Pualam** Quiet losmen, close to the hot springs, with clean, fair rooms set around a pleasant garden. ①

## Songan and the volcano road

At the northern end of the lake, 12km from Penelokan and 4km beyond Toya Bungkah, the village of **SONGAN** is a thriving community of farmers. Not to be confused with the bigger, more important temple of the same name up on the crater rim, **Pura Ulun Danu Batur** in Songan is believed locally to be

## Walks above Songan

Directly behind the temple in Songan, a small **footpath** winds up onto the rim of the outer crater. To the right, the path heads up towards Abang, passing above Trunyan and the cemetery, but this is the hard way to climb Abang and shouldn't be attempted without a guide; see p.300 for the alternative route via Suter.

As you head left, several footpaths pass through small strung-out villages of traditional bamboo huts whose inhabitants farm the steep dry hillsides. There are some fine views down to the north coast, and back to Abang, Agung, and even – on a clear day – Rinjani on Lombok. With a good supply of food and water (it gets hotter the further down you go), a reasonable sense of direction and a bit of Indonesian, you should be able to locate and follow the paths down to the **north coast** where you can pick up public transport west to Air Sanih or east to Tulamben.

Alternatively, follow the tracks on the crater rim for about 3km until a track leads down to the village of **Blandingan**, from where there's a direct path back to Songan.

one of the oldest temples in Bali. A ceremony is held in Songan every ten years to honour the goddess of the lake, involving the ritual drowning of a range of animals (buffaloes, pigs, goats, chickens and geese), all adorned with gold ornaments. Not many bemos serve Songan and you may end up walking to or from Toya Bungkah; either follow the road or take the lakeside track.

From a junction in the middle of Songan, a **road** circles the base of Gunung Batur, passing through **Yehmampeh** on its way round to Penelokan, a trip of about 26km. If you have your own transport, it's worth getting off the tourist track at least part of the way around here to enjoy the different views of the crater rim and Gunung Batur. To the northwest side of the volcano, **Pura Bukit Mentik** is known locally as Lucky Temple, because lava from the 1974 eruption surrounded it but caused no damage. The lava fields from that eruption now supply the grey-black stone *paras*, and sand used in building and ferried continuously from the area.

### Buahan and Abang

The most attractive section of road in the crater follows the eastern shore of Danau Batur beyond Kedisan, offering great views across the lake to Toya Bungkah, with Gunung Batur rising up behind. A couple of hundred metres beyond the village of **BUAHAN**, 2km from the junction with the Penelokan road at Kedisan, *Hotel Baruna* (☎0366/51221; ❶) was barely open at the time of writing and the rooms were terribly neglected, but it's worth considering for the views alone, which are glorious.

From here the road edges between the lake and the cliffs, which rise up into the mass of Gunung Abang, and finally ends at the tiny village of **ABANG**, where a couple of shops sell soft drinks. From Abang, there's a lakeside footpath to Trunyan (4km).

### Trunyan

Inhabited by the Bali Aga people who rejected the changes brought about by the Majapahit invasion in 1343 (see p.444), the village of **TRUNYAN** and its nearby cemetery at Kuban are a well-established tourist attraction. Situated right beside Danau Batur with Gunung Abang rising up sheer behind, there are two routes to the village: by boat from Kedisan or by a three-kilometre footpath from Abang village. The **boat trip** is beautiful but chilly and takes less than an hour. Boats leave from the pier at Kedisan; tourists must charter them, at a cost (advertised as including a guide and all donations) of Rp196,500 for a boat for one, Rp99,500 per person for two people, Rp67,175 per person for three people – and so on, up to a maximum of seven people, at Rp30,335 per person. They complete a circuit from the pier to Trunyan village, on to the cemetery, then Toya Bungkah and back to Kedisan.

The origin of the name "Trunyan" is open to dispute. Some say it derives from *taru*, meaning wood, and *munyan*, meaning perfume, referring to the banyan tree in the cemetery; others claim it derives from *turun hyang*, meaning descendants from heaven. There's no doubt that Trunyan was inhabited in ancient times: ninth-century copper inscriptions refer to a statue of a god named Bhatara Da Tonta that must be bathed, painted and decorated with jewellery. This possibly refers to a four-metre-high **statue** in the village temple, called Da Tonta by the people of Trunyan.

The village keeps many of the ancient **Bali Aga customs**, most notoriously the traditional way of disposing of the dead, which involves bodies being placed in open pits covered only by a cloth and a rough bamboo roof and left to decompose in the air. The banyan tree in Trunyan's tiny **cemetery** at Kabuan, just north of the village and accessible only by boat, supposedly prevents the corpses from smelling. For many tourists, this is the reason for their visit, but all you're likely to see are a few artfully arranged bones and skulls, the towering banyan tree and the covered graves.

Apart from growing cabbages and onions, the village's main source of income is from tourists, and although the boat fee is supposed to include donations you'll be asked for more. Some people have even been pressed for a donation to be allowed to leave. While it's easy to suggest you stand firm on these demands, Trunyan can feel rather isolated and forbidding; you'd do well to make sure you have plenty of small notes to give away.

## Routes to the north coast

It's a long 40km from Kintamani down the busy main road through the foothills to the **north coast** at Kubutambahan, one of the main north–south routes across the island. There's some pretty scenery, with more mountains to the west and verdant valleys and forested ridges gradually descending to the coast. The vegetation changes, too, as the hardier, high-altitude vegetables and crops give way to more tropical growth.

The village of **PENGINYAHAN**, 19km from Kintamani, makes a good stopping place. *Restoran Coffeebreak*, owned by a Balinese–Dutch family, Ketut Widiada and his wife Paula, is just beside the road offering inexpensive Indonesian **food** and drinks. There are two small losmen rooms with hot-water bathrooms in a pretty garden below the road where you can **stay** (no fixed price, discuss with the owners). Down in the valley there are three **waterfalls**, the most impressive being Mesanti, about 40m high and surrounded by lush forest in an unspoiled location; the river isn't suitable for swimming, though. You can trek from the warung to Mesanti (2hr each way), although it's possible to drive part of the way and then walk about half an hour each way. The warung staff can give you directions or provide a guide (Rp50,000 for the short trek or Rp150,000 for the longer one, including some simple food).

From Penginyahan downwards the temperature increases; another forty minutes or so brings you to the north coast at Kubutambahan, from where Singaraja is 11km west and Air Sanih is 6km east.

## The back road to Bondalem

To avoid the busy main road, you can follow a **back road** to the north coast that delivers you to Bondalem, east of Air Sanih. It's a narrow, twisting and very steep 16km, but with private transport it's an attractive road through the countryside with some lovely views. It leaves the main road at the village of Lateng, 13km from the market at Kintamani, and 500m after the end of the village of Dausa; there's a sign pointing to Bondalem. The main road swings left on a sharp bend and there's a row of shops on the right at the start of this side road; it's worth checking if you've got the correct turning (which is known locally as the Tejakula road).

The road initially descends through vegetable gardens and stands of cloves, cocoa, coffee and avocado in the cool highlands, with great views of nearby villages on neighbouring ridges and westwards to the area around Gunung Batukau. There are few villages; **MADENAN** is a neat, cool settlement about 10km of the way down. After this, the temperature rises significantly, and coconut plantations stretch into the distance all the way to the north coast. The road reaches the main north-coast road at the village of **BONDALEM** (see p.321 for information on accommodation in the area). It's 15km west to Air Sanih, and 36km east to Tulamben via Sembirenteng and Tembok.

# The Bedugul region

Neither as big nor as dramatic as the Batur region, the Danau Bratan area, sometimes just known as **Bedugul**, has impressive mountains, beautiful lakes, quiet walks and attractive temples. The area is very much an Indonesian destination: farmers make offerings to Dewi Danu, the goddess of the crater lake, at **Pura Ulun Danu Bratan** on the shores of **Danau Bratan**, while lowland dwellers come to the **Bali Botanical Gardens** in Candikuning for picnics, and to enjoy the watersports on offer at the **Taman Rekreasi Bedugul** (Bedugul Leisure Park) on the shores of Danau Bratan. The entire area is frequently referred to as Bedugul or Bratan, but it's very spread out: Bedugul is, strictly speaking, the small area on the shore of Danau Bratan occupied by the Taman Rekreasi.

Danau Bratan nestles in the lee of Gunung Catur, on the main Denpasar–Mengwi–Singaraja road 53km north of Denpasar and 30km south of Singaraja; no direct route links it to Batur. Approaching from the south, the road rises

## Cloves

It was the search for **cloves**, among other spices, that first drove Europeans to explore the Indonesian archipelago, and for hundreds of years they were one of the region's most lucrative exports. Native to certain islands of the Moluccas (the original "Spice Islands") clove production is now centred in Maluku, Sumatra, Sulawesi and Bali. You'll spot the tall trees in the mountains around Bedugul, and if you're there during harvest time in August and September you'll see huge piles of cloves beside the road – buds that must be picked before the petals open, after which the amount of clove oil declines sharply.

Today, Bali's cloves are shipped to factories in Java where they're used in the manufacture of Indonesia's pungent **kretek cigarettes**. These consist of up to fifty percent cloves mixed with tobacco, and demand is so great that the former clove capital of the world now imports them from Madagascar and Zanzibar to supplement local production.

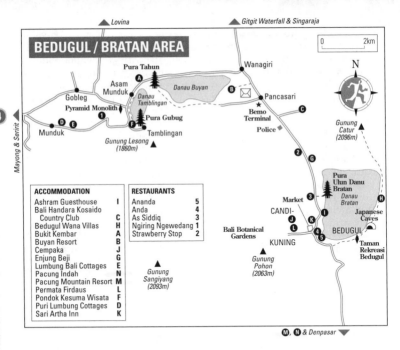

▲ Lovina          ▲ Gitgit Waterfall & Singaraja

# BEDUGUL / BRATAN AREA

0          2km

N

Pura Tahun

Ⓐ          Wanagiri

Asam          Danau Buyan          Ⓑ
Munduk          ✉
Gobleg          Danau          ● Pancasari
Pyramid Monolith          Tamblingan          ★          Ⓒ
Ⓞ          ✚ Pura Gubug          Bemo          Gunung
          Terminal          Catur
Munduk          Ⓓ Ⓔ          Ⓕ          Tamblingan          Police ⚓          (2096m)
Gunung Lesong          Ⓖ
(1860m)          Ⓖ          Pura

          Ⓞ          Ulun Danu
          Bratan
Market          Danau
CANDI-          Bratan
          Ⓗ
          Japanese
          Caves
Bali Botanical          BEDUGUL
Gardens          ⓀⒿ
KUNING          ⒷⓁ          Taman
          Rekreasi
Gunung          Bedugul
Pohon
(2063m)

▲
Gunung
Sangiyang
(2093m)

| ACCOMMODATION | | RESTAURANTS | |
|---|---|---|---|
| Ashram Guesthouse | I | Ananda | 5 |
| Bali Handara Kosaido | | Anda | 4 |
| Country Club | C | As Siddiq | 3 |
| Bedugul Wana Villas | H | Ngiring Ngewedang | 1 |
| Bukit Kembar | A | Strawberry Stop | 2 |
| Buyan Resort | B | | |
| Cempaka | J | | |
| Enjung Beji | G | | |
| Lumbung Bali Cottages | E | | |
| Pacung Indah | N | | |
| Pacung Mountain Resort | M | | |
| Permata Firdaus | L | | |
| Pondok Kesuma Wisata | F | | |
| Puri Lumbung Cottages | D | | |
| Sari Artha Inn | K | | |

Ⓜ, Ⓝ & Denpasar ▼

from the tropical heat into cooler temperatures through a series of small villages. **Pacung** offers accommodation; just north of it, near the market in **Baturiti**, a road is signed to Senganan, which takes a picturesque route through Jatiluwih to the Batukau region (see p.355). The main road completes another steep 8km north to the rim of an ancient volcanic crater at the market village of **Candikuning** from where it descends through the village of **Pancasari**, skirting the western shore of Danau Bratan. It then climbs again to the pass out of the crater at **Wanagiri** (known locally as Puncak), where it begins the steep descent to the northern plains. The smaller, quieter **Danau Buyan** and **Danau Tamblingan** lie about 6km northwest of Danau Bratan.

All the lakes have superbly situated shoreside temples, and the area is dotted with attractive villages. Most tourists visit as part of a roundtrip including

## Trekking around Bedugul

The Bedugul area offers plenty of opportunities for **trekking**; you can ask at your accommodation for a local guide, although they generally don't advertise, or at the ticket offices for Danau Buyan and Danau Tamblingan. Alternatively, agencies in Toya Bungkah run treks in the Bedugul area: Roijaya Wisata (℡0366/51249, ⓔJero_Wijaya@hotmail.com); Bali Sunrise 2001, at the *Volcano Breeze Café* (℡0366/51824 or 0818/552669, ⓦwww.balisunrise2001.com); and *Arlina's* (℡0366/51165). For example, Bali Sunrise 2001 offer a seven-hour trek from **Bedugul** to Gitgit via lakes Buyan and Tamblingan ($85–$100 per person depending where they pick you up) and Roijaya Wisata arrange day-treks in the area ($40 per person) and overnight trips ($100). Sobek also offer jungle trekking around Bedugul (see ⓦwww.99bali .com/adventure/sobek for more information). *Puri Lumbung* and *Lumbung Bali Cottages* (see p.313) in Munduk also arrange treks in the area.

Danau Batur and the north coast; relatively few stay overnight, although there's a reasonable range of accommodation. There are **bus** services to and from Denpasar (Ubung; 1hr 30min) and Singaraja (Sukasada; 1hr 30min); however, having your own transport means you can enjoy the glorious road that passes north of lakes Buyan and Tamblingan before heading to the north coast via Munduk and Mayong, or explore the peaceful backroads to the west of Danau Tamblingan.

## Candikuning and Danau Bratan

The small village of **CANDIKUNING**, situated above the southern shores of Danau Bratan, is home to one of the gems of central Bali, the **Bali Botanical Gardens**.

Candikuning's pretty, little daily **market**, Bukit Mungsu, offers fruit, spices and plants, including orchids. There's a **wartel** (daily 8am–9.30pm) in the market. You can **change money** at the moneychangers in the market or in the car park at Pura Ulun Danu Bratan. For **tourist shuttle bus** tickets (see p.335 for journey details), the Perama office (☎0368/21011) is at the *Sari Artha* losmen, just below the market on the main road in Candikuning. There's one daily service to the north and one to the south (Rp30,000). It's also possible to arrange charter transport (at the *Ashram Guesthouse*, for example); it's around Rp150,000 per car to Lovina, Ubud, Kuta and other southern resorts.

### Accommodation

Most accommodation in the area is in or near Candikuning village, although there are a few options slightly further afield.

**Ashram Guesthouse** ☎0368/21450. Its location on the lakeside makes this large place a winner. There's a range of options from basic rooms boasting shared cold-water bathrooms to comfortable bungalows with hot water. ②–④

**Bali Handara Kosaido Country Club** ☎0362/22646, ⓦwww.balihandarakosaido.com. Accessed from the main road north of Danau Bratan, 6km from Bedugul, the centrepiece of this luxury establishment is its world-famous golf course: a 6434-yard par 72, which claims to be the only one in the world situated in the crater of a volcano. Rooms are well furnished with lots of natural wood, and have heating and fabulous views over the course. Other facilities include tennis courts, a fitness centre and a spa. The view of Danau Buyan from the bar is glorious but, unless you have transport, it's a two-kilometre walk up the drive. It's $100 for a round of golf (guests half-price); equipment rental is extra. ⑦–⑨

**Bedugul Wana Villas** ☎081/734 8866. Enquire at the restaurant down by the lakeside in the Taman Rekreasi Bedugul. These thatched cottages, all with hot water, are on the far side of the lake, clearly visible across the water and accessed by boat from Bedugul. Transport is included in the price. ⑧

**Cempaka** ☎0368/21402. Quiet, budget place just behind *Permata Firdaus* off the road to the Botanical Gardens. Accommodation is in a two-storey block, and pricier rooms upstairs have hot water. ②

**Enjung Beji** ☎0368/21490, ⑦21022. Accommodation in well-furnished cottages set in an attractive garden; less expensive ones are on the way down to the compound. All have hot water. ⑥

**Pacung Indah** ☎0368/21020, ⑦21964. Situated 9km south of Bedugul, just before the village of Pacung. Just four bungalows and suites, all with hot water and some with self-catering facilities, with fine views from the communal terrace. ⑤–⑥

**Pacung Mountain Resort** ☎0368/21038, ⑦21043. Across the road from *Pacung Indah*. More expensive rooms have a fabulous panorama across the local fields and there are top-end bungalows situated down in the ricefields; a cable car brings guests up to the main buildings, and there's also a pretty little swimming pool. It can feel a bit forlorn if there aren't many guests but springs to life when groups pass through. ⑧–⑨

**Permata Firdaus** ☎0368/21531. Just off the road to the Botanical Gardens, offering good-value rooms with hot water. ②

**Sari Artha Inn** ☎0368/21011. Situated north of the market, there's a choice of rooms with or without hot water, all with verandas, set in a pretty garden but with no views. The Perama office is here. ①–②

## Bali Botanical Gardens

A short walk south from the Bukit Mungsu market area in Candikuning, along a small side road by the giant corn-on-the-cob, are the **Bali Botanical Gardens** (Kebun Raya Eka Karya Bali; daily 8am–6pm; Rp3500; parking for cars Rp1500, for motorbikes Rp500; entry for cars Rp6000; motorbikes prohibited). The gardens, a branch of the National Botanical Gardens at Bogor on Java, were set up in 1959 and cover more than 150 hectares on the slopes of Gunung Pohon (Tree Mountain). There are more than a thousand species of plants including **trees**, **bamboo** and **orchids**. The gardens are also a rich area for **bird-watching** (see box, below).

At weekends it gets busy, but during the week you'll see few visitors. There's a map near the entrance and visitors receive an information leaflet detailing the three temples in the grounds, which can be an attractive focus for exploration. The gardens are a centre for the study of the plants of the region, and there's also a herbarium and a library. Serious students should contact the gardens beforehand: Eka Karya Botanic Gardens Bali, Indonesian Institute of Sciences, Candikuning, Baturiti, Tabanan 82191, Bali (☎0368/21273).

## Danau Bratan

Situated at 1200m above sea level and thought to be 35m deep in places, **Danau Bratan** is surrounded by forested hills, with the bulk of Gunung Catur rising sheer behind. The lake becomes frenetic with watersports on holidays and at weekends – although the scenery more than compensates for the buzz of motorboats.

The lake (and its goddess) are worshipped in the temple of **Pura Ulun Danu Bratan** (daily 7am–5pm; Rp3300, cars Rp1500), one of the most photographed temples in Bali and the highly revered *kayangan jagat* (directional temple) for the northwest. Built in 1633 by the raja of Mengwi on a small promontory on the western shore of the lake, it's dedicated to Dewi Danu, source of water and hence fertility for the land and people of Bali. The temple consists of several shrines spread along the shore and perched on small islands. On the mainland, Pura Teratai Bang is the main compound, featuring a seven-roofed *meru* dedicated to Brahma. The real highlights, though, are the island shrines, which appear to float on the surface of the lake, with the mountains

---

### The birds of Bedugul

The Bali Botanical Gardens and the southern shores of Danau Bratan are fringed by montane forest and home to an amazing variety of **birds**. The most common sightings are of the forest-dwelling **grey-cheeked green pigeons** and **blue-crowned barbets**, almost entirely green in colour with a blue crown and yellow forehead. The barbet is found only on Java and Bali, and you'll often hear its monotonous call from high in the forest canopy. You're also likely to see **flycatchers**, especially the snowy-browed flycatcher, which has a distinctive white line above the eye, a slate-blue back and orange breast. It pays to stand near flowering or fruiting trees and watch, as they attract a whole range of different birds: the gregarious **Philippine glossy starling**, with its greenish-purple feathers, feeds in fruiting trees, while the tiny **yellow-throated hanging parrot**, green with a red rump, heads for buds and flowers. The **collared kingfisher** is also a regular in the area, a noisy bird, frequently heard before it is seen, giving a loud "chek chek" call. Iridescent blue-green in colour with white underparts and a white collar, it hunts for lizards, large insects and frogs in open areas near water.

## Climbing Gunung Catur

The path up **Gunung Catur** (2096m), sometimes called Gunung Mangu, is easy to find and as long as you don't visit on a festival day, is unlikely to be overrun by people. To reach it, turn away from the lake just past the third of the Japanese caves and take the short track that zigzags up onto the ridge, about 20m above. It hits another, bigger path heading along the ridge; turn left onto this path and simply follow it – and the trail of litter – to the top of Catur. The climb is through shady forest with some tantalizing glimpses of the lake below; allow two to three hours' fairly unrelenting uphill climb (in a couple of places, you'll need to haul yourself up by the tree trunks). Take plenty of water and some snacks and let somebody responsible know where you're going. It should take about an hour and a half to get down again.

At the **summit**, Pura Pucak Mangu, supposedly built by the first raja of Mengwi, is a small forest temple with three-roofed and five-roofed *meru*, surrounded by yellow canna lilies and inhabited by a troop of grey monkeys. A small path from the back of the temple heads down the other side of the mountain, which eventually descends to the main road above Pancasari, but this is wild and uninhabited country and you'd need a **guide** (ask at your accommodation).

rising behind. Closest to the bank, the eleven-roofed *meru* is dedicated to Wisnu and Dewi Danu, and the three-roofed *meru* just beyond it houses an ancient *lingam* to Siwa.

### Taman Rekreasi Bedugul

The **Taman Rekreasi Bedugul** (daily 8am–5pm; Rp3300, cars Rp1500, motorbikes Rp600), on the southern shores of the lake, is signed "Bedugul" from the main road. You can indulge in waterskiing, parasailing and jet-skiing ($10 for 15min or for one lift if parasailing) or rent a speedboat (Rp65,000 for once round the lake) or rowing boat (Rp70,000 per hour). Private boat operators linger near the Taman Rekreasi and the *Ashram Guesthouse*; with a bit of bargaining you'll get a boat for about Rp50,000 per hour.

From the Taman Rekreasi you can walk around the shoreline (walk to the right facing the lake) for a few hundred metres to three **caves**, supposedly dug by Indonesian labourers for the Japanese during World War II; it's said that when the caves were completed, the labourers were shot. You'll need a torch to see anything (you can just wander in), but there's not much there.

### Eating and drinking

Most **restaurants** in the area cater for the passing **lunchtime** trade. The restaurant at the *Pacung Indah* hotel has the best views in the area, accompanying its buffet for Rp55,000 per person. For less expensive food, a row of stalls lines the road where it runs along the lakeside south of Pura Ulun Danu Bratan, and the warung in the temple car park are worth a try. *As Siddiq*, about 100m north of the car park on the opposite side of the road is a popular place serving Taliwang and Sasak food. In addition, several inexpensive places line the road to the Botanical Gardens. *Strawberry Stop*, 2km towards Pancasari, serves the strawberries that grow in the market garden behind the restaurant – with cream or ice-cream, in milkshakes or in pancakes.

In the **evenings**, most places close around 8pm. In Candikuning, *Ananda* and *Anda* just across the road from the turning to the Botanical Gardens are both a good bet, offering a range of inexpensive Indonesian and Chinese food.

# Danau Buyan

The best way to explore **Danau Buyan**, 6km northwest of Bedugul, is on foot, although you can drive part way on the side road that heads west just to the north of the Pancasari bemo terminal. This is lined with houses with beautifully carved household shrines, and leads just over a kilometre to the parking area and ticket office (Rp3000, parking Rp1000). There are plenty of tracks in the area: Pura Tahun at the western end of the lake makes a reasonable focus for exploration and there's a track over to Danau Tamblingan across a raised shoulder of land. Don't wander too far off the beaten track on your own – it's extremely easy to lose your sense of direction in the densely forested terrain.

The only **accommodation** close to Danau Buyan is *Buyan Resort* (☏0362/21351, 🖷21388; ❽) with two-bedroom, self-catering cottages in lovely gardens at the east end of the lake, accessed from the main road south of Wanagiri.

# Danau Tamblingan and beyond

To reach **Danau Tamblingan**, take the road west from **WANAGIRI**, 2km north of Pancasari, which runs along the ridge above the northern shore of Danau Buyan.

About 4km from Wanagiri, *Bukit Kembar* (☏08523/710 0952, 📧princessdayu@yahoo.com; ❹) has six simple rooms with hot water; there's an attached restaurant and extremely fine views from the sitting area just across the road. This is where the road passes above the shoulder of land separating Danau Buyan and Danau Tamblingan, the site of the spring that feeds them.

About 3km beyond *Bukit Kembar*, the road divides at a monolithic, seemingly granite, **pyramid**, actually built some years ago from recycled plastic. Take the left fork and it's another 2km down to the small village of **TAMBLINGAN**, where people make their living from growing vegetables, fishing for carp and rearing cattle on the *tunjung* (lotus) that grows on the lake. *Pondok Kesuma Wisata* ⚑ (☏0828/365225; ❾) has new bungalows with hot water in a lovely garden. Larger villas for families or groups are also available. A hundred metres or so further on is the parking area and ticket office for **Danau Tamblingan** (Rp3000, parking Rp1000), from where it's ten minutes' walk down to the lakeside. On the shore, **Pura Gubug**, sporting eleven-, nine- and five-roofed *meru*, is dedicated to Dewi Danu. Farmers come here on pilgrimages to the three lakeside temples of Batur, Bratan and Tamblingan to worship the lake goddess and pray for good harvests. Across the lake, in the trees, you can just see **Pura Dalem Tamblingan**, the temple of the dead. The area is particularly renowned for bird-watching, and you may spot babblers, woodpeckers, ground thrushes and malkohas if you take the path around the western edge of the lake to the temple.

### The scenic route to the north coast

Back at the pyramid above Tamblingan, the main road from Wanagiri turns away from the lakes as it continues west and descends through coffee fields and roads lined with clove trees. Just over a kilometre further on you'll come to the restaurant *Ngiring Ngewedang*, a great place to stop, with a glorious panorama across the whole of the west of the island. The restaurant has a small moderately priced menu of Indo-Chinese favourites with a few Western choices. You can also see all the stages of the coffee process here in miniature, from the green beans to the production of the box of ground coffee for sale. The road continues on down to Munduk.

**Munduk activities**

A huge number of **activities** can be arranged at *Puri Lumbung Cottages* in Munduk, including local trekking and sightseeing (US$3–8.50 per hour for a guide for a group). The **treks** on offer take in waterfalls, springs, villages, coffee and clove plantations, rivers, *subak*, lakes and temples. An equally diverse variety of **sightseeing** trips are available, as is **horse-riding**. Other activities and classes include massage ($8–12/hr), Balinese Yoga Meditation (from $35/hr, including translator), cooking ($24 per person for an all-day class), Indonesian language, weaving, fruit and flower arranging, woodcarving, dancing and musical instrument classes ($8.50–20/hr depending on the size of the group) and spiritual discussions ($20/hr). Many of these activities are also available through *Lumbung Bali Cottages*.

An **alternative scenic route**, even further off the beaten track, takes the road signed "Gobleg" from above Danau Tamblingan, 1.8km north of the pyramid. It descends past slopes rich in banana, durian, papaya and jackfruit trees, to Gobleg and then Asah Gobleg and then north down through Selat before reaching the coast at **Anturan** towards the east of Lovina. Take a good-quality road map to explore these byways.

### Munduk and around

Three kilometres down from *Ngiring Ngewedang* there's a small sign for **Munduk waterfall**. The falls are far more impressive than the falls at the more famous Gitgit; this is an attractive spot, only one of several waterfalls in the area – anyone staying at *Puri Lumbung Cottages* or *Lumbung Bali Cottages* (see box) can arrange a trek to the others.

A kilometre north is the village of **MUNDUK**, an excellent base for exploring the area. Munduk's most established **place to stay** is *Puri Lumbung Cottages* (☎0362/92810, ⓦwww.purilumbung.com; ❼–❾), where accommodation is in replicas of traditional *lumbung* (rice-storage barns) that used to stand on the site. They have hot water, fabulous views, are extremely well furnished and sit in lovely grounds. There's a moderately priced **restaurant** attached. *Puri Lumbung Cottages* also administer several local **homestays** (❺) in Munduk village. These aren't luxurious, nor are they cheap, but all have hot water and breakfast included. A few hundred metres south, the more recently established *Lumbung Bali Cottages* (☎0362/92818, ⓦwww.lumbungbali.com; ❼) offer comfortable bungalows set in attractive gardens with an attached restaurant. Significant discounts are often available and a range of activities are on offer here as well. There are several warung in the village as an alternative to eating at the hotels.

### On to Mayong

Heading towards the north coast from Munduk you'll pass through the ridge villages of Gunung Sariand Banyuatis before reaching **MAYONG** (see p.334 for details of a detour inland from here through Bestala), where there's a small restaurant, *Bali Panorama* (☎081/756 3007, ⓔmayong-bali@yahoo.com), beside the road. The views across the local paddy-fields are stunning and this is a great spot. It's generally open 9am to 5pm but will open for dinner on request. It's a lovely little organic restaurant with inexpensive to moderately priced drinks, snacks and main courses. *Bali Panorama* also organize local treks of two or six hours (from Rp50,000 per hour depending on the group size) and three-hour cooking classes (Rp175,000 per person); contact them in advance to arrange these activities. From Mayong, the road continues north to **Seririt** on the north coast.

# The north coast

The **north coast** of Bali is a rugged and, in places, dramatic landscape, the northern flanks of the mountains dropping steeply towards sweeping black-sand beaches. The land is parched towards the east, where lava flows from the last eruption of Gunung Agung are still visible. To the west, more fertile territory supports a greater population density and there are some finely sculpted rice terraces.

The major north-coast settlement is **Singaraja**, once the busiest port on the island. Most tourists, however, come to the north for the beach resort of **Lovina**, west of Singaraja, a great place to relax or to use as a base for exploring the temples, hot springs and inland scenery of the region.

## Some history

While the north coast of Bali has been inhabited for centuries, with local villages mentioned in tenth-century inscriptions, the ascendancy of the area really began at the end of the sixteenth century, when **Ki Gusti Ngurah Panji Sakti** founded Buleleng. In 1604, he built a new palace called Singaraja and went on to gain control of Karangasem, Jembrana and parts of eastern Java, in addition to his own kingdom. These dominions expanded even further when, in 1711, the throne was taken by his son-in-law **Gusti Agung Sakti**, the raja of Mengwi, who established a joint Mengwi–Buleleng kingdom, which flourished for most of the eighteenth century.

In 1846, the invading **Dutch** directed their First Military Expedition against the north of the island. After the Balinese defeat in 1849, the Dutch began to administer Buleleng. This encouraged more Europeans, including journalists, merchants and scholars, to visit and settle in the area, while the south of the island was still battling against the Dutch. In attempting to make the colony profitable, the Dutch built roads, improved irrigation systems and encouraged coffee as a cash crop in the north. However, it was not all plain sailing: in 1864, **Ida Made Rai** rebelled in Banjar, near Seririt, and it took the Dutch until 1868 to subdue him and his followers.

As the Dutch strengthened their hold, the administrative importance of the north grew. When Bali and Lombok were combined in one regency by the Dutch in 1882, their capital was established in Singaraja. During World War II, the invading **Japanese** also made their headquarters here, but when the Dutch subsequently returned to the island, they moved their capital to Denpasar due to its proximity to the new airport and the larger population.

# Singaraja and around

The second largest Balinese city after Denpasar, **SINGARAJA** has an airy spaciousness created by its broad avenues, impressive monuments and colonial bungalows set in attractive gardens. With a population of over 100,000, it's home to a mix of Hindus, Muslims and Buddhists. Behind the old harbour you can still see the shophouses and narrow streets of the original trading area; Jalan Hasanuddin is known locally as Kampung Bugis and Jalan Imam Bonjol as Kampung Arab after the Muslim Bugis settlers from Sulawesi whose descendants still live in the area.

Accommodation isn't great in Singaraja and there aren't many sights, but you can spend a few interesting hours exploring this pleasant, tourist-friendly town, best done as a day-trip from Lovina. There is also straightforward access from Singaraja to all points eastwards, including the fabulous temples of **Pura Meduwe Karang** – best of the bunch – or **Sangsit**, **Jagaraga** or **Bebitin**, and it's easy to carry on round the north coast to Amlapura via the small resort of **Air Sanih** and the diving village of **Tulamben**.

## Arrival, orientation and information

Singaraja has three bus and bemo terminals: **Sukasada** (locally called Sangket) to the south of the town, serving Gitgit, Bedugul and Denpasar (Ubung terminal); **Banyuasri** on the western edge of town serving the west, including Lovina, Seririt and Gilimanuk; and **Penarukan** in the east, for services eastwards along the coast via Tulamben to Amlapura, and inland along the road to Kintamani, Penelokan (for the Batur area) and on to Denpasar via

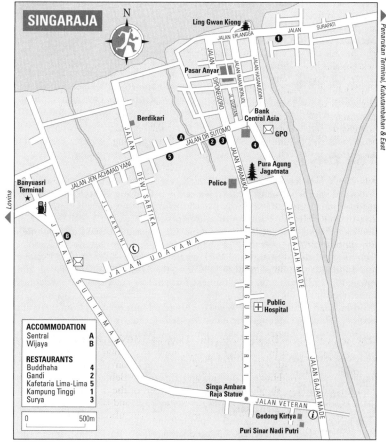

Sukasada Terminal, Beratan & Bedugul ▼

Bangli. For information on travelling to and from **Ngurah Rai Airport**, see the box on p.114.

Small bemos (flat rate Rp2000) ply main routes around town linking two of the terminals – brown between Banyuasri and Penarukan, red between Sukasada and Banyuasri, and blue between Sukasada and Penarukan – with destinations marked on the back of the vehicle. There are no metered taxis in Singaraja, but plenty of dokar; negotiate the destination and price before you get in.

Spread out along the coast and stretching inland for several kilometres, it helps to remember that the town's main thoroughfare of **Jalan Jen Achmad Yani / Jalan Dr Sutomo** is oriented east–west and will eventually take you out onto the road to Lovina, while **Jalan Gajah Made** is oriented north–south and heads, via Sukasada, inland to Bedugul. The area around the major junction where these two main roads meet has hotels, restaurants, banks, post office, telephone office and night market all within walking distance: it feels as much like the town centre as anywhere.

The **tourist office** is south of the town centre at Jl Veteran 23 (Mon–Thurs 8.30am–2pm, Fri & Sat 8.30am–1pm; ℡0362/25141, ⓦwww.northbalitourism.net). Staff may be able to produce a brochure, map and calendar of events. Bemos heading to Sukasada terminal pass the eastern end of Jalan Veteran, 100m from the office.

## Accommodation

Most of the **hotels** in Singaraja cater for Indonesian businesspeople, government officers visiting the city or extramarital assignations. One reasonable option for travellers is *Sentral*, Jl Jen Achmad Yani 48 (℡0362/21896; ❶–❷), with fan or air-con rooms with attached cold-water mandi. The biggest place is *Wijaya*, Jl Sudirman 74 (℡0362/21915, ℻25817; ❶–❹), which has the widest range of rooms and is conveniently close to Banyuasri terminal. There's a choice of air-con or fan, and hot water at the top end.

## The City

Singaraja's best-known attraction is esoteric, but surprisingly interesting. A couple of kilometres south of the town centre is **Gedong Kirtya**, Jl Veteran 20 (Mon–Thurs 7am–2.30pm, Fri 7am–noon, Sat 7am–1pm; contribution expected), the only library of **lontar manuscripts** in the world. These are ancient and sacred texts inscribed on leaves from the *lontar* palm (see box, opposite). The library contains over three thousand texts on religion, customs, philosophy, folklore, medicine, astrology and black magic, written in Balinese, Old Javanese and Indonesian. Established by L.J.J. Caron, the Dutch Resident of Bali, and opened in 1928, this is an establishment for scholars, but visitors are welcome; a member of the library staff will show you around. There are also manuscripts from India and Burma as well as *prasasti*, inscribed bronze plates from the tenth century, which are amongst the oldest written records on Bali.

A few hundred metres west, at the junction of Jalan Veteran and Jalan Ngurah Rai, stands the statue of **Singa Ambara Raja**, the winged lion symbol of Buleleng district. A source of great pride to the citizens of Singaraja, you'll see its image all round the city.

Just behind Gedong Kirtya, **Puri Sinar Nadi Putri** (daily 8am–4pm) is a small **weaving factory** producing attractive weft *ikat* cloth. A larger concern is the more central **Berdikari**, Jl Dewi Sartika 42 (daily 7am–7pm), where they produce top-quality silk and cotton *ikat* and their work is highly regarded nationally. Scarves (from Rp250,000) and sarongs (from Rp450,000) are on sale.

## Lontar manuscripts

The leaves of the **lontar palm** or *punyan ental* are prepared for inscription through a lengthy process. After removal of the central rib, the leaves are soaked in water for three days to destroy the chlorophyll and brushed to remove dirt from the surface, before being boiled with traditional herbal ingredients to increase flexibility and strength. At this stage, the leaves are slow-dried to prevent wrinkling and, after being pressed for ten days, are cut to the required size (35–40cm long and 3–4cm wide), and punched with three holes for threading. The palms are then bound between thin wooden boards, pressed, and their edges coloured red with *kincu* to deter insects. Storing for about six months after binding produces the perfect texture.

The text is engraved on the prepared palm using an iron tool with a sharpened tip, and carbon black from a lamp is rubbed into the inscription to make it visible. Due to the humidity on Bali, the manuscripts only last between fifty and a hundred years, so decaying manuscripts are continuously copied onto new palm leaves, ensuring the survival of this ancient art. To see *lontar* palm being inscribed, head to the village of Tenganan in the hills above Candi Dasa (see p.271).

If you want to watch the weavers, come before 4pm. There's a smaller workshop at *Berdikari Cottages* (see p.393), east of Singaraja.

Almost in the middle of town, on Jalan Pramuka, you can't miss the impressive **Pura Agung Jagatnata**, dedicated in 1993. Built on a grand scale, every available surface is covered in a typically northern style of effusive decoration. The *candi bentar* rises dramatically for 15m, and the main shrine, the *padmasana* to the Supreme God, Sang Yang Widi, in the inner courtyard, is even higher. There's a three-metre-tall Ganesh on the pavement outside, draped in a *kain poleng* cloth.

North along Jalan Pramuka, and over the intersection with Jalan Jen Achmad Yani, alleys run down to the market, **Pasar Anyar**, a two-storey maze of stalls and tiny shops selling pretty much everything needed for everyday life. Continue north and you'll reach Singaraja's **waterfront**, site of the ancient harbour of Buleleng. It's hard to imagine the days when this was the busiest port on Bali. A monument here, Yudha Mandala Tama, shows an independence fighter and commemorates an incident in 1945 during the independence struggle when the Balinese resistance attempted to lower a Dutch flag that was flying on the coast. They succeeded but were spotted and fired on by a Dutch navy vessel offshore, killing one; a tiny shrine to Telah Gugur, the man who died, is just around the corner, opposite the local Chinese temple, Ling Gwan Kiong.

## Eating, drinking and nightlife

The largest concentration of **restaurants** is at Jl Jen Achmad Yani 25, in a small square set back from the road; the Chinese restaurant *Gandi* is a good bet, as is *Surya*, at the entrance to the square, selling Padang food. Further west along the same street there's another cluster of places selling inexpensive rice and noodles: *Kafetaria Lima-Lima* at no. 55a is most obvious. Also worth a look during the day is *Buddhaha* on Jalan Gajah Made, just south of the main post office, with inexpensive Indonesian dishes and drinks. For really cheap eats, *Kampung Tinggi*, just east of the bridge on the main road east out of Singaraja, is lined with food stalls every afternoon (2–8pm), some of which have a basic written menu. At the Western end of Singaraja, the restaurants that line Jalan Pemaron Pura Penimbangan are accessible from the city (see p.330 for details).

As darkness falls, the **night market** in the Jalan Durian area springs into life.

With mountains of fruit and vegetables and plenty of bustling food stalls, this is the only local nightlife and a pleasant way to spend the evening.

## Listings

**Banks and exchange** The most central place to change money is Bank Central Asia on Jl Dr Sutomo (exchange counter Mon–Fri 11am–1pm) where you can also get Visa cash advances. The ATM machine outside accepts Visa, MasterCard and Cirrus cards. There are other ATMs in town, including Bank Danamon on Jl Jen Achmad Yani and BII on Jalan Diponegoro.

**Bus tickets (long-distance)** Menggala, Jl Jen Achmad Yani 76 (☎0362/24374), operates daily night buses to Surabaya (Rp80,000; 8hr), leaving at 7pm, arriving at Probolinggo and Pasuruan in East Java, access points for the Bromo region, in the middle of the night. Safari Dharma Raya, Jl Jen Achmad Yani 84 (☎0362/23460), leaves nightly at 6pm for the 24-hour trip to Jakarta (Rp205,000). Gunung Harta sells tickets through *Hotel Merta Yadnya*, Jl Jen Achmad Yani 2 (☎0362/22791), for

daily buses (6pm; 12hr; Rp65,000) to Yogyakarta.

**Doctors & Hospital** Rumah Sakit Umum (the public hospital), Jl Ngurah Rai ☎0362/41046. Many of Singaraja's medical facilities, including doctors and pharmacies, are concentrated on Jl Diponegoro.

**Internet access** At the GPO, Jl Gajah Made 156 (9am–9pm; Rp6000/hr).

**Phones** The main phone office (daily 24hr) is at the southern end of Jalan Kartini. There are wartels on main roads in the city.

**Post office** The GPO is at Jl Gajah Made 156 (Mon–Thurs 8am–4pm, Fri 8am–2pm, Sat 8am–noon). Poste restante service is to the above address, Singaraja 81113, Bali. This is a Western Union agent. A smaller post office is south of *Wijaya* hotel at Jl Sudirman 68a, a short walk from Banyuasri terminal.

## South of Singaraja

Just to the **south** of the city, the village of **BERATAN**, 2km beyond Jalan Veteran towards the Sukasada terminal, is known locally for its silverwork. The shop/workshop Samayaji, Jl Mayor Metri 89–91, is on the main road. Bemos to Sukasada pass the door.

Further south, 10km along the road to Bedugul, are two well-signposted waterfalls at **Gitgit** (daily 8am–5.30pm; Rp3000). All buses between Singaraja (Sukasada terminal) and Denpasar via Bedugul pass the place. A multi-tiered upper fall descends in fairly unimpressive steps and, 2km further north, is a forty-metre single drop, 500m from the road along a path lined with souvenir stalls. Local belief suggests that if you come to Gitgit with your partner you will eventually separate. There's no reason to **stay** here, but if you get stranded there's *Gitgit Hotel* (☎0362/26212, ⊕41840; ②).

## East of Singaraja

Many of the villages and the wealth of carved temples to the **east of Singaraja** can be visited on a day-trip from Singaraja or Lovina. The main sights all lie on bemo routes.

### Sangsit

Some 8km east of Singaraja, a small road north takes you 200m to the pink sandstone **Pura Beji** of **SANGSIT**. Dedicated to Dewi Sri, the rice goddess, it's justly famous for the exuberance of its carvings. The *candi bentar* and the inner *paduraksa* drip with animals, plants and monsters, and both courtyards are decorated with mask carvings.

About 400m to the northeast across the fields from Pura Beji, you'll be able to spot the red roofs of **Pura Dalem Sangsit**. The front wall of the temple shows the rewards that await the godly in heaven and the punishments awaiting the evil in hell. The punishments are vibrantly clear: stone blocks on the head, babies flung into fires, women giving birth to strange creatures, and sharp penises descending through the tops of skulls. The village of Sangsit straggles 500m north from here to a black-sand beach with fishing boats, shops and warung.

### Jagaraga, Sawan and Bebitin

Back on the main road, 500m east of the Sangsit turning, you come to the road heading inland to Jagaraga, Sawan and Bebitin. Bemos go direct to Bebitin from Singaraja (Penarukan terminal), passing through Jagaraga, 4km from the main road, and Sawan on the way; if you're visiting all these places on public transport go up to Bebitin first and then walk downhill to the others.

Near the small village of **BEBITIN**, Pura Bukit Bebitin is located on a hill with fine views. It has been grandly renovated with some splendid new statuary and carvings, all in the exuberant style so characteristic of northern temples. Bring a sarong and scarf and be prepared to make a donation. To reach the temple, take an ojek the final 2km (Rp5000) uphill from the village.

In the village of **SAWAN**, there are a couple of workshops making gamelan. You won't find the smiths at work every day, but you can try out the gamelan instruments, drums and flutes. The four-kilometre road between Sawan and Jagaraga is lined with mango and rambutan trees overlooking fields of rice in the rainy season and tobacco in the dry. There are several energetically carved temples along the route, including Pura Paninjoan, which is guarded by outstandingly ugly monsters.

**JAGARAGA** was the site of an immense battle between the Balinese and the Dutch during the Second Military Expedition in 1848, which the Balinese, led by their commander Jelantik, won with huge loss of life, their 16,000 troops fighting with lances and kris against 3000 well-armed Dutch. The two forces met here again in 1849, when the Dutch finally took control of Buleleng (see p.447). The famous temple here is **Pura Dalem Jagaraga**, about 1km north of the village, dedicated to Siwa the destroyer and renowned for its front walls, which are a mass of pictorial carvings. Those on the left show village life before the Dutch invasion – kite-flying, fishing, climbing coconut trees. Next to these are the Dutch arriving in cars, boats, planes and on bicycles, destroying the community. On the right-hand side is a much-photographed carving of two Dutch men driving a Model T Ford, being held up by bandits. Nearby are statues of uniformed Dutch officers and the legendary Pan Brayut (see box, p.200).

The only **place to stay** is back on the main road, 200m east of the Jagaraga turning. *Hotel Berdikari* (T & F0362/25195; ❷–❹) appears to get few visitors but has two standards of bungalows; cheaper rooms have cold-water bathrooms and fans, and more expensive ones hot water and air-con. There's a small weaving workshop here (7.30am–4pm), owned by the highly regarded Berdikari company that have a larger workshop in Singaraja (see p.316).

### Pura Meduwe Karang

The most spectacular temple in the area is **Pura Meduwe Karang** at **KUBUTAMBAHAN**, 11km east of Singaraja and 300m east of the junction with the Kintamani road. If you only visit one temple in the north, this is the one to go for. Dedicated to Batara Meduwe Karang (the Lord Possessing the Ground), the temple ensures divine protection for crops grown on dry land, such as coconuts, maize and groundnuts. It's built on a grand scale: the terraces at the front support 34 figures from the *Ramayana* and the centrepiece shows the giant Kumbakarna battling with hordes of monkeys from Sugriwa's army.

Inside, the walls are decorated with **carvings** of Balinese folk, including elderly people and mothers with babies. In the inner courtyard, and typical of northern temples, a large rectangular base links the three central shrines, called the *bebaturan*. On the base of this you'll find one of the most famous carvings on Bali: a cyclist (possibly the Dutch artist W.O.J. Nieuwenkamp, who first visited Bali in 1904 and explored the island on a bicycle) wearing floral shorts, with a rat about to go under the back wheel, apparently being chased by a dog.

## Air Sanih and around

Further east, 6km from Kubutambahan, **AIR SANIH**, also known as Yeh Sanih, is a small beach resort that has grown up around the freshwater springs on the coast, although the accommodation is spread out between Air Sanih and the small village of **BUKTI**, 3km to the east. All public transport between Singaraja and Amlapura passes through here. The freezing cold **springs**, in the centre of the village, are believed to originate in Danau Bratan. They are set in attractive gardens with changing rooms (daily 7am–7pm; Rp2000).

### Accommodation

At the time of writing, much of the older accommodation in the area, with the notable exception of *Cilik's Beach Garden*, had been affected by the downturn in tourism and was looking sadly neglected. Be ready to hunt around a bit for the cleanest room.

**Cilik's Beach Garden** ☎ & ℗0362/26561, ⓦwww.ciliksbeachgarden.com. 200m east of the springs, and the real gem in the area, with two bungalows, one villa and one *lumbung*-style cottage. All have hot water and are set in fabulous gardens overlooking the coast – a truly magical hideaway. ❼–❽

**Cleopatra** ☎0812/362 2232. About 1.5km west of the springs on the south side of the road. New fan and cold-water bungalows, exuberantly decorated and set in a huge garden. ❷

**Puri Rahayu** ☎0362/26565. Just over 200m east of the springs and across the road from the beach, with bungalows in a small compound and a res-

taurant attached. Cheapest rooms have fan, more expensive ones air-con. All have cold water. ❶–❷

**Hotel Puri Sanih** The most convenient place to stay next to the beach and the springs, all rooms with fan and cold water. ❷

**Hotel Tara** ☎0362/26575. On the coast 600m east of the springs, with a row of basic tiled bungalows with a choice of fan or air-con all facing seawards. The location is the big plus here. ❷–❸

**Royal Bali Arsanih** ☎0362/26560. Just over 2km east of the springs, offering hot water and air-con in all bungalows and a small swimming pool. The nicest rooms have a sea view from their verandas. There's an attached restaurant. ❺–❻

### East from Air Sanih

About 12km east of Air Sanih, the road climbs over a headland at **PONJOK BATU** with great views along the coast. The **temple** here was founded by the sixteenth-century Javanese priest **Nirartha** (see pp.142, 345 and 357). According to the story, while sitting on a rock Nirartha saw a wrecked ship below. All the crew were dead on the beach but, using his spiritual powers, he brought them back to life. Following this miracle, the local people noticed that the rock where Nirartha had been sitting shone with a magical light and a temple was founded here. Now, all Balinese drivers stop to pray and receive a blessing for themselves and their vehicle.

About 100m west of the temple, *Puri Bagus Ponjok Batu* is a small **restaurant** linked to the *Puri Bagus* hotel in Lovina, perched on the hillside above the road with lovely coastal views. There's a small menu of moderately priced Indonesian food and plenty of drinks; you can wander a short distance up the hill to a small reservoir with even better views in all directions.

A kilometre west of the temple it's impossible to miss the exuberant decoration on the outside of the **Art Zoo**, the northern gallery of the Balinese artist **Symon** (ⓦ www.symonbali.com), who also has a gallery in Ubud (see p.202).

Less than 1km east of the temple, in the village of **ALASSARI**, *Pondok Sembiran Bungalows* (℡0362/24437, ℻21108; ❺), signed towards the coast from the main road, is an attractive set-up in a quiet location. All accommodation has air-con and hot water, some is by the beach and some about 300m inland, and there's a pretty pool.

Continuing east, the land becomes increasingly dry and barren, and views of the outer rim of the Batur crater dominate the inland skyline. At Pacung, 2km east of Ponjok Batu, a sign points off the main road to **SEMBIRAN**, reached by a narrow lane (3km). This is one of the ancient Bali Aga villages, along with Trunyan (see p.305) and Tenganan (see p.271), but today little distinguishes it from any other village in Bali.

### Bondalem and around

Another kilometre east brings you to **BONDALEM**. On the west side of the village is *Bali Mandala Resort and Bungalows* (℡0362/28508, ⓦwww.balimandala.com; ❻ all inclusive) in a great coastal location with a small swimming pool and good snorkelling off the beach. All bungalows have hot water, and there's a two-storey restaurant, with lovely views, serving Balinese and international food. There are often groups here who come for courses in meditation, yoga and such like, but individuals seeking peace and quiet are also welcome – but do call in advance. There is a **wellness centre**, and **ayurvedic massage** is available. *Bali Mandala* is signposted from the main road, but as it's 800m through a maze of lanes you'll probably need to ask for directions on the way. On the eastern side of Bondalem village a sign indicates a quiet **back road** that leads 26km up to Kintamani.

The small village of **TEJAKULA**, 3km east of Bondalem, is worth a stop for its **horse bath**, a white stone confection of arches and pillars 100m south of the road, no longer used for its original purpose. The village is a sleepy backwater these days but local historians claim that the area had trading links with distant lands as far back as the first century AD, when it far outstripped the later trading ports of Padang Bai and Benoa in fame and influence; numerous local finds of foreign relics support their case. There's excellent accommodation here at *Bali Beach Villas* (℡0362/26561, ⓦwww.cbg-tejakula.com; ❽), an outpost of *Cilik's Beach Garden* in Air Sanih. There are two comfortable, beautifully furnished bungalows right on the beach with fine coastal views. Look out for the sign announcing "*CBG Beach Resort*" pointing seawards at the western end of the village.

A few kilometres beyond here at **LES**, a sign points inland to **Yeh Mempeh**, questionably dubbed the highest waterfall in Bali.

### Sembirenteng and Tembok

About 8km beyond Tejakula, just east of **SEMBIRENTENG**, is *Alam Anda* (℡0812/465 6485, ⓦwww.alamanda.de; ❼–❽), right beside the beach, with a pretty pool and a dedicated **massage** house with ayurvedic massage a speciality. The **restaurant** is cool and breezy, serving a good range of moderate to expensively priced Western and Indonesian food. It's a good place to stop on a drive along the north coast but phone first as they don't open to non-residents if the hotel is busy. The **accommodation** is in bungalows with hot and cold water and fan, or losmen-style rooms with fan and cold water. One bungalow has been modified for wheelchair users. **Diving**, both locally and at other north-coast sites, is available (from $30), as are cookery courses.

About 4km further east at **TEMBOK**, the top-class *Jepun Bali Resort* (℡08133/852 6692, ⓦwww.jepun-bali.com; ❽–❾) offers excellently appointed accommodation in minimalist Bali-modern style. The pool is glorious, landscaping is superb and there's a spa (10am–6pm) where day-visitors are welcome. However, it's pretty isolated. From here, it's 22km east to Tulamben.

# Lovina and around

**LOVINA** stretches along 8km of black-sand beach, the largest resort in Bali outside the Kuta–Legian–Seminyak conurbation. Beginning 6km west of Singaraja, the resort encompasses six villages: from east to west, **Pemaron**, **Tukad Mungga**, **Anturan**, **Kalibukbuk**, **Kaliasem** and **Temukus**. Kalibukbuk is the centre of Lovina and has the greatest concentration of accommodation and restaurants, located on several roads, including one about 1.5km east known as **Banyualit**, leading down to the coast from the main road. While the peak season (June–Aug & Dec) is busy, Lovina remains far less frantic than the southern resorts, although there's some nightlife available.

The potential of the area was spotted by the last raja of Buleleng, Anak Agung Panji Tisna, who built the *Tasik Madu Hotel* at Kaliasem in the 1960s and devised the name Lovina. Today, activity centres on the beach, with **snorkelling**, **diving** and **dolphin-watching** as diversions. There are waterfalls, hot springs and a Buddhist temple nearby, and Singaraja and points east are easily accessible by public transport. The volcanic Bedugul and Batur areas are also within reach.

At Lovina, you can witness the local **buffalo races** (*sapi gerumbungan*), the only place in the country where the colourful tradition can be seen, apart from at Negara. The races were formerly confined to Independence Day (Aug 17), when the biggest event still takes place. However, there are now races staged for tourists in the high season at the track in Kaliasem that are well worth attending.

## Arrival, information and transport

Getting to Lovina is easy: inter-island **buses** from Java to Singaraja pass through, as do Gilimanuk–Singaraja and Amlapura–Gilimanuk services and all local buses and **bemos** from the west of the island. From Denpasar, you can come on Denpasar (Ubung)–Singaraja services via Pupuan or on minibuses to Seririt and then swap onto local bemos. From the east of Bali, you'll come via Singaraja, from whose Banyuasri terminal it's a short bemo ride (Rp1000). **Tourist shuttle buses** also serve the resort from other parts of Bali and Lombok; Perama's office is in Anturan (a short walk from the Anturan accommodation) – it's an additional Rp5000 to be dropped off elsewhere. Check with other shuttle bus operators whether they will drop you off more centrally. As the resort is so spread out, it's well worth pinning down where you want to stay initially, especially if you arrive late in the evening as many of the inter-island buses do. For information on travelling to and from **Ngurah Rai Airport**, see the box on p.114.

Lovina's **tourist office** (Mon–Sat 8am–8pm) is on the main road at Kalibukbuk in the same building as the police post. Getting around the resort on **public transport** is simple during daylight hours as there are frequent bemos between Singaraja and Seririt, but the service dies after dark when you'll need to negotiate with the transport touts, unless your hotel or restaurant offers transport. A huge number of places offer **vehicles for rent** or charter (see "Listings") and charges are on a par with the resorts in the south. There are also

**bicycles** for rent, but the Singaraja–Seririt road is very busy – it's best to use these on the back roads.

# Accommodation

Lovina has **accommodation** options for every budget and taste. Generally, those next to the beach are more expensive, and the places lining the main road the cheapest. The busiest season is from mid-June until late August and again in December.

### Pemaron and Tukad Mungga

*Putri Sari*, on the main road, is the marker for the eastern end of Lovina. The accommodation in **Pemaron** and **Tukad Mungga** (where the beach is known as Pantai Happy) is along side roads leading down to the beach; upmarket places have their own drives from the main road. It's a quiet area, with a range of accommodation options from budget cheapies to top-class choices and with several restaurants. The turning for Pantai Happy is opposite a split gateway and sign for Tukad Mungga. The beach is quite scruffy but there are good coastal views.

**Happy Beach Inn** ☎0362/41017. Four basic, cheap rooms with attached cold-water bathrooms close to the beach. There's a small but pleasant garden and a beachside restaurant. ❷
**Jati Reef** ☎0362/41160. Well located near Pantai Happy, but a bit soulless. The bungalows are spread out behind the beach and have cold water and fan. ❷
🏊 **Kubu Lalang** ☎0362/42207, ⓦhttp://kubu. balihotelguide.com. Traditional but well-furnished bungalows in a pretty garden just behind the beach midway between Pantai Happy and Anturan (5–10min walk in each direction). There's also access from the main road. ❷–❹
**Hotel Permai** ☎0362/41471. A large set-up, home to the Permai dive centre. Rooms (all with balconies or verandas) are in two-storey buildings

around the good-sized pool. Most have fans but a couple of more expensive ones have air-con. ❷
🏊 **Puri Bagus Lovina** ☎0362/21430, ⓦwww. bagus-discovery.com. This is the most luxurious hotel on the Lovina coast, offering large, airy villas located in glorious grounds towards the far eastern end of the resort. There's a lovely pool, a library, an excellent, atmospheric restaurant, and the gorgeous spa is surrounded by pools and fountains. Service is friendly but efficient. Suites with private pools are also available. ❽–❾
**Puri Bedahulu** ☎0362/41731. Next to the beach at Pantai Happy with a pretty garden and a restaurant looking across the sand. Bungalows have elegant carvings and are comfortable; the most expensive ones have air-con. All have hot water. ❷

### Anturan

The tiny fishing village of **Anturan** remains much quieter than Kalibukbuk, although there are still plenty of people around and you'll share the beach with the villagers; they're well-used to tourists wandering around. There are plenty of beach-hawkers but it's all relaxed and amiable. To get there, take the turning almost opposite the petrol station and the Anturan health centre (*Puskesmas*); coming from the east, look out for big signs for *Bali Taman Lovina*, *Yudha* (*Simon Seaside Cottages*) and *Villa Agung*. The Perama office is just west of the turning; all the listed accommodation is within ten minutes' walk of here.

**Bali Taman Beach Resort** ☎0362/41126, ⓦwww.indo.com/hotels/bali_taman. A big operation with a pool near the beach, tennis courts and attractive grounds. All accommodation has hot water and air-con. Lower-end rooms are in a two-storey block, more expensive bungalows are larger and have bathtubs, and the most expensive of all

have ocean views. ❻–❽
**Bayu Mantra** ☎0362/41930. Clean, tiled bungalows in a large garden set back from the beach. All rooms have fans and there is a choice of hot or cold water. ❶–❷
**Gede Homestay** ☎0362/41526. Good-quality accommodation in two rows of neat bungalows

Seririt

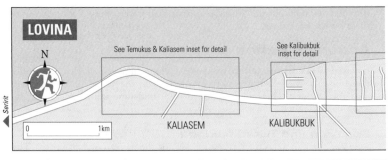

# LOVINA

N

See Temukus & Kaliasem inset for detail

See Kalibukbuk inset for detail

KALIASEM

KALIBUKBUK

0     1km

## ACCOMMODATION

| | | | | | | | | | |
|---|---|---|---|---|---|---|---|---|---|
| Adirama | ee | Bali Taman Beach Resort | U | Harris Homestay | L | Kubu Lalang | X | Pulestis | J |
| Aditya | hh | Bayu Kartika | A | Hotel Banyualit | qq | Lila Cita | ll | Puri Bagus Lovina | bb |
| Agus Homestay | dd | Bayu Mantra | V | Hotel Celuk Agung | tt | Mandhara Chico | Q | Puri Bali | F |
| Aneka Lovina | nn | Billibo | gg | Hotel Permai | cc | Mas | ss | Puri Bedahulu | Z |
| Angsoka | H | Damai Lovina Villas | O | Indra Pura | uu | Mutiara | jj | Puri Manggala | ii |
| Astina | D | Gede Homestay | P | Jati Reef | aa | Padang Lovina | M | Puri Manik Sari | N |
| Bagus Homestay | ff | Happy Beach Inn | Y | Juni Arta | oo | Pondok Elsa | K | Puspa Rama | W |

# KALIBUKBUK

Patung Lumba Lumba

N

Nirwana Seaside

Spice Dive

JALAN BINA RIA

JALAN MAWAR

Spice Dive
Malibu Dive

Biyu Gallery

Nirwana Gallery

Tip Top Shop

Police

Malibu Dive

Kristop Shop

Khi Khi Restaurant

Baruna

Benny Tantra

Postal Agent

0     100m

# ANTURAN

N

Health Centre

0     200m

O, ⑬ & ⑭ ▼

# TEMUKUS & KALIASEM

N

Adjani Office

Spice Dive

Buffalo Races

0     200m

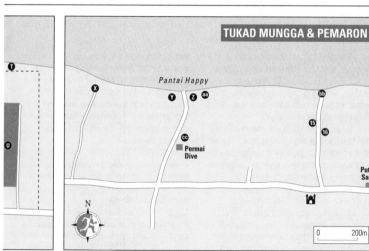

See Banyualit inset for detail

See Anturan inset for detail

See Tukad Mungga & Pemaron inset for detail

*Pantai Happy*

Perama

BANYUALIT

ANTURAN

TUKAD MUNGGA

PEMARON

*Jalan Pemaron Pura Penimbangan Singaraja*

### RESTAURANTS

| | | | | | | | |
|---|---|---|---|---|---|---|---|
| Rambutan | I | Suma | mm | Bali Apik | 8 | Kopi Bali | 4 | Sea Breeze | 3 |
| Ray | rr | Taman Lily's | G | Barakuda | 5 | Kubu Lalang | X | Volcano Club | 18 |
| Rini | E | Villa Agung | S | Bu Warung | 12 | Le Madre | 9 | Waru Bali | 1 |
| Sartaya | pp | Villa Jaya | B | Café Spice | 17 | Le Nasi Goreng | 6 | Warung Bambu Pemaron | 16 |
| Sea Breeze Cottages | C | Yudha | R | Damai | 14 | Poco Bar Evolution | 11 | Zigiz | 10 |
| Sol Lovina | kk | | | Funky Monkey | 2 | Pojok Indah | 13 | | |
| Sri Homestay | T | | | Jasmine Kitchen | 7 | Ranggon Bali | 15 | | |

## TUKAD MUNGGA & PEMARON

*Pantai Happy*

Permai Dive

Putri Sari

N

0    200m

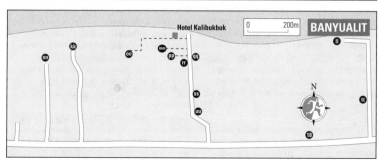

Hotel Kalibukbuk

0    200m

## BANYUALIT

N

facing each other across a small garden right behind the beach. There's a small restaurant and sunbathing area. Cheaper rooms have fan and cold water, more expensive ones air-con and hot water. **②**

**Mandhara Chico** ☎0362/41271. Close to the beach offering tiled rooms, some with hot water and air-con, in a small compound. The best rooms are the two bungalows at the front with verandas facing seawards. **②–③**

**Puspa Rama** ☎0362/42070, ✉agungdayu@yahoo .com. A small row of six clean rooms all with fan and some with hot water, set in a large garden on the lane leading to the beach from the main road. **②**

**Sri Homestay** ☎0362/41135, ✇www .sri-bali.de. A relaxed place in a seafront location where the bungalows, all with fan and cold water, face the ocean. There's a small restaurant,

and Internet access is available. You can get here via a track from the main road or via the beach. **②**

**Villa Agung** ☎0362/41527, ✇www.agungvilla .com. Rooms, all with hot water, are set back from the sea behind the small swimming pool, with fan in the cheaper rooms and air-con in the more costly. There are also cottages sleeping four or five people. However, the real bonus is the seafront restaurant, lounge, sunbathing area and bar; ideally located for the ocean views. **③**

**Yudha** (formerly *Simon Seaside Cottages*) ☎0362/41183, ✉41160. A long-time favourite just beside the beach. There's a pool and a choice of air-con or fan, and hot water is available. All rooms have a balcony or veranda, and there's a restaurant overlooking the beach. Look at several rooms first – they vary a lot. **③**

## Banyualit

The **Banyualit** side-road marks the beginning of the developed part of Lovina, about 1.5km east of Kalibukbuk. There's plenty of accommodation down here, most of it at the budget end, while the mid-range and upmarket options have their own drives off the main road. The beach here is pretty and curved, with a few local fishing boats. There are plenty of restaurants and the *Volcano Club*, Lovina's main nightlife, is also in this area.

**Aneka Lovina** ☎0362/41121, ✇www.aneka-hotels.com. West of the Banyualit turning, fifteen minutes' walk from Kalibukbuk. Rooms are in a two-storey building or thatched bungalows, all set in attractive gardens with a beachside pool. All have air-con and hot water. **②–③**

**Hotel Banyualit** ☎0362/41789, ✇www.banyualit .com. This long-standing Lovina landmark has several standards of bungalows in a lush garden with an attractive pool. The more expensive options are the best value and have air-con and hot water, with top-end villas tucked away near the pool. **③–⑦**

**Hotel Celuk Agung** ☎0362/41039, ✉celukabc@singaraja.wasantara.net.id. On a turning just to the east of the Banyualit turn-off, a few hundred metres from the main road. Excellent option in this price range. All rooms have hot water and air-con, the grounds are extensive and attractive, and there's a large pool (Rp15,000 per day for non-residents), tennis courts, jogging track and a footpath to the beach. **⑥**

**Indra Pura** ☎0362/41560. Straightforward budget choice offering accommodation in fan bungalows with attached cold-water bathrooms, all set in a pretty garden at the main-road end of the Banyualit turning. **②**

**Juni Arta** ☎0362/41885, ✉evyrs_luvy@hotmail.com. Reached via a path behind *Hotel Kalibukbuk*, this is a small row of good-quality, good-value bungalows in a peaceful

spot. All rooms have cold water, and there's a choice of fan or air-con. An excellent budget choice. **②**

**Lila Cita** Right on the beach at the end of a quiet lane, a few hundred metres further on from *Hotel Celuk Agung*, with four upgraded bungalows in a large but rather sad-looking site. There's a choice of fan or air-con. One of the quietest places along the coast. **②–③**

**Mas** ☎0362/41773. Behind an impressive gateway on the Banyualit turning to the beach, and offering simple rooms with hot water, some with fan and some with air-con, decorated with local textiles in a pleasant garden. **②–③**

**Ray** ☎0362/41088. Tiled rooms in a two-storey block with balcony or veranda. All have cold water and fan and are a reasonable budget choice. **②**

**Sartaya** ☎0362/42240. Good-quality, clean, tiled bungalows all with cold water and a choice of fan or air-con. **①–②**

**Sol Lovina** ☎0362/41775, ✉41659. One of the largest hotels in Lovina, with a huge entrance area, attractive grounds and beachside pool. All accommodation has hot water and air-con; cottages are much more attractive than the cheaper rooms. There are also villas with private pool, and there's an attached spa. **⑧–⑨**

**Suma** ☎ & ✉0362/41566. Excellent choice offering clean, well-maintained rooms in a two-storey block a short walk from the beach. There are lots of options, and air-con and hot water are available. **②–④**

## Kalibukbuk

Centred around two side-roads, Jalan Mawar, also known as Jalan Ketapang or Jalan Rambutan, and Jalan Bina Ria, **Kalibukbuk** has a huge number of places to stay and to eat, plus some nightlife and shops, moneychangers, dive shops, travel agents and car rental outlets. The narrow entrance to Jalan Mawar is easy to miss; look out for *Khi Khi Restaurant* on the opposite side of the road. Jalan Bina Ria is the most developed, and several side-roads lead off from it.

**Angsoka** ☎0362/41841, ⊛www.angsoka.com. An enormous variety of accommodation in a spacious compound conveniently located off Jalan Bina Ria. Pleasant swimming pool (Rp20,000 for non-guests). ②–④

**Astina** ☎0362/41187, ⓔselisakadek@hotmail .com. Plenty of standards of accommodation in a large garden compound occupying a quiet spot a short walk from the beach at the end of Jalan Mawar. There are basic rooms with shared bathrooms up to cottages with air-con and hot water. ①–④

**Bayu Kartika** ☎ & ☏41219, ⊛www .bayukartikaresort.com. Boasts one of the best positions in Lovina, on the coast at the end of Jalan Mawar. There is a good range of bungalows, from cheaper ones with fan and cold water and no view to expensive options offering air-con, hot water and ocean views. The pool is huge (Rp20,000 for non-resident visitors) and the restaurant nearby. ③–⑤

🏃 **Damai Lovina Villas** ☎0362/41008, ⊛www.damai.com. Located 4km inland from Kalibukbuk in a beautiful location. Accommodation, service and ambience are all elegantly luxurious and the best in Lovina. The eight superbly appointed bungalows, furnished with antiques and including a DVD player (no TVs), are widely spaced in glorious gardens and have all the character and facilities to be expected at this end of the market. There's a spa and lovely pool on site, plus an amazing pool in the nearby river. The restaurant is one of the delights of northern Bali. Prices start at US$190. ⑨

**Harris Homestay** ☎0362/41152. A popular budget gem tucked away in the back streets off Jalan Bina Ria. Good-value, good-quality rooms, all with fan and attached cold-water bathrooms. ①

**Padang Lovina** ☎0362/41302, ⓔpadanglovina@ yahoo.com. Central accommodation in a two-storey block just off Jalan Bina Ria. The downstairs rooms have hot water; all rooms have fans and good balconies or verandas. Guests here can use the pool at *Pulestis*. ②

**Pondok Elsa** ☎0362/41186. Just off Jalan Bina Ria, with good-quality accommodation in bungalows set in a cosy compound. There's a choice of fan or air-con and more expensive rooms have hot water. ②

**Pulestis** ☎0362/41035, ⓔjokoartawan@hotmail .com. Reached through a grand entrance on Jalan Bina Ria, a very short walk from the beach, the small compound has comfortable rooms with a choice of hot water or cold, fan or air-con, and the pleasant pool has a fun waterfall feature. Excellent value. ②–③

🏃 **Puri Bali** ☎0362/41485, ⊛www.puribalilo vina.com. A variety of rooms, some with thatched roofs, in an attractive garden with an excellent pool; more expensive ones, closer to the pool, have air-con and hot water. Enjoys a quiet location on Jalan Mawar, not far from the beach. ②–④

**Puri Manik Sari** ☎0362/41089. Accessible from the main road and from Jalan Bina Ria, there are several standards of bungalows in a pretty garden, with fan-cooled rooms with cold water at the bottom end and air-con rooms with hot water at the top. It's set far enough back from the road to avoid the noise. ①–③

**Rambutan** ☎0362/41388, ⊛www.rambutan.org . Halfway down Jalan Mawar, this long-standing Lovina favourite is justifiably popular, with well-furnished, clean bungalows set well apart in a beautiful garden. There are five standards of rooms to choose from, two pools, an attractive restaurant and some larger family villas. ③–⑦

🏃 **Rini** ☎ & ☏0362/41386, ⓔrinihotel@telkom .net. Several choices of extremely clean and well-maintained accommodation in an attractive garden location on Jalan Mawar just a short walk to the beach. More expensive rooms have air-con and hot water, and there's a pool with a poolside restaurant. ③–⑤

**Sea Breeze Cottages** ☎0362/41138, ☏24028. Just beside the *Sea Breeze* restaurant on the coast, these attractive wooden bungalows have air-con and hot water and all face seawards. There's a pretty pool (non-residents Rp20,000). ⑤

🏃 **Taman Lily's** ☎ & ☏0362/41307. A row of excellent-value, spotless bungalows, with fans or air-con, and hot water, on Jalan Mawar. ②–③

**Villa Jaya** ☎0362/7001238. New place a short walk along a track from Jalan Mawar. Six rooms in a block, all clean and tiled with hot water and a choice of fan or air-con. There's a small pool and restaurant. ②–④

## Kaliasem and Temukus

As you head west from Kalibukbuk, passing through the villages of **Kaliasem** and **Temukus**, the main road runs much closer to the coast; the places worth considering here are set far enough back from the road to block the noise out. The western end of Lovina is marked by *Agus Homestay* on the coast side of the road although there is one place, *Bagus Homestay*, 1km or so further west, somewhat adrift from the main resort.

**Adirama** ⌾0362/41759, ⊛www.adiramabeach-hotel.com. On the main road at Kaliasem. All rooms have hot water and a choice of fan or air-con and the most expensive rooms have sea views. There's a large pool close to the beach. ❺–❼

**Aditya** ⌾0362/41059, ⊛www.indo.com/hotels/aditya. Large place with a long sea-frontage. There's an attractive raised pool and plenty of accommodation options, all with hot water and air-con; the most expensive are close to the sea. ❼–❽

**Agus Homestay** ⌾ & ⓕ0362/41202. A small place at the far western end of the main Lovina development. Clean, tiled rooms, with verandas that face the ocean. All have air-con and hot water. ❷

🏊 **Bagus Homestay** ⌾0362/93407, ⓕ93406. Situated 1.5km west of its sister operation, *Agus Homestay*, so quite separate from the main Lovina development. Clean bungalows with air-con and hot water in a lovely garden with a good swimming pool beside a pleasant beach. More expensive ones have a bathtub rather than shower. ❸–❺

**Billibo** ⌾0362/42020, ⓕ41355. Tiled bungalows close to the beachfront in a large garden, with a choice of fan or air-con and hot- or cold-water bathrooms. ❶–❷

**Mutiara** ⌾0362/41132. Friendly, family-run place offering basic rooms in a two-storey building, all with fan and cold water. Airier rooms are upstairs. It's a short walk to the beach. ❶

**Puri Manggala** ⌾0362/41371. Simple rooms in a family compound tucked between the beach and the road. There's hot water and air-con in the most expensive rooms. ❶–❸

## The resort

Lovina's long **black-sand beach** fringed by palm trees stretches into the distance where, on clear days, the imposing peaks of East Java look surprisingly close. In many spots, most notably at Anturan, you'll share the sand with local fishing boats. Swimming is generally calm and safe, although there are no lifeguards. There's not a great deal to do other than enjoy the beach and the low-key resort life behind it, but one of Lovina's early-morning **dolphin trips** (see box, over) is almost obligatory. The monument **Patung Lumba Lumba**, at the beach end of Jalan Bina Ria, depicts dolphins complete with black-and-white-checked *kain poleng* headscarves; it's pretty tacky although copied throughout the resort.

### Diving and snorkelling

Situated between the main **diving** areas on the north coast – Pulau Menjangan to the west and Tulamben and Amed to the east – Lovina is an excellent base for diving. The local reef, perhaps unfairly, has a reputation as being a bit uninteresting for experienced divers, though there's an excellent range of fish, and tyres, an old car and a small wrecked boat have been placed on the reef and are encouraging coral growth. Note that the Lovina reef is too far from the shore to swim to; you'll need a boat.

Plenty of **operators** work in the resort, all offering trips for qualified divers, introductory dives and a variety of courses. Two dives in the Lovina area cost US$40–50, to Pulau Menjangan $50–65, to Tulamben $50–55, and to Amed $50–75. Introductory dives and refresher sessions are about $75, a PADI Open Water course $250–285 and a PADI Advanced Open Water $270 – local hotel pools are available for early training. See p.71 for general information about choosing a dive company.

△ Dolphin statue, Lovina

## Dolphin trips

Lovina is famous (or infamous) for dawn trips to see the school of **dolphins** that frolics just off the coast: opinions are fairly evenly split between those who think it's grossly overrated and those who consider it one of the best things on Bali.

A flotilla of simple *prahu* hewn from a single tree trunk with a bamboo stabilizer on each side head out to sea at dawn, providing lovely views of the coast and the central mountains. The ensuing scenario is comical, as one skipper spots a dolphin and chases after it, to be followed by the rest of the fleet, by which time, of course, the dolphin is long gone. If you can see the funny side, it's a good trip, and very, very occasionally **whales** have been spotted.

Expect to **pay** Rp30,000 per person for the two-hour trip; book directly with the skippers on the beach or through your accommodation. Captains are banned from working for long periods if they're discovered to have given discounts or allowed more than four passengers per boat.

Your losmen can also arrange **snorkelling trips,** or you can approach the boat skippers on the beach direct; expect to pay about Rp30,000 for a trip of one and a half or two hours to the local reef. Most of the dive shops will take snorkellers along on dive trips further afield if they have space; this is more expensive ($20–25) but offers greater variety. It pays to shop around and see who is going where. The *Kubu Lalang* restaurant (☎0362/42207) offers **night snorkelling** trips (Rp100,000 per person).

### Dive operators

**Baruna** On the main road in Kalibukbuk ☎0362/41084. A branch of the established operator.

**Malibu Dive** Next to *Malibu* restaurant ☎ & ☎0362/41225 and on Jalan Bina Ria ☎0362/41061. A PADI dive centre operating a full range of dives for certified divers as well as PADI courses.

**Permai Dive** At *Hotel Permai*, Pantai Happy ☎0362/41223. Courses start off in the hotel pool.

**Spice Dive,** Kaliasem ☎0362/41509, ⊛www .balispicedive.com. Also has shops on Jalan Bina Ria and Jalan Mawar. Long-established operator and the resort's only PADI five-star dive centre, offering courses up to Assistant Instructor level. Specializes in PADI Junior Open Water courses with a specifically trained instructor and special gear. Nitrox, with a specifically trained instructor, is also available. Also offers a two-day "Rainbow Tour" ($170 per person) to Baluran National Park in Java via Pulau Menjangan, including five dives. Boat charters are available to put together your own trip.

### Watersports

Spice Dive (see above) organizes **watersports** from their beach location in Kaliasem, where they offer parasailing ($12 for one run) and wakeboarding, kneeboarding and waterskiing (all $15 for 20min), plus banana-boat rides ($7 per person for 20 min, minimum four people). You can watch all the action from the highly recommended *Café Spice* (see "Eating").

**Sailing**, **spear fishing** and **fishing** are all offered at Rp80,000 per person per hour from *Kubu Lalang* restaurant (☎0362/42207).

## Eating, drinking and nightlife

There's a high turnover of **restaurants** in Lovina – the favourite today may well be extinct tomorrow – and a healthy level of competition ensures plenty of good "Happy Hour" deals, especially around Jalan Bina Ria. The quality and variety of food is excellent with something for every taste and pocket. The places recommended below are, unless noted otherwise, in the inexpensive to moderate price range. A couple of kilometres towards Singaraja, Jalan Pemaron Pura Penimbangan, which leads off the main road, hugs the coast for a kilometre or so and then leads back to the main road, is the location of a host of local restaurants specializing in seafood and Indonesian food all at inexpensive to moderate prices, frequented by local people rather than travellers. *Cosy Resto*, *Ranggun Sunset* and *Casablangka* are all worth a try.

**Bali Apik** Tucked away off Jalan Bina Ria and serving an excellent choice of breakfasts as well as a large Indo-Chinese, seafood and Western menu, including steaks. Service is friendly and relaxed.

**Barakuda** On Jalan Mawar, specializing in well-cooked, good-value seafood, including fish, squid, crab, prawns and lobster. Your choice is served with one of eleven Balinese or Chinese sauces. There are plenty of vegetarian, pork and chicken options, as well as pancakes for dessert.

**Bu Warung** Probably the best-value food in Kalibukbuk, this tiny place on the main road has a small menu of around a dozen well-cooked main courses (Rp7500–8500). There are also sandwiches, jaffles, pancakes, and fried bananas and pineapple.

**Café Spice** ☎0362/41969. Located beside the beach at the Spice Dive centre at Kaliasem. The menu includes seafood, Western and Indo-Chinese meals plus plenty of snacks, soups, shakes and juices, with lots of unusual choices including *bruschette*, spinach terrine and excellent homemade bread. Phone for a free pick-up in the Lovina area.

**Damai** ☎0362/41008. The restaurant attached to the luxury *Damai Lovina Villas* offers the most exquisite dining in northern Bali, if not the entire island. The menu is imaginative, innovative, well cooked, fabulously presented and exciting to eat. Meals are meticulously prepared and service is friendly yet discreet. The $38 five-course Gastronomic Dinner is a feast beyond words – and it changes daily. There's an equally appealing à la carte menu.

**Funky Monkey** Shady chill-out spot at the beach end of Jalan Bina Ria. Drinks are cheap and there's a tiny menu of Indonesian and Western food. The nasi campur is a steal at Rp5000 but not for chilli wimps.

**Jasmine Kitchen** Outstanding restaurant serving fabulous Thai food in relaxed surroundings just off Jalan Bina Ria. Desserts and coffees are exceptional, there are magazines to read, and staff are great.

**Kopi Bali** Popular place towards the ocean end of Jalan Bina Ria. Features a big, inexpensive menu of travellers' fare including lots of specials and plenty of breakfasts. This is an excellent place for big appetites with small budgets.

**Kubu Lalang** ☎0362/42207. On the coast at the eastern end of Lovina, with a free boat transfer for lunch or dinner for a minimum of four people from elsewhere in the resort (two hours' notice required and it does depend on the tide). The moderately priced menu is huge, including plenty of vegetarian choices and slightly unusual, imaginative dishes.

**Le Madre** Quiet little Italian spot on Jalan Mawar, but with the usual travellers' fare as well. Service is friendly, and *focaccia* is baked daily.

**Le Nasi Goreng** Located on Jalan Bina Ria. Pleasant decor, friendly staff and the usual travellers' fare, with a few specials. Excellent juices.

**Pojok Indah** ☎0362/41571. Attached to the Bali Fruit Drink winery 6km from Kalibukbuk up in the hills past the *Damai Lovina Villas*. Fabulous steaks and beef stew in the expensive price range (Rp65,000) but worth every rupiah. Dinner is communal so the atmosphere depends on who's dining. A visit to the wine cellars afterwards can be extremely boozey. You need to book and decide what you'll eat beforehand.

**Ranggon Bali** ☎0362/25104. In a pretty location surrounded by a garden and fields on the track leading down to *Puri Bagus Lovina* at the eastern end of the resort. There's a big Indonesian,

## Buffalo races

In the high season, Lovina stages **buffalo races** (*sapi gerumbungan*), in the late afternoon in a field in Kaliasem (Rp40,000). Look out for local flyers advertising the races, which are supplemented by cooking, rice-pounding and martial arts displays. The buffalo are dolled up in ornate yokes and headdresses to prance as quickly as possible along a set course, hampered somewhat by huge bells around their necks, their jockeys perching on painfully narrow seats. Spectators are encouraged to have a go themselves – and this is just as entertaining, especially the funny walks that result from bumpy contact with the aforementioned seats. A much grander, more serious event takes place annually on Independence Day (Aug 17).

Balinese and seafood selection with a smaller Western choice, all in the moderate price range.

**Sea Breeze** Superbly situated on the beach at Kalibukbuk, and good for a sunset drink, with an extensive menu of Western, Indonesian and seafood dishes including excellent soups, salads and sandwiches. There's a fine selection of cakes and desserts – crumble, brownies, lemon meringue pie, lemon cheesecake and chocolate mousse – although beware, they're not all available every day.

**Waru Bali** At the end of Jalan Mawar close to the beach, a relaxed and popular place with a big good-value menu of the usual travellers' fare.

There's a megibuns (*rijsttafel*) available for two people at Rp42,500.

**Warung Bambu Pemaron** ☎0362/27080 or 31455. On the road down to *Puri Bagus Lovina* at the eastern end of Lovina; serves an excellent range of Balinese and Indonesian food. A *rijsttafel* (Rp70,000 per person) and "Romantic Buffet" (Rp85,000 per person) are available for as few as two diners. Balinese dancing accompanies dinner twice a week (Wed & Sun). There is original art for sale and cooking classes are available (see p.333). Free transport in the Lovina area.

### Nightlife

Anybody coming to Lovina expecting energetic **nightlife** is in for a disappointment: after a day relaxing on the beach, most people eat a leisurely dinner and head off to bed. The only established nightspot is the *Volcano Club* on the main road near Banyualit; opening varies with the season – look out for local adverts. There's regular **live music** in the *Poco Bar Evolution* and *Zigiz* bars on Jalan Bina Ria, and occasional **parties** at *Café Spice*, sometimes with live music, run until 3 or 4am; look out for flyers advertising these.

## Shopping

There's no shortage of retail opportunities in Lovina and the **shops** stock a good selection of textiles, clothing and souvenirs in small places along Jalan Bina Ria, Jalan Mawar and the main road in Kalibukbuk, which is also the area for secondhand **books**. The *Jakarta Post* **newspaper** arrives in the afternoon at Kristop Shop on the main road.

One of the most impressive places is Nirwana Gallery on the main road slightly east of the junction with Jalan Bina Ria. It has a vast array of beautifully displayed **textiles, paper** and **wood** items – a fair representation of most of the crafts of Bali – all labelled with fixed prices. Biyu Gallery, on the main road to the west of the junction of Jalan Bina Ria, sells a fantastic selection of stuff from across Indonesia; textiles and statues predominate but it's a real treasure-trove and prices range from Rp50,000 to several millions. Take a look at Durian, next to *Rambutan* on Jalan Mawar, packed full of textiles, carvings and **jewellery**; several other little shops along here are also worth a browse. One place that's out of the ordinary is Benny Tantra, which sells excellent hand-painted and cartoon **T-shirts** (Rp60,000 for printed ones, Rp180,000 for hand-painted ones) and cards (Rp2500). At the top end of the price range, *Damai Lovina Villas* sell their own beautifully packaged exquisite **toiletries** – their prices are on a par with those in the West.

## Massage and treatments

As well as the ladies on the beach offering massages, places offering a broader range of **massages and treatments** have mushroomed in recent years. One of the most established is The Lovina Spa Wellness and Healing (☎0362/27297), on the corner of Jalan Mawar and the main road. Several massages, including ayurvedic (Rp200,000 for 1hr 30min), and spa treatments including *mandi lulur* (Rp150,000 for 2hr) are available as are day-packages and packages including accommodation. At the cosmetic end of the market, Lee's Beauty Care

(☎0812/366 9074), above *Bali Apik* restaurant just off Jalan Bina Ria, has a wide range of facials, manicures, pedicures and hair treatments (from Rp35,000) in relaxed surroundings.

## Cookery courses

Taking a **cookery class** for a few hours is an increasingly popular activity in Lovina. Most courses include a trip to the market and you get to eat the dishes you've cooked. Classes vary in length so check this when you book. Most places can cater to your level of skill and your culinary interests; for example, all have a vegetarian option. The price depends partly on the menu you choose to cook and there's usually a minimum number of participants (usually two) required for the class to run. Adjani (✉ad_janibali@telkom.net) was the first place to offer cookery classes in Lovina. They have an office on the main road in Kaliasem. Prices vary from Rp125–175,000 per person. *Barakuda* restaurant on Jalan Mawar is also well established and offers classes consisting of four main courses (Rp75,000–85,000 per person) or seven main courses (Rp120,000–150,000). *Warung Bambu Pemaron* (☎0362/27080) arranges basic or advanced classes and has a class that concentrates on preparing sweets (Rp250,000 per person). Putu's Cooking (☎08133/856 3705) is also advertised throughout the resort (Rp150,000 per person).

## Listings

**Car, bike and motorbike rental, and charter transport** Available throughout the resort both from established firms and as charters from people who'll approach you on the street. Expect to pay around Rp90,000 a day for a Suzuki Jimney, Rp125,000 for a Kijang. Insurance deals vary and are only available with established companies. Motorbikes are also widely available (Rp30,000–40,000 per day), as are bicycles (Rp10,000–20,000 per day). Established companies include Yuli Transport, at Yuli Shop (☎0362/41184), opposite *Rambutan* on Jalan Mawar, and Dupa, next to Baruna on the main road (☎0362/41397), where Made Wijana (☎08133/856 3027) is a safe, reliable and recommended driver. If you want to charter a vehicle plus driver, you'll be looking at about Rp250,000 per day including petrol. It's also possible to charter a vehicle for a one-way drop to destinations throughout Bali (Rp100,000 to Tulamben, Rp110,000 to Pemuteran, Rp140,000 to Tulamben and Rp160,000–195,000 to Amed, Candi Dasa, Padang Bai or any of the South Bali resorts; if there are several of you, this can be good value.

**Doctor** Dr Handra (☎0812/360 5733) is an English-speaking local doctor. Your hotel or the tourist office can also recommend doctors. The closest hospitals are in Singaraja, although for anything serious you'll have to go to Denpasar.

**Exchange and banks** There are moneychangers every few metres throughout the resort. There's a BCA ATM (Visa, MasterCard and Cirrus) on the main road in Kalibukbuk, and another on Jalan Bina Ria.

**Internet access** Offered by many places (Rp350–400/min). Spice Dive on Jalan Bina Ria and Jalan Mawar also burns CDs (for digital photographs), prints text (Rp2000/page) and can work with any USB devices such as memory sticks.

**Phone** There are wartels throughout the resort, most open from 7.30 or 8am to 10 or 11pm.

**Police** Located in the same building as the tourist office; they'll also try to help you with information if the tourist office is closed.

**Post office** The post office (Mon–Thurs 7.30am–3pm, Fri 7.30am–1pm, Sat 7.30–11.30am) is about 1km west of Kalibukbuk. For poste restante, have mail addressed to you at the Post Office, Jalan Raya Singaraja, Lovina, Singaraja 81152, Bali. Several postal agents in Kalibukbuk sell stamps.

**Tours** Available throughout the resort, at Rp200,000–250,000 per car. The main ones on offer include Singaraja (Pura Beji, Jagaraga, Sawan, Kubutambahan, Ponjok Batu and Hot Springs), Kintamani (Pura Beji, Kubutambahan, Penulisan, Penelokan and Toyah Bungkah), Eastern Bali (Pura Beji, Kubutambahan, Penulisan, Besakih and Tenganan, Candi Dasa and Tirtaganggan) and Sunset (Gitgit, Danau Bratan, Taman Ayu and Tanah Lot). Consider chartering a vehicle and driver and putting together your own itinerary.

**Travel agents/shuttle buses** Perama has an office at Anturan (daily 8am–10pm; ☎0362/41161). There are shuttle buses to destinations on Bali and Lombok and charters (Rp80,000 per person, minimum two people) available to Tulamben, Amed, Tirtagangga and Padang Bai. Perama also book buses to other parts of Indonesia, including Jakarta (Rp180,000), Surabaya (Rp100,000) and Yogyakar- ta (Rp165,000). See p.318 for bus ticket offices in Singaraja. There are plenty of other companies advertising shuttle services.

## Around Lovina

There are plenty of attractions to see around Lovina. Several are accessible on public transport – such as the **Buddhist monastery** and **hot springs** at Banjar – while others in the area inland from Seririt are better explored with your own transport. A kilometre beyond the western limits of Lovina, Jalan Singsing leads 1km south to the **Singsing (Daybreak) waterfalls**, only really worth a look in the rainy season and not nearly as dramatic as other falls in the region.

### Buddhist monastery and hot springs

Bali's only **Buddhist monastery** lies 10km southwest of Lovina and can be combined with a visit to the hot springs at Banjar, which are on a parallel road slightly further west. Catch any westbound bemo to **DENCARIK**, where a sign points inland to the monastery and ojek wait to take you the last, steep 5km.

The **Brahmavihara Arama** (rarely closed; free, donation for sarong rental) was built in 1970 with financial help from the Indonesian and Thai governments. It's a splendidly colourful confection in a wonderful hillside setting. A gold Buddha from Thailand is the centrepiece in the lower temple, carved stone plaques show scenes from Buddha's life on all the main temples and there's a pictorial Buddhist grotto to the left of the top temple.

From the temple you can walk to the **hot springs** (daily 8am–6pm; Rp3000, parking Rp1000). Head back downhill and take the first road to the left. After a few hundred metres – with fine views of the mountains of East Java in the distance – you'll reach a major crossroads and marketplace at the village of **BANJAR TEGA**. Turn left and a highly decorated *kulkul* tower will now be on your right. After about 200m you'll see a sign for the "Air Panas Holy Hot Springs" pointing you to a left turn. From here it's a pleasant one-kilometre walk to the springs where there are three pools with *naga* spouting water, which has a slight sulphur smell and a silky softness. Weekends and holidays can get a bit busy.

The pools are overlooked by a **restaurant** that offers moderately priced food and good views. *Pondok Wisata Griya Sari* (☎0362/92903, ☏92966; Rp100,000–185,000) has comfortable **rooms** with pleasant verandas ranged up the hillside in a lovely garden – although the bathrooms have only cold water.

From the springs you can walk the 3km back down to the main road, or take an ojek from the market. This area is the main grape-growing region in Bali and you'll see the cultivated vines in the fields next to the road.

### Inland from Seririt

With your own transport, you can take an interesting **inland drive** through the countryside south of **Seririt**, 12km west of Lovina, initially along the Denpasar road. The road climbs through paddy-fields and fields of grapes, splitting after 7km at **RANGDU**. The right-hand fork takes you up across the mountains via Pupuan to the south coast, while the left fork goes through **MAYONG**, Banyuatis and Gunungsari to Munduk and on up to the area north of lakes Tamblingan and Buyan.

If you take the left fork and follow the road for just under 3km, you'll reach a small left turn signed "Desa Bestala". This side-road leads to the village of

**BESTALA**, where you should turn left by the statue of the independence fighter. This is a wonderful little road that winds down into the valley, across the river and then zigzags up the other side for a couple of kilometres to the hamlet of **MUNDUK BESTALA**, famous throughout Bali for its durians (Jan and Feb are the main season). There's a tiny market area just before a T-junction in the village; the road deteriorates from here on. You can either go left for about 1.5km to a lookout point with good views over the north coast, or turn right and continue for about 3km to another lookout spot with the entire region laid out before you as far as the Batukau mountains to the south. For guided walks in this area, see *Bali Panorama* restaurant in Mayong (p.313). Continuing on this road and taking a left fork at the next junction brings you to **Pedawa** and **Sidetapa**, two Bali Aga villages, which still retain their narrow lanes, high-walled compounds and gates. For guided treks in the Sidetapa area, talk to Adjani in Lovina (see p.333).

# Travel details

## Bemos and public buses

It's almost impossible to give the frequency with which bemos and public buses run: see Basics, p.49, for details. Journey times given are the minimum you can expect. Only the direct bemo and bus routes are listed; for longer journeys, you'll have to go via either Singaraja or Denpasar.

**Air Sanih** to: Amlapura (2hr); Culik (1hr 30min); Gilimanuk (3hr); Singaraja (Penarukan terminal; 30min); Tirtagangga (2hr); Tulamben (1hr).

**Bedugul** to: Denpasar (Ubung terminal; 1hr 30min); Singaraja (Sukasada terminal; 1hr 30min).

**Kintamani** to: Denpasar (Batubulan terminal; 2hr); Singaraja (Penarukan terminal; 1hr 30min); Ubud (40min).

**Lovina** to: Amlapura (3hr 30min); Gilimanuk (2hr 30min); Jakarta (Java; 24hr); Probolingo (for Bromo; 6hr); Seririt (20min); Singaraja (Banyuasri terminal; 20min); Surabaya (Java; 8hr); Yogyakarta (Java; 12hr).

**Penelokan** to: Bangli (45min); Buahan (30min); Denpasar (Batubulan terminal; 1hr 30min); Gianyar (50min); Singaraja (Penarukan terminal; 1hr 30min); Songan (45min); Toya Bungkah (30min).

**Singaraja (Banyuasri terminal)** to: Gilimanuk (2hr 30min); Lovina (20min); Seririt (40min);

Surabaya (8hr); Yogyakarta (Java; 12hr).

**Singaraja (Penarukan terminal)** to: Amlapura (3hr); Culik (2hr 30min); Denpasar (Batubulan terminal; 3hr); Gianyar (2hr 20min); Penelokan (1hr 30min); Kubutambahan (20min); Sawan (30min); Tirtagangga (2hr 30min); Tulamben (1hr).

**Singaraja (Sukasada terminal)** to: Bedugul (1hr 30min); Denpasar (Ubung terminal; 3hr); Gitgit (30min).

## Perama shuttle buses

*STO = overnight stopover is needed*

**Bedugul** to: Candi Dasa (daily; STO); Kuta/Ngurah Rai Airport (daily; 2hr 30min–3hr); Kuta, Lombok (daily; STO); Lovina (daily; 1hr 30min); Mataram (Lombok; daily; STO); Padang Bai (daily; STO); Sanur (daily; 2hr–2hr 30min); Sengiggi (Lombok; daily; STO); Ubud (daily; 1hr 30min).

**Lovina** to: Bedugul (daily; 1hr 30min); Candi Dasa (2 daily; 3hr–3hr 30min); Kuta/Ngurah Rai Airport (daily; 3hr); Kuta, Lombok (daily; STO); Mataram (Lombok; daily; 7–8hr); Padang Bai (daily; 2hr 45min); Sanur (daily; 2hr 30min–3hr); Sengiggi (Lombok; daily; 7hr 30min–8hr 30min); Ubud (daily; 3hr 30min–4hr).

# 5

# West Bali

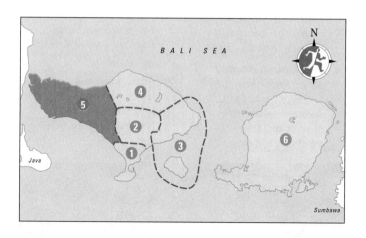

CHAPTER FIVE # Highlights

* **Tanah Lot** Perched like a sea bird on a wave-lashed rock, this is Bali's most famous temple. See p.344

* **Subak Museum, Tabanan** Fascinating insight into Bali's rice-farming culture. See p.348

* **Yeh Gangga** A dramatic stretch of remote black-sand beach with just a couple of exceptional places to stay. See p.350

* **Pura Luhur Batukau** Atmospheric garden-temple at the foot of a sacred mountain, full of wild birds, flowering shrubs and moss-encrusted statues. See p.353

* **Wongayagede and the Jatiluwih road** Enjoy a night in the cool mountain air, then drive through Bali's most famous rice terraces. See p.353

* **Snorkelling off Pulau Menjangan** National-park island with crystal waters and spectacular, abundant shallow reefs. See p.368

* **Pemuteran** Small, relaxed beach haven just outside Bali Barat National Park. See p.370

△ Temple sculptures at, Pura Luhur Batukau

# 5

# West Bali

Sparsely populated, mountainous, and in places extremely rugged, **west Bali** stretches from the northwestern outskirts of Denpasar across 128km to Gilimanuk at the island's westernmost tip. Once connected to East Java by a tract of land (now submerged beneath the Bali Strait), the region has always had a distinct Javanese character. When East Java's Hindu Majapahit elite fled to Bali in the sixteenth century, the Javanese priest Nirartha started his influential preaching tour of Bali from the west – leaving the region with a stunning trinity of clifftop temples at **Tanah Lot**, **Rambut Siwi** and **Pulaki**. More recently, the Muslim faith has made significant inroads into western Bali, too, so much so that in the region to the west of Negara, mosques now seem to outnumber temples and a good percentage of the male population leaves the house wearing a small black *peci*.

Apart from making the statutory visits to the big attractions just west of Denpasar – **Pura Tanah Lot** and **Sangeh Monkey Forest** being the main draws – few tourists linger long in west Bali, choosing instead to rush through on their way to or from Java, pausing only to board the ferry in the port town of Gilimanuk. Yet the southwest coast holds some fine black-sand beaches, and some good surf at **Medewi**, while the cream of Bali's coral reefs lie off the northwest coast around **Pulau Menjangan** (Deer Island), near the little beach haven of **Pemuteran**. Furthermore, Bali's only national park is here: over seventy percent of the land area in the west is preserved as **Bali Barat National Park**, home to the endangered Bali starling and a lot of other unusual birds as well. The island's second highest peak, the sacred **Gunung Batukau**, dominates many west Bali vistas and, although both the extreme west and some stretches of the northwest lie in its rain shadow, which renders the land arid and infertile, the southwest boasts the most fertile paddies in Bali, not least in the area around **Jatiluwih**, focus of a famously scenic drive. Bali's rice-growing culture is celebrated by a special museum in nearby **Tabanan**.

Despite the lack of tourist centres in the west, there are several exceptional **hotels** both on the coast and in inland villages, most of them quiet and well off the usual tourist route. The southwest coast is served by **bemos** from Denpasar's Ubung bemo terminal, and the northwest coast by bemos from Singaraja: both services terminate at **Gilimanuk**, on Bali's westernmost tip, from where car ferries shuttle across the Bali Strait to Java. In addition, there's at least one north–south bemo service, via Pupuan. If you're driving yourself, be warned that traffic along the Denpasar–Gilimanuk road is plagued by thundering trucks heading to and from Java.

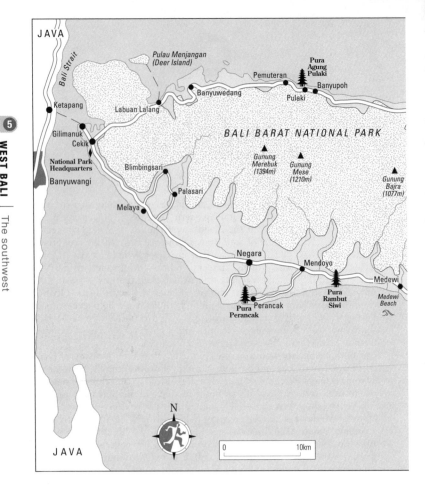

# The southwest

From **Ubung** bemo terminal in the northwest of Denpasar, all westbound
bemos follow the busy main road through an almost continuous urban sprawl
of unexciting small towns. After 15km, the conurbation becomes more distinctive as it shapes into **Kapal**, which, as you can't fail to notice, is one of
the shrine-making centres of Bali: the sidewalks here are lined with every
conceivable permutation in stone, concrete and wood, some roofed with wiry
black *ijuk* thatch made from sugar-palm fibres. The road branches just west of
Kapal, the northbound fork being a major artery for Bedugul and Singaraja
via the seventeenth-century temple complex at **Mengwi**, with a side-road to
the **Sangeh Monkey Forest**. Continuing west towards Gilimanuk, the road
reaches a crossroads at Kediri, access point for the coastal temple of **Pura**

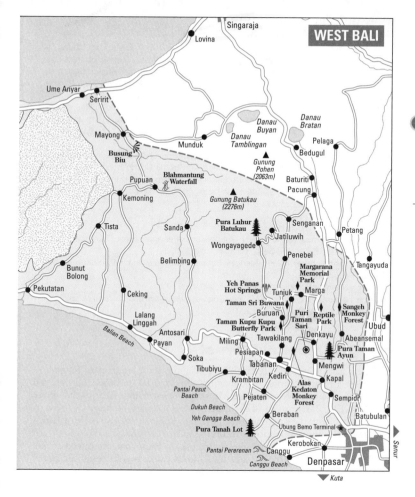

**Tanah Lot**. Each of these three major sights can be visited by public transport in a comfortable day-trip from Denpasar or Kuta, and also feature on the itineraries of every tour operator in south Bali. Kediri lies on the outskirts of **Tabanan**, the regency capital, from where you can get transport to **Yeh Gangga beach** and the royal palace at **Krambitan**.

If you have your own transport and are heading west from Kuta or Sanur, it's worth bypassing Denpasar by taking the more scenic **back road** instead. From Kuta, head north up Jalan Legian, through Seminyak, until you reach the crossroads village of Kerobokan (about 9km from Kuta). The eastern arm takes you to central Denpasar, the western arm to the beach at Canggu. Continuing north, you'll soon reach Sempidi, which lies on the main Denpasar–Kediri road, 5km before the junction at Kapal.

# Sangeh Monkey Forest

Monkeys have a special status in Hindu religion, and a number of temples in Bali boast a resident monkey population, respected by devotees and duly fed and photographed by tourists. The **Monkey Forest** (Bukit Sari) in the village of **SANGEH**, 21km north of Denpasar, is the most atmospheric of these, its unruly inhabitants the self-appointed guardians of the slightly eerie **Pura Bukit Sari** (daylight hours; donation). According to local legend, the forest itself was created when Rama's general, the monkey king Hanuman, attempted to kill off Rama's enemy Rawana, by squashing him between two halves of the sacred Mount Meru. In the process, part of the mountain fell to earth at Sangeh, with hordes of Hanuman's simian retainers still clinging to the trees, creating Bukit Sari and its monkey dynasty. The temple was built here some time during the seventeenth century, in the heart of a forest of sacred nutmeg trees that tower to heights of forty metres. It is best appreciated in late afternoon, after the tour buses have left, when both forest and temple take on an attractive ghostly aspect, missing from the island's other monkey forests. Whatever time you visit, take heed of the signs warning you to beware of the unnervingly confident monkeys: keep cameras and jewellery out of sight and remove all foodstuffs from bags and pockets. There are no paths through the forest, but a track almost circles its perimeter and the temple compound is easy to find. The weathered and moss-encrusted grey-stone temple is out of bounds to everyone except the monkeys, but beyond the walls you can see a huge *garuda* statue, stonecarved reliefs and tiered, thatched *meru*.

Sangeh is on a minor northbound road that connects Denpasar with Kintamani via the junction village of Petang, and is served by **bemos** from the small Wangaya terminal in central Denpasar (see p.95). With your own transport, Sangeh is an easy drive from Mengwi, 15km southwest, or a pleasant forty-minute ride from Ubud. Sangeh also features on every **tour** operator's programme, often combined with Mengwi and Tanah Lot, and sometimes Bedugul.

# Mengwi and around

About 18km northwest of Denpasar, the small village of **MENGWI** has a glittering history as the capital of a once powerful kingdom and is the site of an important, if underwhelming, temple from that era, **Pura Taman Ayun**. From the early seventeenth century until the close of the nineteenth, the wily, battle-strong rajas of Mengwi held sway over an extensive area, comprising parts of present-day Badung, Tabanan and Gianyar districts. Their fortunes eventually waned, however, and in 1885 the kingdom of Mengwi was divided between Badung and Tabanan. Descendants of the royal family still live in the Mengwi area, and one of their palaces, **Puri Taman Sari** in nearby Umabian, now operates as a high-class homestay. Also not far from Mengwi is the important **Margarana memorial**, erected in honour of Bali's anti-Dutch freedom fighters.

### Pura Taman Ayun

The state temple of the former kingdom of Mengwi, **Pura Taman Ayun** (daily during daylight hours; Rp3100, kids Rp1600) was probably built by Raja I Gusti Agung Anom in 1634 as the focus of his newly powerful dynasty. Designed as a series of garden terraces with each courtyard on a different level, the whole Pura Taman Ayun complex is surrounded by a moat – now picturesquely enhanced by weeds and lilies – to symbolize the mythological home of the gods, Mount Meru, floating in the milky sea of eternity. Disappointingly, all this looks far more impressive in aerial photographs than from the ground. The traditional bathing pools on the outer edge of the moat, beside the road, are still used by townspeople every evening. The **inner courtyard** is encircled by its own little moat and is inaccessible to the public except at festival time – although the surrounding wall is low enough to give a reasonable view of the two dozen separate shrines and *bale* within. The north and east sides of the compound are lined with multi-tiered **meru**. The most important of these are the three that honour Bali's holiest mountains; they occupy positions within the temple compound that correspond to their positions on Bali in relation to Mengwi. Thus, the eleven-roofed structure in the far northwest corner represents Gunung Batukau; the nine-roofed *meru* halfway down the east side stands for Gunung Batur; and Batur's eleven-roofed neighbour honours Gunung Agung. The Batur *meru* has only nine tiers because the mountain is significantly lower than the other two.

To the west of Pura Taman Ayun's moat, the **Mengwi Museum** (daily during daylight hours; donation requested) contains a comprehensive if rather faded collection of different palm-leaf offerings made for the hundreds of ceremonies and special days in the Balinese calendar.

Pura Taman Ayun is just east off the main Mengwi–Singaraja road and easily reached by **bemo** from Denpasar's Ubung terminal (30min). Coming from Gilimanuk or other points on the west coast, take an Ubung-bound bemo as far as Tabanan's Pesiapan terminal, then change on to a blue-and-yellow-striped bemo, which will take you straight to the temple complex.

### Puri Taman Sari

One very good reason to visit this area is to stay at the *puri* (palace) of a branch of the Mengwi royal family. *Puri Taman Sari* ✿ (☎0361/281241, ⓦwww .balitamansari.com; ⓺–⓻), in the tiny village of **UMABIAN**, about 5km northwest of Pura Taman Ayun, is built to a traditional design but with modern comforts. The compound features traditional pavilions for sleeping, cooking and ceremonial activities, plus some delightful air-con guest accommodation, but, unusually, is set in expansive grounds overlooking a classic rice-terrace panorama. The ethos behind the *puri* accommodation is that guests should get involved in the normal daily life of this typical high-caste household, where activities include making offerings, watching village girls' dance rehearsals, attending late-night village gamelan practice and helping to cook. You can also do cycle rides and walks through local fields, and to nearby Alas Kedaton Monkey Forest. Access to *Puri Taman Sari* is via Denkayu on the Mengwi–Bedugul–Singaraja road, but phone for directions.

### Reptile and Crocodile Park

Unless you have a real passion for crocodiles, there's little point making the effort to visit the overpriced and poorly designed Taman Buaya dan Reptil, known as the **Reptile and Crocodile Park** (daily 9am–6pm; $10), which is home to four kinds of croc and eight species of lizard but is way inferior to the Reptile Park in Batubulan, described on p.174. This park is 8km north of Mengwi on the Bedugul road and served by all Ubung–Singaraja and Ubung–Seririt bemos.

### Margarana Memorial Park

When Indonesia began fighting for independence from Dutch colonial rule immediately after World War II, resistance in Bali was spearheaded by the young army officer **Gusti Ngurah Rai**, whose plan was to gather forces from all over the island on the slopes of Gunung Agung (see "History", on p.451, for more detail). The most famous battle of this campaign, the Margarana *puputan* (fight to the death), took place in Marga, about 6km north of Mengwi, on November 20, 1946, and resulted in the death of Ngurah Rai and all 96 of his men. The battlefield has now been turned into the **Margarana Memorial Park**, or Taman Pujaan Bangsa Margarana (daily 7am–4.30pm; donation), dedicated to the 1372 independence fighters who died between 1945 and 1950, the vast majority of them from the Tabanan area. Just inside the entrance to its pleasantly landscaped grounds, four statues brandish traditional weapons while a fifth unfurls the flag of independence. At the heart of the park stands a red-brick shrine carrying a small photograph of Ngurah Rai (now a national hero, and the man after whom the airport is named) and the words of his letter of no surrender, which ends with the cry "Freedom or death!". Beyond the shrine stretches row upon row of neat gravestones.

The memorial is visited by almost every schoolchild on the island but few tourists. Access by public transport involves taking any Denpasar (Ubung)–Bedugul–Singaraja **bemo** as close as you can to Marga, then walking the 2km west of the main road to the monument.

## Pura Tanah Lot and around

Dramatically marooned on a craggy wave-lashed rock sitting just off the southwest coast, **Pura Tanah Lot** really does deserve its reputation as one of Bali's top sights. Fringed by frothing white surf and glistening black sand, its elegant multi-tiered shrines have become the unofficial symbol of Bali, appearing on a vast range of tourist souvenirs, while its links with several other coastal temples afford it an especially holy status. Unsurprisingly, the temple attracts huge crowds every day, particularly at sunset, and a busy tourist village has mush-

## The sacred and the profane

The construction in the mid-1990s of the *Nirwana Golf and Spa Resort* so close to Pura Tanah Lot marked a new low in the relationship between **property developers** and Balinese villagers. In Bali, there are long-standing religious laws about how close to a temple one is allowed to build, and about what status the secular building should have in relation to the temple; when it became obvious that the consortium behind the *Nirwana* had managed to circumvent these rules, huge protests erupted in the press and on the streets.

This was the first time there had been such strong and widespread **opposition to tourist development** on Bali. By building a tourist resort here, it was argued, one of the island's most important temples was being treated as nothing more than an ornament for the pleasure of foreign eyes – a serious case of disrespect. In addition, it was reported that farmers who refused to sell their ancestral land to make way for the project were forced out by underhand means (including blocking irrigation channels to make the land infertile) and that several small temples were destroyed. Nonetheless, pragmatism prevailed, and the *Le Meridien Nirwana* is now one of Bali's most successful luxury hotels.

With hundreds of jobs at stake and a desperate desire for the tourist dollar, the *Nirwana* controversy is typical of the tensions that have been dogging Bali ever since the first tourists arrived in the 1930s. As land gets more expensive, it is left to outside investors with little regard for Bali's religious heritage to bankroll new projects and impose their own conditions. On the other hand, cash injections like this are good for the Balinese economy and it's unclear whether local investors would be any more ethical. For a more complete view of the effect of tourist development in Bali, see p.497.

roomed around the approach to the temple, encompassing everything from typical art-market stalls selling sarongs and souvenirs to outlets for Versace and Polo design wear.

Access is fairly easy by public bemo and there are several places to stay around the temple, but most visitors come on **organized day-trips** from Bali's biggest resorts.

### The temples

**Pura Tanah Lot** (daily during daylight hours; Rp3300, kids Rp1800, plus Rp1500 per car) is said to have been founded by the wandering Hindu priest **Nirartha**, who sailed across to Bali from his home in Java during the sixteenth century. Legends describe how the holy man was preaching at Pura Rambut Siwi, about 50km northwest up the coast, when he was distracted by a beaming light from the southeast. Setting off in search of the source, Nirartha arrived at Tanah Lot to find that the light was shining from a holy spring here. He began to preach to the local people of Beraban, but this angered the village priest who demanded that the rival holy man should leave. In response, Nirartha meditated so hard that he pushed the rock he was sitting on out into the sea; this became the Tanah Lot "island". He then dedicated his new retreat to the god of the sea and transformed his scarf into poisonous snakes to protect the place. Ever since then, Pura Tanah Lot has been one of the most holy places on Bali, closely associated with several other important temples along this coast, including Pura Rambut Siwi and Pura Luhur Uluwatu.

Because of its sacred status, only bona fide devotees are allowed to climb the temple stairway carved out of the rock face and enter the compounds; everyone else is confined to the patch of grey sand around the base of the rock (which is under water at high tide). When the waters are low enough, you can take a sip of **holy water** (*air suci*) from the spring that rises beneath the temple rock (donation requested) or stroke the holy coral **snakes** that are kept in nests behind the cliff face. Otherwise, your best option is to climb up to the mainland clifftop in search of the best viewing spot. If you follow the signed **clifftop path** to the southwest (right) of the temple rock you can admire the great panorama that extends as far as the raised plateau of the Bukit on Bali's southernmost tip. When Pura Tanah Lot and the other south-coast temples were built, the aim was to try and make each coastal temple visible from the next one in the "chain", thereby creating a tangible string of shrines honouring the god of the sea. The sixteenth-century builders did well here, as you can certainly make out the location, if not the actual profile, of the next in the chain, Pura Luhur Uluwatu, which stands above the Bukit cliffs.

Continuing along the coast path, you'll pass a string of small weather-beaten **clifftop shrines** perched on the edges of narrow promontories. From the rock shelf that supports tiny **Pura Galuh** you get a fantastic view of Pura Tanah Lot's two *meru*, as well as the curved flight of rock-cut steps that leads up to them. North of Pura Galuh, the jagged coastline juts out into dozens of tiny bays, most of which are accessible from the clifftop, though the grey-sand beaches are prone to strong waves and aren't that inviting for swimming. After about 1km, the path veers inland, through a tiny hamlet and past the imposing **Pura Pekendungan**. Follow the path around to the right of this temple to get back to the Tanah Lot car park, or veer left to rejoin the coastal path that leads to the beach at Yeh Gangga, an hour and a half's walk away (see p.350).

### Practicalities

Though there are occasional bright-blue **bemos** from Denpasar's Ubung terminal direct to Tanah Lot, you'll probably end up having to go via **KEDIRI**, 12km northeast of the temple complex on the main Denpasar–Tabanan road. All Ubung (Denpasar)–Gilimanuk bemos pass through Kediri (about R3000; 30min), whose bemo station is at the crossroads where the road branches left for Tanah Lot, right for central Tabanan and straight on for Gilimanuk. Bright-blue Kediri–Tanah Lot bemos (about Rp5000; 25min) run fairly regularly in daylight hours, more frequently in the morning.

If arriving under your own steam from Kuta, the prettiest **route to Tanah Lot** is via Kerobokan and Beraban, passing through classic rice terraces and traditional small villages. Alternatively, you could come via the *subak* rice museum in nearby Tabanan (see p.348), or make a slight detour to the ceramic-producing village of Pejaten (see opposite).

From Tanah Lot car park, you have the choice of two **approaches to the temple complex**. Usual access is through the corridor of souvenir stalls leading straight to the temple rock; a less crowded and more dramatic route takes you through the back of the car park, via the hamlet described above.

There's an ATM, several **exchange** booths and a wartel in Tanah Lot's tourist village, in front of *Dewi Sinta Cottages* hotel.

### Accommodation and eating

Tanah Lot all but dies after the last tour bus pulls away at about 7.30pm, so there's little incentive to stay here overnight, though there are a few **hotels** to choose from. The most convenient of these is the welcoming, well-managed *Dewi Sinta Cottages*, beside the entrance ticket-booth (☏0361/812933, ⊛www.balinetwork .com/dewisinta.html, ⊜dewisinta@dps.wasantara.net.id; ❹–❻), whose fan and air-con bungalows are set in a soothing tropical garden with swimming pool; the fan rooms have the best views, overlooking the pool and the ricefields beyond. Set well away from the commercial clutter, about 500m back along the access road from the temple car park, *Pondok Wisata Astiti Graha* (☎0361/812955; ❷) is surrounded by ricefields and offers spotless if rudimentary rooms with cold-water bathrooms. On an entirely different scale, the super-swanky *Le Meridien Nirwana Golf and Spa Resort* (☎0361/815900, ⓦwww.lemeridien-bali.com; ❾) is a huge five-star luxury hotel renowned for its quality service, exquisite private villas and much-praised Greg Norman–designed 18-hole golf course ($130). Its extensive grounds enjoy views of Pura Tanah Lot and feature three swimming pools (you can't swim in the sea here) and a spa.

The coastal path overlooking the temple complex is packed with **restaurants** affording prime views and predictably inflated prices, but you get a better menu at the *Dewi Sinta Restaurant* in the tourist village. A more peaceful place to eat is the *Bali Lestari*, located in a tranquil ricefield setting about 100m before the Tanah Lot car park; the food is standard, but the views are nice and staff will drive you back to the temple for free.

### Pejaten

About 6km northeast of Tanah Lot and signed off the Kediri–Tanah Lot road, the ceramic-producing village of **PEJATEN** is famous as the place where most Balinese roof tiles and roof-crown ornaments (*ketu*) are made. Of more interest to tourists is the distinctive Pejaten **ceramic ware**, with its idiosyncratic designs and trademark pastel grey-green, powder blue, and beige glazes. Pejaten ceramicists are especially known for their tiny pots, bowls and stoppered bottles, as well as for earthenware plates and bowls, many of which are decorated with lively figurines of frogs, geckos or monkeys. Although Pejaten ceramics are now sold in most of the big resorts, you should be able to get better prices and a bigger choice in the village itself: Tanteri's Ceramic shop in the centre of the village stocks an impressive variety. There are kilns dotted all over the village, each of them fuelled by coconut husks, which lie in piles along the roadside – about as industrial as rural Bali gets. To have a look inside one of the workshops, follow the signs for CV Keramic.

## Tabanan and around

Despite being the former capital of the ancient kingdom of Tabanan and the administrative centre of one of Bali's most fertile districts, **TABANAN** itself is only a medium-sized town with little to encourage a protracted stop. Its one outstanding feature is the **Subak Museum**, a kind of ethnographic exhibition about rice farming in Bali. Otherwise, Tabanan's main claim to fame is as the home of the outstanding dancer, I Ketut Marya, known as **Mario**, remembered for his astonishing performances of the *kebyar*, which he reinvented and popularized in the 1920s (see p.475).

Historically, the kingdom of Tabanan was always one of the more stable power centres, holding out against the Dutch until the last possible moment when, in 1906, the colonialists launched their offensive on southern Bali and then – irked by the refusal of the Tabanan royal house to outlaw *suttee* (self-immolation of bereaved wives) – marched on Tabanan. The raja of Tabanan and his crown prince had decided to negotiate rather than commit *puputan*, but the Dutch refused to make a deal and, rather than face exile to Lombok or Madura, the regents committed suicide inside Denpasar prison. Little now remains of the former kingdom, as the Dutch sacked Tabanan's main *puri*, leaving only the subsidiary palace at Krambitan, 8km away.

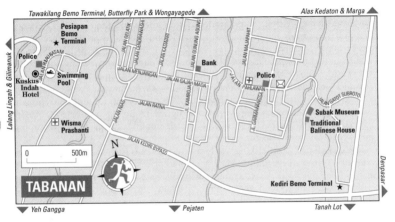

## Practicalities

All Ubung (Denpasar)–Gilimanuk **bemos** bypass Tabanan town centre, dropping passengers at the **Pesiapan terminal**, a major transport hub on the northwest edge of town. Bright-yellow city bemos shuttle from Pesiapan into the town centre (Rp3000), 1.5km east, where you'll find most of the banks, ATMs and currency exchanges, plus Internet access and the post office, on Jalan Gajah Mada and its continuation, Jalan Pahlawan. Several regional bemo services run out of Pesiapan, including to Krambitan (Rp2000), Kediri (for Tanah Lot; Rp3000) and Taman Ayun (Mengwi), plus occasional services to Yeh Gangga. For **accommodation**, you could do worse than the *Kuskus Indah Hotel* (☎0361/815373; ❷), whose clean fan and air-con rooms are located just a few metres west of the Pesiapan bemo station at Jalan Pulau Batam 32 – and there's a public swimming pool across the road (Rp4000). There are much more scenic places for an extended stay, however, at Yeh Gangga beach 8km southwest (see p.350), or further west at Lalang Linggah (Balian beach; see p.356).

## Subak Museum and Traditional Balinese House

Tabanan's two most interesting sights are rarely visited by tourists but are worth a look nonetheless. They're both located on the eastern edge of town, within 100m of each other. The Subak Museum is signposted off the main Tabanan road in **BANJAR SENGGULAN**, 1.5km east of Tabanan town centre and about the same distance west of the Kediri T-junction; the Traditional Balinese House is signed from the Subak Museum itself. Coming from Ubung, either alight at the Kediri junction and walk the 1.5km, or change on to a town-centre bemo at the Pesiapan terminal.

### Subak Museum

Tabanan district has long been a major rice producer, and the **Subak Museum** or Mandala Mathika Subak (Mon–Thurs & Sat 8am–4.30pm, Fri 8am–1pm; donation requested) celebrates the role of the rice-farmers' collectives (the *subak*) by describing traditional farming practices and exhibiting typical agricultural implements.

One of the most interesting displays explains the complex and yet completely unmechanized **irrigation system** used by every *subak* on the island – a process that's known to have been in operation on Bali as early as 600 AD. Fundamental to any irrigation system is the underground tunnel that connects the river water supply to the *subak*. This artificial watercourse then feeds hundreds of small channels that are dug to crisscross the *subak* area. A system of tiny wooden dams regulates the water flow along these channels: small wooden weirs block and divert the water, while lengths of wood with angled castellations carved from them, called *tektek*, determine both the volume and the direction of the flow. Also worth looking out for are the **basket muzzles** that are placed over cows' heads to stop them eating grass while they're towing the plough, the **spiked wooden tweezers** used to catch eels from the waterlogged paddies at night, and the **wooden nets** used to trap dragonflies, which are prized as delicacies by the Balinese.

## Traditional Balinese House

Less than 100m from the Subak Museum, the **Traditional Balinese House** (hours as above; free) was built to give visitors an idea of the typical layout of a village home, comprising a series of thatched *bale* (pavilions) in a walled compound. Each *bale* has a specific function and must be located in a particular spot within the compound, specified by the sacred Balinese direction *kaja* (towards the sacred Gunung Agung mountain) and its counterpoint *kelod* (away from the mountain, or towards the sea). There are no labels or guides here, but for more information on sacred Balinese architecture and an annotated plan of a traditional house compound, see p.491.

True to form, in this house the **family temple** occupies the *kaja* (mountainward) corner, to the far left of the entrance gate. To the right of the temple, the open-sided *bale dangin* is reserved for ceremonial functions, in particular for marriage and funeral rites. The enclosed, windowless pavilion along the left-hand (north) wall of the compound is the *bale daja* for sleeping, and next to that, immediately to the left of the entrance gate, stands the open-sided multifunctional pavilion, which can be adapted for sleeping if necessary. Straight ahead of the entrance gate in the middle of the compound, the only two-storey *bale* has an enclosed rice-storage barn upstairs and a breezy social space or guestroom below. The kitchen pavilion or *paon* stands to the right of the entrance in the *kelod* corner, diagonally opposite the temple, and contains a few traditional cooking implements made from bamboo and coconut wood; the nearby *bale* along the right-hand (south) wall is for rice milling. There's no bathroom, as villagers traditionally do their ablutions outdoors.

## Taman Kupu Kupu Butterfly Park

About 5km north of Tabanan, in the village of **WANASARI** on the road to Gunung Batukau, the **Taman Kupu Kupu Butterfly Park** (daily 8am–5pm, last entry 4pm; Rp40,000, kids Rp20,000) houses an impressive and informatively labelled variety of butterfly species from all over Indonesia in its small but prettily landscaped garden. The best time to visit is in the morning when the butterflies flit around most energetically. All Tabanan–Penebel **bemos** go past Taman Kupu Kupu, departing from the Tawakilang terminal, which is 2km north of Tabanan town centre on the Penebel road and accessed by a town-centre bemo from central Tabanan or Pesiapan terminal.

## Tunjuk

The tiny, very traditional village of **Tunjuk**, about 7km northeast from Tabanan's Tawakilang bemo terminal and junction (or 3km west of the Margarana Memorial), hosts an interesting "village life" programme organized through **Taman Sri Buwana** (reserve ahead on ☎0361/742 5929, ⓦwww .balitreasureisland.com/sribuwana; $39). It features visits to the local elementary school and to a traditional house compound that is home to 29 different families (all related) each with their own kitchen, *lumbung*, general *bale* and sleeping pavilion, as well as a rice-farming demonstration, a walk through the ricefields, and lunch. Contact Taman Sri Buwana or Bali Discovery Tours (℡0361/286283, ⓦwww.balidiscovery.com) for transport.

### Alas Kedaton Monkey Forest

Less interesting than Sangeh Monkey Forest (see p.342), **Alas Kedaton** (daily 8am–6pm; Rp3300, kids Rp1500), 3km north of the Kediri junction, is only worth a visit for the chance to get close to its resident monkeys, who are not as aggressive as many of their cousins elsewhere in Bali. The temple here is a quite recently constructed *pura dalem*, or temple of the dead, out of bounds to tourists, and the monkeys only congregate in the small area of the forest along the temple's perimeters. Beware of getting landed with a guide, who will pester you into visiting their souvenir shop on the edge of the temple car park. Access to Alas Kedaton is via Kediri: either take a bemo from Denpasar's Ubung terminal to Kediri, then charter another one for the final 3km, or drive to Kediri, then follow signs for Marga.

## Yeh Gangga beach

Heading west out of Tabanan, nearly every minor road that branches off south leads straight to the coast, a barely developed stretch of black sand notable for its strong currents and weird offshore rock formations. One of the most appealing sections is at **YEH GANGGA**, 10km southwest of Tabanan, where there are two exceptionally attractive sets of bungalows – a good base from which to explore the area if you have your own transport. The sea gets pretty rough here, and is too dangerous for swimming, but it's a dramatic scene, punctuated by huge eroded rocks, and the beach stretches for miles in both directions. You can walk along the coast to Tanah Lot (see p.346) in under two hours, and the Pejaten ceramics village (see p.347) is within easy cycling distance.

The access road to Yeh Gangga is signposted off the main road about 4km west of the Kediri junction, or you can get there via back roads from Tanah Lot. Occasional Yeh Gangga **bemos** depart Tabanan's Pesiapan terminal (45min) but you may have to charter one (Rp15,000).

At the end of the road you'll come to *Bali Wisata Bungalows* ✈ (℡0361/7443561, ⓦwww.baliwisatabungalows.com; ❸–❺), whose half a dozen large, spacious, fan-cooled **bungalows** are set in a wild shorefront garden of cacti and windblown shrubs, with nothing but the sea and the rice-paddies in sight. Many of the bungalows have separate living areas and some have kitchen facilities; they all have fine views. There's a large salt-water swimming pool, a spa and massage service, plenty of info on local activities, daily transport into Tabanan, and a good restaurant. Call to arrange transport from the airport.

About 1km northwest along the coast, beyond the rock with a hole, is *Waka Gangga* (℡0361/416256, ⓦwww.wakaexperience.com; ❾), perhaps the nicest of the idiosyncratic *Waka* group of small luxury hotels. Its ten exquisite, circular bungalows are scattered across terraced rice-paddies and beautifully constructed from dark woods, rough-cut stone and natural fabrics; each one has a garden bathroom and huge glass windows affording panoramic 270-degree views of the ocean to the south and ricefields to the north. There's a swimming pool, restaurant and spa here, too.

△ Yeh Gangga beach

## Krambitan and around

Midway between the main road and the coast, the village of **KRAMBITAN**, 8km southwest of Tabanan, lacks obvious attractions, but makes a pleasing base for staying in a typically Balinese environment that rarely sees foreign overnight visitors. There are some pretty villages, fine rice-paddy landscapes and empty beaches within cycling distance, and you also get the chance to sleep in a royal palace. Frequent turquoise **bemos** connect Krambitan with Tabanan's Pesiapan terminal, taking about thirty minutes. If driving from Kuta or Denpasar, take the back road via Kerobokan, Beraban and Pejaten for the most scenic route.

In the late seventeenth century, Krambitan became the home of a branch of the **royal family** of Tabanan, and some of their descendants still live here. Deprived of their political role, the rajas' offspring have turned to tourism, transforming part of one of their palaces into compact but elegant guest **accommodation**. The palace compound of *Puri Anyar* (☎0361/812668, ⓕ810885; ⑥) is an impressively grand composition of elaborate carvings and tropical garden courtyards, within which are several *bale* for accommodating paying guests, each one furnished with a huge four-poster bed and garden bathroom; rooms must be reserved ahead as this is still very much a family home. If asked, *Puri Anyar* can also arrange cultural one-day programmes that incorporate demonstrations in dance, traditional games, kite design, and making offerings.

Another descendant of the Tabanan royal family lives just around the corner from *Puri Anyar*, at **Puri Agung Wisata**, which you can visit for a small donation. Though Puri Agung (literally "big" or "main" palace) is the most important of the Tabanan palaces, it seems much less stylish than *Puri Anyar*, but might be worth a look for the special tooth-filing pavilion and family temple compound. Apparently, it's a popular venue for tourists' wedding parties.

Both Krambitan and the neighbouring village of **PANARUKAN** have a reputation for their outstanding dancers, who sometimes give **dance performances** at *Puri Anyar* (call for details). They are particularly renowned for their *calonarang*, a ritual cleansing Barong and Rangda dance in which almost half the village participates (see p.474) and for their *tektekan* bamboo percussion orchestra.

# North to Gunung Batukau

Much of inland southwest Bali lies in the shadow of the massive **Gunung Batukau** (sometimes spelled Bautukaru; 2276m), the second highest mountain on the island (after Gunung Agung) and one of the holiest. All west Bali temples have a shrine dedicated to the spirit of Gunung Batukau, and on the lower slopes of the holy mountain itself stands the beautiful **Pura Luhur Batukau**, Bali's directional temple (*kayangan jagat*) for the west and the focus of many pilgrimages.

Gunung Batukau and its hinterland is the **wettest** region of Bali, and the dense tropical forest that clothes the uppermost slopes has been designated a nature reserve, a particularly rewarding area for **bird-watching**. Lower down, on the gentler slopes that effectively stretch all the way to Tabanan, 21km southeast of Pura Luhur, the superior soil provides some of the most productive agricultural land on the island: the rice terraces around **Jatiluwih** are particularly scenic. Because of Batukau's cool, damp microclimate, it's worth bringing warm clothes and rain gear up here with you, even if you're only making a brief visit to Pura Luhur Batukau (817m above sea level) or are planning to stay in comfort in the nearby village of **Wongayagede**.

### Transport practicalities

From Tabanan, with your own transport, you have a choice of two main **routes to Batukau**. The following account describes a circular tour to Pura Luhur Batukau and back, going up via Penatahan and Wongayagede and returning via Jatiluwih, Senganan and Penebel.

There are no public **bemos** to Pura Luhur Batukau, though there is a service that goes as far as Jatiluwih, via Penebel, and you may be able to charter the same bemo on to Pura Luhur. The Tabanan–Penebel–Jatiluwih bemos leave from the bemo terminal at Tawakilang, 2km north of Tabanan's town centre – approximately hourly in the mornings, less frequently after noon.

Most **tour** operators offer trips to Pura Luhur Batukau, usually in combination with a few hours at the *Yeh Panas Natural Hot Spring and Spa Hotel*, or as part of an itinerary that also takes in the Jatiluwih rice terraces and either the Pura Taman Ayun at Mengwi or Bedugul's Pura Ulun Danu. Sobek (☎0361/287059, ⓦwww.99bali.com/adventure/sobek) run guided **mountain-bike** trips down the side of Gunung Batukau for US$55, and *Paddy Venture* do bicycle and quad-bike tours through the Jatiluwih ricefields (see p.126 for details).

### Tabanan to Wongayagede (via Yeh Panas)

The main **Tabanan–Wongayagede route** follows a well-maintained road all the way from Tabanan town centre: simply keep a lookout for signs to Pura Luhur Batukau. Beyond Tabanan the road passes through several shrub-lined villages, past the butterfly park in Wanasari (see p.349) and on through archetypal

Balinese scenes of rice terraces and tree-shaded roads before reaching a junction at **BURUAN**. The right-hand fork will take you up to Gunung Batukau via Penebel, Senganan and Jatiluwih, and is described in reverse on p.355.

Soon after taking the left-hand fork you pass through the village of **PENA-TAHAN**, site of the **Yeh Panas Hot Springs**. These sulphurous springs have been bought up by the *Yeh Panas Natural Hot Spring and Spa Hotel* (☎0361/262356, ✉espa_yehpanes@telkom.net; ❼) so to enjoy them you either need to stay overnight in the comfortable air-con bungalows built high on the hillside for optimum rice-terrace views, or you can buy a spa package with or without lunch ($15/50). For a soak in a more natural hot spring, continue past the hotel for a few hundred metres, along the road to Pura Luhur, and a tiny sign points you 100m west down a track to a traditional hot-spring pool.

A few kilometres north of Yeh Panas, about 500m before the road enters Wongayagede, you'll see the Catholic church (*gereja*) of St Martinus de Pons, on the northern fringe of the hamlet of **TENGKUDAK**. It's likely to be locked but the facade is quite an interesting example of Balinese Christian architecture: several Christian motifs have been carved on to an otherwise typical red-brick facade and the whole structure is crowned with a four-tiered Hindu-style *meru* tower.

## Wongayagede

If you're planning to climb Gunung Batukau (see box, on p.354), you'll need to spend at least one night in **WONGAYAGEDE**, the village nearest to the trailhead, about 2km south of the temple car park. Even if you're not intending to trek up the mountain, a night or two here would be a rewarding experience – remote and extremely scenic, offering ample opportunity to explore the tranquil countryside.

The poshest **place to stay** in the village is the exceptionally tranquil *Prana Dewi* ⚑ (☎08133/866 0154, ⓦwww.balipranaresort.com; ❻–❼), signed west off the main road through the village (north of the side road to Jatiluwih). Occupying an idyllic, inspirational spot within the ricefields and enjoying wonderful views of majestic Gunung Batukau, *Prana Dewi*'s eight stylish bungalows are thoughtfully designed with traditional features, picture windows, verandas and four-poster beds, and widely spaced amidst the garden's streams and ponds; there are no fans or air-con as it's cool up here at 636m. The **restaurant** is worth visiting in its own right: it shares the same views and serves home-grown red rice, organic vegetables, salads and brown bread as well as curries (from Rp28,000) and pasta. You can arrange **guides** for the Gunung Batukau trek here, as well as for less taxing local walks. *Prana Dewi* also holds regular **yoga retreats** ($180 for three days full-board).

The other place to stay also boasts breathtaking views and a genuine homestay welcome: *Warung Kaja* (☎0811/398052, ✉pkaler@dps.centrin.net.id; ❷) is about 750m east along the Wongayagede–Jatiluwih road and has just two very rustic bungalows, one behind the family home and the other all on its own in the middle of the ricefields. The manager leads local treks through the fields and up to the temple (4hr; Rp60,000 per person).

## Pura Luhur Batukau

Usually silent – except for its resident orchestra of cicadas and frogs – **Pura Luhur Batukau** (donation requested) does full justice to its epithet, the "Garden Temple". The grassy courtyards are planted with flowering hibiscus, Javanese ixora and cempaka shrubs, and the montane forest that carpets the slopes of Gunung Batukau encroaches on the compound's perimeters to the north,

## Climbing Gunung Batukau

Few people **climb** the sacred slopes of Gunung Batukau, and during the leech-ridden rainy season (Nov–March), not even the most sure-footed Balinese would attempt it. If you do decide to climb (July is the best month), you'll definitely need a guide. Although there are fairly well-defined paths nearly all the way to the summit (starting from the outer courtyard of Pura Luhur Batukau), many turn out to be false trails. In addition, the slopes are thickly wooded and offer few clearings from which to work out your bearings. When you finally reach the peak, you'll find a small temple dedicated to the god of the mountain. Constant shade and low-lying cloud also make the atmosphere damp and the paths quite slippery, so you should come prepared with warm clothes, rainwear, and decent shoes. The usual guided climb takes four to six hours to reach the summit (though it has been done in two and a half), and three to five hours to return to ground level. To complete the climb and descent in one day you'll need to start at sunrise, having spent the night in Wongayagede 2km down the road; although this is just about possible, some people like to camp near the top.

You can organize **guides** through *Prana Dewi* or *Warung Kaja* in Wongayagede but both places use the guys who hang around the temple so you could also organize it directly with them. They offer several programmes, including short hikes part way up the slopes to various of the mountain's shrines (1–3hr; Rp100,000 per guide per hour), return day-hikes to the summit (Rp700,000 per guide; bring your own water and food – beef is not permitted on the mountain), and overnight summit treks (Rp1,000,000 per guide; bring your own sleeping bag, food and water). It's also possible to climb Gunung Batukau via the mountain's southwestern flank, beginning near the village of Sanda on the Seririt–Pupuan–Antosari road; a guide can be arranged through *Sanda Butik Villas*, described on p.374.

east and west. Monuments are encrusted with moist green moss, and a web of paths fans out to solitary shrines set further into the forest. Batukau's **bird** population finds plenty to feed on here, so you're likely to see a fair number of forest dwellers, including bright green woodpecker-like barbets, scarlet minivets, olive-green grey-headed flycatchers, and possibly even scarlet-headed flowerpeckers in the temple treetops.

Pura Luhur Batukau is thought to have become a holy site in the eleventh century, and was subsequently consecrated by the rajas of the kingdom of Tabanan who made it into their state temple and dedicated shrines here to their ancestral gods. In 1604, however, the rival rajas of Bululeng razed the shrines to the ground and, although devotees continued to worship at the ruins, the temple was not fully renovated until 1959. Many of the thatched *meru* now standing inside the **inner sanctuary** still represent a particular branch or member of the ancestral family of the rajas of Tabanan. The most important shrine, though, is the unusual seven-tiered pagoda, which is dedicated to Mahadewa, the god of Gunung Batukau. To the east of the main temple compound, a large square **pond** has been dug to represent and honour the gods of nearby Danau Tamblingan, which lies immediately to the north of Gunung Batukau. Only Batukau's priests are allowed access to the tiny island shrine in the middle of the pond, which they reach by means of a makeshift raft on a pulley.

In deference to Pura Luhur's extremely sacred status, visitors are requested to obey the strict **rules of admission** that are posted at the entrance. Aside from the usual prohibitions, such as menstruating women and those who have been recently bereaved, Batukau also bars pregnant women and new mothers (who are considered ritually impure for 42 days after the birth), as well as "mad ladies/gentleman". Pura Luhur Batukau still plays a very important role in the lives of Balinese Hindus. Members of local *subak* groups come here to draw holy water from the pond for use in agricultural ceremonies, and at the annual Galungan festivities truckloads of devotees travel long distances to pay their respects and lay their offerings.

## Wongayagede to Tabanan (via Jatiluwih)

The road to Jatiluwih branches east from Wongayagede about 2.5km south of Pura Luhur, and then proceeds to take you through some of the most famous rice-paddy vistas on Bali, offering expansive panoramas over the broad and gently sloping terraces and, cloud-cover permitting, background shots of Gunung Batukau as well. A short distance along the road, a couple of bends beyond *Warung Kaja* homestay (described on p.353), *Paddy Venture* (☎0361/467947) is the first of several restaurants to make the most of the glorious vistas, and also runs **tours** through the paddies on foot and by bicycle, quad-bike and Land Rover ($40–69). A couple of kilometres further east, the *Naga Puspa* restaurant makes another great vantage point as the road begins to wend through ever more lush landscapes, dense with banana trees, *kopi bali* coffee plantations, fields of chilli peppers and tomato plants, ferns and *dadap* trees, plus the occasional chicken farm; you may be charged a village tax to pass through here (Rp3300 per person, plus Rp1500 per car). This whole area is known as **JATILUWIH**, after the hamlet of the same name, where the long-running *Café Jatiluwih* (7.5km from the Wongayagede junction) is another welcoming spot for a scenic break.

About 11km from Wongayagede, the road arrives at the **SENGANAN** road junction. The quickest route to the north or south coasts is the northeast (left) fork, a good, fast 7.5-kilometre road that feeds into the main Denpasar–Bedugul–Singaraja artery at Pacung, 6km south of Bedugul and 25km north of Mengwi. For the slower, more scenic route to Buruan and Tabanan, take the southbound (right) fork that runs via the sizeable market town of **PENEBEL**.

# The coast road to Negara

Few tourists venture further west than Tanah Lot, but the stretch of coast beyond Tabanan holds some nice surprises at the black-sand beaches of **Balian** and **Medewi**. The spectacular cliff-side temple of **Pura Rambut Siwi**, almost as stunningly located as Tanah Lot but far less crowded with visitors, provides a cultural focus for this area, while **Negara** really only merits a visit for its twice-yearly traditional buffalo races.

The main road divides 16km west of Tabanan at the village of **ANTOSARI**, splitting the thundering westbound Gilimanuk and Java traffic from the vehicles heading to Seririt and the north coast. The northbound road, served by Ubung (Denpasar)–Seririt–Singaraja buses and dark-red bemos, climbs through some pretty impressive mountain scenery and is described on p.374.

## Lalang Linggah and Balian beach

Heading west through Antosari and along the base of the mountain ridge, the road to Gilimanuk drops right down to the coast, affording fine sea views with shadows of southeast Java on the horizon, along with tantalizing inland panoramas of paddy-fields. You can make more of these views by stopping off at *Soka Indah* (☎0361/246004; ❷), located in **Soka** at the point where the road hits the coast. The large, tour-group-oriented restaurant here is better than it looks and, if you follow the path down from the car park to the sea (Rp1000 for non-guests), you'll find a couple of large, surprisingly secluded, comfortable bungalows with fine sea views.

About 10km west of Antosari, the Gilimanuk road zips through **LALANG LINGGAH**, the village closest to **Balian beach**, a spiritually charged spot at the mouth of the Balian River, whose caves and headlands are frequented by priests and shamen and whose three surf breaks attract committed waveriders. It's a pleasantly low-key place to hang out, with some inviting accommodation, though take local advice on the vicious current, which can make it too dangerous for casual swimmers. Fields of rice run down to the grey-sand beach, spiked by occasional cashew trees and stands of clove, cinnamon and cocoa bushes, and there are a few tracks to explore here and inland, up the course of the river, or you can just head west along the thirty-kilometre-long beach.

All Ubung (Denpasar)–Gilimanuk **bemos** and buses pass through Lalang Linggah; they take about an hour and a quarter from Ubung or about half an hour from Medewi. Coming from the north coast you can take any Seririt–Pulukan or Singaraja–Seririt–Antosari bemo and then change onto the Ubung–Gilimanuk service.

### Accommodation

Lalang Linggah has a small but enticing range of **accommodation** options. Signed from the Gilimanuk road on the west side of the Balian River estuary, *Sacred River Retreat* (*Sungai Suci*; ℡0361/814993; ⑥–⑦) is an alternative resort with an emphasis on spiritual activities. You can join the regular meditation and yoga sessions here, learn silk painting, dancing, bamboo gamelan or singing, and request an audience with a local *dukun* (traditional faith healer). The eleven two-storey bungalows are simple and mellow; some have upstairs bedrooms and downstairs garden bathrooms, and there are three pools and a vegetarian restaurant (bring your own alcohol). About 400m west of *Sacred River*, signs take you 400m south off the main road to *Gajah Mina* ☂ (℡0812/381 1630, ⓦwww.gajahminaresort.com; ⑧), a chic little walled hideaway of seven artfully designed bungalows and a couple of family suites, each with French windows on to its own very private garden terrace, and easy access down to the mouth of the Balian River and its three beaches. There's a luxurious pool here, a bar, and a restaurant serving outstanding French-influenced cuisine. Nearby *Pondok Pisces* ☂ (℡08133/879 7722, ⓦwww.pondokpisces.com; ②–⑤) is a lovely, welcoming little homestay just 300m from the sea (follow signs for *Gajah Mina* from the main road) and run by an Australian–Indonesian couple. Its five fan-cooled rooms and bungalows are comfortably designed and all slightly different, the most distinctive being the authentic hand-carved wooden house shipped over from Timor; guests can use the pool at *Gajah Mina*.

## Medewi beach

As it skirts the coastline, the 25km stretch of road between Lalang Linggah and Medewi beach crosses more than a dozen rivers, each one streaming down from the Batukau mountain range, watering kilometre after kilometre of stunningly lush land en route. Rice-paddies dominate the landscape, some even dropping right down to the shoreline, but this area is also a major coconut-growing region as well as a big producer of vanilla pods, cloves, cocoa beans and coffee.

**MEDEWI** village sits on the main Tabanan–Gilimanuk road, served by frequent bemos (about 2hr from Ubung), and consists of little more than a mosque and a string of houses in among coconut groves and paddy-fields. It was first settled in 1912, when the whole area was covered in thorny *ketket* trees; the Balinese word for "thorny" is *meduwi*, hence the name of the village, though the trees have all been cleared now. The black-sand shore is primarily a fishing beach, but there's a small enclave of shorefront bungalows catering mainly to **surfers**: the light current and fairly benign waves makes this a popular spot for novices. You can also rent boats here, either to go snorkelling or for a spot of fishing.

The most popular **accommodation** is the friendly, surfer-oriented *Homestay G'de* (℡0812/397 6668; ●), whose exceptionally cheap warung right on the shore serves huge portions at tiny prices and gives access to eight primitive but perfectly acceptable en-suite rooms in a two-storey block. The cheapest rooms at the adjacent *Hotel Pantai Medewi*, also known as *Medewi Beach Cottages* (℡0365/40029, ℻41555; ●–●), are twice as pricey and half as nice, though their more expensive air-con cottages occupy seafront positions and are set in pleasant gardens with a swimming pool. The *Pantai Medewi* also organizes day-trips and diving excursions to Pulau Menjangan. About 200m further west along the beach, or a bit further by road, the slightly run-down *Hotel Tin Jaya* (℡0365/42945; ●) has en-suite rooms in rice-barn-style cottages set beside a beachfront lawn. Twenty minutes' walk east along the shore from *Homestay G'de*, or about 5km by road, there's attractive, rather luxurious accommodation at seafront *Puri Dajuma Cottages* (℡0365/43955, 🌐www.dajuma.com; ●), where the bungalows are surrounded by a tropical garden, with pool, spa and *hammam*, and are pleasingly furnished with four-poster beds and garden bathrooms. *Puri Dajuma* also runs a programme of interesting trips around this untouristed area of Bali; the hotel is signed off the main Gilimanuk road in the village of Pekutatan.

## Pura Rambut Siwi

When the sixteenth-century Hindu priest Nirartha sailed to Bali from Java, he paused at a spot 16km west of modern-day Medewi and, impressed by its rugged coastline and views across to his homeland, he claimed it as holy and began preaching the Hindu doctrine. On leaving to continue his tour of Bali, Nirartha donated a lock of his hair to the villagers, who duly erected a temple and named it **Pura Rambut Siwi**, "the temple for worshipping the hair". This temple is now the most important in Jembrana district and is easily reached by the Denpasar–Gilimanuk **bemo** and then a 750-metre side-road through the paddy-fields to the coast. You'll be asked by the Brahman temple caretakers to wear a sash and give a donation, and in return they will offer to guide you around the temple.

Nirartha's sacred hair is enshrined, along with some of his clothing, in a sandalwood box buried deep inside the central three-tiered *meru*. This shrine is the focus of the **inner courtyard**, which is inaccessible to casual visitors but can be admired from alongside its south-facing **paduraksa**. Built in tiers of solid red brick and ornamented with fierce stonecarvings of open-mouthed Bhoma, the gateway gives direct access to the cliff face and frames a stunning view of the Bali Strait. From here you pass between an assortment of guardian statues to the outer *candi bentar*, which is protected by two mythical tigers. The figure that stands in the middle of the stairway, staring out to sea with his right arm raised, is said to be looking sorrowfully at Java (you can see Mount Bromo quite distinctly from here), bemoaning the ascendance of Islam over the Hindu kingdom of Majapahit. Gently stepped garden terraces of frangipani and stubby palm trees connect the *candi bentar* with the **shrine to Dewi Sri**, goddess of rice and of water and hence of prosperity, that balances on the cliff edge.

Descending the rock-cut steps to the charcoal-black-sand beach, you'll find a string of small shrines tucked into the cliff face to the left of the stairway. The first, a cave temple known as **Pura Tirta**, houses a holy freshwater spring that rises just under the cliff and is guarded by a statue of Nirartha. A series of dank, bat-infested caves links Pura Tirta to **Goa Mayan Sati** (the Cave of the Holy Tiger), 50m further east, but the underground complex is out of bounds to visitors as all new priests of Pura Rambut Siwi meditate here before becoming fully ordained. A one-hundred-metre walk further up the beach brings you to **Pura Penataran**, dedicated to the god of the sea, Baruna, and protected by a couple of underwater snake deities, or *naga* – white for Siwa, black for Wisnu.

## Negara

Formerly the home of the Jembrana royal family and still the administrative capital of Jembrana district, **NEGARA** is graced with wide boulevards, a large number of mosques and a noticeably Islamic feel. Historically, this was a major port of entry for the Javanese and Madurese, who would sail across the Bali Strait to the river estuary at Perancak and then head up the Ijo Gading River into the town, 7km further north. **Pura Perancak**, at the mouth of the estuary, commemorates the landing of the influential Javanese Hindu priest Nirartha here in the sixteenth century. Negara's Muslims, already well established here by the nineteenth century, came mostly from southern Sulawesi, many of them people of Bugis origin, descendants of a seafaring race with a reputation as fearsome pirates. Traditional Bugis-style housing – raised, elongated wooden structures – still features in the area, notably in the hamlet of **Loloan Timor**, 6km up the river estuary and about 1km south of Negara town centre.

Negara's one significant attraction are its traditional **buffalo races** or *mekepung*, which are organized by the Jembrana authorities and held here every dry season, usually in August and then again between September and November (check with any Balinese tourist office for the dates and exact location; most tour agents sell all-inclusive trips to the races). The buffalo and their jockeys come from all parts of Jembrana district, divided into two teams according to whether they live east or west of the Ijo Gading River. Decked out in strings of bells and decorative harness, their horns painted in bright colours, the buffalo pairs are paraded in front of the spectators before the competition begins. The races last all day and take place along a two-kilometre stretch of Negara's back roads. Buffalo pairs, both hauling along a *cikar* cart, are pitted against each other,

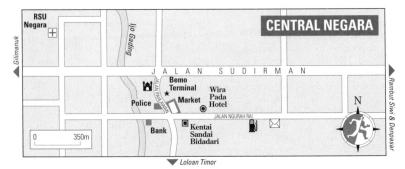

encouraged by whip-happy jockeys. Every winning pair gains points for its team, but stylish contenders are also awarded bonuses; the victors are announced at the end of the day. It's thought that the games were introduced to Negara by the farmers who emigrated from the island of Madura, off northeast Java, where similar races are still held; the only other traditional buffalo races in Bali are held in Lovina on the north coast (see p.331). During the rest of the year, **buffalo-race practices** are held every Sunday morning (7–9am), with alternate Sundays being competition day, in **Delod Berawah**, which is signed off the Denpasar–Negara highway at Mendoyo, about 7km east of the town centre. *Puri Dajuma Cottages* and *Hotel Pantai Medewi* in Medewi organize weekly outings to the practices.

### Practicalities

All Denpasar–Gilimanuk **bemos** pass through Negara town centre, calling in at the bemo terminal north of the market on Jalan Pahlawan. Hardly any tourists **stay** here, but those that do usually choose the *Wira Pada Hotel* (☎0365/41161; ❷–❸), which is centrally located at Jl Ngurah Rai 107 and has decent enough air-con rooms plus some fairly grim windowless fan rooms set around a courtyard. It also runs a reasonably priced streetside **restaurant**, which serves Chinese and Indonesian standards. Across the road and about 150m further west, *Kentai Sandai Bidadari* at no. 22 supplements its Indonesian fare with hearty breakfasts, pancakes and sandwiches.

# The far west

Almost as soon as you leave Negara, the landscape of the **far west** changes dramatically, becoming noticeably drier and more rugged. The thickly forested, cloud-capped mountain slopes shelter very few villages and much of the land is conserved as **Bali Barat National Park**. Few tourists explore the park – the only one on the island – but it's particularly rewarding for bird-watchers and also harbours some of Bali's best coral reefs, around the fringes of **Pulau Menjangan (Deer Island)**.

If you're arriving overland from Java, the port town of **Gilimanuk** will be your first introduction to Bali. Although there's little to detain you in the town itself, the national park is just a few kilometres away, and good transport connections enable you to head either straight to Lovina and the north coast or to Denpasar and the south.

## Palasari and Blimbingsari

While Muslims have long been welcomed into western Balinese society, **Christians** have historically had a frostier reception. When the Dutch gained full control over Balinese affairs in 1908, they extended their policy of undiluted cultural preservation to include barring all Christian missionaries from practising on the island. But attentions relaxed over the next two decades, and by 1932 Tsang To Hang, a Chinese representative of the American Christian and Missionary Alliance (CMA), had made several hundred converts on Bali, mostly within Bali's Chinese community but also some of "pure Balinese" ethnicity. The CMA's fundamentalist approach created hostility between the converts and their neighbours, however, as converts were encouraged to destroy Hindu temples and to question the iniquities of the entrenched Hindu caste system. Hindu leaders responded by forbidding Hindus from having any contact with Balinese Christians.

The Dutch soon banned the CMA, and in 1939 concluded that the best way to ease growing tensions between Balinese Christians and Hindus was to isolate the Christians in a remote, inhospitable area of uninhabited jungle high up in the mountains of west Bali, some 30km northwest of Negara. Against massive odds and with an amazing pioneering spirit, the Protestants hacked the cross-shaped village of **BLIMBINGSARI** out of the jungle and built a huge modern church at its core, the mother church for Bali's entire Christian community. Some 5km southeast, the Catholics did the same for their community at **PALASARI**. Both missions were founded on the principle of contextualization within Balinese culture, so many elements of Balinese Christian practice have distinctly Balinese-Hindu roots, including church architecture, dress, and thanksgiving offerings, an interesting achievement given that Balinese culture has long been held as inextricable from Balinese religion. Balinese music and dance, for example, are taught in Blimbingsari and Palasari, but the characters and stories are taken from the Bible rather than from the *Ramayana* and *Mahabharata*, and the churches up here are quite astonishing, blending Balinese and Western European architecture to dramatic effect. Both modern-day settlements are, however, in decline, with populations of little more than two thousand apiece, and a younger generation forced to seek employment elsewhere.

The two communities are accessible, and signed, via a road that runs inland from near Melaya on the main Tabanan–Gilimanuk road. There's no regular bemo service to either place, though gangs of **ojek** usually hang around the main road turn-offs. Several families in Blimbingsari offer informal homestay accommodation to visiting Christians, but the only **hotel** here is the ultra-luxurious *Taman Wana Villas* (T0365/40970, Wwww.bali-tamanwana-villas .com; published rates from $250; o), just beyond Palasari, and clearly signed all the way from the main Gilimanuk road 8km away. Its circular villas occupy a breathtaking spot overlooking the Palasari reservoir, surrounded by ricefields and palm groves, with the distant peaks of Gunung Klatakan and Gunung Bakingan and the waters of the Bali Strait all visible from the restaurant.

## Gilimanuk

Situated on the westernmost tip of Bali, less than 3km from East Java, the small, ribbon-like town of **GILIMANUK** is used by visitors mainly as a transit point for journeys to and from Java. A 24-hour ferry service crosses the Bali Strait so few travellers bother to linger in the town, and anyway there's nothing to see here except the silhouettes of Java's great volcanoes across the water. The one attraction is the chance to go **muck-diving** in the cold, shallow, silty waters of Gilimanuk's **Secret Bay**, just east of the port, where juvenile fish and rare marine species are prolific and especially rewarding for macro-photographers. Any dive operator in Pemuteran (see p.372) or the south (see p.158) can organize a trip here; contact them in advance if you want to be met off the Java ferry.

**Bemos and buses** run to Gilimanuk from Denpasar's **Ubung** terminal, 128km away, via the southwest coast (dark-green bemos; see p.342), and from **Singaraja**, 88km away, via **Lovina** (dark-red; see p.315). It's also possible to get buses here from **Padang Bai** and **Amlapura** on the east coast (see p.278). Gilimanuk's main bus depot is behind the ferry terminal, but bemos run from in front of the market, near the mosque on Jalan Raya Gilimanuk.

**Accommodation** in Gilimanuk is not at all tourist-oriented, as losmen here are intended mainly for minimal overnight stops (which includes the brothel trade) or for long-stay contract workers. One of the better options is *Hotel Sampurna* (❶–❷), which has half a dozen fan and air-con rooms opposite the mosque on Jalan Raya Gilimanuk, about 900m south from the ferry terminal. There's a slightly more tourist-friendly place on the edge of town at *Pondok Wisata Lestari* (☎0365/61504; ❶–❷), about 2km southeast of the port along the road to Cekik, or 1.5km north of the Bali Barat National Park headquarters. Its eighteen typical losmen rooms range from very cheap and

Sari, Pondok Wisata Lestari, ▼ Cekik, Singaraja & Negara

very basic to more comfortable air-con options, and there's a restaurant here, too. About 50m north of *Lestari*, a sign leads you 250m down a side-road to *Sari* (☎0365/61264; ❶–❷), which has more attractive accommodation in two-storey bamboo bungalows (some with hot water, but no air-con) set round a courtyard, a couple of hundred metres from the shore.

## Crossing to Java

Crossing the Bali Strait between Bali and Java is as easy as hopping on a bemo: there are no formalities, and onward transport facilities from both ports are frequent and efficient. If you're travelling quite a way into Java, to Probolinggo (for Mount Bromo), for example, or to Surabaya, Yogyakarta or Jakarta, the easiest option is to get an all-inclusive ticket from your starting point in Bali. The cheapest **long-distance buses** (from Rp180,000 to Jakarta, or Rp120,000 to Yogyakarta) run out of Denpasar's Ubung station, with pick-up points in Tabanan, Negara and sometimes Gilimanuk, but there are also more expensive **tourist shuttle buses** and **bus-and-train** combinations operating from major tourist centres across the island (from about Rp250,000/165,000). All these services include the ferry crossing in the ticket price.

Ferries shuttle between Gilimanuk and Ketapang (East Java) and back again 24 hours a day (every 20min; 30min including loading and docking). **Tickets** are issued as you board: for foot-passengers they cost Rp3300 (Rp2200 for kids), for motor-bikes Rp9000–20,000 (including riders), and cars Rp55,000 (including driver and passengers). Note that most car rental agencies on Bali prohibit tourists from taking their vehicles to other islands (see p.50 for more).

Arriving in **Ketapang**, the Banyuwangi Baru train station is about 100m north of the ferry terminal and runs services to Surabaya Kota, Probolinggo and Yogyakarta. The central bus stations for cross-Java travel are in the much larger nearby town of **Banyuwangi**, 8km south of Ketapang and served by frequent bemos from the ferry terminal.

## The Bali Strait

The **Bali Strait** is a notoriously difficult stretch of water to negotiate: although Bali and East Java are 3km apart here, the water is just 60m deep, and the current extremely treacherous. A regular ferry service across the Strait was only inaugurated in the 1930s, before which the crossing was made on light wooden fishing *prahu* all the way round to the Perancak estuary on the southwest coast, and then north up the Ijo Gading River to Negara (some 33km east of Gilimanuk).

According to **legend**, Bali was once connected to East Java, and its great mountain, Gunung Agung, was a holy place of pilgrimage for spiritually minded Javanese. One such was a Brahman named Sidi Mantra who, plagued by a gambling addict of a son, set off to ask for help from the great dragon of Gunung Agung, Naga Besukih. The *naga* agreed to pay off the family's debts and, shaking his body a little, let precious stones fall from his scaly skin. But the gambling continued, and Sidi Mantra was obliged to return to the *naga* several more times. Eventually, the son, Manik Angkeran, decided to bring back some of the treasure for himself and, characteristically greedy, sliced off the *naga*'s tail. The *naga* retaliated by reducing him to a pile of ashes. Manik's father eventually came looking for his son and struck a deal, promising to restore the *naga*'s tail in return for his son being brought back to life. The deal done, Sidi Mantra wanted to ensure that his son wouldn't cause him any more trouble, and so with his magic staff, he scored a line across the land between where he and his son stood facing each other. Within seconds, the earth cracked and filled with water, and this was how the Bali Strait came into being.

Geologists corroborate some of the Bali Strait legend, as it's generally agreed that a **land bridge** did once connect Gilimanuk with East Java. Both Java and Bali rest on a continental plate known as the Sunda shelf, which is sunk deep below the Java Sea. However, during the glacial age approximately one million years ago, sea levels across the world dropped, temporarily exposing the Bali Strait land bridge and enabling people from East Java to walk quite easily into Bali and back again. This may become a reality once more, if the controversial plans to construct a **Bali–Java bridge** ever come to fruition.

# Bali Barat National Park

Nearly the whole of west Bali's mountain ridge is protected as **Bali Barat National Park (Taman Nasional Bali Barat)**, a 760-square-kilometre area of savannah, rainforest, monsoon forest, mangrove swamp and coral reef, which is home to a range of small animals, prolific marine life and approximately 160 species of bird – including the elusive and endangered **Bali starling**, Bali's one true endemic creature (see box, p.365). This was also once the province of the Bali tiger, but the last one was shot here in the 1930s.

Just a fraction of the national park is open to the public, and its biggest attraction by far is **Pulau Menjangan** (Deer Island), whose spectacular coral reefs draw snorkellers and divers from all over Bali. On dry land, the handful of rarely-trekked **trails** are reasonably rewarding for birdwatching, or you can take a boat trip through the shoreline mangroves.

### Practicalities

All dark-green Ubung (Denpasar)–Gilimanuk **bemos** pass the national park headquarters at Cekik, 3km south of Gilimanuk, as do all dark-red Singaraja–Gilimanuk bemos; both routes are also useful for access to trailheads.

Anyone who enters Bali Barat National Park must be accompanied by a park guide and must also have a permit. Both can be arranged through either the national park headquarters or the branch office at the Labuan Lalang

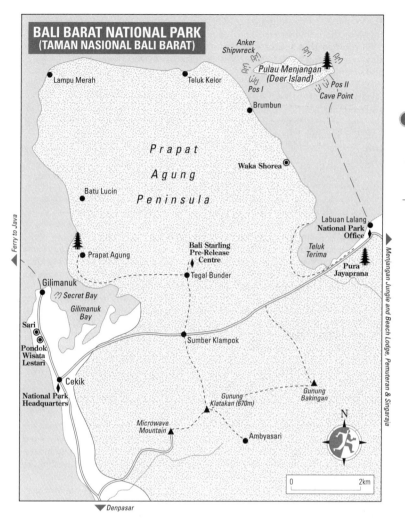

**BALI BARAT NATIONAL PARK**
**(TAMAN NASIONAL BALI BARAT)**

Anker Shipwreck

Lampu Merah

Teluk Kelor

Pulau Menjangan
(Deer Island)

Pos I

Pos II
Cave Point

Brumbun

*P r a p a t*

Waka Shorea

*A g u n g*

Batu Lucin

*P e n i n s u l a*

Labuan Lalang
National Park
Office

Ferry to Java

Prapat Agung

Teluk
Terima

Bali Starling
Pre-Release
Centre

Pura
Jayaprana

Tegal Bunder

Gilimanuk

Secret Bay

Gilimanuk
Bay

Sari

Sumber Klampok

Pondok
Wisata
Lestari

Cekik

National Park
Headquarters

Gunung
Klatakan (670m)

Gunung
Bakingan

Microwave
Mountain

Ambyasari

N

0          2km

Denpasar

Menjangan Jungle and Beach Lodge, Pemuteran & Singaraja

jetty. The **national park headquarters** (daily 7am–5pm) is conveniently located at **CEKIK**, beside the Denpasar–Gilimanuk–Singaraja T-junction, 3km south of Gilimanuk; for details on the branch office at the Labuan Lalang jetty, see p.367.

Most of the **guides** are English-speaking and conversant in the flora and fauna of Bali Barat; they don't necessarily need to be booked in advance. The basic fee is Rp150,000 for a two-hour hike for up to two people (Rp250,000 for three to five people), or Rp400,000/500,000 for a seven-hour hike. Specialist-interest treks can also be arranged on request. If you don't have your own transport you'll also be expected to pay for any necessary bemo or boat charters. Having arranged a guide, you'll be granted a **permit**, which currently costs Rp2500 per person, though there are rumours of a possible price-hike to

Rp20,000. Permits are good for only one day, unless you make other arrangements at the headquarters.

All the hotels in Pemuteran, 28km northeast of Cekik (see p.373), organize **day-trips** to the park, and most tour agencies in Kuta, Sanur and Ubud can also arrange tours.

## Accommodation and eating

Although it's possible to ask the rangers' permission to **camp** in the park, they do a good job of dissuading visitors with stories of snakes and scorpions; if you're determined, however, you'll need to provide your own tent, carry your own water, and should expect to pay Rp300,000 per person for the whole day and overnight experience. If student and other groups aren't in residence, you can usually also pitch your own tent at the Cekik national park headquarters, though there are few facilities and you'll have to pay extra for a shower. Otherwise, the closest decent **guesthouses** are *Pondok Wisata Lestari* and *Sari*, about 1.5km north of the park headquarters on the road into Gilimanuk; see p.361 for details. Alternatively, make for the appealing accommodation at Pemuteran (see p.371), 28km along the road towards Singaraja.

Despite the national park status, there are also a couple of upmarket **resorts** inside the confines of the park, both of them closer to Labuan Lalang than Cekik, and both offering guided walks and diving and snorkelling excursions. The fourteen elegantly simple bungalows at *Waka Shorea* (☎0362/94666, ⓦwww.wakaexperience.com; ⑨) are just across the water from Pulau Menjangan on the shore of the Prapat Agung Peninsula, only accessible by hotel shuttle-boat from the Labuan Lalang jetty area. A couple of kilometres east of Labuan Lalang, at Km 17, the *Menjangan Jungle and Beach Resort* (☎0362/94700, ⓦwww.menjangan.net; ⑨) was reportedly built under such strictly enforced restrictions that many of its buildings incorporated existing trees rather than having them cut down. It's a huge resort, constructed entirely from Kalimantan timber, with spectacularly indulgent rooms in luxury sea-view villas (from $350) and some disappointingly ordinary terraced "monsoon forest" rooms set around a swimming pool near the resort's riding stables.

Other than at the two resorts, there are no warung or **food** hawkers inside the national park, so you'll need to take your own supplies for the hikes. A *bakso* and noodle cart sets up outside the Cekik park headquarters every day. The nearest restaurant is at *Pondok Wisata Lestari*, 1.5km north up the road to Gilimanuk, or there are several warung at the Labuan Lalang jetty, 13km east of Cekik.

### The Tegal Bunder trail

If your main interest is bird-spotting, then you should opt for the **Tegal Bunder trek** (1–2hr; best in the early morning), a 25-minute drive from Cekik. The focus of this trek is the monsoon forest around the Bali Starling Pre-Release Centre in the northwestern reaches of Bali Barat. If you don't have your own transport, you can get a dark-red bemo to the access road at Sumber Klampok and then walk 2km, or you could begin with a jaunt through the mangrove forests of Gilimanuk Bay (see below) and start the trek from the coast.

Driving from Cekik, you'll pass through extensive areas of fairly dull, often leafless, **dry monsoon forest**, much of which sheds its greenery in order to survive the long dry periods between monsoons. Among the more interesting trees here are the thorny knobbed crocodile trees (*panggal buaya*), whose hard white "satin" wood is very popular with carvers, and the gnarled, twenty-metre-high rosewood trees (*sonokeling*), which produce fine wood for furniture. Grey macaques and rarer black monkeys live in these forests and can often be seen by the roadside.

## The Bali starling

With its silky, snow-white feathers, black wing and tail tips and delicate soft crest, the **Bali starling** or Rothschild's Myna (*leucopsar Rothschildi*) is a strikingly beautiful bird and the provincial symbol of Bali. It's Bali's only remaining endemic creature and survives in the dry monsoon forests and savannah grasslands that characterize the northwestern peninsula of Bali Barat National Park. Very few people get the chance to see the bird in its natural habitat: the last census in March 2004 recorded just four Bali starlings left in the wild, so all its known haunts have been made out of bounds to casual observers. It is also fairly easily confused with the much more common black-winged starling, whose wings and tail are almost completely black; the Bali starling has a blue patch of bald skin around each eye, but the black-winged starling's patches are yellow.

The Bali starling (*jalak putih Bali* in Bahasa Indonesia) was probably never a very common creature, and forest clearance in the first half of the twentieth century, followed by excessive hunting for the pet trade since the 1970s, has brought the species to the verge of extinction in the wild. In the 1930s, naturalists reported seeing "hundreds of birds", but by 1966 numbers were considered sufficiently low for the Bali starling to be put on the official list of **endangered species**. In contrast, the captive population has risen sharply. Bali starlings make docile and very pretty pets and, despite being notoriously nervous birds, they have flourished in captivity and sell for as much as US$2000.

Experts agree that the wild population needs to number at least a thousand if the species is to survive without the risk of inbreeding, and various agencies have established a breeding programme to try and ensure that this target is reached. Under this project, captive Bali starlings are mated at the **Bali Starling Pre-Release Centre** on Bali Barat's Prapat Agung Peninsula. At the centre, the young birds are taught how to survive in the wild before being released at the end of the rainy season (Feb/March), when fruit and insects are plentiful, into known habitats further north on the peninsula, where it's hoped they'll breed with the dwindling wild population. Unfortunately, the project was robbed in 2000, so visitors now need a permit to see the birds at the Pre-Release Centre; the only other places you can see Bali starlings in Bali are at the Bali Bird Park in Batubulan (see p.174) and at the *Begawan Giri* hotel in Ubud, which is also sponsoring a captive breeding programme, the Bali Starling Foundation Project.

The Bali starling is exceptionally sensitive to changes in its surroundings and requires a very stable habitat to survive. During the **breeding** season, the entire population is found in a small, extremely arid area of less than three square kilometres around Brumbun on the northeastern edge of the Prapat Agung Peninsula. During the dry season (April–Oct), the birds seek roosting trees a little further afield, flying 8 to 9km to the south and southwest of the breeding ground. Park authorities are worried that if the plans to build a Bali–Java bridge ever come to fruition, a dangerously large swathe of the starlings' habitat would be lost, thus reversing the good work achieved by the breeding programme. Certainly, the construction of an upmarket hotel on the fringes of their habitat can't have done much for the poor creatures' nerves.

Once through the ranger checkpoint at **SUMBER KLAMPOK**, a sidetrack leads to the **Bali Starling Pre–Release Centre** (see box). If you've gained permission to enter from park headquarters, you should get to see a few members of this rare and pretty species while they're being trained for new lives in the wild. When they're ready to leave, the young birds are encouraged to settle around Brumbun, northeast of Batu Lucin, which is why most of the Prapat Agung Peninsula is closed to visitors.

The forests of Tegal Bunder harbour a large **bird population**, including flocks of the common yellow-vented bulbul, and the loud-chirping black-naped orioles. Other possible sightings include parakeets and fantails; the green jungle fowl; the pinky-brown spotted dove, which has a distinctive call; the black drongo, completely black save for its red eyes; and the tiny bright-yellow-breasted olive-backed sunbird.

### Gilimanuk Bay boat trip

The Tegal Bunder trail combines nicely with a boat trip round mangrove-lined **Gilimanuk Bay**. Tiny *jukung* for two people for two hours cost Rp70,000 and should be arranged through the national park guides; you have to pay the standard guide fee on top.

**Mangroves** are best seen at low tide, when their exposed aerial roots form knotted archways above the muddy banks. Not only are these roots essential parts of the trees' breathing apparatus, but they also reclaim land for future mangroves by trapping debris into which the metre-long mangrove seedlings can fall. In this way, mangrove swamps also stabilize shifting muds and protect coastlines from erosion and the impact of tropical storms.

Boat skippers should be able to get you close enough to the mangroves to spot resident **fiddler crabs**, named after the male's massive reddish claw that it uses to threaten and to communicate, and is said to be so strong it can open a can of beans. You might see **mudskippers** as well, specially adapted fish who can absorb atmospheric oxygen when out of the water, as long as they keep their outsides damp – which is why they spend a lot of time slithering through the mangrove mud. **Crab-eating or long-tailed macaques** hang out along the shore, too, filling their outsized cheek pouches with fruit, mussels, small mammals and crabs (they're very good swimmers and divers).

On the exposed reef you'll see **sea cucumbers**, **sea horses**, and various species of **crab**, as well as heaps of seashells. You might also spot some elegant dark-grey **Pacific reef egrets**. The current off this shore is dangerously strong so it's not advisable to swim here, and you probably won't want to sunbathe, as the beaches seem to end up with all the plastic bottles and other debris washed in across the Bali Strait.

### Teluk Terima

The two-hour walk around **Teluk Terima**, the bay to the west of the Labuang Lalang jetty and park office, passes through monsoon forest and coastal flats fairly similar to those at Tegal Bunder. It's a fruitful area for early-morning sightings of sea eagles, dollar birds and even the rufous-backed kingfisher, plus monkeys and deer.

### The Gunung Klatakan trail

The **Gunung Klatakan**–Gunung Bakingan trail (7hr) is the most popular and strenuous of the Bali Barat hikes. It starts at the Sumber Klampok ranger post and ascends the slopes of Gunung Klatakan and Gunung Bakingan, before descending to the main road a few kilometres east of Sumber Klampok. En route you pass through an area known as Watu Lesung, where grinding stones, possibly dating back to prehistoric times and now considered to be holy, were found. For the most part, the trail follows a steep incline, via the occasional sheer descent, through **tropical rainforest** that leaves few clearings through which to view the surrounding peaks. The forest is thick with ferns, vines, spiky-stemmed rattan and viciously serrated pandanus palms, plus lots of different epiphytic orchids, including the strikingly elegant long-stemmed, white-sepalled madavellia orchid. You're unlikely to spot much **wildlife** on this trail, but you'll probably hear the black monkeys swinging through the uppermost canopy, and you may stumble across a fearsome-looking wild boar – short-sighted and a bit stupid, boars tend to charge in a straight line until they hit an obstacle, regardless of where their prey happens to be, so if one starts galloping towards you, just run away in zigzags. The most dramatic of the **birds** up here are the southern pied hornbill, which has a black head, a white breast and tail feathers, and a pronounced casque on its yellow beak, and the wreathed hornbill, which has a much smaller casque on its beak and no white breast. Other commonly sighted birds include the multicoloured banded pitta, the bluey-grey dollarbird with its distinctive red beak, the talking mynah, and the red and green jungle fowl.

### Pulau Menjangan (Deer Island)

By far the most popular part of Bali Barat National Park is **Pulau Menjangan (Deer Island)**, a tiny uninhabited island 8km off the north coast, whose shoreline is encircled by some of the most spectacular **coral reefs** in Bali. Most visitors rate this as the best snorkelling spot on Bali, and divers place it high on their list, too. The majority of divers and snorkellers come on organized **tours** from the south or Candi Dasa (prices average US$95 for two dives, $40 for snorkellers, or $190 for a two-day excursion), though it's cheaper and much more convenient to arrange trips from the nearby north-coast resorts of Pemuteran or Lovina ($70 for two dives or $30 for snorkellers). Or you could base yourself in Gilimanuk (see p.360) or at one of the resorts built within the national park (see p.364). Unless you have your own diving equipment, tours are the only way for divers to explore the reefs. However, for snorkellers it can often work out cheaper to turn up at Labuan Lalang, the access port for Menjangan, and club together with other tourists to hire a boat. As the island comes under the jurisdiction of the national park, you have to go with a guide, but you can arrange both the guide and boat transport at the jetty in Labuan Lalang without first checking in at the Cekik headquarters.

Menjangan practicalities

The departure point for Pulau Menjangan is **LABUAN LALANG**, just east of Teluk Terima, 13km from Cekik and 15km west of Pemuteran. To get there, take any Singaraja-bound bemo or bus from Gilimanuk (30min) or Cekik (20min), or any Gilimanuk-bound bemo or bus from Lovina (2hr) or Pemuteran (30min). If you're coming from the southwest coast, take any Ubung (Denpasar)–Gilimanuk bus or bemo to Cekik, then change onto the Singaraja-bound service. There's a small national park office at Labuan Lalang (daily except national holidays 8am–3pm), as well as several warung.

The **hiring of boats** to Pulau Menjangan is well organized and should be arranged through the national park office in the Labuan Lalang car park. Boats can be hired at any time of day up to about 3pm (underwater visibility is best in the morning); they hold up to ten people and prices are fixed at Rp250,000 for a round trip of up to four hours, which includes thirty minutes journey-time each way. All snorkelling boats anchor off Menjangan's southeastern corner: if you take lunch (there's no food or water on the island), you can picnic on the beach there (which has some shade) between snorkelling. In addition to boat rental, you must pay Rp60,000 for a national park guide, who usually snorkels with you, plus Rp2500 per person for the national park entry fee (the entry fee is slated to rise soon, perhaps to as much as Rp20,000). The boat can be hired for as many extra hours as you like for Rp20,000 per hour (plus extra for the guide), and you can rent mask, fins and snorkel from the warung by the jetty

## Life on the reef

Coral reefs are living organisms composed of a huge variety of marine life forms, but the foundation of every reef is its ostensibly inanimate **stony coral** – hard constructions such as boulder, cabbage patch, mushroom, bushy staghorn and brain coral. Stony coral is composed of colonies of polyps – minuscule invertebrates that feed on plankton, generally depend on algae and direct sunlight for photosynthesis, and extract calcium carbonate (limestone) from sea water in order to reproduce. The polyps use this calcium carbonate to build new skeletons outside their bodies – an asexual reproductive process known as budding – and this is how a reef is formed. It's an extraordinarily slow process, with colony growth averaging somewhere between 0.5cm and 2.8cm a year.

Fleshy, plant-like **soft coral**, such as dead man's fingers and elephant's ear, is also composed of polyps, but a variety with flaccid internal skeletons built from protein rather than calcium. The lack of an external casing means the polyps' vivid colours are much more visible, and as they do not depend on direct sunlight they flourish at greater depths, swaying with the currents and using tentacles to trap micro-organisms. **Horny coral**, or gorgonians, like sea whips and sea fans, are a cross between stony and soft coral, while **sea anemones** have much the most obvious, and poisonous, tentacles of any member of the coral family, using them to trap fish and other large prey.

The algae and plankton that accumulate around coral colonies attract a catalogue of **reef fish**. Most are small in stature, with vibrant and exotically patterned skins for camouflage against the coral, and flattened bodies, broad tails and specially adapted fins for easy manoeuvring around the tiniest of reef crannies. **Butterfly fish** are typically well designed: named for the fluttering movements of their thin, flat, yellow, white and black bodies, they can swim backwards and some also have elongated snouts for nosing into crevices. **Moorish idols** are also much in evidence and are easily recognized by the long pennant fin that trails from the dorsal fin, their pronounced snout, and dramatic black, yellow and white bands of colour. **Surgeon-fish** are another common sight: there are around one hundred different species, each with its own distinctive markings, but they all share the feature that gives them their name – a sharp blade on either side of the tail-base, which becomes erect when antagonized and can inflict serious damage. A lot more streamlined, the slender, pipe-like **trumpetfish** grows up to 75cm long, has elongated jaws and is a skilful and

for Rp40,000 a set. There are occasional reports of **thefts** from the boats while snorkellers are underwater, so leave valuables in the car or the hotel and bring minimal money out with you, or keep it in a waterproof neck-pouch.

### The Menjangan reefs

The clear, shallow water between Labuan Lalang and Pulau Menjangan is protected from excessive winds and strong currents by the Prapat Agung Peninsula, and its reefs form a band 100m to 150m around the coastline, offering seven different **dive** sites, with drop-offs of 40m to 60m, first-class wall dives, and superb visibility ranging from 15m to 50m. Two of these sites, off the southeastern corner of the island, offer outstanding **snorkelling**: at Pos II, the extensive reef wall drops down around 50m but tops out very near the surface and is a phenomenally rich trove of sea fans and soft and hard corals visited by masses of reef fish, parrot fish, clams, nudibranchs and all manner of other reef dwellers (see box). At nearby Cave Point, the reef features lots of nooks and crannies, some of which are accessible to snorkellers. Elsewhere, in among the expansive sea fans, enormous barrel sponges and black tree corals so distinctive of this area, the reefs teem with all sorts of frequently spotted daytime predator. With the help of a bird-like beak, which is in fact several teeth fused together, the ubiquitous **parrot fish** scrapes away at the coral, leaving characteristic white scars, and then grinds the fragments down with another set of back teeth – a practice that can do quite a lot of damage to a reef.

Larger, less frequent visitors to Bali's and Lombok's reefs include the **moray eel**, whose elongated jaws of viciously pointed teeth make it a deadly predator; it hunts mainly at night and often holes up in coral caves during the day. The similarly be-fanged **barracuda** can grow to two metres and is the world's fastest-swimming fish. **Sharks** are more common, and it's also sometimes possible to swim with a **manta ray**, whose extraordinary flatness, strange wing-like fins, and massive size – up to 6m across and weighing some 1600kg – make it an astonishing presence. Weighing up to twice as much as rays, **oceanic sunfish** (sometimes known as **mola mola**) are phenomenal sights, measuring some 3m top to bottom and about 2.5m end to end. They are extremely rare, but are occasionally spotted off Nusa Lembongan (see p.256); they're very short-sighted so can often be inspected at close quarters. **Turtles** occasionally paddle around reef waters, too, but the two local species – green and hawksbill – are fast becoming endangered in Bali (see p.146).

Bali's and Lombok's reefs also support countless species of **invertebrates**, includ-ing all sorts of multi-celled, multi-hued **sponges**, both encrusting and free-stand-ing; and a thousand-plus species of hermaphroditic, shell-less mollusc known as **nudibranchs** or sea slugs, which come in an arresting array of patterns and shapes and live in shallow waters. The hideous slug-like **sea cucumber** lies half-buried on the sea bed where it constantly ingests and excretes so much sand and mud that the combined force of those sea cucumbers in a three-square-kilometre area can together redistribute one million kilogrammes of sea-bed material a year.

Of the reef's numerous spiny echinoderms, the commonest **sea urchins**, which also tend to live in shallow areas near shore, are those with evil-looking black spines up to 35cm in length, though some varieties are covered in short, blunt spines or even excruciatingly painful flower-like pincers. The magnificent **crown-of-thorns starfish** is also protected by highly venomous spines, which sheath the twenty or so "arms" that extend from a body and can measure up to 50cm in diameter. Disas-trously for many reefs, the crown-of-thorns starfish feeds on coral, laying waste to as much as fifty square centimetres of stony coral in a 24-hour period.

marine life including yellowback fusiliers, puffer fish, barracuda and silvery jacks. There's also an old **shipwreck** lying 45m deep off the western tip of the island, frequented by sharks and rays as well as by Moorish idols, sweetlips and snappers. It's a small *prahu*, known as the "Anker", but is rarely visited because it's too deep for normal PADI divers. The wreck's anchor is only about 6m deep, and features on some dive excursions, but is some way from the ship itself.

Although some of the reefs were showing signs of **damage** in the late 1990s, caused in part by the El Niño effect warming the seas and bleaching the shallower reefs, the whited-out areas are confined to a few surface spots, and the walls and deeper reefs have maintained their rich colours and vitality. In addition, national park guides and local dive operators have banded together to patrol the reefs and prevent further destruction from dynamite fishing and ill-placed anchors.

### The island

Snorkelling boats from Labuan Lalang moor just off the **southeastern shore** of Pulau Menjangan, within a few strokes of the fabulous Pos II drop-off. There's a ranger post on the beach here, and some shade, but the beach itself is nothing special. To explore the island's interior, head up the steps on the eastern edge of the beach to reach a small shrine, which is close by a freshwater spring. Brahmans from the mainland make pilgrimages here in search of medicinal herbs that grow in the area between the shrine and the spring. A path runs round the rest of the flat, sandy-soiled island, which can be circled in about an hour. Few animals live on Pulau Menjangan, save for a herd of barking deer, which occasionally swim across to the mainland. Three rarer species are also said to inhabit Pulau Menjangan: the Java deer, the Bali starling (see box on p.365) and the tiny yellow-breasted, greeny-yellow-backed mangrove white-eye, which in Bali is found only here and on Nusa Penida.

### Pura Jayaprana

For the best aerial view of Pulau Menjangan, stop off at **Pura Jayaprana** (donation), 12km east of Cekik and 1km west of Labuan Lalang. The temple itself is unimpressive, but its location at the top of a long flight of steps is superb, with panoramas that take in the island, its translucent waters, and even the shadows of the coral reefs beneath. Pura Jayaprana enshrines the grave of an eponymous local seventeenth-century folk hero who was murdered so that the king could have free access to the young man's wife. The woman in question, Layonsari, remained faithful to the memory of her dead husband and chose suicide over marriage to the king. The young couple's grave is enclosed in a glass case in the shrine's inner courtyard, watched over by kitsch doll-like statues representing Jayaprana and Layonsari.

# The northwest coast

East of Cekik, the main Gilimanuk–Singaraja road emerges from Bali Barat National Park at Teluk Terima and runs along the narrow strip of the **northwest coast** between the sea and the mountains, passing Labuan Lalang, access point for Pulau Menjangan (Deer Island; described above), and 8km further east, the uninspiring hot springs at **Banyuwedang**. The terrain gets more interesting beyond Banyuwedang, with dramatic mountain slopes dominating inland views as far as **Pemuteran**, a peaceful beach haven offering plenty of opportunities for snorkelling and diving. East again and you soon reach an even smaller hideaway at **Ume Anyar**, before the road divides: east for Lovina and Singaraja (covered in Chapter 4) or south for the cool, refreshing hills around **Sanda** and **Belimbing**.

## Pemuteran and around

East of Banyuwedang, the great craggy folds of Bali Barat's north-facing ridges rise almost perpendicular from the roadside, and in the foreground of this amazing setting sits the little fishing village of **PEMUTERAN**, 28km east of Cekik. It's a pleasantly low-key area to stay and a good place to base yourself for diving and snorkelling (both nearby and at Pulau Menjangan), plus the small cluster of lovely, if mostly rather pricey, hotels here make a conscious effort not to upset the village ambience. You can swim and snorkel in the safe, calm waters off the tree-shaded black-sand beach and there's horse-riding and outings to the national park.

### Practicalities

All dark-red Gilimanuk–Singaraja **bemos** pass through Pemuteran and will drop you in front of your chosen hotel; they take about thirty minutes from Labuan Lalang (or 1hr 20min from Lovina). If coming from Ubud or the south-coast resorts, your fastest option is to take a **tourist shuttle bus** to Lovina and then hop on to a bemo. Some tiny private charter planes use the airstrip in Pegamatan, 4km west of Pemuteran.

Nearly all Pemuteran accommodation occupies beachfront land, with access being via the Gilimanuk–Singaraja road. *Taman Sari*, *Pondok Sari* and *Taman Selini* are in a small cluster at the western end of Pemuteran, within a minute's walk of each other along the shore, a bit further by road. About 1km further east along the road, you reach *Jubawa Homestay*, *Matahari Beach* and *Aneka Bagus*; *Segara Bukit* is out on its own in Banyupoh, another 4km further east.

There's a well-provisioned local store on the main road near *Taman Selini* and (very slow) **Internet** access at *Jubawa Homestay*. Mobile-phone reception in this area is patchy as Simpati is the only network currently operating here. The nearest banks and ATMs are in Gilimanuk, but you can **change money** and travellers' cheques at the pharmacy near the *Pondok Sari* entrance. The Pemuteran Clinic (T0362/92623), 100m east of *Taman Selini*, is open 24 hours, but for any major ailments you'll have to go to one of the hospitals in Singaraja or Denpasar.

### Accommodation

In high season, all **hotels** get booked up by diving tours, so it's best to reserve as far ahead as possible. Note, however, that **phone lines** in this area are extremely unreliable and few hotels have on-site email, so reservation requests can take time to be answered. Pre-booked customers at the Reef Seen Aquatics dive school and riding school (see p.372) can stay at their simple bungalows (❻).

**Aneka Bagus Resort and Spa** About 400m east of *Matahari Beach* T0362/94798, Wwww .anekahotels.com. Small, upmarket place comprising thirteen large, air-con Bali-style deluxe villas, with garden bathrooms, facing each other across a garden that runs down to the pebbly beach. Nearer the road, the standard air-con rooms in a two-storey block are nothing special. There's an attractive infinity pool and a spa on the premises. ❼

**Jubawa Homestay** 1km east of *Taman Selini*, 200m west of *Matahari Beach* T0362/94745. Although this is the only place in Pemuteran not built on the shore, the eight immaculate bungalows are set back from the road, in a neat little garden beneath the mountains, about 300m from the beach. The interiors are smart and sparkling with dark-wood furniture and nice bathrooms. Rooms with fan ❸, with air-con ❹

**Matahari Beach Resort and Spa** 1.2km east of *Taman Selini* T0362/92312, Wwww.matahari -beach-resort.com. Accommodation in this luxury beachfront complex comprises 32 very classy private villa compounds furnished with four-poster beds and pretty garden bathrooms. But the real attraction is the exceptionally elegant spa complex, reminiscent of a Roman bathhouse, with its own lotus-pond tea pavilion, as well as private massage rooms and a gym. The hotel also has a swimming pool and a beachfront bar. ❾

**Pondok Sari** Between *Taman Sari* and *Taman Selini* T0362/94738, Wwww.

pondoksari.com. A lovely, good-value set of twenty large, stylishly designed, semi-detached cottages spaced around a beautiful mature tropical garden that runs down to the black-sand beach. Some cottages have air-con, and they all have attractive open-roofed garden bathrooms, plus there's a pool and a spa. ❻

**Segara Bukit Seaside Cottages** 5km east of *Taman Selini* in Banyupoh T0362/94749, F94647. One of the cheapest places to stay in the area, with just a dozen perfectly pleasant fan and air-con rooms ranged around a small garden beside a sandy beach, not far from a fish farm. Also has a pool, a restaurant, a small dive centre, and car rental. Rooms with fan ❷, with air-con ❺

**Taman Sari** Western end of Pemuteran T0362/93264, Wwww.balitamansari.com. Another lovely place to stay, with attractive terraced bungalows, appealing, spacious, detached air-con bungalows with shady verandas and garden bathrooms, plus several deluxe suites. Has a pool and a good Thai restaurant. ❻–❾

**Taman Selini** Immediately east along the shore from *Pondok Sari* T0362/94746, Wwww.tam -anselini.com. Tiny, elegant outfit with eleven rather chic bungalows, all furnished with four-poster beds, large garden bathrooms, and day beds on the spacious verandas. Mango trees grow in the beachfront garden, and there's an inviting sea-view pool and a Greek restaurant. ❽

## Eating

All the hotels have **restaurants** serving freshly caught seafood, as well as the usual range of tourist and Indonesian standards. *Taman Selini*'s menu includes a huge range of traditional Greek dishes (the owner is from Greece and also runs the *Pantarei* restaurant in Legian), and *Taman Sari* restaurant serves a famously good Thai menu. For cheap and cheerful Balinese standards, there are several small warung alongside the main road, including *Warung Small*, across the road from *Taman Selini*, where it's hard to spend more than Rp10,000.

The *Matahari Beach* stages frequent classical Balinese **dance** performances for diners at its very expensive restaurant, or you can watch a similar performance by local village girls at Reef Seen Aquatics dive centre, next to *Taman Selini*, on most Saturday evenings at 7pm (they also rehearse there Sat 3–5pm & Sun 9am–noon).

### Snorkelling and diving

The chief activity in Pemuteran – apart from lying on the black-sand beach – is **snorkelling and diving**. Although there are some impressive reefs within easy reach of Pemuteran's shore, most divers and snorkellers agree that they are outclassed by those at nearby **Pulau Menjangan**.

### Pemuteran reefs

As at Menjangan, some of the **Pemuteran reefs** have suffered considerable damage over the last decade, ascribed to a similar combination of bad practices by local fishermen and unavoidable environmental factors. In an attempt to try and do something about this, local hotels and dive operators have set up a very successful **coral-growing experiment**, the award-winning Karang Lestari Pemuteran Project (ⓦwww.balitamansari.com/reef.html), just off the Pemuteran shore. Using the pioneering "Biorock" process of electrical mineral accretion, this involves encouraging new growth by continuously passing a low electrical current through the stony coral, causing minerals to build up at about four times the normal speed. Any snorkeller can observe the experiment – the largest of its kind in the world – in the reefs in front of *Pondok Sari* and *Taman Sari*, where more than forty large, differently configured, cage-like steel structures lie on the sea bed, bound with wires; here, in amongst the groves of deathly grey coral, you can see the quite abundant new growth, which is much more colourful. See p.406 for more on the Biorock process.

There are a number of healthier, more interesting **reefs** within fifteen minutes' boat ride of the Pemuteran shore, where divers and snorkellers can expect to encounter a huge variety of reef fish, including bright blue dancers, black-and-white-striped damsel fish, and shoals of silver fusiliers, as well as snappers and the occasional white manta ray or shark. Reef Seen Aquatics dive centre has mapped out the most rewarding areas, with Napoleon (5m) and Tunkad (3m) best for snorkellers but also good for deep dives.

### Dive centres

Pemuteran's **dive centres** all run diving and snorkelling trips to local reefs as well as to Pulau Menjangan; some also go to Gilimanuk's Secret Bay and to Tulamben on Bali's east coast. On the beach in front of the hotels, you'll find Reef Seen Aquatics (☎0362/93001, ⓦwww.reefseen.com) beside *Taman Selini*; Werner Lau at *Pondok Sari* (☎08133/851 8512, ⓦwww.wernerlau.com); and Archipelago Dive (☎0362/93264, ⓦwww.archipelagodive.com) at *Taman Sari*. Yos Marine Adventures is across the road from *Taman Selini* (☎0365/61600, ⓦwww.yosdive.com).

A single boat **dive** on the Pemuteran reefs averages US$40 including all equipment; two dives around Pulau Menjangan or in Secret Bay cost about $70 inclusive. Dive courses average $310 for the four-day PADI Open Water. **Snorkelling** trips cost Rp100,000 per person to the Pemuteran reefs (2hr), or 300,000 per person to Menjangan (6hr), though small groups of snorkellers will probably find it cheaper if less convenient to arrange boats from Labuan Lalang (see p.367). All snorkelling equipment is rented through the village association booth on the beach between *Pondok Sari* and *Taman Sari* (Rp40,000 for three hours).

### Other activities

All the Pemuteran hotels organize day-trips to local sights, including hikes through Bali Barat National Park. Reef Seen Aquatics dive centre runs sunrise cruises for dolphin watching (Rp100,000 per person for 2hr) but, although the early-morning skies are worth the early start, don't count on seeing dolphins here. You can also go **horseback riding** (Rp290,000 for 2hr; kids Rp190,000 for 30min), and take riding lessons ($30 for 1hr).

Reef Seen also runs a **turtle-hatching** project (Rp25,000 donation, plus Rp75,00 to release a turtle) at its dive centre. Green, Olive Ridley and hawksbill turtles all have nesting sites in the Pemuteran area, but all three species are fast becoming endangered (see box on p.146), and their eggs are particularly prized, so the idea here is to buy the eggs from fishermen and then hatch and rear them at Reef Seen. When old enough, the youngsters are released off the Pemuteran coast, but at most times of the year there'll be at least a couple of turtles in the holding pens at Reef Seen, which staff will be happy to show you.

## To Seririt and the road south

Just beyond the eastern edge of Pemuteran, the stark charcoal-grey stone of **Pura Agung Pulaki** peers down from a weatherworn cliff face, making for a good viewpoint. The temple's history dates back to the days of the sixteenth-century Javanese priest Nirartha, but the buildings are modern and overrun by a band of grey macaques. Most bemo drivers stop here on their first trip of the day to make an offering at the roadside shrine and get sprinkled with holy water dished out by the attendant priest.

Much of the coastal land between Pulaki and Seririt, 30km to the east, has been set aside for **viticulture**. With its cool sea breezes, temperate climate and moderately fertile soil, this stretch of the northwest coast is ideal for vines: local growers make sweet red wine from some of the juicy black grapes, and dry the rest for export.

The town of **SERIRIT** is chiefly of interest to travellers as a junction and for its banks and ATMs. The main north-coast road slices through the town centre, travelled by frequent dark-red Gilimanuk–Lovina–Singaraja bemos (Lovina is 13km to the east); this is also the departure point for the scenic back road to Munduk, Danau Bratan and Bedugul (see p.312). Most importantly, though, Seririt stands at the head of the most westerly route between the north and south coasts, described below.

About 1.5km west of Seririt, 33km east of Pemuteran, in the village of **UME ANYAR**, a couple of signs point you north off the main road down a lane to two quite different **places to stay**. Creatively managed by a Canadian–Indonesian couple, *Zen Lifestyle Energy Resort* (T0362/93578, Wwww.zenbali.com; 8), 600m from the road, commands fine views over surrounding vineyards and to the sea beyond and makes an idyllic retreat (though it is unsuitable for under-

14s). The emphasis here is on rest and rejuvenation, with a stunningly sited infinity pool and an impressive menu of massage and spa treatments, which includes the signature Ayurvedic balancing massage. The fifteen air-con rooms are stylishly contemporary, the food is exceptional, and there are daily yoga sessions plus dolphin-watching and mountain tours; the local beach is scruffy but fine for swimming. Some 700m further down a rough track, the rather remote *Ratu Ayu Villas* (T0362/93612, Wwww.travelideas.net/bali.hotels/sacred–sanctuary .html; ●) are secluded in a hollow, five minutes' walk from the sea, on a site that's imbued with great spiritual history and power. The three two-storey bungalows are simply but artistically designed, with balconies offering inspiring views of the ricefields, the sea and the distant mountains. Established by one of the owners of *Puri Lumbung* in Munduk (see p.313), *Ratu Ayu* also emphasises cultural, spiritual and educational tourism and arranges workshops with local musicians.

## To the south coast

The road from Seririt to the south coast commands some breathtakingly lovely views as it crosses through the mountains, rice-growing valleys and small hilltop villages that lie just beyond the eastern limits of Bali Barat National Park. Seven kilometres south of Seririt the road branches southeast for Mayong and Danau Tamblingan, an area that's described on p.313. On the southbound road, the first great viewpoint comes 12km south of Seririt, after **BUSUNG BIU**, where you can stop in a lay-by to admire the spectacular vista of rice terraces tumbling down into the valley, framed by the peaks of Gunung Batukau to the southeast.

The road divides at the village of **PUPUAN**, 22km south of Seririt, the site of a hundred-metre-high waterfall called **Blahmantung**. Despite the height, the falls are less than spectacular, only really worth visiting in February or March when water levels are high from several months of rain. The 1.7-kilometre-long access road is steep and rutted, signed just beyond the southernmost limit of Pupuan; you can walk it in about half an hour.

### Pupuan to Pekutatan (via Tista)

From Pupuan, the more westerly route takes you on a slow, twisty course west via the ridgetop settlements of **KEMONING** (where you can veer off south, via Ceking and Bangal, down a road that ends just west of Balian beach; see p.356) and **Tegalasaih**, and then south through clove plantations to **TISTA**. Beyond Tista, the road parallels the Pulukan River and soon passes right through the middle of an enormous fig tree at **Bunut Bolong** (a famous local sight but not worth a special trip). About 10km south of the tree, the road comes to a T-junction at **PEKUTATAN** on the main Tabanan–Gilimanuk road, 2km east of Medewi beach (see p.356).

### Pupuan to Antosari (via Sanda)

The easterly branch of the road from Pupuan drops down through similarly eye-catching mountainscapes, affording especially impressive views of Gunung Batukau to the east. On the way, you'll pass dozens of **coffee plantations** (the *robusta* variety, known and drunk locally as *kopi bali*), many of them protected by liberal plantings of spindly looking **dadap ("coral") trees**. The almost-circular leaves of the fast-growing *dadap* are commonly used in offerings, but those that are allowed to fall provide vital fertilizer for the coffee plants, while the roots simultaneously anchor the soil and prevent erosion.

In the village of **SANDA**, about 30km from Seririt, one former coffee plantation has been turned into a small, charmingly colonial-style **hotel** and **restaurant**, *Sanda Butik Villas* (T0828/369137, Wwww.sandavillas.com; ●), whose eight stylish rooms are tastefully decorated in Balinese style and all have enormous enclosed verandas that overlook the neighbouring plantations. A small patch of the original coffee plantation has also been incorporated into the hotel garden and there's a pool here, too, though the 700m elevation on the slopes of Gunung Batukau means the temperature in Sanda is always refreshingly cool. In the early mornings you get grand views of Batukau, and it's possible to hire a guide here for the climb from the village to the summit and back (see p.354 for more on Gunung Batukau), as well as for other local trips.

Some 10km further south, overlooking a gorgeous valley in the village of **BELIMBING**, sits the delightful little award-winning **hotel** *Cempaka Belimbing* (℡0361/7451178, ⓦ www.cempakabelimbing.com; ❼). The best rooms here are the valley-view villas, which enjoy a breathtaking panorama of palm groves, paddy-fields and the peaks of Gunung Batukau, but all sixteen rooms have fine outlooks and are spacious and smartly outfitted; there's a swimming pool and spa services, and the place has an appealingly cosy feel to it, right in the heart of the village. Even if you don't stay, it's worth stopping for a drink at the nearby roadside *Café Belimbing* to soak up the glorious views.

About 10km south of Belimbing, the road meets the Denpasar–Gilimanuk highway at **Antosari** (see p.355), 16km west of Tabanan.

# Travel details

## Bemos and public buses

It's almost impossible to give the frequency with which bemos and public buses run: see Basics, p.49, for details. Journey times given are the minimum you can expect. Only direct bemo and bus routes are listed; for longer journeys, you'll have to go via either Denpasar's Ubung terminal (see p.342), Gilimanuk (see p.360), or Singaraja's Banyuasri terminal (see p.315). The nearest **shuttle bus** service runs out of Lovina on the north coast (see p.322).

**Gilimanuk** to: Antosari (2hr 15min); Cekik (10min); Denpasar (Ubung terminal; 3hr 15min); Kediri (for Tanah Lot; 2hr 45min); Medewi (1hr 45min); Labuan Lalang (for Pulau Menjangan; 25min); Lalang Linggah (for Balian beach; 2hr 15min); Negara (1hr); Pemuteran (1hr); Lovina (2hr 15min);

Seririt (1hr 30min); Singaraja (Banyuasri terminal; 2hr 30min); Tabanan (2hr 30min).

**Pemuteran** to: Cekik (50min); Gilimanuk (1hr); Labuan Lalang (for Pulau Menjangan; 30min); Lovina (1hr 15min); Seririt (45min); Singaraja (Banyuasri terminal; 1hr 30min).

**Ubung (Denpasar)** to: Antosari (1hr); Cekik (3hr); Gilimanuk (3hr 15min); Jakarta, Java (24hr); Kediri (for Tanah Lot; 30min); Lalang Linggah (for Balian beach; 1hr 15min); Medewi (1hr 30min); Mengwi (30min); Negara (2hr 15min); Singaraja (Sukasada terminal; 3hr); Solo (Java; 15hr); Surabaya (Java; 10hr); Tabanan (35min); Yogyakarta (Java; 15hr).

## Boats

**Gilimanuk** to: Ketapang (East Java; every 20min; 30min).

# Lombok and the Gili Islands

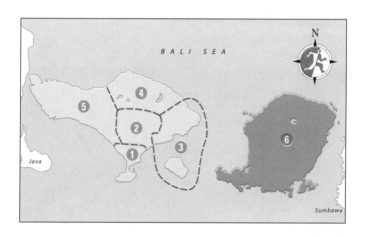

CHAPTER SIX # Highlights

* **Crafts** Pottery, textiles, wood-carving and basketware are on sale in craft villages scattered across Lombok. See p.429

* **Senggigi** Lombok's relaxed main resort, with some of the island's best hotels and restaurants. See p.394

* **Gili Islands** Three perfect islands off the northwest coast, each very different in character from its neighbours. See p.401

* **Gunung Rinjani** Highest mountain on the island, offering adventurous and rewarding trekking. See p.416

* **Sembalun valley** Picturesque upland valley far off the tourist trail, surrounded by impressive mountain peaks. See p.418

* **Sapit** Pretty village on the southern slopes of Rinjani, ideal for chilling out for a while. See p.425

* **South-coast beaches** Hidden coves nestle between rocky headlands all along Lombok's south coast, while big swells attract surfers. See p.435

△ Tanjung Aan, Lombok

# 6

# Lombok and the Gili Islands

About 35km east of Bali at its closest point, **Lombok** is inevitably compared with its better-known western neighbour, although it differs considerably in almost every aspect – physically, culturally, linguistically and historically. It also contrasts quite markedly for the visitor, with lots of wide-open spaces, plenty of unspoilt beaches and less traffic and pollution. Things are changing fast, but Lombok's appealing character remains intact and accessible to visitors rather than buried beneath a veneer of tourist development.

The majority of Lombok's 2.5 million inhabitants are the indigenous Muslim **Sasak** people. About ten percent of the population are Balinese, mostly settled in the west of the island and easily recognizable from their distinctive temples and household architecture. The two cultures appear to coexist relatively amicably, but it doesn't take too long to discern less amiable emotions below the surface – perhaps not surprising given historical events and the fact that a lot of the economic advantages of increased tourism have eluded the native Sasak.

From the seventeenth century onwards, Lombok came increasingly under **Balinese influence**, after the Balinese had helped the Sasak aristocracy defeat invaders from Sumbawa. Infighting among the rajas of the four Lombok principalities – Pagasangan, Pagutan, Mataram and Cakranegara – further weakened the hold of the Sasak rulers. In 1830, **Ratu Agung** acceded to the throne of Mataram, and over the next thirteen years brought the whole of Lombok under his rule. In 1849, he also gained control of Karangasem in East Bali in return for supplying troops to the Dutch. His brother, Ratu Agung Ngurah, succeeded him in 1872 and, seeking to serve his own ambitions in Bali, pushed his demand for his subjects to serve as soldiers too far. The residents of Praya **rebelled** in 1891, and unrest quickly spread. The Dutch intervened, eventually invading Lombok in 1894 and bringing the entire island under colonial rule until Indonesian independence.

Measuring 80km by 70km, Lombok is slightly smaller than Bali and divides into three geographical regions. The mountainous **north** is dominated by the bulk of **Gunung Rinjani**, at 3726m one of the highest peaks in Indonesia and, until late 1994, believed to be dormant; trekking up Rinjani is easily organized and highly satisfying. The **central plains**, about 25km wide, contain the most population centres and most productive agricultural areas as well as the major

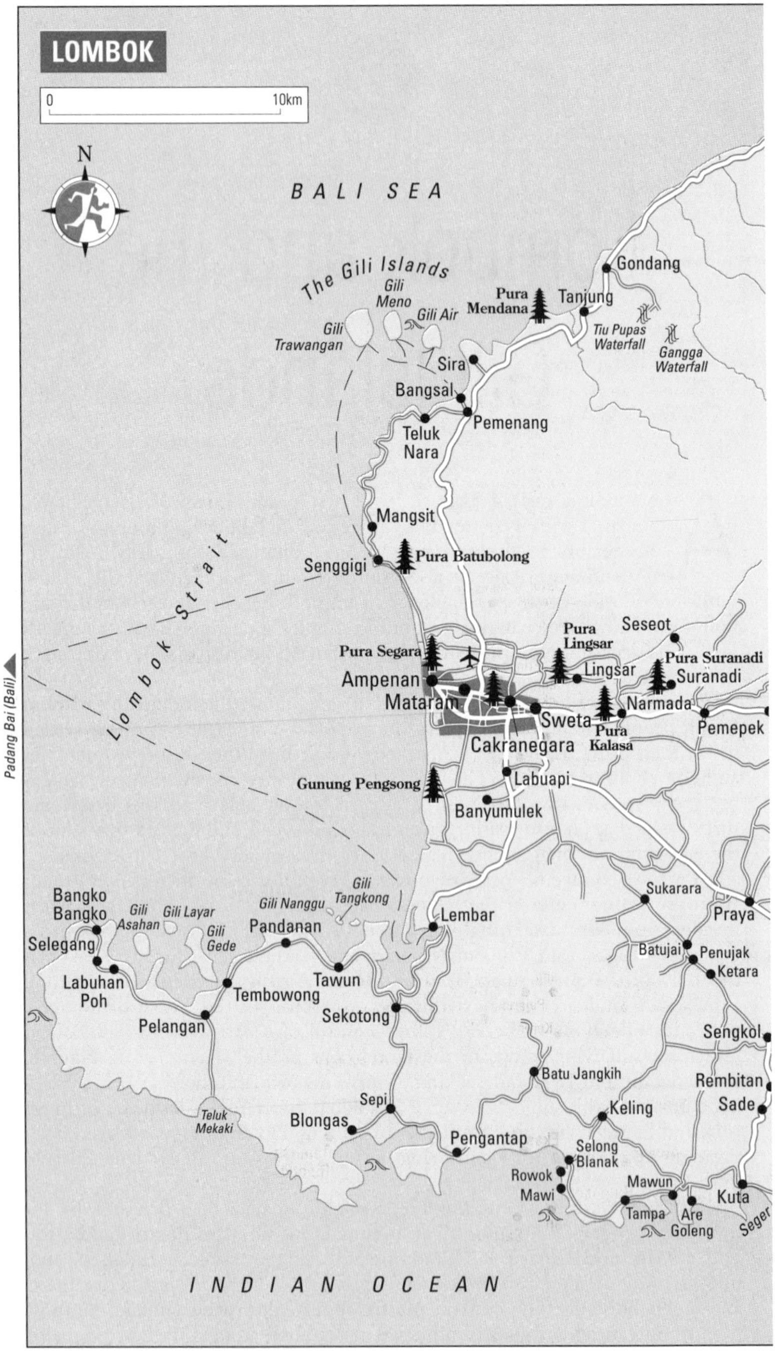

**LOMBOK**

0             10km

N

*BALI SEA*

*The Gili Islands*

Gili Meno
Gili Air
Gili Trawangan

Pura Mendana
Tanjung
Gondang

Tiu Pupas Waterfall
Gangga Waterfall

Sira
Bangsal
Pemenang

Teluk Nara

Mangsit

*Lombok Strait*

Senggigi
Pura Batubolong

Pura Lingsar
Seseot

Pura Segara
Lingsar
Pura Suranadi
Suranadi

Ampenan
Mataram
Sweta
Narmada
Pemepek

Cakranegara
Pura Kalasa

Gunung Pengsong
Labuapi

Banyumulek

*Padang Bai (Bali)*

Gili Tangkong

Bangko Bangko
Gili Asahan
Gili Layar
Gili Nanggu
Pandanan
Lembar
Sukarara
Praya

Selegang
Gili Gede

Labuhan Poh
Tembowong
Tawun
Batujai
Penujak
Ketara

Pelangan
Sekotong

Sengkol

Batu Jangkih
Rembitan
Sade

*Teluk Mekaki*
Sepi
Keling

Blongas
Pengantap
Selong Blanak

Rowok
Mawun
Mawi
Kuta

Tampa
Are
Goleng
Seger

*INDIAN OCEAN*

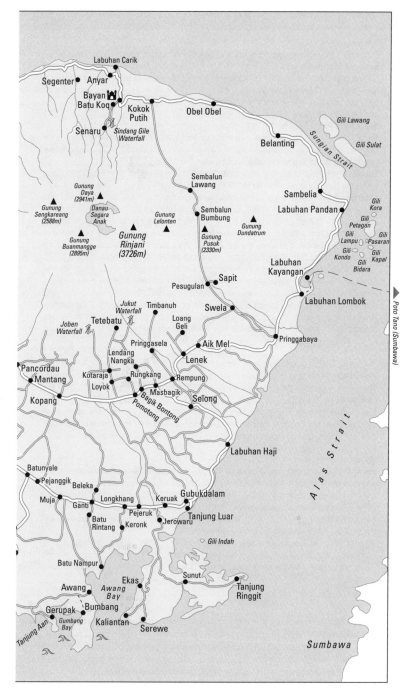

Labuhan Carik

Segenter • Anyar

Bayan
Batu Koq

Kokok
Putih

Obel Obel

Senaru

Sindang Gile
Waterfall

Belanting

Gili Lawang

Sungian Strait

Gili Sulat

Gunung
Daya
(2941m)

Sembalun
Lawang

Gunung
Sengkareang
(2588m)

Danau
Segara
Anak

Gunung
Lelonten

Sembalun
Bumbung

Sambelia

Labuhan Pandan

Gili
Kora

Gunung
Buanmangge
(2895m)

Gunung
Rinjani
(3726m)

Gunung
Pusuk
(2330m)

Gunung
Dundatrum

Gili
Petagan

Gili
Lampu

Gili
Pasaran

Labuhan
Kayangan

Gili
Kondo

Gili
Kapal

Gili
Bidara

Pesugulan

Sapit

▶ Poto Tano (Sumbawa)

Jukut
Waterfall

Timbanuh

Swela

Labuhan Lombok

Joben
Waterfall

Tetebatu

Loang
Geli

Aik Mel

Pringgabaya

Pringgasela

Pancordau
Mantang

Lendang
Nangka

Lenek

Kotaraja

Rungkang

Rempung

Loyok

Kopang

Bagik Bontong

Masbagik

Selong

Pomotong

Alas Strait

Labuhan Haji

Batunyale

Pejanggik

Beleka

Muja

Ganti

Longkhang

Keruak

Gubukdalam

Pejeruk

Tanjung Luar

Batu
Rintang

Keronk

Jerowaru

Gili Indah

Batu Nampur

Ekas

Sunut

Awang

Awang
Bay

Tanjung
Ringgit

Gerupak

Bumbang

Gumbang
Bay

Kaliantan

Tanjung Aani

Serewe

Sumbawa

### By plane

Mataram's Selaparang Airport is the only one on the island, and its only direct **international flights** are from Singapore on Silk Air. Regular **internal flights** with Garuda, Citilink, Merpati and Lion Air link Lombok with other international hubs in Indonesia (see Basics, p.33, for more details).

### By boat from Bali

**Slow ferry** From Padang Bai to Lembar.

**Ferry** Every 1hr 30min; takes 4hr–4hr 30min. Rp15,000. An extra charge is made for bicycles (Rp17,600), motorbikes (Rp36,400) and cars (from Rp225,000). See p.50 for information on taking rental vehicles between the islands.

**Tourist boat** Perama run a daily boat at 9am direct to Senggigi (4hr; Rp100,000) and on to the Gili islands (6–7hr; Rp150,000).

**Charters** From Amed to the Gili Islands. Be aware that the boats are often small with single engines, don't carry radios, and that mobile phones may well be out of range in the middle of the Lombok Strait. If you're still interested, contact I Nengah Suande through the *Diver's Café and Bungalows* in Jemeluk (see p.286). You'll be looking at Rp750,000-plus per boat. For the return trip, Din (☎08133/950 9859) is one of the boat captains on Gili Meno; he's often in front of the Blue Marlin dive shop.

*Note that the bemo drivers at Lembar port are hard bargainers: most tourists end up paying far more to get to Bertais/Mandalika/Sweta terminal than the correct fare of about Rp5000. These hassles are one reason to book directly to Mataram or Senggigi with Perama or another tourist shuttle company; if you haven't booked in advance, you could try negotiating with the driver/conductor on the buses that meet the ferries. Metred taxis serve the port; a typical fare from Lembar is Rp25,000 to Cakranegara, Rp40,000–45,000 to Sengiggi.*

### By boat from Sumbawa and other islands

**Ferry** From Poto Tano (Sumbawa) to Kayangan, Labuhan Lombok (every hour; takes 1hr 30min; Rp9000). Bicycles cost extra (Rp7500), as do motorbikes (Rp15,000) and cars (from Rp114,000).

**From other islands** The Indonesian passenger line, Pelni (🌐www.pelni.co.id) operates services between the islands of the archipelago, calling at Lembar on Lombok. See p.33 for details of routes and p.390 for details of the Pelni office on Lombok.

### By bus

**Java, Bali, Sumbawa and Flores to Bertais/Mandalika/Sweta terminal**. Several services daily. Sample fares include Rp275,000 for air-con and reclining seats from Jakarta (Java) to Lombok (32hr), Rp200,000 from Yogyakarta (Java; 22hr). Other fares include Denpasar (Bali; 6–8hr; Rp85,000); Surabaya (Java; 20hr; Rp135,000); Sumbawa Besar (6hr; Rp55,000); Bima (12hr; Rp85,000); Sape (all Sumbawa; 14hr; Rp95,000); and Labuhanbajo (Fores; 24hr; Rp125,000).

**Tourist shuttle buses** Operate from Bali to the main tourist destinations on Lombok: Mataram, Senggigi, the Gili Islands and Kuta, Lombok. Perama (🌐www .peramatour.com) are the most established company with offices in all major tourist areas.

road on the island, linking the west and east coasts. Attractive villages perched in the southern foothills of Rinjani, such as **Tetebatu** and **Sapit**, and many of the island's craft centres, are easily accessible from this cross-island corridor. Further south again is a range of dry, low inland hills, around 500m high, behind the sweeping bays and pure white sands of the **southern beaches**, all of which can be explored from **Kuta**, the accommodation centre of the south and surfing focus of the island.

The main resort is **Senggigi**, easily accessible from Bali by sea or air, and strung out along a rugged stretch of the west coast. Several groups of islands lie off the Lombok coast. The trio of **Gili Islands** – Trawangan, Meno and Air – off the northwest coast, are well known to tourists in search of sea, sun and sand. Those off the southwest peninsula and the northeast coast are also becoming more accessible.

Lombok's economy is based on **agriculture**, with production of rice, cassava, cotton, tobacco (a major export), soya beans and chilli peppers. In recent centuries the island has found it impossible to support its burgeoning population, and thousands have died in **famines**, reportedly 50,000 in one as recently as 1966. Consequently, many people have left to settle on other Indonesian islands as part of the government's **transmigrasi scheme** (see p.453). The government is also trying to moderate the island's dependence on agriculture: **pumice**, **cultivated pearls**, **seaweed** and **sea cucumber** are growing in economic importance, and income from the increasingly well-known pottery industry and tourism is rising annually.

The **tourist** presence on Lombok is nowhere near as pervasive as in Bali. Most visitors stick to a relatively well-beaten track, making it easy to find less popular routes, remote villages, unspoilt coastline and villagers still living traditional lives.

**Accommodation** is widespread but in some areas choices may be limited; five-star luxury is confined to Senggigi, the Gili Islands, the *Oberoi* on the northwest coast and *Novotel Lombok* in the south. Elsewhere choices are fewer and simpler, although in many cases no less appealing.

Lombok's tourist industry was left in tatters following **riots** in Ampenan in January 2000. Apparently based on religious differences, the riots – which were extinguished within a couple of days – were later thought to have been fired by political agitation. Tourism gradually recovered, only to be decimated again following September 11, 2001, and then again after the Bali bombing in October 2002. Any signs of an early recovery were dashed in 2003 as the SARS epidemic in Asia and the war in Iraq convinced many potential visitors that they'd rather stay home. By late 2004, visitor numbers were up and the corner appeared to have been turned; however, perhaps not surprisingly, many people on Lombok are cautious having seen their hopes dashed too many times in recent years to give in to unbridled optimism.

# West Lombok

**West Lombok** – stretching from the remote southwest peninsula, through the port of **Lembar**, to the four-city conurbation of **Ampenan–Mataram–Cakranegara–Sweta**, then north to **Senggigi** and the small village of **Bangsal** (access port for the Gili Islands) – offers by far the best facilities for tourists. With Lombok's only airport and its major port and bus station all in this area, most visitors pass through at some point during their stay, and a high

## Lombok tours

If time is very limited, you may want to join a **tour of Lombok**. The biggest range of options is available in Senggigi, but it's also extremely easy to devise your own itinerary and charter a vehicle and driver to take you around (see p.401). If you're interested in arts and crafts, you'll definitely be better off visiting independently, as tour guides receive a commission from craft showrooms (thus bumping up the price you pay) and only take you to the places that they have an agreement with.

Typically, the tours on offer are either **half-day** (4hr) or **full day** (8hr). Prices vary enormously; when making enquiries find out whether prices quoted are per person or for the vehicle, and whether lunch is included. Check the itinerary, the size of the group, and whether you'll be travelling by bus, minibus or car.

**Four-cities tour** Half-day, including Nusa Tenggara Provincial Museum, Mayura Water Palace, Pura Meru, Narmada, Lingsar and a shopping centre or market.

**Southern tour** Full day, including Narmada, Sukarara, Penujak, Rembitan or Sade, Kuta and Tanjung Aan.

**Northern tour** Full day to Senaru stopping at Pusuk, Segenter, Sindang Gile waterfall and Senaru.

**Central/Eastern tour** Full day taking in the Sembalun valley, Puncak Pass, Sapit and Masbagik.

**Gili Islands** Full day to the islands, usually for snorkelling. If travelling from Senggigi, check whether you go by boat all the way to the islands – it's an attractive ride.

**Gili Nanggu** By boat from Senggigi or road to Lembar or Tawun, and then boat to the island for snorkelling.

### Tour operators

**Citra Lombok Indah** Senggigi
ⓣ0370/693921, ⓦhttp://
citralombokindah.blogspot.com
**Coconut Cottages** Gili Air
ⓣ0370/635365, ⓦwww
.coconuts-giliair.com
**Gora** Senggigi ⓣ0370/693477
**Ideal** Pasar Seni, Senggigi
ⓣ0370/693656, ⓔidealtour@indo
.net.id

**Lotus Asia Tours** Senggigi
ⓣ0370/636781, ⓦwww
.lotusasiatours.com
**Perama** Senggigi ⓣ0370/693007,
ⓦwww.peramatour.com
**Rinjani Trekking Club** ⓣ0817/573
0415, ⓦwww.geocities.com/
info2lombok

proportion come to Lombok purely for the established resorts of Senggigi and the Gili Islands.

# Ampenan–Mataram–Cakranegara–Sweta and around

The conurbation of **AMPENAN–MATARAM–CAKRANEGARA–SWETA**, with a population of around 250,000, comprises four towns that merge one into the next over 8km from west to east. A straightforward local transport system contributes to this user-friendly city, with markets, shops, restaurants and banks – although if you want any nightlife, you'll have to head to Senggigi.

The conurbation is laid out around three parallel roads, which stretch from **Ampenan** on the coast through **Mataram** and **Cakranegara** to **Sweta** on

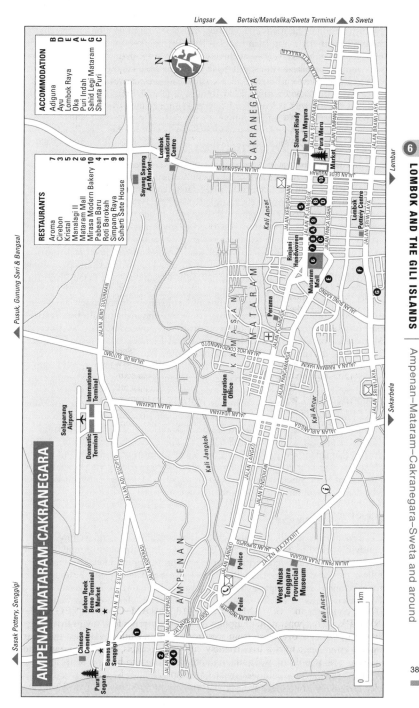

# AMPENAN–MATARAM–CAKRANEGARA

**ACCOMMODATION**

| | |
|---|---|
| Adiguna | B |
| Ayu | D |
| Lombok Raya | E |
| Oka | A |
| Puri Indah | F |
| Sahid Legi Mataram | G |
| Shanta Puri | C |

**RESTAURANTS**

| | |
|---|---|
| Aroma | 7 |
| Cirebon | 3 |
| Kristal | 5 |
| Manalagi II | 2 |
| Mataram Mall | 6 |
| Mirasa Modern Bakery | 10 |
| Pabean Baru | 4 |
| Roti Barokah | 1 |
| Simpang Raya | 9 |
| Suharti Sate House | 8 |

Pusuk, Gunung Sari & Bangsal ▲

Sasak Pottery, Senggigi ▲

Lembar ▼

Sekarbela ▼

Lombok Handicraft Centre

Sayang Sayang Art Market

Slamet Riady

Puri Mayura

Pura Meru

Market

Lombok Pottery Centre

Rinjani Handwoven

Perama

Mataram Mall

Immigration Office

Selaparang Airport

International Terminal

Domestic Terminal

Kali Jangkok

Kali Ancar

Police

Pelni

West Nusa Tenggara Provincial Museum

Chinese Cemetery

Kebon Roek Bemo Terminal & Market

Bemos to Senggigi

Pura Segara

AMPENAN

MATARAM

CAKRANEGARA

1km

0

**6**

**LOMBOK AND THE GILI ISLANDS** | Ampenan–Mataram–Cakranegara–Sweta and around the eastern edge. The roads change their names several times along their length, the most northerly being Jalan Langko–Jalan Pejanggik–Jalan Selaparang, which allows travel only in a west–east direction for an extensive stretch. Its counterpart running parallel to the south, Jalan Tumpang Sari–Jalan Panca Usaha–Jalan Pancawarga–Jalan Pendidikan, allows only east–west travel for a part of its length. The third major route, Jalan Brawijaya–Jalan Sriwijaya–Jalan Majapahit, two-way for most of its length, skirts to the south of these and is the site of the central post office and tourist office.

## Arrival and information

**Selaparang Airport** is on Jalan Adi Sucipto at Rembiga, a couple of kilometres north of Mataram. There's an exchange counter, open for all international arrivals, and a **taxi** counter with fixed-price fares (to Mataram Rp15,000; central Senggigi Rp30,000; north Senggigi Rp40,000; Bangsal Rp60,000; Sekotong Rp75,000-110,000; Tetebatu Rp105,000; Labuhan Lombok Rp135,000; Senaru Rp175,000; Sembalun Rp200,000; maximum four people). All the luxury hotels have booking counters here; discounts vary from day to day, so shop around. There's also a **wartel** (daily 7am–9pm). A few black **bemos** serving Kebon Roek terminal in Ampenan (heading to the right) pass along the road in front of the airport. See p.403 for public transport details from the airport to Bangsal (for the Gili Islands).

If you're arriving in the city by bus or bemo from pretty much anywhere except Senggigi and Pemenang, you'll come into the island's main **bus terminal** on the eastern edge of the conurbation, known variously as **Bertais**, **Mandalika** or **Sweta**, where local bemos and Lombok buses jostle for space beside long-distance services to Sumbawa, Flores, Bali, Java and Sumatra. Arriving **from Senggigi**, and on some of the bemos from Pemenang, you'll come into the **Kebon Roek terminal** in Ampenan. These two bus terminals are linked by the frequent yellow bemos that zip around the city.

The most helpful **tourist office** is the Provincial Tourist Service for West Nusa Tenggara, which is rather out of the way off Jalan Majapahit in the south of the city, at Jl Singosari 2 (Mon–Thurs 7.30am–2pm, Fri 7.30–11.30am, Sat 7.30am–1pm; ℡0370/634800, ℻637233). There are shorter opening hours during Ramadan (see p.64). They offer leaflets, a map of Lombok and advice about travel in Lombok and Sumbawa. Yellow bemos heading via "Kekalik" pass the end of Jalan Singosari as they run along Jalan Majapahit between Bertais/Mandalika/Sweta terminal and Kebon Roek terminal.

## City transport

All **bemo** trips within the four-cities area cost Rp1300, and yellow bemos constantly ply the route between Kebon Roek terminal in Ampenan and Bertais/Mandalika/Sweta terminal from early morning until late evening. Most follow the Jalan Langko–Jalan Pejanggik–Jalan Selaparang route heading west to east, and Jalan Tumpang Sari–Jalan Panca Usaha–Jalan Pancawarga–Jalan Pendidikan heading east to west, although there are plenty of less frequently served variations.

The horse-drawn carts here, unlike the ones on Bali, have small pneumatic tyres and are called **cidomo**; they aren't allowed on the main streets, covering the back routes that bemos don't work. Always negotiate a fare beforehand.

There are plenty of easily identifiable official metered **taxis**. Flagfall is Rp3000 for the first kilometre, then Rp1250 per kilometre; a trip across the city is unlikely to be more than Rp12,000.

# Accommodation

There's a large range of **accommodation**, although relatively few tourists stay here since Senggigi is only a few kilometres up the road. **Cakranegara** is the best area to stay – it's the commercial heart of the city, has accommodation options for every budget and is convenient for transport links and sights.

**Adiguna** Jl Nursiwan 9 ☎0370/625946. A good budget choice, situated in a quiet, convenient street near the bemo routes, and featuring reasonable rooms in a small garden. **❶**

**Ayu** Jl Nursiwan 20 ☎0370/621761. This losmen has buildings on both sides of the road, and is popular with businesspeople, Indonesian families and foreign tourists. The cheaper rooms have mandi and squat toilets, the more expensive ones Western toilets. **❶**

**Lombok Raya** Jl Panca Usaha 11 ☎0370/632305, Ⓔlombokraya_htl@telkom.net. Yellow bemos from Bertais/Mandalika/Sweta terminal pass by the door of this upmarket place. It has clean tiled rooms overlooking an attractive pool and garden. All rooms have air-con and hot water. Discounts of more than fifty percent are often available. **❻–❼**

**Oka** Jl Repatmaja 5 ☎0370/622406. Five fan rooms with attached mandi and good verandas set in a convenient and quiet location. **❶**

**Puri Indah** Jl Sriwijaya 132 ☎0370/637633, Ⓕ637669. A bit out of the way, but excellent value and very popular. There's an attractive pool with rooms, offering a choice of fan or air-con but no hot water, ranged around it. **❶–❷**

**Sahid Legi Mataram** Jl Sriwijaya 81 ☎0370/636282, Ⓔsahid@mataram.wasantara .net.id. Comfortably furnished, elegant hotel with lovely gardens, good rooms with air-con, hot water and satellite TV, and an excellent pool. Free airport transfers. Large discounts usually available. **❻–❼**

**Shanta Puri** Jl Maktal 15 ☎0370/632649. The largest travellers' place in Cakranegara, offering a wide range of rooms: the most expensive with air-con and hot water. Upstairs rooms lead off a pleasant balcony. **❷**

# The City

In the far west of the city, the old port town of **AMPENAN** flourishes around the mouth of the Kali Jangkok. It's the liveliest part of the city, with bustling narrow streets, a busy **market** and an atmosphere of business and enterprise that some of the enormous tree-lined roads further east lack. The descendants of early Chinese and Arab traders settled here in a maze of shophouses, although trading has long since ceased and Ampenan is now home to a fishing community. It's also a secondary transport hub, the jumping-off point to Senggigi a few kilometres up the coast, and has a selection of **restaurants** (see p.388). It's easy to spend a few hours exploring the narrow lanes and market area behind the main crossroads and then wandering out to the coast.

The **West Nusa Tenggara Provincial Museum**, Jl Panji Tilar Negara 6 (Mon–Thurs 8am–2pm, Fri 8–11am, Sat 8am–12.30pm, Sun 8am–2pm; Rp100), is worth a brief visit. The exhibits, with only a few labelled in English, range from displays about the geological formation of Indonesia and the various cultural groups of Nusa Tenggara to household, craft and religious items.

It's a pleasant walk out to the coast at the end of Jalan Pabean. A few hundred metres' walk north is the Balinese **Pura Segara**, the temple of the sea. It's often locked, although it's possible to see the *kulkul* tower over the wall. Inland and north from here, between the sea and the main road, the extensive **Chinese cemetery** is both a reminder of the large Chinese population of the area who were persecuted in the purges in 1965 (see p.452) and a visible symbol of the affluence of many of the Chinese community today.

## Mataram and Cakranegara

Merging into Ampenan to the east, **MATARAM** is the capital of West Nusa Tenggara province as well as of the district of Lombok Barat (West Lombok).

It's full of imposing government buildings set in spacious grounds on broad, tree-lined avenues, but there's little of tourist interest.

East again, **CAKRANEGARA**, usually known as Cakra (pronounced *chakra*), was the capital of Lombok in the eighteenth century during the height of the Balinese ascendancy on the island, and was the site of the savage fighting during 1894 that culminated in Dutch victory. Today, it's the commercial capital of Lombok, with shops, markets, workshops and hotels. The **market** is worth a visit (see below).

Built in 1744 during the rule of the Balinese in West Lombok, the **Puri Mayura** (Mayura Water Palace), on Jalan Selaparang (daily 8am–5pm; Rp2000), is set in well-maintained grounds, which get busy on Sundays. It's pleasant enough if you're looking for a bit of relaxation in the city. The centrepiece of the palace was the *bale kambang* (floating pavilion), the meeting hall and court of justice, set in the middle of a large artificial lake, which has now been replaced by a modern version reached by a small causeway. The Pura Jagatnatha within the grounds houses some exuberant carvings and is especially popular with worshippers at the time of the full moon.

Across the main road, **Pura Meru**, also known as Pura Mayura, is the largest Balinese temple on the island, built in 1720 by Prince Anak Agung Made Karang in an attempt to unite the various Hindu factions on Lombok. The *candi bentar* displaying scenes from the *Ramayana* is the highlight of the temple, which bustles and brims with activity on festival days but is otherwise deserted.

## Eating and drinking

There's a wide range of great-value **places to eat** offering **Chinese**, **Padang** and **fast food**. If you're really watching the rupiah, head for the food stalls in the Kebon Roek terminal. Although Lombok is predominantly Muslim, visiting **during Ramadan** does not mean hours of daylight fasting. Most of the places below remain open during the day at this time, with a curtain at the window discreetly hiding diners.

All the places below are in the inexpensive to moderate price range.

**Aroma** Jl Palapa I 2, Cakranegara. A long-standing favourite with residents and visitors alike, serving superb Chinese food, with seafood a speciality.

**Kristal** Jl Pejanggik 22a, Cakranegara ✆0370/627564. Air-con place convenient for the Cakranegara losmen with a huge Chinese, Indonesian and seafood menu, including lots of choice for vegetarians. Will take phone orders and deliver in the Cakra area.

**Mataram Mall** Jl Pejanggik, Cakranegara. There's a *McDonald's* on the ground floor and a *Swensen's* ice-cream stall inside, but the top-floor food court is more interesting, lined with small stalls selling local food; order at the stalls, collect the ticket you'll be given when they bring your food, and pay at the cash desk.

**Mirasa Modern Bakery** Jl Gede Ngurah, Cakranegara. Takeaway only. A huge selection of excellent savouries, pastries, sweet breads and cakes

– although the lurid doughnuts are probably only for real sugar junkies.

**Pabean Baru** Jl Yos Sudarso 111, Ampenan. Small Chinese restaurant with large servings of well-cooked food. There are several other good options in this street if it's full; the closest is *Cirebon* next door, or *Manalagi II* is across the street at no. 128.

**Roti Barokah** Jl Saleh Sungkar 22, Ampenan. About 100m south of the turning to Kebon Roek terminal. A little bakery and snack bar with a few tables where you can enjoy tasty pizzas, doughnuts and cakes. Also does takeaway.

**Simpang Raya** Jl Pejanggik 107, Cakranegara. A large range of well-cooked Padang food.

**Suharti Sate House** Jl Maktal 9, Cakranegara. With a selection of satés plus seafood and chicken options, this place is just along the road from the *Shanta Puri* and is convenient for all the Cakra losmen. Only a few vegetarian options.

## Shopping

**Shopping** can be fun in the city – whatever you're after and whether you prefer to shop in bustling markets or small, specialized shops. Tourist shops throughout Lombok can arrange packing and shipping, but beware the costs of shipping stuff before you fall in love with too much. A cubic metre is the smallest amount that can be sent and precise costs depend on the destination within each country; as a guide, prices to Australia are from AUS$210, Canada from CA$240, New Zealand from NZ$250, UK from £100 and USA from $220.

### Markets

The **markets** surrounding the Bertais/Mandalika/Sweta bus terminal, at Kebon Roek terminal in Ampenan, and in Cakranegara (just behind Jalan Gede Ngurah just south of the crossroads with Jalan Pejanggik and Jalan Selaparang) are all worth a look for a taste of pretty much everything that Lombok has to offer, from foodstuffs via household goods to crafts. Take a flashlight if you are interested in buying – some of the alleyways can be too dark to make out detail clearly. See p.391 for the markets in Gunung Sari.

### Crafts and textiles

There's a craft shopper's paradise at the **Lombok Handicraft Centre** (daily 9am–6pm), also known as Sayang Sayang, which is just beyond the Kali Jangkok river, about 2km north of Cakranegara along Jalan Hasanudin at Rungkang Jangkok. It has dozens of shops selling every type of craftwork imaginable, some with workshops attached. Ratna, in the middle of the complex, offers a huge variety and is as good a place as any to start. You'll need to get a cidomo from Cakranegara. There's a more accessible, slightly less overwhelming offshoot at Sayang Sayang Art Market around the corner on Jalan Jend Sudirman with stalls ranged around a huge car park; bemos from Kebon Roek terminal pass here.

There are a couple of local factories producing **ikat** cloth; both have shops attached. Rinjani Handwoven (☎0370/633169; Mon–Thurs & Sat 8.30am–8.30pm, Fri 8.30am–11am) is at Jl Pejanggik 44–46 in Cakranegara; and Slamet Riady (☎0370/631196; daily 8am–6pm, but the weavers don't work on Sunday) is at Jl Tanun 10, just off Jalan Hasanudin in Cakranegara, with a small sign just north of the *Pusaka* hotel. The process is the same as that used in Bali (see p.488), and the *ikat* is very similar.

### Pottery

Lombok **pottery** has an international reputation for style and beauty, and it's possible to get a good idea of the range and quality of the products in the city. **Lombok Pottery Centre**, Jl Sriwijaya 111a, Ampenan (☎0370/640351, ⓦwww.lombokpottery.com; Mon–Fri 8am–5pm, Sat noon–4pm) is the shop and showroom of the Lombok Craft Project, which was established in 1988 in Banyumulek, Penakak, east of Masbagik, and Penujak, and has largely fuelled the renaissance of pottery on the island. The showroom stocks a range of products from the three villages and has information about the project itself; they also have a showroom in each of the three villages. Even the most gigantic pots won't set you back much more than Rp150,000 and there are plenty of small items.

On the road north from Ampenan, **Sasak Pottery**, Jl Koperasi 102, Ampenan (☎0370/631687, ⓦwww.sasak-pottery.com), is a couple of kilometres before the southern edge of Senggigi. This is a huge showroom with designs for every taste, prices for every pocket and sizes for every suitcase.

## Pearls and jewellery

An increasingly popular souvenir is jewellery made from the **pearls** cultivated in the farms dotted along the Lombok coastline. They're sold by weight and come in a variety of sizes, shapes and colours. The centre for shopping is Sekarbela, a couple of kilometres south of Mataram: there's a new two-storey shopping centre, Komplex Pertokan MCC, at the junction of Jalan Gajah Made and Jalan S Kaharudin, and shops also line the main road in the village about a kilometre west.

For **gold** and **silver jewellery**, head for Kamasan (see map, p.385), north of Mataram, where pretty much every family works in the business. Workshops and shops around Jalan H.O.S.Cokroaminoto are responsible for quite a lot of the jewellery on sale in Bali and Lombok. Look out for Miza Silver at Jalan H.O.S.Cokroaminota 61.

# Listings

Airlines The airlines serving Lombok have ticket counters at the airport and/or offices in the city area. Citilink, Selaparang Airport ☎0370/622987 ext 246, and at *Hotel Lombok Raya*, Jl Panca Usaha 11, Cakranegara ☎0370/649999; Garuda, Selaparang Airport ☎ & ℱ0370/664 6846 and at *Hotel Lombok Raya*, Jl Panca Usaha 11, Cakranegara ☎0370/638259 (Mon–Fri 8am–5pm, Sat, Sun & hols 9am–1pm), Indonesia-wide call centre ☎08071/427832; Lion Air at *Sahid Legi Mataram* hotel ☎0370/629111, ℱ636213 (Mon–Sat 8.30am–5pm, Sun 9am–2pm); Merpati, Jl Pejanggik 69 ☎0370/621111 (Mon–Sat 8am–5.30pm, Sun 9am–3pm), 24hr information line ☎0800/101 2345, ⓦwww.merpati.co.id; Silk Air, *Hotel Lombok Raya*, Jl Panca Usaha 11, Cakranegara ☎0370/628254, ℮silkair-lombok@mataram. wasantara.net.id. For details of international airline offices in Bali, see box, p.115.

Banks and exchange All the large Mataram and Cakra banks change money and travellers' cheques. The most convenient are the Bank of Central Asia, Jl Pejanggik 67 ☎622587; BNI, Jl Langko 64 ☎0370/622788; Bank Danamon, Jl Pejanggik ☎0370/622408; BII, Jl Gede Ngurah 46b ☎0370/635027. All have Visa, MasterCard and Cirrus ATMs, and there's a row of ATMs outside the back entrance to the Mataram Mall. The main post office is a Western Union agent.

Boats Pelni, Jl Industri 1, Ampenan ☎0370/637212, ⓦwww.pelni.co.id (Mon–Fri 8am–3pm, Sat 8am–2pm).

Buses You'll get the best choice of inter-island departures out at the bus station at the Bertais/ Mandalika/Sweta terminal. Perama can advise on fares and timings and can book tickets for you.

Car rental The biggest firm is Toyota Car Rental, Jl Adi Sucipto 5, Mataram ☎0370/626363, ⓦwww .trac.astra.co.id. Rinjani Rent Car is at Jl Panca

Usaha 7b ☎0370/632259. You'll get a better choice and deal in Senggigi.

Consulates The closest consulates are all on Bali (see p.35).

Dentist Dr Darmono, Jl Kebudayan 108, Mataram (☎081/836 7749), speaks good English. Speak directly to him to make an appointment. If you can't get through on his mobile, contact him from 8am–4pm on ☎0370/636852 and from 4–9pm on ☎0370/643483. Clinic opening times are 8am–noon & 5–9pm.

Departure tax Leaving Lombok by air: Rp15,000 (domestic), Rp75,000 (international).

Hospitals The public hospital, Rumah Sakit Umum, Jl Pejanggik 6, Mataram ☎0370/623498, has an English-speaking "tourist doctor", Dr Felix.

Immigration office *Kantor Imigrasi*, Jl Udayana 2, Mataram ☎0370/632520.

Internet access The main concentration of places is on Jalan Panca Usaha along the back of the Mataram Mall. Also convenient is Wartel Jenny, Jl Penjanggik 69 (8am–midnight). All are significantly cheaper than Senggigi.

Motorbike rental The main rental place is at the roadside at Jl Gelantik 21, Cakranegara, 200m west of the *Srikandi* losmen on Jl Kebudayaan; if you are going to rent here, you'll need to be confident that you can identify a reasonable bike. Insurance isn't available. See p.51 for general advice.

Opticians Several good-value places in Mataram: Optik Melawai (☎0370/629884, ⓦwww.melawai .com) in the Mataram Mall, and International Optik, Jl Pejanggik 24 (☎0370/631854).

Phones The main phone office is at Jl Langko 23, Ampenan (daily 24hr). There are plenty of wartels in town, including Wartel Jenny, Jl Penjanggik 69 (6am–midnight), which is convenient for the Cakra losmen.

Police Jalan Langko, Ampenan ☎0370/631225.

## Out of the city

There are several worthwhile and easy **excursions** from the four-city conurbation; to the north, the road to Pemenang via Pusuk and, to the south, places that lie on or near the road to Lembar. All are accessible by bus or bemo from the Bertais/Mandalika/Sweta bus terminal.

Other feasible excursions inland, to Narmada and Lingsar, are covered in the Central Lombok section (see p.420).

### To the north

Heading north out of Mataram on the Pemenang road, it's a couple of kilometres to **GUNUNG SARI**, the location of a vibrant daily morning market selling every variety of produce and goods that Lombok can offer. From here the road climbs through fields and into forest, twisting up the far western slopes of the central volcanic mass of the island. After another 8km, there's basic accommodation at *Pusuk Permai* (☏0370/634922; ❷), although the attached *Villa Air Batu* (❻–❼) has a *lumbung*-style place, plus a fabulous two-storey villa overlooking the river. About 1.5km beyond, the **Pusuk Pass** is marked by a restaurant and fabulous views down to the north coast – the aggressive monkeys make eating here a dubious pleasure. From here, it's another 10km down to the plains and the village of **Pemenang**. On this road it's usually possible to buy *tuak manis*, a local drink made from palm sap, and from February to April the durian sold here are regarded as especially sweet.

### To the south

The *pura* on the summit of **Gunung Pengsong**, 6km south of Mataram, is one of the prettiest Balinese temples in Lombok. The complex begins at the bottom of the hill with an extensive outer compound from where it's a twenty-minute climb to the tiny temple at the top. A traditional story, that the earliest Balinese settlers on Lombok landed at the base of the hill, makes the temple the focus of regular ceremonies for the Balinese community on the island. One of the main **festivals** held here is Bersih Dasa, following the harvest in March or April, when Dewi Sri, the rice goddess, is honoured. There are good views across the fields to the coast.

### Labuapi and Banyumulek

About 7km south of Mataram, on the main road that leads to Lembar and along the side-roads from it, the small village of **LABUAPI** is lined with workshops and showrooms selling crafts. They specialize in woodcarving, and are especially well known for masks. You can see them being painted and varnished in the workshops behind the shops. *Rumah Makan Hajat*, just south of the BRI bank on the main road, is famed for its goat saté, *sate kambing*.

The village of **BANYUMULEK**, 2km south of Labuapi, is one of the three main **pottery** centres on the island. Stretching west of the main road to Lembar, it's an easy one-kilometre walk from the junction, marked by traffic lights and a monument, rather crumbling these days, composed of a tower of pots, to the pottery workshops and showrooms; cidomo serve the route. An extensive range of earthenware goods is produced in all sizes and all styles. Fashions change fast; currently, designs incorporating sections of engraving, eggshells and rattan are especially popular.

# Lembar and the southwest peninsula

With enticing offshore islands and a glorious coastline, the **southwest peninsula** is alluring if you want to get off the beaten track – a million miles away from the bustle of **Lembar** or the city area. **Bangko Bangko** at the tip of the peninsula is legendary among surfers as the location of the Desert Point break, regarded as the best in the world by some. Even if you follow only part of the road to Bangko Bangko, you'll get a feel for this arid land whose sparse population makes its living from the sea. The road is suitable for cycling, as it is pretty free of traffic; however, parts are very hot and you should carry food and plenty of water.

## Lembar

**LEMBAR**, the gateway to the peninsula and the port for Bali, is 22km south of Mataram. There's little **accommodation** here and no advantage in staying. *Tidar* (☎0370/681444; ●–❷) has five rooms with fan and attached bathrooms, and a restaurant with a small menu of inexpensive Indonesian food. It's about 300m along the road to the port from the junction with the main road from the city.

---

### The Wallace Line

Bali and Lombok are separated by a 35-kilometre stretch of water, the Lombok Strait, over 1300m deep in places, through which runs an imaginary boundary, the **Wallace Line**, marking a division between the distribution of Asian and Australasian wildlife.

Between 1854 and 1862, the British naturalist **Sir Alfred Russell Wallace** travelled throughout the Indonesian archipelago. Encountering differences between the wildlife on Bali and that on Lombok, he suggested that during the Ice Ages, when the levels of the world's oceans dropped, animals ranged overland from mainland Asia down through Sumatra and Java to Bali. However, reaching the waters of the Lombok Strait, they could go no further. Similarly, animals from the land masses to the south roamed as far as Lombok on the other side of the strait.

Some evidence does support this idea. Bali and the islands to the west have creatures mostly common to mainland Asia (rabbits, monkeys, tigers), while the wildlife on Lombok and the islands to the east is more characteristic of Australia and New Guinea (parrots, marsupials, platypus and lizards). For example, the **yellow-crested cockatoo**, a native of Australia, and the **rainbow lorikeet** and **red-cheeked parrot** are found no further west than Lombok.

However, later research shows that many animal species are common to both Bali and Lombok; you're likely to see **crab-eating macaques** and **silvered leaf monkeys** both in Bali Barat National Park and on the slopes of Gunung Rinjani. Opinion has now shifted away from the clear-cut migration theory devised by Wallace and today naturalists refer not to Wallace's Line but to a **zone of transition** from the Asian type of animal life to the Australasian; in honour of Sir Alfred, this is known as "Wallacea".

**Bemos** run between the Bertais/Mandalika/Sweta terminal and the port at Lembar, connecting with the ferry service to Bali (for details, see p.382). Public bemos to the southwest peninsula leave from the large terminal 500m north of the port, at the junction of the main road and the turning to Bangko Bangko via Sekotong (this turn is marked with hotel signs, including notices for *Hotel Bola Bola Paradis* and *Hotel Sekotong Indah*). Bemos operate from Lembar to Selegang during the day, although you may need to change on the way. A metered **taxi** from Lembar port to Tawun will cost about Rp40,000.

# The southwest peninsula

As the crow flies, it's around 23km from Lembar to Bangko Bangko, at the tip of the peninsula, where the road ends. However, the journey by road is at least 50km, meandering around the picturesque north coast. The road is tarmacked to Selegang, 3km before Bangko Bangko, after which you're on sand tracks. The scenery is great: many of the **beaches** are glorious and clusters of **islands** are visible offshore.

Out of Lembar, you've a choice of two roads. The longer route traces the outline of the massive harbour, much of which is black sand lined with mangroves, while the shorter, busier one winds inland through rolling hills – all distances below assume you take this road. The small village of **SEKOTONG**, 11km from Lembar, marks the junction of the Bangko Bangko road with a tiny road that heads 11km south to Sepi on the south coast (see p.436).

## Tawun and around

Past Sekotong, the scenery improves dramatically and the views of the offshore islands become more enticing as you reach the village of **TAWUN**, 19km from Lembar. This is a sweeping white-sand bay, from where you can look across to Gili Sudak, Gili Tangkong and Gili Nanggu. There are charter boats (there's no public boat service) to **Gili Nanggu** (20min; Rp60,000 per boat). The boat captains rent out **snorkelling** gear (Rp40,000 per set), and snorkelling trips to Gili Nanggu (Rp160,000) or to several of the islands (Rp170,000) are also possible. The only accommodation on the islands is at *Gili Nanggu Cottages* (☎0370/623783, ⓦwww.gilinanggu.com; ❸–❺) with a choice of fan or air-con, and a moderately priced **restaurant** attached. It's ideal for total relaxation or trips to nearby islands: Gili Tangkong to the east and Gili Poh, the miniscule desert-island lookalike, to the west.

Just 2km around the coast from Tawun, in the village of **LABU**, *Hotel Sekotong Indah* (☎0818/362326; ❷) has bungalows just across the road from the beach. Most rooms have fan and attached cold-water bathroom but there is one with air-con.

Moving further west you'll be unable to miss the gigantic, new blue-roofed *Sundancer* development, which will include residential villas, holiday homes and eventually a hotel, ranging up the hillside at **PANDANAN**, 23km from Lembar.

## Tembowong to Bangko Bangko and Pandana

At the village of **TEMBOWONG**, 10km from Tawun, *Putri Duyung Home-stay* (☎0812/375 2459; ❶) is a family-run place owned by Pak Gede Patra. Rooms are extremely simple with attached mandi and squat toilet. This is an ideal base from which to explore **Gili Gede**, the largest offshore island visible from here, and the surrounding six smaller islands; the family rent out a **boat** at Rp200,000 per day.

A further 2km west, **PELANGAN** is the largest village in this part of the peninsula. An enticing side-road heads south for about 5km to the bay of Teluk Mekaki on the south coast; ask about the condition of this road before trying it. *Hotel Bola Bola Paradis* (☎0370/623783, ✉batuapi99@hotmail.com; ③–④) boasts a great coastal location 2km beyond Pelangan. All rooms have fan and hot water is available. They get packed out from April to September (when you need to book ahead), and you should ring at other times to let them know you're coming, as things do go very quiet. **Boat** trips are available (Rp200,000 for 3hr).

From here, the coast road is lined with more and more mangrove. It turns inland before arriving at the bay at **SIUNG**, 7km from Pelangan, from where the coastline of Bali becomes distantly visible. The road follows the shore for another 3km to **LABUHAN POH**, where the lovely bay appears almost circular, enclosed by hills, headlands and islands, all fringed with white sand.

About 3km west of Labuhan Poh, the blacktopped road ends at **SELEGANG**, a small hamlet of a few houses. A dirt road winds among the arid coastal hills for another 3km, emerging onto a white-sand bay lined with fishermen's huts and colourful sail boats. This is **BANGKO BANGKO**, which from mid-May to September, and again in December, draws hundreds of **surfers** from across the globe in search of the elusive, ultimate wave that is **Desert Point** just offshore here. Alternatively, access is on a liveaboard boat charter from Bali.

The track continues around the bay and up the hill to look down on the next hamlet of **PANDANA**. This is a harsh landscape: the place buzzes when the surfers hit town but it's otherwise as remote and isolated spot as you'll find in Lombok. From here, you've no alternative but to turn around and head back the way you've come.

# Senggigi and the northwest coast

Covering a lengthy stretch of coastline, **SENGGIGI**, with sweeping bays separated by towering headlands, is an attractive and laid-back beach resort, offering a wide range of accommodation and restaurants, and low-key nightlife. Parts of the area are packed wall-to-wall with hotels, many of them pretty luxurious, but it's perfectly possible to have an inexpensive and relaxing stay here, and proximity to the airport makes it an ideal first- or last-night destination. There are, however, plenty of hawkers in the central areas (see box, p.398).

## Arrival and orientation

Easily accessible by public transport, Senggigi is served by **bemos** from Ampenan throughout the day (every 15–20min); pick them up on Jalan Saleh Sungkar just north of the turn-off to Kebon Roek terminal in Ampenan. Metered taxis zip between the city and the resort. From the **airport**, fixed-price taxis charge Rp30,000 to central Senggigi, Rp40,000 to the north of the resort. Perama **tourist shuttle buses** and **boat services** operate to Senggigi from the main Bali tourist destinations; see "Travel details", p.438.

The southern end of Senggigi is 5km north of Ampenan, and a few places are spread out along the next 4km until the main concentration of hotels, which stretches for roughly 1km from the *Graha Senggigi* to the *Sheraton*. Low-density development continues for another 7km to the most northerly development, *Bulan Baru* at Lendang Luar. **Bemos** ply the coastal road as far as here during the day, and metered blue **taxis** operate throughout the area from early

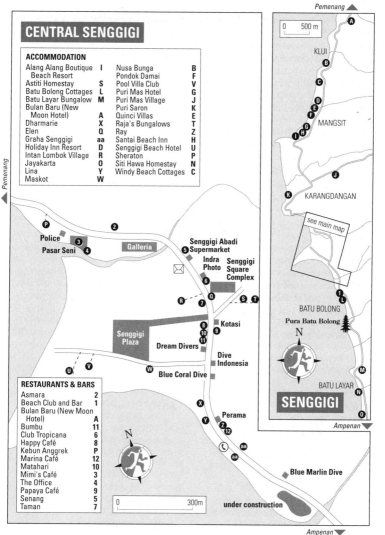

## CENTRAL SENGGIGI

### ACCOMMODATION

| | | | |
|---|---|---|---|
| Alang Alang Boutique Beach Resort | I | Nusa Bunga | B |
| Astiti Homestay | S | Pondok Damai | F |
| Batu Bolong Cottages | L | Pool Villa Club | V |
| Batu Layar Bungalow | M | Puri Mas Hotel | G |
| Bulan Baru (New Moon Hotel) | A | Puri Mas Village | J |
| | | Puri Saron | K |
| Dharmarie | X | Quinci Villas | E |
| Elen | Q | Raja's Bungalows | T |
| Graha Senggigi | aa | Ray | Z |
| Holiday Inn Resort | D | Santai Beach Inn | H |
| Intan Lombok Village | R | Senggigi Beach Hotel | U |
| Jayakarta | O | Sheraton | P |
| Lina | Y | Siti Hawa Homestay | N |
| Maskot | W | Windy Beach Cottages | C |

Police

Pasar Seni

Galleria

Senggigi Abadi Supermarket

Indra Photo

Senggigi Square Complex

Kotasi

Senggigi Plaza

Dream Divers

Dive Indonesia

Blue Coral Dive

### RESTAURANTS & BARS

| | |
|---|---|
| Asmara | 2 |
| Beach Club and Bar | 1 |
| Bulan Baru (New Moon Hotel) | A |
| Bumbu | 11 |
| Club Tropicana | 6 |
| Happy Café | 8 |
| Kebun Anggrek | P |
| Marina Café | 12 |
| Matahari | 10 |
| Mimi's Café | 3 |
| The Office | 4 |
| Papaya Café | 9 |
| Senang | 5 |
| Taman | 7 |

Perama

N

0        300m

under construction

Pemenang

KLUI

MANGSIT

6

KARANGDANGAN

see main map

BATU BOLONG

Pura Batu Bolong

N

BATU LAYAR

SENGGIGI

Ampenan

LOMBOK AND THE GILI ISLANDS | Senggigi and the northwest coast

0      500 m

Pemenang

Blue Marlin Dive

Ampenan

morning to late at night; a ride from central Senggigi to Lendang Luar costs about Rp11,000.

There's no **tourist office** in Senggigi; the nearest one is in Mataram (see p.386). The resort is lined with "tourist information" places, but these are commercial companies primarily offering tours and vehicle rental.

## Accommodation

The full range of **accommodation** is available in Senggigi. The most attractive part of the coast is **north Senggigi**, with hotels more spread out and great

Various travel agencies on Lombok and the Gili Islands advertise boat trips via **Sumbawa** and **Komodo** to **Flores**, including several **snorkelling** stops, some **trekking**, sightseeing and a visit to see the Komodo dragons. Conditions on board can be pretty basic and comforts few. Prices vary, starting at Rp550,000 per person for a five-day trip. If possible, go by personal recommendation, and be clear where the trip ends and how you'll move on from there (air transport out of Labuanbajo can be difficult to arrange). The following sell trips: Perama – contact any office; Citra Lombok Indah, Senggigi (☎0370/693921), Gora Tour & Travel, Senggigi (☎0370/693477).

views across to Bali. In **central Senggigi**, there's plenty happening, with bars, restaurants and good shopping. **South Senggigi** has the advantage of being closer to the city area and airport.

## South Senggigi

**Batu Bolong Cottages** ☎ & ℱ0370/693198. Just north of Pura Batu Bolong, these are attractive, clean cottages with good-quality furnishings in pleasant gardens, on both sides of the road; the more expensive ones have air-con and hot water, and the deluxe seafront rooms have fine coastal views. ❷–❺

**Batu Layar Bungalow** ☎0370/692235, ⊕http:// lombokbg.hp.infoseek.co.jp. Clean, tiled bungalows with fans and hot water in an attractive garden. It's about 200 metres' walk through a coconut grove to the beach, and there's free transport to central Senggigi. ❷

**Jayakarta** ☎0370/693048, ⊕www .jayakarta-lombok.com. Marking the southern end of Senggigi, the imposing *lumbung* foyer is the most impressive part of the hotel, although the garden is pleasant and the pool lovely. The accommodation is comfortable, all with air-con and hot water, without being plush. Significant discounts are often available. ❼–❾

**Siti Hawa Homestay** ☎0370/693414, ⒺPon-dok_sitihawa@hotmail.com. Small, basic rooms, some with attached bathroom, all with mosquito net, in a family compound about 4km south of central Senggigi. ❶

## Central Senggigi

**Dharmarie** ☎0370/693050, ℱ693099. Attractive bungalows in a central location next to the beach. All have air-con and hot water, more expensive ones with sea views. Staff are helpful. Good choice in this price range. ❹–❺

**Elen** ☎0370/693077. Tucked away up an alleyway opposite *Taman* restaurant, a reasonable central budget choice. All rooms have cold water, and air-con is available. ❶–❷

**Graha Senggigi** ☎0370/693101, ⊕www .grahasenggigi.com. Located on both sides of the road, at the southern end of the central area. Accommodation is comfortable, all rooms have air-con and hot water, there are two restaurants, a large pool (open to non-guests for Rp17,000) and a high waterslide (guests Rp14,000, non-guests Rp27,000). ❼–❽

**Intan Lombok Village** ☎0370/693090, ⊕www .intanhotels.com/lombok. Accommodation is in the heart of the central area and available in rooms, bungalows and cottages, all set in extensive grounds. The highlight is the pool, reputedly the largest in Lombok (non-guests Rp25,000). There are several bars and restaurants. ❽–❾

🏃 **Lina** ☎0370/693237. This long-standing Senggigi favourite is justifiably popular. All the rooms in this tiny compound, right on the seafront in central Senggigi, just opposite the Perama office, have air-con, but only the more expensive ones have hot water. There's a large restaurant, too. ❷–❸

**Maskot** ☎0370/693365, ℱ693236. Central place behind a lengthy stretch of beach, although there's no pool. The bungalows all have air-con, hot water and huge verandas. ❻

🏃 **Raja's Bungalows** ☎0812/377 0138, ⒺRajas22@yahoo.com. Tucked away off the road to the mosque, four clean, tiled budget bungalows with fan and attached cold-water bathrooms set in a lush garden. If this is full, then *Astiti Homestay* (☎0370/693041, ❶), on the same track, is a slightly cheaper alternative. ❷

**Ray** ☎0370/660 5599. Ranged up the hillside in central Senggigi, close to the Perama office, a short walk from the beach. Rooms are good value. The more expensive ones have air-con. Be aware it's right next door to the *Marina Café*, which has loud, sometimes live, music until late. ❶–❷

**Senggigi Beach Hotel and Pool Villa Club**
☎0370/693210, ⊛http://senggigibeach
.aerowisata.com. Large place in grounds that
occupy an entire promontory in central Senggigi
surrounded by beach. The rooms are comfortable,
and there's an attractive pool plus several bars
and restaurants, tennis courts and a spa. Prices
in the hotel start at US$80. The *Pool Villa Club*
(☎0370/693210, ⊛http://poolvillaclub.aerowisata
.com) is part of the same establishment but set
in its own grounds and is super-plush. There are
sixteen fabulously appointed two-storey villas with
direct access to the elegant pool. Published prices
in the *Pool Villa Club* start at $380. Hotel ❽–❾
Club ❾

**Sheraton** ☎0370/693333, ⊛www
.sheraton.com The best luxury hotel in
Senggigi offers all the facilities, comfort and service to be expected at this end of the market. It is a
peaceful enclave but convenient for central Senggigi facilities. The swimming pool is brilliant (non-
guests must pay admission), the grounds are lush
and top-class restaurants cater for all tastes; the
breakfast buffet is a real feast. There's a seafront
spa, health club, shopping gallery and Kiddy's Club.
Published prices start at $170, and private villas
with their own pools are available. ❾

## North Senggigi

### Alang Alang Boutique Beach Resort
☎0370/693518, ⊛www.alang-alang-villas
.com. An atmospheric choice about 1km north of
central Senggigi. All rooms and bungalows have
air-con and hot water and are furnished with
local artefacts. The gardens are glorious, with
a pretty pool. Free evening transport to central
Senggigi. ❽

**Bulan Baru (New Moon Hotel)**
☎0370/693785, ⊜bulanbaru@hotmail.com.
Situated at Lendang Luar, 7km north of central Senggigi. Spotless bungalows with air-con and hot water
situated in a pretty garden with a lovely pool. It has
a "no children" policy. It's fabulously peaceful, and
Setangi beach is nearby, with decent snorkelling off
the coast. There's an excellent restaurant attached
and service is friendly and efficient. ❸

**Holiday Inn Resort** (from early 2006 *Holiday
Resort Lombok*) ☎0370/693444, ⓕ693092. Some
5km north of central Senggigi, this upmarket place
has five standards of rooms in extensive grounds.
Two-bedroom self-catering villas are located
across the road from the main hotel and are excellent value at $200 per week if you stay more than
a month. There's a giant swimming pool, a range
of daily activities, a spa, and several bars and
restaurants. ❽–❾

**Nusa Bunga** ☎0370/693034, ⊛www.nusabunga
.com. Over 5km north of the centre, offering
simple, tiled thatch-roofed brick cottages all with
air-con and hot water facing seawards in their own
bay, with a small swimming pool and an attractive
garden. ❼

**Pondok Damai** ☎ & ⓕ0370/693019. On the
coast 4km north of central Senggigi, this is a quiet
spot with good-value accommodation in bamboo
and thatch bungalows built on a tiled base in a
lovely garden. Hot water in the more expensive
ones. ❷–❸

**Puri Mas Hotel** ☎0370/693831, ⊛www
.boutiquevilla.com. Attractive bungalows, all with
hot water, air-con and antique furnishings, set in
a lush garden with a fine pool next to the beach
at Mangsit, 4km north of central Senggigi. *Puri
Mas Village* (☎0370/693596) is set inland with a
fabulous pool, spa and restaurant, although some
guests may not enjoy the caged tropical birds and
captive animals here. ❼–❾

**Puri Saron** ☎0370/693424, ⓕ693266. Several
standards of room with air-con and hot water are
available at this place, 2km north of central Senggigi. There's an attractive pool and nearby restaurant. Large discounts are often available. ❼–❾

**Quinci Villas** ☎0370/693800, ⊛www
.quincivillas.com. Designer accommodation
abounding in natural materials in Bali Modern
style decorated with original art. Welcoming gay
as well as mixed-sex couples and aiming to cater
equally well for both, this place is 4km north of
central Senggigi, with a brilliant pool and beachside restaurant. ❼–❽

**Santai Beach Inn** ☎0370/693038, ⊛www
.santaibeachinn.com. On the coast at Mangsit,
these popular thatched bungalows are set in
a wonderfully overgrown garden. Meals can
be provided (booking needed) and are eaten
communally; the menu is ideal for fish-eating
vegetarians but they can also cater for vegans
– carnivorous guests are welcome to dine elsewhere. All rooms have fan and cold water, but
there are a couple of larger family rooms with
hot water. Bookings are only accepted for the
large rooms, but phone ahead, as they do get
full. ❷–❹

**Windy Beach Cottages** ☎0370/693191,
⊜lidya@mataram.wasantara.net.id.
Bamboo, wood and thatch bungalows, in a lovely
spot on the coast at Mangsit, 5km north of central
Senggigi. All rooms have hot water and the more
expensive have air-con. You can book shuttle bus
tickets and tours here and rent snorkelling equipment – there are a couple of good spots off the
beach. ❷–❸

## They don't mean to spoil your holiday

Walk along the street or beach at any time in central Senggigi or eat at a beach-side or streetside restaurant and the chances are you'll be approached by one or more of the local **hawkers** selling T-shirts, sarongs, watches, jewellery, paintings, bookmarks, tours, transport and pretty much anything else you can imagine. It can be irritating, but it's worth bearing a few things in mind. Despite the tourist gloss, many people in Lombok are poor and the opportunities for young people are few. Jobs in hotels and restaurants are like gold dust, government jobs depend on having connections, and there are simply not enough jobs in the commercial sector to meet demand. Farming is a harsh life and family land is often insufficent to feed all the people dependent on it. Youngsters come to Senggigi in the hope of scraping a living and getting a toe-hold in the tourist industry – and perhaps meeting a future husband or wife from overseas. And the only way they can sell things is to approach tourists.

Suggestions for coping:

* Acknowledge people but remain polite and calm. A simple "No, thank you" is enough.

* If you say you'll look at things tomorrow or later, then you should do so – they'll remember.

* If you start bargaining and the seller agrees your price, you are then obliged to buy.

* Even if you don't want to buy, talk to the sellers and find out about their lives; after all, you've come to Lombok to meet the people.

## The resort and around

Life in Senggigi centres on the **beach** or swimming pool during the day and the restaurants and bars in the evening. Senggigi is an excellent base for exploring further afield, although the only local "sight" is **Pura Batu Bolong**, 1km south of the centre of Senggigi. The shrines are spread around a rocky promontory with fabulous views along the coast. The main part of the temple is built over an archway in the rock, the hole through which virgins were once supposedly sacrificed to appease the gods. Nowadays, this is a peaceful spot, a favourite with local fishermen.

### Diving and snorkelling

There are plenty of operators in the resort, most also with offices in the Gili Islands, for people who want the comforts of Senggigi and don't mind the additional cost and travel time to **dive** around the islands. Most companies keep their boats at Teluk Nara, about 20km north of Senggigi, and transport you there by road. See p.71 for general guidelines on choosing an operator.

The dive sites closer to Senggigi (Nipah Slope, Malimbu Cave and Alang-Alang Wall) are dived less often than the sites further afield.

Qualified divers will **pay** US$45–65 for two dives; a PADI Open Water course is around $300, a PADI Advanced Open Water course $225, a Scuba Review around $50 and Discover Scuba about $70. Check whether equipment rental is included in the price.

Most operators run **snorkelling** trips to the Gili Islands; you go along with the divers and have to be fairly self-reliant in the water. Expect to pay $15–25, including equipment and lunch.

### Dive operators

See p.406 for more details on the operators who are Gili-based.

**Bagus Divers** at *Jayakarta Hotel* ☎0370/693045 ext 819, ⊛www.bagusdivers.if.tv. In addition to the usual, offers diving trips to east Lombok ($65 per person, minimum two people).

**Blue Coral** ☎0370/693441, ℱ634765. Daily dive and snorkelling trips and PADI courses.

**Blue Marlin** ☎0370/692003, ⊛www.diveindo.

com. Also at *Alang-Alang* ☎0370/692004 and *Holiday Inn Resort* ☎0370/693719. See p.406.

**Dive Indonesia** ☎0370/693521, ⊛www .diveindonesiaonline.com. See p.407.

**Dream Divers** ☎0370/692047, ⊛www .dreamdivers.com. Also at *Intan Lombok Village*; see p.396. In addition to the usual courses and fun dives, they dive sites closer to Senggigi, and offer diving in southern Lombok for highly experienced divers (see p.407 for details) as well as liveaboards to the Gilis, Sumbawa and Komodo.

### Adventure trips

Lombok certainly won't excite the juices of hard-core adrenaline junkies, but there are a couple of activities on offer. Lombok Biking Tour (☎0370/6605792), with an office next to *Bumbu* restaurant, offer a range of guided **cycle tours** that take in Lingsar, Pusuk Pass, Gunung Pengsong or Sekotong, from $18 per person including equipment and transport to the start. Sea Kayak Adventures (☎0370/692003, ⊛www.diveindo.com), attached to Blue Marlin, offer guided **kayaking** trips up the coast or around the islands in single-person or two-seater kayaks (from $45) with boat back-up. Manta Dive and Blue Marlin on Gili Trawangan offer **water-skiing and wakeboarding** (see p.407).

### The road north

With your own transport, **the road north** from Senggigi to Pemenang (24km), hugging the spectacular coastline, makes a great day out. As you travel through the bays of Karangdangan, Mangsit, Malimbu, Teluk Kodek, Nippah and Teluk Nara, there are fine views of the Gili Islands – tiny white specks atop a turquoise sea – and across to Gunung Agung, Gunung Abang and even Gunung Batukau on Bali when the weather is clear. However, the road is steep, with bad bends and sheer drops, and is especially hazardous at night. Huge expanses of the coast are totally undeveloped, with a few villages dotted amidst sweeping bays amidst stands of coconut palms. This remains an area where you can find total relaxation.

Pemenang marks the turn-off to Bangsal, from where boats depart to the Gili Islands. Only a couple of kilometres beyond Pemenang lies the stunning beach at Sira.

## Eating, drinking and nightlife

A wide range of **restaurants** in Senggigi offer high-quality international cuisines, mostly at inexpensive or moderate prices. For real budget eating, street carts selling local food congregate on the main stretch in central Senggigi after dark, and there's a row of sellers along the road as it climbs up beyond the *Sheraton*. During the month of Ramadan all tourist places remain open.

For something a bit different, Perama's **Sunset Dinner Cruise (**Rp250,000 per person, minimum two people) leaves at 1pm on Monday, Wednesday and Friday for snorkelling and the sunset, followed by dinner on board. Guests can either sleep on the boat or return to Senggigi.

**Asmara** ☎0370/693619. This tasteful, relaxed restaurant in central Senggigi serves a huge menu of excellent Western, Indonesian and seafood dishes. There's good home-made bread for breakfast (from 7am), and also baby and children's

meals. Free pick-up throughout Senggigi. Booking recommended. Moderate to expensive.

**Beach Club and Bar** A small beachside place south of the centre. There's a pool table, satellite television, a tiny menu of well-cooked, moderately priced Western food and a huge drinks list.

**Bulan Baru (New Moon Hotel)** At Lendang Luar, 7km north of central Senggigi. Well-cooked and nicely presented, moderately priced Indonesian, Thai and Western dishes (including bangers and mash for homesick travellers) are all described on the menu in mouth-watering detail. This is a good spot for lunch, with lots of soups, salads, sandwiches and rolls, and Setangi beach a short walk away. Staff are pleasant and welcoming.

**Bumbu** Small, justifiably popular place in central Senggigi. Thai food is the speciality and the best choice, but tell the waiters if you can't cope with industrial quantities of chilli. There are plenty of other options, including steaks and sandwiches.

**Happy Café** Offering excellent live music in a friendly atmosphere, with a gigantic bar and an excellent menu of moderately priced Indonesian, Thai, Chinese and Western food.

**Kebun Anggrek** At *Sheraton* hotel ☎0370/693333. Senggigi's most upmarket dining experience. The menu ranges across Asian-Pacific, Indonesian and Western dishes in the expensive price range, up to the Fisherman's Platter (Rp195,000) and the Degustation menu of five courses (Rp185,000).

**Matahari** One of a row of places in central Senggigi selling the usual travellers' fare at reasonable prices. Examine the menus in other places along the street to find more in the same mould.

**Mimi's Café** A relaxed spot in the *pasar seni* (art market) with good Indonesian and Western meals at moderate prices. They do have some expensive options, up to barbecued lobster at Rp339,500.

**Papaya Café** Quality live music in a welcoming atmosphere. There's an Indonesian, Western and Chinese menu – the Chinese dishes come in small, medium or large servings. There's plenty of seafood, peaking with the King of Seafood for two for Rp220,000, and thin and crispy pizzas are a speciality.

**The Office** Beachside spot in the *pasar seni* with a good menu of Indonesian and Western food at moderate to expensive prices. There's a huge drinks list and a vast television screen.

**Senang** No-frills, central Senggigi place offering a small Indonesian menu featuring simple rice, noodle and soup options. Everything is good, plentiful and inexpensive: main courses from Rp7000.

**Taman** Imposing place in central Senggigi; excellent and atmospheric with a great deli/bakery.

## Nightlife

The **nightlife** in Senggigi, the only on mainland Lombok, is very low-key, in keeping with the sensibilities of the local Muslim population, and venues are limited. *Marina Café*'s live music, sometimes featuring big bands from Jakarta attracts a mix of local people, expats and tourists onto its decent dancefloor; there's also a garden area and quiet bar for less exuberant fun. *Club Tropicana* (Rp25,000, which includes a drink) is also open nightly, but Friday and Saturday are busiest. It's popular with local people, who swell the crowd, which includes some of the increasing number of tourists from other parts of Indonesia who spend the weekend in Senggigi, boosting Saturday-night numbers.

## Shopping

Senggigi boasts plenty of shops selling Lombok **crafts** including textiles, jewellery, basketware and items from across the archipelago, as well as Western clothes and bags aimed at the tourist market. If you need a big dose of retail therapy, though, head for the shops in nearby Ampenan–Mataram–Cakranegara–Sweta (see p.389). There are also plenty of shops along the road from Senggigi to Ampenan, although smaller stuff is rather overwhelmed by furniture.

**Alxih** On the main road near the *pasar seni*; worth a look for its jewellery.

**Asmara Collection** Attached to *Asmara* restaurant, selling an excellent range of good-quality items big and small, including boxes, toiletries and furniture.

**Bayan Lombok** In the same row of shops as the Senggigi Abadi supermarket, selling an excellent selection of wooden handicrafts, including masks, boxes and trays, all at great prices. They have a workshop in Mataram if you want to see more.

Oleh Oleh On the main street, with a selection of good-quality souvenirs.
Pasar seni The collection of tiny stalls that make up the art market sell a great selection of stuff.

Sudirman On the main street, almost opposite *Happy Café*. Long established in Senggigi, selling a variety of mostly wooden items from across Indonesia.

## Listings

Airlines See p.390 for details of airlines serving Lombok. Information on international airline offices in Bali is on p.115.

Boats Perama (℡0370/693007, ⊛www.perama-tour.com) operate a daily boat to Gili Trawangan at 1.30pm (1hr 30min; Rp30,000). If you're interested in chartering a boat to the Gili Islands or for local fishing or sightseeing along the coast, head to the beach and negotiate with the captains. You'll be looking at Rp250,000–300,000 per day.

Buses Perama (℡0370/693007, ⊛www.perama-tour.com), Anjani (℡0370/693587) and Gora (℡0370/693477) offer tourist shuttles to Bali and Lombok destinations and prices are comparable; they advertise along the main street. They have a daily departure and serve smaller destinations by charter. Perama can advise on inter-island bus journeys and book tickets. See p.438 for inter-island buses from the Bertais/Mandalika/Sweta terminal. See p.439 for details of Perama services.

Car and bike rental Plenty of places rent vehicles with and without drivers. Kotasi is the local transport cooperative. Check the insurance at the time of renting. It's worth shopping around, but general prices are: Suzuki Jimneys (Rp150,000/day), Kijangs (Rp200,000–225,000), motorbikes (Rp30,000–35,000 without insurance) and bicycles (Rp15,000–20,000). Expect to pay around Rp50,000 per day for a driver. Chartering a vehicle including driver and fuel (from Kotasi, travel agents or street touts) costs Rp250,000–300,000 per day all-in, depending on where you want to go. It's best to go by personal recommendation. One highly recommended local driver is Hasan Nur

(℡081/854 8227, ⊜hsn_y@yahoo.com), who can also be contacted through *Bulan Baru* (see p.397).

Dentist You'll need to go to Mataram-Ampenan-Cakranegara-Sweta (see "Listings". p.390).

Doctor Some of the luxury hotels have clinics: the *Sheraton* ℡0370/693333 (3–11pm with a paramedic and a doctor on call 24hr), *Senggigi Beach Hotel* ℡0370/693210 (24hr) and *Holiday Inn* ℡0370/693444 (9am–5pm daily except Fri). See p.390 for hospitals in Ampenan-Mataram-Cakrane-gara-Sweta.

Exchange BCA and BNI banks both have central ATMs for Visa, MasterCard and Cirrus. There are exchange counters (daily 10am–10pm) on the main street.

Internet access Several Internet cafés along the main street (daily 8am–10pm; Rp300/min).

Left luggage Perama (Rp10,000/item/day, maximum one week), or most accommodation will store stuff if you're coming back to them.

Phones A couple of wartels in the centre; the one above Indah Photo is as good as any (daily 8am–11pm).

Police On the road in Senggigi ℡0370/632733.

Post office In the centre of Senggigi (Mon–Thurs 7.30am–5pm, Fri & Sat 7.30am–4pm). Poste restante is available; get mail addressed to yourself at Post Office, Senggigi, Lombok 83355, West Nusa Tenggara.

Supermarkets A couple in the centre, including Senggigi Abadi (daily 8.30am–9.30pm), which sells necessities, postcards and souvenirs. The English-language *Jakarta Post* arrives in the afternoon.

Tour companies See p.384 for information on Lombok tours and operators.

# The Gili Islands

Strikingly beautiful, with white-sand beaches lapped by brilliant blue waters and circled by coral reefs hosting myriad species of fish, each of the **Gili Islands** has its own character – although on each of them there's a range of accommodation to suit every pocket and food for every palate.

Of the three, **Gili Trawangan** best fits the image of "party island". With its

## Boats to and from the Gili Islands

Whichever boat you use to get to the Gili Islands, you'll get your feet wet at either end of the journey; the boats anchor in the shallows and passengers wade to and fro.

### From Bangsal
**Public boats** leave Bangsal throughout the day when full (7.30am–4.30pm; journey time 20–45min). **Shuttle boats** depart at 10am from the islands and 4.30pm from Bangsal, with an additional shuttle at 2pm from Bangsal to Gili Meno (Rp8000). You can also **charter** a boat, for a maximum of ten people, for single or return, or trips to more than one island. Prices are fixed and displayed in the ticket office.

|                     | To Gili Air | To Gili Meno | To Gili Trawangan |
|---------------------|-------------|--------------|-------------------|
| Public boat         | Rp3500      | Rp4000       | Rp4500            |
| Shuttle boat        | Rp10,000    | Rp11,000     | Rp12,0000         |
| Charter (one way)   | Rp68,000    | Rp78,000     | Rp88,000          |

### From Senggigi and elsewhere
**From Senggigi** There's a daily Perama boat at 9am (Rp30,000; 1hr 30min). Charters are available from the Kotasi cooperative in Senggigi (see p.401) or approach the boat captains on the beach. It's a great trip but the boats are small – you won't be able to travel if the winds and tides make the sea too rough.

**From Amed on Bali** Increasing numbers of skippers arrange charters to the islands. Be aware that the boats are often small with single engines, don't carry radios, and mobile phones may well be out of range in the middle of the Lombok Strait. If you're still interested, contact I Nengah Suande through the *Diver's Café* near Jemeluk (from Rp750,000 per boat).

**Tourist shuttle bus** Tickets for the Gili Islands are available from all main tourist destinations on Bali. Perama customers swap on to the Perama boat either at Padang Bai or Senggigi – other companies use public ferries.

### Returning to Lombok or Bali
The times, frequencies and fares on the **public boats** to Bangsal are the same for the return journey as for the outward-bound trip. **Shuttle boats** leave Gili Meno and Gili Trawangan at 8.15am and Gili Air at 8.30am; note there is only one departure a day. You can arrange a one-way **charter to Senggigi** at any of the ticket offices on the islands (Rp250,000 per boat).

Several operators on the islands offer **tourist shuttle tickets** to Lombok or Bali destinations; whichever operator you use, there is no direct boat to Senggigi – you go to Bangsal and proceed overland. You'll walk from the port at Bangsal to the gate on the main road, where you'll be collected by the tour operator. You can also buy shuttle bus tickets from the travel agents lining the road at Bangsal. There's also a fixed-price **taxi** service (to Mataram, Senggigi or the airport Rp60,000; Lembar Rp100,000; Senaru Rp100,000; Tetebatu Rp200,000; Kuta/Labuhan Lombok Rp250,000) – but you'll almost certainly get a better deal if you head for Pemenang and negotiate directly with the drivers to charter a bemo from there.

If you're interested in chartering a boat direct to **Amed** in Bali, talk to Din (☎081339/509859) on Gili Meno, but see the warning on p.382.

---

vast array of accommodation, restaurants and nightlife, it attracts the liveliest visitors. If you want to get away from it all, head for the smallest of the islands, **Gili Meno**, which has absolutely no nightlife and much less accommodation. Closest to the mainland, **Gili Air** sits somewhere between the two, with plenty of facilities in the south, and more peace and quiet the further round the coast you go. All the island beaches are public. The local people are more used to seeing scantily clad Western women than in any other part of Lombok, but you should definitely cover up when you move away from the beach.

**Accommodation prices** vary dramatically depending on the season and are more fluid than anywhere else on Bali or Lombok. A bungalow costing Rp50,000 in February or October will cost Rp100,000 or more in July, August and December, hovering somewhere in between if the crowds arrive early or leave late.

## Pemenang and Bangsal

The access port for the Gili Islands is **BANGSAL**, 25km north of Senggigi, a 1.5-kilometre cidomo ride or a shadeless walk from **PEMENANG**, 26km beyond the Ampenan–Mataram–Cakranegara–Sweta area. Pemenang is served by **bemos** and **buses**: all transport between Ampenan–Mataram–Cakranegara–Sweta and points around the north coast passes through. **From the airport**, turn left on the road at the front of the terminal, head straight across the roundabout and, 500m further on, at traffic lights on a crossroads, turn left and catch any bus heading north, which will drop you at Pemenang. **From Senggigi**, though, there's no public bemo service along the coastal road north to Pemenang; see below for details of the boat service from Senggigi direct to the islands. A gate at Bangsal stops all vehicles 500m from the harbour itself, so prepare to **walk** the final bit or bargain with the cidomo drivers (Rp5000 per cidomo is fair).

Sadly, Bangsal has developed a reputation as a place full of aggravation and **hassle** for tourists; there have even been punch-ups. Keep your cool: the Gilis are worth it. The **ticket office** (8am–4.30pm) for all boats to the islands is on the seafront; it's organized, and there's a printed price-list covering public boats, shuttles and charters. Go directly there and buy your ticket; ignore touts along the road who'll try to persuade you to buy from them. It's also useful to know that, despite anything you might be told, everything on sale in Bangsal is also on sale on the Gili Islands, including water, mosquito coils and return boat tickets. Ideally, you should get your own bag onto and off the boats; if you cannot manage this, you should negotiate with the porters before you let them touch the bags – and be clear whether you're talking about rupiah, dollars, for one bag or for the whole lot.

Bangsal has a few **restaurants**, some moneychangers, several travel agents and, should you need a **place to stay**, the losmen *Taman Sari* (☎0370/646934; Rp30,000–75,000), just by the gate. They have two standards of accommodation opening onto a small garden. All rooms have attached bathroom, the cheaper ones with squat toilet.

## Island transport and practicalities

If you wish to **charter** a boat on the islands, prices (displayed at the ticket offices) are fixed: it's currently Rp80,000–90,000 one way between any of the islands and Rp155,000–175,000 return.

None of the islands has a particular **crime** problem, although some years ago there were attacks on women during and after the parties on Gili Trawangan. Do take reasonable precautions (see p.409). Many of the bungalows feature locking drawers or safe deposit boxes for your valuables. There are no **police** on the islands, although SATGAS on Gili Trawangan have a role in tourist security: it's the role of the *kepala desa*, the headman who looks after Gili Air (where he lives) and Gili Meno, and the *kepala kampung* on Gili Trawangan, to deal with

## "Hopping island" boat service

The **"hopping island"** boat service between all three Gili Islands does one circuit, Air–Meno–Trawangan–Meno–Air, in the morning, and another in the afternoon. It's fast and conveniently timetabled, and so makes a day-trip to another island straightforward. The **fare** for any one leg of the route is Rp12,000; for a two-leg journey (Air–Trawangan), it's Rp15,000.

**Gili Air to Gili Meno** Departs 8.30am & 3pm.
**Gili Meno to Gili Trawangan** Departs 8.45am & 3.15pm.
**Gili Trawangan to Gili Meno** Departs 9.30am & 3.30pm.
**Gili Meno to Gili Air** Departs 9.45am & 4.15pm.
It's also possible to charter a boat between the islands. See p.402.

any problems. You should be taken to make a report to police on the mainland (at Tanjung or Ampenan).

## Snorkelling and diving

The **snorkelling** and **diving** around the Gili Islands is some of the best and most accessible in Lombok. All the islands are fringed by **coral reefs**, which slope down to a sandy bottom at around 25m, although there are some coral walls. Visibility is generally around 15m. The **fish** life here is the main attraction and, with more than 3500 species estimated to live in the Indonesian waters, there's certainly plenty of variety; species include white- and black-tip reef sharks, sea turtles, cuttlefish, moray eels, lobster, manta rays, Napoleon wrasse and bumphead parrotfish. There are good snorkelling spots just off the beaches of all the islands, and there are well over a dozen easily accessible **sites** around the islands, with exotic names such as Shark Point, Deep Turbo, Turtle Heaven, Deep Halik and Manta Point. Talk to the dive guides on the island to find out the best site depending on local conditions at the time of your dive.

There are **dive operations** on all the islands, and many of their **diving instructors** are from overseas, offering tuition and dive-guiding in all European languages. Most operators have PADI materials in several languages.

There's a price agreement, with operators charging identical rates; however, they vary in approach and atmosphere and you should choose carefully (see p.71 for general advice). Check at the time of booking whether the price includes equipment rental. If you're a qualified diver, expect to pay $25 per dive, $35 per night dive and $50 for Scuba Review; Discover Scuba, for unqualified divers, also costs $50. A PADI Open Water course is $300; PADI Advanced Open Water course $200–235. Some operators are qualified to take people on the Instructor Development Course, which costs $900–1000.

Dive companies take **snorkellers** on trips for about $10. Snorkel gear is widely available for Rp15,000–20,000 per day; check it carefully before you take it. You can buy good-quality gear on the islands in the dive shops.

All divers off the Gili Islands pay a one-off **reef tax** of Rp30,000 (snorkellers pay Rp10,000) to the Gili Eco Trust, which works to protect the reefs around the islands.

Be careful over **safety precautions**. The nearest hospital is in Mataram and the nearest recompression chamber in Denpasar on Bali. Note, too, that **offshore currents** around the islands are hazardous. Dive operators are aware of this and on the alert. However, if you're snorkelling or swimming off the beach you're potentially at risk: it's easy to get carried out further than you intend and then be unable to get back. There have been drownings.

# Gili Trawangan

**GILI TRAWANGAN**, the furthest island from the mainland and the largest, attracts the greatest number of visitors and is very developed. The southeast of the island is wall-to-wall bungalows, restaurants and dive shops, although it is still low-key and relaxing. For quieter surroundings, head to the laid-back northeast, northwest or southwest coasts.

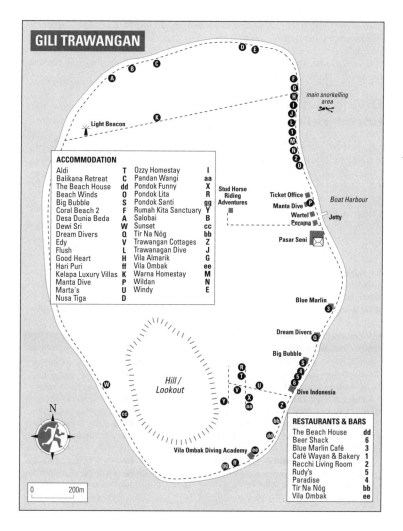

GILI TRAWANGAN

Light Beacon

main snorkelling area

**ACCOMMODATION**

| | | | | |
|---|---|---|---|---|
| Aldi | T | Ozzy Homestay | I | |
| Balikana Retreat | C | Pandan Wangi | aa | |
| The Beach House | dd | Pondok Funny | X | |
| Beach Winds | O | Pondok Lita | R | |
| Big Bubble | S | Pondok Santi | gg | |
| Coral Beach 2 | F | Rumah Kita Sanctuary | Y | |
| Desa Dunia Beda | A | Salobai | B | |
| Dewi Sri | W | Sunset | cc | |
| Dream Divers | Q | Tir Na Nóg | bb | |
| Edy | V | Trawangan Cottages | Z | |
| Flush | L | Trawanagan Dive | J | |
| Good Heart | H | Vila Almarik | G | |
| Hari Puri | ff | Vila Ombak | ee | |
| Kelapa Luxury Villas | K | Warna Homestay | M | |
| Manta Dive | P | Wildan | N | |
| Marta's | U | Windy | E | |
| Nusa Tiga | D | | | |

Stud Horse Riding Adventures

Ticket Office
Manta Dive
Boat Harbour
Wartel
Perama
Jetty

Pasar Seni

Blue Marlin

Dream Divers

Big Bubble

Hill / Lookout

Dive Indonesia

N

**RESTAURANTS & BARS**

| | |
|---|---|
| The Beach House | dd |
| Beer Shack | 6 |
| Blue Marlin Café | 3 |
| Café Wayan & Bakery | 1 |
| Recchi Living Room | 2 |
| Rudy's | 5 |
| Paradise | 4 |
| Tír Na Nóg | bb |
| Vila Ombak | ee |

Vila Ombak Diving Academy

0          200m

Until a few decades ago, Gili Trawangan was uninhabited. In the late 1800s it had been a penal colony for 350 Sasaks exiled here for rebelling against the raja of Lombok in 1891. Hunters came irregularly from Lombok for deer (now extinct). Then, in the 1970s, ten or twelve Bugis families from Sulawesi settled here, **tourists** discovered the islands, and the new settlers built cottages for their visitors. The rest, as they say, is history.

Island **transport** is by cidomo. Ask about renting bicycles at your guesthouse, or there's a stall near the jetty; prices vary but so does the quality of the bike. Only a tiny section of road in the southeast corner is paved, so be prepared for some sandy cycling.

A **walk** around the island, less than 3km long by 2km at the widest part, takes four hours or less. There's not much to see on the west side other than the occasional monitor lizard and giant cacti, ixorea, eucalyptus and palms. Whether you're cycling or walking, take plenty of water; there's a stretch of coast (about 35min on foot) between *Desa Dunia Beda* in the north and *Dewi Sri* in the southwest where there's nowhere to get a drink. Inland, the 100m **hill** is the compulsory expedition at sunset – follow any of the tracks from the southern end of the island for views of Gunung Agung, Gunung Abang and Gunung Batur on Bali, with the sky blazing behind.

## Diving, snorkelling, watersports and horse-riding

The northern end of the east coast is the most popular for **snorkelling**: most people hang out here during the day, and there are plenty of warung behind the beach here for refreshment. Local boat captains offer **glass-bottomed boat** and snorkelling trips to sites around all three islands (10am–4pm; Rp45,000 per person including equipment).

### Dive operators

All the operators offer **dives** for qualified divers and courses, and most have their own pools for the early stages of learning. They're all close together in the southeast corner of the island, so it's easy to check them out first.

**Big Bubble** ☎ 0370/625020, ⊛ www.bigbubble .com. Small, friendly place owned by two British women, they keep groups small and dive at times to suit guests or when the sites are quiet.

**Blue Marlin** ☎ 0370/632424, ⊛ www.diveindo .com. A PADI Five-Star IDC Dive Centre. Offers a full range of courses up to PADI IDC (Instructor Development Courses) and IANTD (International

### Biorock

The waters off Gili Trawangan are the location of some Biorock installations aimed at stimulating **coral growth** in the area and rejuvenation of the reef. The equipment consists of steel bars, plus copper wiring that is attached to electrodes. A small current is transmitted through the wiring, crystallizing the minerals in the seawater into limestone, the building block of reefs, on the bars. This becomes a perfect breeding ground for coral, which can also be stimulated by the introduction of live coral fragments. The trial here is still in its early stages, but measurements elsewhere have shown that coral growth can occur three to five times faster than when nature is left to her own devices. With the support of the islands' dive shops and local communities, it is hoped to introduce the installations in many locations in the waters off the Gili Islands. For more information on Biorock, check out the Global Coral Reef Alliance (⊛ http://globalcoral.org).

Association of Nitrox and Technical Divers) Instructor Training Course level and have a developed expertise in technical diving. They've explored wrecks off the Lombok coast as well as new sites closer to Gili Trawangan. Diver propulsion vehicles can be hired ($25 per dive), and they've a 65-foot Indonesian *pinisi*, the *Ikan Biru*, that departs weekly for a five-day liveaboard trip or private charter.

**Dive Indonesia** ☎0370/644174, ⓦwww .dive.indonesia.com. Courses up to PADI IDC level; all divers are loaned dive computers to use. They also feature liveaboards.

**Dream Divers** ☎0370/634496, ⓦwww .dreamdivers.com. A PADI Five-Star IDC Centre offering German in addition to English. For those with more than fifty dives who can cope with currents and surge, they offer a two-day diving trip to southern Lombok, to one of the very few places in the world where it's possible to see schools of a

hundred or more hammerhead sharks (April–Oct). IANTD run dives and courses as well.

**Manta Dive** ☎0370/643649, ⓦwww.manta-dive .com. Under British ownership and with highly respected local dive guides who have thousands of dives on the local reefs. Courses up to PADI Divemaster level are on offer, and there's always lots of Divemaster trainees around who give the place a good buzz. A decent water depth just outside the dive shop makes access to the boat easy. Also offers two-day trips to east Lombok, diving in the channel between Gili Lawang and Gili Sulat.

**Vila Ombak Diving Academy** ☎0370/638531. A PADI Five-Star IDC Centre. Don't be deterred by the location in one of the smartest hotels on the island – prices here are similar to those elsewhere. All divers are provided with a computer attached to their regulator. There are also very good-value "Dive and Stay" packages on offer with *Vila Ombak* hotel.

## Watersports and horse-riding

There are a couple of **watersports** places to try. Manta Dive offer water-skiing and wakeboarding (Rp600,000 per hr); Blue Marlin do the same (Rp200,000 for 20min), as well as wakeboarding lessons (Rp400,000 per hr) and courses (4 days $300, 14 days $800). Sea Kayak Adventures (☎0370/692003, ⓦwww .diveindo.com), attached to Blue Marlin, offer guided **kayaking** trips around the islands in single-person or two-seater kayaks ($45) with boat back-up. *Vila Ombak* also rents out kayaks ($10 per half-day, $15 per day).

A new development on the island is **horse-riding**. Stud Horse Riding Adventures (☎0370/639248) offer lessons (30min; Rp75,000) or guided riding around the island (Rp150,000 per hour).

# Accommodation

The traditional **accommodation** of bamboo and thatch bungalows have been almost completely replaced by concrete-and-tile bungalows, although all come with attached bathrooms with a Western-style toilet. Hot water and air-con are widely available, although only those at the top of the scale pay much attention to ambience. *Vila Almarik*, *Vila Ombak* and *Desa Dunia Beda* provide the real hotel options; everything else is much simpler.

The north end of the island is quiet, while the southeast corner is closest to the restaurants and parties, though many here lack views and sea breezes. A lot of good-value places are in the village behind the main drag here and behind the warung on the northeast coast. There are also some quiet spots around the southern tip and on to the west coast, but the beach is nothing special and you're a long walk from anything.

Given the local climate, gleaming new bungalows quickly fade unless they're vigilantly maintained. For that reason, it's worth keeping an eye out for **new places**, whether or not they're listed here: they're likely to be a good, clean bet.

Unlike anywhere else on Lombok, **villas** are now an option on Gili Trawangan. *The Beach House* (see below) has a four-bedroomed house with private pool at Rp2,000,000 a night; *Hari Puri* (contact in Singapore is ⒺEira@singnet.com.sg) is a four-bedroomed villa at $300; and *Kelapa Luxury Villas* (☎370/632424, ⓦwww .kelapavillas.com) have one- to four-bedroomed villas from $250–450 per night.

**Balikana Retreat** ☎0370/622386, ⓦwww
.balikanaretreat.com. Located in the quiet north.
There are simpler rooms with seaview at the front
and others clustering around the large pool. Air-con
available. ④–⑥

**The Beach House** ☎0370/642352,
ⓔbeachhouse@dps.centrin.net.id. Bungalows with
air-con and hot water, which can be interconnected
for families. Two are disabled-friendly. ⑥

**Beach Winds** ☎0812/376 4347. Good-value
fan or air-con bungalows in the northeast. Prices
include breakfast, which, party-goers may appreciate, is available at any time of day. ⑤

**Big Bubble** ☎0370/625020, ⓦwww
.bigbubblediving.com. A row of good-quality
bungalows behind the dive shop.

**Coral Beach 2** ☎0812/376 8534. A fair option in
the northeast with straightforward fan bungalows
just behind the beach. ②

**Desa Dunia Beda** ☎0370/641575, ⓦwww
.desaduniabeda. Six gorgeous wooden bungalows
with fabulous traditional furniture widely spaced
in a large garden with a stylish pool and attached
spa. All have fans but no air-con. This is the most
far-flung accommodation on the island, there are
no televisions, and it's Rp25,000–30,000 for a
cidomo from the harbour. ⑧

**Dewi Sri** ⓔsliehchelet@hotmail.com. On the
west coast, thirty minutes' walk from the main
restaurant area. Some accommodation is in basic
wood, bamboo and thatch bungalows with squat
toilet but the newer, tiled rooms are the best ones
in the area. Nearby *Sunset* (☎0812/378 5290,
ⓔlily_karyani@hotmail.com ①–②) is also worth
a look. ①–②

**Dream Divers** ☎0370/634496, ⓦwww
.dreamdivers.com. Bungalows behind the dive
shop in the main restaurant area. Hot water and
air-con in the pricier rooms. ⑤–⑥

**Good Heart** ☎0812/2395 170. Two great wood
and palm bungalows in the northeast, with good
beach views, air-con, satellite TV and hot water.
Among the most stylish on the island. ⑥

**Manta Dive** ☎0370/643649, ⓦwww
.manta-dive.com. Behind the dive shop.
Gorgeous, stylish wooden bungalows, with all
mod-cons, based loosely on a traditional Lombok
rice-barn design. ⑥

🏃 **Marta's** ☎0812/372 2777,
ⓔmartas_trawangan@yahoo.com. Good-
quality two-storey accommodation in the village,
all with air-con and hot water, and lovely verandas looking out into an attractive garden. ⑤

**Nusa Tiga** ☎0370/643249. On the north coast,
with basic tiled bungalows. In the same price
range, *Windy* next door is also worth a look. ②

**Ozzy Homestay** ☎0812/371 8039. Small place
with good-quality fan rooms. Next door, *Trawa-
nagan Dive* is similar in price and facilities, while
*Flush*, further south, has a two-storey, traditional
place, same price code. ③

🏃 **Pondok Lita** ☎0370/648607. An excellent, clean budget choice – tucked away
in the village, about five minutes' walk from the
beach (follow the track between Dive Indonesia
and *Trawangan Cottages*). Rooms, set around a
small garden, have fan and cold-water attached
bathroom. *Aldi*, *Pondok Funny*, *Edy* and *Pandan
Wangi* are all close by, and in the same vein at
price category. ②

**Pondok Santi** ⓔnans95_5@hotmail.com. Well-
built traditional bungalows with a brick mandi, in
a coconut grove in the south. A popular option, as
the bungalows have large verandas, and it's only
a five- to ten-minute walk to the main restaurant
area. ②

**Rumah Kita Sanctuary** Three bamboo and
thatch bungalows in the village. They have fans
and attached cold-water bathrooms, plus a
more spacious garden than many places in this
area. ②

**Salobai** ☎0370/643152, ⓕ643151. Pleasant
bungalows (fan or air-con), all with cold water,
around on the north coast. ④–⑤

**Tir Na Nog** ☎0370/639436,
ⓔtirnanog@mataram.wasantara.net.id. Rooms in
two-storey buildings behind the restaurant; all have
hot water and a choice of fan or air-con. Right in
the middle of the action. ③–④

**Trawangan Cottages** ☎0370/639282. Two rows
of clean, tiled simple cottages in the southeast
corner, close to the action. One set is further away
from the beach along a track. Air-con and hot
water in the more expensive. ③–⑤

**Vila Almarik** ☎0370/638520, ⓦwww
.almarik-lombok.com. A hotel in the quiet northeast corner offering rooms with air-con, hot water
and stylish furnishings, set in a small garden. The
swimming pool is pretty (non-residents can use it
🏃 eat meals at the restaurant). ⑦

🏃 **Vila Ombak** ☎0370/642336, ⓦwww
.hotelombak.com. The best hotel on the island is
a central, stylish place with a choice of accommodation in two-storey *lumbungs* (with excellent
terraces and verandas) or bungalows, all with
air-con and hot water. The garden is lovely, the pool
(Rp75,000 for non-residents) comes complete with
waterfall, and there's an attached spa. ⑧

**Warna Homestay** ☎0370/623859. Just south of
*Café Wayan & Bakery*, a row of good-quality tiled
bungalows tucked behind a warung. *Wildan*, slightly
further south, is similar in style and price. ②

# Eating, drinking and nightlife

The east coast is lined with **restaurants** and **warung**. In the northeastern area, simple warung provide cold drinks and inexpensive Indo-Chinese food in basic surroundings, and are favourite hangouts in the middle of the day. The places in the southeast, from the jetty south, are more upmarket, prices are higher and tables and chairs are just above the beach. Wherever you eat, the quality and variety of the food is good and prices are reasonable, with **seafood** the best option. Unless stated, all are moderately priced.

**The Beach House** The menu of this stylish beachside restaurant is small but covers all bases; sandwiches, soups, pasta, seafood and Indonesian food sit comfortably beside English-style fish and chips. The attached deli has an excellent range of wine, coffee, chocolate and other treats.

**Beer Shack** Attached to Dive Indonesia. Located right on the beachfront, with an excellent breakfast menu and plenty of snacks and main meals on offer later in the day, including salads and nachos.

**Blue Marlin Café** Attached to the Blue Marlin dive shop. Either dine near the pool at the front or up in the two-storey building behind. The menu is large and food well cooked. All the usual favourites are here, plus a selection of Thai food, hot plates, baked potatoes and all-day breakfasts.

**Café Wayan and Bakery** Worth a visit for its bread, croissants, cinnamon rolls and other highly ¿ but excellent baked goods.

**Recchi Living Room** Up in the northeast of the island, the surroundings are simple but the food is possibly the best on the island – the chef worked in five-star hotels before seeking out the quiet island life. There's a big menu of Western and Indonesian dishes, but all are carefully and intricately prepared and presented, and the service is lovely. Food of this standard would cost a fortune across the Lombok Strait on Bali.

**Tír Na Nóg** Extremely popular Irish bar with good beer, darts, movies and CNN news. There's an ambitious menu with plenty of barbecued seafood and Indonesian and Western food, including steaks, pizzas, Irish stew, bangers and mash, and apple pie. The drinks list includes bottled Guinness, draught Bintang and Carlsberg in high season, and Irish whiskey. Outdoor *bale* all have individual screens and each can watch its own choice of DVD movie from a vast selection.

**Vila Ombak** The island's most upmarket dining experience, with two moderate to expensive restaurants, one on the beachfront and the other in a grand two-storey building. There are plenty of delightful desserts and the wine list is long, stretching to champagne.

## Nightlife

Gili Trawangan is renowned for its high-season **parties**, which get going at about 11pm and last until they finish. Venues are advertised on flyers around the island: currently, Monday is *Blue Marlin Café*, Wednesday *Tír Na Nóg*, Friday *Rudy's*, Saturday *Dive Indonesia* and Sunday *Paradise*. Monday and Wednesday are the biggest nights and likely to draw revellers from the other islands and Lombok. *Tír Na Nóg* doesn't close until around 2am and, apart from the parties, is the late-night venue of choice.

Please note that, for reasons of **personal safety**, women should not leave late-night venues alone, even to go to the bathroom.

# Listings

**Bus tickets** Perama (daily 7am–10pm) is close to the jetty.

**Exchange** Moneychangers line the main strip.

**Internet** Several places offer Internet access (about Rp400/min; minimum 5min), including the wartel, which has the advantage of air-con.

**Medical** Clinic Vila Ombak, just south of the hotel of the same name (daily 8am–5pm).

**Phones** The wartel is open 8am–11pm.

**Post** There's a postal agent in the *pasar seni*.

**Shopping** Several shops sell and exchange second-hand books in European languages, there's a small art market, and you can buy clothes, crafts and everyday necessities at various shops and stalls. Beach hawkers offer pearl jewellery.

# Gili Meno

**GILI MENO**, a small oval about 2km long and just over 1km wide, is the most tranquil of the three islands, with a local population of just 350 and no nightlife. There's no island-wide electricity generator; most places have their own, which they operate part-time.

It takes a couple of hours to stroll around the island, which has a picturesque salt lake in the centre, surrounded by a few sets of salt-making paraphernalia (see p.432). The only "sight" is **Gili Meno Bird Park** (daily 9am–5pm; Rp30,000; Ⓦwww .balipvbgroup.com) in the middle of the island; its collection of hornbills, orioles, cockatoos and parrots, plus a wallaby, deer and Komodo dragon, may leave animal and bird lovers feeling rather depressed, though.

Boats arrive at the **harbour** on the east coast. You can **change money** at two kiosks, one south of *Mallia's Child* and one just north of the harbour. There's a **wartel** (daily 8am–10pm) near the harbour, with **Internet** access, but phone lines aren't totally reliable. There's no Perama office, although you can book by calling the Senggigi office (Ⓣ0370/693007), and shuttle bus tickets with Gora are widely available.

**GILI MENO**
0    250m
N

Beacon

Salt Lake

Gili Meno Bird Park

Boat Harbour

Wartel

Blue Marlin Dive

Disused Bounty Jetty

| ACCOMMODATION | | | |
|---|---|---|---|
| Amber House | D | Kontiki | P |
| Biru Meno | Q | Mallia's Child | L |
| Lumba-Lumba | N | Pondok Santai | C |
| Casablanca | E | Rawa Indah | J |
| Fantastic Cottages | I | Royal Reef Resort | F |
| Gazebo | O | Rust Bungalows | H |
| Good Heart | A | Tao' Kombo' | M |
| Jali Bungalows | G | Villa Nautilus | K |
| Karang Biru (Blue Coral) | B | | |
| **RESTAURANTS** | | | |
| Balenta | 2 | Jali Restaurant | 4 |
| Bibi's Café | K | Rust | 5 |
| Lumba Lumba | N | The Jungle Bar | M |
| Diana | 1 | Ya Ya | 3 |
| Good Heart | A | | |

The **snorkelling** is good along the east coast; go in at *Royal Reef Resort* and drift down to *Kontiki* in the south. Take care as there may be boat traffic in the harbour. The other option is to go in at the yellow lighthouse in the north of the island, turn left and let the current take you round to the west coast over the Meno Wall and down to the Bounty jetty. See p.404 for a warning about **offshore currents**. Chartering a boat allows you to venture further afield; ask on the beach (about Rp160,000 per boat for four people). Equipment is available on the island but a lot has seen (far) better days. Blue Marlin has some decent sets (Rp30,000 per day). For **diving**, consult Blue Marlin Dive (Ⓣ0370/639979, Ⓦwww.diveindo.com); prices are the same as Gili Trawangan and they offer courses up to Divemaster. For **boat trips**, search out Din (Ⓣ081339/509859), one of the boat captains; he's often in front of the Blue Marlin dive shop. He'll take you out on fishing trips, to see dolphins (best in March–Aug & Nov), to a shipwreck off the Lombok coast and to see spring water in the sea off the north coast of Lombok. Prices are generally from Rp200,000 for the boat (2–4 people). You can charter him to Amed in eastern Bali, but see the warning on p.382.

# Accommodation

Budget through to luxury **accommodation** is available on Gili Meno, mostly spread along the east coast. Most places have their own electricity generator, except one or two at the northern end, which is where you'll get the best budget value.

**Amber House** ☎0370/643676, ✉amber_house02pm@hotmail.com. Traditional thatch and bamboo bungalows in a shady garden, set slightly back from the beach towards the north of the island. ❶

**Biru Meno** ☎081/736 1915. In a great location at the southern end of the island, ten minutes' walk from the harbour, with good-quality bamboo and thatch bungalows on a tile base, plus attached cold-water bathrooms. Fans can be rented from the village for Rp5000 a night. ❷

**Café Lumba-Lumba** Book through *Casablanca*. Three tiled bungalows on the west coast, with the two at the front having fine views to the sea. A great spot for the sunset. ❸

**Casablanca** ☎0370/633847, ✉lidyblanca@mataram.wasantara.net.id. Offering four standards of room set about 100m back from the beach with a pretty garden. Accommodation ranges from basic fan and cold-water rooms to large ones with air-con and hot water. There's a tiny pool (check its condition) and a restaurant. ❸–❺

**Fantastic Cottages** ☎081339/509859. Wood, thatch and bamboo bungalows with attached mandi set back from the beach near the harbour. There are large verandas for relaxing. *Rawa Indah* is nearby and similar in style and price. ❶

**Gazebo** ☎0370/635795. Ten comfortable bungalows set in a shady grove, with fan or air-con but no hot water. There's a pretty pool near the beach. ❻–❼

**Jali Bungalows** ☎0370/639800. Simple bungalows with attached bathrooms convenient for the harbour. ❶–❷

**Karang Biru (Blue Coral)** ☎0812/378 2030. This row of traditional bungalows, in an isolated location in the north of the island, has attached bathrooms facing seawards. *Good Heart*, further west, and *Pondok Santai*, to the southeast, both offer similar accommodation and equal isolation. ❶

**Kontiki** ☎0370/632824. Close to a good beach, bungalows are tiled, with fans and attached cold-water bathrooms. There's one with air-con. ❹–❺

**Mallia's Child** ☎0370/622007, ⓦwww.gilimeno-mallias.com. Well-built bungalows in a good location near a fine beach, with fine sea views from the verandas. ❷–❸

**Royal Reef Resort** ☎0370/642340. Very close to the harbour, these good-quality wood, bamboo and thatch bungalows, set in a large garden, have fans and good verandas. ❸

**Rust Bungalows** ☎0370/642324. Traditional wood and thatch bungalows with attached bathrooms behind the restaurant of the same name just near the harbour. ❶–❷

**Tao' Kombo'** ☎0812/372 2174, ✉tao_kombo@yahoo.com. Set in a shady spot about 200m behind the beach in the south, with a large bar and communal area. Three good bungalows have bathroom, fan and a fresh-water shower. There are also four *brugak* (open-sided sleeping platforms) with lockable cupboards, mattress, screen, mosquito net and shared bathrooms. *Brugak* ❶ Bungalows ❷

**Villa Nautilus** ☎0370/642443, ⓦwww.villanautilus.com. The most modern and stylish, light and airy rooms on any of the three islands. Front walls are made of glass doors that can be opened onto the deck, and there's an abundance of natural materials. All have air-con and hot water. ❼

# Eating and drinking

There are plenty of **places to eat**. For local food *Balenta* and *Ya Ya* are both good choices, while *Rust* restaurant is excellent for fresh fish. *Bibi's Café* attached to *Vila Nautilus* serves the best pizzas on the island – but is good for pretty much everything. The location of *Jali Restaurant* looking out onto the harbour, Gili Air and the Lombok mountains rising behind, is excellent, and over the other side of the island *Good Heart*, *Diana* and *Café Lumba Lumba* are ideal for drinks on the way round the island or at sunset. In the **evening**, the *Jungle Bar* at *Tao' Kombo'* is the place to hang out, with cool music and plenty of drinks.

# Gili Air

Closest to the mainland, **GILI AIR** stretches about 1.5km in each direction. Atmospherically, it sits between lively, social Gili Trawangan and peaceful Gili Meno. It takes a couple of hours to complete a circuit on foot, and there are great views across to Sira beach on the mainland. Although accommodation is spread around most of the coast, it's concentrated in the southeast corner where the **beach** is the most popular, with good **snorkelling**. Snorkelling gear is available for rent: try Ozzy Shop (Rp15,000 per day). For snorkelling further afield, **glass-bottomed boat trips** (Rp40,000 per person, minimum of six; 9.30am–3pm), which take in sites off all three islands, are advertised pretty much everywhere, or ask at Ozzy Shop or on the beach.

Dive operators on the island include Dream Divers (☎0370/634547, ⓦwww .dreamdivers.com) and Blue Marlin (☎0370/634387, ⓦwww.diveindo.com). Yan's Bookshop and Ozzy Shop on the east coast rent **bicycles** (Rp15,000 for 24hr).

There are plenty of **moneychangers** around the island. There's a **wartel** (daily 8am–10pm) behind *Hotel Gili Indah* and another at Ozzy Shop, where there is also **Internet access** (Rp400 per min, minimum Rp4000). The Perama office (8am–10pm; ☎0370/637816) is near the harbour, where tourist shuttle tickets to destinations throughout Bali and Lombok can be booked. Postcards and stamps are available from the shops; mail is taken to the mainland by Perama.

## Accommodation

There's a selection of good-value **accommodation**, with the quietest spots on the north and west coasts. It makes sense to engage a cidomo to reach the more far-flung spots when you arrive with your bags; it'll be about Rp10,000 from the harbour to *Abdi Fantastik*, Rp15,000 to *Lombok Indah*.

**Abdi Fantastik** ☎0370/636421. In a great location looking seawards on the east coast; the wood and thatch bungalows are simple but well-built and clean, and have fans and mosquito nets, and there are sitting areas overlooking the water. ❷

**Coconut Cottages** ☎0370/635365, ⓦwww.coconuts-giliair.com. Attractive, clean and well-maintained bungalows in a garden haven set back from the east coast, about 25 minutes' walk from the harbour. There are several standards of bungalows, some with hot water. Tours can also be arranged here. ❷–❹

**Gili Air Santay** ☎0370/641022, Ⓔgiliair-santay@yahoo.com. Popular, good-quality traditional cottages set 100m back from the east coast in a shady garden. *Brugak* on the beach for relaxing. ❸

**Gita Gili** ☎0812/372 4813. In a good location near the coast and convenient for the harbour, with thatch, wood and bamboo bungalows facing the sea. All have attached cold-water bathroom. ❸

**Gusung Indah** ☎0812/378 9054. Pleasantly located, close to the east coast, with two standards of bungalows facing seawards, some with squat toilets. *Sandi Cottages*, just north, is also worth a look, with similar facilities and price. ❷

**Hotel Gili Air** ☎0370/634435, Ⓔgiliair@mataram.wasantara.net.id. The most upmarket option on the island, with four standards of bungalows, all with hot water and air-con in the more expensive. The swimming pool is fabulous (Rp25,000 for non-residents). Negotiate big discounts when it's quiet. ❻–❼

**Hotel Gili Indah** ☎0370/637328, Ⓔgili_indah@mataram.wasantara.net.id. With a big compound near the harbour, and several standards of bungalows (from fan and cold water to air-con and hot water). All are reasonably furnished, and the ones at the front have good sea views. ❸–❺

**Legend** ☎0812/376 4552. Relaxed, popular spot on the northeast coast. Bungalows are traditional, and the smaller ones have squat toilets. The attached warung holds weekly parties. ❷

**Lombok Indah** ☎0812/373 6746. Budget place on the northeast coast, set just behind the beach (nearby *Legend* has weekly parties). There are older, more basic rooms and larger better-quality ones. ❶–❷

**Lucky's** ☎0812/378 2156. A good choice over on the west side of the island (5–10min walk from the harbour). Rooms are simple but perfectly OK, and there are many *bale* to sit and relax in. *Salabose*

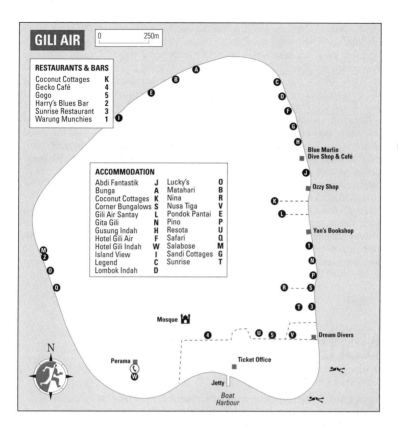

**GILI AIR**

0 ___ 250m

**RESTAURANTS & BARS**

| | |
|---|---|
| Coconut Cottages | K |
| Gecko Café | 4 |
| Gogo | 5 |
| Harry's Blues Bar | 2 |
| Sunrise Restaurant | 3 |
| Warung Munchies | 1 |

**ACCOMMODATION**

| | | | |
|---|---|---|---|
| Abdi Fantastik | J | Lucky's | O |
| Bunga | A | Matahari | B |
| Coconut Cottages | K | Nina | R |
| Corner Bungalows | S | Nusa Tiga | V |
| Gili Air Santay | L | Pondok Pantai | E |
| Gita Gili | N | Pino | P |
| Gusung Indah | H | Resota | U |
| Hotel Gili Air | F | Safari | Q |
| Hotel Gili Indah | W | Salabose | M |
| Island View | I | Sandi Cottages | G |
| Legend | C | Sunrise | T |
| Lombok Indah | D | | |

Blue Marlin Dive Shop & Café

Ozzy Shop

Yan's Bookshop

Mosque

Dream Divers

Perama

Ticket Office

Jetty

Boat Harbour

and *Safari* are both nearby and have some rooms worth considering. ❷

**Matahari** Decent choice on the far northwest coast. The bungalows are slightly better quality than others nearby – but things can change. Nearby options are *Bunga*, *Pondok Pantai* and *Island View*, all in the same price category. ❶–❷

**Nina** ☎08180/362 2893. Justifiably popular cottages reached by walking through *Corner Bungalows* which, for the same price, are also worth a look, in the southeast of the island. Bungalows are simple but good quality, with attached bathroom with Western toilet. ❷

**Nusa Tiga** Traditionally built bungalows with Western toilets in the attached bathrooms and deep

verandas with hammocks for relaxing. A reasonable budget choice in this area, set back from the coast in the south of the island. *Resota*, nearby, is similar. ❶–❷

**Pino** Good bamboo, thatch and wood cottages in a neat garden just on the edge of the island's southeast corner. The sitting places on the beach have brilliant views, and you can also snorkel off the beach here. ❷

🏃 **Sunrise** ☎ & ☎0370/642370. On the southeast corner. Accommodation is in two-storey *lumbung* barns with sitting areas upstairs and down. The ones at the front have excellent sea-views. All have cold-water attached bathrooms and fans. There are some bigger family rooms. ❸–❺

## Eating, drinking and nightlife

There's a good range of **restaurants**, offering Indonesian and Western food at inexpensive to moderate prices. The most popular places to hang out in the day are the **bars** and restaurants that line the southeast coast, from *Dream Divers* in the south up to *Warung Munchies* (afternoon specials with cake are excellent). All have fine views across to Sira beach on the mainland and the foothills of Gunung Rinjani behind. *Sunrise Restaurant* is as pleasant as any. It is worth moving inland to *Gecko Café* (closed Friday) for its small but excellently cooked menu of Western and Indonesian food, including home-made bread and cakes. There's a weekly special dinner for Rp35,000–50,00 per person (booking essential).

The most imaginative dining is at *Coconut Cottages*, with seating in the main restaurant or in *brugak* in the garden. It has appetizing and well-presented Western and local cuisine and seafood. **Sasak buffets** can be organized for a minimum of ten people with two days' notice (Rp40,000 per person): Sasak dishes include *gedang kelak santen* (green papaya soup with coconut milk), *pergadel kentang* (spicy potato and coconut cakes), *daging gape* (spicy beef stew with coconut) and *olah olah* (beans in coconut milk).

*Harry's Blues Bar*, attached to *Salabose* on the west coast, is an excellent spot for a sunset drink. At the time of writing, **parties** were only permitted twice a week: *Legend* on Wednesday and *Gogo* on Saturday. During the high season, **full-moon parties** arranged by bars in the southeast of the island have also become popular; enquire at your guesthouse about the current situation.

# North Lombok

Dominated by the volcanic mass of Gunung Rinjani and its neighbours, the villages in **north Lombok** nestle in the foothills of the mountains or perch along the black-sand coastline.

Most tourists either visit the area on a day-trip around the island or come to climb **Gunung Rinjani**, an easily arranged adventure, although only possible in the dry season (May–Oct). The area offers plenty of accommodation, and there are also attractive **waterfalls** and **traditional villages** to tempt the less energetic.

This area is easily accessible, with **buses** to Anyar from the Bertais/Mandalika/Sweta terminal or to Bayan from Labuhan Lombok in the east. The main advantage of having your own transport is to get to the Sembalun valley more easily; there are buses through the valley between Pringgabaya on the cross-island road and Kokok Putih in the north, but services aren't frequent. You'll find very few **exchange** facilities after you leave Bangsal.

## The north-coast road

From Pemenang, the coast road heads north. Just 2km beyond the village, a small road opposite the local school is signed to "Lombok Golf Kosaido Country Club". This leads three kilometres to **SIRA**, the longest white-sand **beach** on Lombok. Glaringly beautiful, with views across to the Gili Islands, it's deserted, with no facilities. Just before you reach the beach, a left turn brings you to Lombok Golf Kosaido Country Club (☏0370/640138, ✉siregolf@mataram

.wasantara.net.id), where verdant fairways gleam between the coconut palms (green fees are $80, excluding cart, shoe and club rental). Golfers may like to know that Manta Dive on Gili Trawangan (see p.407) has a deal with the club.

Just under 4km from Pemenang, a side-road leads to the coast and the **Oberoi** (℡0370/638444, 🅦www.oberoihotels.com; ❾), Lombok's most luxurious hotel and winner of several prestigious awards. Accommodation and ambience is fabulously luxurious and service superb; published prices start at $240, while villas with private swimming pool are $500. There's a **dive centre**, tennis court, library and **spa**. Several **restaurants** provide top-class, imaginative Western and Indonesian cuisine in gorgeous surroundings.

If you can't afford this but appreciate comfort, *Medana Resort* (℡0370/628000, 🅦www.lombokmedana.com; ❸) is about 500m before you reach the *Oberoi*. There are six luxurious bungalows with deep verandas in a lush garden, plus a pretty pool. There's Internet access plus TV and VCD players, snorkelling gear, mountain bikes, a sailboat and glass-bottomed boat for rent. The beach is a few minutes' walk away.

## Tanjung and around

Back on the main road, 4km further east, **TANJUNG** is the largest settlement around the north coast. It's an attractive town with a daily morning market of stalls overflowing with local produce.

About 4km beyond, in the small village of **GONDANG**, a sign to **Tiu Pupas waterfall** points inland, although it's further than the 4km claimed. The track is rough and narrow and the area is a maze of confusing lanes, but the falls are glorious, tumbling 40m down a semicircular sheer rock face into a deep pool. However, in the dry season (May–Nov) the water reduces to a trickle and the pool becomes a muddy puddle. **Gangga waterfall**, also known as **Selelos**, is a trek for the adventurous, about an hour's walk beyond Tiu Pupas. There are two paths; you can ask the young man who looks after the visitors' book for directions or engage him as guide, or you can access the falls from the signed turning 2km east of Gondang. A couple of hundred metres west of this second turning, a sign points seawards to *Pondok Pantai* ⚐ (℡0812/375 2632, 🅦www .pondok-pantai.com; ❷), a hidden gem almost a kilometre from the main road in a pretty garden on the coast. Accommodation is wood, thatch and bamboo, and moderately priced meals are available. It doesn't get much more peaceful than this.

About 5km beyond Gondang in a hamlet called **MONTONG FAL**, just as the road turns inland, *Pondok Nusa Tiga* (℡08133/956 5818; ❶) comprises four rooms in a two-storey building with bathrooms just outside. The views from the verandas are good, and the upstairs rooms catch a fine breeze. The owners can give you directions for local walks taking in waterfalls, coffee and cocoa plantations and traditional villages; fields of soya and peanuts and cashew orchards dot the landscape, and the population is sparse.

The village of **TAMPES**, 10km beyond Montong Fal, is a sleepy place that bursts into activity every Wednesday morning for a traditional market. A kilometre west of the village there's a large jetty for the export of pumice. It's a twisty 27km from here to Anyar.

## Segenter, Anyar and around

Almost at the northern tip of the island, 4km west of Anyar, the welcoming traditional village of **SEGENTER** is signed 2km inland. Park just outside the gate of the fenced village and a guide will meet you. You'll be taken inside one of the houses to see the eating platform, stone hearth and the *inan bale*, a small house-within-a-house where newlyweds spend their first night, but which is otherwise used to store rice. At the end of the visit you'll be expected to make a **donation** to the village and sign the visitors' book.

The road from here to Anyar touches the coast here and there at pretty beaches lined with *jukung*, but much of it passes inland through cashew orchards with great views across the lower slopes of Gunung Rinjani.

It's widely believed that the Majapahit prime minister, Gaja Made, landed at Labuhan Carik on the coast near **ANYAR** in the fourteenth century, although details of the Majapahit role on the island have largely been lost (see p.446). Today, it's a small, sleepy village with nothing to detain you. **Buses** from the Bertais/Mandalika/Sweta terminal terminate at Anyar, from where **bemos** go on to Ancak, Bayan, Batu Koq and Senaru.

The small village of **BAYAN**, 4km south of Anyar, is the site of Masjid Kuno Bayan Beleq, the **oldest mosque** on Lombok, said to be pre-1700, 1km east of the junction with the road to Batu Koq. You can't go in, but even from outside it's striking: a traditional bamboo and thatch building atop a circular stone and concrete citadel. Many of Lombok's more orthodox Muslims are uncomfortable that this ancient symbol of their religion is located in an area dominated by the Wetu Telu religion (see p.468). Buses from Labuhan Lombok and Sembalun Lawang via Kokok Putih terminate in Bayan.

East of Bayan, the road winds for 8km through the foothills of Gunung Rinjani, offering fine views of the volcano. The ricefields of Bayan soon give way to the much drier terrain of the east of Lombok. From **KOKOK PUTIH**, also known as Kalih Putih, a small junction with a few shops, buses run via the Sembalun valley, an alternative access-point for treks up Rinjani, to Pringgabaya or Aik Mel on the cross-island road. The main road around the north coast continues for another 10km to Obel Obel and on to the east coast (see p.428).

# Gunung Rinjani and around

Despite deforestation across much of Lombok, an extensive area of forest does remain on the slopes of **Gunung Rinjani** (3726m), and stretches for over 65km across the north of the island. From a distance, Rinjani appears to rise in solitary glory from the plains, but in fact the entire area is a throng of soaring summits. Invisible from below, the most breathtaking feature of the area is **Danau Segara Anak**, the magnificent crater-lake, measuring 8km by 6km.

The **climb** up Rinjani is the most energetic and the most rewarding trek on either Bali or Lombok. Ascent is from either **Senaru** or **Sembalun Lawang**, which are both set up for tourists, although there are other access points for local pilgrims.

## Batu Koq and Senaru

The small villages of **BATU KOQ** and **SENARU**, south of Bayan (about 86km from Mataram), are at an altitude of 600m: their cool temperatures in refreshing contrast to the north-coast heat. Both are reached by bemo (Rp5000) or ojek (Rp10,000) from Anyar, a few kilometres to the north.

Just south of *Bukit Senaru*, a small path heads east to the river and **Sindang Gile waterfall** (Rp2000). It's a lovely spot, the main fall about 25m high. **Tiu Kelep** is another waterfall a further hour beyond the first, where the water pours down in a double horseshoe shape. You should probably take a dip here; local

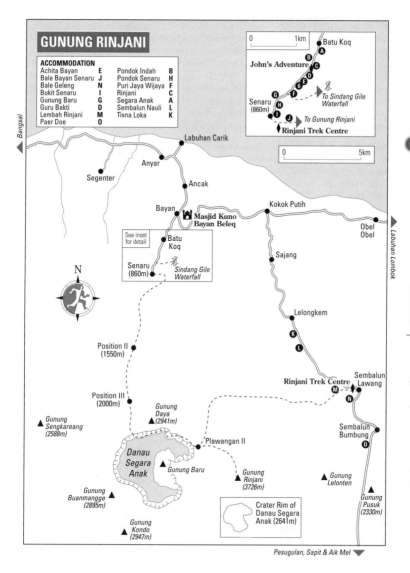

**GUNUNG RINJANI**

**ACCOMMODATION**

| | | | |
|---|---|---|---|
| Achita Bayan | **E** | Pondok Indah | **B** |
| Bale Bayan Senaru | **J** | Pondok Senaru | **H** |
| Bale Geleng | **N** | Puri Jaya Wijaya | **F** |
| Bukit Senaru | **I** | Rinjani | **C** |
| Gunung Baru | **G** | Segara Anak | **A** |
| Guru Bakti | **D** | Sembalun Nauli | **L** |
| Lembah Rinjani | **M** | Tisna Loka | **K** |
| Paer Doe | **O** | | |

*Pesugulan, Sapit & Aik Mel* ▼

belief is that you become a year younger every time you swim behind the falls.

It's worth visiting the **traditional village** in Senaru, a fenced compound with houses of bamboo and thatch next to *Bale Bayan Senaru*. The villagers still live a very simple life. Someone will appear to show you around, and you'll be expected to make a donation and sign the visitors' book.

For gentle exercise through the immediate area, the **Senaru Panorama Walk** (Rp45,000; 4hr) or **Rice Terraces and Waterfalls Walk** (Rp35,000; 1hr) are guided by local women. Ask at your accommodation or the Rinjani Trek Centre. Minimum numbers apply.

## Accommodation

The **accommodation** is spread for several kilometres along the road through Batu Koq and Senaru. *Segara Anak* is the most northerly (furthest from the mountain), while *Bale Bayan Senaru* lies at the end of the road where the path up the mountain begins. Most are basic concrete and tile with attached cold-water bathrooms; breakfast is usually included in the price. Places on the east of the road generally have the best views towards the mountain. All these places will store your stuff while you climb, and many have small **restaurants** attached, serving simple Indonesian and Sasak meals.

**Achita Bayan** ☎0817/577 3878. Concrete-floored bungalows with verandas both back and front for mountain and garden views. Some squat and some Western toilets. ❶

**Bale Bayan Senaru** ☎0817/579 2943. At the top of the road, tiled, basic bungalows in a small garden with attached mandi and squat toilet. ❶

**Bukit Senaru** ☎086812/104252. Well-spaced bungalows in a pleasant garden with good verandas. They're bigger than many in the area, and have Western toilets. ❶

**Gunung Baru** ☎0817/572 4863. Small set-up, not far from the start of the trail, with a few basic bungalows. ❶

**Guru Bakti** ☎08180/362 8240. Ignore the tumbledown options visible from the road there's a good row of places further back with great views of the waterfall from the verandas. ❶

**Pondok Indah** ☎08180/363 6058. Clean bungalows, with fine north-coast views in the more expensive ones. ❶

**Pondok Senaru** ☎086812/104141. The biggest set-up in the area, offering good-quality accommodation, all with great verandas, set in a pretty garden, with a huge restaurant offering fine views from the *bale* at the far end. Hot water in a bucket on request. ❷–❸

**Puri Jaya Wijaya** Small place with verandas overlooking the garden, rather than the great views behind. ❶

**Rinjani** ☎0817/575 0889. Doesn't take advantage of the views, but the four bungalows are clean and tiled and better quality than many. ❶

**Segara Anak** ☎0817/575 4551. The first place on the road from Bayan. There are fine panoramas from the verandas of the more expensive bungalows. ❶

# Sembalun Lawang and Sembalun Bumbung

A steep road twists 16km south from Kokok Putih to **SEMBALUN LAWANG**, set in countryside that is unique in Lombok – a high, flat-bottomed mountain valley virtually surrounded by hills. It's said locally that the people of this area are directly descended from the Majapahit dynasty of Java. There has recently been a renaissance of **handweaving** in the village and it's possible to visit local weavers – ask locally. It's also possible to arrange the leisurely and interesting Sembalun Village Walk (4hr; Rp100,000 per person, minimum two people). For those who want gentle trekking, the Sembalun Wildflowers Walk involves one night camping and is best from May to October (from Rp900,000 for one person to Rp225,000 per person in a group of six or more). Ask at the Rinjani Trek Centre.

There are several **places to stay** in the area. Five kilometres north of Sembalun Lawang on the road to Kokok Putih, *Tisna Loka* (✉tisnaloka@yahoo.com; ❷) offers rooms in a large house with shared bathroom. A kilometre further towards Sembalun Lawang, *Sembalun Nauli* (☎0818/362040, ✉sembalunnauli@lycos .com; ❷–❸) has four brick rooms with thatched roofs and verandas that face Rinjani. Just 200m up the track at the start of the Rinjani trek, *Lembah Rinjani* (☎08180/362 0918; ❷–❸) has a choice of rooms: basic ones with shared mandi, or large tiled rooms with attached showers and Western toilet plus verandas facing the mountain. *Bale Geleng* (☎0868/1210 9271; ❶) is on the main road 600m beyond the entrance to the trek. They offer wood, thatch and bamboo *lumbung*s on stilts with outside bathrooms all set in a pretty garden.

South of the village is a vast patchwork plain of fields and vegetable gardens before the valley closes in, the mountain walls rising steeply on all sides. Some

4km south of Sembalun Lawang is **SEMBALUN BUMBUNG**, an attractive village with houses clustered around the mosque in the shadows of the surrounding mountains. At the far southern end of the village, *Paer Doe* (●) is a tiny **homestay** with basic rooms.

From Sembalun Bumbung, the mountain road winds for 15km across Gunung Pusuk to Pesugulan, the turn-off for Sapit, Swela and on to Pringgabaya or Aik Mel on the cross-island road. This road is prone to closure due to landslides; check on its status before heading out. There's **public transport** on this route and also via Kokok Putih from Bayan and from Labuhan Lombok to the valley.

It is possible to arrange one-way **charters** from the valley (Rp200,000–250,000 to most Lombok destinations) at *Lembah Rinjani* (see above).

## Climbing Gunung Rinjani

The **summit of Gunung Rinjani** is reached by relatively few trekkers; the majority are satisfied with a shorter, less arduous trip to the **crater rim** – from where you can see the turquoise crater-lake, **Danau Segara Anak** (Child of the Sea), and the perfect cone of **Gunung Baru** (New Mountain) rising from it. The lake is considered to be the abode of the gods, and Wetu Telu pilgrims come on nights of the full moon while Balinese Hindus make offerings to the lake during the Pekelem festival (during the full moon of the fifth Balinese month).

Having lain dormant since 1906, Gunung Baru **erupted** in August 1994, closing the mountain for several weeks. Gunung Rinjani itself has been inactive since 1901, apart from a few puffs of smoke in 1944 and 1951. However, the mountain should be treated with respect, and the weather here is notoriously unpredictable. **Trekking** on Rinjani is not for the frail or unfit and shouldn't be attempted without adequate food and water. Although not all the treks need a porter or guide, you should definitely let somebody know where you're going and when you'll be back; you should report to the Rinjani Trek Centres at either Senaru or Sembalun Lawang when you set off.

### Routes

The shortest trek is **from Senaru**, climbing to the **crater rim**. At the Rinjani Trek Centre, at the top of the village, you pay Rp25,000 for **admission** to the national park, and register. The route takes you from the top of the village at 860m (marked on some maps as **Position I**), up through the forest to further **rest positions** (*plawangan*) with small *bale*; beware the precocious monkeys at the *bale* who will rifle through your stuff and take what they want. **Position II** is at 1550m and **Position III** at 2000m; you then leave the forest for the steep slog up to the rim at 2641m. Most people take six to seven hours (or more), not allowing for rests, to get to the rim from Senaru. A tent is vital to sleep on the crater rim.

From the rim, a path (2hr) descends into the crater to **the lake**, at 2050m. It is steep and rather frightening at the top, but gets better further down. You can bathe in the lakeside hot springs.

From the lake, you can return the same way or there's a different path (3hr plus) to the rim on the Sembalun side at 2639m and a site called **Plawangan II**, and from there up to the **summit of Rinjani** (another 3hr plus). Try to reach the summit for sunrise; it clouds over and gets very windy soon after.

A shorter route to Plawangan II and then to the summit is to climb **from Sembalun Lawang** on the northeast side of the mountain, starting on the track next to the Rinjani Trek Centre and passing *Lembah Rinjani*. This takes seven to eight hours to Plawangan II (where you'll overnight) and then another three hours-plus to get to the summit the next morning.

## Rinjani practicalities

There are three main **climbs**: to the crater rim **from Senaru** (2 days), to the rim and then down to the lake from Senaru (two nights/three days) and, the hardest of all, to the summit – the shortest summit trips start and finish in **Sembalun Lawang** (3 days) while the longer version (4 days) heads up from Sembalun and then back down via the lake and crater rim to Senaru.

If you're climbing from Senaru to the rim or down to the lake, you don't need a **guide**, although a **porter** is a great advantage. The path leaves to the left just beyond *Bale Bayan Senaru* in Senaru, and is difficult to lose. There's spring **water** at Positions II and III from the Senaru side during and just after the rainy season, and also around the lakeshore, but you should check on this locally before setting out. It's vital to carry adequate **food and water** for the climb.

For the longer treks, you'll definitely need a guide. Each of the losmen in the area has a local trek organiser who should have printed information about the different treks and prices, which, in theory, are fixed. Alternatively, contact John's Adventures in Senaru (☎0817/578 8018, ⊛www.rinjanimaster.com), who also arrange lengthier explorations of the entire area including caves, hot springs and Gunung Baru. Prices depend on the trek and the numbers climbing but should include guide, porters, equipment (including sleeping bags) and meals. Prices below are per person.

|  | 1 person | 2 people | 3+ people |
|---|---|---|---|
| Rim (2 days) | Rp1,190,000 | Rp714,000 | Rp606,900 |
| Lake (3 days) | Rp1,400,000 | Rp840,000 | Rp714,000 |
| Summit (3 days) | Rp1,610,000 | Rp966,000 | Rp821,000 |
| Summit (4 days) | Rp1,820,000 | Rp1,092,000 | Rp928,200 |

### All-inclusive Rinjani trips

Although it's easy to arrange your own climb up Rinjani from Senaru, Batu Koq or the Sembalun valley, many companies on Lombok offer **inclusive trips** to climb the mountain – useful if time is short, but expensive. Prices include transport in both directions, guides, porters, food and equipment. Costs vary, and it pays to shop around. Contact Perama (any office), Gora Tour & Travel, Senggigi (☎0370/693477), Citra Lombok Indah, Senggigi (☎0370/693921, ⊛www.citralombokindah.blogspot.com) or Rinjani Trekking Club, Senggigi (☎0817/573 0415, ⊛www.geocities.com/info2lombok).

The most complete exploration of the mountain involves a round trip, ascending from either Senaru or Sembalun Lawang, taking in the summit and the lake, and descending to the other. You can make arrangements in Senaru or Sembalun Lawang. For even more extensive trips, up to six days and five nights in length, contact John's Adventures in Senaru (see box, above).

# Central Lombok

The broad corridor of **central Lombok**, stretching from west to east coasts between, to the north, the mass of Gunung Rinjani and its neighbours, and, to the south, the lower range of coastal hills, is the densely populated agricultural heartland of the island.

Stretching for 74km from Ampenan–Mataram–Cakranegara–Sweta to Labuhan Lombok, the main highway on the island passes close to many of the most attractive destinations. Tourist facilities have developed in the hills – there's accommodation in the pretty villages of **Tetebatu** and **Sapit** – while down on the plains **Lendang Nangka** has become a pilgrimage for travellers seeking the "real" village experience. The culturally minded make stops at Hindu sites at **Narmada**, **Pura Lingsar** and **Suranadi**, while the craft villages dotted throughout the area offer the chance to see potters, weavers and blacksmiths at work.

Well served by **bemos and buses**, much of the centre is accessible without your own transport. Note that there are very few moneychangers east of Sweta.

# Narmada and around

Built in 1805 by the raja of Mataram, Anak Gede Karangasem, the grounds of **Taman Narmada** (daily 7am–6pm; Rp2000, swimming Rp2000), are served by frequent bemos from the Bertais/Mandalika/Sweta terminal just 10km away. It includes a replica of Gunung Rinjani and its crater-lake, made for the raja when he became too old to climb the real volcano to make his offering to the gods. More cynical commentators claim that he built the lake to lure local women to bathe while he sat in his pavilion and watched.

The gardens lie on the south side of the main road through **NARMADA**, opposite the bemo terminal and daily market; they're popular with local families and included on many organized tours. However, if you have more time this is a good place to wander: the terraces and the lake are extensive, and there's a swimming pool. The Balinese temple here, **Pura Kalasa**, is the focus of the celebration of Pujawali (usually in Nov or Dec), when offerings of ducks are made to the lake. The aqueduct at the side of the lake is one of the few remnants of Dutch development on the island during their period of occupation (1894–1942).

### Pura Lingsar

A few kilometres north of Narmada and easily reached by bemo from there, **Pura Lingsar** (daily 7am–6pm; admission by donation) was built around 1714 and rebuilt in 1874. Local guides will approach you; Rp15,000–20,000 is a fair price. The temple is a focus of worship for the Hindu religion as well as Muslims – including the Wetu Telu (see p.468). The furthest north, and highest, courtyard is the Hindu one guarded by fierce monsters at the *candi bentar*, while the Wetu Telu area has a pond overlooked by a vivid statue of Wisnu, home to some well-fed eels, which emerge for hard-boiled eggs brought by devotees. The Pujawali festival is also celebrated here (Nov or Dec), and is followed by a mock battle between Hindus and Muslims throwing *ketupat* (rice wrapped in leaves) at each other.

Not many tourists stay, but there is **accommodation**. About 1.5km west of the turning to the temple on the back road from Narmada to Cakranegara is *Puri Lingsar Bungalows* (⊕0370/671652; ❶), with basic bungalows offering fan, attached bathroom and deep verandas in an attractive garden. Some 500m beyond the turning to the temple, *Losmen Ida* (⊕0812/3708119; ❶) is newer and has tiled rooms with fan and attached mandi and squat toilet.

## Suranadi

Situated about 300m above sea level, **SURANADI** is 7km north of Narmada at the site of a freshwater spring. The temple here, **Pura Suranadi**, is a holy pilgrimage site for Hindus: the Hindu saint Nirartha is believed to have located the springs while in a trance. Almost next to the temple is a small forest area, the **Hutan Wisata Suranadi** (Rp3000), a reasonable picnic spot.

*Suranadi Hotel* (T0370/636411, F635630; ❷–❹) has **accommodation** situated above a swimming pool (non-residents Rp8000). It's rather overpriced, although the top-end bungalows are attractive and have hot water. Meals in the attached **restaurant** are moderately priced. A good budget option is *Hotel Jati* (T0370/6606437; ❶), 200m up the road between Pura Suranadi and *Suranadi Hotel*. It's new and has few frills (there's squat toilets) but is perfectly adequate. Almost a kilometre beyond here, along the same road, *Teratai Cottages* (T0812/370 0936; ❶–❷), is in a great rural location. There are several standards of accommodation (with air-con and hot water at the top end), in cottages in a large garden with a pool and terrace, boasting fabulous views.

## Seseot

If you have your own transport, you can reach the attractive village of **SESEOT** from Suranadi. Head up the road that goes past the Hutan Wisata Suranadi, turn right at the T-junction and continue uphill. After about 5km you'll reach Seseot, where the presence of a temple as well as a mosque testifies to the mixed religion of this small but bustling village in the hills. For the casual visitor, it's the village's location next to the river that's the draw, with good views across the fields and plenty of places for a quiet picnic beside the river – either follow the path beside the mosque down to the river or cross the road bridge at the top of the village to the other side. Bemos also run to Sesoet from Narmada.

For an altogether different atmosphere, the *GEC Rinjani Country Club* (T0370/633488, Wwww.lombokgolf.com; ❼), also known as *Padang Golf*, sits about 1km from the main cross-island road at **Golong** (there's a sign at Sedau, 5km east of Narmada), or about 3km by the back road from Suranadi. All accommodation is excellent quality (hot water and air conditioning), and there are tennis courts, a spa and a large swimming pool (Rp10,000 for non-residents). This is one of only two 18-hole **golf courses** on the island. Green fees are $50 during the week, $70 at weekends including caddy fee; guests get thirty-percent discount. Equipment rental is extra.

# Tetebatu and around

**TETEBATU** is situated on the southern slopes of Gunung Rinjani, 50km from Sweta (11km north of the main cross-island road), with stunning views of the volcano across terraced fields lush with rice in the rainy season and tobacco in the dry. At an altitude of 400m, the area is cool but not cold and it's excellent for a few days' relaxation or as a base from which to explore the centre of the island.

On public transport, get off the **bemo** or **bus** at Pomotong on the main road and either take an ojek straight up to Tetebatu or a bemo to Kotaraja and an ojek on to Tetebatu. Alternatively, you can reach Tetebatu by Perama charter from Senggigi (Rp60,000 per person, minimum two people).

From Tetebatu, you can explore nearby waterfalls and craft villages: the *Green Orry* and *Pondok Tetebatu* (see below) rent motorcycles (Rp30–45,000 per day)

or vehicle charters (Rp150,000–200,000 per day including driver and petrol), and *Green Orry* can arrange a cidomo charter (Rp50,000 per day). Guides for local treks (Rp30,000–50,000 for 4hr) can be arranged here, too. These places can also supply **charter transport** to other Lombok destinations: sample prices are Rp150,000 to Senggigi, Rp125,000 to Labuhan Lombok, Rp175,000 to Kuta or Bangsal, Rp300,000 to Senaru.

It isn't easy to change money locally. There's a **wartel** just above the *Salabuse* restaurant on the road up to *Wisma Soedjono* but no Internet access.

## Accommodation and eating

**Accommodation** is on the main road up to the *Wisma Soedjono* from Kotaraja and the road off to the east, Waterfall Street. At the time of writing, a lot of it was looking sad – the area has suffered badly in the tourist downturn of the last couple of years so it pays to look at a few places. Most have **restaurants** attached, although a few simple restaurants have also sprung up, all serving the usual inexpensive to moderately priced Indo-Chinese and travellers' fare, plus some Sasak options. *Warung Harmony* and *Salabuse*, on the main road, are both worth a try.

**Cendrawasih** Accommodation, in four two-storey traditional *lumbung*-style barns, is charming and set in a great garden on Waterfall Street, and the attached thatched restaurant has fine views. ❶

**Green Orry** ☎0376/632255, ℱ632233. Tiled, clean bungalows in a pleasant compound on Waterfall Street, plus a restaurant. ❷

**Hakiki** Set in the middle of paddy-fields at the eastern end of Waterfall Street, accommodation is in very basic two-storey traditional *lumbung* with excellent verandas and attached mandi and squat toilet. There's a fine view of Gunung Rinjani from here. ❶–❷

**Nirwana Cottages** Some 200m off Waterfall Street. Two basic brick and thatch cottages whose verandas give brilliant views of Rinjani. ❶

**Pondok Bulan** ☎0376/632581. Located on Waterfall Street, with good views south, there are traditional bamboo and thatch *lumbung*-style bungalows as well as bigger, less traditional, family rooms. ❶–❷

**Pondok Tetebatu** ☎0376/632572, ℱ632622. Good-quality, clean, tiled rooms in two rows facing across a small garden. ❶

**Wisma Soedjono** ☎ & ℱ0376/21309. This used to be the home of Dr Soedjono, the first doctor in eastern Lombok, and is still owned by his family. It offers a range of accommodation set in great grounds at the far north end of the village and is the most upmarket option in the area, and the only place offering hot water. There's also a swimming pool. ❶–❷

## Jukut and Joben waterfalls

With your own transport you can follow the road east from Tetebatu to **KEMBANG KUNING**, from where it's six kilometres to **Jukut waterfall** (Rp2000, parking Rp1000). You have to complete the last couple of kilometres on foot, along a steep path with little shade, so you should take drinking water. The water pours over a sheer cliff about 20m high into a circular pool surrounded on all sides by towering walls covered in undergrowth. It's cool and shady, you can picnic near the river, and during the week it's fairly quiet. Talk to local people about the advisability of setting off alone for a trek up here, as there were one or two robberies some years ago. From Kembang Kunung, a seven-kilometre back road leads to Lendang Nangka.

Northwest of Tetebatu, **Joben waterfall**, also known as Otak Kokok Gading, is much less dramatic. The water falls only a short distance and is fed into an open-air shower block. It's believed locally, however, that this is a sacred place and that the water will turn cloudy if you're ill.

## Kotaraja, Loyok and Rungkang

The village of **KOTARAJA**, 5km south of Tetebatu, is a local transport hub. The name means "City of Kings", referring to ancient times when the kingdom of Langko fell to Balinese invaders and the royal family fled here. The area is known for its blacksmiths, but you'll have to ask for directions and come early to see them at work. From time to time, Kotaraja is the setting for the traditional *peresehan*, fights in which male opponents attack each other with long rattan canes with only buffalo-skin shields to defend themselves. If you're in the area when this is due to take place, you'll hear about it.

A centre for bamboo basketware, **LOYOK** is just a few kilometres south of Kotaraja. Several handicraft shops here sell a range of local goods including bags, lamps and boxes, and even the children plait basketware as they walk along the road.

Pottery is produced at **RUNGKANG**, just east of Loyok. Arrive early in the workshops to see the pots being moulded over stones and beaten into shape with a flat stick. Made from the local grey clay, the pots turn an attractive mottled orange-black colour when fired, and are surprisingly light.

# Lendang Nangka and beyond

Developed single-handedly as a tourist destination by local teacher Haji Radiah, **LENDANG NANGKA** is a small farming community 2km north of the main cross-island road, and served by cidomo and ojek from Bagik Bontong. Pressure on the land is huge and many villagers have moved to West Papua as part of the government's *transmigrasi* policy (see p.453). Although the scenery is not as picturesque as Tetebatu, the atmosphere in the village is welcoming and this is a great place to experience village life and to practise your Indonesian or Sasak. There's a wealth of walks through the ricefields around the village, and the local people are used to strangers wandering around.

Established in 1983, *H.Radiah's* (☎0376/631463, @soul-lenka@hotmail.com; ❶ full board) is a **homestay** in the real sense of the word. It's in the middle of the village, but tucked away behind the school, so ask for directions. You can stay in rooms in the family compound or in larger, newer rooms in a house in the local fields. It's great to be part of a household and have the rare opportunity of coming into contact with Sasak women in their home environment. Many visitors enjoy an afternoon walk in the area with Radiah. Sannah, Radiah's wife, cooks traditional Sasak food and she's used to visitors in the kitchen. There's a *bale* in the garden where you can while away a few hours, and you get a map with plenty of suggestions for local excursions. There's a **wartel** with **Internet access** across the road.

## Penakak and around

Further east, the hamlet of **PENAKAK** lies just off the main road, 1.5km east of the domes, spires and minarets of the mosque, Masjid Al-Jami Al-Akbar, on the main cross-island road in the centre of **Masbagik**. Look out for a pottery shop and wartel on the north side of the main road: the turning to Penakak is opposite. Penakak is one of the three main pottery villages on Lombok, and the road through the village is lined with potteries. The range of goods produced is enormous; the potteries will ship goods overseas.

The **waterfalls** at **PANCOR KOPONG** and **PANCOR BULING** are accessible by cidomo from Masbagik to Nibas (3km) and then walking the last kilometre from Nibas, or you can walk from Pringgasela (2km); either way it's best to ask for directions. The falls are not especially high, but they're impressively wide and set in the midst of attractive ricefields with pleasant walks round about.

### Pringgasela and Timbanuh

Some 5km north of **REMPUNG** on the cross-island road is the local weaving centre of **PRINGGASELA**. Local women make both *songket* and *ikat* cloth on simple backstrap looms (see p.488 for details of production), and there are plenty of workshops in the village. *Glose Homestay* (☎0376/631594, ⓔyoungartshop@yahoo.com; ❷ full board) is behind Young Art Shop, just west of the main crossroads in the centre of the village and marked by a white monument. Rooms are simple and part of the family compound. Access to Pringgasela is from Rempung by ojek or cidomo. For an excursion well off the beaten track, the road up to **TIMBANUH**, 8km north of Pringgasela via Pengadangan, ascends to the southern foothills of Rinjani through coffee, banana and rambutan plantations. It's a shady, picturesque trip until the road ends on a ridge with spellbinding views across to Sumbawa. You need your own transport to get here.

### Loang Geli

Back on the main road at **LENEK**, another small road heads north and, after about 3km, a wide dirt track, just past the school and opposite the *kepala desa*'s office, leads a further 1km to **LOANG GELI**, the site of a cold freshwater **spring**, often listed as a local sight. From the parking spot, it's 100m down a gently sloping path to the swimming area where the spring flows into a deep concrete pool – pleasant without being exceptional. The pool is surrounded by a **Monkey Forest**, but weekend and holiday crowds keep the monkeys away.

# Sapit

Situated at 1400m on the southern slopes of Gunung Pusuk, the small village of **SAPIT** is a quiet retreat with wonderful views. It's 15km from Sembalun Lawang (2–3hr by daily bus), but the road is very steep and prone to being washed away; check in Sembalun or Sapit on the current condition before setting off on your own. It's the same distance from the cross-island road, either via Aik Mel or Pringgabaya. There's **accommodation** at *Hati Suci* (☎0818/545655, ⓦwww.hatisuci.tk; ❷) and nearby *Balelangga* (same contact; ❷), which are both run by the same family: *Balelangga* offers simpler accommodation with outside toilet while *Hati Suci* has bungalows with attached bathrooms, some with squat toilets. Both have lovely gardens and great views across the paddy-fields to the coast and Sumbawa. Each has a small **restaurant** offering a basic menu, and staff here will point you in the right direction for local walks and, for the hardy, the fifteen-kilometre trek across to the Sembalun valley (see p.418).

# East Lombok

With a much drier climate, smaller population and fewer facilities than the west of the island, **east Lombok** attracts few visitors, although if you're heading to or from Sumbawa you'll pass through the small port of **Labuhan Lombok**. While there's little to detain you here for long, to the north of Labuhan Lombok the land is dramatically arid, giving striking views inland to the mountains, and the accommodation at **Labuhan Pandan** offers the ultimate in relaxation and the opportunity for trips to the uninhabited islands off the coast. **Labuhan Haji**, south of Labuhan Lombok, is an attractive seaside town, with lush scenery inland. Accommodation options here are gradually increasing, although they are still limited.

## Labuhan Lombok and around

**LABUHAN LOMBOK**, 74km east of Mataram, is probably the least interesting town in Lombok, although its near-circular bay is attractive. Boats to Sumbawa depart from the **ferry terminal**, Labuhan Kayangan, a three-kilometre shadeless walk around the south side of the bay; take a local bemo if you can (Rp1000). **Kayangan Hill**, on the south side of the bay, has good views inland and across to Sumbawa; the path up the hill leaves from the road to the ferry terminal, and it's a short, dusty climb.

**Buses** run regularly along the cross-island road between Labuhan Lombok and the Bertais/Mandalika/Sweta terminal, with some continuing on to the ferry terminal. Buses also run between Labuhan Lombok and Sembalun Lawang; change at Kokok Putih for Batu Koq or Senaru. Travelling between Kuta and Labuhan Lombok involves changing at Praya and at Kopang, on the main road.

### Moving on to Sumbawa

The **ferry to Sumbawa** departs Labuhan Lombok around the clock (every hour; Rp9000, bicycle Rp7500, motorbike Rp15,000, cars from Rp114,000) and takes ninety minutes to two hours to reach Poto Tano on Sumbawa's northwest coast, a few kilometres from the main road across the island. Buses meet the ferries bound for Taliwang (30km south), Alas (22km east), Sumbawa Besar and, occasionally, Bima. Alternatively, you can book **long-distance bus** tickets in Mataram (see p.390) through to destinations on Sumbawa.

A decent **place to stay** is *Hotel Melati Lima Tiga*, Jl Kayangan 14 (☎0376/23316; Rp55,000), about 150m from the town centre on the road to the ferry terminal. The rooms are a bit box-like and lack fans but are adequate, although bathrooms, with mandi and squat toilet, are shared. Several **warung**, fine for basic Indonesian food, line the same road; *Warung Kelayu* is very popular. There's a **wartel** at *Hotel Melati Lima Tiga* and, if you head to the main road and turn left, the **post office** is 100m along on the right.

## South of Labuhan Lombok

**SELONG**, 20km southwest of Labuhan Lombok and the capital of Lombok Timur (East Lombok), is a thriving market town, although the travel hub for the area is a couple of kilometres west at **Pancor**. It has a **tourist office**, on Jalan Lalu Muchdar (☎0376/21894), and **accommodation** at *Erina*, Jl Pahlawan 164 (☎0376/21297; ❷), on the north side of the main road – but there's little reason to linger.

About 7km southeast is **LABUHAN HAJI**, a port (served by bemos from Pancor) from where Muslim pilgrims traditionally departed on the *hajj*, or pilgrimage to Mecca. The village is a maze of alleyways clustered behind the black beach but, apart from a small port office, there's little evidence of the once-thriving trading community. The Chinese here suffered particularly badly during the civil conflict following the attempted coup in 1965 (see p.452); around forty were killed and the remainder fled to Sumbawa to the west of Lombok. The only **accommodation** is at *Meliwis Beach Hotel* (❶), which has basic wood, bamboo and thatch bungalows with fan and attached bathrooms, close to the beach, to the north of the main harbour area. There is a new foreign-owned hotel planned for the area, so options may increase. The beach is rather scruffy but there are good views. It's quiet during the week, but gets busy at weekends.

## North of Labuhan Lombok

Travelling north from Labuhan Lombok, the scenery quickly becomes parched and villages are few and far between. The time to see this area round to Obel Obel at its best is at the end of the rainy season in April/May – for much of the year, it is extremely arid. The towering mahogany trees 5km from Labuhan Lombok are welcome shade and are widely believed to be the largest such specimens in Lombok.

### Labuhan Pandan and the islands

In the area of **LABUHAN PANDAN**, 13km north of Labuhan Lombok, look out for **Pantai Pulo Lampu** beach – popular at weekends but otherwise peaceful. Bemos (Rp2000) and ojek (Rp10,000) run here from Labuhan Lombok. The best **accommodation** is 3km further north at *Pondok Matahari* ⚓ (☎0812/374 9915; ❷), which has a choice of bungalows on the seafront or larger rooms set further back in a two-storey block. All are clean and tiled, with Western toilets, and the garden is excellent. There is an attached **restaurant**. There is **snorkelling** off the beach here; you can rent snorkelling gear at the accommodation (Rp15,000–20,000). Just south, *Siola Cottages* (☎08133/951 6723; ❶; closed during Ramadan) is much more basic. *Ma Jena's* is a simple warung by the roadside a few hundred metres further south.

There are two groups of **islands** off the northeast Lombok coast. The most southerly are **Gili Petangan** and its satellites, Gili Lampu and Gili Pasaran, which have beaches as well as coral walls and attract many varieties of fish;

further north (and a longer boat trip away) are the larger islands **Gili Sulat** and **Gili Lawang**, surrounded by coastal mangrove, without any beaches but with a large array of offshore coral. All are uninhabited and preserved from buildings by a government ban, although some boat trips from Lombok east to Sumbawa and Flores use them for camping. Japanese scientists are involved in a mangrove study on Gili Lawang, Gili Petangan and Gili Sulat, and have built a walkway in the swamp that can be used for jungle walks without disturbing the area. You can arrange **snorkelling** and **fishing** expeditions to the islands from both *Pondok Matahari* and *Siola Cottages*. A day-trip out to Gili Lampu and the surrounding islands costs Rp180,000; to Gili Sulat and Gili Lawang costs Rp200,000. Overnight **camping** trips are also possible. The dive operator Bagus Divers (see p.399) organizes dives in the area, as does Lombok Marine Adventures, the dive company at the *Novotel Lombok* hotel (see p.434). **Buses** using this road head to the Bertais/Mandalika/Sweta terminal via Labuhan Lombok (if they're heading south) and Sembalun Lawang (heading north).

### Sambelia and around

Just north of Labuhan Pandan, the village of **SAMBELIA** is a traditional Bugis settlement with some houses built on stilts – although they're gradually being replaced by concrete and brick dwellings. The views of Gili Sulat and Gili Lawang from here around to **BELANTING** are enticing, as the islands shimmer in the heat across the Sungian Strait.

Moving on around the coast towards Obel Obel, the countryside gets even drier, traffic is rare and the road twists and turns through the hills, which slope right down to the black-sand shore. **OBEL OBEL**, about 45km from Labuhan Lombok, is a tiny oasis among the folds of the barren hills. There are very few tourists here, but you should be able to buy a drink somewhere. About 10km further on is the junction of Kokok Putih, where a road branches south to Sembalun Lawang; the coast road continues west to Bayan.

# South Lombok

The largely undeveloped **south coast** of Lombok is extraordinarily beautiful, with mile upon mile of picturesque bays of pure white sand separated by rocky headlands. Known to surfers for several years, **Kuta** is a low-key development with a choice of accommodation. From here you can explore the bays to the west and to the three glorious inlets that pierce the coast to the east. **Awang Bay** and the **southeast peninsula** are dotted with villages making a living from the sea and from desperately dry farmland. Well off the beaten track, and accessible only with private transport, this is a part of the island largely unseen by visitors. If you're restricted to public transport, you can still reach the inland villages specializing in pottery, weaving, basketware and carving, such as **Beleka**, **Sukarara**, **Penujak** and **Sukaraja**, and the traditional villages of **Sade** and **Rembitan**.

A new **international airport** has been proposed for the area around Praya for some years. After years in limbo it looks as though it may actually happen,

Celebrated on Lombok and the more distant islands of Sumba and Savu, this annual festival centres around a seaworm, *eunice viridis*, which is known locally as *nale* or **nyale**. The worms live attached to rocks in the ocean, but at roughly the same time every year, February to March, they begin their sexual cycle and release male and female sexual parts, which rise to the surface ready for fertilization, turning the ocean into something resembling a seething mass of spaghetti. The number of worms is believed to indicate the success of the next rice harvest, and it is estimated that around 100,000 people travel to the south coast of Lombok at this time to gather the worms (they are believed to be aphrodisiacs), to enjoy traditional songs and to watch the re-enactment of the *Putri Nyale* or *Mandalika* legend. This tells how a beautiful princess, distraught because of the number of suitors who were fighting over her hand in marriage and loath to upset any by refusing them, flung herself into the sea where her hair was changed into *nyale* seaworms.

Nyale is celebrated in Kuta, Kaliantan and some of the villages on the shores of Awang Bay.

although exactly when is anyone's guess. However, there's no doubt that if and when it happens, the entire south of the island will open up – perhaps changing beyond all recognition, perhaps not.

The issue of **safety for tourists** in the south of Lombok periodically gains a high profile. The vast majority have a great trip with no problems, but there have been reports of robberies and attacks on the back roads west of Kuta. Ask in Kuta about the current situation and consider taking a local person with you as a driver or passenger – they'll also keep an eye on the vehicle while it's parked. It is also worth heeding local advice and avoiding the village of Ketara, on the road from Sengkol to Praya via Penujak, after dark – take the road via Batunyale instead.

# Praya and the craft villages

The busy market town and transport hub of **PRAYA**, 22km southeast of Sweta, is the capital of Central Lombok (Lombok Tengah), although it lies well to the south of the island. It's a pleasant place, easily accessible by **bus** or **bemo** from the Bertais/Mandalika/Sweta terminal, its administrative buildings set in broad streets. However, with the bus terminal 3km northwest of the centre, most visitors will bypass the town completely. The only **accommodation** is the functional *Hotel Dienda Hayu*, Jl Untung Surapati 26 (☎0370/654319; ❶–❷), which has air-con in its more expensive rooms. It's looking a bit frayed these days, but if you're stranded this is the only option. To find it, turn left at the traffic lights on the main road, Jalan Jend Sudirman, which are about 300m east of BCA and BNI banks; the hotel is up on the right. The **tourist office** is at Jl Gajah Made 125 (☎0370/653766), about 500m west of the bus terminal on the main road. There are BCA and BNI **bank** ATM machines for Visa, MasterCard and Cirrus on Jl Jend Sudirman in the town centre and BRI is a few hundred metres west of the junction of the main road with the road in from Kuta. There are several **wartels** on the main road. Most visitors change in Praya for local transport to Sengkol and Kuta without stopping; however, if you need a **place to eat**, *Ria*, opposite the banks on Jalan Jend Sudirman, on the west corner of a new shopping centre, is an inexpensive little spot. It is famed in southern Lombok for goat saté, which appears on the menu as *nasi gudeg* – you'll get a plate of rice, saté and sauce, and a bowl of mutton soup. However, there are also plenty of vegetarian options.

## South and west of Praya

On the road to Selong Blanak, **PENUJAK**, 6km southwest of Praya, is one of the three major pottery villages on Lombok. Most workshops are on or near the main road to Sengkol, at the southern end of town; you'll see a sign for the Lombok Crafts Project just south of the large bridge across the river. There are plenty of designs and patterns available, in all shapes and sizes, up to 1m tall, and you can watch the potters at work if you come early in the day.

Directly west of Praya, although the route is via Puyung or Batujai, the weaving village of **SUKARARA** is firmly on the tour-bus circuit and has some enormous showrooms offering the widest range of textiles on Lombok. Slick salesmen work the customers, while out on the veranda the weavers produce *ikat* and *songket* cloth using backstrap looms (see p.488); the latter tends to be more aggressively colourful than the former, whose subtle shades are produced by vegetable dyes from indigo, betel nut, pineapple and bay leaves. The weavers begin learning from the age of seven and take many years to master the huge number of designs, which they weave from memory. Local girls have to be skilled at weaving in order to be considered marriageable; men do not weave, as it is believed it will make them sterile. A sarong and scarf set can take anywhere from a month to more than three months to weave, depending on the thread and quality, and the weaver receives a percentage of the price when it's sold. There are also a few smaller shops in the village, which have a more relaxed feel to them. Prices are generally reasonable, but you need to shop around – which you may not have time to do if you come on an organized tour.

## East of Praya

East of Praya, the road to Gubukdalam is the main road across the south of the island, and most of the **villages** of interest are near it. With bemos plying the route, access to most is straightforward.

Turning south at **Ganti**, 13km east of Praya– the turn isn't signed but it's in the middle of the village with a wartel on the corner – the road passes through Batu Rintang and down to the northern end of Awang Bay and the coastal village of **BATU NAMPAR**, where people make their living from fishing and seaweed cultivation; see p.262 for an alternative route to the bay. Just inland, a huge area of **salt ponds** provides another source of income (see box, p.432). The views of the bay from here are excellent: you can see clearly across to Ekas on the southeast peninsula. The large rock called **Linus**, just off the shore, plays an important role in local weddings – the bride and groom sail around it together as part of the ceremony.

To reach **BELEKA**, known for the production of rattan basketware, turn north at Ganti, 200m east of the Batu Nampar turning; it's a busy junction, with cidomo waiting to take you the 3km. There's a large number of shops and workshops here, and the local specialities are wares made from grass, rattan, *ketak* (a thin rattan) and bamboo in a huge range of shapes and sizes, up to laundry baskets large enough for you and your clothes.

### East of Ganti

Back on the main road, 7km east of Ganti at Longkhang, a turning leads for several kilometres to the village of **Keronk** where pretty much every household

△ Lombok textiles, Sukarara

## Making salt

On many parts of the Lombok coast, particularly around Awang Bay (and on Bali, at Kusamba and Amed), you'll see the salt beds and piles of white salt that are evidence of one of the most backbreaking occupations on the islands – **salt-making**. Vast quantities of salt water are hauled from the sea in buckets and poured into specially dug ponds, close to the shore. When the water has evaporated, the salty, sandy residue is placed in hollowed-out palm-tree trunks and mixed with more seawater. The water becomes saturated with salt and the thick brine is poured off and evaporated to form salt crystals. Further stages of purification take place, and you may see large bamboo baskets suspended from frames at salt-making sites: the liquid from the wet salt crystals, which contains soluble impurities, drips down a string hanging from the baskets, leaving pure salt crystals behind.

The rainy season brings salt production to a halt and high tides can also flood the salt pools. A typical family of salt producers can make around 25kg of salt a day, but salt is cheap to buy and many former salt-producing areas are now turning to seaweed farming as a more lucrative way of earning a living.

is involved in woodcarving. The turning from the main road isn't signed but is just west of some tobacco kilns beside the road. The dirt road leads 1.5km past a local dam to the village. One carving that you'll see everywhere shows three figures climbing on top of each other. Legend tells how three brothers were hunting deer in the forest. One of them, Doyan Medaran, was waiting for his brothers beside a deer that he had killed when a giant appeared. Doyan Medaran was so frightened that he climbed up a massive tree to hide from the giant who, after devouring the deer, disappeared into the forest. Doyan Medaran remained stuck in the tree until his brothers came along and rescued him by climbing on to each others' shoulders.

Known for its canoe-making, the village of **KERUAK**, another 5km east, has a few workshops east of the village in the hamlet of Batu Rimpang, to the south of the road to Tanjung Luar. You can watch work in progress as hand tools are used to create dugout canoes from vast tree trunks. On completion, the boats are taken by road to the coast. About 500m east of Keruak, *Warung Sekarmulya* is an inexpensive, friendly Javanese place to eat nasi campur.

The right turn to **TANJUNG LUAR** is just under 6km east of Keruak, on a tight left-hand bend opposite a school, from where it's a couple of kilometres to the coastal village. This is a fishing village with Bugis houses built on stilts and a harbour packed full of boats, where you can watch cormorants diving for fish and admire the great views around the wide sweep of the coastline. You can charter a boat here to take you to Tanjung Ringgit on the southeast peninsula.

From the turning to Tanjung Luar, it's 10km north up the coastal road to Labuhan Haji.

# Kuta and around

The only village with significant tourist development on the south coast is **KUTA**, 54km from Mataram and 32km from Praya, a tiny fishing village situated just behind the west end of the sweeping, white-sand beach. It's the choice of travellers seeking a few days by the sea a bit further off the beaten track than Senggigi or the Gili Islands and especially suitable if you like wild coastal

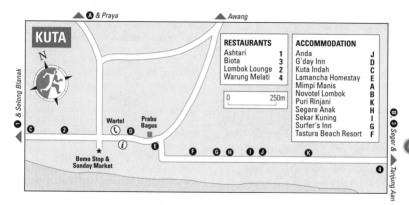

&#9650; **A** & Praya     &#9650; Awang

&#9664; **1** & Selong Blanak

**B** **3** Seger & &#9654; Tanjung Aan

**KUTA**

N

| RESTAURANTS | |
|---|---|
| Ashtari | 1 |
| Biota | 3 |
| Lombok Lounge | 2 |
| Warung Melati | 4 |

0       250m

| ACCOMMODATION | |
|---|---|
| Anda | J |
| G'day Inn | D |
| Kuta Indah | C |
| Lamancha Homestay | E |
| Mimpi Manis | A |
| Novotel Lombok | B |
| Puri Rinjani | K |
| Segare Anak | H |
| Sekar Kuning | I |
| Surfer's Inn | G |
| Tastura Beach Resort | F |

Wartel   Prabu Bagus

Bemo Stop & Sunday Market

**6**

scenery and turbulent surf. The beach is framed by rocky headlands, and **Seger** and **Tanjung Aan** beaches are within walking or cycling distance. Apart from Sunday, when the lively **market** takes place, the area is extremely quiet. Prabu Bagus (☎0370/655207) arranges 4–5hr fishing and sightseeing **boat trips** east and west along the coast – a fabulous way to see the coastline (Rp400,000 for a maximum of 4 people; you'll need to negotiate).

Kuta is an ideal base for **surfing** with breaks off the beach in Kuta and Tanjung Aan beach. West of Kuta, most of the bays are worth a look, from Mawun through Mawi as far west as Blongas, although they vary in accessibility and the surf can be erratic. East of Kuta there are breaks off the coast of the southeast peninsula near **Serewe**, inside the southern headlands of **Awang Bay**, also known as Ekas Bay, and **Gumbang Bay**, which some people call Grupuk Bay, a short drive from Kuta. You can charter boats from Gerupak and Awang or base yourself out at Ekas.

Coming from the west, **buses** and **bemos** run to Praya from the Bertais/Mandalika/Sweta terminal. From Praya, bemos run either to Sengkol, where you can change, or right through to Kuta. From the east of Lombok, bemos run to Praya via Kopang on the main cross-island road. Perama offer **tourist charters** to Kuta from their offices in Senggigi and Mataram (Rp60,000 per person, minimum two people). There's a **tourist office** in the village (☎0370/655269) but its opening hours are a bit vague.

## Accommodation

Kuta's **accommodation** has something for all tastes and pockets, from simple budget places through mid-range options to the luxury *Novotel Lombok*. In Kuta itself, the road runs about 50m inland from the beach; accommodation is spread for about 500m on the far side of the road, so don't expect cottages on the beach. There are also places in the village.

**Anda** ☎0370/654836. This is a good budget choice; all rooms are clean and tiled, with fans and mosquito nets, and set in a shady garden setting on the road along the beach. **1**

**G'day Inn** ☎0370/655342. Five well-kept rooms with attached bathrooms in a friendly family compound in the village. **1**

**Kuta Indah** ☎0370/653781, ⓕ654628. Located

at the western end of the bay with fan rooms at the bottom end and hot water and air-con at the top. There's a good garden and excellent pool. Depending which room you're in, there's free or discounted transport to Tanjung Aan and Mawun beaches. **5**–**6**

**Lamancha Homestay** ☎ & ⓕ0370/655186. Family place in the village, a short walk from the beach comprising three rooms with attached mandi and squat toilet. **❶**

🏃 **Mimpi Manis** ☎ 081/836 9950, 🌐 www
.mimpimanis.com. Just over 1.5km north of the
beach on the way to Sade, this spotless place is run
by a Balinese–English family. Choose between air-con
or fan rooms or a two-storey house; bathrooms have
cold-water shower and Western toilet. Rooms also
have DVD players and an extensive choice of films. **❷**

🏃 **Novotel Lombok** ☎ 0370/653333, 🌐 www
.novotel-lombok.com. Stunningly located
3km east of Kuta on the fabulous Seger beach,
this is the only luxury development along this
coast. Accommodation is in low-rise buildings or
bungalows in lovely grounds with four pools. All
rooms have garden rather than ocean views; you'll
pay more for an outside veranda. The top-end villas
are glorious. It's a fairly isolated spot, but there are
several bars and restaurants, a business centre, a
dive centre, plenty of organized activities, and a
wonderful spa above the beach. **❽–❾**

**Puri Rinjani** ☎ 0370/654849, 🖷 654852. Six
rooms in a big garden; all are clean and tiled, with

cold water. There's one room with air-con. **❷**

🏃 **Segare Anak** ☎ & 🖷 0370/654846,
🖃 segaranakcottage@hotmail.com. Set in
the middle of the accommodation strip along the
beach road, this long-standing favourite has a big
choice of rooms set in a lovely garden. Safe deposit
boxes are available. **❶–❷**

**Sekar Kuning** ☎ 0370/654856. There are a few
very cheap, very basic rooms; however, with new
building going on in the compound, quality and
prices may well rise. **❶**

**Surfer's Inn** ☎ 0370/655582, 🖃 lombok_
hotel@yahoo.com. Surrounded by an unmissable
pink wall, this new place has rooms ranged around
a pretty pool. All have cold water, and there's a
choice of fan or air-con. **❷–❻**

**Tastura Beach Resort** ☎ 0370/655540,
🖃 tastura@mataram.wasantara.net.id. Bungalows
are widely spaced in a huge garden with a good
pool. All rooms have air-con, hot water and lovely
deep verandas. Negotiate discounts up to sixty
percent. **❼–❽**

## Eating, drinking and entertainment

All Kuta's losmen have **restaurants** attached, offering inexpensive or moderately priced travellers' fare; seafood is the speciality. *Puri Rinjani* has well-cooked
food, *Segare Anak* a vast menu, while *Warung Melati* and *Biota* at the eastern end
of the beach strip offer the best beach views. In the village, *Lombok Lounge* is a
friendly little place near *Kuta Indah*. For stunning views, *Ashtari* 🏃, at the top of
the hill on the road west from Kuta, is unbeatable.

Nobody comes to Kuta for the **nightlife**, which is just as well, as there isn't
any, although you may find some live music in the high season. Alternatively, if
you've a TV in your hotel room you can rent a DVD player (and get unlimited
access to their exhaustive DVD collection) from *Mimpi Manis* for Rp25,000 a
night (refundable deposit of Rp250,000).

## Listings

**Books** Big second-hand book selection at *Mimpi
Manis*.

**Changing money** *Kuta Indah* and *Segare Anak*
bungalows change money.

**Charter transport** Ask at your accommodation or
at *Segare Anak*. It costs around Rp250,000 per day
for a car (including driver and fuel). Motorcycles are
available at *Mimpi Manis* at Rp30,000 per day, but
there's no insurance in Kuta. Decent cycles cost
Rp20,000 per day from *Mimpi Manis* or *Segare
Anak*.

**Internet access** Available in *Segare Anak* and
*Anda* (Rp400–500/min).

**Phones** There are wartels in the village (daily
7am–10pm) and at *Segare Anak* (7am–9pm).

**Post** *Segare Anak* is a postal agent and you can use
them for poste restante; get mail addressed to you
at *Segare Anak*, Kuta Beach, Lombok Tengah, Nusa
Tenggara Barat 83573. The nearest post office is in
Sengkol.

**Shuttle bus tickets** *Segare Anak* are Perama
agents.

## Inland from Kuta

The traditional village of **SADE**, 6km north of Kuta, is a stop on most day-trips
to the south of the island. It lies close to the Kuta–Sengkol road and is used to

visitors (donation expected).Young lads will offer to guide you; they speak good enough English to explain all the delights, such as the buffalo-dung foundations of the houses. It's certainly picturesque, and the *lumbung* barns and traditional houses are faithfully preserved, but it does feel a bit like a theme park and you'll be approached to buy things or to take photographs of people – all at a price.

Just up the road, 2km to the north, **REMBITAN** seems less artificial and is close to a site of Muslim pilgrimage. One of the Nine Walis believed to have brought Islam to Indonesia is supposedly buried here at **MAKAM NYATO**, and on Wednesdays pilgrims come to worship at the grave, shaded by frangipani and banyan trees. Rembitan is regarded in some quarters as having the oldest mosque on the island (although Bayan in the north is more widely accepted to have that honour; see p.416). About fifteen years ago, there was a big fire near the ancient mosque. It did not burn, however, and children later reported having seen figures clad in white surrounding and protecting the building. The belief in the mystical properties of the mosque grew, and when the roof was repaired many local people took part of the old one as protection for their homes.

There are a couple of **batik workshops** on the road between Sade and Rembitan: at Telage Art Shop and Rembitan Sasak Art Gallery (both daily 8am–6pm), you can watch batik painting in progress. The variety of images is huge, including classical characters from the *Ramayana*, primitive motifs, traditional scenes and a huge selection of modern designs. Prices range from about Rp80,000 for the small pieces up to Rp650,000 or more for the biggest – but you do need to bargain.

## West of Kuta

Along the coast **west of Kuta** you can explore some of the loveliest beaches on the island, backed by rolling hills and tiny villages. However, bemos are rare, so you'll need your own transport. There are few signs and not many landmarks, so be prepared for a leisurely trip and some wrong turnings. The road deteriorates the further west you go – west of Keling was barely passable in late 2004; check the state it's in before setting off. Allow at least four hours travelling time for the trip from Kuta around to Sekotong, southwest of Lembar.

The road out of Kuta, past *Kuta Indah*, climbs up steeply for a couple of kilometres. The views from the *Ashtari* restaurant at the top of the hill back across the entire Kuta area is one of the most dramatic in southern Lombok.

Some 5km out of Kuta you'll pass the "MTR 64" road marker (indicating 64km to Mataram). Just under 1km west of this, look out for a dirt track heading off to the coast. After 2km, it reaches the coastal village of **ARE GOLENG**. The beach here is about 400m long, and the seaweed beds in the shallows are clearly visible. A tiny island, **Gili Nungsa**, sits out in the bay, with an attractive little beach visible from the shore. Villagers' huts line the area just behind the beach; wend your way east through the coconut grove for a few hundred metres to find a more secluded part of the bay.

The next beach west is **Mawun**, 8km from Kuta and reached by a five-hundred-metre-long sealed road a couple of hundred metres beyond the "MTR 66" marker. The bay is almost semicircular, enclosed on both sides by rocky headlands, with the water fading from turquoise to a deep, vibrant blue, enhanced by the white of the waves crashing onto the rocks on either side. Don't expect this paradise to be deserted: there are usually a few other tourists here. You'll pay Rp4000 for parking a car, Rp2000 for motorbikes, and there are cold-drink sellers plying their wares.

About 3km further west, the main road reaches the coast and runs a few hundred metres inland from the gently curving **Tampa** beach. The beach is backed by flat scrub and there isn't much shade – but it's pretty deserted.

Access to the beach at **Mawi**, about 4km west of Tampa, isn't easy. Take the next sealed road branching off seaward (if you reach the "MTR 75" marker, you've gone too far). After 1.5km it ends in a stand of banana, coconut and kapok trees with a couple of houses. It's a few hundred metres' walk to the lovely white-sand beach, a favourite with surfers, and separated from nearby **Rowok** by a rocky outcrop. From here, there are great views, plus the impressive sight of Gili Lawang – three pinnacles sticking sheer out of the ocean.

### Selong Blanak and around

Back on the road, after 1.5km you reach **SELONG BLANAK**, 15km from Kuta, also accessible via Penujak from Praya (24km). The bay here is a fabulous curving beach a couple of kilometres long with rocky headlands at each end. There are superb views west along the coast, and it's popular with local people on Sundays and holidays when the local lads enjoy motorcycle racing along the sand while families feast at the nearby food and drink stalls. For a more peaceful location, the two beaches visible to the west are **Tomangomang**, nearest to Selong Blanak, and **Serangan**, both accessible by tracks.

From Selong Blanak, the road west to Pengantap curves 18km inland and is a bit of an adventure. It climbs up very steeply into the coastal hills through mahogany and teak stands with fine views of the surrounding countryside. About 3km from Selong Blanak it reaches the tiny village of **KELING** where it splits. The right fork leads north to Penujak while the left fork continues on westwards through tiny hamlets of bamboo and thatch houses, reaching the village of **Montong Sapah** after another 6km. The road surface deteriorates the further west you get but the views on the descent back to the coast make the whole enterprise worthwhile, with fabulous panoramas spread out ahead. Another 9km brings you to the village of **PENGANG-TAP**, a row of thatched houses just behind the beach. This is a working beach and the turquoise shallows are filled with the frames for seaweed farming as the harvest dries on the beach. From Pengangtap, the road again curves away from the coast, arriving at **SEPI** after 5km, another tiny coastal hamlet, which is served by bemos from Lembar via Sekotong, and by trucks east to Keling. There's accommodation at *PS Bungalows* (❼, full board), which have fans and cold-water bathrooms in a totally rural spot. Book through Dream Divers in Senggigi (see p.399), who can also arrange transport for $25 per person return. From Sepi, you can continue 1km west to **BLON-GAS**, where there's good snorkelling, diving and surfing and equally isolated accommodation at *Belongas Bay Lodge* (℡0370/693690 or 086812/104135; ❽) located just behind the beach, with its own generator for fans and hot water. There's a choice of the lodge or smaller bungalows, and full board is available. They have an information and booking office in Senggigi just opposite *Sudirman*. Transport can be arranged here, too. The "road" (here, no more than a rough, impassable track most of the time) heads west from here to Teluk Mekaki before curving north to Pelangan on the north coast of the southwest peninsula (see p.394).

Alternatively, follow the steep road that climbs northwards from Sepi through the coastal hills. The road very gradually improves, the density of population increases and, after 11km, you reach Sekotong where you can turn west to Bangko Bangko or north to Lembar.

## East of Kuta

The glorious beaches of **Seger** and **Tanjung Aan** are easily accessible from Kuta and, at a push, walkable if you have no transport (bicycles are a good idea). Seger is closest to Kuta (1km) and is now the location of the luxury *Novotel Lombok*. Tanjung Aan, 5km from Kuta, comprises two perfect white-sand beaches, **Aan** to the west and **Pedau** to the east, separated by a rocky outcrop, Batu Kotak. As their popularity has grown, the beaches now host hawkers and drinks stalls, but no other facilities.

Past Tanjung Aan, the small fishing village of **GERUPAK**, just under 8km from Kuta, perches on the western shores of Gumbang Bay. **Lobster** is one of the local specialities and buyers come here from all the big hotels on Lombok and sometimes from Bali. Seaweed is the other main source of income (see p.262 for information on seaweed farming). *Kelapa Bungalows* (☎0818/545034; ❶), on the road in from Kuta, about 300m before the beach, are wood, bamboo and thatch, with mattresses on the floor, but they have attached bathrooms and fans and are set in a large garden. It's a ten- to fifteen-minute walk to nearby Molok beach and a slightly longer walk to Tanjung Aan. Bungalows in this spot seem to come and go; you'd do well to check they're open before lugging your stuff out. There are bemos (Rp2000) or ojek (Rp5000) from Kuta. At Gerupak, the *Surfer's Café* is right on the edge of the beach and catches a great breeze.

From Gerupak, there are fine views across the bay to **BUMBANG** on the eastern shore, and you can rent a boat for sightseeing in the bay (Rp50,000 per boat for two people for two hours, Rp20,000 for each additional person). The more adventurous can charter a boat around to Ekas from here (Rp200,000 for a day-trip for two people), which takes at least an hour each way.

The thriving fishing village of **AWANG**, 16km east of Kuta, is well worth the trip for the views of **Awang Bay**, a massive inlet, 10km long and 8km wide in parts. As the road descends into the village, you'll be able to spot the island of Linus, just off Batu Nampar at the northern end of the bay, the tiny settlement of Ekas across on the southeast peninsula, and see all the way south to the open sea. You can charter boats from Awang across to Ekas, a much easier option than tackling the rough roads (Rp100,000–150,000 each way). Wooden bugis-style houses on stilts line the shore, and the bay is full of boats of all shapes and sizes, from large ocean-going fishing vessels down to tiny dugout canoes. The **beach** here spreads magnificently both north and south from the village, and on the way down into Awang the view is stunning.

# The southeast peninsula

Lombok's isolated **southeast peninsula** is worth exploring for the startling scenery of Awang Bay, the totally rural lifestyle of the villagers down here, the rarity of visitors making the trip and the fact that this is as far off the beaten track as it is possible to get on Lombok. There's only one place to stay, but exploring the area properly isn't feasible on a day-trip or on public transport. The only road to the peninsula leaves the southern main road at **SEPAPAN**, about 500m west of Keruak, and is signposted to "Jerowaru, Tanjung Ringgit, Kaliantan and *Heaven on the Planet*". There is a petrol station on the main road about 400m west of the turning to the peninsula. Make sure you fill up with fuel before leaving the main road, and bear in mind that travel is slow, as the road surfaces deteriorate the further south you go.

The first village, after about 3km, is **JEROWARU**, where the road splits – turn right at the southern end of the village, 4km from the main road. The landscape is dry and scrubby but with some glimpses of the east coast as the road completes a dogleg around it. To continue south, turn left after another 1.5km at the Masjid Al-Muntaha mosque in the village of Tutuk. Carry on south to the village of Pemongkang and head on through it. South of the village, just over 5km from the turn by the mosque, there's a major junction. Signs point left to Tanjung Ringgit and Pantai Cemara and right to Ekas and Pantai Surga.

Following the Ekas road, after another 6km, *Heaven on the Planet* (☏0812/370 5393, ⓦwww.heavenontheplanet.co.nz; ❸–❻), the only accommodation on the peninsula, is signed off the main road, way up on a cliff with footpaths to two local beaches; the track to the hotel is diabolical: steep, rutted and rocky. There's a range of accommodation, from small bungalows with outside bathroom, to bigger ones with attached bathrooms offering better views, up to a large bungalow with an attached lounge, a DVD player and the most remarkable views from its veranda. Booking is essential, and transport can be arranged from Senggigi. Access to the hotel is only by boat from Awang in the rainy season and more comfortable by that route at any time. There's an attached moderately priced restaurant, and snorkelling and diving are available. Motorbikes are available for rent. The local dive site is Walls of Heaven, an underwater cliff dropping sheer to 50m. Nearby, at the tiny fishing village of **EKAS**, built just behind the shoreline, people make their living from fishing and seaweed farming. A few **bemos** link Ekas and the main road at Sepapan, but they're very irregular.

Down towards the southern tip of the peninsula the road splits again, right to **KALIANTAN** and left to **SEREWE**, both tiny fishing and seaweed-farming villages. There are good views around the coast, but they don't compare with the grand panorama you get from Ekas.

Taking the left fork back at Pemongang, the road to **TANJUNG RINGGIT**, the southeastern tip of Lombok, is long and rough, and you'll need to check en route to be sure of finding the right turning – consider renting a boat from Tanjung Luar on the east coast (see p.432) rather than endure the drive. Tanjung Ringgit is reputed to be a magical place, with large caves believed to be the home of a demon. There are some startling coastal views, including across to Sumbawa, which appears very close from here, and some old canons from World War II, but the long trek back the way you've come is the only option at the end of the day.

# Travel details

## Buses and bemos

It's almost impossible to give the frequency with which bemos and public buses run: see Basics, p.49, for details. Journey times given are the minimum you can expect. Only direct bemo and bus routes are listed.

**Ampenan** to: Senggigi (20min).

**Bertais/Mandalika/Sweta terminal** to: Bayan (for Gunung Rinjani; 2hr 30min); Bima (Sumbawa; 12hr); Denpasar (Bali; 6–8hr); Dompu (Sumbawa; 10hr); Jakarta (Java; 32hr); Labuanbajo (Flores; 24hr); Labuhan Lombok (2hr); Lembar (30min);

Pemenang (for the Gili Islands; 50min); Pomotong (for Tetebatu; 1hr 15min); Praya (for Kuta; 30min); Ruteng (Flores; 36hr); Sape (Flores; 14hr); Sumbawa Besar (Sumbawa; 6hr); Surabaya (Java; 20hr); Yogyakarta (Java; 22hr).

**Labuhan Lombok** to: Bayan (2hr); Bertais/Mandalika/Sweta terminal (2hr); Kopang (for Praya; 1hr); Sembalun Lawang (2hr 30min).

**Lembar** to: Bertais/Mandalika/Sweta terminal (30min); Sekotong (1hr); Selegang (3hr); Taun (2hr); Tembowong (2hr 30min).

**Praya** to: Bertais/Mandalika/Sweta terminal (30min); Gubukdalam (1hr 30min); Kuta (1hr).

**Sapit** to: Aik Mel (1hr); Pringgabaya (1hr); Sembalun Lawang (2hr).

**Sembalun Lawang** to: Bayan (3hr); Labuhan Lombok (3hr); Sapit (2hr).

**Senggigi** to: Ampenan (20min).

## Perama shuttle buses

*STO = overnight stopover is needed*

**Mataram** to: Bedugul (Bali; daily; STO); Candi Dasa (Bali; daily; 5hr–5hr 30min); Kuta, Bali/Ngurah Rai Airport (Bali; daily; 8hr 30min); Lovina (Bali; daily; STO); Padang Bai (Bali; daily; 4hr 30min–5hr); Sanur (Bali; daily; 8hr); Senggigi (daily; 30min); Ubud (Bali; daily; 8hr).

**Senggigi** to: Bedugul (Bali; daily; STO); Candi Dasa (Bali; daily; 5hr–5hr 30min); Kuta, Bali/Ngurah Rai Airport (Bali; daily; 8hr 30min); Lovina (Bali; daily; STO); Padang Bai (Bali; daily; 4hr 30min–5hr); Sanur (Bali; daily; 8hr); Mataram (daily; 30min); Ubud (Bali; daily; 8hr).

**Gili Islands** to: Bedugul (Bali; daily; STO); Candi Dasa (Bali; daily; 5hr–5hr 30min); Kuta, Bali/Ngurah Rai Airport (Bali; daily; 8hr 30min); Lovina (Bali; daily; STO); Padang Bai (Bali; daily; 4hr 30min–5hr); Sanur (Bali; daily; 8hr); Mataram (daily; 30min); Senggigi (daily; 2hr); Ubud (Bali; daily; 8hr).

## Perama shuttle boat

**Senggigi** to: Padang Bai (Bali; daily; 4–5hr); Gili Islands (daily; 2hr).

## Pelni ferries

**Lembar** Fortnightly services to:

*KM Awu:* Ende (Flores; 34hr); Kalabahi (Alor; 59hr);

Kupang (Timor; 46hr); Larantuka (Flores; 7D+2hr); Makassar (Sulawesi; 95hr); Maumere (Flores; 72hr); Nunukan (Kalimantan; 6D+20hr); Parepare (Sulawesi; 4D+18hr); Tarakan (Kalimantan; 6D+12hr); Waingapu (Sumba; 24hr).

*KM Tilongkabila:* Baubau (Sulawesi; 61hr); Benoa (Bali; 4hr); Bima (Flores; 15hr); Bitung (Sulawesi; 4D+20hr); Kendari (Sulawesi; 3D+1hr); Kolonedale (Sulawesi; 3D+20hr); Labuanbajo (Flores; 24hr); Luwuk (Sulawesi; 4D+1hr); Makassar (Sulawesi; 37hr); Raha (Sulawesi; 66hr).

## Other ferries

**Bangsal** to: Gili Islands (several times daily; 20–45min).

**Gili Air** to: Bangsal (daily; 20min); Gili Meno (daily; 20min); Gili Trawangan (daily; 40min).

**Gili Meno** to: Bangsal (daily; 30min); Gili Air (daily; 20min); Gili Trawangan (daily; 20min).

**Gili Trawangan** to: Bangsal (daily; 45min); Gili Air (daily; 40min); Gili Meno (daily; 20min).

**Labuhan Lombok** to: Poto Tano (Sumbawa; every hour; 1hr 30min).

**Lembar** to: Padang Bai (Bali; every 90min; 4hr–4hr 30min).

**Senggigi** to: Gili Islands (2 daily; 2hr); Padang Bai (Bali; daily; 4–5hr).

## Planes

**Selaparang Airport** (Mataram) to: Denpasar (Bali; 12 daily; 30min); Jakarta (Java; daily; 3hr); Singapore (6 weekly; 2hr 30min); Surabaya (Java; 4 daily; 50min); Yogyakarta (Java; daily; 1hr 15min).

# Contexts

# Contexts

# History

Two tiny islands, Bali and Lombok have been buffeted by powerful empires throughout their history, and their fortunes have often been tied to those of their larger neighbours, Java and Sumbawa. Relations between Bali and Lombok have been uneasy at the best of times, but more often turbulent and bloody. The origins of their present cultural, religious and economic differences are firmly rooted in past events.

## Beginnings

**Homo erectus**, a distant ancestor of modern man, lived in Indonesia around half a million years ago during the Ice Ages. Fossilized bones of "Java Man" from this period were found in Central Java and stone axes and adzes have been discovered on Bali.

As the earth cooled during the **Ice Ages**, glaciers advanced from the polar regions and the levels of the oceans fell. Many of the islands of Indonesia became joined to the land masses of Southeast Asia and Australia by exposed **land bridges** across which the early humans moved. There were two main routes into Indonesia from the mainland: one down through Thailand into Malaysia, the other via the Philippines.

**Homo sapiens** appeared around 40,000 years ago, hunter-gatherers who lived in caves, and whose rock paintings have been found on some of the far eastern islands of the archipelago. The **Neolithic** era, around 3000 BC, is marked by the appearance of more sophisticated stone tools, agricultural techniques and basic pottery. Remains from this period have been found at Cekik, in the far west of Bali.

From the seventh or eighth centuries BC, the **Bronze Age** began to spread south from southern China. Famed for their bronze casting, decorated drums have been found throughout the Indonesian archipelago, as have the stone moulds used in their production. The most famous example in Bali, and the largest drum found anywhere in Southeast Asia, is the **Moon of Pejeng**, nearly 2m wide, housed in a temple just east of Ubud. Discoveries of carved **stone sarcophagi** from this period are on display in the Bali Museum in Denpasar and the Museum Arkeologi in Pejeng.

## Early traders and empires

From at least 200 BC, **trade** was a feature of life across the archipelago. The earliest written records in Bali, metal inscriptions or prasasti dating from the ninth century AD, reveal significant Buddhist and Hindu influence from the Indian subcontinent, shown also by the statues, bronzes and rock-cut caves at Gunung Kawi and Goa Gajah.

The most famous event in early Balinese history occurred towards the end of the tenth century when a princess of East Java, Princess **Mahendratta**, married the Balinese king **Udayana**. Their marriage portrait is believed to be depicted in a stone in the Pura Tegeh Koripan near Kintamani. Their son, **Erlangga**, born around 991 AD, later brought the two realms together until his death in 1049.

In the following centuries, the ties between Bali and Java fluctuated. In 1284, Kertanegara, the ruler of the Singasari empire in Java, conquered Bali for a time, but by the turn of the century Bali was again being ruled domestically, by **King Bedaulu**, based in the Pejeng district, east of Ubud.

Little is known of the ancient history of **Lombok**, which was divided into kingdoms, although it is known that the kingdom of Selaparang controlled an area in the east of the island for a period.

## The Majapahit

One of the most significant dates in Balinese history is 1343 AD, when the island was colonized by **Gajah Mada**, the prime minister of the powerful Hindu **Majapahit** kingdom of East Java. Establishing a court at Samprangan in eastern Bali, and granting lands to members of the aristocracy, the first Majapahit ruler of Bali was **Sri Dalem Kapakisan**. This brought about massive changes in Balinese society, including the introduction of the caste system. Balinese who did not accept these changes established their own villages in remote areas. Their descendants, known as the **Bali Aga** or *Bali Mula*, the "original Balinese", still live in separate villages, such as Tenganan near Candi Dasa and Trunyan on the shores of Danau Batur, and adhere to ancient traditions.

Kapakisan was succeeded by his son, **Dewa Ketut Ngulesir**, who set up his court in **Gelgel**, in east Bali. Throughout the fifteenth century, the power of the Majapahit empire on Java declined as the influence of Islam expanded. It finally fell in 1515, and the many small Islamic kingdoms in Java coalesced into the Islamic Mataram empire. Many Hindu followers of the Majapahit – priests, craftsmen, soldiers, nobles and artists – fled east to Bali, flooding the island with **Javanese cultural ideas** and reaffirming Hindu practices.

Given the huge influence of **Islam** at this time, it is unclear why the faith did not spread to Bali, especially as it moved further east to Lombok, Sulawesi and Maluku. One reason could be that the religion spread along trade routes: with poor harbours and few resources, Bali was largely bypassed and the tide of Islam swept east, although there are small Muslim communities on the island.

An ancient text detailing the history of the Majapahit dynasty lists **Lombok** as part of its empire, and the villages in the Sembalun valley on the eastern flanks of Gunung Rinjani consider themselves directly descended from the Majapahit dynasty, claiming that the brother of a Majapahit raja is buried in the valley.

### Bali's Golden Age

Dewa Ketut Ngulesir was succeeded by his eldest son, **Batu Renggong**, who became king, or **dewa agung** (literally meaning "great god"), in 1550. The title of *dewa agung* continued through the succeeding generations of the Gelgel, and later Klungkung, dynasty until the twentieth century. During Batu Renggong's reign, the Gelgel kingdom achieved remarkable military successes, from Blambangan in Java in the west to Sumbawa in the east. This period coincided with a cultural renaissance in Bali and, as a result, is often referred to as the **Golden Age**. The Javanese Hindu priest **Nirartha**, who encouraged the renaissance, achieved a great following on Bali.

Gradually, the glory faded. Batu Renggong's grandson, **Di Made Bekung**, lost Blambangan, Lombok and Sumbawa. Eventually, the chief minister, Gusti Agung Maruti, rebelled against Bekung, who fled and died in exile. Gusti Agung Maruti reigned from 1650 to 1686, eventually being killed by Di Made Bekung's son, **Dewa Agung Jambe**, who moved the court to **Klungkung**, calling his new palace the Semarapura (Abode of the God of Love).

As the Golden Age faded other kingdoms within Bali rose to prominence, most notably **Gianyar** under Dewa Manggis Kuning in 1667.

# Foreigners and trade

Lacking the spices of the eastern isles, Bali appears not to have been in the mainstream of the archipelago's early trading history. The **Chinese** visited Bali, which they knew as Paoli or Rice Island, in the seventh century, but by this time trade had been established on nearby islands for a thousand years. Bali became known to **Europeans** at the end of the fifteenth century when numerous Portuguese, Spanish and English explorers came in search of the lucrative Spice Islands. They marked Bali on their maps as Balle, Ilha Bale or Java Minor, but rarely stopped, although Sir Francis Drake is reported to have visited in 1580.

During the sixteenth century, the Balinese first came into contact with Europeans. The **Portuguese**, having won the race for the Spice Islands, turned their eyes towards Bali, and in 1588 dispatched a ship from Malacca, aiming to construct a fort and trading post on the island. The ship hit a reef just off Bali and sank with huge loss of life. The survivors were treated kindly by the *dewa agung* but not permitted to leave the island. Portuguese attempts at establishing contact were not repeated.

On April 2, 1595, four **Dutch** ships under the command of Commodore Cornelius Houtman left northern Holland to explore the east. His ships anchored off Bali and three sailors landed at Kuta on February 9, 1597, for reconnaissance, including Aernoudt Lintgens, whose report of his experiences is the first account by a Westerner of the island. The other two crew members were so entranced that they did not return to the ship. One eventually returned to Holland, but the other settled permanently in Bali.

The second visit by the Dutch came in 1601, when Cornelis Heemskerk arrived with an official letter from the prince of Holland requesting **formal trade relations**. The *dewa agung* replied on a *lontar* palm letter accepting friendly relations between the countries and agreeing to mutual trade. The VOC, or **Dutch East India Company**, was formed in 1602, and its head-quarters founded in Batavia (modern-day Jakarta) in 1619, from where the Dutch trading empire expanded as far afield as Sumatra, Borneo, Makassar and the Moluccas.

In 1633, the Dutch sent a mission to Bali offering the *dewa agung* assistance in his fight against the kingdom of Mataram in Java, but the *dewa agung* rejected their overtures.

From then on until the beginning of the nineteenth century, Bali was largely ignored by Europe, as it produced little of interest to outsiders. The exception was **slaves**, who were sold by the princes of the island through the port of Kuta to Dutch merchants from Batavia and French merchants from Mauritius.

# The situation in Lombok

During the seventeenth century, Lombok came under influence from the **Balinese** and the **Makassarese** of Sulawesi. The Balinese from Karangasem, in the far east of Bali, arrived in the early seventeenth century across the Lombok Strait, and settled in the west of Lombok, gradually achieving political control over the area. At roughly the same time, the Makassarese, who had conquered Sumbawa in 1618, invaded the east of the island. The first major conflicts between the two invaders occurred in 1677 when the Balinese, assisted by the indigenous **Sasak** aristocracy, defeated the Makassarese.

From the end of the seventeenth to the mid-nineteenth century, the Balinese struggled to secure control over Lombok. In 1775, **Gusti Wayan Tegah**, who had been placed on the throne by the raja of Karangasem, died, and disagreements over the succession by his two sons led to the formation of two rival principalities in the west, with further disputes around 1800 leading to more splits. By the beginning of the nineteenth century, there were four rival Balinese principalities vying for control: Pagasangan, Pagutan, Mataram and Cakranegara. With their Balinese overlords fighting among themselves, the Sasak aristocracy in the east of the island faced little interference in their affairs.

In 1838, the Balinese factions were reunited when the raja of Mataram, **Ratu Agung K'tut**, who had already conquered Pagasangan and Pagutan, moved against Cakranegara, which was supported by the enterprising Danish trader **Mads Lange**. With Lange unable to prevent the supply of reinforcements for Mataram crossing the Lombok Strait from Karangasem, Ratu Agung K'tut eventually triumphed, and brought the east of Lombok under his control.

His greatest victory occurred in 1849. The Dutch, at that time involved in their Third Military Expedition against Bali, wanted to move against the east Balinese kingdom of Karangasem. Providing four thousand troops to supplement the Dutch, Ratu Agung K'tut ensured the defeat of the ruling dynasty in Karangasem and, in payment for his help, won the right to put his own nominee on the throne.

## European turmoil and Dutch interest

Conflicts in Europe at the turn of the nineteenth century had massive repercussions in Bali. In 1795, **French** troops under Napoleon successfully invaded the Netherlands, thus acquiring **Dutch** possessions overseas. By the turn of the century, the Dutch colonies in Southeast Asia were under the control of a governor-general appointed by Napoleon. This governor was subsequently defeated by the **British**, who had their own interests in the area to protect, and in 1811 the British also defeated the Dutch forces in Java. The British Lieutenant-Governor of Java, **Sir Thomas Stamford Raffles**, administered the region, but British rule in the area was short-lived. Napoleon was defeated at Waterloo in 1815 and, as part of the peace settlement, the Indies were returned to the Dutch.

## Dutch incursions

By the mid-1830s, Dutch concerns had become political. The Danish trader **Mads Lange** had set up a trading post in Kuta; this trade, to which the Dutch were not party, was largely in rice, which both Bali and Lombok produced to excess, and it was traded directly with British-held Singapore. The Dutch evolved a plan to start trading with Bali, with the aim of gaining political control before the British. They visited Badung and Klungkung and, in 1839, established an agent in Kuta with the agreement of the raja of Badung. In 1840, the Dutch envoy, **Huskus Koopman**, began a series of visits with the aim of persuading the Balinese to agree to Dutch sovereignty over the island.

Another major Dutch aim was to resolve the issue of *tawan karang* or reef rights, which had caused them long-term grievance. The Balinese had always asserted their right to goods salvaged from shipping wrecked on the island's reefs, much of which was Dutch. The plundering of the Dutch vessel *Overijssel*, wrecked on the Kuta reef on July 19, 1841, particularly outraged the Dutch.

By 1843, Koopman, a skilled operator, had made **treaties** with the regencies of Badung, Klungkung, Buleleng, Karangasem and Tabanan, agreeing to a Dutch trade monopoly. The rajas failed to realize that they had also agreed to give the Dutch sovereignty over their lands and to abolish reef rights. Following Koopman's retirement, a new commissioner arrived in 1844 to finalize the treaties, but it soon became apparent that there were huge differences in Dutch and Balinese understandings. Most regencies did ratify the treaties, but **Buleleng** and **Karangasem** stood firm. A further Dutch mission came the following year, including a military officer whose brief was to assess the Buleleng defences. At a meeting in Singaraja in May 1845, Gusti Ketut Jelantik, brother of the rajas of Buleleng and Karangasem, stated, "Not by a mere scrap of paper shall any man become the master of another's lands. Rather let the kris decide." The Dutch returned to Java.

## Dutch military victory

On June 26, 1846, the **First Dutch Military Expedition** arrived off the Buleleng coast with 3500 men and issued an ultimatum to the raja of Buleleng to comply with all the Dutch demands. On June 28, the military force landed and marched into Singaraja to find it deserted, the Balinese troops having withdrawn to the village of Jagaraga. The rajas of Buleleng and Karangasem came to Singaraja to negotiate with the Dutch and eventually signed a surrender, agreeing to Dutch sovereignty and to paying costs for the victor's military expedition.

The Dutch departed, believing they had achieved their objectives, and left behind a small garrison until the compensation was paid. However, this fitted in with Jelantik's plan, and he continued to prepare for future battle. Meanwhile, nothing was paid to the Dutch, and ships that foundered continued to be plundered by the Balinese. On March 7, 1848, the governor-general of the Dutch East Indies sent ultimatums to Buleleng, Karangasem and Klungkung demanding compensation, payment of war debts, the destruction of defence works and, in the case of Buleleng, the delivery of Jelantik to them. The ultimatums were ignored, and the **Second Dutch Military Expedition** arrived off the northern coast at Sangsit on June 8, 1848, with almost three thousand troops. Having quickly overcome the defences on the coast, the well-armed force marched towards **Jagaraga** where Jelantik had organized his army of around 16,000, armed largely with kris and lances. The Dutch were eventually put to flight, at a cost of around two hundred dead and wounded. The Balinese suffered over two thousand casualties but on June 10, 1848, the Dutch sailed back to Batavia.

The following year, in the **Third Dutch Military Expedition**, the Dutch used almost their entire military force in the Indies to overcome the Balinese. Around seven thousand troops landed in Buleleng on April 4, 1849. The Balinese asked to negotiate and despatched 12,000 troops in full military uniform for the meeting at Singaraja between the rajas of Buleleng and Karangasem and General Michiels, the commander-in-chief of the expedition. Both this meeting and a later one at Sangsit on April 13 failed to reach any agreement. On April 15, the Dutch attacked the fortress at Jagaraga and defeated the Balinese with the loss of only about thirty men to the Balinese thousands.

Jelantik and the rajas of Buleleng and Karangasem fled east to continue the fight from there, while the Dutch set up new headquarters at Padang Bai. With four thousand additional troops from Lombok, the Dutch decided to attack Karangasem first. On their arrival at the palace on May 20, the raja of Karangasem, Gusti Gde Ngurah Karangasem, his family, and followers, all committed **puputan** (ritual suicide). The raja of Buleleng, accompanied by Jelantik, fled to the mountains of Seraya, where they were killed in further fighting.

Dutch troops then headed west towards Klungkung, with the village of Kusamba their first objective. However, the Balinese still occupied the surrounding villages and, during the night of May 25, they attacked, mortally wounding General Michiels. This episode is known as the **Kusamba War**. The death of Michiels from what is generally regarded as a non-fatal injury is ascribed to the influence of a magical bullet, **I Seliksik**, today an heirloom of the rajas of Klungkung.

With demoralized, sick and massively outnumbered troops reluctant to march against the *dewa agung* in Klungkung, Mads Lange was employed as go-between, and an **agreement** was drawn up on July 13, 1849. The Balinese recognized Dutch sovereignty and accepted that *tawan karang* was prohibited, and in return the Dutch agreed to leave the rajas to administer their kingdoms and not to base garrisons in the areas they had conquered. A feast on July 15 put the seal on the agreement.

## The strengthening of the Dutch position

Initially, the Dutch left matters pretty much alone. However, during the 1850s they strengthened their hold and placed Dutch controllers over the rajas of Buleleng and Jembrana.

From their administrative capital in **Singaraja**, the Dutch made some improvements to irrigation, planted coffee as a cash crop and outlawed slavery and the tradition of *suttee*, whereby widows would throw themselves on the funeral pyres of their dead husbands. Further military expeditions quelled **local rebellions**, such as one in 1864 when Ida Made Rai led an uprising in the village of Banjar, close to modern-day Lovina.

Meanwhile, with the Dutch concentrated in the north, the internal politics in the **south** of the island grew extremely complex. The kingdoms of Klungkung, Badung, Gianyar, Mengwi, Bangli and Tabanan were all weakened by internal conflicts and fighting with each other. They turned more and more to the Dutch, seeking protection to save themselves from extinction by their neighbours.

### Rebellion and the Dutch in Lombok

In Lombok, meanwhile, Ratu Agung K'tut continued to rule until his death in 1872, when he was succeeded by his younger brother, **Ratu Agung Ngurah**.

In the **west** of the island, relations were relatively harmonious, but in the **east** the situation was different: Balinese power had been re-established only in the 1840s and the frustrated Sasak aristocracy deeply resented their Balinese masters. There were rebellions in 1855 and 1871, which the Balinese quashed, but the **rebellion of 1891** proved more serious. For many years, Ratu Agung Ngurah had vied with the *dewa agung* of the Balinese kingdom of Klungkung over claims to the title of Supreme Ruler of Bali. In 1891, he decided to take action, but his demand for several thousand Sasak troops was met with resistance in **Praya**, and a local Sasak aristocrat was executed. On August 7, 1891, several thousand Sasaks surrounded and burned the palace of the Balinese district chief. A huge force of West Lombok troops was sent to the scene but the rebellion could not be crushed. It quickly spread and by September 22, 1891, Balinese rule had been overthrown throughout East Lombok.

At this point, the **Dutch** became involved. They blockaded the coast so that the raja of Lombok could not import weapons, and cut communications with Karangasem in Bali, so he could not send for reinforcements. The situation dragged on for years, gains being made and then lost, until July 1894, when the Dutch army landed in West Lombok. Faced with this huge threat close to home, the raja recalled all his troops, and the Sasaks from the east reoccupied their land.

On the night of August 25, 1894, there were reprisals. Balinese forces attacked the Dutch camp in the **Mayura Palace** at Cakranegara, where around nine hundred soldiers were camped. The Dutch escaped with heavy casualties, but they soon received reinforcements and, aided by the Sasaks from the east, proved too strong for the raja. Mataram was razed to the ground and Cakranegara attacked. Some members of the royal family surrendered while others committed *puputan*. The Dutch took control of the entire island, including the district of Karangasem on Bali, which had been under the raja's control.

## Further confrontation in south Bali

The Dutch had wanted to extend their control to the **south of Bali** for many years, but it wasn't until the turn of the twentieth century that they made their move. On May 27, 1904, a schooner, the *Sri Kumala,* under Dutch protection, hit the reef just off Sanur. The owner complained to the Resident in Singaraja that copper and silver coins had been stolen from the ship. The Resident decreed a **blockade** of Badung and ordered that the raja of Badung, Gusti Gde Ngurah, should pay compensation.

The raja of Tabanan defused the blockade by allowing goods to be imported through ports further north, and the situation dragged on until July 1906, when the Dutch delivered ultimatums threatening military action. Dutch forces landed at Sanur, and by September 20, 1906, had advanced to **Badung** (modern-day Denpasar). Gusti Gde Ngurah realized defence was useless and arranged the traditional **puputan**. An eye-witness account from a Dutch observer, Dr van Weede, in his book *Indies Travel Memories*, describes the event:

The ruler and the princes with their followers, dressed in their glittering attire, with their krises girded on, of which the golden hilts were in the form of Buddha statues and studded with precious stones; all of them were dressed in red or black and their hair was carefully combed, moistened with fragrant oils. The women were wearing the best clothes and accessories that they had; most of them wore their hair loose and all had white cloaks. The prince had his palace burned down and had everything that was breakable destroyed.

When at nine o'clock it was reported to him that the enemy had penetrated Denpasar from the North, the tragic procession of 250 people started to move; each man and woman carried a kris or long lance, also the children who had the strength to do it, while the babies were carried in their arms. Thus they walked to the north along the wide road bordered by tall trees, meeting their destruction.

The prince walked in front, carried on the shoulders by his followers according to custom, and silently ... until all of a sudden, at a turning in the road, the dark line of our infantry was visible before them. Immediately a halt was commanded and Captain Schutstal ordered the interpreters to summon the arriving party to a halt with gestures and with words. However these summons were in vain, and in spite of the repeated warnings the Balinese went over to a trot.

Incessantly the Captain and the interpreters made signs, but it was in vain. Soon they had to realize that they had to do with people who wanted to die. They let them approach to a hundred paces, eighty, seventy paces, but now they went over to a double quick step with couched lances and raised krises, the prince always in front.

A longer delay would have been irresponsible in view of the safety of our men, and the first salvo was given; several killed men remained at the place. One of the first to fall was the ruler; and now one of the most horrible scenes one could imagine took place.

While those who were saved continued the attack, and the shooting on our part for self-defence remained necessary, one saw lightly wounded give the death-blow to the heavily wounded. Women held out their breasts to be killed or received the death blow between their shoulders, and those who did this were mowed down by our rifle fire, other men and women got up to continue the bloody work. Also suicides took place there on a big scale, and all seemed to yearn for their death: some women threw as a reward for the violent death which they desired from them gold coins to the soldiers, and stood straight up in front of them, pointing at their heart, as if they wanted to be hit there; if no shot was fired they killed themselves. Especially an old man was busily stepping over the corpses, and used his kris left and right until he was shot down. An old woman took his task and underwent the same fate, however, nothing helped. Always others got up to continue the work of destruction.

This scene was repeated later the same day at the palace of the prince of **Pamecutan**. Estimates of the number of people killed that day vary between four hundred and two thousand. Having defeated Badung, on September 27, the Dutch marched on to **Tabanan**, where the raja and crown prince surrendered and were imprisoned, where they both committed suicide rather than face exile. The following month, the Dutch forced **Klungkung** and **Bangli** to sign agreements with them in which they became colonial vassals in all but name.

## The completion of Dutch control

On April 28, 1908, Dutch troops in **Klungkung** witnessed a scene similar to the Badung *puputan* two years earlier. Oral reports tell how the *dewa agung* stabbed his royal kris into the ground at his feet expecting the power of the regalia to rent the ground asunder or bring torrential rain to destroy the enemy. Nothing happened and, sensing Klungkung's time was up, around two hundred members of the royal household committed suicide that day; the remainder were exiled and did not return for many years.

With Klungkung under direct Dutch administration, the raja of **Bangli** felt it was only a matter of time before a pretext was found to attack him and, in October 1908, requested that his kingdom should have the same status as Gianyar and Karangasem and become a Dutch Protectorate. When this was approved in January 1909, the whole of the island of Bali came under **Dutch control**.

## Colonial rule

The *puputan*s of 1906 and 1908 caused a stir in Europe and the United States and pressure was put on the Dutch to moderate their policies. Having gained control of the island, the Dutch ruled with a philosophy they called the Ethical Policy, which they claimed upheld Balinese values. Traditional rulers were left in place as regents under the authority of the Dutch administration, although not all of the old royal families were amenable to this; in Buleleng, it was not until several generations after the Dutch conquest that an obliging member of the royal family could be found.

Under the Dutch, engineers, doctors and teachers were introduced to the colony. In addition, Bali was spared the less enlightened **agricultural policies** that had turned large parts of Java into plantations. Big businesses were discouraged from Bali, although the steamship line KPM began encouraging **tourism** on the island. The first visitors landed in the 1920s, and by the 1930s about a hundred visitors a month were arriving. Many were artists, musicians, anthropologists and writers, who made their homes on the island, some following in the footsteps of the artist **Walter Spies** and settling in the Ubud area, others in Iseh near Klungkung, with more maverick souls, such as K'tut Tantri and Louise and Bob Koke, preferring the then rarely visited Kuta area.

## Lombok under the Dutch

The situation of the people of **Lombok** began to deteriorate following the Dutch victory in 1894, and continued to do so for the next fifty years, bringing the population to the point of starvation more than once. The aim of the Dutch was to rule profitably: they taxed the population to the hilt and introduced **compulsory labour** for projects such as road-building. In addition to land tax, there were **taxes** on income and on the slaughter of animals. These were initially payable in local currency, but the system changed and they were demanded in Netherlands Indies currency (NIC). The Chinese rice exporters were one of the few groups on the island who traded in NIC, and increasing amounts of rice started to be sold to them to raise money for taxes. Consequently, a high proportion of food grown on the island was exported, and local rice consumption dropped by a quarter. By 1934, it was estimated that a third of the population were **landless and destitute**.

# World War II and independence

Following the bombing of the American Fleet in Pearl Harbour on December 7, 1941, Japan entered **World War II** and moved quickly through Asia. The Japanese fleet arrived off Sanur on February 18, 1942, and moved through Bali, occupying it without a fight. The larger islands to the west, Java and Sumatra, had fallen by March 9.

The Japanese **occupation** was hard but short-lived. It also had significant political effects within the archipelago, as it showed that the Dutch colonialists were, in fact, vulnerable and could be defeated.

Throughout the war years, the idea of liberation grew and, on August 17, 1945, just three days after the Japanese surrender, Indonesia made its **Declaration of Independence** in an announcement by President **Sukarno**, who had established the Indonesian Nationalist Party in 1927. Some Balinese were strong supporters of independence but many were uncertain about joining a republic dominated by Muslim Java.

## The fight for independence

Returning to retake their colony in March 1946, the **Dutch** faced ferocious fighting on Java but initially little opposition on Bali. However, the guerrilla forces, the most famous of which was led by **Gusti Ngurah Rai**, harried the Dutch relentlessly, despite suffering massive losses in a famous battle near Marga in Tabanan. Ngurah Rai is remembered as a hero: Bali's airport is named after him, as is the island's main bypass road, on which stands a commemorative statue, and the Marga battlefield, where he died, is now a memorial park.

The status quo returned to Bali, with local rulers overseen by Dutch administrators. However, the Dutch were fighting a lost cause. The US questioned the sense of the Dutch expenditure of Marshall Plan aid (money allocated to European countries for reconstruction after the war) on fighting to keep the Indies. The Australian government was sympathetic towards Indonesia, and the other European colonial powers could offer the Dutch no support. Finally, in January 1949, under pressure of world opinion, the UN Security Council ordered the

Dutch to withdraw their troops and negotiate. In December 1949, the United States of Indonesia was legally recognized, dissolving the following year to form the **Republic of Indonesia**, with Sukarno as president.

## The Sukarno years

The early years of independence were not kind to Indonesia. The economic situation was disastrous as inflation, corruption and mismanagement ran riot. Martial rule was instituted, and parliament was abolished in 1959 with the introduction of **guided democracy**. The economic situation went from bad to worse as inflation soared and Western investment dried up. 1963 saw a catastrophic war against Malaya to try to prevent the creation of the Federation of Malaysia.

Although Sukarno's mother was Balinese, the Balinese felt neglected by the government in Jakarta, which, in turn, was suspicious of Balinese Hinduism. Sukarno visited his palace at Tampaksiring regularly, with a massive entourage that demanded to be fed, entertained and then sent away with gifts. During the 1960s, a groundswell of resentment against the government grew in Bali. The Balinese began to believe that a state of spiritual disharmony had been reached, and a huge purification ceremony, **Eka Dasa Rudra**, was held in 1963 against the backdrop of a rumbling Gunung Agung, which eventually blew its top and laid waste to much of the east of the island.

Later events in Jakarta piled disaster upon disaster in Bali. During the night of September 30, 1965, a group of young left-wing army officers kidnapped and killed six high-ranking generals who they claimed were planning to overthrow the president. It is generally claimed that the attack on the generals was an attempted communist coup that failed when **Major-General Suharto** took control of the army and set about seizing political power amid a media blitz against the communist party (PKI). The entire incident, dubbed the **Gestapu** affair, has been the subject of enormous speculation, as the communists could never have hoped to take over and were doing well politically in any case. Also, Suharto was not on the hit list although he was of higher rank than some of the generals who were killed.

A wave of killings across Indonesia began in December 1965, continuing until March 1966, although there were sporadic outbursts up to 1969. Estimates suggest that 100,000 people were killed on Bali and 50,000 on Lombok, with actual or suspected members of the communist party (PKI) and their sympathizers the main targets, along with the Chinese population on both islands. Tens of thousands were also taken into military detention, and they and their families have been stigmatized ever since – an issue that is gaining some prominence as the victims begin to publicize their plight. On the whole, though, it's a period of history that nobody will discuss these days.

Following the attempted coup, Sukarno lost much of his power to Suharto, and, by March 1966, with most of Suharto's political opponents out of office, the **New Order** was in place. Suharto officially became the second president of Indonesia in March 1968, a position that he held for over thirty years.

## Indonesia under Suharto

Following the dramatic ending of the Suharto regime in May 1998, the history of his rule began to be written, and will no doubt occupy scholars for many years to come. What now seems clear is that, in some respects, his rule was beneficial to the country. The New Order policy of attracting foreign investment, curbing inflation and re-entering the global economy was largely successful. It was helped enormously by Indonesia's massive natural resources of copper, tin, timber and oil, and foreign investment enabled manufacturing industries to be opened up in the archipelago. The economic situation of the country improved and figures looked good: the 1993 GNP per head of population was estimated at US$680, an annual increase of five percent per year since 1985.

An unspoken but clearly understood **social contract** appeared to be in place throughout the Suharto years. Ordinary Indonesians saw their material prosperity rise, which Suharto took credit for. However, in return they allowed the government almost complete freedom. The **political** situation remained fairly stable up until 1997, largely by limiting opposition. In July 1971, in the first election since 1955, the government party, Sekretariat Bersama Golongan Karya, known as **Golkar**, won the majority of seats in the House of Representatives (*Dewan Perwakilan Rakyat*) and, in March 1973, Suharto was re-elected as president. Despite the two main opposition parties, **Partai Demokrasi Indonesia** (PDI), the Indonesian Democratic Party, and **Partai Persatuan Pembangunan** (PPP), the Muslim-based United Development Party, this pattern was repeated in general elections until 1997, with Suharto re-elected five times from 1978 to 1998.

In 1996, the government engineered a special party congress of the PDI and expelled the popular and charismatic PDI leader, **Megawati Sukarnoputri**, daughter of Sukarno, behind whom opposition to the government appeared to gather. Following her removal, Jakarta suffered its most serious **riots** for two decades; violence and open disaffection escalated throughout the country in 1996 and 1997. Spoken opposition to the government, effectively silenced for decades, grew, as did ethnic tensions across the archipelago.

The **economic crisis** of the late 1990s that decimated the economies of

## Transmigrasi and separatism

Initially introduced as a policy during Dutch colonial times, the Indonesian government continued the practice of transmigration, or **transmigrasi** – the relief of population pressure in some parts of the archipelago, most often Java, by settling other, less-populated islands. The scheme has received criticism from human rights' groups and environmentalists, who claim that land has been taken from indigenous peoples and massive deforestation has occurred; they also say that it is an attempt to "Javanize" the ethnically diverse Indonesians. Some of the most violent incidents against settlers have occurred in West Kalimantan where Dayak tribesmen turned against Madurese settlers.

The Indonesian government was notorious overseas for its annexation of **East Timor** in 1976, and its brutal suppression of the independence movement there in the following decades, involving, some estimates suggest, the deaths of 200,000 people out of a population of 650,000. During and after the downfall of Suharto, East Timor was one of the most violent areas of the country with huge tension and strife between Muslims, Chinese, anti-Indonesian Timorese Catholics and pro-Indonesian militia. It is now acknowledged that the Indonesian army played an active and violent part in this gruesome melange. East Timor's achievement of independence in May 2002 added determination and hope to separatist movements across Indonesia. At the other end of the vast archipelago, the **Free Aceh Movement** (GAM) has been active in the north of Sumatra since 1990, with thousands killed so far. In **West Papua** the Organisasi Papua Merdeka (OPM, or Free Papua Movement) has been in active opposition to the government since 1977.

Southeast Asia savaged Indonesia as well. In August 1997, a dollar bought around Rp2400; by early 1998, it had passed Rp10,000. In late 1997 and early 1998, almost a million workers lost their jobs as companies went bust or cut back. Prices of imports (including food) rose sharply, and a series of riots in the early part of the year, centred on Java, targeted Chinese businesses – long the scapegoats of Indonesian unrest. Gradually, Indonesian anger turned against President Suharto and his family, who were seen to have been the biggest winners in the Indonesian economic success story.

Student rioting in May 1998 was the catalyst for change, at a cost of several deaths, leading to more widespread unrest and, eventually, to **Suharto's resignation** on May 21 and the appointment as president of **B.J. Habibie**, a friend of Suharto and a man many felt came from the same mould.

## After Suharto

President Habibie was blamed for losing East Timor and became embroiled in financial scandal. The results of the June 1999 general **elections** were unequivocal: the PDI, led by **Megawati Sukarnoputri**, won 37 percent of the vote; the old ruling party Golkar led by Habibie got twenty percent; and the PKB (National Awakening Party), led by the relatively unknown Muslim cleric **Abdurrahman Wahid**, received twenty percent, with the remainder shared between smaller contenders. By October 1999, these three party leaders had emerged as candidates for the presidency. The election of Wahid brought violent protests to the streets of both Denpasar and Singaraja in outrage that Megawati Sukarnoputri – who many felt was owed the presidency – was not in power.

President Abdurrahman Wahid, popularly known as **Gus Dur**, was forced from office after just 21 months, surrounded by accusations of corruption.

### Mega and beyond

On July 23, 2001, **Megawati Sukarnoputri** became president. Megawati – darling of the Balinese, to whom she is known simply as Mega – was regarded in Bali with something approaching fanaticism, based on the fact that her maternal grandmother (Sukarno's mother) was Balinese. Starting her presidency on a wave of optimism, she proved to be ineffectual, less charismatic in leadership than she had been in opposition and unable to tackle Indonesia's problems.

However, Indonesia hit the world headlines on **12 October, 2002**, for far more tragic reasons than its political situation, when bombs planted in the heart of tourist Bali, at the *Sari Club* and *Paddy's Irish Bar* in Kuta, exploded, killing more than two hundred people, the majority of them tourists but with dozens of Indonesian victims also. A third bomb exploded outside the US consulate in Denpasar but caused little damage and no injuries. The attacks are widely believed to have been carried out by Jemaah Islamiyah, advocates of an Islamic state across Southeast Asia. One of the bombers, most of whom were Javanese, was later quoted as saying: "It was a place of sin, it deserved to be demolished." Another testified that the bombings were to "avenge the killings of muslims by the United States and its allies". The perpetrators included Amrozi bin Nurhasyim, who gained global notoriety when he punched the air after being sentenced to death; he was one of three who received the death penalty – dozens of others received prison sentences. Balinese tourism collapsed overnight but had begun its recovery while the wheels of Indonesian justice continued to grind on. By mid-2005, none of the death sentences had been carried out. Meanwhile, the bombing of the *Marriot Hotel* in Jakarta in

May 2003 and the Australian Embassy in Jakarta in 2004 brought home to Indonesians and the wider world that fundamentalist forces are at large in the largest Muslim nation in the world.

Whatever Megawati's failings, she did, however, lay the foundations for Indonesia's **first-ever direct presidential election** in 2004, in which 114 million voters across 14,000 islands voted her out of the job in favour of **Susilo Bambang Yudhoyono**, commonly known as **SBY**.

While early signs were positive – and with 61 percent of the vote he was a popular winner – the problems for Indonesia (and, in turn, Bali and Lombok) remain colossal. The separatist struggles in West Papua and Aceh are unresolved; corruption, terrorism and nepotism are the concerns of every Indonesian; more than sixteen percent of Indonesians live below the poverty line; and, just a few months after SBY entered office, the Indian Ocean tsunami in December 2004 devastated northern Sumatra, followed by smaller disasters in early 2005. Time will tell whether the new president has more success, or longevity, than his last three predecessors.

# Religion

O ver 87 percent of Balinese are Hindus. In contrast, Lombok is only three percent Hindu and the vast majority of its inhabitants are Muslim.

Religious activity permeates almost every aspect of **Balinese** life. Every morning, tiny palm-leaf offerings are laid down for the gods and spirits who need 24-hour propitiation; in the afternoons, processions of men and women parade the streets en route to temple celebrations, towers of offertory fruit and rice cakes balanced on their heads. Temple compounds dominate the horizons of every village, and the desire to entice and entertain the deities inspires daily performances of dance and gamelan music.

While Islam is as pervasive on **Lombok** as Hinduism is on Bali, it has a much more austere presence. You'll hear the call to prayer five times a day, and streets are often deserted on Fridays around noon, when a large proportion of the population go to the mosque. Marriage and circumcision are celebrated, but the exuberant and frequent festivals of Balinese Hinduism have no Muslim equivalents.

## Balinese Hinduism

Though it's not a proselytizing faith, **Balinese Hinduism** is a demanding one, which requires participation from every citizen. Despite certain obvious similarities, Balinese Hinduism differs dramatically from Indian and Nepalese Hinduism. Bali's is a blend of theories and practices borrowed from Hinduism and Buddhism, grafted onto the far stronger indigenous vision of a world that is overrun by good and bad spirits. The Balinese have practised ancestor worship and followed animist cults ever since the Stone Age and, consequently, only the most complementary aspects of the newer Asian theologies have been adopted.

### Early influences

The **animism** of the Stone- and Bronze-Age Balinese probably differed very little from the beliefs of their twenty-first-century descendants, who worship certain sacred mountains and rivers and conduct elaborate rituals to ensure that the souls of their dead ancestors are kept sweet. In among these animist practices are elements borrowed from the **Mahayana Buddhism** that dominated much of Southeast Asia in the eighth century – certain Buddhist saints, for example, some of which are still visible at Goa Gajah, and a penchant for highly ornate imagery. The strongest influences arrived with the droves of **East Javanese Hindu priests** who fled Muslim invaders en masse in the early sixteenth century. High-caste, educated pillars of the Majapahit kingdom, these strict followers of the Hindu faith settled in all corners of Bali and quickly set about formalizing Bali's embryonic Hindu practices. Balinese Hinduism, or **agama Hindu** as it's usually termed, became Bali's official religion, and the Majapahit priests have, ever since, been worshipped as the true Balinese ancestors.

As Bali's Hinduism gained strength, so its neighbouring islands turned towards Islam, and now Bali is a tiny Hindu haven in an archipelago that contains the biggest Islamic population in the world. Hindu Bali's role within the predominantly Muslim Indonesian state has always been problematic. As part of its code of national law (*Pancasila*), the Jakarta administration requires that all Indonesian faiths be monotheistic and embrace just one God – a proviso that doesn't sit easily with either Hindu or animist tenets. After concerted theological and political wranglings, however, Bali's Hindu Council came up with an acceptable compromise. By emphasizing the role of their supreme deity, **Sanghyang Widi Wasa** (who manifests himself as the Hindu Trinity of Brahma, Siwa and Wisnu), the Council convinced the Ministry of Religion that Bali was essentially monotheistic, and in 1962 Balinese Hinduism was formally recognized by Jakarta. As a result, a host of new Balinese temples were dedicated to a unifying force – Jagatnata or "Lord of the World"; two typical examples of modern *pura Jagatnata* can be seen in Denpasar and Singaraja.

## The beliefs

At the root of *agama Hindu* lies the fundamental understanding that the world – both natural and supernatural – is composed of opposing forces. These can be defined as good and evil, positive and negative, pure and impure, order and disorder, gods and demons, or as a mixture of all these things, but the crucial fact is that the forces need to be balanced. The desire to achieve **equilibrium** and harmony in all things dictates every spiritual activity. **Positive forces**, or *dharma*, are represented by the gods (*dewa* and *bhatara*), and need to be cultivated, entertained and honoured with offerings, dances, beautiful paintings and sculptures, fine earthly abodes (temples) and ministrations from ceremonially clad devotees. The **malevolent forces**, *adharma*, which manifest themselves as earth demons (*bhuta*, *kala* and *leyak*) and cause sickness, death and volcanic eruptions, need to be neutralized with elaborate rituals and special offerings.

To ensure that malevolent forces never take the upper hand, elaborate purification rituals are undertaken for the exorcism of spirits. Crucial to this is the notion of **ritual uncleanliness** (*sebel*), a state which can affect an individual (during a woman's period, for example, or after a serious illness), a family (after the death of a close relative, or if twins are born), or even a whole community (a plague of rats in the village ricefields, or a fire in village buildings). The whole island can even become *sebel*, and **island-wide exorcisms** are held every new year (*Nyepi*) to restore the spiritual health of Bali and all its people. The 2002 Kuta bombing caused the whole island to become ritually unclean, and as well as a huge purification ceremony at Ground Zero a month after the attack, exorcism rites were also performed simultaneously across the island. Other regular, very elaborate island-cleansing rituals are performed every five, ten and twenty-five years, climaxing with the centennial *Eka Dasa Rudra* rite, which is held at the holiest temple, Besakih. In addition, there are all sorts of **purification rituals** (*yadnya*) that Balinese must go through at various significant stages in their lives (see p.494).

The focus of every purification ritual is the ministering of **holy water** (*agama Hindu* is sometimes known as *agama tirta*, the religion of holy water). Ordinary well or tap water can be transformed into holy water by a *pedanda* (high priest), but water from certain sources is considered to be particularly sacred – the springs at Tirta Empul in Tampaksiring and on Gunung Agung, for example, and the water taken from the lakeside Pura Danu Batur.

As the main sources of these life-giving waters, Bali's three great **mountains** are also worshipped: the highest, and the holiest, of the three is Gunung Agung, associated with the sun god Surya, and site of Bali's most sacred mother temple, Besakih; and Gunung Batur and Gunung Batukau also hold great spiritual power, as do the lakes that fill their volcanic craters. Ever since the Stone Age, the Balinese have regarded their mountains as being the realm of the deities, the sea as the abode of demons and giants, and the valleys in between as the natural province of the human world. From this concept comes the Balinese sense of direction and **spatial orientation**, whereby all things, such as temples, houses and villages, are aligned in relation to the mountains and the sea: **kaja** is the direction towards the mountains, upstream, and is the holiest direction; **kelod** is the downstream direction, the part that is closest to the sea and therefore impure.

An important practical tenet of *agama Hindu* is **Tri Hita Karana**, the need to constantly work towards harmony between the three dimensions of daily life – spiritual, social and environmental – fostering a three-way balance between humans and God, humans and humans, and humans and the environment (both cultural and physical). This philosophy is even applied within the tourist industry, which runs a Tri Hita Karana award system for hotels that achieve this balance in design and operation.

Finally, there are the notions of karma, reincarnation, and the attaining of enlightenment. The aim of every Hindu is to attain **enlightenment** (*moksa*), which brings with it the union of the individual and the divine, and liberation from the endless painful cycle of death and rebirth. *Moksa* is only attainable by pure souls, and this can take hundreds of lifetimes to attain. Hindus believe that everybody is **reincarnated** according to their **karma**, karma being a kind of account book that registers all the good and bad deeds performed in the past lives of a soul. Karma is closely bound up with caste and the notion that an individual should accept rather than challenge their destiny.

## The gods

All Balinese **gods** are manifestations of the supreme being, **Sanghyang Widi Wasa**, a deity who is often only alluded to in abstract form by an empty throne-shrine, the *padmasana*, that stands in the holiest corner of every temple. Sanghyang Widi Wasa's three main aspects manifest themselves as the Hindu trinity: Brahma, Wisnu and Siwa. Each of these three gods has different roles and is associated with specific colours and animals.

**Brahma** is the Creator, represented by the colour red and often depicted riding on a bull. His consort is the goddess of learning, **Saraswati**, who rides a white goose.

As the Preserver, **Wisnu** is associated with life-giving waters; he rides the *garuda* (half-man, half-bird) and is honoured by the colour black. Wisnu also has several avatars, including **Buddha** – a neat way of incorporating Buddhist elements into the Hindu faith.

**Siwa**, the Destroyer, or more accurately, the Dissolver, is associated with death and rebirth, with the temples of the dead and with the colour white. He is sometimes represented as a phallic pillar or lingam, and sometimes in the manifestation of **Surya**, the sun god. Siwa's consort is the terrifying goddess **Durga**, whose Balinese personality is the gruesome widow-witch **Rangda**, queen of the demons. The son of Siwa and Durga is the elephant-headed deity **Ganesh**, generally worshipped as the remover of obstacles.

Brahma, Wisnu and Siwa all have associated lesser deities or *dewi* (*dewa* if male), many of them gods of the elements and of the physical world. **Dewi Sri** is the goddess of rice, worshipped at tiny shrines in every group of paddy-fields, and honoured at significant stages throughout the agricultural year. **Dewi Danu** (more formally known as Ida Batara Dewi Ulun Danu) is the equally important goddess of the crater lake – honoured with temples on the shores of the three volcanic lakes Bratan, Batur and Tamblingan, and so important to the rice-growers of Bali as a source of vital irrigation that annual pilgrimages are made to all three temples. **Dewa Baruna** is the unpredictable god of the sea, and **Dewi Melanting** the goddess of commerce and prosperity.

## The demons

**Demons** also come in a variety of manifestations. The forces of evil are personified by a cast of **bhuta** and **kala**, invisible goblins and ghosts who inhabit eerie, desolate places like the temples of the dead, cemeteries, moonless sea-shores and dark forests. Their purpose on earth is to wreak havoc in the human world, causing horrible lingering illnesses and ruinous agricultural and economic disasters, preying on the most vulnerable babies, and entering villagers' minds and turning them insane. But their power is not invincible, and they can be appeased and placated with **offerings** just as the gods can – the difference being that the offerings for these demons consist mainly of dirty, unpleasant, unattractive and mouldy things, which are thrown down on the ground, not placed respectfully on ledges and altars. Demons are notoriously greedy, too, and so the Balinese will always throw a dash of *arak* (rice liquor) on the ground before drinking, or drop a few grains of rice to the floor when eating.

Various other strategies are used to repel, confuse and banish the *bhuta* and *kala*. Most entrance gates to temples and households are guarded by fierce-looking statues and demonic images designed to be so ugly as to frighten off even the boldest demon. Many gateways are also blocked by a low brick wall, an **aling-aling**, as demons can only walk in straight lines, and so won't be able to negotiate the necessary zigzag to get around the wall. *Bhuta* and *kala* get particular pleasure from entering a person's body via their various orifices, so certain temples (especially in the north) have covered their walls in pornographic carvings, the theory being that the demons will have so much fun penetrating the carved simulation orifices on the outside walls that they won't bother to try their luck further inside the temple compound.

In addition to the unseen *bhuta* and *kala*, there are the equally fearful **leyak**, or witches, who take highly visible and creepy forms, transforming themselves into headless chickens, bald-headed giants, monkeys with rows of shiny gold teeth, fireballs and riderless motorbikes. *Leyak* can transform themselves effortlessly from one form to another, and most assume the human form during the daytime, leading outwardly normal lives. Only at night do they release their dark spirits to wreak havoc on unsuspecting villagers, while their human shell remains innocently asleep in bed. Even in their human form, *leyak* cannot be killed with knives or poisons, but they can be controlled and disempowered by harnessing white magic, as practised by shamanic *balian* (traditional healers; see p.495), or by priests.

# The temples

The focus of every community's spiritual activity is the **temple**, or *pura*, a specially designed temporary abode for the gods that's open and unroofed so as to invite easy access between heaven and earth. Major religious ceremonies take place inside the *pura*, and members of the community spend a great deal of their time and income beautifying the sanctuary with carvings, and consecrating offerings at its altars.

At first glance, visitors can find Balinese temples rather confusing, and even unimpressive, in appearance. Many of them seem to be rather bland affairs: open-roofed compounds scattered with a host of shrines and altars, built mainly of limestone and red brick, and with no paintings or treasures to focus on. But

## Bali's top ten temples

Certain Balinese **temples** have acquired a special status because of their history, their association with a certain priest or raja, or from the sheer beauty of the carvings inside them or their stunning physical situation. The ten that are most worth visiting are (in alphabetical order):

Besakih p.246
Pura Dalem, Jagaraga p.319
Pura Agung Jagatnata,
  Denpasar p.103
Pura Luhur Batukau p.353

Pura Meduwe Karang,
  Kubutambahan p.319
Pura Puseh, Batubulan p.174
Pura Rambut Siwi p.357
Pura Saraswati, Ubud p.194
Pura Tanah Lot p.344

many of Bali's numerous temples – there are at least 20,000 on the island – do reward closer examination. Every structure within a temple complex is charged with great symbolic significance, often with entertaining legends attached, and many of the walls and gateways are carved with an ebullience of mythical figures, demonic spirits and even secular scenes. (Note that when **visiting a temple**, you must be appropriately dressed, even if there's no one else in the vicinity; see p.79 for details.)

The reason there are so many temples in Bali is that every *banjar* and small village is obliged to build at least three, each one serving a specific role within the community. At the top of the village – the *kaja*, or holiest end – stands the **pura puseh**, the temple of origin, which is dedicated to the founders of the community. For everyday spiritual activities, villagers worship at the **pura desa**, the village temple, which always lies at the heart of the village, and often doubles as a convenient forum for community meetings and other secular activities. (In some communities, the *pura puseh* and the *pura desa* are combined within a single compound.) The essential trio is completed by the **pura dalem**, or temple of the dead, at the *kelod* (unclean) end of the village, which is usually dedicated either to Siwa, or to the widow-witch Rangda. Larger villages will often have a number of other temples as well, perhaps including a **pura melanting** for the gods of wealth and commerce, and a small agricultural temple or shrine, a **pura subak**, dedicated to the rice goddess, Dewi Sri.

Bali also has nine directional temples, or **kayangan jagat**, which are regarded as extremely sacred by all islanders as they protect the island as a whole and all its people. The *kayangan jagat* are located at strategic points across the island, especially on high mountain slopes, rugged cliff faces and lakeside shores: Pura Ulun Danu Batur is on the shores of Danau Batur (north); Pura Pasar Agung on Gunung Agung (northeast); Pura Lempuyang Luhur on Gunung Lempuyang (east); Goa Lawah near Candi Dasa (southeast); Pura Masceti near Lebih (south); Pura Luhur Uluwatu on the Bukit (southwest); Pura Luhur Batukau on Gunung Batukau (west); Pura Ulun Danu Bratan on the shores of Danau Bratan (northwest); and Besakih on Gunung Agung (centre). The most important of these is Besakih – the mother temple – as it occupies the crucial position on Bali's holiest, and highest, mountain, Gunung Agung; the others are all of equal status, and dutiful islanders are expected to attend the anniversary celebrations (*odalan*) of the one situated closest to their home.

### Temple layout

Whatever the size, status or particular function of a temple, it will nearly always follow a prescribed layout (see temple plan on p.462), adhering to the precepts of

**religious architecture** minutely described in the ancient *lontar* texts. All Balinese temples are oriented *kaja–kelod*, and are designed around two or three courtyards, each section divided from the next by a low wall punctuated by a huge, and usually ornate, gateway.

In many temples, particularly in north Bali, the **outer courtyard** (*jaba*) and **middle courtyard** (*jaba tengah*) are merged into one. These courtyards represent the transition zone between the human and the divine worlds, containing special pavilions for the preparation of offerings and the storing of temple paraphernalia, as well as for cockfights and the less sacred dance performances (such as those for tourists). The extremely sacred **inner courtyard**, *jeroan*, houses all the shrines, and is the focus of all temple rituals. All offerings are brought here, prayers are held in front of the shrines, and the most sacred dances are performed within its confines. The *jeroan* is quite often out of bounds to the lay community and opened only during festivals.

Every *pura* contains a whole collection of small structures, each one devoted to a specific purpose. **Bale** are open-sided pavilions, usually built of wood, raised on small stilts, and thatched with black sugar-palm fibre. These are practical buildings for seating devotees or gamelan players, and for storing things. **Gedong** is the generic term for the squat, often cube-shaped shrines that are generally made of brick, with thatched roofs. Each *gedong* is dedicated to a particular deity or ancestor, and sometimes contains a symbolic image. The elegant pagoda-style shrines that tower over every temple wall are known as **meru**, after the sacred Hindu peak Mount Meru, home of the gods. Each *meru* has a small wood or brick base beneath a multi-tiered roof thatched with thick black sugar-palm fibre. There's always an odd number of roofs (three, five, seven, nine or eleven), the number indicating the status of the god to whom the *meru* is dedicated.

## Priests

The only people who are conversant with all the rituals of *agama Hindu* are the **high priests**, or *pedanda*, men and a few women of the Brahman caste who spend years studying the complex theology. This knowledge gives them such special power that they are considered to be quite aloof from the other villagers; the *pedanda* and his or her family usually live in a special compound (*griya*) that stands slightly apart from the rest of the community.

Only the most important ceremonies are presided over by a *pedanda*. Wreathed in clouds of incense and dressed all in white, save for bejewelled mitres on their heads and multiple strings of beads around their necks, the *pedanda's* role is to invoke the spirit of the supreme deity with a complicated ritual performance of chanting, hand gestures and the periodic ringing of a small handbell. With legs folded into a half-lotus and eyes closed, the *pedanda* can spend hours chanting the appropriate mantras in an ancient tongue – either the old Javanese language, Kawi, or the similarly esoteric Sanskrit – which mean nothing to the lay people who generally just pause for a brief prayer before moving on. The scholarly *pedanda* are also traditionally the only people to understand the complexities of the Balinese calendar system and so they are consulted over the timing for major events – such as the most auspicious day for laying the foundation stone of a house or office, for example, or for holding a cremation ceremony.

It is the job of the **village priest**, the *pemangku*, to attend to the more mundane spiritual activities of the community. *Pemangku* are nearly always male, though their wives also help. Easily recognized by his white apparel and formal white *udeng* headdress, the *pemangku* spends a great deal of time at the temple, sweeping

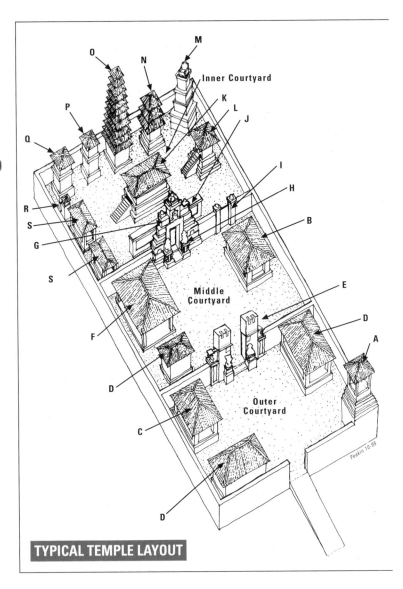

**TYPICAL TEMPLE LAYOUT**

the grounds, repairing the buildings and, in the run-up to the *odalan* and other local celebrations, preparing the *pura* for the reception of offerings and necessary rituals. At the time of the *odalan*, it is the *pemangku* who invites the gods to partake of the offerings, and he and his wife then dispense holy water to the worshippers. Their other main duty is to advise the community on appropriate offerings and rituals for every occasion: if a household is struck down by sickness, for example, or if a family suddenly has some good fortune, they will ask the *pemangku* to help them express their sorrow or thanks. It is the *pemangku* who appears at the

**A – kulkul** Drum tower. Tall roofed tower that contains the drum (*kulkul*) used to summon members of the *banjar* to festivals, to community meetings and, in the past, into battle. More accurately described as a wooden bell, the drum itself is made from a hollowed-out log slit down the middle and suspended by a rope from the roof.

**B – wantilan** Performance pavilion. Large *bale* used for cockfights and for dance performances.

**C – bale gong** Gamelan pavilion. Sizeable open-sided, thatched pavilion in which the gamelan instruments are stored; this is where the musicians sit and play at festivals.

**D – bale** All-purpose pavilion, used for village meetings and for resting devotees.

**E – candi bentar** The split temple gate. Looks like a tower that has literally been sliced down the middle. Its spiritual symbolism can be interpreted in several ways: the material world has been split so that the human body can enter the spiritual realm; the left side represents femaleness, the right, maleness; if an evil spirit tries to pass through, the two halves will come together to crush it.

**F – paon** Kitchen. Open-sided pavilion where the offerings are prepared before an *odalan* or other important festival.

**G – paduraksa** (or **kori agung**) Central covered gateway to the inner courtyard. Often the temple's most imposing structure, the *paduraksa* is usually approached by a flight of steps and crowned with a sculpted tower. The central wooden door is usually kept locked (except at festival times), so devotees and casual visitors generally use a side door to the inner courtyard. The archway over the central door is always crowned by a carving of a grotesque fanged head – **Bhoma**, child of the earth or son of the forest, whose role is to ward off demons.

**H – raksasa** Metre-high demon statues. Usually appearing in pairs on either side of gateways, *raksasa* wield clubs, have aggressive, scary faces, and act as another deterrent to malevolent spirits.

**I – side gate** Kept open to allow access to the inner courtyard, as the central main gate is officially only for the use of the deities and their representatives.

**J – aling-aling** Low freestanding stone or brick wall. Located directly in front of the *kori agung*'s central doorway, this is the last line of defence against unwanted demons: evil spirits can only walk in straight lines, so the *aling-aling* will block their path.

**K – gedong paruman** or **pepelik** Empty pavilion nearly always located right in the middle of the inner courtyard, where the gods are invited to assemble and to watch temple festivities.

**L – gedong pesimpangan** The principal shrine honouring the village founder or important local deity.

**M – padmasana** Lotus throne. An empty stone throne built into the summit of a tall (sculpted) tower, which is reserved for the supreme deity Sanghyang Widi Wasa who is invited to sit here whenever he descends to earth. Always located in the corner that's closest to the holiest mountain, Gunung Agung (usually the northeast corner), with its back towards the peak. The tower structure is always supported by the cosmic turtle, Bedawang, and two *naga*, or mythological sea serpents, which are part of the Balinese creation myth. **Bedawang** is the creature who carries the world on his back (when he gets restless, he shakes the earth's foundations, so causing earthquakes), while **Naga Basukih** and **Naga Anantaboga** act as his steadying agents, simultaneously representing human needs, namely food, shelter, clothing and security.

**N – meru Gunung Agung** Three-roofed (occasionally eleven-roofed) shrine, dedicated to Bali's holiest mountain.

**O – meru Sanghyang Widi Wasa** Eleven-roofed shrine dedicated to the supreme deity.

**P – meru Gunung Batur** One-roofed (occasionally nine-roofed) shrine dedicated to the sacred Batur mountain.

**Q – gedong Maospahit** Shrine honouring the Javanese Majapahit (or Maospahit) people, who are considered the spiritual ancestors of the contemporary Balinese. This shrine is often distinguishable by a sculpture of a deer's head, or a carved or real pair of antlers set over the shrine's (locked) door – the deer is the symbol of these ancestral gods.

**R – taksu** Stone pillar. The seat for the interpreter of the gods, who occasionally descends to inhabit the bodies of certain worshippers, sending them into a trance so that they can convey messages between the gods and the humans.

**S – bale piasan** Pavilions where offerings are laid.

beginning of every dance performance (even the tourist ones) to bless the performers with sprinklings of holy water, and it is his job, too, to awaken the dancers of the *sanghyang dedari* and *sanghyang jaran* out of their trances.

## Temple festivals

Aside from the daily propitiation of the household spirits, *agama Hindu* requires no regular act of collective worship from its devotees – no daily mass or weekly

## Temple dress

It is customary for Balinese men and women to wear **traditional dress** whenever they attend temple festivals, cremations, weddings, birth-rites and other important rituals; men also wear temple dress if playing in a gamelan orchestra and occasionally for *banjar* meetings, too.

The traditional outfit for **women** is a lacy, close-fitting, long-sleeved blouse (*kebaya*) and a tightly wound sarong (*kain kamben*), set off by the all-important sash (*selempot*) around the waist, which symbolically contains the body and its physical appetites. Some women don flamboyant hair-pieces and conspicuous jewellery as well. For some big festivals, women from the same community will all wear the same-coloured *kebaya* to give their group a recognizable identity.

**Men** also wear a type of sarong (*kamben sarung*) and a formal, collared shirt as well (generally white but sometimes batik) or maybe even a starched jacket-like shirt. The man's sash (*selempot*) is often hidden under the shirt, but the more important item for him is the hip-cloth (*saput*), which is often yellow and usually knee-length and is worn over the sarong. Men also wear a headcloth (*udeng*), which they tie in whatever way they like, but generally leaving a triangular crest on top (shops sell ready-tied *udeng*). As with the sash, the *udeng* symbolically concentrates the mental energies and directs the thoughts heavenwards, via the perky cockscomb at the front.

service – and so, for much of the year, Bali's 20,000 temples remain deserted, visited only by the village *pemangku* and perhaps the occasional curious tourist. But this all changes on the occasion of the temple's anniversary celebrations, or **odalan**, a three-day devotional extravaganza held at every temple either once every 210 days (every Balinese calendar year; see p.63 for an explanation of this) or once every 365 days (the *saka* year). With at least three temples gracing every sizeable community in Bali, any visitor who spends more than a week on the island will be certain to see some kind of festival. Most temples welcome tourists to the celebrations, provided they dress respectably (see p.79) and wear the temple sash, and that they don't walk in front of praying devotees.

As well as the temple anniversary celebrations, there are numerous island-wide religious festivals to mark sacred days according to both Balinese calendars; the most important of these are the *Nyepi* and *Galungan-Kuningan*, described on p.64. Although the majority of the other rituals – birth celebrations, toothfiling, marriage and death – that punctuate every Balinese Hindu's life also have strong religious ramifications, most of these are conducted within the confines of the family's own compound, and are described on pp.495–496.

The larger, wealthier and more important the temple, the more dramatic the *odalan* celebrations. Whatever the size, the purpose is always the same: to invite the gods down to earth so that they can be entertained and pampered by as many displays of devotion and gratitude as the community can afford. In the days before the *odalan*, the *pemangku* dresses the temple statues in **holy cloths**, either the spiritually charged black and white *kain poleng*, or a length of plain cloth in the colour symbolic of that temple's deity. Meanwhile, the women of the community begin to construct their offering towers, or *banten* (see opposite), and to cook ceremonial food.

*Odalan* are so important that everyone makes a huge effort to return to their home village for their own temple festival, even if they live and work far away; most employers will automatically give their Balinese staff time off to attend. **Celebrations** start in the afternoon, with a procession of ceremonially clad women carrying their offerings to the temple. Sometimes the gods will temporarily inhabit the body of one of the worshippers, sending him or her into a trance and conveying its message through gestures or words. Elsewhere in the temple compound, there might be a cockfight and some gamelan music, and sacred dances are often performed as well. After dark, a shadow play, *wayang kulit*, is often staged.

## Offerings

The simplest **offerings** are the ones laid out every day by the women of each house, and placed at the household shrine, at the entrance gate, and in any nooks and crannies thought to be of interest to *bhuta* and *kala*. These offerings, called **canang**, are tiny banana-leaf trays, pinned together with bamboo splinters and filled with a symbolic assortment of rice, fruit, flowers and incense. The flowers are always red or pink, to represent the Hindu god Brahma, and white for Siwa, with the green of the banana leaf symbolizing Wisnu. Though it's still common, especially in the villages, for women to make their own *canang*, an increasing number buy theirs at the market. Offerings for the gods are always placed in elevated positions, either on specially constructed altars or on functional shelves, but those meant for the demons are scattered on the ground. When she lays the offering for the gods down, the devotee sprinkles a few drops of holy water over the *canang* and wafts the incense smoke heavenwards. This sends the essence of the *canang* up to the appropriate god and ensures that he comes down immediately to enjoy it. Once the essence has been extracted, the *canang* loses its holiness and is left to rot.

When there is a community festival or an island-wide celebration, the women of each *banjar* will band together to make great sculpted towers of fruit and rice cakes, tiny rice-dough figurines, and banners woven from palm fronds. The most dramatic of these are the magnificent **banten**, built up around the trunk of a young banana tree, up to three metres high. *Banten* cannot be reused, but once they've done service at the temple they can be dismantled and eaten by the families who donated them.

On the occasion of major island-wide festivals, such as *Galungan-Kuningan*, or at the Balinese New Year, *Nyepi*, Bali's villages get decked out with special banners and ornamental poles, designed to attract the attention of the deities living on Gunung Agung and invite them onto the local streets. The banners, known as **lamak**, are amazing ornamental mats, often up to three metres long and woven in bold symbolic patterns from fresh green banana leaves. The most common design centres round the **cili** motif, a kind of stylized female figure with a body formed of triangles and other simple geometric shapes, wearing a spiky looking headdress; *cili* are thought by some to represent the rice goddess Dewi Sri. Seven days before the great *Galungan* festival begins, special bamboo poles, or **penyor**, are erected along the streets of every village, each one bowed down with intricately woven garlands of dried flowers and palm leaves, which arch gracefully over the roadway. Attached to the *penyor* are symbolic leafy tassels, and offerings of dried paddy sheaves and coconut shells.

# Bali's other faiths

**Islam** is Bali's second religion – albeit one that's practised by just under ten percent of the population. Bali has around two thousand mosques, the majority of which are in the west and north of the island, in the communities of people who have moved across the Bali Strait from Java.

The tiny **Christian** population (1.8 percent), many of whom live in two Christian communities on a remote mountainside in west Bali (see p.359), have adapted a number of Hindu traditions, such as dance performances, replacing the central characters with biblical ones but retaining the tone of the originals. Roman Catholics and Protestants together make up around one percent of the Balinese population and both communities have built huge churches in their west-Bali villages.

Bali has nine **Buddhist** temples, the most famous of which is the Thai-style Theravada Buddhist sanctuary in the north-Bali village of Banjar (see p.334). Although the 2000 census shows that only half a percent of the population is Buddhist, mainstream Balinese Hinduism incorporates a number of Buddhist teachings and practices. Because **Confucianism** is not monotheistic, it's not officially recognized by the Indonesian government and so is effectively illegal. Most Chinese temples on Bali are therefore Theravada Buddhist, but suffused with enough Confucian elements to retain a distinctly Chinese character. The major Chinese temples are located near the coast and in the biggest commercial centres – close to the homes of the original Chinese traders and settlers; the most notable are in Kuta, Tanjung Benoa and Singaraja.

# Lombok and Islam

Indonesia is the largest **Muslim** nation in the world, and ninety percent of its population follow the faith. On Lombok, 97 percent of the islanders are Muslim, with a tiny minority adhering to the Wetu Telu branch (see below). As Wetu Telu is not officially recognized, numbers of followers are uncertain, but most estimates suggest around 28,000.

Within Indonesia, the practice of Islam varies from area to area. On Lombok, women are expected to dress modestly, but are not strictly veiled; the centre and east of the island are the most devout, but even here you'll see women with and without head-coverings, and relatively few with their entire body covered. The **mosque** is the centre of the Muslim faith, with Friday as the most religious day, when the noon service pretty much empties the villages (see p.80 for etiquette required when visiting a mosque).

It is still unclear exactly how Islam came to Indonesia, but it seems likely that it spread along trade routes, probably via traders from Gujarat in India who had converted to Islam in the mid-thirteenth century. In the fourteenth century, it spread from Sumatra, down into Java and, by the sixteenth century, had arrived in Lombok. Traditionally, the arrival of Islam in Java is thought to have more exotic roots, brought by nine Islamic saints or *wali sangga*, one of whom is believed to be buried near Rembitan in the south of Lombok.

## Wetu Telu

Followers of the **Wetu Telu** religion – the title translates as "three times", referring to the number of daily prayer-times – adhere to the central tenets of Islam, such as belief in Allah as the one God and Muhammad as his prophet, but diverge significantly from the practices of other Muslims, who, because they pray five times a day, are known as "Wetu Lima".

For the Wetu Telu, the older traditions of **ancestor worship** and **animism** are as important as the more orthodox ideas of Islam, and many follow their own three-day observation of the fast in the holy month of Ramadan, rather than the full month. The most important rituals associated with Wetu Telu are **life-cycle events** such as birth, death, marriage and circumcision, as well as rituals connected with agriculture and house-building. Their most important annual festival is **Maulid**, Muhammad's birthday.

Throughout their history, the Wetu Telu have been subjected to varying degrees of pressure. During the nineteenth century, some Muslims, many of whom had completed the *hajj*, or pilgrimage to Mecca, sought to ensure a wider orthodox adherence to the faith, and only the Dutch takeover of the island moderated the more zealous among them. Following the Indonesian declaration of independence and the subsequent war against the Dutch, a local movement, **Nahdatul Wahtan**, was formed in Selong in East Lombok, led by Haji Zainuddin Abdul Majid, which persecuted the followers of the Wetu Telu religion. In more recent times, during the civil unrest in 1965, anyone less than scrupulously orthodox was in danger of being regarded as Communist, and there were some attacks against the Wetu Telu at that time. Today, it's almost certain that numbers are falling, for while it is possible to convert to Islam, you must be born Wetu Telu to belong to the faith.

In many ways, Wetu Telu practices have more in common with those of Balinese Hinduism: both faiths worship at Pura Lingsar, and some adherents believe that **Gunung Rinjani** is the dwelling place of the ancestors and the Supreme God and make pilgrimages to the mountain. Some Muslims dislike the fact that **Bayan**, in the north of Lombok, one of the first centres of Islam on Lombok and site of the oldest mosque on the island, is now a stronghold of Wetu Telu belief.

# Traditional music and dance

Music and dance play an essential part in daily Balinese life, and as a visitor you can't fail to experience them, either at a special tourist show, in rehearsal or at a temple festival. You can even learn the rudimentaries at introductory classes in Ubud (see p.214). There's a vibrant tradition of music and dance on Lombok, too, rarely witnessed by casual visitors to the island, since it's associated almost exclusively with religious practices.

## Balinese performing arts

Traditionally, **Balinese** dancers and musicians have always learnt their craft from the experts in their village and by imitating other performers. Since the 1960s, however, arts students have also had the option of attending a government-run high school and college dedicated to the performing arts. The month-long Bali Arts Festival (⊛www.baliartsfestival.com; see p.105), held every summer in Denpasar, showcases the best in the performing arts, staging both new and traditional works performed by professional arts graduates as well as village groups.

### Balinese gamelan music

The national music of Bali is **gamelan**, a jangly clashing of syncopated sounds once described by the writer Miguel Covarrubias as being like "an Oriental ultra-modern Bach fugue, an astounding combination of bells, machinery and thunder." The highly structured compositions are produced by a group of 25 or more musicians seated cross-legged on the ground at a variety of bronze percussion instruments – gongs, metallophones and cymbals – with a couple of optional wind and stringed instruments. All gamelan music is written for instruments tuned either to a five- or (less commonly) a seven-tone scale, and most is performed at an incredible speed: one study of a gamelan performance found that each instrumentalist played an average of seven notes per second.

"Gamelan" is the Javanese word for the bronze instruments, and the music probably came over from Java around the fourteenth century; the Balinese duly adapted it to suit their own personality, and now the sounds of the Javanese and Balinese gamelan are distinctive even to the untrained ear. Where Javanese gamelan music is restrained and rather courtly, Balinese is loud and flashy, boisterous and speedy, full of dramatic stops and starts. This modern Balinese style, known as **gong kebyar** (*gong* means orchestra, *kebyar* translates, aptly, as lightning-flashes), has been around since the early 1900s, emerging at a time of great political upheaval on the island, when the status of Bali's royal houses was irreparably dented by Dutch colonial aggression. Until then, Bali's music had been as palace-oriented as Javanese gamelan, but in 1915 village musicians from north Bali gave a public performance in the new *kebyar* style, and the trend spread like wildfire across the island, with whole orchestras turning their instruments in to be melted down and recast in the new, more exuberant, timbres.

Gamelan orchestras are an essential part of village life. Every *banjar* that can afford to buy a set of instruments has its own *seka* or **music club**, and there are said to be 1500 active *gong kebyar* on the island. In most communities, the *seka* is open only to men (the all-female gamelan of Peliatan is a rare exception), but has no restrictions on age, welcoming keen players of any standard and experience between the ages of about eight and eighty. **Rehearsals** generally happen after nightfall, either in the *bale banjar* or in the temple's *bale gong* pavilion. There's special *gong* music for every occasion – for sacred and secular dances, cremations, *odalan* festivities and *wayang kulit* shows – but players never learn from scores (in fact, few *gong* compositions are ever notated), preferring instead to have it drummed into them by repetitive practice. Whatever the occasion, *gong* players always dress up in the ceremonial uniform of their music club, and make appropriate blessings and ritual offerings to the deities. Like dancers, musicians are acutely conscious of their role as entertainers of the gods.

## Gamelan instruments

The type of music that a *seka* plays depends on the make-up of its particular gamelan orchestra, and every single *gong* on the island sounds slightly different. Balinese can supposedly find their way around the island in the dark by recognizing the distinctive tones of the various local gamelan.

Although the *gamelan kebyar* is by far the most popular style of music in Bali – and therefore the most common type of orchestra – there are over twenty other different ensemble variations on the island. The smallest is the four-piece **gender wayang**, which traditionally accompanies the *wayang kulit* shadow-play performances; the largest is the old-fashioned classical Javanese-style orchestra comprising fifty instruments, known as the **gamelan gong**. Most gamelan instruments are huge and far too heavy to be easily transported, so nearly every *banjar* also possesses a portable orchestra known as a **gamelan angklung**, specially designed around a set of miniature four-keyed metallophones, for playing in processions and at unusual venues – at cremations for example, or at sea-shore festivals. The classic sounds of the Balinese gamelan are produced mainly by bronze instruments, but there are also a few orchestras composed entirely of bamboo instruments – split bamboo tubes, marimbas and flutes. These ensembles are a particular speciality of western Bali, where they're known as **gamelan joged bumbung** and **gamelan jegog**.

The *gong kebyar* is composed of at least 25 instruments, and always features half-a-dozen tuned *gongs*, several sets of metallophones, two drums, a few sets of cymbals and one or more flutes. The leader of the orchestra is always one of the two **kendang** players (a double-ended cylindrical drum), whose job it is to link the different elements of the orchestra, as well as to take leads from the dancers during performances. Cast in bronze and set in beautifully carved jackfruit-wood frames – often painted red and decorated with gold leaf – metal xylophones or **metallophones** create the distinctive clanging and shimmering gamelan sound. They come in a variety of forms, but the principle is the same for all versions. A series of bronze bars or keys are strung loosely together (the smallest metallophone has four keys, the biggest fourteen) and suspended over bamboo resonators. Players strike each key with a small wood- or metal-tipped mallet held in the right hand, while simultaneously dampening the last key with the finger and thumb of the left hand. Since the *kebyar* is often played incredibly fast, metallophone players need phenomenal coordination to move up and down the "keyboard", striking and dampening two different keys at the same time. The most common metallophones used for the *kebyar* are the three types of **gangsa**. The largest and deepest toned is the **ugal**, which carries the melody, while the higher-pitched **pemade**, and a corresponding number of **kantilan**, pitched higher still, add trills and melodies.

The *gangsa's* hallmark sound is produced by the **kotekan** technique, generally translated as "the use of interlocking parts", which requires two instruments to play a single part. In many cases, there are only split-second differences between the two parts. To add further depth, all pairs of Balinese instruments are tuned to slightly different pitches, a practice that produces the characteristic *vibrato* sound.

Centre-stage is nearly always dominated by the long row of ten or more linked bronze kettle-*gongs* (flattened bells with knobs on the top): the **trompong**. The large bronze **gong**, suspended from a frame at the back of the orchestra, gives structure to every musical composition, its mellow tones marking off the beginning and end of each melody. Other minor and occasional instruments include different-sized cymbals (**cengceng**), bamboo flutes (**suling**), and the classical two-stringed violin, the **rebab**. Some orchestras also enliven their performances with guest spots from the **genggong**, a simple palm-wood jew's-harp, whose haunting vibrations sound a bit like the didgeridoo and are most popularly used for the frog dance.

## Discography

### CDs and cassettes from Bali

Most of the tourist CD shops on the island have pretty good selections of Balinese music; the compilations are often the best buy. Ubud's Ganesha Bookshop (ⓦwww.ganeshabooksbali.com) offers an online ordering service for its stock of Balinese and Indonesian CDs.

**Angklung Sidan** (Bali Stereo). The smaller, lighter, processional gamelan orchestra from the village of Sidan plays ceremonial classics.

**The Best of Gamelan Bali Parts 1 and 2** (Rick's/Maharani). Compilation of various different gamelan styles, including the music that accompanies the Jauk demon dance, and a piece for the rarely heard wooden xylophone, the *gambang*.

**Degung Instrumental: Sabilungan** (SP Records). Not strictly Balinese, but played in every hotel, restaurant and CD shop, this is a classic tape of Sundanese (west Javan) *degung* music. The softer gamelan

is fronted by a strong part for the bamboo flute, which lends a lovely dreamy quality to this exceptionally sensual music.

**The Exotic Sounds of Bali** (Rick's/Maharani). Compilation of different styles played by Ubud musicians, including pieces for the *genggong* (jew's-harp) and the *gong suling* (gamelan orchestra with bamboo flute), and excerpts from the *a cappella kecak* and the electrifying *kebyar duduk* dance.

**The Very Best of Kecak Dance** (Rick's/Maharani). The haunting *a cappella* vocals of the all-male choir that accompanies the spectacular *kecak* (monkey) dance.

### CDs available outside Indonesia

**Bali: Gamelan and Kecak** (Nonesuch, US). A fine cross-section of gamelan and other music, including

*gong kebyar, gender wayang* ensemble for shadow plays, *kecak* and frog dance *genggong*.

**Gamelan Batel Wayang Ramayana** (CMP, Germany). Village gamelan from Sading perform music from the shadow puppet play.

**Gamelan: Gamelan Gong Kebyar of "Eka Cita" Abian Kapas Kaja** (World Music Library). A terrific example of the Balinese *kebyar* style. The group is from a small village near Denpasar.

**Gamelan Semar Pegulingan: The Heavenly Orchestra of Bali** (CMP, Germany). A beautifully sonorous recording of the gentle, older

gamelan from the east-Bali village of Kamasan.

**Jegog of Negara** (World Music Library). A bamboo ensemble from the village of Negara in the west of Bali. Wonderful textures, both percussive and sonorous.

**Music for the Gods** (Rykodisc, US). Fascinating examples of gamelan, *kecak*, log drum and other music from the 1940s, recorded by American anthropologists Bruce and Sheridan Fahnestock.

# Traditional dance-dramas of Bali

Most Balinese **dance-dramas** have evolved from **sacred rituals**, and are still performed at religious events, with full attention given to the offertory and devotional aspects. Before the show begins, a *pemangku* (village priest) will always sprinkle the players and the performance area with holy water, and many performances open with a *pendet*, or welcome dance, intended for the gods. The exorcist Barong–Rangda dramas continue to play a vital function in the **spiritual practices** of every village, and the *baris* dance re-enacts the traditional offering up of weapons by village warriors to the gods to invest them with supernatural power. Some of the more secular dance-dramas tell ancient and **legendary stories**, many of them adapted from the epic Hindu morality tales (the *Ramayana* and the *Mahabharata*) that came from India more than a thousand years ago. Others are based on **historical events**, embellishing the romances and battles that characterized the royal courts of Java and Bali between the tenth and the fourteenth centuries.

With the advent of mass tourism, however, it's becoming less easy to see a traditional performance staged in its natural environment, at a temple festival or village event for example, rather than as a commercial performance. Nonetheless, some of the **tourist shows** are very good, performed by expert local troupes with traditional finesse. Practical information on where to see the best dancers is given on p.65.

There are few professional **dancers** in Bali; most performers don costumes and make-up only at festival times or for the regular tourist shows. Almost every Balinese boy and girl is taught to dance – small boys learn the *baris* (warrior dance), girls the *legong* – and the most adept are then chosen to perform at community functions, as part of the established local troupe. Dancers learn by **imitation and repetition**, the instructor often holding the pupil against his or her body and manipulating limbs until the exact angles and tensions are reproduced to perfection. Personal expression has no place in the Balinese theatre, but the skilful execution of traditional moves is always much admired, and trained dancers enjoy a high status within the village.

**Female dancers** keep their feet firmly planted on the ground, their legs and hips encased in restrictive sarongs that give them a distinctive forward-angled posture. They express themselves through a vocabulary of controlled **angular movements** of the arms, the wrists, the fingers, the neck and, most

## The Mahabharata

Like its companion piece the *Ramayana*, the **Mahabharata** is an epic moral narrative of Hindu ethics that came originally from India in the eleventh century. Written during the fourth century AD by the Indian poet Vyasa, the original poem is phenomenally long, with over 100,000 verses in all. The **Balinese version** is translated into the ancient poetic language of Kawi and written on sacred *lontar* books kept in the Gedong Kirtya library at Singaraja.

At the heart of the story is the conflict between two rival branches of the same family, the Pandawas and the Korawas, all of them descendants of various unions between the deities and the mortals. The five **Pandawa brothers** represent the side of virtue, morality and noble purpose, though they each have idiosyncrasies that are not entirely snowy white. The eldest is **Yudhisthira**, a calm and thoughtful leader with a passion for justice, whose one vice – an insatiable love of gambling – nonetheless manages to land the brothers in a fair amount of trouble. Then comes **Bhima**, a strong, courageous and hot-headed fighter, whose fiery temper and earthy manner make him especially appealing to the Balinese. The third brother, **Arjuna**, is the real hero; not only is he a brave warrior and an expert archer, but he's also handsome, high-minded, and a great lover. Arjuna's two younger brothers, the expert horse-man **Nakula** and the learned **Sahadeva**, are twins. Their rivals are their cousins the **Korawas**, who number a hundred in all, and are led by the eldest male **Durodhana**, a symbol of jealousy, deviousness and ignoble behaviour.

An early episode in the *Mahabharata* tells how the Pandawa boys are forced by the Korawas to give up their rightful claim to the kingdom's throne, and are banished to the mountains for a minimum of thirteen years. The Pandawa brothers grow up determined to regain their rightful heritage. Meanwhile, both families engage in all sorts of minor adventures, the best of which recur in carvings, *wayang kulit* dramas and dances. A particular favourite is the exploit known as **Bhima Swarga**, in which Bhima is dispatched to Hell to rescue the souls of his dead father and stepmother. While there, he witnesses all sorts of horrible tortures and punishments many of which are graphically depicted on the ceilings of Klungkung's Kerta Gosa. When Bhima returns to earth with the souls of his relatives, he's immediately sent off to Heaven in search of the holy water needed to smooth his dead parents' passage into Heaven. This episode is known as **Bhima Suci** and features the nine directional gods, as well as a dramatic battle between Bhima and his own godly (as opposed to earthly) father, Bayu.

Finally, a full-scale battle is declared between the two sets of cousins. On the eve of the battle, Arjuna suddenly becomes doubtful about the morality of fighting his own family, and confides as much to his friend and charioteer Krishna. Krishna, who is actually an avatar of the Hindu god Wisnu, then launches into a long theological lecture, in which he explains to Arjuna that the action is the all-important factor, not the result, and that because Arjuna is of the warrior caste, his duty is to fight, to act in a manner that's appropriate to his destiny. This episode of the *Mahabharata* is known as the **Bhagavad Gita**, and encapsulates the core Hindu philosophy of caste, and the notions of karma and destiny. Duly persuaded, Arjuna joins his brothers in battle, and at the end of eighteen bloody days the Pandawa brothers are victorious.

beguilingly, the eyes. Each pose and gesture derives from a movement observed in the natural rather than the human world. Thus, a certain type of flutter of the hand may be a bird in flight, a vigorous rotation of the forearms the shaking of water from an animal's coat. Dressed in pantaloons or hitched-up sarongs, the **male dancers** are much more energetic, and whirl about a lot, emphasizing their manliness by opening shoulders and limbs outwards, keeping their knees bent and their heads high.

Most dramas are performed in superb natural settings, either within a temple compound, or in the outer courtyard of a noble family's palace. The **costumes and masks** give immediate clues to the identity of each character – and to the action that is to follow. Some dramas are performed in a combination of contemporary Bahasa Indonesia and the ancient poetic language known as Kawi, while others stick to modern speech – perhaps with a few humorous English phrases thrown in for the tourists.

In the last sixty years, the Balinese dance repertoire has expanded quite considerably, not least because of the efforts of one of the island's most famous performers, the late I Ketut Marya. Better known as **Mario**, he was also a highly imaginative choreographer, adapting old forms to suit the modern mood, and most famously to fit the modern *kebyar* gamelan style in the 1920s.

## Baris

The **baris** or **warrior dance** can be performed either as a solo or in a group of five or more, and either by a young woman, or more commonly a young man. Strutting on stage with knees and feet turned out, his centre of gravity kept

### The Ramayana

Written in Sanskrit around the fourth century BC, the 24,000 verses that comprise the **Ramayana** have since fired the imaginations of writers, artists, dramatists, theologians and sculptors right across Southeast Asia. Like the other great Hindu epic, the *Mahabharata*, the *Ramayana* has been translated into the classical Javanese Kawi language and transcribed on to sacred *lontar* texts.

It's essentially a morality tale, a dramatization of the eternal conflict between the forces of good (*dharma*) and the forces of evil (*adharma*). The forces of good are represented by Rama and his friends. **Rama** is the hero of the piece, a refined and dutiful young man, handsome, strong and courageous, who also happens to be an avatar of the god Wisnu. Rama's wife, **Sita**, epitomizes the Hindu ideals of womanhood – virtue, fidelity and love – while Rama's brother, **Laksmana**, is a symbol of fraternal loyalty and youthful courage. The other important member of the Rama camp is **Hanuman**, the general of the monkey army, a wily and athletic ape who is unfailingly loyal to his allies. On the opposing side, the forces of evil are mainly represented by the demon king **Rawana**, a lustful and devious leader whose retainers are giants and devils.

The story begins with Rama, the eldest son of the king, being banished to the forests for thirteen years, having been cheated out of his rightful claim to the throne by a scheming stepmother. Sita and Laksmana accompany him, and together the trio have various encounters with sages, giants and seductresses.

The most crucial event in the epic is the **abduction of Sita** by Rawana, a crime that inspires the generally easygoing and rather unwarlike Rama to wage battle against his enemy. A favourite subject for dances and carvings, the episode starts with Sita catching sight of a beautiful golden deer and imploring her husband Rama to catch it for her. The golden deer turns out to be a decoy planted by Rawana, and the demon king duly swoops down to abduct Sita as soon as Rama and Laksmana go off to chase the animal.

The distraught Rama determines to get Sita back and, together with Laksmana, he sets off for Rawana's kingdom. En route he meets Hanuman, the monkey general, who agrees to sneak him into Sita's room at Rawana's palace and **give her Rama's ring** (another popular theme of pictures and dramas). Eventually, Rama, Laksmana, Hanuman and his monkey army all arrive at Rawana's palace and, following a big battle, Sita is rescued and Rawana done away with.

low, the *baris* cuts an impressive figure in a gilded brocade cloak of ribboned pennants, which fly out dramatically at every turn. In his performance, he enacts a young warrior's preparation for battle, goading himself into courageous mood, trying out his martial skills, showing pride at his calling and then expressing a whole series of emotions – ferocity, passion, tenderness, rage – much of it through the arresting movements of his eyes.

Traditionally, the solo *baris* has always improvised a lot, leading the gamelan rather than following it. In its original sacred form, known as the *baris gede*, this was a devotional dance in which soldiers dedicated themselves and their weapons to the gods.

## Barong–Rangda dramas

Featuring the most spectacular costumes of all the Balinese dances, the **Barong–Rangda dramas** are also among the most sacred and most important. Essentially a dramatization of the eternal conflict between the forces of good and evil, the dramas can take a variety of forms but nearly always serve as ritualized exorcisms.

The mythical widow-witch character of **Rangda** represents the forces of evil, and her costume and mask present a duly frightening spectacle (see p.235 for Rangda's story). The **Barong** cuts a much more lovable figure, a shaggy-haired creature with a bug-eyed expression and a mischievous grin on his masked face, something like a cross between a pantomime horse and a Chinese dragon. The Barong Ket (lion) is by far the most common persona adopted by this mythical creature, but you might also see Barong Macan (tiger), Barong Bangkal (wild boar) and Barong Celeng (pig). All Rangda and Barong **masks** are invested with great sacred power and treated with due respect and awe. When not in use, the masks are kept wrapped in "magic" cloth and stored in the temple.

Barong–Rangda dramas can be self-contained, as in the *calonarang* (see below), or they can appear as just one symbolic episode in the middle of a well-known story like the *Mahabharata*. Whatever the occasion, the format tends to be fairly similar. Rangda is always called upon by a character who wants to cause harm to a person, family or village (unrequited love is a very common cause). She generally sends a minion to wage the first battles, and is then forced to appear herself when the opposition calls in the Barong, the defender of the good. In this final confrontation, the Barong enters first, occasionally joined by a monkey who teases him and plays tricks. Suddenly, Rangda appears, fingernails first, from behind the central gateway. Flashing her white magic cloth, she harasses the Barong, stalking him at every turn. When the Barong looks to be on his last legs, a group of village men rush in to his rescue, but are entranced by Rangda's magic and stab themselves instead of her. A priest quickly enters before any real injury is inflicted. The series of confrontations continues, and the drama ends in stalemate: the forces of good and evil remain as strong and vital as ever, ready to clash again in the next bout.

The story of the **calonarang** is basically an embellished version of the Barong–Rangda conflict, grafted on to an ancient legend about the daughter of a witch queen whom no one will marry because they're scared of her mother. The witch queen Calonarang is a manifestation of Rangda who, furious at the lack of suitors for her daughter, demands that her followers wreak destruction in all the villages. This drama is acted out on a regular basis, whenever there are considered to be evil forces and impurities affecting the community, and sometimes the whole neighbourhood takes part, the men parading with hand-held *kulkul* drums and the women filing in to make offerings at the temple shrines.

There's also an unusual human version of the Barong, called **Barong Land-ung** (literally "tall barong"). These are huge puppets, one male and one female, each one operated by a single performer. The male puppet looks forbidding, his masked face is black, and he has a fanged mouth and grimacing features. As a representation of the legendary Jero Gede, a giant from Nusa Penida who brought disease and misfortune to Bali, this enormous figure is also meant to scare away any similar giants. Jero Gede is always accompanied by a far sweeter-looking female puppet, known as Jero Luh, who wears a white mask with a smiling face and faintly Chinese eyes. Together they act out a bawdy comic opera, which has exorcist purposes as well.

## Kebyar

A great wave of artistic experimentation hit Bali in the 1920s, particularly in north Bali, where a group of young musicians started playing around with the traditional gamelan form (see p.468). They came up with a vibrant and much brasher type of music, the **kebyar**, whose energetic rhythms inspired the talented young dancer Mario to choreograph a new piece. He performed this dance while seated on the ground and so called it **kebyar duduk** (seated *kebyar*). It's a stunningly camp piece of theatre, starring just one man, who alternately flirts with the gamelan, plays the kettle-*gongs* (*trompong*) that are placed in front of him, and flutters his fan in beguiling self-dramatization. Some years later, a slightly different version of this dance was invented, the **kebyar trompong**, in which the dancer sits and plays the *trompong* for only part of the performance, in between mincing coquettishly about the stage and making eyes at the audience.

## Kecak

Sometimes called the **monkey dance** after the animals represented by the chorus, the **kecak** gets its Balinese name from the hypnotic chattering sounds made by the a cappella choir. Chanting nothing more than "cak cak cak cak", the chorus of fifty or more men uses seven different rhythms to create the astonishing music that accompanies the drama. Bare-chested, and wearing lengths of black-and-white-check *kain poleng* cloth around their waists and a single red hibiscus behind the ear, the men sit cross-legged in five or six tight concentric circles, occasionally swaying or waving arms and clapping hands in unison. The **narrative** itself is taken from a core episode of the *Ramayana*, centring around the kidnap of Sita by the demon king Rawana, and is acted out in the middle of the chorus circle, with one or two narrators speaking for all the characters.

Although frequently attributed to the German artist and musician Walter Spies, the main creative force behind the *kecak* was the famous *baris* dancer **I Wayan Limbak**, who lived in Bedulu in Gianyar. In 1931, he developed the chants from the *sanghyang* trance dances, in which the chorus chants the "cak cak cak" syncopation as part of the trance-inducing ritual, and created accompanying choreography to flesh out the episode from the *Ramayana*.

## Legong

Undoubtedly the most refined of all the temple dances, the quintessentially Balinese **legong** is rather an acquired taste, which can seem tiresome to the uninitiated because of its restrained movement and lack of dramatic narrative. Its beauty is all in the intricate weavings of arms, fingers, torsos and heads. The *legong* is always performed by three pre-pubescent girls who are bound tightly in sarongs and chest cloths of opulent green or pink, with gilded crowns filled with frangipani blossoms on their heads. When village elders and former dancers are selecting aspiring *legong* dancers, they look not only for agility and vitality, but also for grace and poise, as the spirit of the *legong* is considered the acme of Balinese femininity. As a result, *legong* dancers have always enjoyed a special status in their village, a reputation that endures long after they retire at the onset of menstruation. In the past, many a *legong* dancer has ended up as a raja's wife or, latterly, as an expatriate artist's muse and subsequent partner.

The dance itself has evolved from a highly sacred *sanghyang* trance dance and takes several different forms. By far the most common is the **legong keraton** (dance of the court), based on a classical twelfth-century tale from Java. It tells the story of King Laksem, who is holding a princess, Rangkesari, captive against her will. Rescue is on the way in the form of Prince Daha, who plans to wage battle against King Laksem. The princess tries to dissuade the king from going to war, encouraging him to set her free instead of risking lives, but the king is adamant and sets off. As he leaves, he is attacked by a raven, an extremely bad omen, after which he duly loses the battle and is killed.

The **performance** begins with a solo dance by a court lady, known as the *condong* (dressed in pink and gold). She picks up two fans from the ground in anticipation of the arrival of the two *legong* (literally "dancer"). Dressed identically in bright green and gold, the two *legong* enact the story, adopting and swapping characters with no obvious warning. The *condong* always returns as the raven, with pink wings attached to her costume. The final fatal battle is never shown on stage.

### Mahabharata dance-dramas

Many of the stories from the Hindu epic, the **Mahabharata**, are known by every Balinese and repeated endlessly in paintings, sculpted reliefs and dramatizations (see p.472 for an introduction). The basic *Mahabharata* narrative tells of the extended rivalry between the Pandawa brothers and their usurping cousins the Korawas, and features all sorts of battles between the two sides, as well as confrontations with gods and demons, long journeys, seductions and practical jokes. The most popular *Mahabharata* characters are the second Pandawa brother, **Bhima**, a passionate, tempestuous man with a good heart and a slightly coarse, earthy manner, and his younger, far more refined brother, **Arjuna**, an expert archer and all-round romantic hero.

### Oleg tambulilingan

Translated as the **bumblebee dance**, the *oleg tambulilingan* is one of the most vivacious, humorous and engaging dances of the Balinese repertoire but, unfortunately, it doesn't get performed that often. It's a flirtation dance, performed by a man and woman who act as courting bumblebees sipping honey in a flower garden, the man sexually obsessed with the female, desire burning in his eyes, the female coquettish and eventually compliant.

The *oleg tambulilingan* is one of several dances invented by the late great dancer Mario, who created it in 1952 as a commission for a world tour. The female role is complicated, needing a highly skilled performer, and so is often taken by a former *legong* dancer.

### Ramayana dance-dramas

The great Hindu epic, the *Ramayana*, is a popular inspiration for all sorts of dance-dramas (see p.473 for more on the story). By far the best-loved episode of the whole tale is the act in which Rama's queen Sita is kidnapped by the demon king Rawana, and whisked off to his palace. The kidnapping features prominently in two of the most frequently performed tourist dance shows, the *kecak* and the **Ramayana Ballet**.

Although the storyline is fairly simple, things can get confusing if you're unable to differentiate between characters. **Sita** always wears her hair long and is distinguishable from assorted maidservants and female friends by the two long red scarves that hang from her waist. The hero, **Rama**, is played by a woman, and in the opening scenes always wears a golden crown with a quiver full of arrows on his back. Confusingly, Rama's brother, **Laksmana**, is also played by a woman, but he generally sports a black headdress. The demon king, **Rawana**, on the other hand, has a very masculine presence, strutting around in flamboyant battle dress. It's pretty easy to recognize Rama's chief aide, the monkey general **Hanuman**, by his distinctive white monkey mask and long white tail – he always wears white, while his simian retainers dress in different colours. The monkeys are the main source of the drama's jokes and slapstick humour.

## Sanghyang: trance dances

The state of **trance** lies at the very heart of traditional Balinese dance. In order to maintain the health of the village, the gods are periodically invited down into the temple arena to help in the exorcism of evil and sickness-inducing spirits. When the deities descend, they reveal themselves by possessing certain people and using them as their medium. Sometimes the deities communicate in verbal form, which may or may not have to be interpreted by the priests, and sometimes the whole physical being is taken over and the devotee is moved to dance or to perform astonishing physical feats. The chosen medium is put into a trance state through a combination of special priestly chants and protective mantras, intoned exhortations by the a cappella choir, and great clouds of pungent incense wafted heavenwards to attract the gods' attention. Trance dances are traditionally only performed when the village is suffering from a particularly serious bout of sickness or bad weather – the versions that are reproduced at tourist shows have none of the spiritual dynamism of the real thing, though it is said that performers do sometimes slip into trance even then.

One of the most common trance dances is the **sanghyang dedari** (angel deity), which is widely believed to have been the inspiration for the popular courtly dance, the *legong*. In the *sanghyang dedari*, the deities possess two young girls who perform a complicated duet with their eyes closed and, in part, while seated on the shoulders of two male villagers. Although they have never learnt the actual steps, the duo almost invariably performs its movements in tandem and sometimes continues for up to four hours. When they finally drop to the floor in exhaustion, the priest wakes them gently with a sprinkle of holy water. In the *sanghyang dedari* performed at tourist shows, however, the girls have almost certainly rehearsed the dance beforehand and probably do not enter a trance state at all. They wear the same tightly bound green and gold sarongs as the *legong* dancers, and dance to the haunting backing vocals of an a cappella chorus of men and women.

In the **sanghyang jaran** (horse deity), one or more men are put into a trance state while the temple floor is littered with burning coconut husks. As they enter the trance, the men grab hold of wooden hobbyhorse sticks and then gallop frantically back and forth across the red-hot embers as if they were on real horses. The all-male *kecak* chorus fuels the drama with excited a cappella crescendos until, finally, the exhausted hobbyhorse riders are awoken by the priest.

## Topeng: mask dances

In the **topeng** or **mask dance**, the performer is possessed by the spirit of the mask. Balinese masks are extremely sacred objects, carved and painted with great reverence to the gods and spirits (see p.486). Before every entrance, the *topeng* actor sprinkles holy water on his mask and recites a mantra. Women never participate in *topeng*: female roles are played by men, and most actors play several characters in each drama.

The **storylines** of most *topeng* dramas are much more important than in most other Balinese dance-dramas. They usually centre around popular folk tales or well-known episodes from history, and every character wears a mask that makes him or her immediately recognizable. Refined and **noble characters** always wear full masks, usually painted white with almond-shaped eyes, and thick black eyebrows for the men. They communicate with elegant gestures of the hands, arms and head, and move with rather grand, often swaggering bravado. A royal servant always acts as a narrator figure, speaking on behalf of the voiceless nobles, and he, like the coarser characters, the **clowns** and the **servants**, wears a half-mask and baggy shapeless clothing in which to roll about the floor and engage in comic antics.

One of the most popular mask dances is the **topeng tua**, a solo performance by the character of an old man, a retired first minister, who recalls his time in the king's service. The mask is always shrouded in straggly white hair and a beard, and the actor hobbles about with shaky legs and wavering fingers. Another classic tourist *topeng* is the **frog dance** – performed to the evocative music of the Balinese jew's-harp or *genggong* – which tells how a frog turns into a prince. The **jauk** is a masked dance of a slightly different nature, in which the solo dancer portrays a terrifying demon-king. His red or white mask has huge bulging eyes, a horribly goofy smile and a thick black moustache, and his hands are crowned with foot-long fingernails, which he flashes menacingly throughout the dance. To the clashing strains of the full-blown gamelan who take their cues from the exuberant dancer, the *jauk* leaps mischievously about the stage as if darting from behind trees and pouncing on unsuspecting villagers.

## Wayang kulit: shadow puppet shows

On an island where cinema screens and TVs haven't quite percolated through to the smallest villages, a **wayang kulit** performance, or **shadow puppet drama**, still draws in huge crowds and keeps them entertained well into the early hours. The stories and techniques are familiar to all, but the sheer panache, eloquence and wit of a good *dalang* (puppet master) means the show is as likely to break news, spread gossip and pass on vital information as it is to entertain.

A typical *wayang kulit* show takes place after sundown on the occasion of a wedding, a cremation or a temple *odalan*, staged either in the outer courtyard of the village temple, or in the *bale banjar* meeting area. The *dalang* (nearly always a man) sets up a white cloth screen, lights flaming rags dipped in paraffin for his illumination and assembles his collection of puppets (*wayang*). It's not unusual for a *dalang* to own 150 different **wayang**, each of them fashioned from flat lengths of buffalo hide, carved and perforated to create a lacy effect before being painted and mounted on a stick. (You can see the workshops of some well-known *dalang* in Sukawati, described on p.176.) As in many other Balinese dramas, *wayang* characters can be divided into those belonging to the refined and noble camp (royal personages, holy men and women, heroes and heroines) and those that are coarse and vulgar (clowns and servants). The refined characters speak in the ancient courtly language of Kawi, while the coarse characters use Balinese. One character may be represented by a number of different puppets, each one showing him or her in a particular mood or stance.

The **dalang** mobilizes all the puppets behind the screen, speaking for each of them and moving each one in character as well. Well-educated and humorous, with a quite astonishing memory for lines, not to mention an impressive range of different voices, the *dalang* also conducts the special four-piece orchestra that accompanies his performances, the *gender wayang*. Not surprisingly, *dalang* are greatly revered by other villagers, who see them as being invested with great spiritual power.

From the complete *wayang* cast, the *dalang* selects between thirty and sixty puppets for any one show. The torch-lit **screen** represents the world in micro-cosm: the puppets are the humans that inhabit it, the torch stands in for the sun, and the *dalang* acts as god. Puppets who represent good characters always appear to the right of the *dalang*, and those who are evil appear on his left. A leaf-shaped fan-like puppet, symbolizing the tree of life, marks centre stage and is used to indicate the end of a scene as well as to represent clouds, spirits and magical forces. The most popular *wayang kulit* **stories** are taken from the *Mahabharata*.

# Lombok music and dance

**Lombok** has a rich heritage of music and dance, linked to religious occasions on the island. The indigenous Sasak traditions have been subject to many influences, both Hindu and Islamic, direct from Bali and Java, and through Buginese and Makassarese traders. The resulting melange of puppetry, poetry, song and dance is huge and varied, but largely inaccessible to tourists. There are **no cultural shows** such as you will find on Bali, but you may happen across a wedding or other celebration on your way around the island.

There is some conflict on Lombok between the traditional forms of music and dance and the more modern Islamic ones. Some religious leaders have tried to **ban** traditional gamelan because of its association with earlier beliefs, such as animism and ancestor worship (the bronze instruments of traditional gamelan are sometimes described as "the voice of the ancestors"). The **wayang Sasak** puppets, introduced in the seventeenth century to help the spread of Islam on the island, have now also been forbidden by more conservative Muslims, on the grounds that Islam prohibits the depiction of the human form.

## Lombok's gamelan music

Lombok's traditional **gamelan** music is similar to Bali's. Several common types of ensemble accompany dances and songs, comprising the familiar drums, chimes, cymbals and gongs. The **gamelan gong Sasak** resembles the Balinese *gamelan gong* in instruments and repertoire, but may be combined with the rather unusual **gamelan grantang**, consisting of bamboo xylophones. The **gamelan oncer** is also widely used, and best known for its use in the *kendang belek* dance, in which two instrumentalists carry and play large drums and dance a dramatic and confrontational duet.

**Gamelan tawa–tawa** and **barong tengkok** are two musical ensembles used in processions during life-cycle celebrations or other festivities such as national holidays. The usual gongs and drums are accompanied by eight sets of cymbals attached to decorated lances for marching with. The gamelan *barong tengkok* from central Lombok actually has gongs suspended within a Barong figure, and traditionally plays at wedding ceremonies, while the bride and groom are paraded on wooden horses.

**Muslim ensembles** were developed about a century ago in an attempt to stamp out the traditional orchestras. **Gamelan rebana** consists of up to twenty different drums, which mimic the traditional sound of gamelan music, but without the use of bronze instruments. More unusual is the **gamelan klentang**, made up entirely of iron instruments. Other Muslim ensembles, **kecimol** and **cilokaq**, consist of an oboe (*preret*), flutes, lutes, violins and drums, and often accompany Sasak poetry.

## Lombok's dances

Compared with the huge artistic academic interest in Balinese performance art, Lombok has been largely ignored, although several Lombok **dances** are recognizably similar to traditional Balinese ones. The **Gandrung**, for instance, which is performed mainly in central Lombok by a solo female dancer who selects a man to join her in the performance, has a counterpart on Bali.

Lombok also has examples of rare **trance dances**. The **suling dewa**, accompanied by flutes and song, is found in the north of the island, and used to induce spirits to enter the local shaman and bless the village. The **pepakon**, from east Lombok, causes the sick to become possessed so that their illness can be removed from them.

**Processional dances** also occur. The **batek baris** is performed in Lingsar, among other places, the dancers wearing costumes mimicking Dutch army uniforms and carrying wooden rifles while they lead a procession to the sacred springs. The **tandang mendet** takes place rarely, and only in the mountain village of Sembalun Bumbung, and heads a procession to the grave of a Majapahit ancestor buried in the valley.

As in Bali, some dances in Lombok are based on **legends**. The **telek** is based very broadly on the tale of a princess who falls in love with a humble man; and the **kemidi rudat** on the *Thousand and One Nights* stories, complete with colourful characters and clowns.

# Arts and crafts

The desire to make things look good – and to make beautiful things – is so ingrained in the Balinese way of life that there is no separate Balinese word for "art" or "artist". Villagers have traditionally considered it their unquestioned duty to honour both their gods and their rajas with attractive objects and buildings.

Lombok lacks the dynamic artistic heritage of Bali, and as a predominantly Islamic island that forbids the depiction of the human form, has virtually no indigenous fine art. However, there is a thriving crafts tradition.

For general information on **where to buy** arts and crafts in Bali and Lombok, see p.76. For details of workshops and classes in traditional Balinese arts and crafts, see Ubud, p.214, and Kuta, p.134.

# Balinese arts and crafts

Although highly skilled, the **carvers**, **sculptors**, **weavers** and **painters** who decorated Bali's temples and palaces were never paid for their work, and would earn their living as farmers or traders, just like everybody else. They worked as **artists** only when summoned by the raja or the high priest – and they never signed their work. By the 1930s, however, the rajas had lost a great deal of their power to the Dutch colonials (many had in fact lost their lives, or at least their homes), and foreign tourists were gradually taking their place as **patrons of the arts** – and paying for the work. Over time, this encouraged a whole variety of changes: artists began to carve and paint secular subjects, to experiment with new materials, to express themselves as individuals and to sign their own work. Making paintings and carvings became a full-time, and relatively lucrative, job, and the arts and crafts industry is now one of the most profitable on Bali. See "Basics", p.77, for a guide to where to shop for arts and crafts.

## Painting

Art historians group traditional **Balinese painting** into five general **schools**: *wayang* (also known as classical or Kamasan), Ubud, Batuan, Young Artists, and Modern or Academic. Inevitably the categories are broad and over-generalized, but Balinese painters, like artists working in other media, are not shy about copying good ideas or even reproducing successful work, so it's not difficult to pinpoint representative features or techniques. One notable and extremely prolific artist who really can't be fitted into any of the above categories is the late **I Gusti Nyoman Lempad** (see p.195 for more on his work).

### Wayang or Kamasan style

The earliest Balinese painters drew their inspiration from the *wayang kulit* shadow plays, re-creating puppet-like figures on their canvases and depicting episodes from the same religious and historical epics that were played out on the stage. Variously known as the **wayang style**, the **classical style** or the **Kamasan style** (after the village most noted for its *wayang*-style art), this is the most traditional genre of Balinese art, and the one that's been the least influenced by Western techniques and subjects. The oldest-known examples date

## Art galleries

Ubud is the centre for all things arty and not only houses the majority of Bali's best art museums but is also home to dozens of artists' studios, both local and expat. The best collection of Balinese painting on the island is housed in the **Neka Art Museum** in Ubud (ⓦ www.museumneka.com; see p.198), where you'll get an excellent introduction to all the major styles, and see some of the finest Balinese pictures in existence. Other worthwhile Ubud art museums include the **Seniwati Gallery of Art by Women** (ⓦ www.seniwatigallery.com; see p.195), which is dedicated to paintings by women living in Bali; the Agung Rai Museum of Art, **ARMA** (ⓦ www.armamuseum.com; see p.206), whose collection covers choice works from the past three hundred years; and the **Museum Puri Lukisan** (ⓦ www.mpl-ubud.com; see p.193), which features select paintings and woodcarvings from the 1930s on. Outside Ubud, head for the collections at the **Gunarsa Museum of Classical and Modern Art** near Klungkung (ⓦ www.gunarsamuseum.com; see p.243), and the **Taman Budaya Cultural Centre** in Denpasar (see p.105). For unrivalled examples of classical Balinese art, visit the old **Taman Gili** palace in Klungkung (see p.242).

back to the mid-seventeenth century, when *wayang*-style figures were painted on to decorative temple scrolls, curtains that hung in royal sleeping pavilions, and astrological charts. None of these has survived, however, except in descriptions from contemporary literature.

The most dramatic and famous *wayang*-style pictures – those covering the ceilings of two buildings within the old palace of Klungkung, the **Kerta Gosa** (Law Courts) and the Bale Kambung (Floating Pavilion) – are in fact less than two hundred years old and have been retouched several times. Probably painted in the early decades of the nineteenth century, the Kerta Gosa pictures are considered the yardstick of classical Balinese art (see p.242 for a full description).

All *wayang*-style pictures are packed full of people painted in **three-quarter profile** (both eyes visible), with caricature-like features and angular, puppet-like poses. There is no perspective, and stylized symbols are used to indicate the location; in lengthy narratives, the pictures are divided into scenes by borders composed of rows of mountains, flames or walls. Traditional *wayang* artists use only a limited palette of five different **colours** – red, blue, yellow, black and white – creating the characteristic muted effect. Because of all the stages involved in a *wayang*-style picture, most modern paintings are produced by a team, with the senior artist drawing the outlines in black while assistants fill in the colours.

Like the *wayang* puppets, the **characters** that people classical paintings are instantly recognizable by their facial features and hairstyles, by the clothes that they wear and the objects that they hold, and by their stance and their size. Convention requires, for example, that "refined" characters (heroes, heroines and other people of noble birth) have a slightly supercilious expression on all occasions (in love, in battle, in anger or in joy), and that their bodies be svelte and elegantly posed. "Coarse" characters, on the other hand, like clowns, servants and demonic creatures, have bulbous eyes, gaping mouths with prominent teeth, and chunky bodies.

The *wayang* style is still popular with modern artists: some stick faithfully to classical themes, while others experiment more freely. The traditional school is centred on the village of **Kamasan** near Klungkung, the home of the original Kerta Gosa artists and source of subsequent generations of restorers ever since.

Probably the most famous living artist of the Kamasan school is **I Nyoman Mandra**, whose works can be bought in his Kamasan showroom. Commercially minded Kamasan artists now apply their talents to more portable artefacts, such as small cloth pictures and reproductions of traditional calendars.

## Ubud style

Although *wayang*-style pictures were occasionally peppered with incidents taken from everyday life, few artists took much interest in secular subjects until the early decades of the twentieth century. In the 1930s, however, Balinese painters started to experiment with more realistic **techniques**, including perspective, relative proportions and the use of light and shadow, and to reproduce in acrylics the events witnessed at the market, the temple, the village and the ricefields. As tourists and expatriate artists began showing a commercial interest in the works, so the painters started to reduce their pictures to a more portable size, and to frame them as well.

The epicentre of the artistic experimentation was the village of Ubud and its neighbouring hamlets, and so this naturalistic style has been dubbed **Ubud style**. Despite its numerous innovative elements, the Ubud style still retains many typical *wayang* features. The most obvious is the overwhelming sense of **activity** that characterizes the canvases (a concept described in Balinese as *rame*), with each character engaged in some transaction or chore or conversation, and any intervening space taken up with detailed miniature reproductions of offerings or scavenging dogs. This **attention to detail** is another traditional feature: every palm leaf and blade of grass is painstakingly delineated, every sarong pattern described. People, however, are rarely given much individuality, their faces usually set in a rather stylized expression.

The two expatriate artists most commonly associated with the emergence of the Ubud style are the German **Walter Spies** and the Dutchman **Rudolph Bonnet**. Both men lived in the Ubud area in the 1930s, and both spent a great deal of time with local painters, swapping ideas and inspirations. Most significantly, they were involved in setting up the arts group Pita Maha (see p.193).

Most of the best-known Ubud-style artists are represented in the Neka Art Museum, the Agung Rai Museum of Art (ARMA), and the Museum Puri Lukisan, all in Ubud, and in the Taman Budaya Cultural Centre in Denpasar. The paintings of **Anak Agung Gede Sobrat** are particularly worth looking out for: his *Bumblebee Dance* is a perfect example of the Ubud style; the original is on show in the Neka Art Museum, and it's reproduced on cards and posters all over the island. The only Walter Spies painting currently on display in the whole of Bali is his *Calonarang*, which you can see at ARMA.

## Pengosekan style

During the 1960s, a group of young painters working in the Ubud style and living in the village of Pengosekan on the outskirts of Ubud came up with a new approach, subsequently known as the **Pengosekan style**. From the Ubud-style pictures, the Pengosekan school isolated just a few components, specifically the **birds, butterflies, insects** and **flowering plants**, and magnified these elements to fill a whole canvas. The best Pengosekan paintings look delicate and lifelike, generally depicted in soothing pastels, and slightly reminiscent of classical Japanese flower and bird pictures. To see some of the finer pictures, you can either go to the showroom run by the descendants of the original Pengosekan artists, in their village, to the Seniwati Gallery in Ubud or the commercial Agung Rai Gallery in Peliatan.

**C**

**CONTEXTS** | Arts and crafts

## Batuan style

In contrast to the slightly romanticized visions of village events being painted by the Ubud-style artists in the 1930s, a group of painters in nearby Batuan were coming up with more thought-provoking interpretations of Balinese life. Like the *wayang* artists, **Batuan-style** painters filled their works with scores of people, but on a much more frantic and wide-ranging scale. A single Batuan-style picture might contain a dozen apparently unrelated scenes – a temple dance, a rice harvest, a fishing expedition, an exorcism, and a couple of tourists taking snapshots – all depicted in fine detail that strikes a balance between the naturalistic and the stylized. By clever juxtaposition, the best Batuan artists (such as the Neka Art Museum exhibitors **I Wayan Bendi**, **I Made Budi** and **Ni Wayan Warti**) can turn their pictures into amusing and astute comments on Balinese society. Works by their precursors, the original Batuan artists, **Ida Bagus Made Togog** and **Ida Bagus Made Wija**, focused more on the darker side of village life, on the supernatural beings that hung around the temples and forests, and on the overwhelming sense of men and women as tiny elements in a forceful natural world.

## Young Artists style

A second flush of artistic innovation hit the Ubud area in the 1960s, when a group of teenage boys from the hamlet of **Penestanan** started producing unusually expressionist works, painting everyday scenes in vibrant, non-realistic colours. They soon became known as the **Young Artists**, a tag now used to describe work by anyone in that same style. The inspiration for the boys' experiments is generally attributed to the interest of Dutch artist **Arie Smit**, who settled in Penestanan in the 1960s, gave the boys materials and helped them organize exhibitions. The style is indisputably child-like, even naive: the detailed, mosaic-like compositions of scenes from daily life are crudely drawn with minimal attention to perspective, outlined in black like a child's colouring book, and often washed over in weird shades of pinks, purples and blues.

All the major museums have works by some of the original Young Artists from the 1960s, the most famous of whom include I Ketut Tagen, I Wayan Pugur, I Nyoman Londo, I Nyoman Mundik and I Nyoman Mujung. The Neka Art Museum in Ubud devotes a whole gallery to Arie Smit's outstanding body of work.

## Academic and other modern styles

Modern artists whose work doesn't fit easily into the other major schools of Balinese painting are often labelled as **Academic**, meaning that they've studied and been influenced by Western techniques. The best-known Academic painters tend to be graduates from the Yogyakarta Academy of Fine Arts who have settled in Bali and painted Balinese subjects in a non-traditional style. Many of the most influential Academics are or have been part of the **Sanggar Dewata Indonesia** art movement, whose style – loosely defined as Balinese Hindu abstract expressionism – has been the dominant form of modern Balinese painting since the 1970s. Although the style has been somewhat devalued by the countless poor-quality abstracts sold in souvenir shops across Bali, works by the most famous Academics – including **Affandi**, **Anton H** and **Abdul Aziz**, all from Java, the Sumatran-born **Rusli**, and from Bali, **Made Wianta**, **Nyoman Gunarsa** and **I Nyoman Tusan** – are on show in both the Neka Art Museum and ARMA, as well as in the Gunarsa Museum near Klungkung and in the Museum Rudana in Teges. Of these important modern artists, Made Wianta is probably the best-known internationally; famous for his multimedia pieces and performance art, he represented Indonesia in the Venice 2003 Biennale, with a video installation on the Kuta bombings.

# Woodcarving

The oldest and most traditional forms of Balinese **woodcarvings** are those that grace the pillars, panels, doors and lintels of temples and palaces. For centuries, woodcarvers have been commissioned to decorate the most important structures of these buildings, such as the gorgeous pillars that support one of the *bale* at the Pura Desa in Sebatu. The Sebatu pillars represent *raksasa*, or demon guardians, and like certain other traditional wooden figurines are designed to repel undesirable intruders and to protect the building from evil influence. You can see some fine examples of traditional carved doors, pillars and protective figures in the reproduction palaces constructed in Denpasar's Bali Museum, and also in the former palace of Ubud's ruling family, Puri Saren, now a hotel.

### Modern carvings

The idea that woodcarvings could be purely ornamental or expressive artefacts didn't gather credence until the early years of the twentieth century, when Balinese carvers began both to take a greater interest in **secular subjects** and

△ Wooden garuda

to court the burgeoning tourist market with carvings of sensually posed naked women, praying girls, and lifelike animals and birds. It also became fashionable to do without the layers of bright paint that characterized traditional carvings, and instead to expose the fine grains of the timber. The most popular styles were quickly copied, and a whole new artistic genre evolved in just a few years.

By the mid-1930s, however, certain influential artists and collectors perceived a significant lowering of artistic standards across the island, which they attributed to the increased commercialization of the traditional arts. In response, they set up the **Pita Maha arts movement** (see box on p.193), which encouraged and inspired some of Bali's most respected carvers. One of these was **Ida Bagus Nyana**, from the village of Mas, who, from the 1930s to the 1960s, produced works in a range of innovative styles, including abstract elongated human figures, erotic compositions of entwined limbs, and smooth, rounded portraits of voluptuously fat men and women. His son, **Ida Bagus Tilem**, has continued to experiment and is particularly famous for using contorted roots and twisted branches to make highly expressive pieces. Works by father and son are displayed, and sold, at the Njana Tilem Gallery in Mas (see p.177). The Jati artist **I Nyoman Cokot** also experimented with bizarre cuts of wood, developing a "free-form" style that made wholesale use of monstrous great branches, fashioning them into weird, otherworldly creatures. Cokot's son, **Ketut Nongos**, lets his supernatural beings emerge from the contours of weatherworn logs and gnarled trunks.

The legacy of these innovative artists can be seen in almost every souvenir shop in Bali, many of which sell goods that suffer from the exact same lowering of artistic standards that hit Bali in the 1930s. Aside from a few notable exceptions, few young artists have attained the same status as the stars of the Pita Maha, and carvers are now more often grouped by village rather than by individual reputation. The village of **Mas**, for example, is renowned for its unvarnished figurines, as well as for traditional *topeng* and *wayang wong* masks (see below). **Nyuhkuning** has long been the established centre of polished wooden animals carved in uncannily natural poses, while **Tegalalang** specializes in fanciful, brightly painted birds and fish, and in huge simulacra of fruit trees. **Pujung** carves *garuda* figures, ranging from a few centimetres to several metres in height.

One of the most common and easily carved Balinese woods is the soft, pure white timber known as **crocodile wood** (*panggal Buaya*), which comes from trees whose trunks are covered with spiny mounds. The dark wood of the **hibiscus** tree (*waru*) and the lemony yellow to pale brown wood of the **jackfruit** tree are also relatively easy to work with, as is the lovely tan-coloured timber from the flowering **poinciana** or *suwar*. Most of the "free-form"-style carvings are made from the gnarled trunks and branches of **frangipani** trees.

## Masks

Carved wooden **masks** play a hugely significant role in traditional Balinese dance-dramas. Many of them are treated as sacred objects, wrapped in holy cloth and stored in a high place within the temple compound when not being used, and given offerings before every public appearance. There's even an annual festival day for all masks and puppets, called Tumpek Wayang, at which actors and mask-makers honour their masks with special chants and offerings. Such is the power generated by certain masks, that some mask-makers enter a trance while working.

The undisputed centres of mask-making on Bali are the villages of **Mas** and **Singapadu**. Although the masks sold to tourists in these villages lack the spiritual power of their holy prototypes, most are still fashioned in the same way.

The best **material** for masks is the very pale wood of the *pule* (milkwood) tree. The mask-maker nearly always cuts the timber himself, making special prayers of apology and thanks to the tree before sawing away at its branches or trunk. The carving of any mask usually takes the best part of two weeks. Old-school mask-makers still make their own paints from natural substances, but most now rely on commercial pigments; hair is either goat's hide or horsehair, and tusks are carved from the bones of wild boars or from water-buffalo horns.

Traditional masks fall into three basic categories: human, animal and super-natural. Most **human** masks are made for performances of the *topeng*, literally "masked drama" (see p.478), and have a sacred, a symbolic and a narrative role. In *topeng*, the particular features of a mask are meant to indicate personality type. **Animal** masks feature very strongly in the *wayang wong* dance-dramas, which take most of their stories and characters from the Hindu epic the *Ramayana*. Most sacred of all are the fantastical Barong and Rangda masks, worn by the **mythical creatures** who represent the forces of good and evil and who appear in almost every drama to do battle with each other.

## Stonecarving

**Stonecarvings** are Bali's most public art form, gracing doorways, walls, towers, shrines and gardens all over the island. Bali's best stonecarvers come from a small area around the village of **Batubulan**, still the best place to see the craftspeople at work.

Chiselled mainly from the local volcanic tuff or *paras*, a soft grey material that yields well to pressure but disintegrates rather speedily in wind and rain, the prime function of stonecarvings has always been to entice and entertain the gods and to ward off any undesirable spirits and evil forces. The **temples** in the south are generally quite restrained in their use of carved ornamentation, being built mainly from red brick with just a few sections of carved *paras* (though Batubulan's Pura Puseh is a remarkable exception), but the northern temples, which are often built entirely from *paras*, flounder beneath a riot of reliefs and curlicues. Many of the classic northern temples are just a short bemo ride from Singaraja, and include the Pura Dalem in Jagaraga, Pura Beji and the Pura Dalem in Sangsit and, most famously, Pura Meduwe Karang at Kubutambahan.

Rajas and high-ranking nobles also commissioned fantastic carvings to embel-lish their **palaces** (*puri*). Unfortunately, many of these did not survive the early twentieth-century battles with the Dutch, but one notable exception is the Puri Saren Agung (Ubud Palace). This was once the home of the culturally refined Sukawati family, and they employed Bali's most skilful stonecarver, I Gusti Nyoman Lempad (see p.195), to decorate the walls, gateways and shrines in the *puri* compound.

Interestingly, there's little to distinguish the basic **iconography** that graces religious and secular buildings. **Gateways** are normally the focus of the most elaborate carvings, as these have a symbolic as well as a practical function, divid-ing the outer from the inner world, whether they're leading to the inner temple courtyard, or giving access to palace compounds. Surprisingly, the Hindu trinity (Brahma, Wisnu and Siwa) are rarely depicted in stone, but a number of their spiritual relatives and manifestations do crop up regularly. Temple carvings are not solely confined to deities and demons, however, and surfaces are often enli-vened by playful, even risqué scenes taken from **secular** life. In the renowned temples of north Bali, you'll find beautifully observed scenes covering everything from love-making to beer-drinking parties, from car breakdowns to cartoon-style aeroplanes. Many of these were inspired by the antics of the Dutch citizens who lived in Bali in the early 1900s.

## Traditional textiles

Over half a century after Western fashions started filtering into Bali, cloth still has a **ritual purpose** on the island – worn, given or hung at important rites-of-passage ceremonies such as first hair-cutting and tooth-filing. Bali's indigenous textile industry has always focused on the **ikat** technique, particularly the weft *ikat* or *endek* of Gianyar and the double *ikat* or *geringsing* of Tenganan. It's possible to see weavers at work in both these places, as well as at the smaller weaving factories of Singaraja. Their fabrics are worn and sold all over the island, along with a whole range of **batik** textiles, which come mainly from Java. In addition, Bali has also become something of an entrepôt for the textiles of outlying Indonesian islands, particularly Sumba and Flores. For some of the finest examples of locally woven cloth, check out the **displays** in the Bali Museum in Denpasar and at the informative Threads of Life Textile Arts Center and Gallery in Ubud (see p.197), where you can also take workshops in traditional textile appreciation.

### Ikat

Easily recognized by the fuzzy-edged motifs it produces, the **ikat** weaving technique is common throughout Indonesia, woven either on backstrap or foot-pedal looms (or, increasingly in the wealthier areas, on semi-automatic looms) from either silk, cotton or rayon. The distinctive feature of *ikat* is, however, not so much the weaving process as the dyeing technique. The word *ikat* derives from the Indonesian verb "to tie" or "to bind", and the technique is essentially a sophisticated tie-dye process that has three variations. In **warp-ikat**, it is the warp yarn (the threads that run lengthwise through the material) that's tie-dyed in several stages before the weft is woven in; in **weft-ikat**, the warp threads are left plain and the weft yarn (the threads running across the fabric) is dyed to the finished design; and in double *ikat*, both warp and weft are dyed before weaving begins.

Nearly all the *ikat* woven in Bali is weft-*ikat*, also known as **endek**, recognizable by its predominantly geometric and abstract motifs. The art of embroidered *ikat*, or supplementary weft weaving, is also practised to fine effect in Bali, where it's known as **songket**. *Songket* fabric uses threads of gold and silver metallic yarn to add decorative tapestry-like motifs of birds, butterflies and flowers onto very fine silk (or, increasingly, rayon or artificial silk). *Songket* sarongs are worn by the wealthiest Balinese at major ceremonial occasions, and the brocaded sashes worn by performers of traditional Balinese dance are always made from *songket*.

Bali is quite unusual in its favouring of weft-*ikat*; warp-*ikat* is the most widely practised technique in almost every other Indonesian island. Although it's hard for a non-expert to tell the difference, you can usually hazard a guess from the textile design, which in warp-*ikat* tends to be larger and more figurative. The warp-*ikat*s of **east Sumba** are particularly distinctive, and very popular in the shops of Bali, woven with bold humanoid motifs and images of real and mythological creatures and usually dyed in combinations of indigo and deep red. Warp-*ikat*s from **Flores** also use a distinctive blend of natural indigo and deep red dyes that generally results in lovely combinations of brown, ochre and dark red; typically, these are woven into intricate non-figurative and geometric patterns. The warp-*ikat*s of Flores tend to be quite small, because of the restrictive size of the backstrap loom used to weave them. Crocodiles, fish and stylized human forms feature most frequently on the warp-*ikat*s of **Timor**, often in simple tones of indigo and white or deep red and white.

Warp- and weft-*ikat* are complicated and time-consuming processes, but are nothing compared to double *ikat*, or **gringsing** as it's known in Bali. The *geringsing* technique involves the dyeing of both the warp and the weft threads into their final designs before they're woven together: a double *ikat* sarong can take five years to complete. There are just three areas in the world where this highly refined weaving method is practised – India, Japan, and the Bali Aga village of **Tenganan** in eastern Bali. Not surprisingly, *gringsing* is exceedingly expensive to purchase, and over the centuries it has acquired an important ritual significance. At first glance, the *geringsing* of Tenganan is quite easily confused with the warp-*ikat* of Flores, for the Flores weavers use the same combinations of natural dyes, but the Tenganan motifs have a highly charged spiritual significance, and their geometric and floral designs are instantly recognizable to the people of Bali.

### Batik

Despite being far more fashionable than *ikat* for everyday wear, nearly all **batik** fabric is imported from Java, as there's very little traditional batik produced in Bali.

The essential batik **technique** involves drawing patterns in dye-resistant wax on to lengths of fabric, dyeing the fabric, then stripping off the wax to expose the undyed areas. Wax is then often reapplied in different places, and the fabric dyed with a different colour, repeating the process until the finished design is achieved. The refined royal Javanese cities of **Yogyakarta** and **Solo** have long been centres of high-quality batik: coloured mainly with rust brown and indigo dyes against a cream or white background, the patterns adorning Yogyakarta/Solo batik tend to be either abstract, or compositions of graceful birds and flowers, though mythological figures do sometimes feature. Birds and flowers also feature a lot in the batiks that come from Java's other main batik-producing area, **Pekalongan**, on the north coast, but these artists use a greater variety of colours, particularly blues, pinks and greens, and the designs show more Chinese and Arabic influences.

While batik is perfectly acceptable attire for most ceremonial occasions, there's a particular type of batik called **perada** that is used only for ceremonial outfits and ornaments. This is the gold-painted cloth that you'll see fashioned into temple umbrellas, adorning some sacred statues, and worn by *legong* dancers and other performers of religious dances. The background colour of *perada* fabric is nearly always bright green or yellow, sometimes purple, and on to this is painted or stamped a symbolic design (usually stylized birds or flowers) in either gold-leaf paint or, more commonly today, a bronze- or gold-coloured pigment imported from Europe.

# Lombok crafts

Lombok's only native **fine art** can be found at two batik workshops near Rembitan in the south of the island. **Crafts**, however, abound, including textiles, pottery and basketware. If you want to buy crafts on Lombok with minimal effort and little travelling, head for the Lombok Handicraft Centre, the tourist shops in Senggigi, the Lombok Pottery Centre in Mataram, or to local markets. However, the best way to compare quality, styles and price is to go to the villages where the crafts are made, and buy from the producers.

# Textiles

The *ikat* and *songket* **cloth** produced in Bali is also made in Lombok with similar colours and motifs. Footlooms are used in the workshops of **Cakranegara**, while backstrap looms predominate in the villages of **Sukarara**, **Pringgasela** and **Penjanggik**.

Certain cloths are unique to Lombok, some with religious uses, but you won't find them for sale. The **kain usap** is a square cotton cloth either covered in geometric motifs or with alternating wide bands of floral patterns and narrow bands of geometric ones, used to cover the face of the dead. The **lempot**, a rectangular stole with a simple striped pattern and fringed ends, is used to carry small children. A coarsely woven cotton striped cloth, called **kombang**, is particularly sacred; made with a continuous warp, which is cut through in the course of religious ceremonies such as the naming of a child or hair-cutting, the fringes are tied with old Chinese coins for good fortune.

# Pottery

**Pottery** is a traditional craft that is centred in the pottery villages of **Banyumulek** and **Penujak** and in the hamlet of Penakak in **Masbagik Timur**. The potters, traditionally women who pass their techniques on to their daughters, use the local grey clay, worked by hand using a round stone and a wooden paddle to form the pots, which are often very large. As well as traditional water vessels, you'll see an enormous range of bowls, vases, lamp bases, pots and boxes.

Before firing, the pots are left for half a day to dry in the sun and are then stacked in a pile together with firewood and coconut husks. When the fire is under way, the whole pile is covered with rice straw and rice husks. This covering burns, too, but leaves a thick layer of ash, which retains the heat for the final stages of firing, producing temperatures in the region of 800°C. A slip made from a mixture of fine clay, water and an oily plant extract is then applied to the surface of the pot and polished to a deep shine by rubbing with a smooth stone or piece of glass or shell. Patterns are often etched on to the surface of the pot at this stage.

# Basketware

Lombok is also known for its **basketware** made of rattan, bamboo, palm leaves, cane and grass. The boxes, bags and baskets produced are often decorated with beads, shells or wooden carving, and many pots are also covered with a decorative cane lattice. Different villages specialize in particular materials; **Beleka**, for example, produces often enormous rattan baskets, many in a distinctive bulbous style, while **Sayang-Sayang** specializes in palm-leaf boxes, **Loyok** in bamboo, and **Karang Bayan** in grass boxes with carved wooden lids.

# Carving

While the **carving** of small items to decorate woven boxes is common, many of the wooden items you'll see in the art shops on the island are actually from further east in Nusa Tenggara. The distinctive wooden boxes with interlocking lids, *tongal*, are from Sumba, and the animistic hunkered and standing carved figures from islands further east. On Lombok, **Senanti** and **Sukaraja** are the island centres for woodcarving.

# Village life

The majority of people on Bali and Lombok live in villages and earn their living from agriculture. People employed in the cities or tourist resorts may well commute from their village homes each day, and even those whose villages are far away still identify with them and return on particular festivals each year.

## Balinese village layout

Orientation in Bali does not correspond to the compass points of north, south, east and west. Gunung Agung, dwelling place of the gods and highest peak on Bali, is the reference point, and the main directions are **kaja** (towards the mountain) and **kelod** (away from the mountain, which in practice usually means towards the sea). Direction is therefore relative: in the south of the island, *kaja* will be roughly to the north, and in the north of Bali, *kaja* is roughly to the south. The other directions are *kangin* (from where the sun rises), and its opposite, *kauh* (where the sun sets).

All Balinese villages are oriented *kaja–kelod* and the locations of the three village temples, *pura dalem*, *pura puseh* and *pura desa* (see p.460) are determined on this axis.

### House compounds

Each Balinese house compound is built within a confining wall, with variations depending on the caste and wealth of the family. When a son of the family marries, his wife will usually move into his compound, so there are frequently several generations living together, each with their own sleeping quarters, but otherwise sharing the facilities. Given the climate, most domestic activities take place outside or in the partial shelter of **bale**, raised platforms with a roof thatched with grass (*alang-alang*). Outside the *kelod* wall, families have their garbage tip and pig pens. The different structures of the compound are believed to reflect the human body: the family shrine (*Sanggah Kemulan*) is the head, the *bale* are the arms, the courtyard is the navel, the kitchen and rice barn are the legs and feet, and the garbage tip is the anus. The Traditional Balinese House museum in Tabanan (see p.349) is a good example of a typical compound.

When building a compound, a set of rules laid down in ancient texts must be adhered to. The architect or master builder (*undagi*) takes a series of **measurements** from the body of the **head of the household**. For the walls of the compound, he measures the distance between the tips of the middle fingers with the arms stretched out sideways, the distance from the elbow to the tip of the middle finger, and the width of the fist with the thumb stretched out. All these measurements are added together to give a unit length, the *depa asti musti*, and the texts specify how many of these lengths are suitable for the compound.

Prior to calling in the *undagi*, the prospective householder consults an expert in the Balinese calendar, to choose an auspicious day for buying

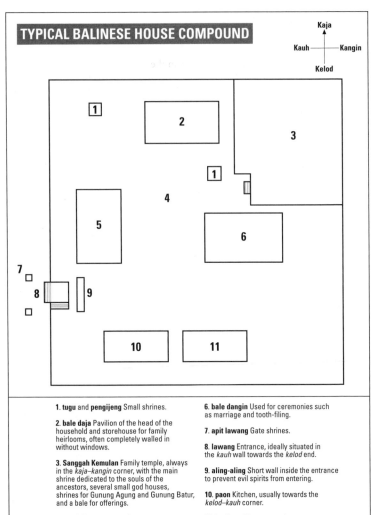

**TYPICAL BALINESE HOUSE COMPOUND**

Kaja

Kauh ——+—— Kangin

Kelod

1. **tugu** and **pengijeng** Small shrines.

2. **bale daja** Pavilion of the head of the household and storehouse for family heirlooms, often completely walled in without windows.

3. **Sanggah Kemulan** Family temple, always in the *kaja–kangin* corner, with the main shrine dedicated to the souls of the ancestors, several small god houses, shrines for Gunung Agung and Gunung Batur, and a bale for offerings.

4. **natah** Open courtyard.

5. **bale dauh** Guest pavilion, parallel to the *kauh* wall.

6. **bale dangin** Used for ceremonies such as marriage and tooth-filing.

7. **apit lawang** Gate shrines.

8. **lawang** Entrance, ideally situated in the *kauh* wall towards the *kelod* end.

9. **aling-aling** Short wall inside the entrance to prevent evil spirits from entering.

10. **paon** Kitchen, usually towards the *kelod–kauh* corner.

11. **lumbung** Rice storage barn, next to the kitchen.

*Note: House compounds in the north of the island are a mirror image of this*

land and beginning construction. Before building starts, a **ceremony** takes place in which an offering, usually a brick wrapped in white cloth sprinkled with holy water, is placed in the foundation of each building so that work will proceed smoothly. When the building work is finished, a series of ceremonies must take place before the compound can be occupied. The final ceremony is the **melaspas**, an inauguration ritual that "brings the building to life".

# Sasak villages

Balinese people who live on Lombok retain their traditional house compounds and *bale*, and the Bugis people, who have settled in coastal areas in the east and south of Lombok, live in their traditional wooden houses, constructed on tall piles with slatted floors and a large number of windows or shutters. The indigenous **Sasak** people of Lombok also have their own architectural style.

**Sasak villages** are traditionally walled enclosures, with a gateway that can be closed at night. There is usually an animal enclosure within the village so the local livestock can be brought in at the end of the day. The usual style of **mosque** is a rectangular bamboo-and-thatch building with a pyramid-shaped roof. **Houses**, made of bamboo with a thatch roof that slopes down steeply almost to the ground, are built on a thick base of mud and dung, and may have none or only a few windows, with a veranda on at least one side. Traditionally, the cooking hearth and eating area are inside the house, along with a walled-off room, the *inan bale*, generally used for storage, although this is also the place where newlyweds spend their first night.

The symbol of Lombok, the **lumbung rice barn**, with its bonnet-shaped roof, is a feature of only the south of the island. They are generally built close together in rows, on four piles, with a thatched roof and only one small opening high up. A circular wooden disc, the *jelepreng*, on each post stops rats climbing up to the rice. Underneath each post, old Chinese coins (*kepeng*) are buried for good luck and protection. In the north, the rice barns are rectangular, their size and number of pillars indicating the wealth of the owner.

# Village organizations

The smallest unit of social organization in each village is the **banjar** or neighbourhood. Each adult male on Bali joins the local *banjar* when he marries; his wife and children are also members but only the adult men attend meetings. The size of *banjar* varies enormously – the largest ones in Denpasar may have five hundred heads of household, while the small rural ones as few as fifty.

Typically, the *banjar* meets monthly in the meeting house, the **bale banjar**, to discuss anything of relevance to the *banjar*: land issues, temple ceremonies, the gamelan orchestra, and so on. Although there is a head of the *banjar* (*kliang*), all decisions are reached by consensus.

The *banjar* has considerable authority. If residential land in the area is left vacant for a period of time, it will revert to the *banjar* for redistribution. If members neglect their duties, they can be fined or even expelled from the village. This is a particularly powerful threat among people where communal life is at the heart of their existence. Expulsion also means the loss of the right to burial and cremation within the village.

## The subak

Much of the daily life of a village revolves around the *sawah*, or **ricefields**, and complex rituals accompany all the stages of rice cultivation encapsulated in the worship of Dewi Sri, the goddess of rice and prosperity.

The local organization in charge of each irrigation system is the **subak**, which have existed on Bali since the ninth century, and are made up of all the farmers who use the water in that system. Membership of the *subak* cuts across village and *banjar* lines. The maintenance of the irrigation system, along with planning that ensures every farmer gets adequate water, is coordinated by the *kliang subak*. Any *subak* with plans that have a wider impact or cause potential conflict with another *subak* – such as changing dry fields to wet – consults the regional water temples and, ultimately, the **Jero Gede**, chief priest of Pura Ulun Danu Batur, whose decision is final.

The **Subak Museum** on the outskirts of Tabanan (see p.348) is well worth a visit for more information on this unique aspect of Balinese life.

# Balinese life-cycle celebrations

On **Bali**, rituals and ceremonies are carried out at important points in an individual's life to purify them, and make sure they maintain sufficient spiritual energy for good health.

The first life-cycle ritual, **pegedong-gedongan**, takes place about six months after conception, when the fetus has a definite human form; the ritual emphasizes the hope of a long healthy life for the child. Subsequent **birth rituals** focus on the placenta (*ari-ari*), which is washed and buried inside a coconut wrapped in sacred white cloth near the gateway of the parents' household. A rock is placed over the spot to protect it, and regular offerings are made there.

Following the birth of a baby, the parents and child are regarded as unclean (*sebel*), and cannot participate in religious practices. For the mother and baby, this lasts 42 days; for the father, it lasts until the baby's umbilical cord drops off, when the **kepus pungsed** ritual is carried out. The cord is wrapped in cloth, placed in an offering shaped like a dove and suspended over the baby's bed, along with a small shrine dedicated to Sanghyang Panca Kumara, son of Siwa. Twelve days after birth, the ceremony of **ngelepas hawon** takes place, with offerings made for the baby in the kitchen, the well and the family temple, followed by the **tutug kambuhan**, 42 days after the birth, which marks the end of the *sebel* period for the mother. After 105 days, **telubulan** is a large, elaborate ceremony at which the child is named, and may be given an amulet to guard against evil spirits.

The child's **first birthday**, *oton*, occurs after 210 days (a Balinese year according to the *wuku* calendar; see p.63), and is celebrated with feasting. This is the first occasion that the baby is allowed contact with the ground, and may be accompanied by a ritual hair-cutting ceremony. The next ceremony, **maketus**, takes place when the child's milk teeth fall out, and prayers are offered to ensure that the adult teeth will be strong. Sanghyang Panca Kumara, who has been protecting the child since birth, is relieved of her duties, and the child is now guarded by the family ancestors.

The next life-cycle ceremonies occur at **puberty**, with *manggah daa* rituals for a girl and *manggah teruna* for a boy, although the male ritual is often omitted.

The **tooth-filing ritual**, *mapandes*, takes place between six and eighteen years of age, preferably before marriage, but after puberty for girls, and is a huge celebration with guests, music and lavish offerings. It is considered to be a vital ritual, and the elderly, and even the dead, have been known to have their teeth filed. The aim of the ritual is to remove coarse, uncontrolled behaviour from the person by filing down the upper canine teeth or fangs – *caling*, as the Balinese call them

– and the four teeth in between; six in total. Rituals are also performed to rid the person of lust, greed, anger, drunkenness, confusion and jealousy, in order that the person will lead a better life and be assured a more favourable reincarnation.

**Marriage**, *pawiwahan* or *nganten*, is the final life-cycle ceremony for most Balinese. There are two options when getting married. The most correct is *mamadik*, when the marriage is agreed between the two sets of parents and a huge financial outlay for ceremonies is involved. Much more common is *ngero-rod* or *malaib* – elopement. The man and woman run off and spend the night together, not so secretly that nobody knows, but with sufficient subterfuge that the girl's parents can pretend to be outraged. The following morning a simple, private ceremony (*makala-kalaan*) is carried out, and the couple are married. More elaborate rituals and a reception may be hosted later the same day by the boy's parents. The girl's parents will not be invited as there is supposed to be bad feeling between the two sides. However, three days later the two sets of parents meet at the *ketipat bantal* ceremony, and are reconciled.

# Cremation

The ceremony that visitors to Bali are most likely to witness is **cremation** (*pengabenan* or *palebonan*). The Balinese believe that the soul inhabits a temporary receptacle, the body, during life on earth. Following death, the body must be returned to the five elements of solid, liquid, energy, radiance and ether to become ready for reincarnation. The complex rituals and magnificent objects make this the most picturesque manifestation of religious observance on the island.

Following death, the body is usually buried, sometimes for years, while the **preparations** for the cremation are made. Poorer families will often share in the cremation ceremonies of wealthier families. The entire extended family and *banjar* is involved in building temporary shelters for shrines and preparing offerings. Animals must be slaughtered, holy water acquired and gamelan, dancers and puppet shows organized. An animal-shaped, highly decorated sarcophagus is built to hold the body. The cremation tower, representing the Balinese universe, supported by the turtle, Bedawang, and the two *naga*, Basuki and Anantaboga, is also built, with tiers similar to the roofs on the *meru* in temples. A *bale* at the base of the tiers houses an effigy of the dead person and the body itself.

The event itself is joyful, accompanied by the music of the bamboo **gamelan**

## Traditional healers

Known as *balian* in Bali and *dukun* in Lombok, **traditional healers** are a vital adjunct to Western medicine on the islands. Illness is believed to stem from a lack of balance between the patient and the spirit world; for example, a patient may have paid insufficient respect to a god or may be the target of black magic. There are many different kinds of *balian*, ranging from the most practical *balian tulang* (bonesetters), *balian manak* (midwives) and *balian apun* (masseurs), to the more spiritual, including *balian taksu*, mediums who enter a trance to communicate with the spirit world and *balian kebal*, who work with charms and spells, making love potions and magical amulets to protect the wearer against spiritual attack. *Balian* are also consulted to find out which ancestral souls have been reincarnated in the bodies of newborn babies, and which days are auspicious for certain events.

**angklung**. The sarcophagus and cremation tower are carried to the cemetery and twirled around many times to ensure the soul is confused and cannot find its way back home to cause mischief for the family. At the cremation ground, the body is transferred from the tower into the sarcophagus, which is anointed with holy water and set alight. The tower is burned in a separate fire. After burning, the ashes are carried to the sea or to a stream that will carry them to the ocean. A further purification ceremony takes place three days after the cremation, another at twelve days, finishing with the ritual of *nyagara-gunung*, when the family take offerings to important sea and mountain temples.

# Sasak life-cycle ceremonies

Some of the ceremonies performed in Sasak communities on **Lombok** are associated with the more orthodox adherents to Islam, while others are associated only with the smaller numbers of Wetu Telu followers. The Wetu Telu **birth ceremony** of *adi kaka* is similar to the Balinese one. A few days after birth, the **naming ceremony** of *buang au* or *malang mali* takes place. A ritual **hair-cutting ceremony**, *ngurisang*, is also obligatory for a young child, although the age it takes place is variable.

The most important ceremony for a Muslim boy is his **circumcision** (*nyuna-tang*), which often takes place in the Muslim month of the Prophet Muhammad's birthday, accompanied by ceremony and feasting.

There are three **marriage** options in Sasak culture: a marriage arranged by the families concerned, one between cousins, or an elopement. The man's family must pay a price for the bride, who will afterwards live in their house. This is negotiated between the families and will depend on the caste differences between the couple. Traditionally, payment is made in cows, money and rice, but also includes betel nut, coconut, a white sarong and old Chinese coins. During the wedding ceremony, the couple are often carried on a type of sedan chair, and accompanied by a gamelan orchestra.

Under the laws of Islam, the dead are **buried**, rather than cremated. According to Wetu Telu custom, the dead are ritually washed and wrapped in a white sarong, carried to the cemetery, and buried with the head towards Mecca. A death in the family sets in motion a whole cycle of possible rituals, the most important being **deena nitook**, seven days after the death, **nyatus** after a hundred days, and the final event, **nyiu**, a thousand days after death, when the grave is sprinkled with holy water and commemorative stones are placed on it.

# The impact of tourism

There is little middle ground in the debate about the effects of tourism on Bali and Lombok. Since the 1930s, when just a few thousand foreign tourists a year visited the island, through to the present day, when it hosts well over 1.5 million visitors annually, one side has argued that Bali will be ruined, its culture destroyed by the tourist influx, while the other side has claimed that the Balinese are well able to protect their traditional culture. The Kuta bomb in October 2002 threw the entire debate into stark relief, as many Balinese viewed the bomb as a spiritual punishment for how they had lost sight and control of their own moral and ethical base in the face of mass tourism. Following the bomb, many Balinese people were adamant that things had to change.

**Tourism** within the archipelago began in 1908, the year the Dutch took control over the whole of Bali. The Dutch colonial government opened a tourist promotion bureau in Batavia (now Jakarta) to encourage tourism to the Netherlands Indies, initially limited to Java, but later extended to Bali, described in brochures as the "Gem of the Lesser Sunda Isles". However, it wasn't until 1924 that tourism in Bali began in earnest. KPM, the Royal Packet Navigation Company, established weekly **steamship services** connecting Bali with Batavia, Singapore, Semarang, Surabaya and Makassar (now Ujung Pandang), with visitors to Bali using the government rest houses dotted around the island. The steamships either anchored at Padang Bai for a couple of days, allowing their passengers quick sorties ashore, or landed them at Buleleng (Singaraja) on Friday morning, collecting them again on Sunday evening.

In 1928, KPM opened the first **hotel** on the island, the *Bali Hotel* in Denpasar, and by the 1930s several thousand tourists each year were visiting Danau Tamblingan and Danau Buyan, the Bali Museum, Goa Gajah, Tampaksiring, Gunung Kawi, Goa Lawah, Gunung Batur, and the temples at Kubutambahan and Sangsit.

Following the establishment of an air link to Surabaya in 1933, a daily ferry to Java from Gilimanuk in 1934 and the opening of the airport at Tuban, near Denpasar, in 1938, Bali began to see the arrival of **independent visitors**, some of whom settled on the island. Many visitors were artists, such as Walter Spies and Miguel Covarrubias, and anthropologists, including Margaret Mead and Gregory Bateson. They focused on the artistic and religious aspects of Balinese life, encouraging the Balinese to produce works of art that would appeal to tourists and, through their writing, painting, photography and film-making, enhancing the image of Bali as a paradise.

The Japanese invasion during World War II, followed by the struggle for independence, halted the tourist influx, but under President Sukarno's rule the **promotion of tourism** became official government policy. Until the late 1960s, though, the poor state of the Balinese economy, the island's limited infrastructure, political disturbance and an ambiguity among the authorities towards mass tourism meant that this was restricted. Part of the war reparation money paid to Indonesia was used to construct the **Bali Beach Hotel** in Sanur, inaugurated in 1966 at a time when the political upheavals following the attempted coup of September 30, 1965, had closed the entire country to foreigners.

With the arrival of General Suharto and the New Order in 1967, economic development, in which tourism was to play a major part, was the primary objective for the nation, and major bodies such as the World Bank, the International Monetary Fund and the United Nations Development Project advocated tourism as a means of development. The inauguration of **Ngurah Rai Airport** on August 1, 1969, marked the beginning of mass tourism on the island; it is now the second-busiest airport in the country, after Jakarta.

In 1972, the government-owned **Bali Tourist Development Corporation (BTDC)** was formed on the recommendations of overseas consultants; its first project was to build a major resort of a dozen hotel complexes, **Nusa Dua**, on poor agricultural land, aimed at closeting visitors away from local people and attracting high-spending tourists at the luxury end of the market. Profits were to be split between the BTDC, the foreign hotel chains who were to manage the hotels, and the consortia who had built them, thus giving no guarantees about how much of the profits were to remain on Bali. The market soon responded to Bali's enticements, the number of visitors climbing from 30,000 in 1969 to 700,000 in 1989. By 1994, there were more than 30,000 rooms and 500 restaurants. Many resort areas have mushroomed dramatically in recent years, in particular Kuta–Legian–Seminyak and Lovina. Taking into account tourists from within Indonesia, who are as fond of Bali as a holiday spot as people from outside the country, it is estimated that over 2.5 million visitors a year arrive on the island.

There is no doubt, however, that in recent years many potential visitors to Indonesia have been frightened off; religious strife and economic instability across Indonesia in the late 1990s had an impact but, inevitably, the main hammerblow happened following the Kuta bombing on 12 October, 2002, when the island virtually emptied of foreign tourists within the following few days. With an estimated eighty percent of the population relying on tourism for their living in some way or another, the economy nose-dived overnight. By June 2003, a World Bank report estmated that the average Balinese income had dropped by forty percent. The fate of Lombok, inextricably linked to that of its more famous neighbour, mirrored Bali exactly. Gradually, tourism has recovered on both islands, despite the obvious ambivalence of Western governments who periodically issue travel warnings against travel to Indonesia – many Balinese point out, correctly, that following the New York and Madrid bombings no government warned against travel to those two places.

## Economy versus culture

The Balinese themselves have long been ambivalent about, and even openly critical of, the **effects of tourism** on Balinese society. In studies by Universitas Udayana, the University of Bali, some Balinese people described tourism as a tempest battering their coasts or an infectious disease spreading discord and defilement through the villages. They are particularly critical when tourism touches on **religion**, condemning the desecration of temples by tourists, the commercialization of dances, and the fact that Balinese involved in the industry neglect their religious duties. However, they acknowledge the financial benefits that tourism has brought; the challenge they have given themselves is to maximize these, while avoiding the wide-ranging cultural costs. As one commentator noted, "Tourism is the fire that cooks your breakfast and the fire that burns down your house."

While there's no doubting the Balinese dependence on the tourist dollar, yen or euro, it's easy to see that, even when tourism is thriving, many of the financial advantages benefit those off, rather than on, the island. The worst-case scenario sees the profits from multinational hotel chains flooding out of the island to Jakarta and abroad, with middle-management jobs within these organizations beyond the reach of the average Balinese, who are often reduced to low-paid, unskilled employment. Jobs are also threatened by Indonesians from across the archipelago who are flooding to Bali, lured by the prospect of work in the tourism industry. A recent Balinese study found that seventeen percent of jobs in the prestigious Nusa Dua complex were held by non-Balinese, and it's also believed that up to ninety percent of the Balinese coast is owned by non-Balinese. Some tourist businesses prefer to employ non-Balinese rather than adapt to the need of Balinese staff to attend their own villages for traditional ceremonies.

However, as families grow and land-holdings are divided among more and more family members, many people in Bali can no longer earn a living from agriculture; the burgeoning tourist sector offers opportunities as masseurs, touts, guides, chambermaids, gardeners and small businesspeople. With the average annual income of the Balinese greater than that of Indonesians in other parts of the country, some benefits from tourism are clear. Indeed, some commentators have noticed that the increased wealth of the Balinese is very often spent in highly traditional ways – in particular, by sponsoring extremely elaborate traditional religious ceremonies.

# Environmental concerns

Tourism also generates major **environmental concerns**. It is estimated that around ten square kilometres of irrigated ricefields are lost to tourist development every year. As an agricultural economy based on the cultivation of rice, **water** is a life or death issue on the island. One five-star hotel room alone is estimated to consume 500 litres of water each day. Recent research by the Japan International Cooperation Agency estimates that unless water conservation becomes a priority on the island, there will be serious water shortages within twenty years.

Particular concerns have arisen about the effects of tourist developments on the island's **coral reefs**, with efforts to reverse damage already underway in the waters off Pemuteran and the Gili Islands. Global awareness of the environmental problems of **golf courses** is growing, and the tourist downturn has meant that previously approved courses on Bali have not become reality.

In general, Balinese objections to tourist developments have managed to produce compromises rather than a halt to plans. At the time, the develop-

---

## Responsible tourism organizations

Many organizations are working to raise awareness of the impact of tourism throughout the world, and encourage responsible travelling. They all have sections devoted to Bali or Lombok or deal with issues that are directly relevant to the islands.

**Ethical Traveler** @ www.ethicaltraveler.com

**Global Anti-Golf Movement** @ www.antigolf.org/english.html

**Indigenous Tourism Rights International** @ www.tourismrights.org

**Indonesian Ecotourism Network** @ www.indecon.or.id

**Partners in Responsible Tourism** @ www.pirt.org

**Tourism Concern** @ www.tourismconcern.org.uk

ment of *Le Meridien Nirwana* near Tanah Lot, the building of the Garuda Wisnu Kencana (GWK) statue near Jimbaran, and the land reclamation around **Pulau Serangan** (Turtle Island) all evoked loud objections – all, however, have gone ahead regardless. As tourist numbers rise again and investors' confidence grows, new proposals undoubtedly appear, some of them with serious environmental impact – time will tell whether opposition voices are heard any more clearly than in the past.

# Social changes

Social change has inevitably followed the influx of tourism. Michel Picard, author of *Bali: Cultural Tourism and Touristic Culture*, presents the idea that Bali has now become a **"touristic culture"** whereby the Balinese have adopted the tourists' perceptions of themselves and their island as their own, and have "come to search for confirmation of their 'Balinese-ness' in the mirror held to them by the tourists".

There are also concerns about **HIV/AIDS** (more than 3000 cases are estimated on Bali) and **drug addiction** among the young men working in the informal sex industry in the tourist areas (there are relatively few female prostitutes). Recent highly publicized cases have raised the profile of **child sex tourism**, while Child Wise, the Australian representative of ECPAT (@www.ecpat .net), recently stated that research shows that since the Bali bombing "the island has become one of the preferred destinations of Australian child sex tourists, with evidence that some offenders are now moving into communities".

However, many of the problems are those of any developing country and, while many Westerners and Balinese intellectuals articulate the negative side of tourism, many of the people in the villages are keen to develop tourist facilities that will bring visitors, and their money, to them.

# The situation in Lombok

On **Lombok**, part of East Indonesia, one of the poorest areas of the whole archipelago, there has been chronic poverty for generations. A few tourists started coming in the 1980s and, by 1987, local people had set up a few small losmen around Senggigi, the Gili Islands and, later, around Kuta. By 1989, over 120,000 were visiting annually, and by 1993 there were many times that number. Fairly early on, government and big businesses, largely from outside the island, began to buy land for the construction of luxury hotels. In practice, many of the developers sat, and continue to sit, on the land they had bought and, outside the Senggigi area, there was little development for several years apart from the *Oberoi* in the north, the golf course near Sire beach, and *Novotel Lombok* near Kuta in the south.

Sasak people are aware that in the battle for tourist jobs, where tourist school **qualifications** are increasingly necessary to get anything but the most basic work in the industry, they do not measure up well against their Balinese neighbours, as poverty has forced them prematurely from formal education.

Plans to build a new **international airport** outside Praya have been on and off for years, and at one point were shelved following huge local protest and the reoccupation of the land by its previous owners.

Local feeling runs higher on Lombok than on Bali: the developments are new and the people poorer, many locals feel that the gap between Muslim morals and those of their Western visitors is unacceptably wide, and they have seen the effects of mass tourism on Bali. However, in recent years the collapses in tourism have brought home to the islanders just how volatile the tourist business is; many were brought to the verge of ruin following the events of September 11, 2001, and the Kuta bombing the following year. Concern has been repeatedly expressed about the island's over-reliance on tourism, but with few resources to draw upon, there's little chance of change.

# Books

While plenty has been written on the culture, temples, and arts and crafts of Bali, there has been little coverage of Lombok.

We have included publishers' details for books that may be hard to find outside Indonesia; other titles should be available worldwide. Ganesha (ⓦwww .ganeshabooksbali.com) in Ubud offer an online ordering service. Titles marked are particularly recommended; "o/p" means out of print.

The recently established Ubud Writers and Readers Festival (ⓦwww .ubudwritersfestival.com), held in October, provides a unique chance to hear writers about Bali discuss their work.

## Travel

**Vicki Baum** *A Tale from Bali*. Occasionally moving, and always interesting, semi-factual historical novel based on the events leading up to the 1906 *puputan* in Denpasar.

★ **William Ingram** *A Little Bit One o'Clock: Living with a Balinese Family* (Ersania Books, Ubud, Bali). Warm, funny, warts-and-all portrait of the author's life with an Ubud family in the 1990s. Both the author and his adoptive family still live in Ubud and are involved in the Threads of Life Textile Arts Center and Gallery.

★ **Louise G. Koke** *Our Hotel in Bali* (Pepper, Singapore). The engaging true story of two young Americans who arrived in Bali in 1936 and built a hotel on Kuta beach, the first of its kind. The book includes black-and-white photos, some of which are now displayed in Ubud's Neka Art Museum.

★ **Anna Mathews** *Night of Purnama*. Evocative and moving description of village life and characters of the early 1960s, focusing on events in Iseh and the surrounding villages from the first eruption of Gunung Agung until the Mathews left in 1963. Written with affection and a keen realization of the gap between West and East.

**Hickman Powell** *The Last Paradise*.

Highly readable account of an American traveller's experiences in Bali in the late 1920s. Interesting descriptions of village customs and temple festivals plus a few spicy anecdotes.

**Annabel Sutton** *The Islands in Between*. Covers a sea voyage across Indonesia. The chapters on Bali and Lombok are informative and amusing, and the whole book gives a good flavour of the variety of life within Indonesia, and a vivid insight into community life on the different islands.

★ **K'tut Tantri** *Revolt in Paradise*. The extraordinary story of an extraordinary woman. British-born artist and adventurer Muriel Pearson – known in Bali as K'tut Tantri and in Java as Surabaya Sue – tells the astonishing tale of her fifteen years in Bali and Java. First living in close association with the raja of Bangli, then building one of the first hotels on Kuta beach, K'tut Tantri finally became an active member of the Indonesian independence movement, operating an underground radio station and smuggling arms and other supplies between the islands, for which she suffered two years' imprisonment and torture at the hands of the Japanese invaders. A fascinating, if in places somewhat embellished, account of Bali and Java between 1932 and 1947.

Adrian Vickers (ed) *Travelling to Bali: Four Hundred Years of Journeys*. Thought-provoking one-stop anthology that includes accounts by early Dutch, Thai and British adventurers, as well as excerpts from writings by the expat community in the 1930s, and the musings of late twentieth-century visitors.

## Travellers' health

Jude Brown *Aromatherapy for Travellers*. Comprehensive and inspirational pocket-sized book, explaining how aromatherapy can help prevent and then treat travel problems. Plenty of practical details on what to do and where to get supplies and further information.

Dr Jane Wilson Howarth *Bugs, Bites and Bowels*. Outlines nasty tropical illnesses, together with likely symptoms and what to do about them. Small enough to take with you.

Dr Nick Jones *The Rough Guide to Travel Health*. Pretty much everything you need to know, in a pocket-sized, pack-friendly format.

# Culture and society

Jean Couteau *Bali Today: Real Balinese Stories, Vol 1* (Spektra Communications, Bali). A juicy little anthology of the anthropologist author's almost gossipy columns in the *Bali Post*. Topics range from the role of the peeping tom and the use of sexual innuendo in the Balinese language to true tales of cross-cultural romance.

★ Miguel Covarrubias *Island of Bali*. The Mexican artist and amateur anthropologist describes all aspects of life on Bali in the 1930s, from the daily routines of his adopted village household to the religious and philosophical meanings behind the island's arts, dramas and music. An early classic (first published in 1937) that's still as relevant and readable now.

▣ Dr A.A.M. Djelantik *The Birthmark: Memoirs of a Balinese Prince* (Tuttle Publishing). Fascinating, lively autobiography of the son of the last raja of Karangasem, who was born in east Bali in 1919, became Bali's most influential doctor, and still lives on the island today. Includes first-hand accounts of Dutch rule, World War II, the eruption of Gunung Agung and the communist killings.

★ Fred B. Eiseman Jr *Bali: Sekala and Niskala Vols 1 and 2*. Seminal, essential, wide-ranging anthologies of cultural and anthropological essays by an American who has lived in Bali for over thirty years. His attention focuses on everything from the esoteric rituals of Balinese Hinduism to the popularity of the clove cigarette.

David J. Fox *Once a Century: Pura Besakih and the Eka Dasa Rudra Festival* (Penerbit Sinar Harapan, Citra, Indonesia). Fabulous colour pictures, and an erudite but readable text, make this the best introduction to Besakih both ancient and modern. Also includes careful and sympathetic accounts of the 1963 Eka Dasa Rudra festival and the eruption of Gunung Agung.

A.J. Bernet Kempers *Monumental Bali: Introduction to Balinese Archaeology and Guide to the Monuments*. A fairly highbrow analysis of Bali's oldest temples and ruins.

Gregor Krause *Bali 1912* (January Books, New Zealand). Reprinted edition of the original black-and-white photographs that inspired the first generation of arty expats to visit Bali. The pictures were taken by a young German doctor and give unrivalled insight into Balinese life in the early twentieth century.

**J. Stephen Lansing** *Priests and Programmers: Technologies of Power in the Engineered Landscapes of Bali*. Scholarly account of the *subak* system of water control and of the role of the local and regional water temples. Also includes a report on the "Green Revolution" in Bali.

**Hugh Mabbett** *The Balinese* (Pepper, Singapore). Accessible, anecdotal essays on modern Balinese life, from the role of women in Bali to a discussion of the impact of tourism.

**Hugh Mabbett** *In Praise of Kuta* (o/p). Enjoyably affectionate portrait of Kuta in the 1980s, with lots of attention paid to the characters who lived, worked and visited Bali's most exuberant resort during the decade when mass tourism took off.

⭐ **Michel Picard** *Bali: Cultural Tourism and Touristic Culture*. Fascinating, readable but ultimately depressing analysis of the effects of tourism upon the people of Bali.

**Adrian Vickers** *Bali: A Paradise Created*. Detailed, intelligent and highly readable account of the outside world's perception of Bali, the development of tourism, and how events inside and outside the country have shaped the Balinese view of themselves as well as outsiders' view of them.

## History

**Ide Anak Agung Gde Agung** *Bali in the Nineteenth Century*. Meticulous account of the most eventful years in Balinese history, when conflict with the Dutch was at its most violent. Evocatively illustrated with an excellent collection of black-and-white photographs that you won't find elsewhere.

**Alfons van der Kraan** *Lombok: Conquest, Colonization and Underdevelopment 1870–1940*. A detailed investigation into Lombok's complex relationship with Bali, its neighbour and conqueror, and subsequently with its Dutch rulers. A scathing

attack on colonialism and its devastating effect on the local populace.

⭐ **Robert Pringle** *A Short History of Bali*. An incisive, readable history of Bali from the prehistorical era to the 2002 bomb, with plenty of focus on social, cultural and environmental developments.

**Margaret J. Weiner** *Visible and Invisible Realms: Power, Magic and Colonial Conquest in Bali*. Academic and densely written account of Balinese history leading up to the climactic Klungkung *puputan*, as detailed in Balinese historical sources and legends.

## Art, crafts and music

**Philip Cornwel-Smith** *Property of the Artist: Symon* (PT Sang Yang Seni, Ubud, Bali). Lively, innovatively designed monograph of the expat Ubud artist Symon (see p.202).

**Fred and Margaret Eiseman** *Woodcarvings of Bali* (o/p). Slim but

interesting look at the history of woodcarving and the types of wood used.

**Edward Frey** *The Kris: Mystic Weapon of the Malay World*. Small but well-illustrated book outlining the history and making of the kris, along with some of the myths associated with this magical weapon. Although intended more for the collector than the visitor, this is an excellent introduction to help you appreciate what you see in the museums.

**John Gillow and Barry Dawson** *Traditional Indonesian Textiles*. Beautifully photographed and accessible introduction to the *ikat* and batik fabrics of the archipelago; a handy guide if you're thinking of buying cloth in Bali or Lombok.

**Brigitta Hauser-Schäublin, Marie-Louise Nabholz-Kartaschoff and Urs Ramseyer** *Balinese Textiles*. Thorough and gloriously photographed survey of Balinese textiles and their role within contemporary society. Includes sections on the more common fabrics such as *endek*, *songket* and *kain poleng*, as well as introductions to some of the much rarer weaves, including the *geringsing* of Tenganan.

★ **Garret Kam** *Perceptions of Paradise: Images of Bali in the Arts* (Yayasan Dharma Seni Neka Museum, Bali). Ostensibly a guide to the paintings displayed in Ubud's Neka Art Museum, this is actually one of the best introductions to Balinese art, with helpful sections on the traditions and practices that have informed much of the work to date.

★ **Jean McKinnon** *Vessels of Life: Lombok Earthenware*. Exhaustive and fabulously photographed book about Sasak life, pottery techniques and the significance of the items they create in the lives of the women potters.

**Idanna Pucci** *Bhima Swarga: The Balinese Journey of the Soul*. Fabulously produced guide to the *Mahabharata* legends depicted on the ceiling of Klungkung's Kerta Gosa. Illustrated with large, glossy colour photographs and a panel-by-panel description of the stories, which makes the whole creation much easier to interpret.

**Hans Rhodius and John Darling** *Walter Spies and Balinese Art* (Tropenmuseum, Amsterdam). Biography of the German expatriate artist and musician, which takes up the debate over the extent of Spies' influence on modern Balinese art, asking whether the received view is actually a colonialist take on art history.

**Anne Richter** *Arts and Crafts of Indonesia*. General guide to the fabrics, carvings, jewellery and other folk arts of the archipelago, with some background on the practices involved.

**Michael Tenzer** *Balinese Music*. Well-pitched introduction to the gamelan, covering theory, practice and history, as well as anecdotes from Balinese musicians.

## Lifestyle

**Gianni Francione and Luca Invernizzi Tettoni** *Bali Modern: The Art of Tropical Living*. A celebration of modern Balinese architecture, from the tasteful to the ostentatious, via expat hideaways and the *Hard Rock Hotel*.

**Rio Helmi and Barbara Walker** *Bali Style*. Sumptuously photographed

paean to all things Balinese, from bamboo furniture to elegant homes.

**William Warren and Luca Invernizzi Tettoni** *Balinese Gardens*. Gorgeously photographed homage to (mostly) modern gardens in the south of the island, with informed introductions to classical gardens,

Balinese flora, offerings, and the role of the garden in Balinese culture.

**Made Wijaya and Isabella Ginanneschi** *At Home in Bali*. The beautiful homes of Bali's beautiful (mainly expatriate) people are here presented in enviable tropical splendour.

## Food and cookery

**Janet de Neefe** *Fragrant Rice*. The Australian co-founder of Ubud's *Casa Luna* restaurant and cooking classes paints an enticing picture of life with her Balinese husband and family, interweaving her cultural observations with recipes for some three dozen local dishes, from gado-gado to smoked duck.

**Heinz von Holzen and Lother Arsana** *The Food of Bali* (Tuttle Publishing). Sumptuously illustrated paperback on all aspects of Balinese cuisine, including the religious and cultural background. The bulk of the book comprises recipes for local specialities – everything from snail soup to unripe-jackfruit curry.

**Jacqueline Piper** *Fruits of South-East Asia: Fact and Folklore*. Although only 94 pages long, this is an exhaustive, well-illustrated book, introducing all the fruits of the region together with the influence they have had on arts and crafts, and the part they have played in religious and cultural practices.

## Natural history

**Guy Buckles** *Dive Sites of Indonesia*. Exhaustively researched, attractive and up-to-date guide for potential divers, with good sections on Bali and Lombok. Especially good on the practical details.

**Fred and Margaret Eiseman** *Flowers of Bali* (o/p). Slim, fully illustrated handbook describing fifty of the most common flowers growing in Bali.

**John MacKinnon** *Field Guide to the Birds of Borneo, Sumatra, Java and Bali*. The most comprehensive field guide of its kind, with full-colour plates and detailed descriptions of the 820 species found on the four islands.

★ **Victor Mason** *Bali Bird Walks* (o/p). Delightful, highly personal offbeat guidebook to over a dozen walks in the Ubud area, with the focus on flora and fauna, particularly birds.

**Victor Mason and Frank Jarvis** *Birds of Bali*. Informal, illustrated introduction to the 120 most commonly sighted birds in Bali.

**Kal Muller et al** *Diving Indonesia*. This is the top handbook for anybody wanting to dive in Indonesia. Written by experts, it is also exquisitely photographed and supplemented with clear, useful maps. Bali and Lombok are only part of this book, but it will inspire you to venture further afield.

★ **David Pickell and Wally Siagian** *Diving Bali: The Underwater Jewel of Southeast Asia*. Beautifully photographed and detailed account of everything you'll ever need to know about diving in Bali. Full of anecdote, humour, advice and practical knowledge, as well as plenty of detailed maps.

# Fiction

**Vern Cook** (ed) *Bali Behind the Seen: Recent Fiction from Bali* (Darma Printing, NSW, Australia). Insightful collection of short stories by modern Balinese and Javanese writers, many of whom explore the ways in which Bali is changing, highlighting different outlooks on traditions, families and Westernization.

**Diana Darling** *The Painted Alphabet*. Charming, sophisticated reworking of a traditional Balinese tale about young love, rivalry and the harnessing of supernatural power.

**Garrett Kam** *Midnight Shadows* (Trafford Publishing, Victoria, Canada). A teenage boy's life in 1960s Bali is turned upside down first by the devastating eruption of Gunung Agung and then by the vicious, divisive, anti-communist violence that swept the island.

**Odyle Knight** *Bali Moon: A Spiritual Odyssey* (Sandstone Publishing, NSW, Australia). Riveting tale of an Australian woman's deepening involvement with the Balinese spirit world as her romance with a young Balinese priest draws her onto disturbing ground. Apparently based on true events.

**Christopher J. Koch** *The Year of Living Dangerously*. Set in Jakarta in the last year of President Sukarno's rule and climaxing in the days leading up to the 1965 takeover by Suharto and the subsequent violence, this story compellingly details ethnic, political and religious tensions that are still apparent in Indonesia today, and is required reading for anyone trying to understand modern Indonesia.

**Claire Messud** *When the World was Steady*. Bali is just one of several locations in this rich, elegant portrayal of two sisters, their relationship with each other and their differing approaches to life. However, the island is skilfully evoked in all its beauty and mystery, as is the cast of expatriates who came to the island to disrupt its peace, when "*dugas gumine enteg*" (the world was steady).

**Putu Oka Sukanta** *The Sweat of Pearls: Short Stories about Women of Bali* (Darma Printing, NSW, Australia). All the stories in this slim volume were written by a man, but the vignettes of village life and traditions are enlightening, and the author is a respected writer who spent many years in jail because of his political beliefs.

# Language

# Language

# Bahasa Indonesia

The national language of Indonesia is Bahasa Indonesia, although there are also over 250 native languages and dialects spoken throughout the archipelago. Until the 1920s, the lingua franca of government and commerce was Dutch, but the emerging independence movement adopted a form of Bahasa Malay as a more suitable revolutionary medium; by the 1950s, this had crystallized into **Bahasa Indonesia**. Now taught in every school and widely understood in Bali and Lombok, Bahasa Indonesia was a crucial means of unifying the new nation. The indigenous languages of Bali and Lombok are still spoken in the islands' villages, and brief vocabularies are given below.

Bahasa Indonesia is written in Roman script, has no tones and uses a fairly straightforward grammar – all of which makes it relatively easy for the visitor to get to grips with. *The Rough Guide to Indonesian* is a pocket-sized **phrasebook** that includes an exhaustive dictionary of useful words as well as pronunciation details, some cultural hints, and information on grammar. Of the numerous **teach yourself** options, Sutanto Atmosumarto's *Colloquial Indonesian: The Complete Course for Beginners* (Routledge) includes a book plus cassette tape and CD, and *Learn Indonesian* euroTalkinteractive CD-ROM (ⓦ www.eurotalk .com) is a beginner's course that has a printable dictionary and allows learners to compare their voices with those of native speakers. Several dictionaries are available: outside Indonesia, the *English-Indonesian Dictionary* and *Indonesian-English Dictionary* by Echols and Shadily (Cornell University Press) are comprehensive; inside the country, you might want to get hold of the more portable, though not pocket-sized, **dictionary** *Kamus Lengkap Inggeris-Indonesia, Indonesia-Inggeris* (Hasta Penerbit).

## Grammar and pronunciation

For **grammar**, Bahasa Indonesia uses the same subject-verb-object word order as in English. The easiest way to make a question is simply to add a question mark and use a rising intonation. **Nouns** have no gender and don't require an article. To make a noun **plural** you usually just say the noun twice, eg *anak* (child), *anak-anak* (children). **Adjectives** always follow the noun. **Verbs** have no tenses: to indicate the past, prefix the verb with *sudah* (already) or *belum* (not yet); for the future, prefix the verb with *akan* (will).

### Vowels and diphthongs

a is a cross between father and cup

e as in along; or as in pay; or as in get; or sometimes omitted (selamat pronounced "slamat")

i as in boutique; or as in pit

o as in hot; or as in cold

u as in boot

ai as in fine

au as in how

Most are pronounced as in English, with the following exceptions:

c as in cheap

g is always hard, as in girl

k is hard, as in English, except at the end of the word, when you should stop just short of pronouncing it. In written form, this is often indicated by an apostrophe; for example, beso' for besok.

# Useful words and phrases

## Greetings and basic phrases

The all-purpose greeting is **Selamat** (derived from Arabic), which communicates general goodwill. If addressing a married woman, it's polite to use the respectful term Ibu or Nyonya; if addressing a married man use Bapak.

| | |
|---|---|
| Selamat pagi | Good morning (5–11am) |
| Selamat siang | Good day (11am–3pm) |
| Selamat sore | Good afternoon (3–7pm) |
| Selamat malam | Good evening (after 7pm) |
| Selamat tidur | Good night |
| Selamat tinggal | Goodbye |
| Sampai jumpa lagi | See you later |
| Selamat jalan | Have a good trip |
| Selamat datang | Welcome |
| Selamat makan | Enjoy your meal |
| Selamat minum | Cheers (toast) |
| Apa kabar? | How are you? |
| Bagus/Kabar baik | I'm fine |
| tolong | please (requesting) |
| silakan | please (offering) |
| Terima kasih (banyak) | Thank you (very much) |
| Sama sama | You're welcome |
| Ma'af | Sorry/excuse me |
| Tidak apa apa | Never mind/no worries |
| Siapa nama anda? | What is your name? |
| Nama saya... | My name is... |
| Dari mana? | Where are you from? |
| Saya dari... | I come from... |
| Bisa bicara bahasa Inggris? | Do you speak English? |

| | |
|---|---|
| Saya tidak mengerti | I don't understand |
| Ada...? | Do you have...? |
| Saya mau... | I want/would like... |
| Tidak mau | I don't want it/No thanks |
| Apa ini/itu? | What is this/that? |
| satu lagi | another |
| cantik | beautiful |
| besar/kecil | big/small |
| pacar | boyfriend or girlfriend |
| bersih/kotor | clean/dirty |
| dingin | cold |
| mahal/murah | expensive/inexpensive |
| sepat/lambat | fast/slow |
| turis | foreigner |
| teman | friend |
| bagus/buruk | good/bad |
| panas | hot (water/weather) |
| pedas | hot (spicy) |
| berapa? | how? |
| lapar/haus | hungry/thirsty |
| sakit | ill/sick |
| kawin/bujang | married/single |
| laki-laki | men |
| bukan | no (with noun) |
| tidak (or tak) | not (with verb) |
| buka/tutup | open/closed |
| lelah | tired |
| banyak | very much/a lot |
| apa? | what? |
| kapan? | when? |

| | | | |
|---|---|---|---|
| dimana? | where? | perempuan or | |
| siapa? | who? | wanita | women |
| mengapa? | why? | ya | yes |

## Getting around

| | | | |
|---|---|---|---|
| Dimana...? | Where is the...? | datang/pergi | to come/go |
| Saya mau pergi ke... | I'd like to go to the... | mengendarai | to drive |
| | | masuk/keluar | entrance/exit |
| Berapa kilometre? | How far? | ferry | ferry |
| Berapa jam? | How long? | bensin | fuel (petrol) |
| Berapa harga karcis ke...? | How much is the fare to...? | dokar/cidomo | horse cart |
| | | rumah sakit | hospital |
| Kemana bemo pergi? | Where is this bemo going? | losmen | hotel |
| | | pasar | market |
| Bila bemo/bis berangkut? | When will the bemo/ bus leave? | sepeda motor | motorbike |
| | | ojek | motorbike taxi |
| Dimana ini? | Where is this? | dekat/jauh | near/far |
| estop! | stop! | apotik | pharmacy |
| disini | here | wartel/kantor telkom | phone office |
| kanan | right | | |
| kiri | left | kantor polisi | police station |
| terus | straight on | kantor pos | post office |
| lapangan terbang | airport | restoran/rumah makan/warung | restaurant |
| bank | bank | | |
| pantai | beach | toko | shop |
| terminal | bemo/bus station | taksi | taxi |
| sepeda | bicycle | karcis | ticket |
| bis | bus | kantor turis | tourist office |
| mobil | car | desa | village |
| kota | city/downtown | jalan kaki | to walk |

## Accommodation and shopping

| | | | |
|---|---|---|---|
| Berapa harga...? | How much is...? | uang | money |
| kamar untuk satu orang | a single room | apakah ada...? | is there...? |
| | | ac | air conditioning |
| kamar untuk dua orang | a double room | kamar mandi | bathroom |
| | | makan pagi | breakfast |
| Ada kamar yang lebih murah? | Do you have a cheaper room? | kipas | fan |
| | | air panas | hot water |
| Boleh saya lihat kamar? | Can I look at the room? | kelambu nyamuk | mosquito net |
| | | kolam renang | swimming pool |
| tidur | to sleep | kamar kecil/wc | (pronounced |
| membeli/menjual | to buy/sell | | "waysay") toilet |

## Bahasa Bali

The Balinese language, **Bahasa Bali**, has three main forms (and dozens of less widespread variations): High (*Ida*), Middle or Polite (*Ipun*), and Low (*Ia*). The speaker decides which form to use depending on the caste of the person he or she is addressing and on the context. If speaking to family or friends, or to a low-caste (Sudra) Balinese, you use **Low Balinese**; if addressing a superior or a stranger, you use **Middle or Polite Balinese**; if talking to someone from a high caste (Brahman, Satriya or Wesya) or discussing religious affairs, you use **High Balinese**. If the caste is not immediately apparent, then the speaker will traditionally open the conversation with the euphemistic question "Where do you sit?", in order to elicit an indication of caste, but in the last couple of decades there's been a move to popularize the use of the polite Middle Balinese form, and disregard the caste factor wherever possible. For more on castes and how to recognize them, see p.80.

Despite its numerous forms, Bahasa Bali is essentially a **spoken language**, with few official rules of grammar or syntax and hardly any textbooks or dictionaries. However, there's a useful, if rather basic, English-language **primer**, called *Bali Pocket Dictionary* by N. Shadeg (Yayasan Dharma Bhakti Pertiwi), available from some bookshops on the island. All phrases and questions given below are shown in the Middle or Polite form, unless otherwise stated.

| | | | |
|---|---|---|---|
| Sira pesengan ragane? | What is your name? | switra | friend |
| | | lunga | to go |
| Lunga kija? | Where are you going? | becik | good |
| | | jeroan | house |
| Kija busan? | Where have you been? | rabi | husband |
| | | tan, nente | no |
| Kenken kebara? | How are you? | pantu, beras, ajengan | rice |
| Napa orti? | How are things? | | |
| Becik | (I'm/everything's) fine | sirep sare | to sleep |
| | | alit | small |
| Tiang gele | I am sick | timpal, isteri | wife |
| Napi punika? | What is that? | inggih, patut | yes |
| corah | bad | siki, diri | 1 |
| ageng | big | kalih | 2 |
| putra, putri | child | tiga | 3 |
| rauh, dateng | to come | pat | 4 |
| ngajeng, nunas | to eat | lima | 5 |
| jaen | delicious | nem, enem | 6 |
| panyaman, pasa metonan | family | pitu | 7 |
| | | kutus | 8 |
| ajeng-ajengan, tetedan | food | sia | 9 |
| | | dasa | 10 |

## Sasak

The language of Lombok is **Sasek**, a purely oral language that varies quite a lot from one part of the island to another. Realistically, Bahasa Indonesia is a more practical option for travellers, but even a few words of Sasak are likely to be greeted with delight. The following should get you started.

There's no Sasak equivalent to the Indonesian **greetings** Selamat pagi and the like. If you meet someone walking along the road, the enquiry "Where are you going?" serves this purpose even if the answer is blatantly obvious.

| | | | |
|---|---|---|---|
| Ojok um bay? | Where are you going? | betjat/adeng-adeng | fast/slow |
| Lampat-lampat | Just walking around | kantje | friend |
| | | takoot | frightened |
| Rinjani wah mo ojok um bay | I'm going to Rinjani | berat/ringan | heavy/light |
| | | beneng | hot |
| Um bay tao...? | Where is...? | lapar | hungry |
| Berem bay khabar? | How are you? | semame/senine | husband/wife |
| Bagus/solah | I'm fine | ndarak | nothing |
| Berem bay seeda? | And you? | goro | thirsty |
| Upa gowey de? | What are you doing? | telah | tired |
| | | djelo sine | today |
| Pira kanak de? | How many children do you have? | djema | tomorrow |
| | | sirutsin | yesterday |
| Yak la low | See you (I'm going) | ndarak | none |
| Nday kambay kambay | No problem | skek | 1 |
| | | dua | 2 |
| Nyeri too! | Go away! | telu | 3 |
| belek/kodek | big/small | empat | 4 |
| semeton mama/ semeton nine | brother/sister | lima | 5 |
| | | enam | 6 |
| kanak/bai | child/grandchild | pitook | 7 |
| peteng/tenang | dark/light | baluk | 8 |
| kanak nine/ kanak mame | daughter/son | siwak | 9 |
| maik | delicious | sepulu | 10 |

## Numbers

| | | | |
|---|---|---|---|
| nol | 0 | sepuluh | 10 |
| satu | 1 | sebelas | 11 |
| dua | 2 | duabelas, tigabelas, empatbelas | 12, 13, 14, etc |
| tiga | 3 | | |
| empat | 4 | duapuluh | 20 |
| lima | 5 | duapuluh satu, duapuluh dua, duapuluh tiga | 21, 22, 23, etc |
| enam | 6 | | |
| tujuh | 7 | | |
| delapan | 8 | tigapuluh, empatpuluh, limapuluh | 30, 40, 50, etc |
| sembilan | 9 | | |

| | | | |
|---|---|---|---|
| seratus | 100 | seratusribu | 100,000 |
| duaratus, tigaratus, empatratus | 200, 300, 400, etc | dua ratusribu, tiga ratusribu, empat ratusribu | 200,000, 300,000, 400,000, etc |
| seribu | 1000 | | |
| duaribu | 2000, 3000, 4000, etc | sejuta | 1,000,000 |
| sepuluhribu | 10,000 | dua juta, tiga juta, empat juta | 2,000,000, 3,000,000, 4,000,000, etc |
| dua puluhribu, tiag puluhribu, empat puluhribu | 20,000, 30,000, 40,000, etc | | |

## Time and days of the week

| | | | |
|---|---|---|---|
| Jam berapa? | What time is it? | bulan | month |
| Kapan dia buka/ tutup? | When does it open/ close | tahun | year |
| | | hari ini/besok | today/tomorrow |
| jam tiga | 3.00 | kemarin | yesterday |
| jam empat lewat sepuluh | 4.10 | sekarang | now |
| | | belum | not yet |
| jam lima kurang seperempat | 4.45 | tidak pernah | never |
| | | sudah | already |
| jam setengah tujuh | ("half to seven") 6.30 | Hari Senin | Monday |
| | | Hari Selasa | Tuesday |
| ... pagi | ... in the morning | Hari Rabu | Wednesday |
| ... sore | ... in the afternoon | Hari Kamis | Thursday |
| ... malam | ... in the evening | Hari Jumaat | Friday |
| menit/jam | minute/hour | Hari sabtu | Saturday |
| hari | day | Hari Minggu | Sunday |
| minggu | week | | |

# Menu reader

## General terms

| | | | |
|---|---|---|---|
| makan | to eat | piring | plate |
| makan pagi | breakfast | gelas | glass |
| makan siang | lunch | minum | drink |
| makan malam | evening meal | tolong tanpa es | without ice, please |
| daftar makanan | menu | tolong tanpa gula | without sugar, please |
| Saya seorang vegetaris | I am vegetarian | dingin | cold |
| | | panas | hot (temperature) |
| Saya tidak makan daging | I don't eat meat | pedas | hot (spicy) |
| | | asam manis | sweet-and-sour |
| pisau | knife | goreng | fried |
| garpu | fork | enak | delicious |
| sendok | spoon | Saya injin bayar | I want to pay |

# Meat, fish and basic foods

| | | | |
|---|---|---|---|
| ayam | chicken | kecap asam | sour soy sauce |
| babi | pork | kecap manis | sweet soy sauce |
| bakmi | noodles | kepiting | crab |
| buah | fruit | nasi | rice |
| es | ice | petis | fish paste |
| garam | salt | sambal | hot chilli sauce |
| gula | sugar | sapi | beef |
| ikan | fish | soto | soup |
| itik | duck | telur | egg |
| jaja | rice cakes | udang | prawn |
| kambing | goat | udang karang | lobster |
| kare | curry | | |

## Everyday dishes

| | | | |
|---|---|---|---|
| ayam goreng | fried chicken | nasi campur | boiled rice served with small amounts of vegetable, meat, fish and sometimes egg |
| bakso | soup containing meat balls | | |
| bakmi goreng | fried noodles mixed with vegetables and meat | nasi goreng | fried rice |
| | | nasi putih | plain boiled rice |
| botok daging sapi | spicy minced beef with tofu, tempeh and coconut milk | pisang goreng | fried bananas |
| | | rijsttafel | Dutch/Indonesian dish made up of six to ten different meat, fish and vegetable dishes with rice |
| cap cai | mixed fried vegetables | | |
| es campur | fruit salad and shredded ice | | |
| gado-gado | steamed vegetables served with a spicy peanut sauce | rujak | hot, spiced fruit salad |
| | | rujak petis | vegetable and fruit in spicy peanut and shrimp sauce |
| kangkung | water-spinach | tahu goreng telur | tofu omelette |
| krupuk | rice or cassava crackers, usually flavoured with prawn | saté | meat or fish kebabs served with a spicy peanut sauce |
| lalapan | raw vegetables and sambal | sayur bening | soup with spinach and corn |
| lontong | steamed rice in a banana-leaf packet | sayur lodeh | vegetable and coconut-milk soup |
| lumpia | spring rolls | urap-urap/urap timum | vegetables with coconut and chilli |

## Balinese specialities

| | | | |
|---|---|---|---|
| babi guling | suckling pig roasted on a spit: the Balinese national dish | betutu bebek | smoked duck |
| | | ebat | a meal of five dishes, including saté, served on a tray |

| | | | |
|---|---|---|---|
| lawar | ceremonial dish: raw meat, blood and spices ground down | | to a pulpy mash, often served with babi guling |

## Sasak specialities

| | | | |
|---|---|---|---|
| ayam taliwang | fried or grilled chicken served with a hot chilli sauce | olah olah | mixed vegetables and coconut cream |
| beberuk | raw eggplant and chilli sauce | otak | brains |
| | | pangan | coconut milk and sugar dessert |
| cerorot | rice flour, palm sugar and coconut milk sweet, wrapped into a cone shape | paru | lungs |
| | | pelecing | chilli sauce |
| | | satay pusut | minced beef and coconut saté |
| geroan ayam | chicken liver | sayur nangka | young jackfruit curry |
| gule lemak | beef curry | sum-sum | bone marrow |
| hati | liver | tumbek | rice flour, coconut milk and palm sugar dessert, wrapped in coconut leaves |
| kelor | vegetable soup | | |
| lapis | rice flour, coconut milk and sugar dessert, wrapped in banana leaves | usus | intestines |
| | | wajik | sticky rice and palm-sugar sweet |

## Fruit

| | | | |
|---|---|---|---|
| apel | apple | mangga | mango |
| buah anggur | grapes | manggis | mangosteen |
| jeruk manis | orange | nanas | pineapple |
| jeruk nipis | lemon | nangka | jackfruit |
| kelapa | coconut | pisang | banana |
| | | semangkha air | watermelon |

## Drinks

| | | | |
|---|---|---|---|
| air jeruk | orange juice | kopi | coffee |
| air jeruk nipis | lemon juice | kopi bal | black coffee |
| air minum | drinking water | kopi susu | white coffee |
| arak | palm or rice spirit | susu | milk |
| bir | beer | teh | tea |
| brem | local rice beer | tuak | rice or palm wine |

# Glossary

**adat** Traditional law and custom.

**aling-aling** Low, freestanding wall built directly behind a house or temple gateway, in order to confuse evil spirits and deter them from entering.

**Arjuna** The most famous of the five heroic Pandawa brothers, stars of the epic Hindu tale, the *Mahabharata*.

**bale** Open-sided pavilion found in temples, family compounds and on roadsides, usually used as a resting place or shelter.

**balian** (or **dukun**) Traditional faith healer, herbalist or witch doctor.

**banjar** Village association or council to which all married men in the neighbourhood are obliged to belong; membership averages 100 to 500.

**Barong Ket** Mythical lion-like creature who represents the forces of good; frequently appears in religious rituals and dance performances.

**Barong Landung** Ten-metre-high humanoid puppets used in temple rituals and dances.

**bemo** Local minibus transport.

**Bhoma** (or **Boma**) The son of the earth, who repels evil spirits and is most commonly represented as a huge open-mouthed face above temple gateways.

**bhuta** (and **kala**) Invisible demons and goblins, the personification of the forces of evil.

**calonarang** Exorcist dance-drama featuring the widow-witch Rangda.

**candi** Monument erected as a memorial to an important person, also sometimes a shrine.

**candi bentar** Split gateway built at the entrance to a temple compound.

**cidomo** Horse-drawn cart used as a taxi on Lombok.

**dalang** Puppet master of wayang kulit shadow plays.

**danau** Lake.

**Dewi Pertiwi** Earth goddess.

**Dewi Sri** Rice goddess.

**dokar** Horse-drawn cart used as a taxi in major Balinese towns.

**dukun** See **balian**.

**endek** (or **ikat**) Cloth in which the weft threads are dyed to the final pattern before being woven.

**Erlangga** (sometimes **Airlangga**) Eleventh-century king from East Java, son of the mythical widow-witch Rangda.

**Galungan** The most important Bali-wide holiday, held for ten days every 210 days in celebration of the triumph of good over evil.

**gamelan** Orchestra or music of bronze metallophones.

**Ganesh** Hindu elephant-headed deity, remover of obstacles and god of knowledge.

**gang** Lane or alley.

**Garuda** Mythical Hindu creature, half-man and half-bird, and the favoured vehicle of the god Wisnu; featured in numerous sculptures and temple reliefs and as a character in several dance-dramas.

**gedong** Building.

**genggong** Crude bamboo wind instrument, played like a jew's-harp and most commonly heard in the frog dance.

**geringsing** Weaving technique and cloth, also known as double ikat because both the warp and the weft threads are dyed to the final design before being woven.

**Hanuman** Monkey-god and chief of the monkey army in the *Ramayana* story; an ally of Rama's.

**Ida Batara Dewi Ulun Danu** (also just **Dewi Danu**) The goddess of the lakes in the centre of the island.

**ikat** See **endek**.

**jukung** Traditional wooden fishing boat with outriggers.

**kain poleng** Black-and-white checked cloth used for religious purposes, symbolizing the harmonious balancing of good and evil forces.

**kaja** Crucial Balinese direction (opposite of **kelod**), which determines house and temple orientation; towards the mountains, upstream.

**kala** same as **bhuta**.

**kantor pos** General post office.

**kantor telkom** Government telephone office.

**Kawi** Ancient courtly language of Java.

**kayangan jagat** Highly sacred directional temple.

**Kebo Iwa** Mythical giant who features in numerous legends as the builder of some of Bali's oldest monuments.

**kecak** Spectacular dance-drama often referred to as the monkey dance.

**kelod** Crucial Balinese direction (opposite of **kaja**), which determines house and temple orientation; towards the sea, downstream.

**kepeng** Old Chinese coins with holes bored through the middle.

**ketu** Terracotta crown-shaped roof ornament.

**kori agung** See **paduraksa**.

**Kumakarma** Brother of the demon king, Rawana, in the *Ramayana* story.

**Kuningan** The culmination day of the important ten-day Galungan festivities.

**kris** Traditional-style dagger, with scalloped blade edges, of great symbolic and spiritual significance.

**kulkul** Bell-like drum made from a large, hollow log slit down the middle and suspended high up in a purpose-built tower in temples and other public places. Used to summon banjar members to meetings and other public events, and also to raise the alarm.

**legong** Classical Balinese dance performed by two or three pre-pubescent girls.

**leyak** Witches who often assume disguises.

**lontar** Palm-leaf manuscripts on which all ancient texts were inscribed.

**losmen** Homestay or guesthouse.

**Mahabharata** Lengthy Hindu epic describing the battles between representatives of good and evil, and focusing on the exploits of the Pandawa brothers – the inspiration for a huge number of dance-dramas, paintings and sculptures.

**mandi** Traditional scoop-and-slosh method of showering, often in open-roofed or "garden" bathrooms.

**meru** Multi-tiered Hindu shrine with an odd number of thatched roofs (from one to eleven), which symbolizes the cosmic Mount Meru.

**moksa** Spiritual liberation for Hindus.

**naga** Mythological underwater deity, a cross between a snake and a dragon.

**odalan** Individual temple festival held to mark the anniversary of the founding of every temple on Bali.

**ojek** Motorcycle taxi.

**padmasana** The empty throne that tops the shrine-tower, found in every temple and dedicated to the supreme god Sanghyang Widi Wasa. The shrine is often supported by the cosmic turtle, Bengan, and two naga.

**paduraksa** (or **kori agung**) Temple gateway to the inner sanctuary, like the candi bentar, but joined together rather than split.

**pancasila** The five principles of the Indonesian constitution: belief in one supreme god; the unity of the Indonesian nation; guided democracy; social justice and humanitarianism; and a civilized and prosperous society. Symbolized by an eagle bearing a five-part crest.

**paras** Soft, grey volcanic sandstone used for carving.

**pasar** Market.

**pasar seni** Literally art market, usually sells fabrics and non-foodstuffs, and sometimes artefacts and souvenirs.

**pawukon** See **wuku**.

**peci** Black felt or velvet hat worn by Muslim men.

**pedanda** High priest of the Brahman caste.

**pemangku** Village priest.

**perada** Traditional gold, screen-printed material used for ceremonial garb and temple umbrellas.

**prahu** Traditional wooden fishing boat.

**prasasti** Ancient bronze inscriptions.

**pulau** Island.

**puputan** Suicidal fight to the death.

**pura** Hindu temple.

**puri** Raja's palace, or the home of a wealthy nobleman.

**Raksasa** Mythical Hindu demon-giant with long teeth and a large club, often used to guard temple entrances.

**Ramayana** Hugely influential Hindu epic, essentially a morality tale of the battles between good and evil; the source material for numerous dance-dramas, paintings and sculptures.

**Rangda** Legendary widow-witch who personifies evil and is most commonly depicted with huge fangs, a massive lolling tongue and pendulous breasts;

features in carvings and in Balinese dance performances.

**Rawana** The demon king who represents the forces of evil (Rama's adversary in the *Ramayana*).

**raya** Main or principal ("Jalan Raya Ubud" is the main Ubud road).

**saka** Hindu calendar, which is divided into years made up of between 354 and 356 days; runs eighty years behind the Western Gregorian calendar.

**Sanghyang Widi Wasa** The supreme Hindu god; all other gods are a manifestation of him.

**Saraswati** Goddess of learning and of water.

**sarong** The anglicized generic term for any length of material wrapped around the lower body and worn by men and women.

**sawah** Ricefields.

**sebel** Ritually unclean.

**shophouse** Shuttered building with living space upstairs and shop space on ground floor.

**Siwa (Shiva)** Important Hindu deity; "The Destroyer" or, more accurately, "The Dissolver".

**songket** Silk brocades often woven with real gold thread.

**subak** Irrigation committee or local farmers' council.

**suttee** Practice of widows choosing to burn themselves to death on their husbands' funeral pyres.

**Swastika** Ancient Hindu and Buddhist symbol representing the wheel of the sun.

**taji** Sharp blade attached to the leg of fighting cocks.

**teluk** Bay.

**topeng** Masked dance-drama, performed with human masks.

**tuak** Rice or palm wine.

**wantilan** Large pavilion, usually used for cockfights and dance performances.

**wartel** Phone office.

**warung** Foodstall or tiny streetside restaurant.

**wayang kulit** Shadow puppet play.

**Wisnu (Vishnu)** Important Hindu deity – "The Preserver". Usually shown with four arms, holding a disc, a conch, a lotus and a club, and often seated astride his vehicle, the garuda.

**wuku (or pawukon)** Complex Balinese calendar system based on a 210-day lunar cycle.

# small print and
# Index

# A Rough Guide to Rough Guides

In the summer of 1981, Mark Ellingham, a recent graduate from Bristol University, was travelling round Greece and couldn't find a guidebook that really met his needs. On the one hand there were the student guides, insistent on saving every last cent, and on the other the heavyweight cultural tomes whose authors seemed to have spent more time in a research library than lounging away the afternoon at a taverna or on the beach.

In a bid to avoid getting a job, Mark and a small group of writers set about creating their own guidebook. It was a guide to Greece that aimed to combine a journalistic approach to description with a thoroughly practical approach to travellers' needs – a guide that would incorporate culture, history and contemporary insights with a critical edge, together with up-to-date, value-for-money listings. Back in London, Mark and the team finished their Rough Guide, as they called it, and talked Routledge into publishing the book.

SMALL PRINT

That first *Rough Guide to Greece*, published in 1982, was a student scheme that became a publishing phenomenon. The immediate success of the book – with numerous reprints and a Thomas Cook prize shortlisting – spawned a series that rapidly covered dozens of destinations. Rough Guides had a ready market among low-budget backpackers, but soon also acquired a much broader and older readership that relished Rough Guides' wit and inquisitiveness as much as their enthusiastic, critical approach. Everyone wants value for money, but not at any price.

Rough Guides soon began supplementing the "rougher" information about hostels and low-budget listings with the kind of detail on restaurants and quality hotels that independent-minded visitors on any budget might expect, whether on business in New York or trekking in Thailand.

These days the guides – distributed worldwide by the Penguin Group – offer recommendations from shoestring to luxury and cover more than 200 destinations around the globe, including almost every country in the Americas and Europe, more than half of Africa and most of Asia and Australasia. Our ever-growing team of authors and photographers is spread all over the world, particularly in Europe, the USA and Australia.

In 1994, we published the *Rough Guide to World Music* and *Rough Guide to Classical Music*; and a year later the *Rough Guide to the Internet*. All three books have become benchmark titles in their fields – which encouraged us to expand into other areas of publishing, mainly around popular culture. Rough Guides now publish:

- Travel guides to more than 200 worldwide destinations
- Dictionary phrasebooks to 22 major languages
- History guides ranging from Ireland to Islam
- Maps printed on rip-proof and waterproof Polyart™ paper
- Music guides running the gamut from Opera to Elvis
- Restaurant guides to London, New York and San Francisco
- Reference books on topics as diverse as the Weather and Shakespeare
- Sports guides from Formula 1 to Man Utd
- Pop culture books from *Lord of the Rings* to Cult TV
- World Music CDs in association with World Music Network

Visit **www.roughguides.com** to see our latest publications.

## Rough Guide credits

**Text editor:** Keith Drew
**Layout:** Dan May, Keith Drew
**Cartography:** Katie Lloyd-Jones, Maxine Repath
**Picture editor:** Sarah Smithies
**Production:** Tiina Wastie
**Proofreader:** Diane Margolis
**Cover design:** Chloë Roberts
......................................

**Editorial: London** Kate Berens, Claire Saunders, Geoff Howard, Ruth Blackmore, Polly Thomas, Richard Lim, Clifton Wilkinson, Alison Murchie, Sally Schafer, Karoline Densley, Andy Turner, Ella O'Donnell, Edward Aves, Nikki Birrell, Helen Marsden, Alice Park, Sarah Eno, Joe Staines, Duncan Clark, Peter Buckley, Matthew Milton, Daniel Crewe; **New York** Andrew Rosenberg, Richard Koss, Steven Horak, AnneLise Sorensen, Amy Hegarty, Hunter Slaton, April Isaacs
**Design & Pictures: London** Simon Bracken, Diana Jarvis, Mark Thomas, Jj Luck, Harriet Mills; **Delhi** Madhulita Mohapatra, Umesh Aggarwal, Ajay Verma, Jessica Subramanian, Amit Verma, Ankur Guha

**Production:** Julia Bovis, Sophie Hewat, Katherine Owers
**Cartography: London** Ed Wright; **Delhi** Manish Chandra, Rajesh Chhibber, Jai Prakash Mishra, Ashutosh Bharti, Rajesh Mishra, Animesh Pathak, Jasbir Sandhu, Karobi Gogoi
**Online: New York** Jennifer Gold, Suzanne Welles, Kristin Mingrone; **Delhi** Manik Chauhan, Narender Kumar, Shekhar Jha, Rakesh Kumar, Chhandita Chakravarty
**Marketing & Publicity: London** Richard Trillo, Niki Hanmer, David Wearn, Demelza Dallow, Louise Maher; **New York** Geoff Colquitt, Megan Kennedy, Katy Ball; **Delhi** Reem Khokhar
**Custom publishing and foreign rights:** Philippa Hopkins
**Manager India:** Punita Singh
**Series editor:** Mark Ellingham
**Reference Director:** Andrew Lockett
**PA to Managing and Publishing Directors:** Megan McIntyre
**Publishing Director:** Martin Dunford
**Managing Director:** Kevin Fitzgerald

SMALL PRINT

## Publishing information

This fifth edition published November 2005 by **Rough Guides Ltd,**
80 Strand, London WC2R 0RL
345 Hudson St, 4th Floor,
New York, NY 10014, USA
14 Local Shopping Centre, Panchsheel Park,
New Delhi 110017, India
**Distributed by the Penguin Group**
Penguin Books Ltd,
80 Strand, London WC2R 0RL
Penguin Putnam, Inc.
375 Hudson Street, NY 10014, USA
Penguin Group (Australia)
250 Camberwell Road, Camberwell
Victoria 3124, Australia
Penguin Books Canada Ltd,
10 Alcorn Avenue, Toronto, Ontario,
Canada M4V 1E4
Penguin Group (New Zealand)
Cnr Rosedale and Airborne Roads
Albany, Auckland, New Zealand

Typeset in Bembo and Helvetica to an original design by Henry Iles.
Printed in Italy by LegoPrint
© Lesley Reader and Lucy Ridout 2005

536pp includes index
A catalogue record for this book is available from the British Library
ISBN 1-84353-509-2

1   3   5   7   9   8   6   4   2

## Help us update

We've gone to a lot of effort to ensure that the fifth edition of **The Rough Guide to Bali & Lombok** is accurate and up to date. However, things change – places get "discovered", opening hours are notoriously fickle, restaurants and rooms raise prices or lower standards. If you feel we've got it wrong or left something out, we'd like to know, and if you can remember the address, the price, the time, the phone number, so much the better.

We'll credit all contributions, and send a copy of the next edition (or any other Rough

Guide if you prefer) for the best letters. Everyone who writes to us and isn't already a subscriber will receive a copy of our full-colour thrice-yearly newsletter. Please mark letters: **"Rough Guide Bali & Lombok Update"** and send to: Rough Guides, 80 Strand, London WC2R 0RL, or Rough Guides, 4th Floor, 345 Hudson St, New York, NY 10014. Or send an email to **mail@roughguides.com**

Have your questions answered and tell others about your trip at **www.roughguides.atinfopop.com**

## Acknowledgements

The authors would like to thank the following people:

From **Lesley** – thanks to the following for expertise, calmness and patience well beyond the call of duty: Hasan Nur, Ketut Lagun, Made Wijana, Wayan Artana and Yopi. For answering endless questions, for hospitality and for determined efforts to help me understand what Bali and Lombok are all about there are Mel, Barbara, Don and Shaufan Husnika in Senggigi; Gemma, Made and Ketut in Kuta; Barbara and Prihanto in Tirtagangga; Bob and Sue still chatting in Candi; Axel and Sigi at Tauch; Joan on Gili Meno; and all the many folks along the way who made the trip so pleasant. Special thanks as always to Yau Sang Man; this time, his stroll was invaluable.

From **Lucy** – special thanks to Wayan Artana, Gusti Ngurah Beratha, Claude Chouinard and Iyan Yaspriyana, Peter and Gina Falkenburg, Dominique Guiet, Ted and Lillen Kruuse-Jensen, Elizabeth McCusker, Meghan Pappenheim, and Annabel Thomas.

Many thanks also to the staff at Rough Guides.

## Readers' letters

Thanks to all the readers who have taken the time to write in with comments and suggestions (and apologies if we've inadvertently omitted or misspelt anyone's name):

Barry Acott, Barrie Lie-Birchall, Nicholas Bull, Kenneth Alan Collins, Joseph Copeland, Bob Dixon, Kristin Eichhorn, Justin Ellis, Jim Fogden, Wendy Glamocak, Peter Kempinsky & Katarina Ulfstdotter, Eric Kloor, Anne Krawic, Willem Lindeijer, Peter McCarthy, Fred Moss, Carol Pimentel, Rosalyn, HH Saffery, Martha and Louis Savelkoul, Kerry Start & Tony Shilling, Astrid Stenzel, Michael Williams, Jenny Wilson.

## Photo credits

### Cover
Main front picture: Pura Ulun Danu, Danau Bratan © Getty
Small front top picture: Temple detail © Getty
Small front lower picture: Ceremonial umbrellas © Getty
Back top picture: Pantai Klotok © Corbis
Back lower picture: Hindu temple © Getty

### Title page
Gili Islands © Sang Man

### Full page
Gunung Batur © Jon Arnold Images/Photolibrary.com

### Introduction
Fishing boat © Gavin Hellier/Photolibrary.com
Morning market © J. Garrett/Trip
Planting rice © John Wright
Family on motorcycle © T. Bognar/Trip
Surfing Kuta beach © Mark A. Johnson/Corbis
Garden bathroom, Damai Lovina Villas © Lesley Reader
Kintamani © Jim Holmes/Axiom
Sunset in Padang Bai © Jim Holmes © Axiom
Early morning, Pura Lempuyang Luhur © Jim Holmes/Axiom

### Things not to miss
01 Prana Dewi hotel, Wongayagede © Lucy Ridout
02 Kuta beach, Lombok © Lesley Reader
03 Nusa Penida's south coast © Lesley Reader
04 Bali Museum, Denpasar © Robert Harding Picture Library
05 Gunung Batur sunrise © Lesley Reader
06 Rice terraces © Jerry Dennis
07 Tenganan craftwork © Lesley Reader
08 Pemuteran © J Marshall/Tribaleye Images/Alamy
09 Kerta Gosa painting © Lesley Reader
10 Bounty Discotheque, Kuta © Dimas Ardian/Getty Images
11 Gunung Agung © Jim Holmes/Axiom
12 Pura Pursering Jagat, Pejeng © T. Bognar/Trip
13 Tirtagangga Water Palace © Jim Holmes/Axiom
14 Rujak seller, Sanur © John Wright

15 Seafood barbecues, Jimbaran © Sang Man
16 Gili Islands © Lesley Reader
17 Jalan Bisma, Ubud © Lucy Ridout
18 Kecak dance © Free Agents Limited/Corbis
19 Lombok pots © Sang Man
20 Hyatt hotel garden, Sanur © Robert Harding Picture Library
21 Painted hats © Jim Holmes/Axiom
22 Gamelan orchestra © Adina Tovy/Robert Harding Picture Library
23 Gili Trawangan © Lesley Reader
24 Painter © Rolf Richardson/Robert Harding Picture Library
25 Spa © Sylvain Grandadam/Robert Harding Picture Library
26 Tanah Lot © Geoff Goodman/Travel Ink
27 View of Gunung Rinjani from Tetebatu © Lesley Reader
28 Pura Meduwe Karang © Lesley Reader
29 Seaweed farming at Nusa Lembongan © Lesley Reader
30 Barong–Rangda dance, Ubud © Lesley Reader
31 *Ritual flirtation dance* by Dewa Putu Bedil courtesy of the Neka Art Museum

### Black and white photos
p.68 Washing the salt off, Kuta beach, Bali © Jim Holmes/Axiom
p.92 Match of the day, Kuta beach, Bali © Chris Humphrey
p.160 *Jukung*, Sanur © Glen Allison/Alamy
p.170 Gunung Kawi © Reinhard Eisele/Corbis
p.184 Museum Puri Lukisan, Ubud © Jim Holmes/Axiom
p.228 Lagoon, Candi Dasa © Lesley Reader
p.284 Fishing boats, Amed © Photolibrary.com
p.294 Canoes, Danau Batur © Craig Brown/Photolibrary.com
p.329 Dolphin statue, Lovina © Martyn Evans/Alamy
p.338 Stone statues at Pura Luhur Batukau © Lesley Reader
p.351 Yeh Gangga beach © J Marshall/Tribaleye Images/Alamy
p.376 Tanjung Aan © Michael S. Yamashita/Corbis
p.429 Lombok textiles, Sukarara © Lesley Reader
p.485 Wooden *garuda* © G. R. Nichols/Trip

# Index

Map entries are in colour.

**INDEX**

**INDEX**

**INDEX**

# R

INDEX

# Map symbols

maps are listed in the full index using coloured text

MAP SYMBOLS

| | | | | |
|---|---|---|---|---|
| – – – – | Chapter division boundary | ⊠ | Gate |
| ═══ | Main road | ⊙ | Statue |
| ═══ | Minor road | ◉ | Accommodation |
| ◄═══ | One-way street | ▣ | Restaurant/bar |
| ▬▬▬ | Pedestrianized street | *(i)* | Information office |
| - - - - - | Path | ℂ | Telephone |
| ——— | River | @ | Internet access |
| – – – | Ferry route | ⊠ | Post office |
| ✈ | Airport | ⊞ | Hospital |
| ♦ | Point of interest | ⊞ | Clinic |
| ♠ | Temple | ⬧ | Swimming |
| ♜ | Mosque | ⛽ | Fuel station |
| ♠ | Chinese Temple | Ⓟ | Parking |
| ⚮ | Waterfall | ♣ | Golf course |
| ⋀⋁ | Spring | ▬ | Building |
| ▲ | Mountain peak | ▬ | Hotel compound |
| ⬇ | View point | ⊞ | Church |
| ◠ | Cave | ░ | Park |
| ⌒ | Surfing beach | ⚬ | Mangrove swamp |
| ⨝ | Snorkelling area | ⋯ | Beach |
| ★ | Bemo stop | | |